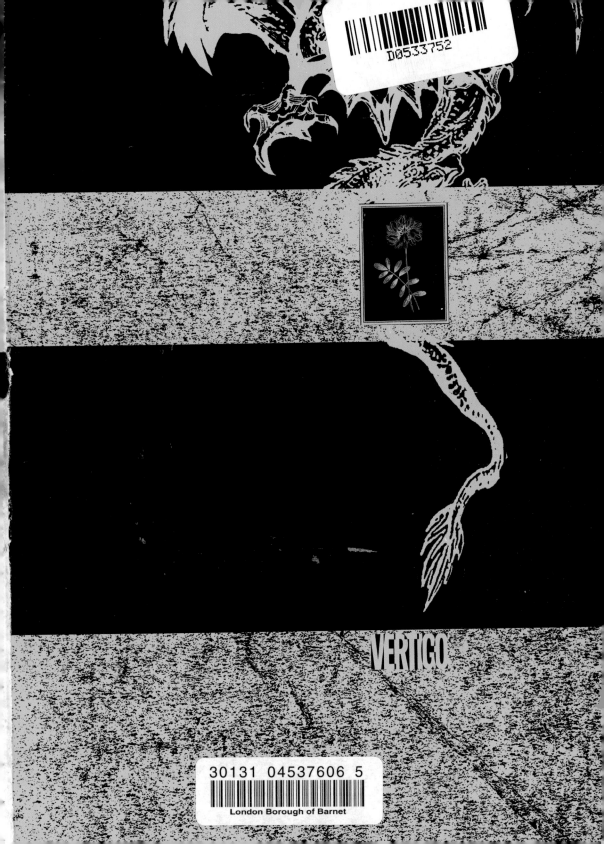

VERTIGO

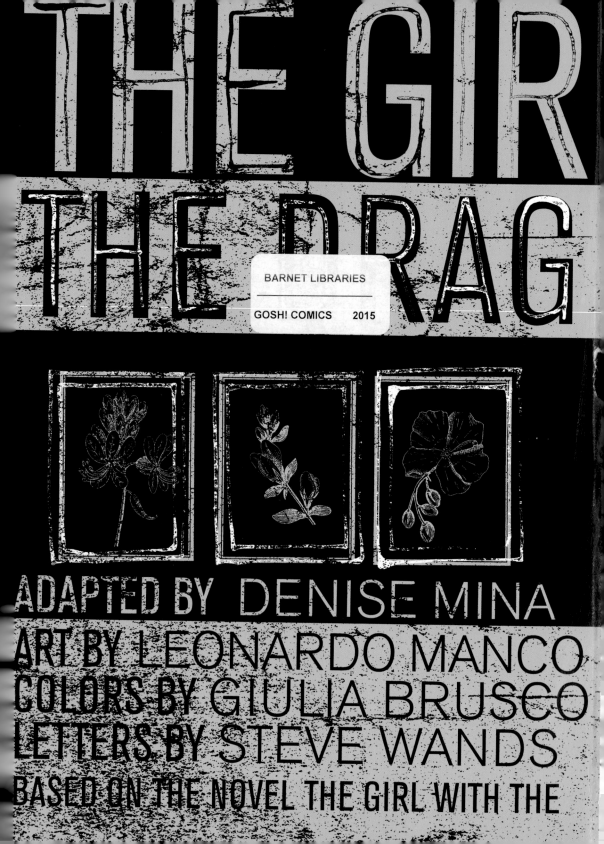

THE GIR
THE DRAG

ADAPTED BY DENISE MINA
ART BY LEONARDO MANCO
COLORS BY GIULIA BRUSCO
LETTERS BY STEVE WANDS
BASED ON THE NOVEL THE GIRL WITH THE

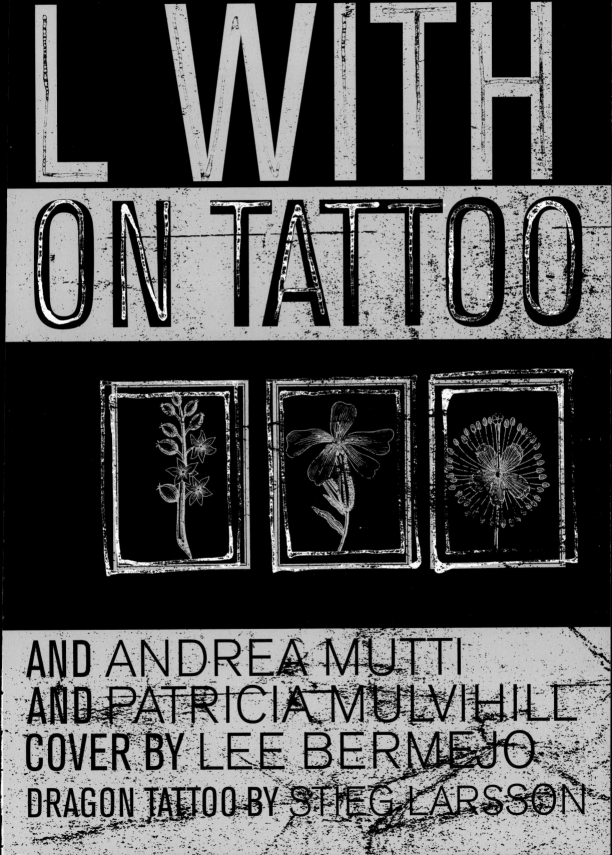

L WITH

ON TATTOO

AND ANDREA MUTTI
AND PATRICIA MULVIHILL
COVER BY LEE BERMEJO
DRAGON TATTOO BY STIEG LARSSON

Will Dennis Editor Mark Doyle Associate Editor Robbin Brosterman Design Director – Books Louis Prandi Publication Design

Shelly Bond Executive Editor – Vertigo Hank Kanalz Senior VP – Vertigo & Integrated Publishing

Diane Nelson President Dan DiDio and Jim Lee Co-Publishers Geoff Johns Chief Creative Officer John Rood Executive VP – Sales, Marketing & Business Development
Amy Genkins Senior VP – Business & Legal Affairs Nairi Gardiner Senior VP – Finance Jeff Boison VP – Publishing Planning Mark Chiarello VP – Art Direction & Design
John Cunningham VP – Marketing Terri Cunningham VP – Editorial Administration Alison Gill Senior VP – Manufacturing & Operations
Jay Kogan VP – Business & Legal Affairs, Publishing Jack Mahan VP – Business Affairs, Talent Nick Napolitano VP – Manufacturing Administration
Sue Pohja VP – Book Sales Courtney Simmons Senior VP – Publicity Bob Wayne Senior VP – Sales

SUSTAINABLE
FORESTRY
INITIATIVE
Certified Chain of Custody
At Least 20% Certified Forest Content
www.sfiprogram.org
SFI-01042
APPLIES TO TEXT STOCK ONLY

Library of Congress Cataloging-in-Publication Data

Mina, Denise.
The girl with the dragon tattoo. Book 1 / Denise Mina, Leonardo Manco, Andrea Mutti.
p. cm.
ISBN 978-1-4012-3557-4 (alk. paper)
1. Crime—Sweden—Comic books, strips, etc. 2. Graphic novels. I. Manco, Leonardo. II. Mutti, Andrea, 1973- III. Larsson, Stieg, 1954-2004. Girl with the dragon tattoo. IV. Title.
PN6737.M57657 2012
741.5'942—dc23
2012030613

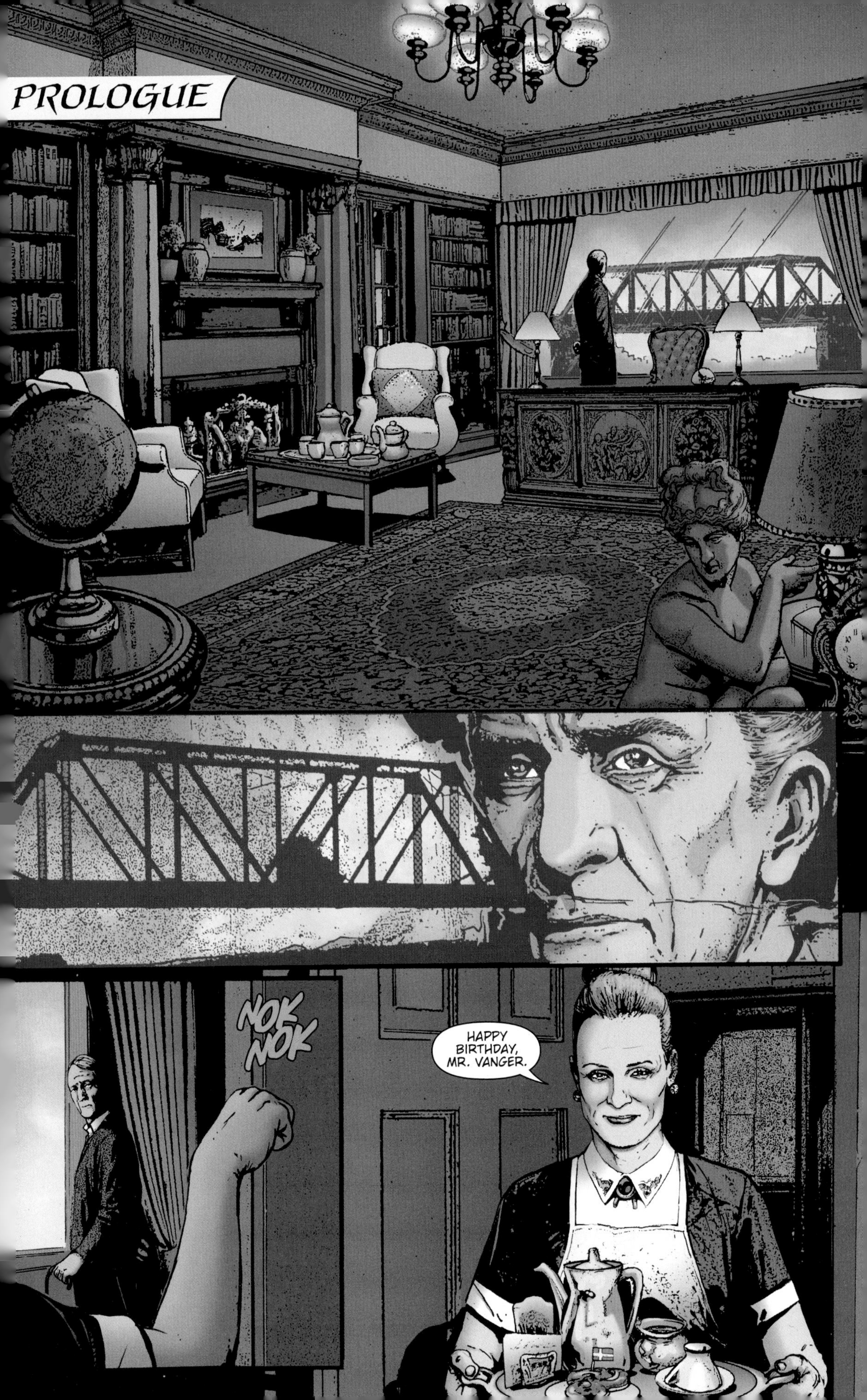
PROLOGUE
NOK NOK
HAPPY BIRTHDAY, MR. VANGER.

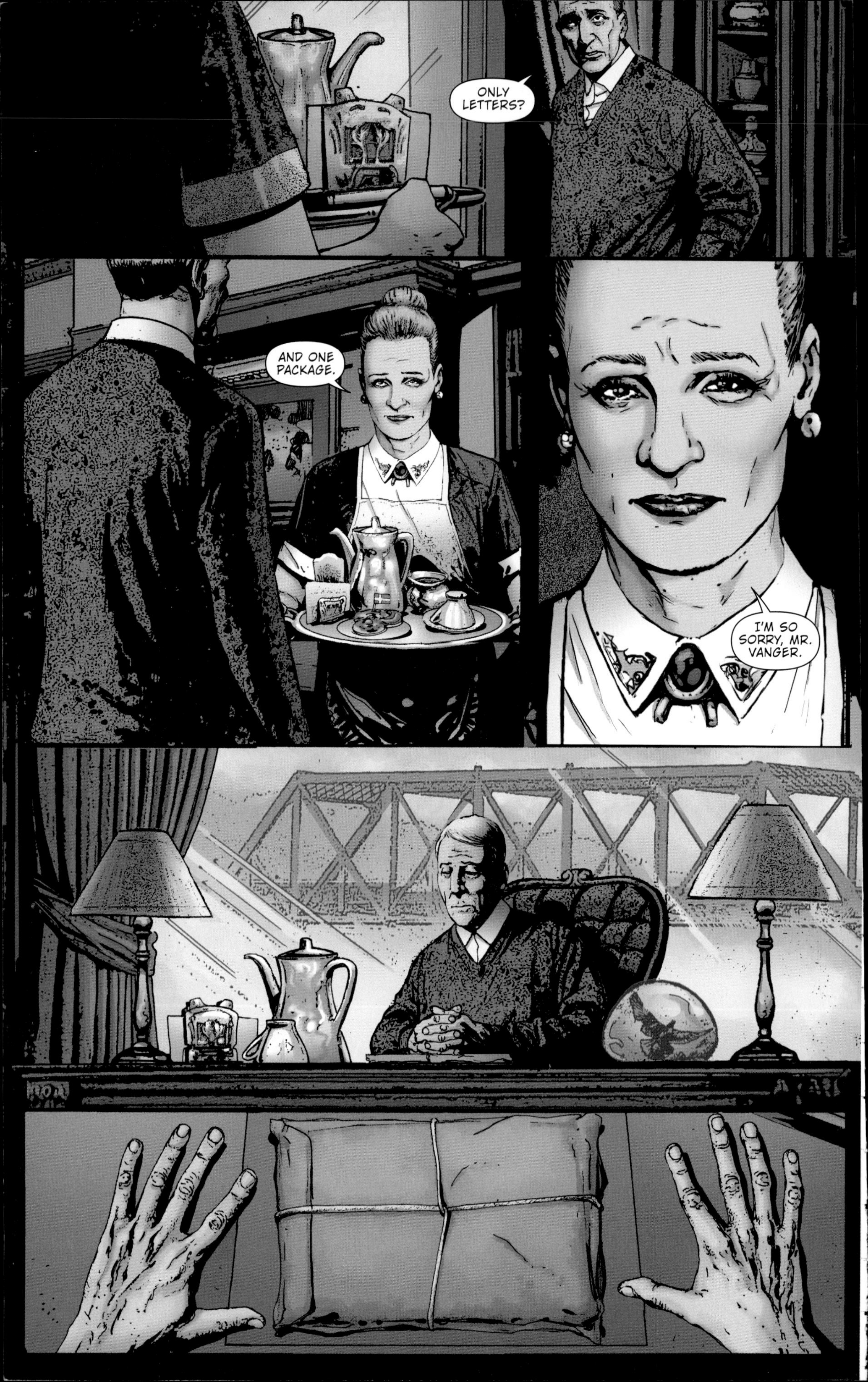
ONLY LETTERS?
AND ONE PACKAGE.
I'M SO SORRY, MR. VANGER.

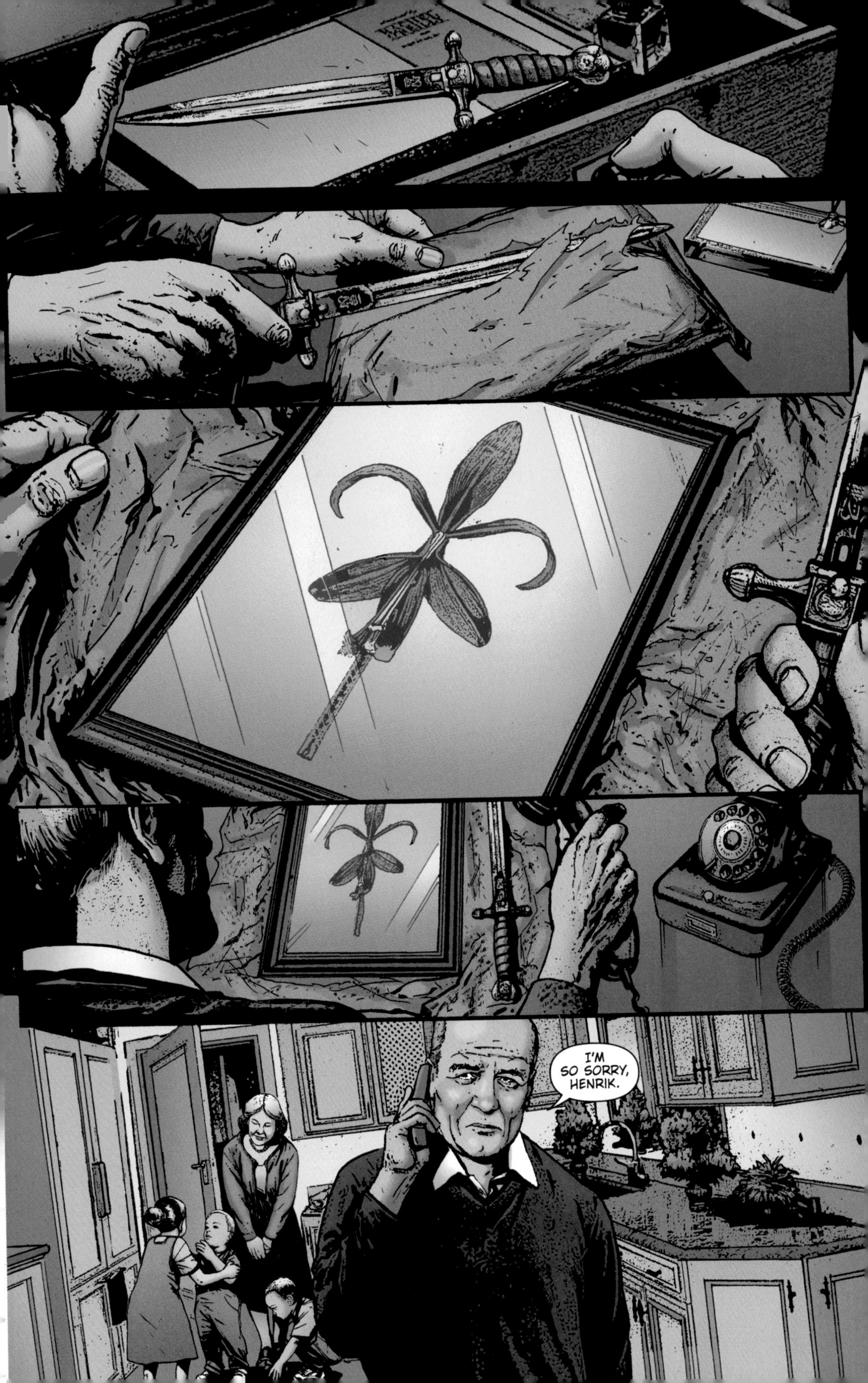
I'M SO SORRY, HENRIK.

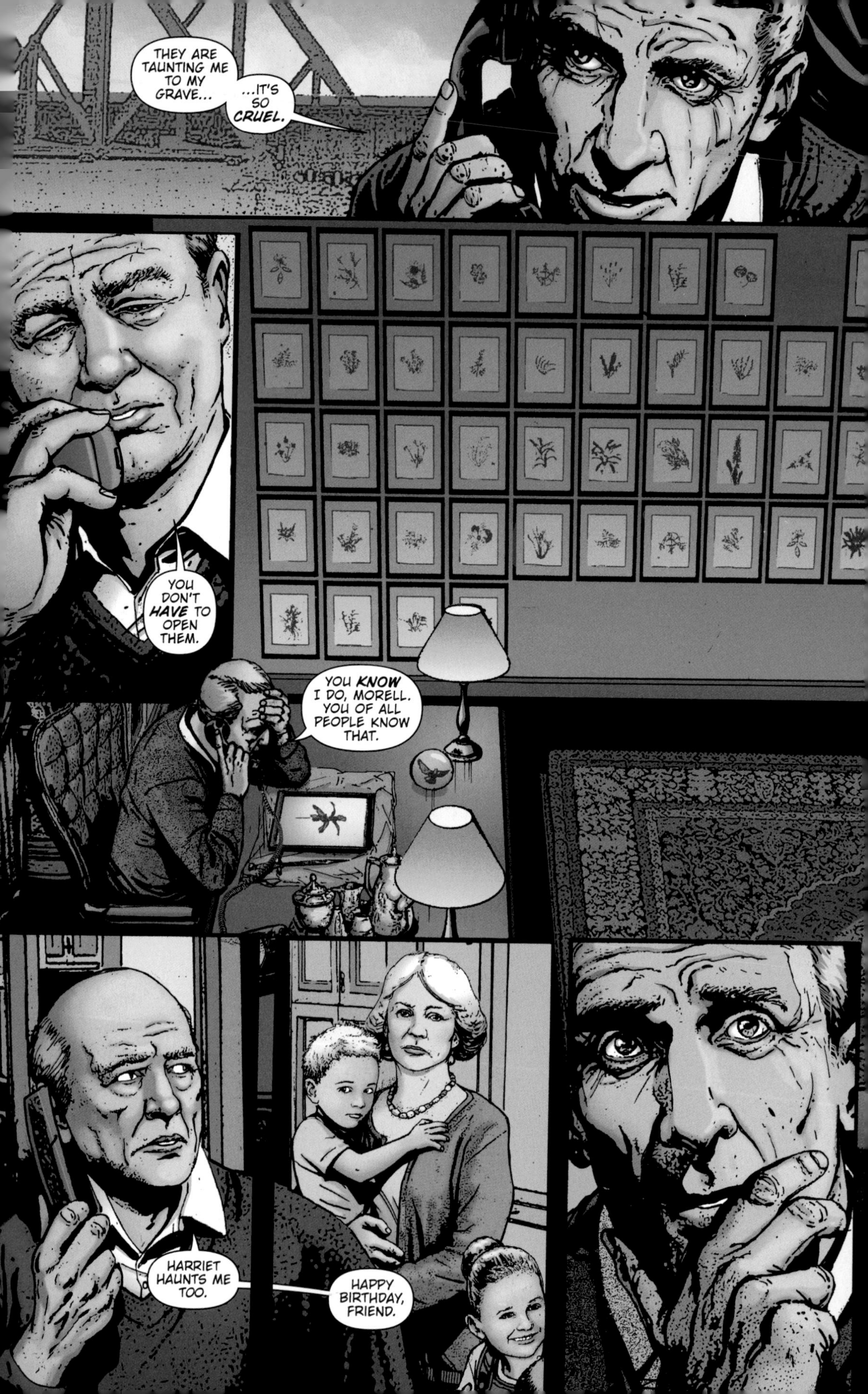
THEY ARE TAUNTING ME TO MY GRAVE...
...IT'S SO CRUEL.
YOU DON'T HAVE TO OPEN THEM.
YOU KNOW I DO, MORELL. YOU OF ALL PEOPLE KNOW THAT.
HARRIET HAUNTS ME TOO.
HAPPY BIRTHDAY, FRIEND.

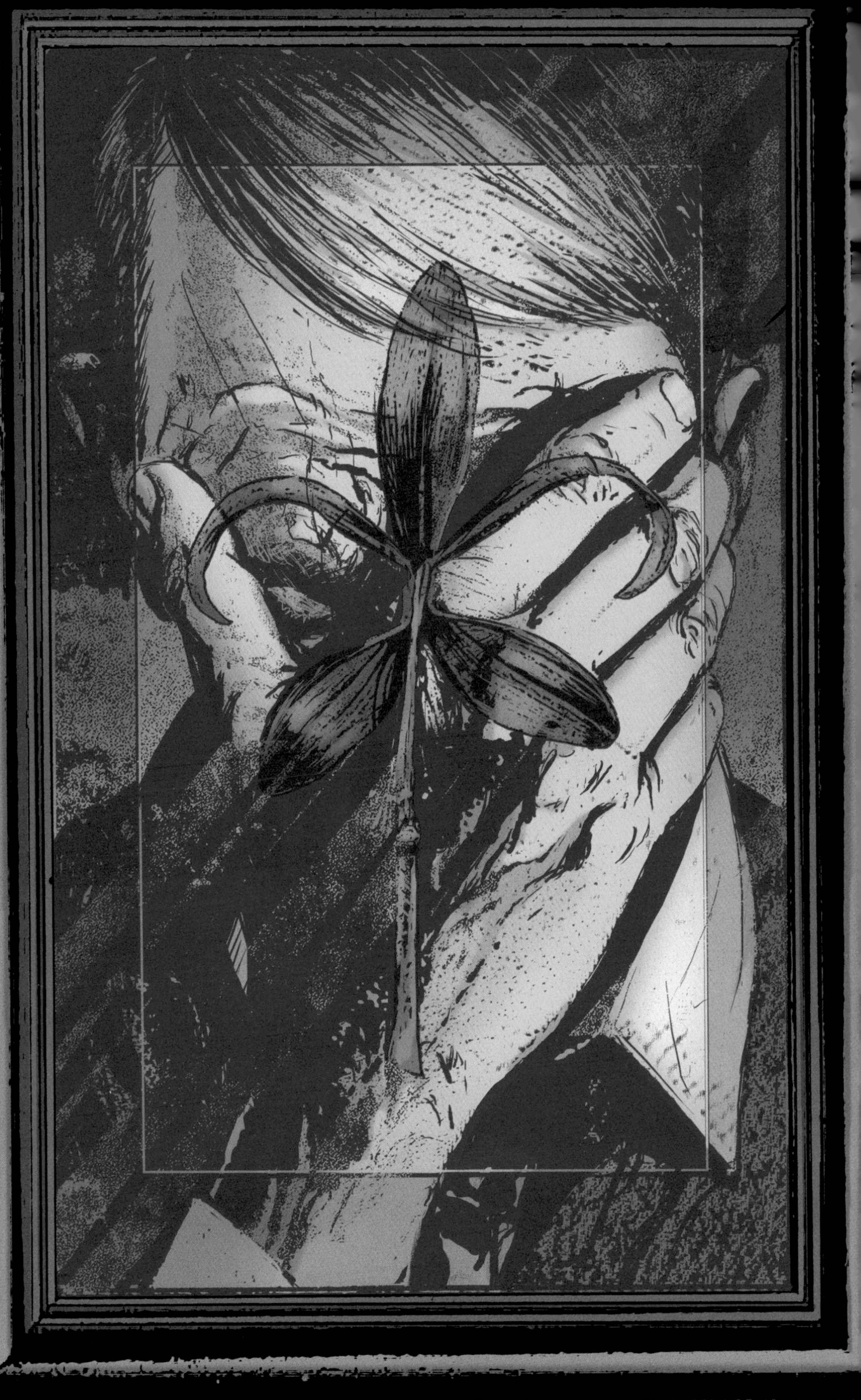

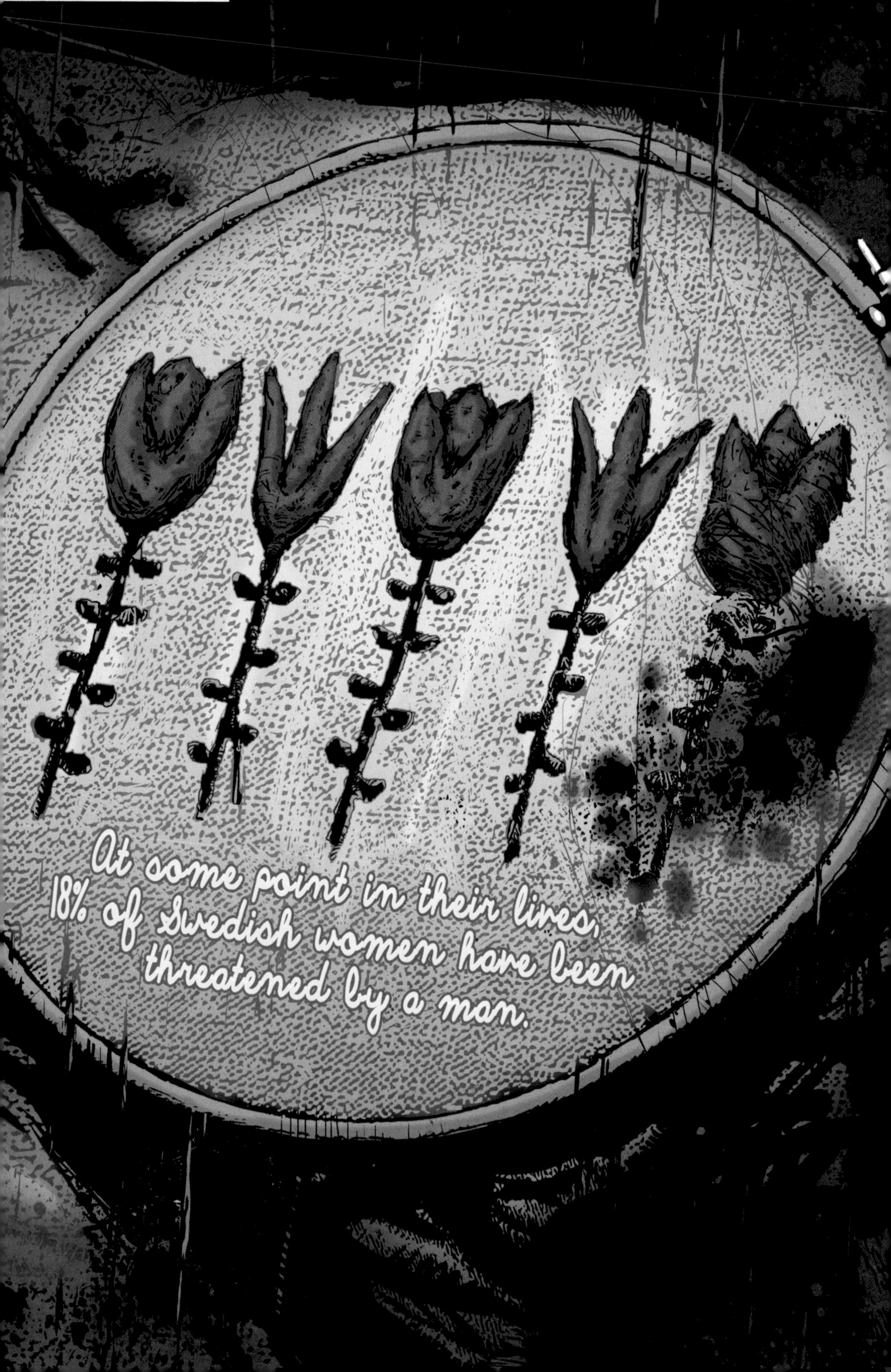
At some point in their lives, 18% of Swedish women have been threatened by a man.

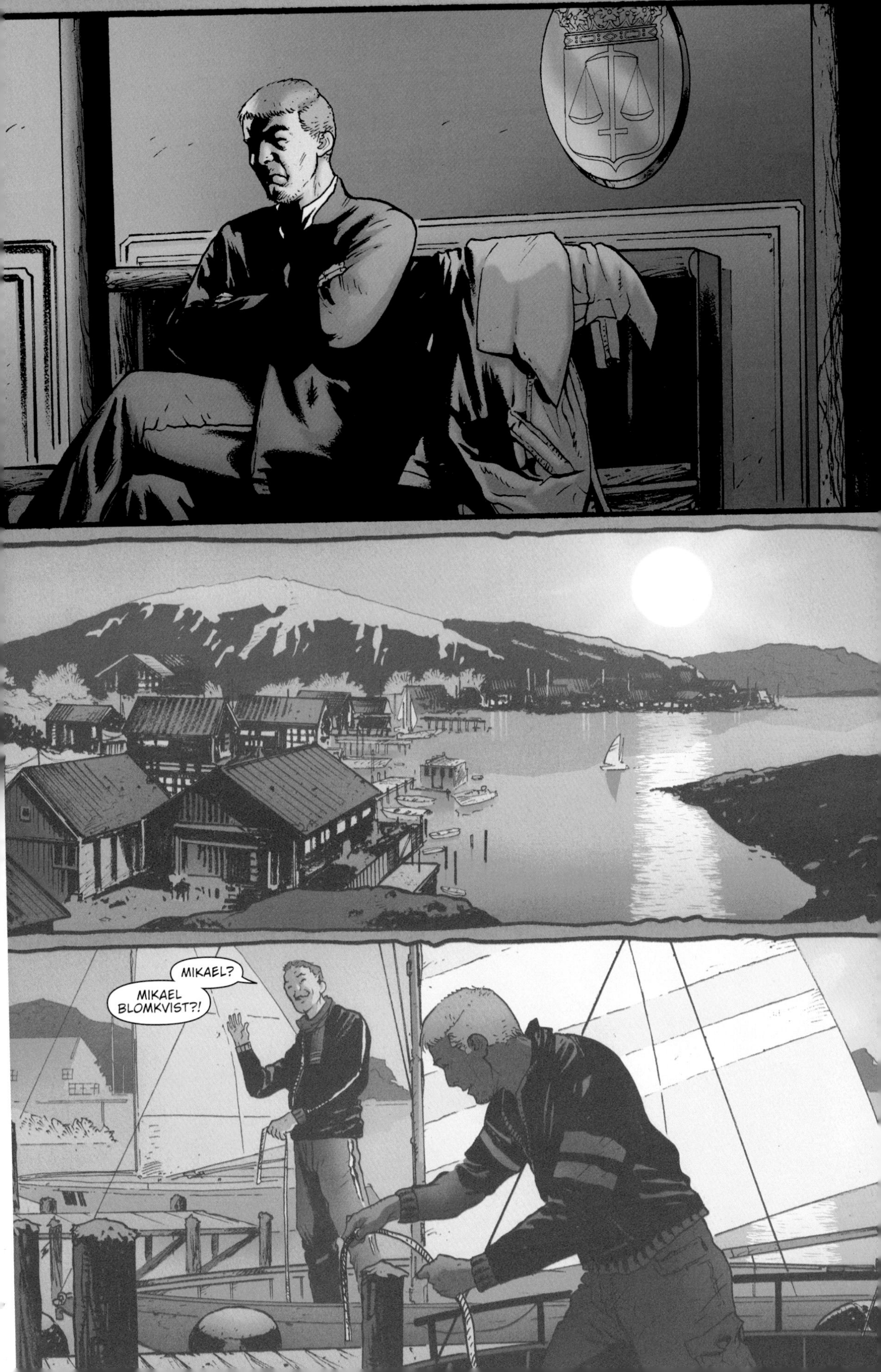
MIKAEL?
MIKAEL BLOMKVIST?!

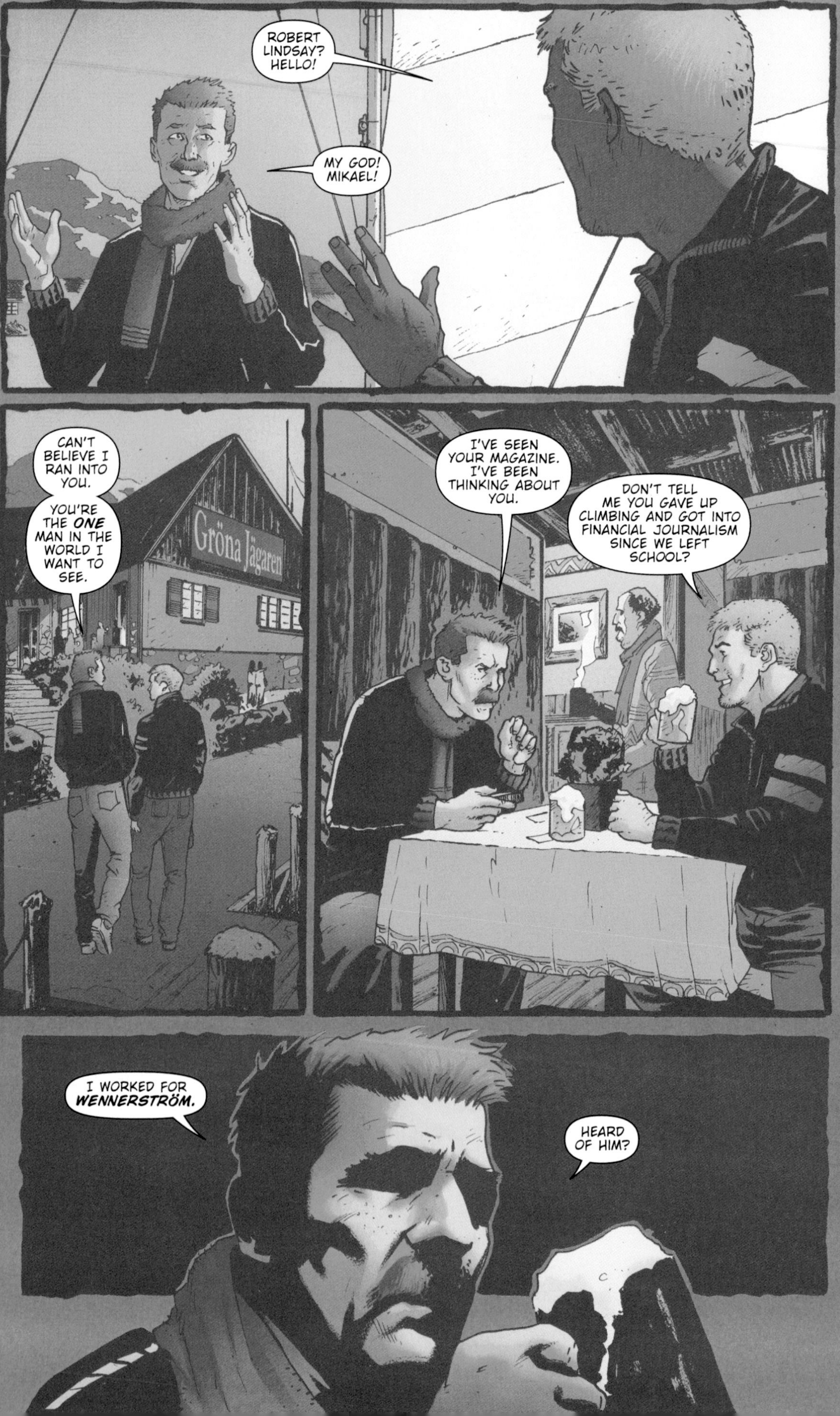
ROBERT LINDSAY? HELLO!
MY GOD! MIKAEL!
CAN'T BELIEVE I RAN INTO YOU.
YOU'RE THE ONE MAN IN THE WORLD I WANT TO SEE.
Gröna Jägaren
I'VE SEEN YOUR MAGAZINE. I'VE BEEN THINKING ABOUT YOU.
DON'T TELL ME YOU GAVE UP CLIMBING AND GOT INTO FINANCIAL JOURNALISM SINCE WE LEFT SCHOOL?
I WORKED FOR WENNERSTRÖM.
HEARD OF HIM?

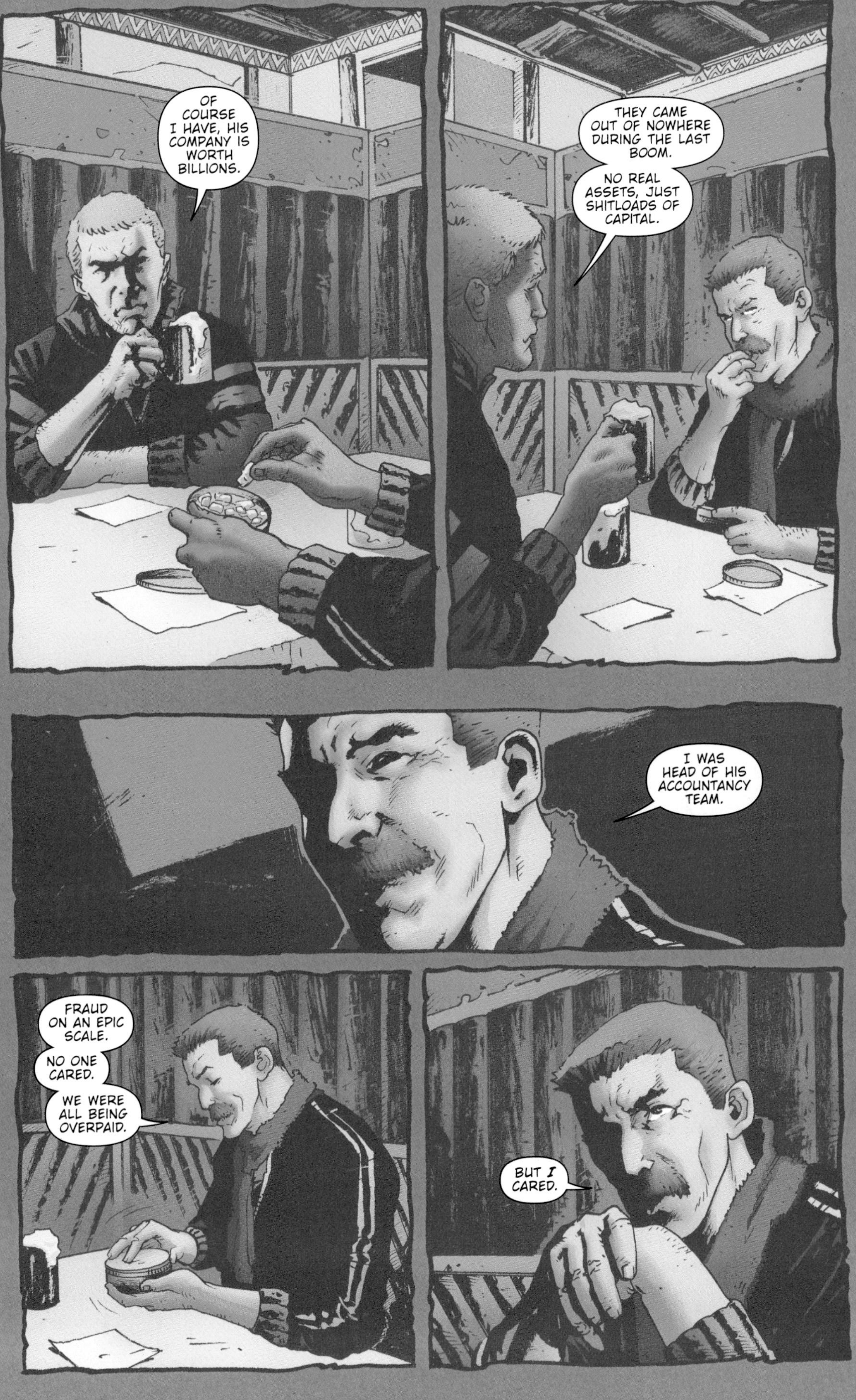
OF COURSE I HAVE, HIS COMPANY IS WORTH BILLIONS.
THEY CAME OUT OF NOWHERE DURING THE LAST BOOM.
NO REAL ASSETS, JUST SHITLOADS OF CAPITAL.
I WAS HEAD OF HIS ACCOUNTANCY TEAM.
FRAUD ON AN EPIC SCALE.
NO ONE CARED.
WE WERE ALL BEING OVERPAID.
BUT *I* CARED.

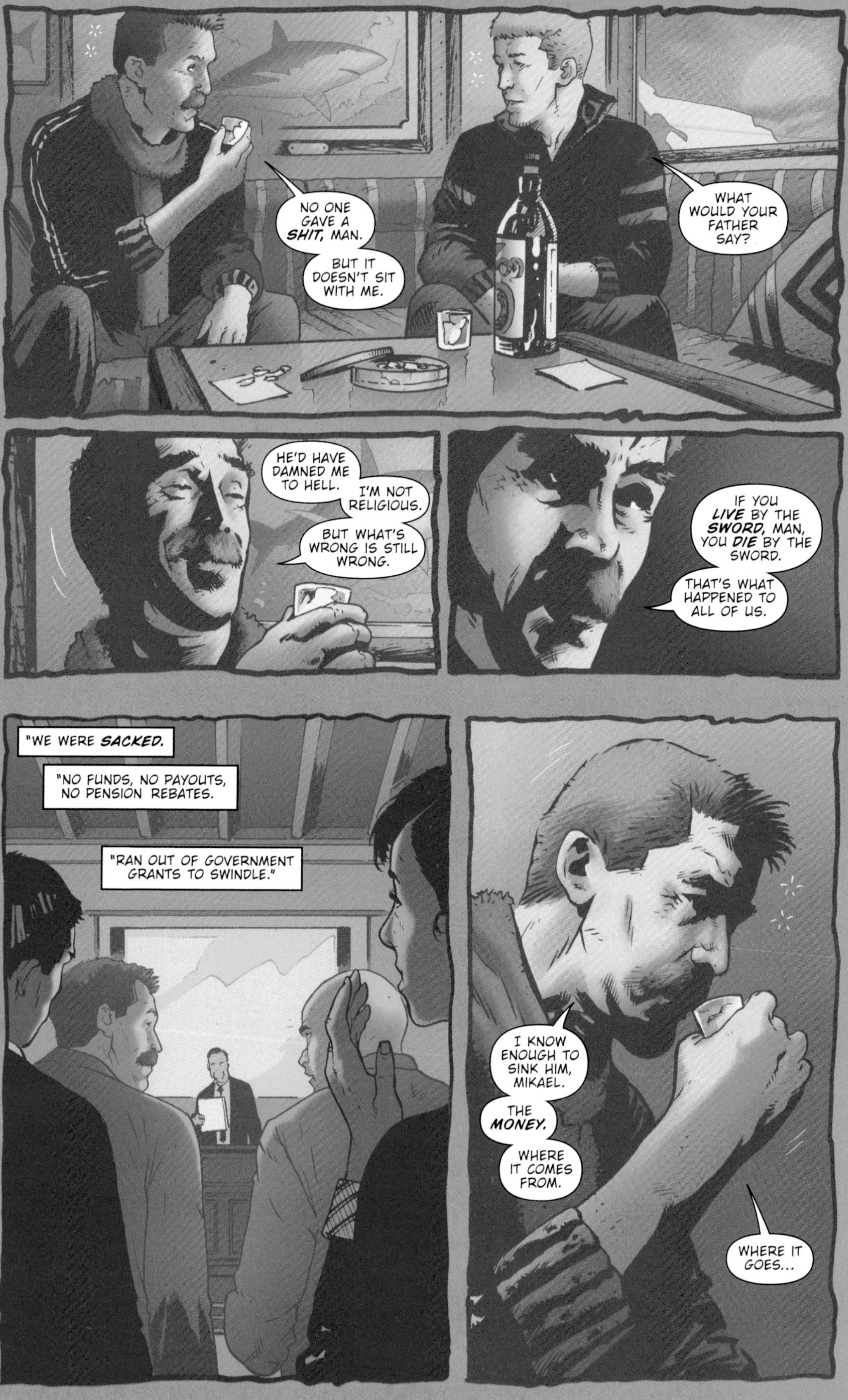

NO ONE GAVE A *SHIT,* MAN.
BUT IT DOESN'T SIT WITH ME.
WHAT WOULD YOUR FATHER SAY?
HE'D HAVE DAMNED ME TO HELL.
I'M NOT RELIGIOUS.
BUT WHAT'S WRONG IS STILL WRONG.
IF YOU *LIVE* BY THE *SWORD,* MAN, YOU *DIE* BY THE SWORD.
THAT'S WHAT HAPPENED TO ALL OF US.
"WE WERE *SACKED.*
"NO FUNDS, NO PAYOUTS, NO PENSION REBATES.
"RAN OUT OF GOVERNMENT GRANTS TO SWINDLE."
I KNOW ENOUGH TO SINK HIM, MIKAEL.
THE *MONEY.*
WHERE IT COMES FROM.
WHERE IT GOES...

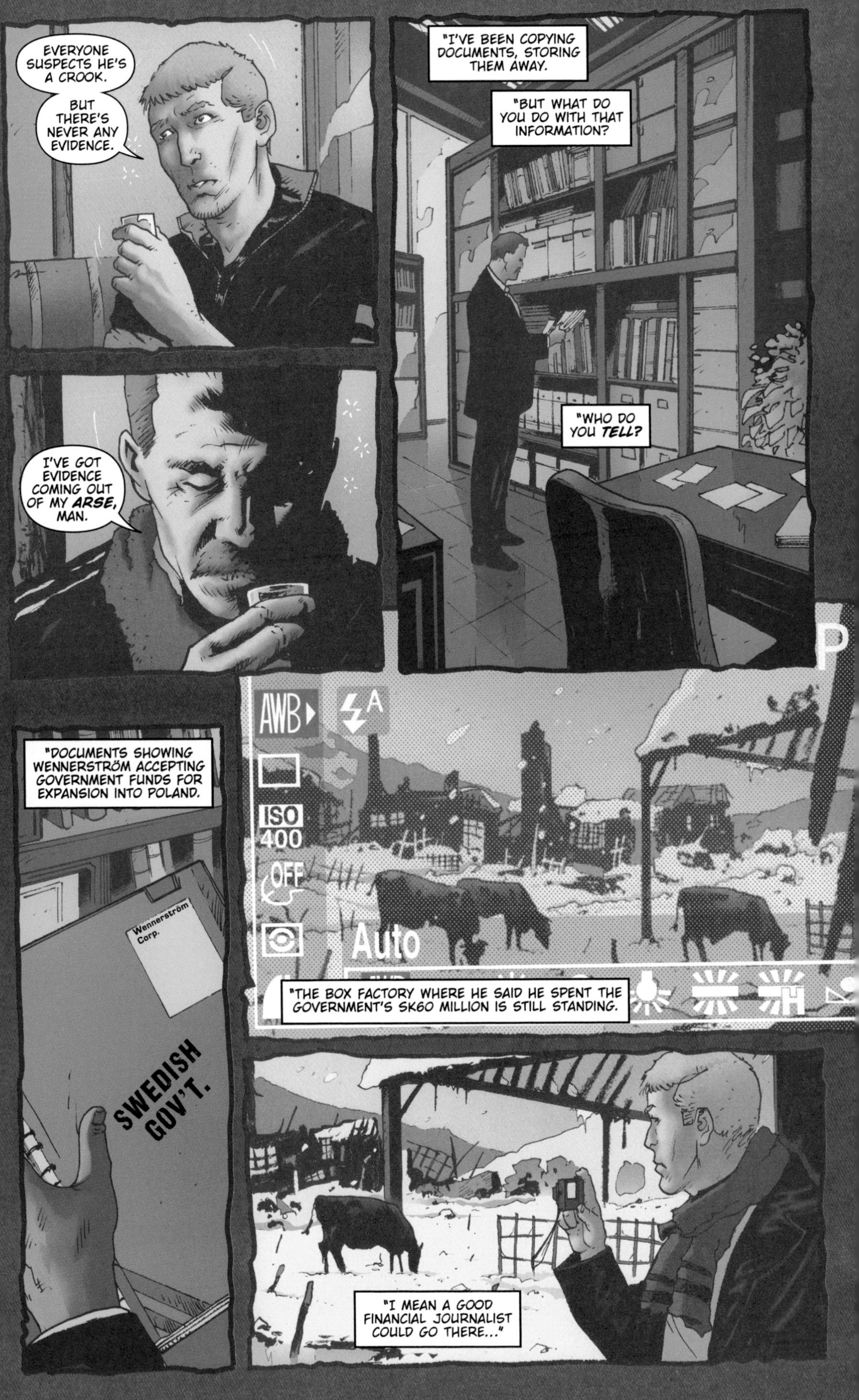
EVERYONE SUSPECTS HE'S A CROOK.
BUT THERE'S NEVER ANY EVIDENCE.
"I'VE BEEN COPYING DOCUMENTS, STORING THEM AWAY.
"BUT WHAT DO YOU DO WITH THAT INFORMATION?
"WHO DO YOU TELL?
I'VE GOT EVIDENCE COMING OUT OF MY ARSE, MAN.
"DOCUMENTS SHOWING WENNERSTRÖM ACCEPTING GOVERNMENT FUNDS FOR EXPANSION INTO POLAND.
Wennerström Corp.
SWEDISH GOV'T.
AWB
ISO 400
OFF
Auto
"THE BOX FACTORY WHERE HE SAID HE SPENT THE GOVERNMENT'S SK60 MILLION IS STILL STANDING.
"I MEAN A GOOD FINANCIAL JOURNALIST COULD GO THERE..."

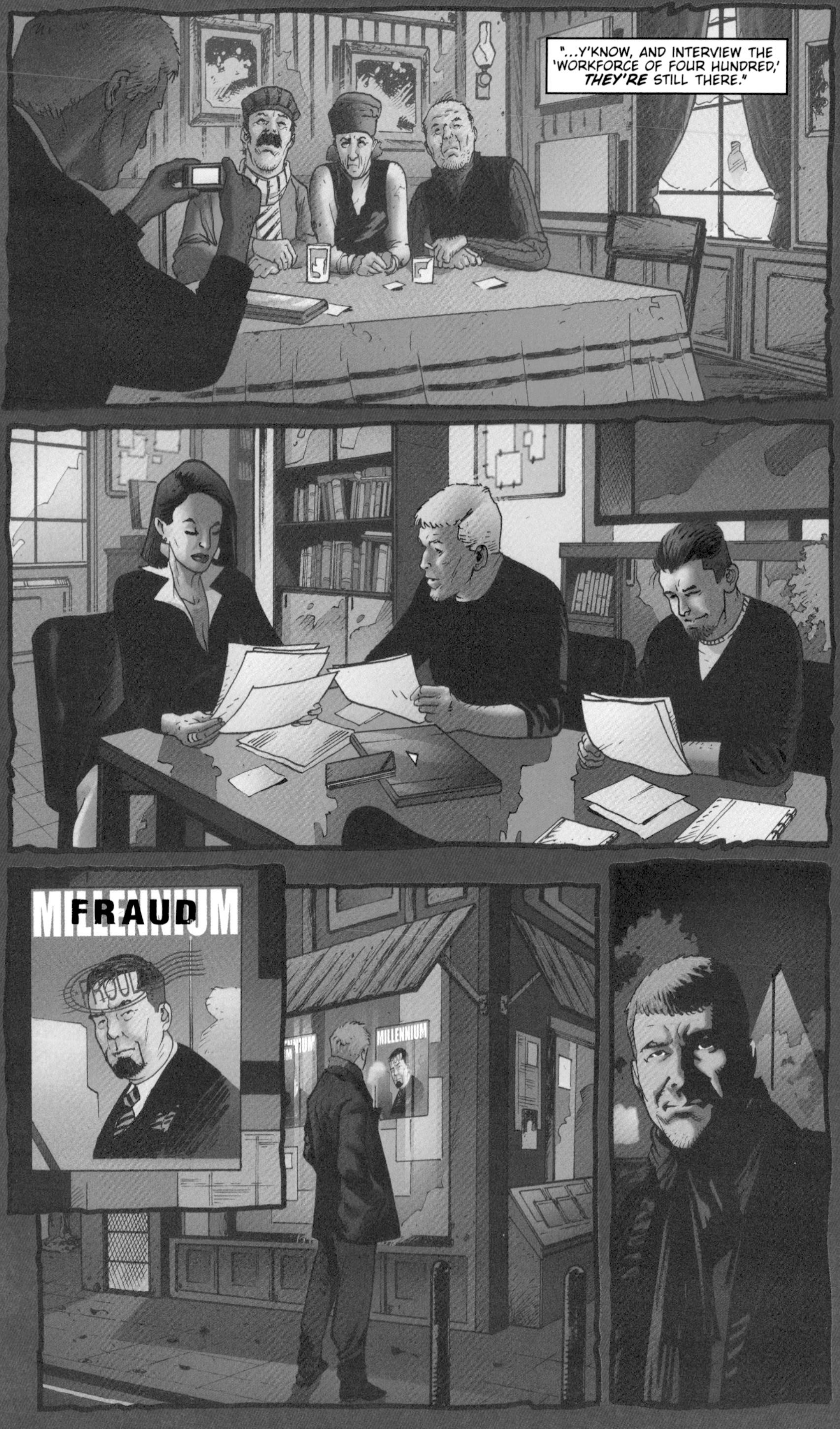
"...Y'KNOW, AND INTERVIEW THE 'WORKFORCE OF FOUR HUNDRED,' *THEY'RE* STILL THERE."
MILLENNIUM
FRAUD
MILLENNIUM

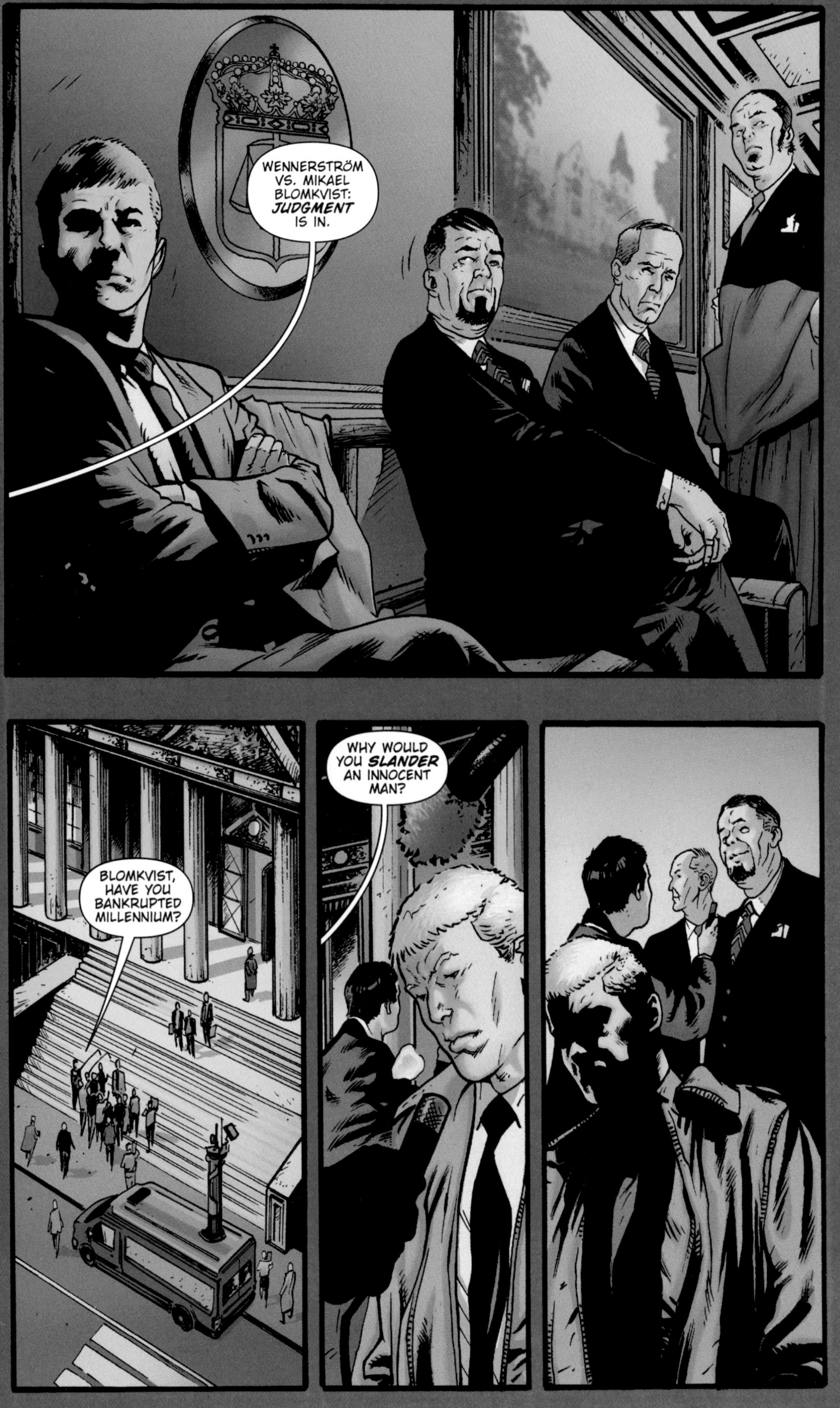
WENNERSTRÖM VS. MIKAEL BLOMKVIST: **JUDGMENT** IS IN.
BLOMKVIST, HAVE YOU BANKRUPTED MILLENNIUM?
WHY WOULD YOU **SLANDER** AN INNOCENT MAN?

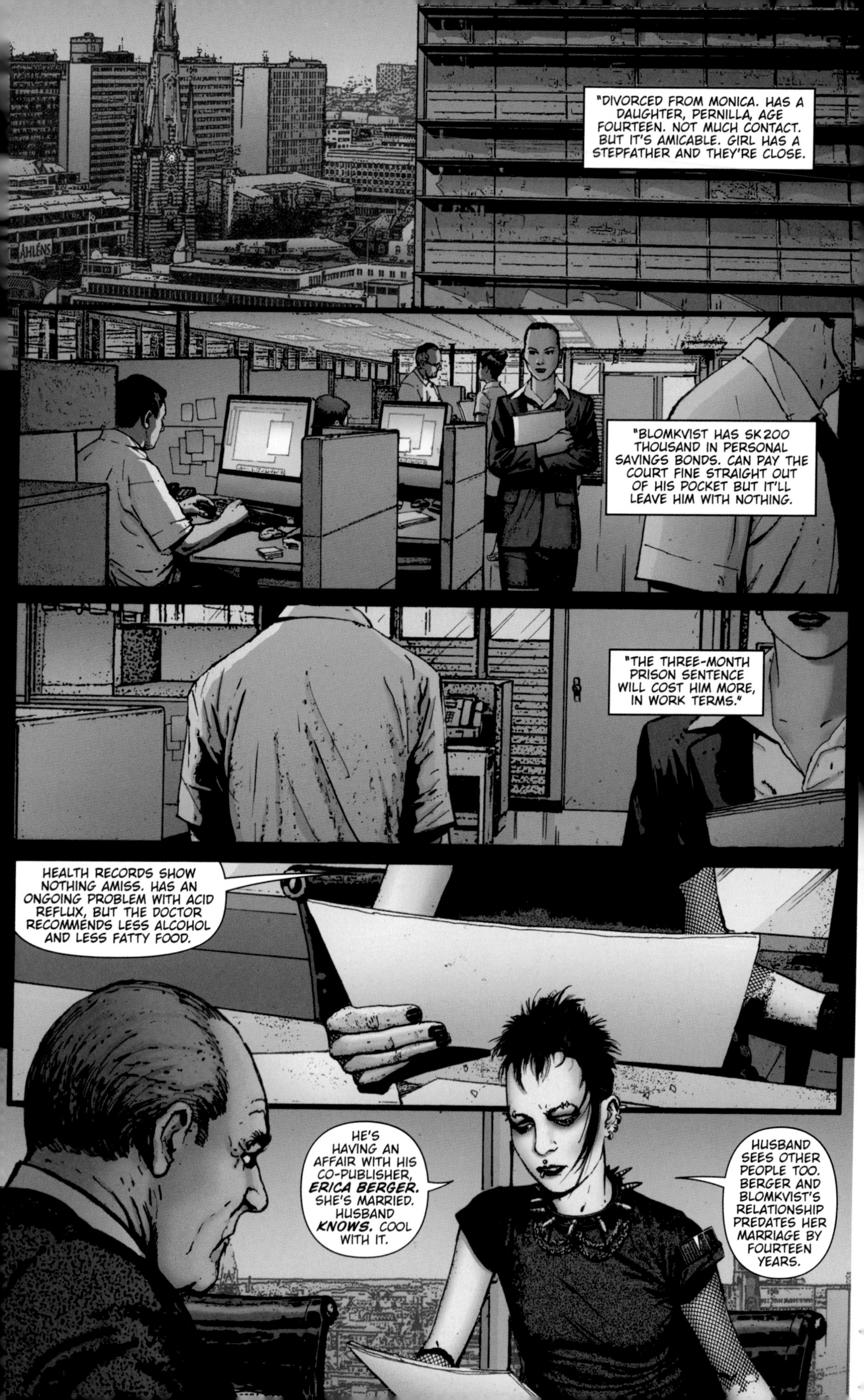
"DIVORCED FROM MONICA. HAS A DAUGHTER, PERNILLA, AGE FOURTEEN. NOT MUCH CONTACT. BUT IT'S AMICABLE. GIRL HAS A STEPFATHER AND THEY'RE CLOSE.
ÅHLÉNS
"BLOMKVIST HAS SK200 THOUSAND IN PERSONAL SAVINGS BONDS. CAN PAY THE COURT FINE STRAIGHT OUT OF HIS POCKET BUT IT'LL LEAVE HIM WITH NOTHING.
"THE THREE-MONTH PRISON SENTENCE WILL COST HIM MORE, IN WORK TERMS."
HEALTH RECORDS SHOW NOTHING AMISS. HAS AN ONGOING PROBLEM WITH ACID REFLUX, BUT THE DOCTOR RECOMMENDS LESS ALCOHOL AND LESS FATTY FOOD.
HE'S HAVING AN AFFAIR WITH HIS CO-PUBLISHER, ***ERICA BERGER.*** SHE'S MARRIED. HUSBAND ***KNOWS.*** COOL WITH IT.
HUSBAND SEES OTHER PEOPLE TOO. BERGER AND BLOMKVIST'S RELATIONSHIP PREDATES HER MARRIAGE BY FOURTEEN YEARS.

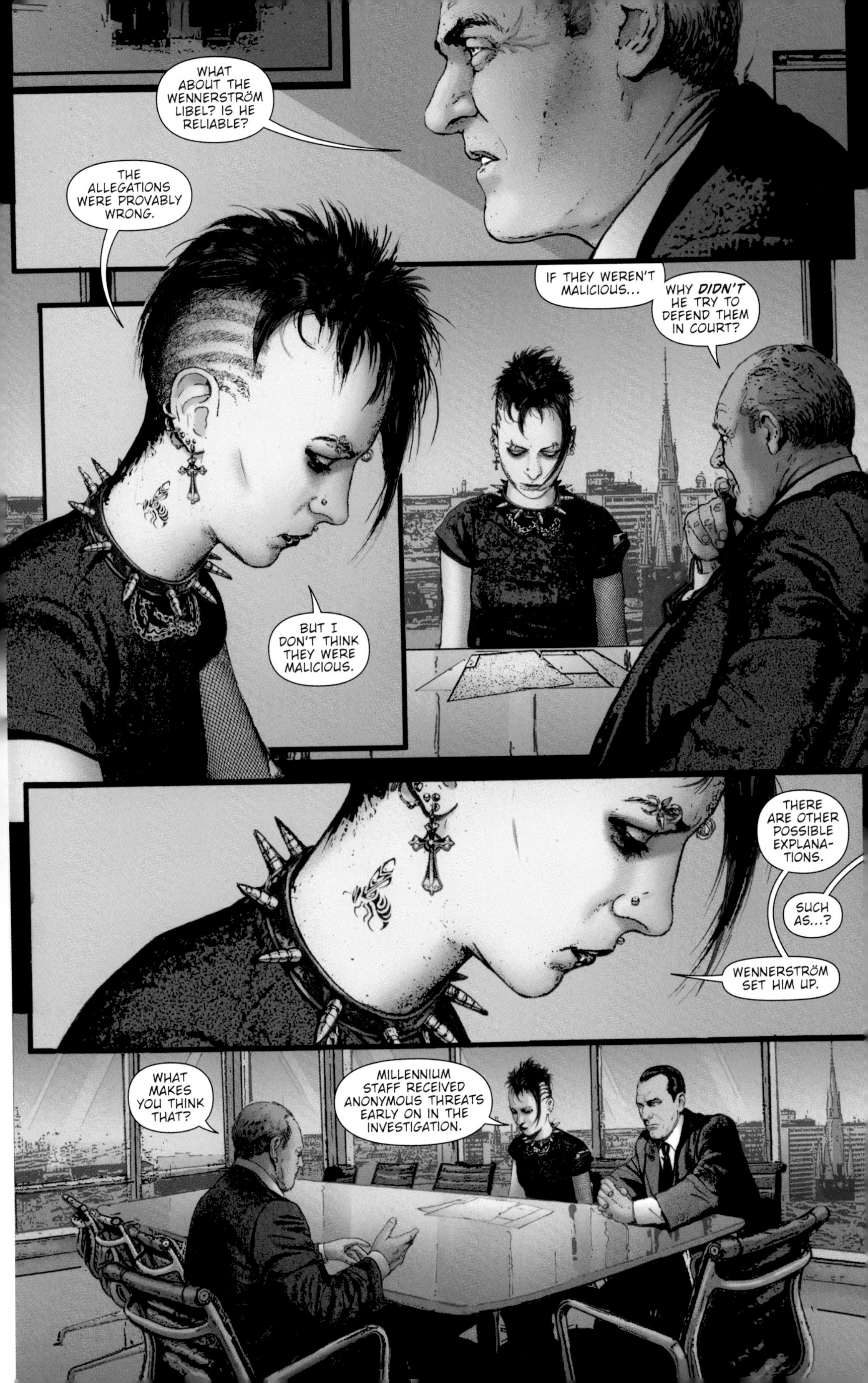
WHAT ABOUT THE WENNERSTRÖM LIBEL? IS HE RELIABLE?
THE ALLEGATIONS WERE PROVABLY WRONG.
BUT I DON'T THINK THEY WERE MALICIOUS.
IF THEY WEREN'T MALICIOUS...
WHY *DIDN'T* HE TRY TO DEFEND THEM IN COURT?
THERE ARE OTHER POSSIBLE EXPLANA-TIONS.
SUCH AS...?
WENNERSTRÖM SET HIM UP.
WHAT MAKES YOU THINK THAT?
MILLENNIUM STAFF RECEIVED ANONYMOUS THREATS EARLY ON IN THE INVESTIGATION.

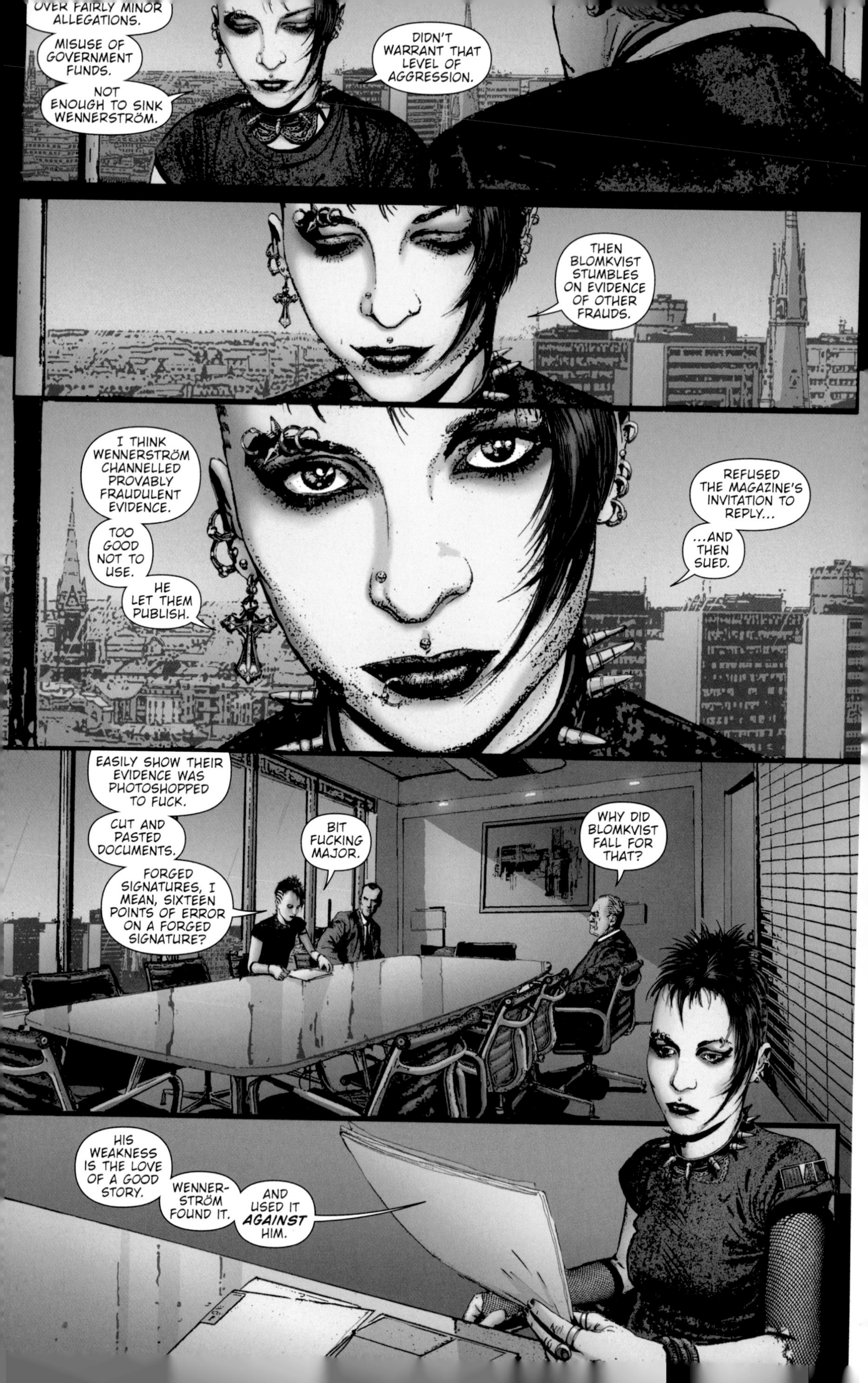
OVER FAIRLY MINOR ALLEGATIONS.
MISUSE OF GOVERNMENT FUNDS.
NOT ENOUGH TO SINK WENNERSTRÖM.
DIDN'T WARRANT THAT LEVEL OF AGGRESSION.
THEN BLOMKVIST STUMBLES ON EVIDENCE OF OTHER FRAUDS.
I THINK WENNERSTRÖM CHANNELLED PROVABLY FRAUDULENT EVIDENCE.
TOO GOOD NOT TO USE.
HE LET THEM PUBLISH.
REFUSED THE MAGAZINE'S INVITATION TO REPLY...
...AND THEN SUED.
EASILY SHOW THEIR EVIDENCE WAS PHOTOSHOPPED TO FUCK.
CUT AND PASTED DOCUMENTS.
FORGED SIGNATURES, I MEAN, SIXTEEN POINTS OF ERROR ON A FORGED SIGNATURE?
BIT FUCKING MAJOR.
WHY DID BLOMKVIST FALL FOR THAT?
HIS WEAKNESS IS THE LOVE OF A GOOD STORY.
WENNER-STRÖM FOUND IT.
AND USED IT *AGAINST* HIM.

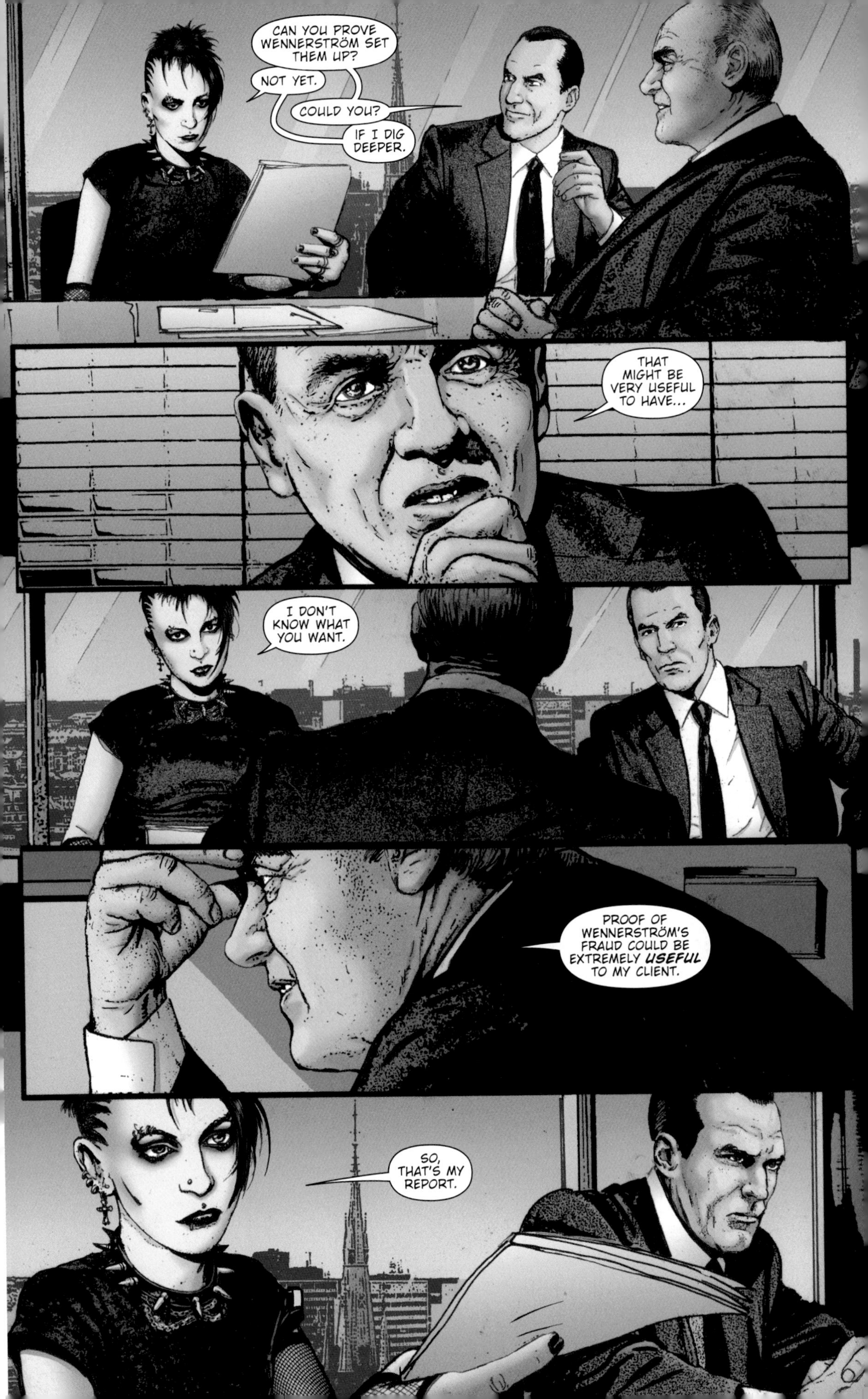
CAN YOU PROVE WENNERSTRÖM SET THEM UP?
NOT YET.
COULD YOU?
IF I DIG DEEPER.
THAT MIGHT BE VERY USEFUL TO HAVE...
I DON'T KNOW WHAT YOU WANT.
PROOF OF WENNERSTRÖM'S FRAUD COULD BE EXTREMELY *USEFUL* TO MY CLIENT.
SO, THAT'S MY REPORT.

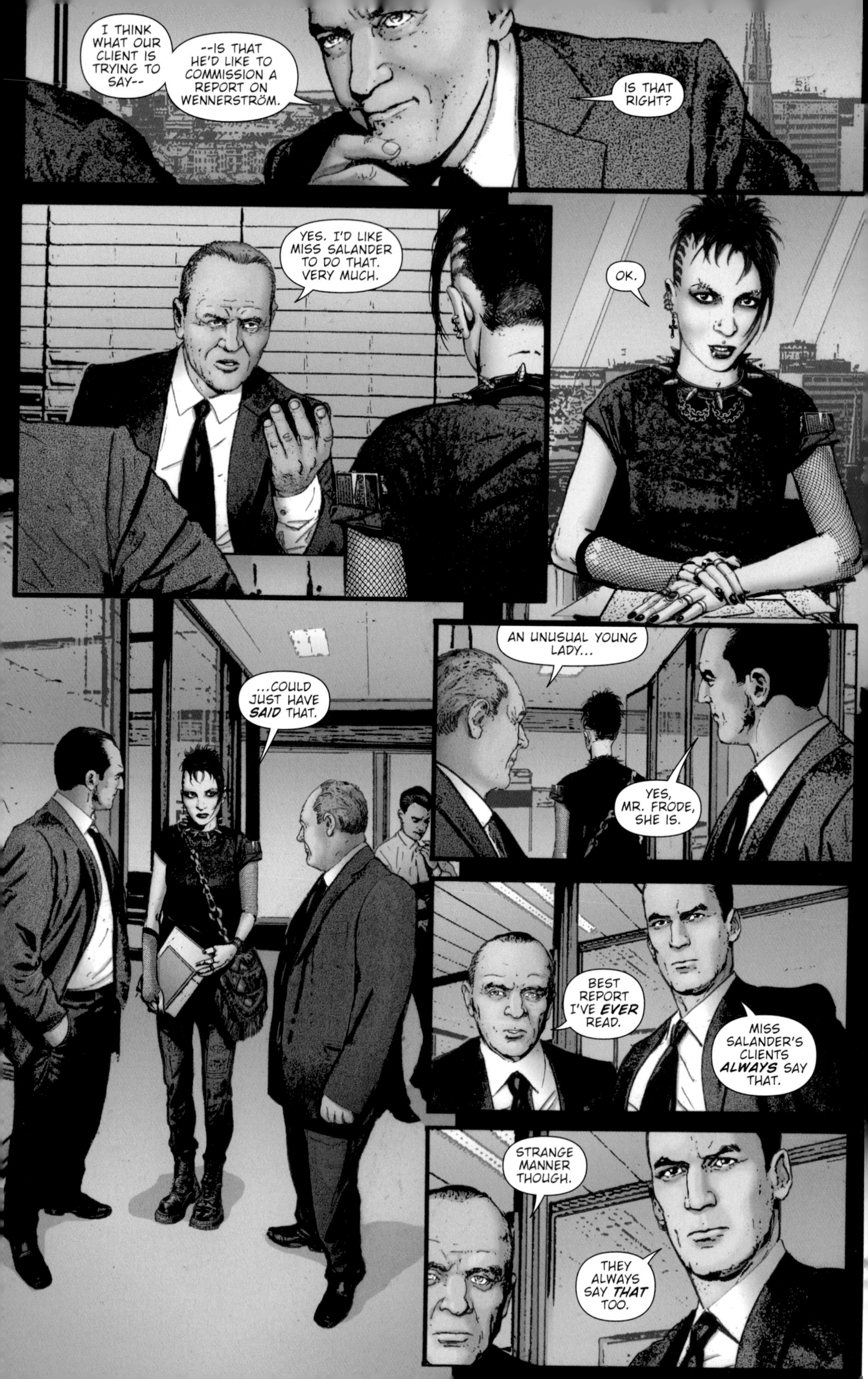
I THINK WHAT OUR CLIENT IS TRYING TO SAY--
--IS THAT HE'D LIKE TO COMMISSION A REPORT ON WENNERSTRÖM.
IS THAT RIGHT?
YES. I'D LIKE MISS SALANDER TO DO THAT. VERY MUCH.
OK.
...COULD JUST HAVE *SAID* THAT.
AN UNUSUAL YOUNG LADY...
YES, MR. FRODE, SHE IS.
BEST REPORT I'VE *EVER* READ.
MISS SALANDER'S CLIENTS *ALWAYS* SAY THAT.
STRANGE MANNER THOUGH.
THEY ALWAYS SAY *THAT* TOO.

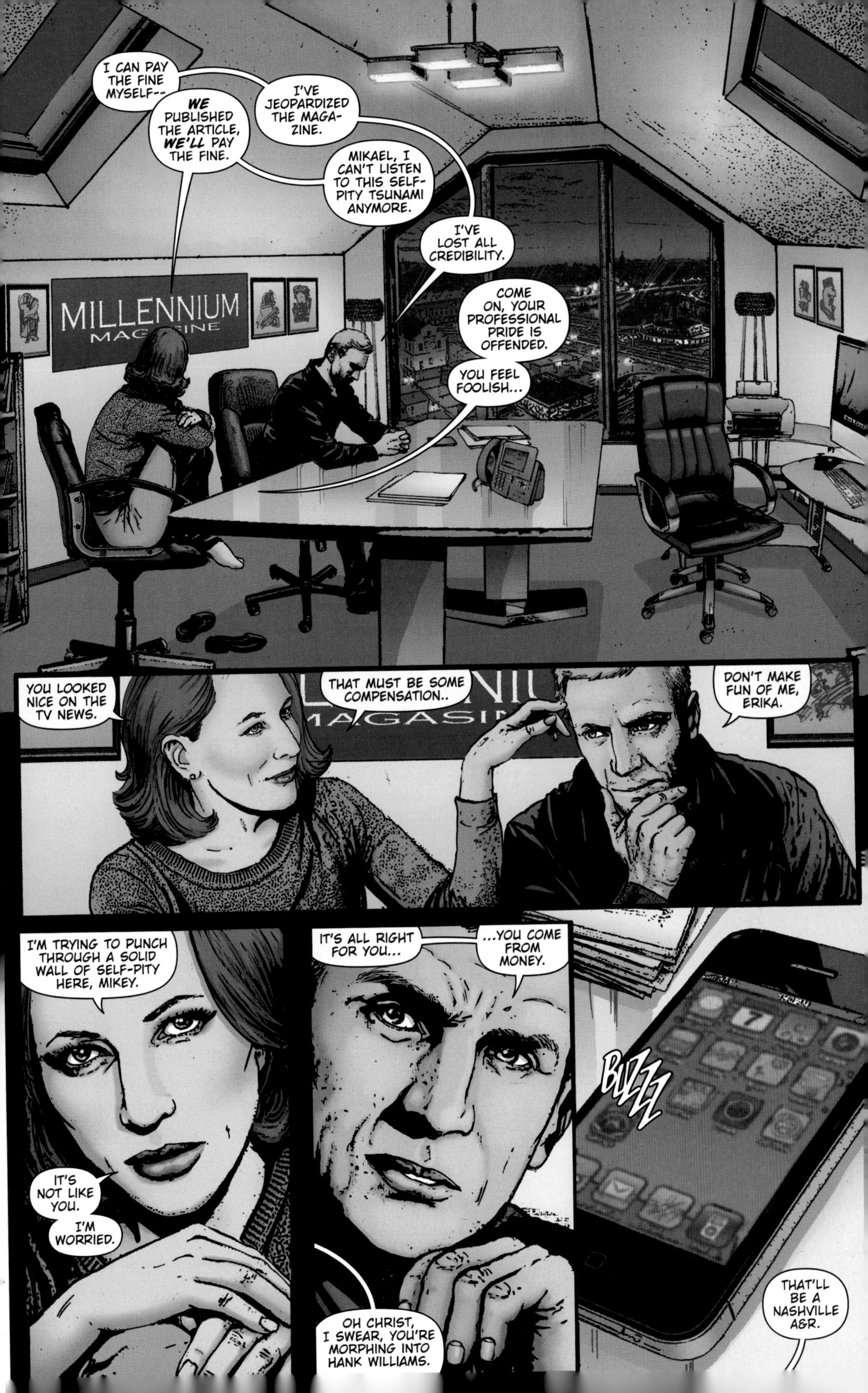
I CAN PAY THE FINE MYSELF--
WE PUBLISHED THE ARTICLE, WE'LL PAY THE FINE.
I'VE JEOPARDIZED THE MAGAZINE.
MIKAEL, I CAN'T LISTEN TO THIS SELF-PITY TSUNAMI ANYMORE.
I'VE LOST ALL CREDIBILITY.
COME ON, YOUR PROFESSIONAL PRIDE IS OFFENDED.
YOU FEEL FOOLISH...
MILLENNIUM MAGASINE
YOU LOOKED NICE ON THE TV NEWS.
THAT MUST BE SOME COMPENSATION..
DON'T MAKE FUN OF ME, ERIKA.
I'M TRYING TO PUNCH THROUGH A SOLID WALL OF SELF-PITY HERE, MIKEY.
IT'S NOT LIKE YOU.
I'M WORRIED.
IT'S ALL RIGHT FOR YOU...
...YOU COME FROM MONEY.
OH CHRIST, I SWEAR, YOU'RE MORPHING INTO HANK WILLIAMS.
BUZZZ
THAT'LL BE A NASHVILLE A&R.

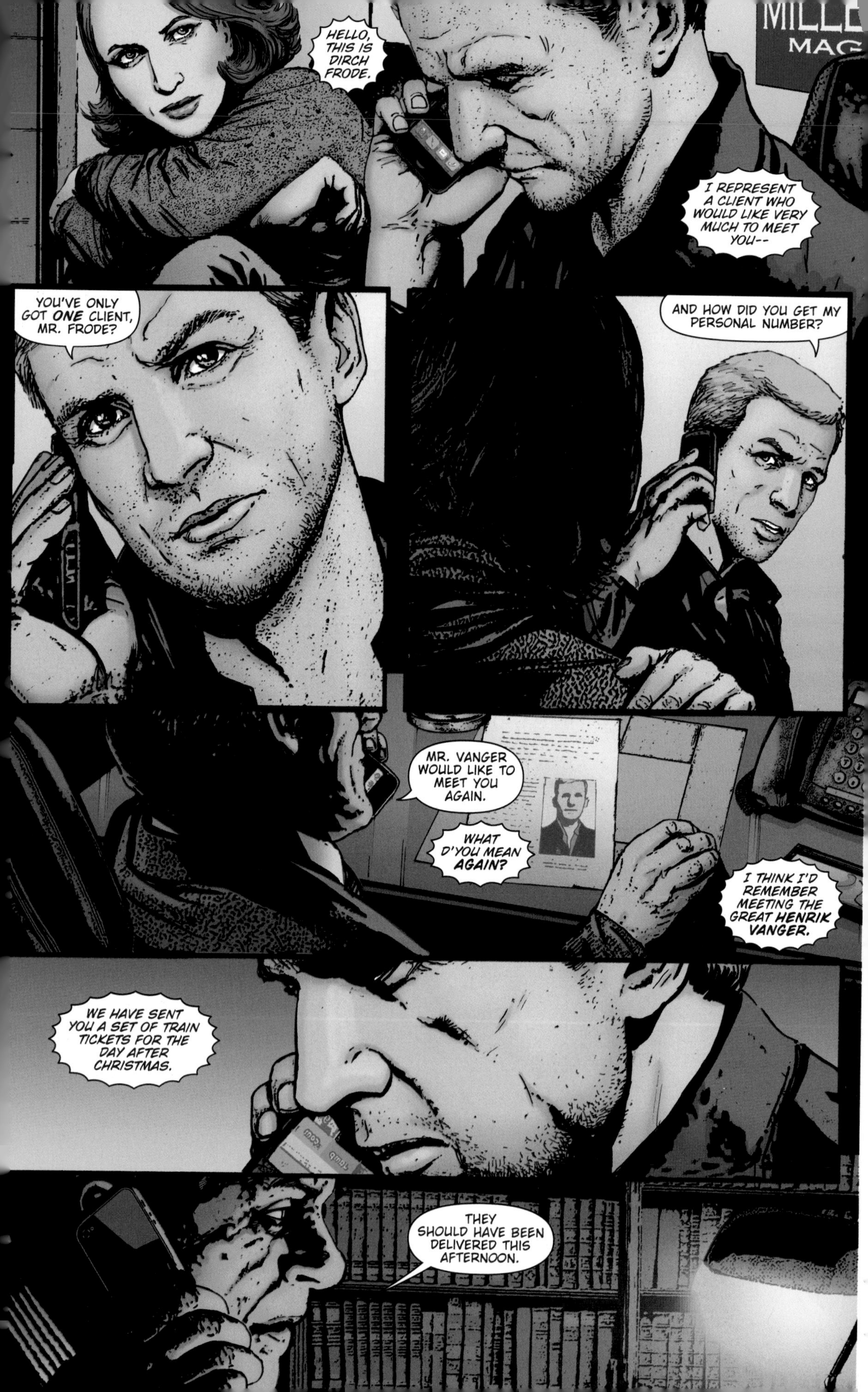
MILLE
MAG
HELLO, THIS IS DIRCH FRODE.
I REPRESENT A CLIENT WHO WOULD LIKE VERY MUCH TO MEET YOU--
YOU'VE ONLY GOT ONE CLIENT, MR. FRODE?
AND HOW DID YOU GET MY PERSONAL NUMBER?
MR. VANGER WOULD LIKE TO MEET YOU AGAIN.
WHAT D'YOU MEAN AGAIN?
I THINK I'D REMEMBER MEETING THE GREAT HENRIK VANGER.
WE HAVE SENT YOU A SET OF TRAIN TICKETS FOR THE DAY AFTER CHRISTMAS.
THEY SHOULD HAVE BEEN DELIVERED THIS AFTERNOON.

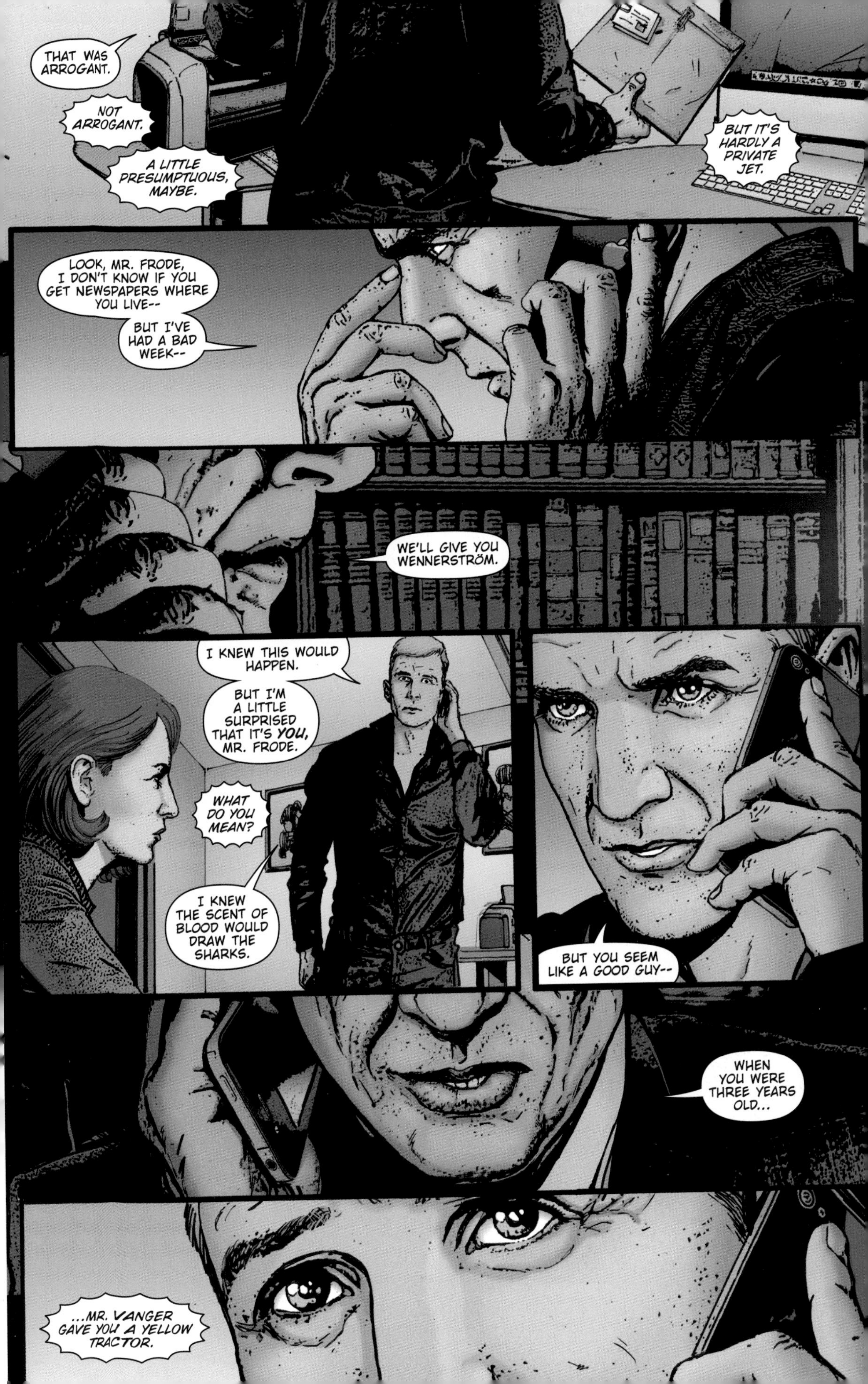
THAT WAS ARROGANT.
NOT ARROGANT.
A LITTLE PRESUMPTUOUS, MAYBE.
BUT IT'S HARDLY A PRIVATE JET.
LOOK, MR. FRODE, I DON'T KNOW IF YOU GET NEWSPAPERS WHERE YOU LIVE--
BUT I'VE HAD A BAD WEEK--
WE'LL GIVE YOU WENNERSTRÖM.
I KNEW THIS WOULD HAPPEN.
BUT I'M A LITTLE SURPRISED THAT IT'S YOU, MR. FRODE.
WHAT DO YOU MEAN?
I KNEW THE SCENT OF BLOOD WOULD DRAW THE SHARKS.
BUT YOU SEEM LIKE A GOOD GUY--
WHEN YOU WERE THREE YEARS OLD...
...MR. VANGER GAVE YOU A YELLOW TRACTOR.

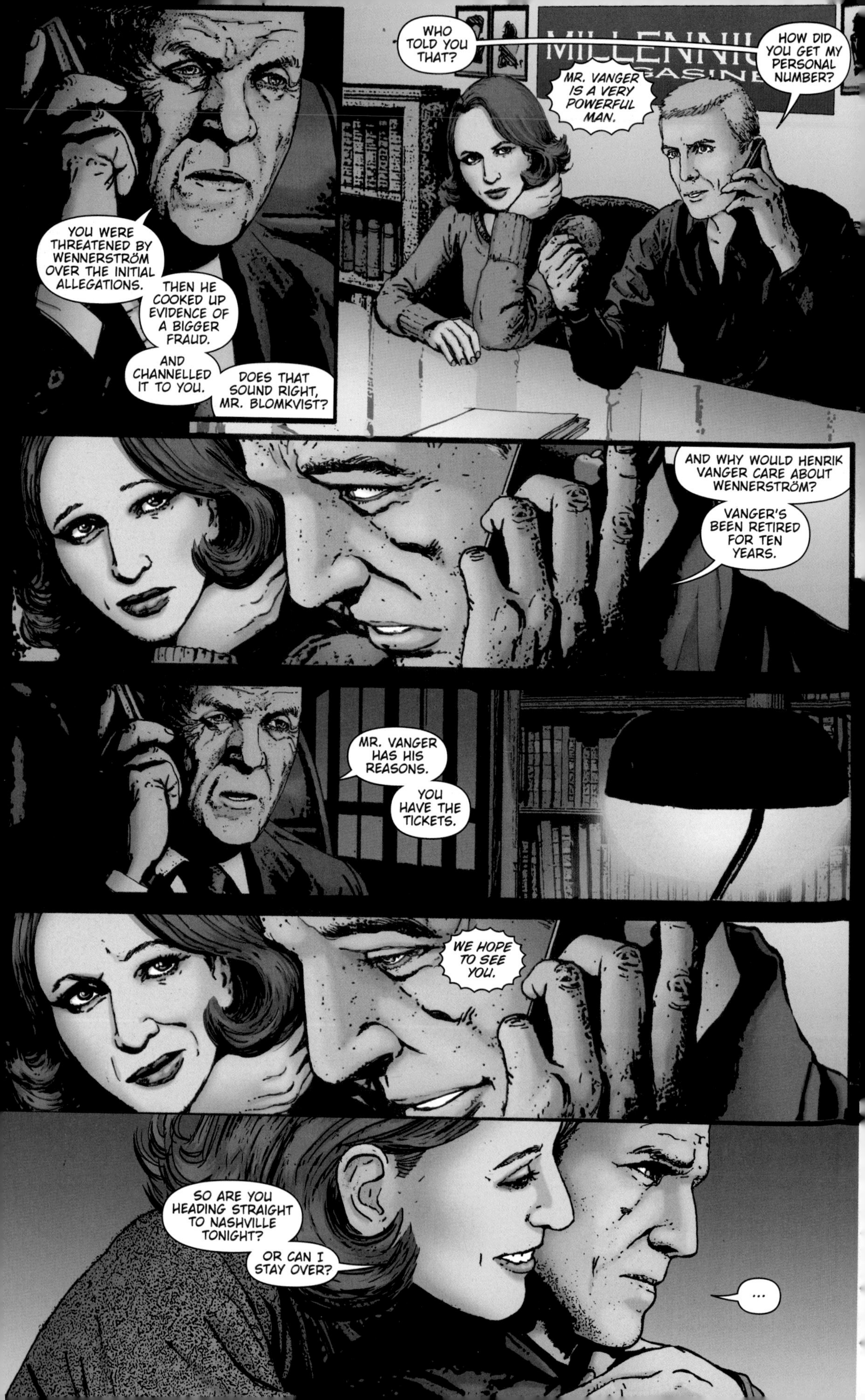
YOU WERE THREATENED BY WENNERSTRÖM OVER THE INITIAL ALLEGATIONS.
THEN HE COOKED UP EVIDENCE OF A BIGGER FRAUD.
AND CHANNELLED IT TO YOU.
DOES THAT SOUND RIGHT, MR. BLOMKVIST?
WHO TOLD YOU THAT?
MR. VANGER IS A VERY POWERFUL MAN.
HOW DID YOU GET MY PERSONAL NUMBER?
AND WHY WOULD HENRIK VANGER CARE ABOUT WENNERSTRÖM?
VANGER'S BEEN RETIRED FOR TEN YEARS.
MR. VANGER HAS HIS REASONS.
YOU HAVE THE TICKETS.
WE HOPE TO SEE YOU.
SO ARE YOU HEADING STRAIGHT TO NASHVILLE TONIGHT?
OR CAN I STAY OVER?
...

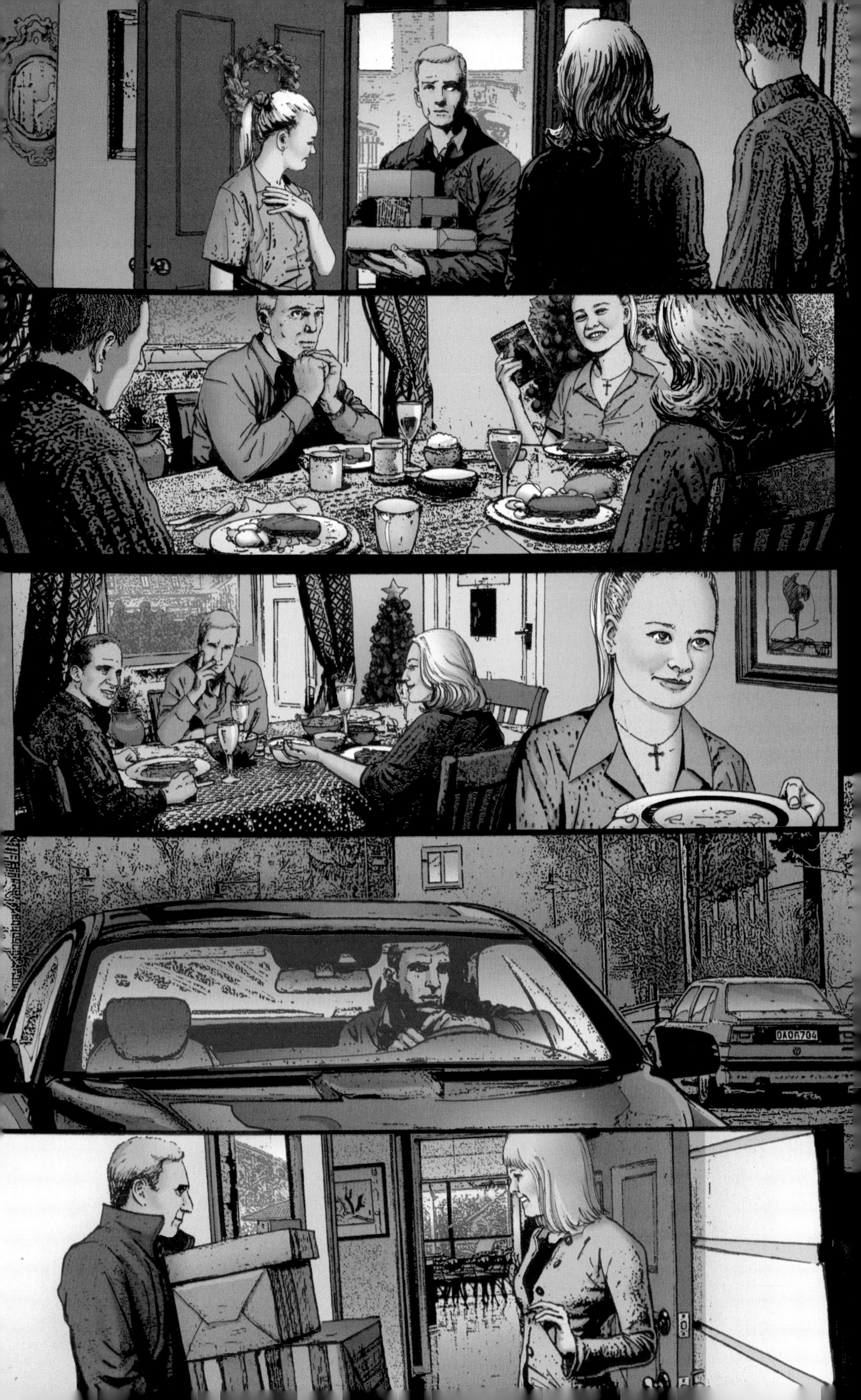

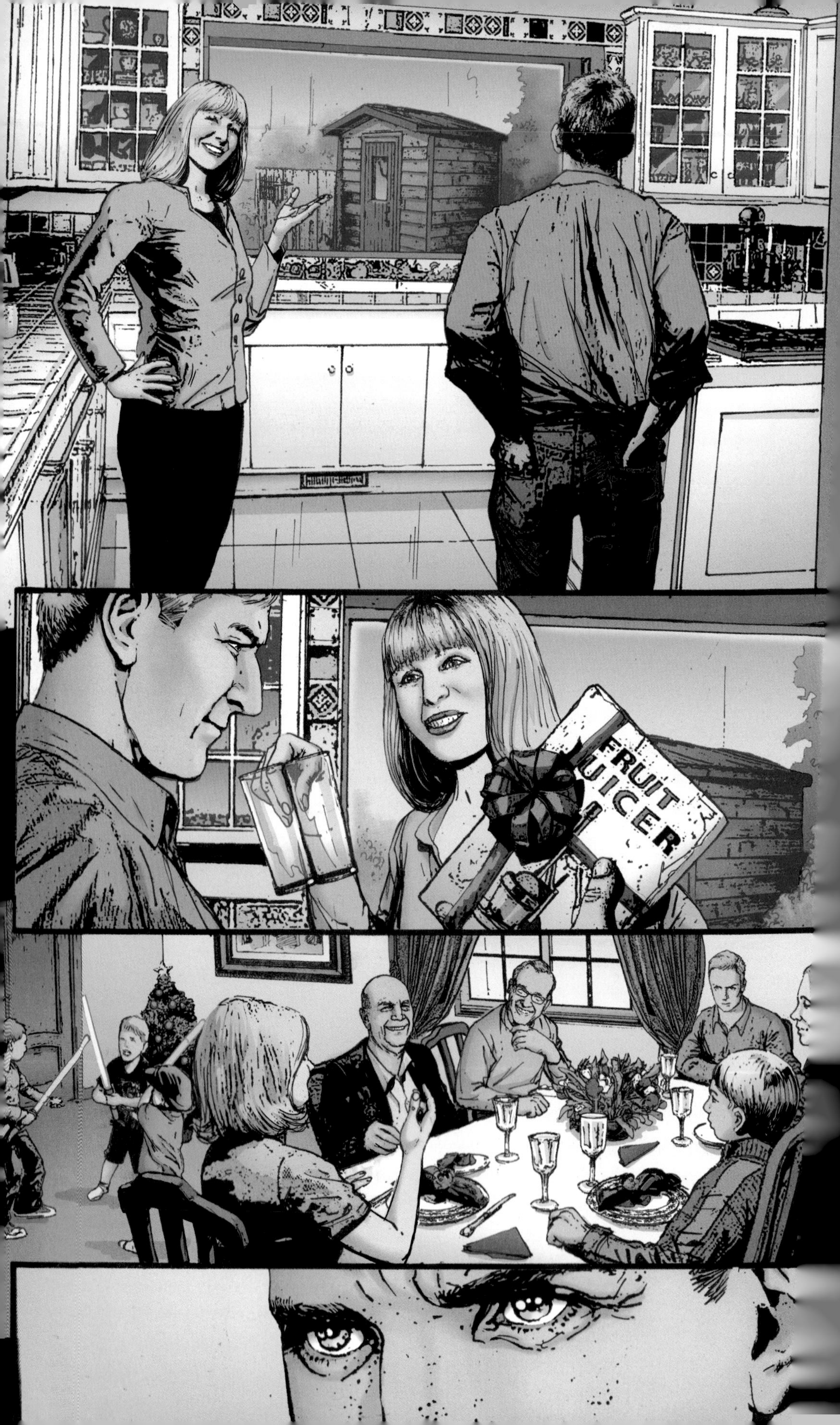
FRUIT
UICER

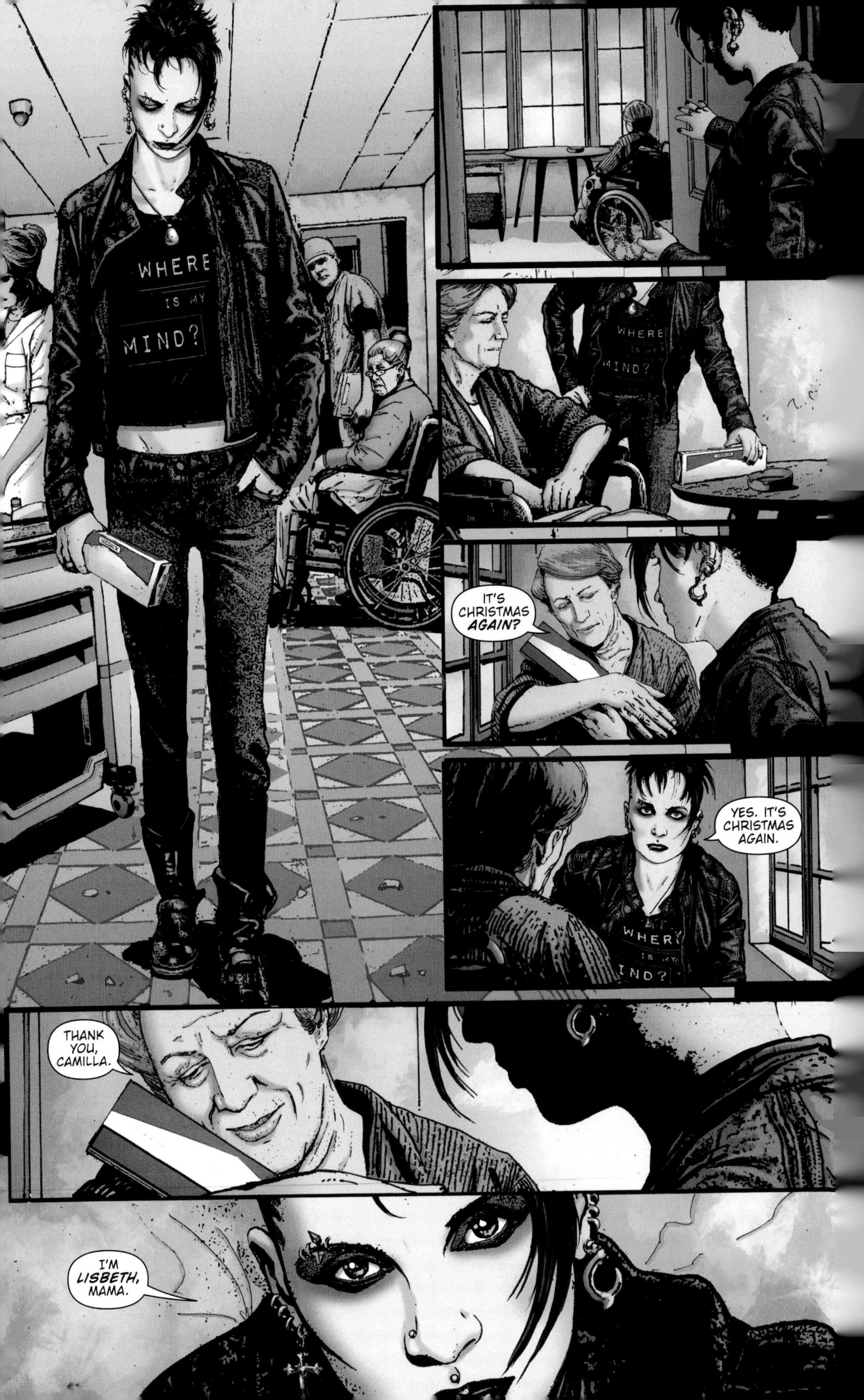
WHERE IS MY MIND?
WHERE IS MY MIND?
IT'S CHRISTMAS *AGAIN?*
YES. IT'S CHRISTMAS AGAIN.
WHERE IS MY MIND?
THANK YOU, CAMILLA.
I'M *LISBETH,* MAMA.

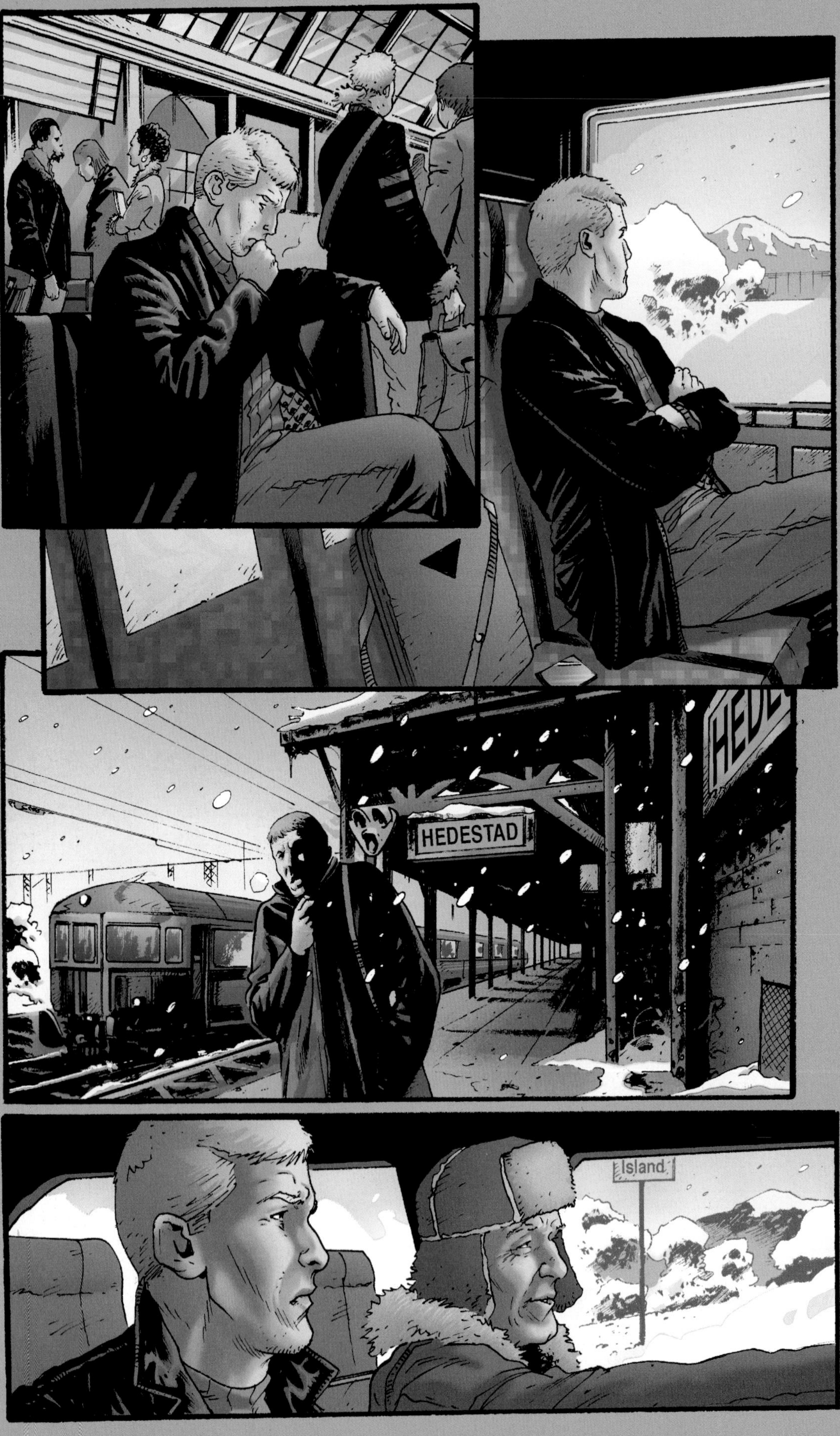
HEDESTAD
Island

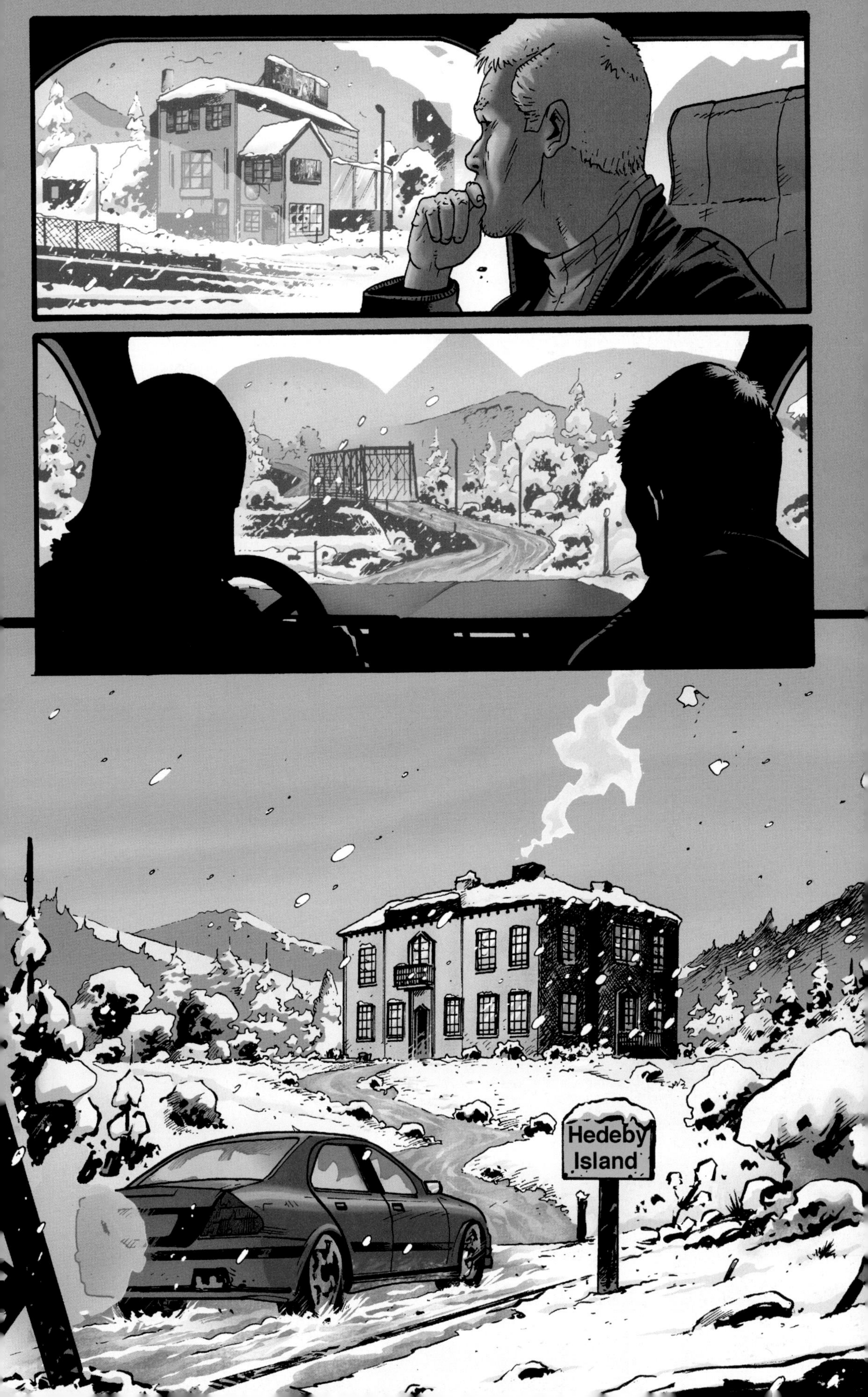
Hedeby Island

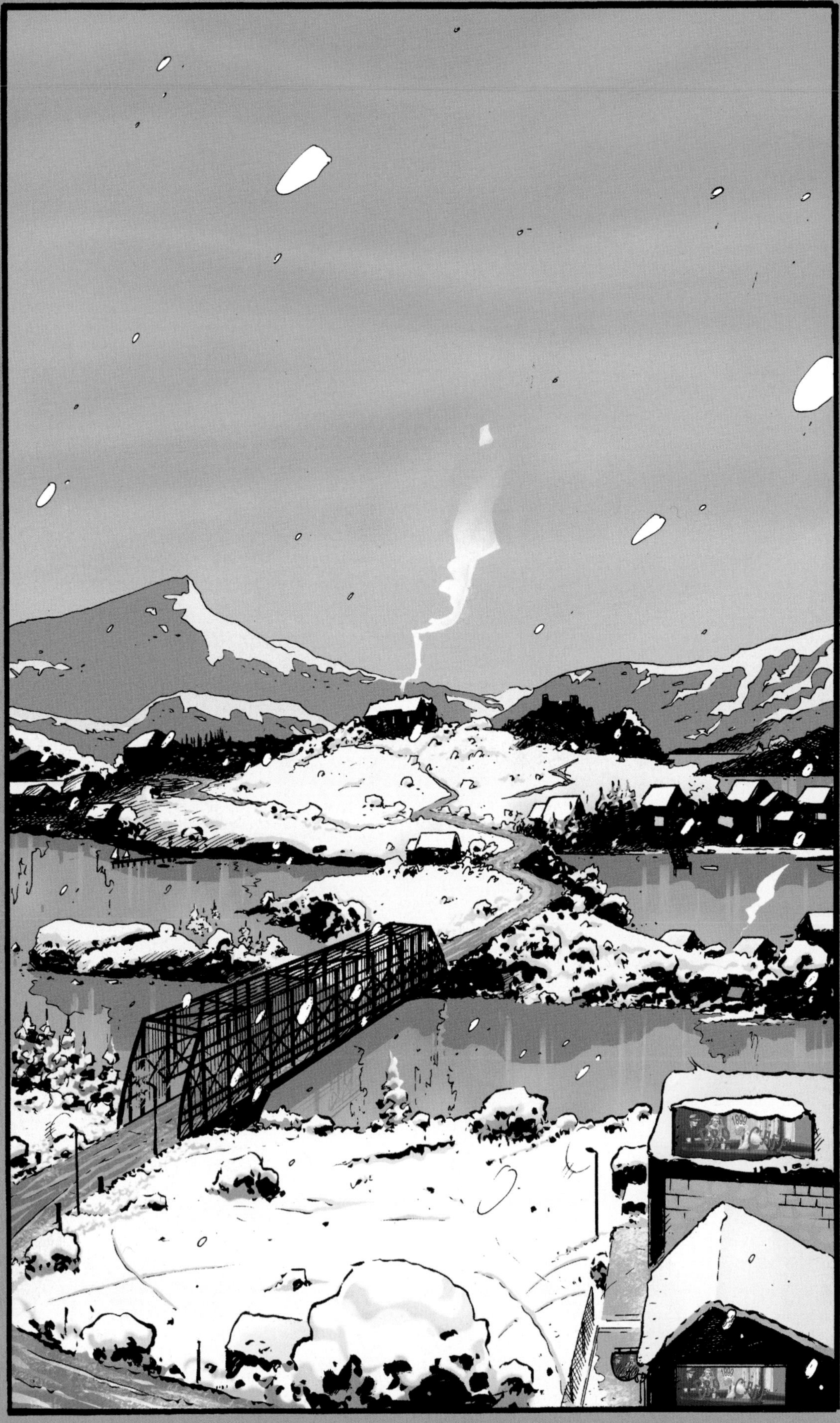

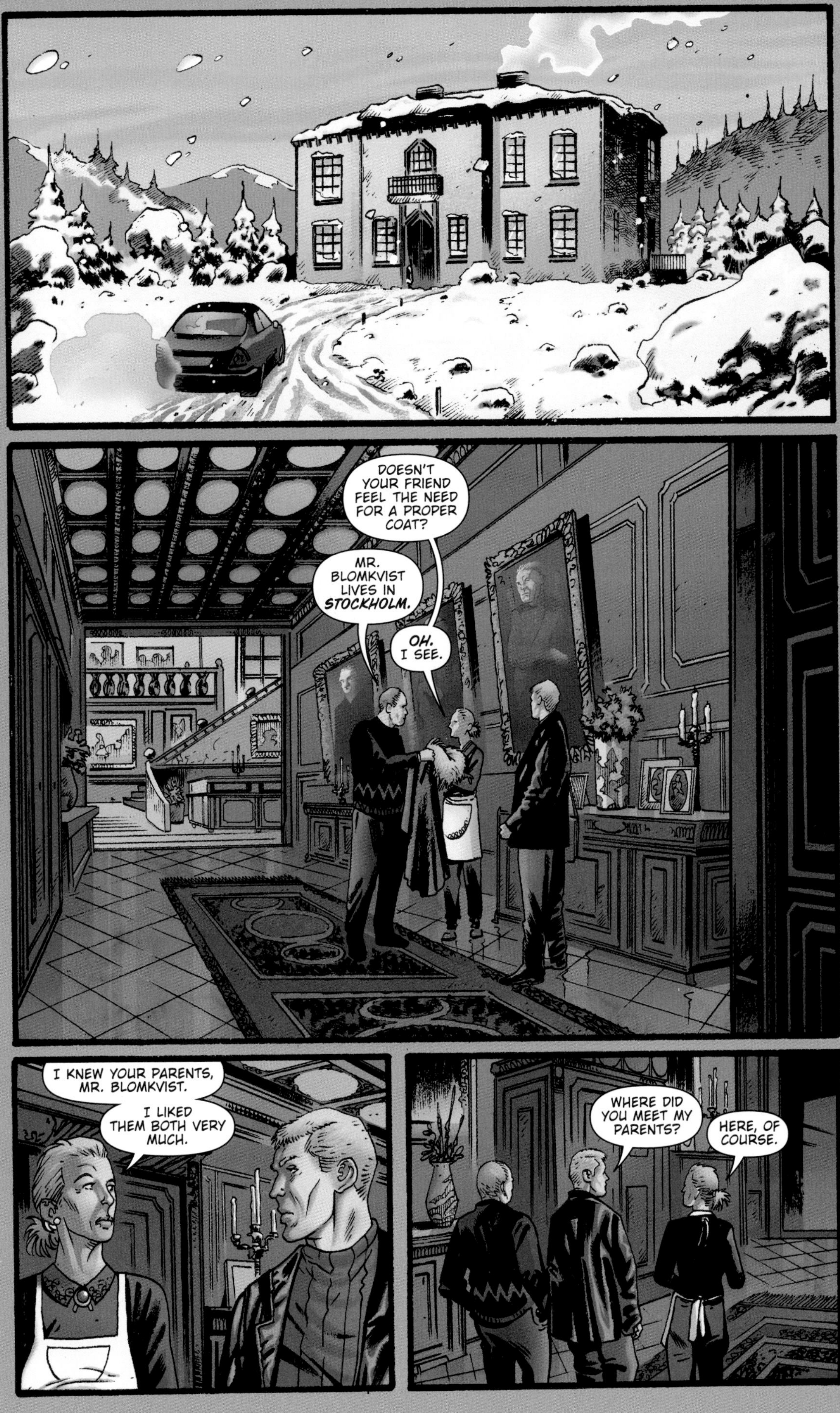
DOESN'T YOUR FRIEND FEEL THE NEED FOR A PROPER COAT?
MR. BLOMKVIST LIVES IN **STOCKHOLM.**
OH. I SEE.
I KNEW YOUR PARENTS, MR. BLOMKVIST.
I LIKED THEM BOTH VERY MUCH.
WHERE DID YOU MEET MY PARENTS?
HERE, OF COURSE.

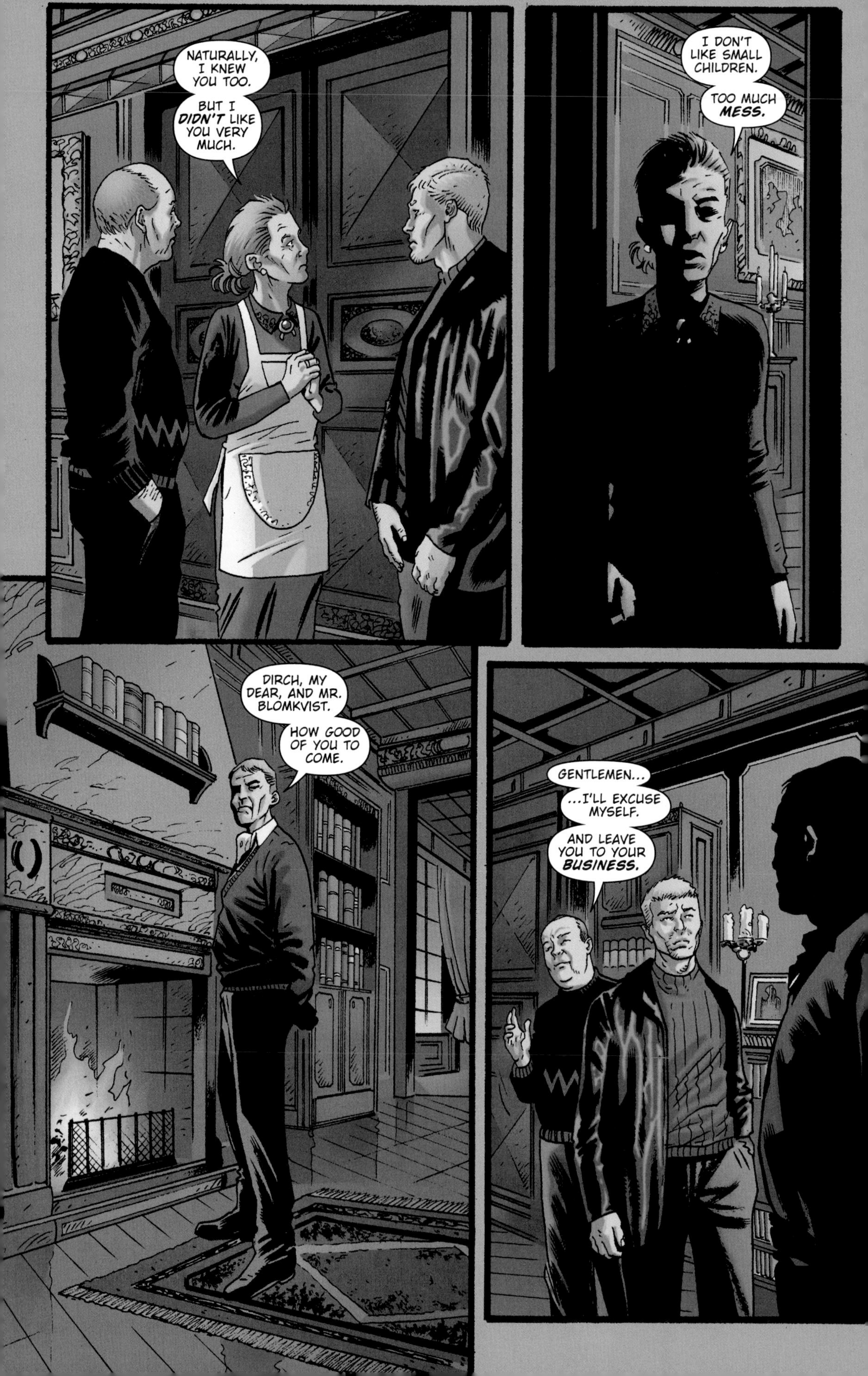
NATURALLY, I KNEW YOU TOO.
BUT I *DIDN'T* LIKE YOU VERY MUCH.
I DON'T LIKE SMALL CHILDREN.
TOO MUCH **MESS.**
DIRCH, MY DEAR, AND MR. BLOMKVIST.
HOW GOOD OF YOU TO COME.
GENTLEMEN...
...I'LL EXCUSE MYSELF.
AND LEAVE YOU TO YOUR ***BUSINESS.***

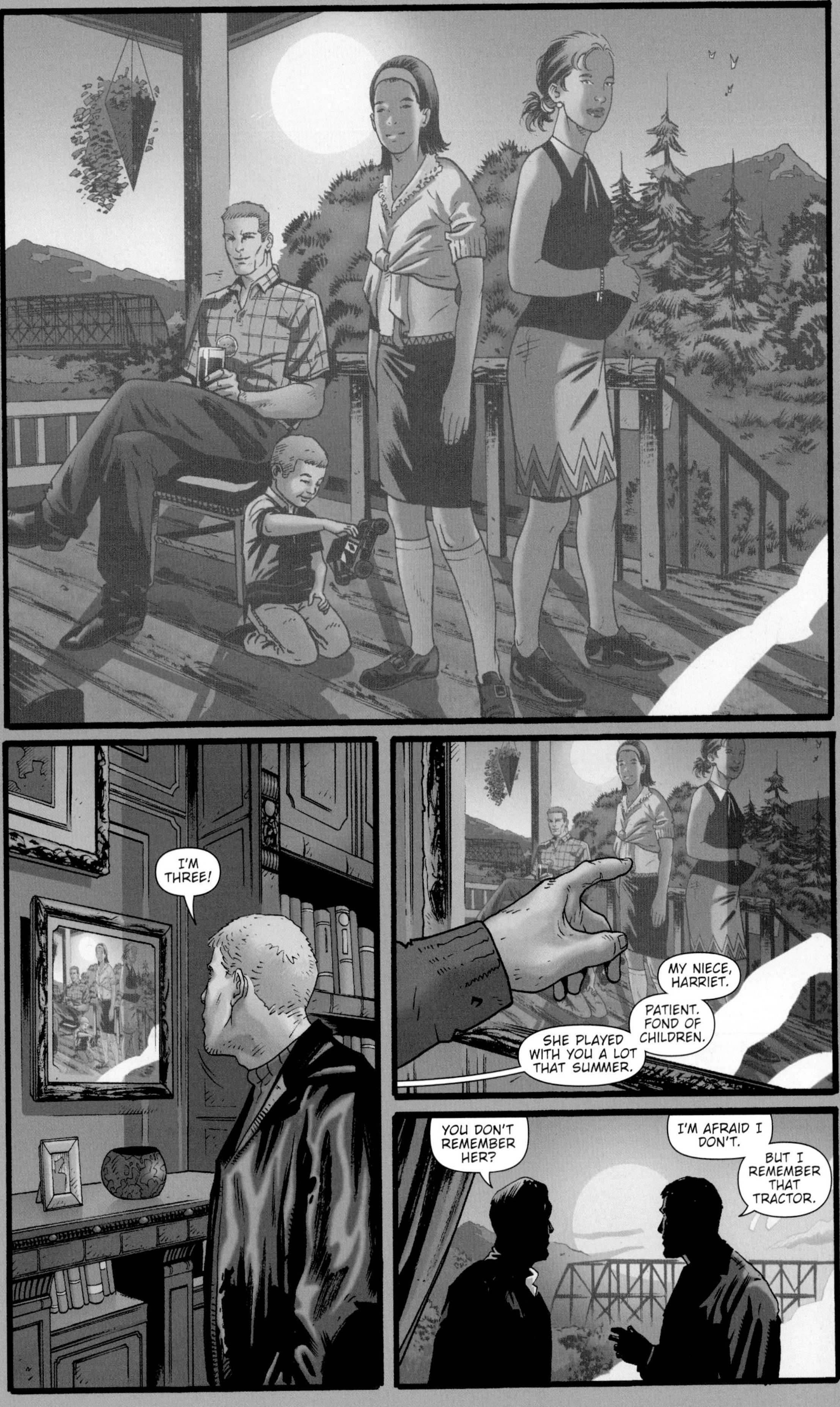
I'M THREE!
MY NIECE, HARRIET.
PATIENT. FOND OF CHILDREN.
SHE PLAYED WITH YOU A LOT THAT SUMMER.
YOU DON'T REMEMBER HER?
I'M AFRAID I DON'T.
BUT I REMEMBER THAT TRACTOR.

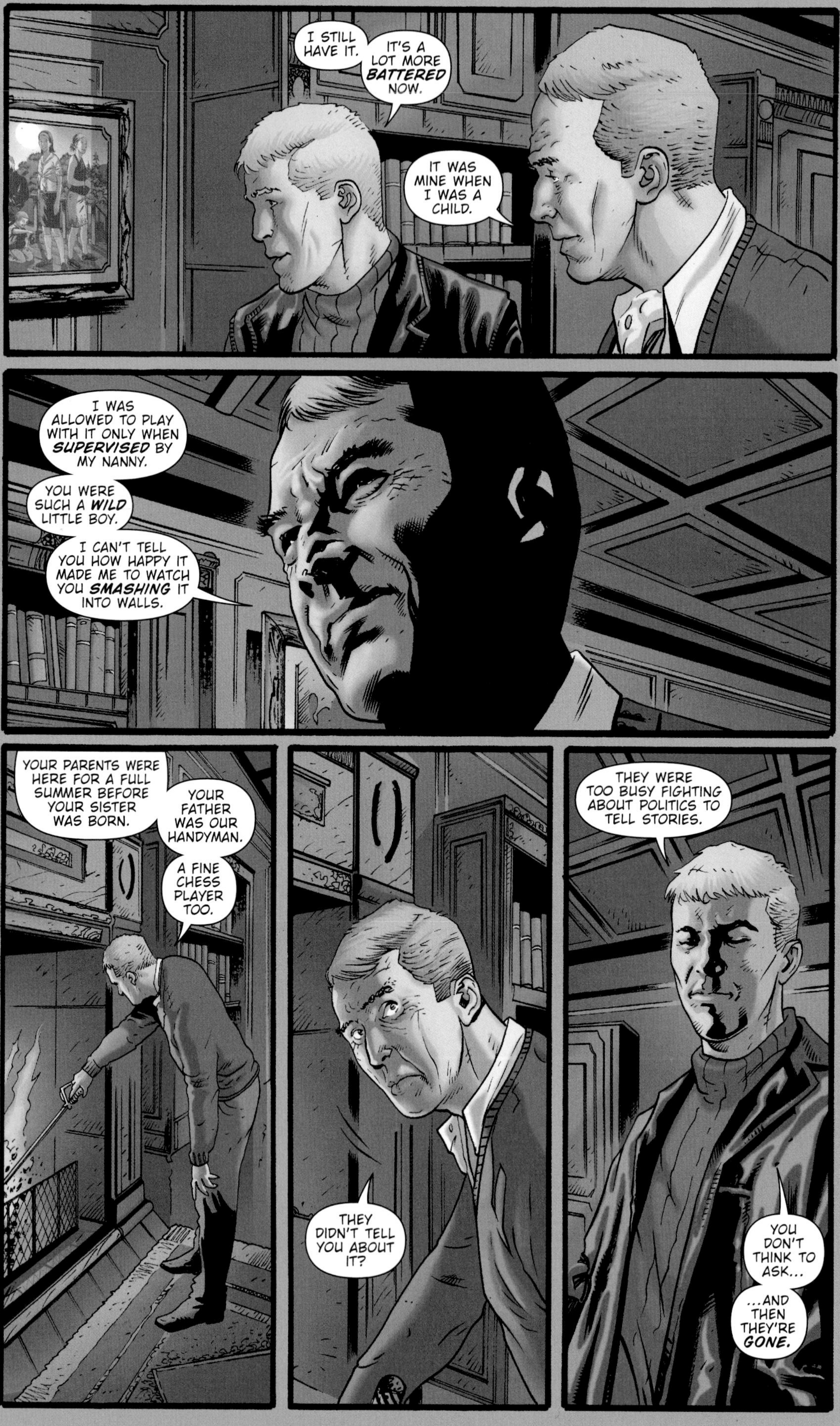
I STILL HAVE IT.
IT'S A LOT MORE **BATTERED** NOW.
IT WAS MINE WHEN I WAS A CHILD.
I WAS ALLOWED TO PLAY WITH IT ONLY WHEN **SUPERVISED** BY MY NANNY.
YOU WERE SUCH A **WILD** LITTLE BOY.
I CAN'T TELL YOU HOW HAPPY IT MADE ME TO WATCH YOU **SMASHING** IT INTO WALLS.
YOUR PARENTS WERE HERE FOR A FULL SUMMER BEFORE YOUR SISTER WAS BORN.
YOUR FATHER WAS OUR HANDYMAN.
A FINE CHESS PLAYER TOO.
THEY DIDN'T TELL YOU ABOUT IT?
THEY WERE TOO BUSY FIGHTING ABOUT POLITICS TO TELL STORIES.
YOU DON'T THINK TO ASK...
...AND THEN THEY'RE **GONE.**

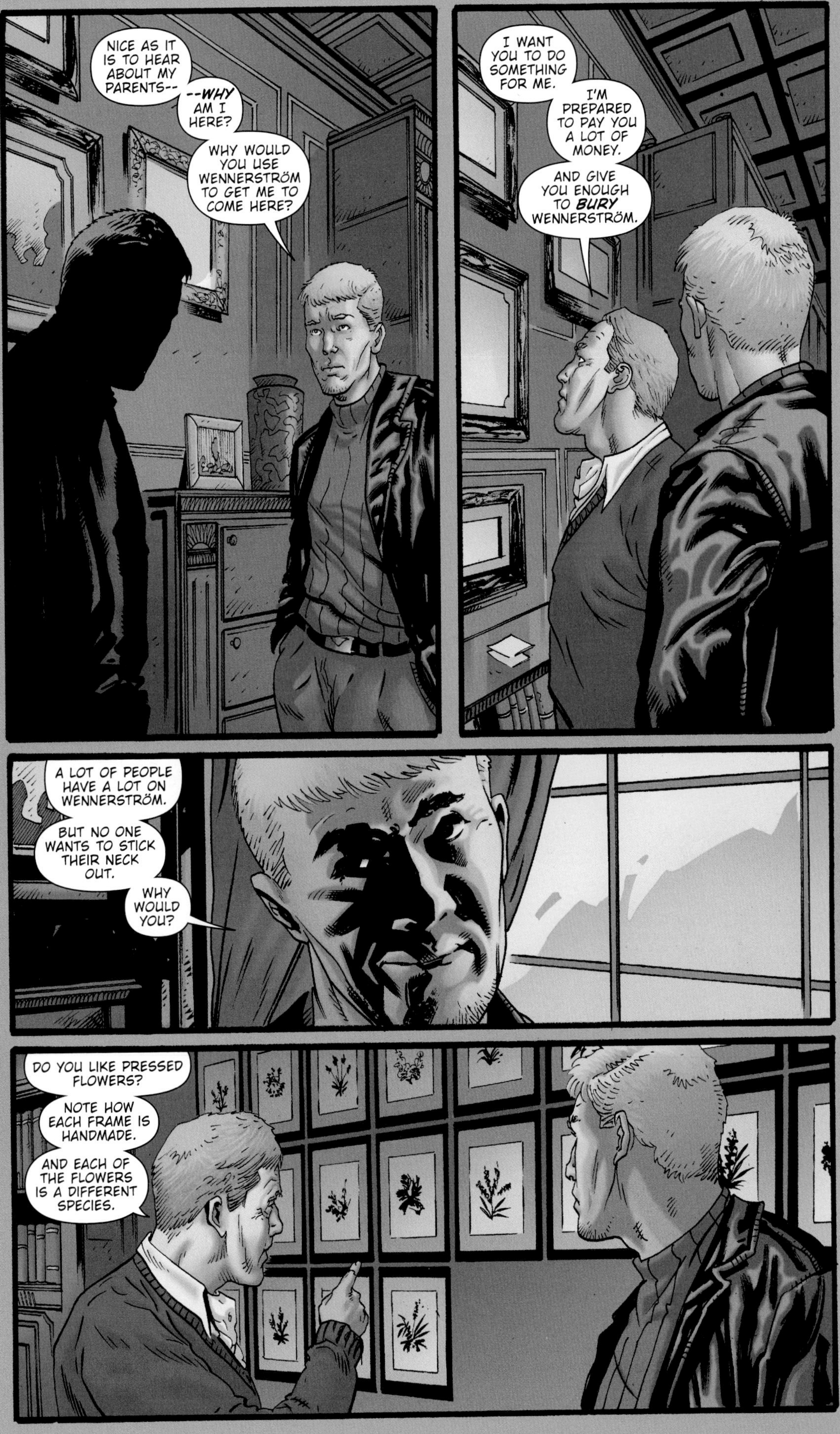
NICE AS IT IS TO HEAR ABOUT MY PARENTS--
--WHY AM I HERE?
WHY WOULD YOU USE WENNERSTRÖM TO GET ME TO COME HERE?
I WANT YOU TO DO SOMETHING FOR ME.
I'M PREPARED TO PAY YOU A LOT OF MONEY.
AND GIVE YOU ENOUGH TO BURY WENNERSTRÖM.
A LOT OF PEOPLE HAVE A LOT ON WENNERSTRÖM.
BUT NO ONE WANTS TO STICK THEIR NECK OUT.
WHY WOULD YOU?
DO YOU LIKE PRESSED FLOWERS?
NOTE HOW EACH FRAME IS HANDMADE.
AND EACH OF THE FLOWERS IS A DIFFERENT SPECIES.

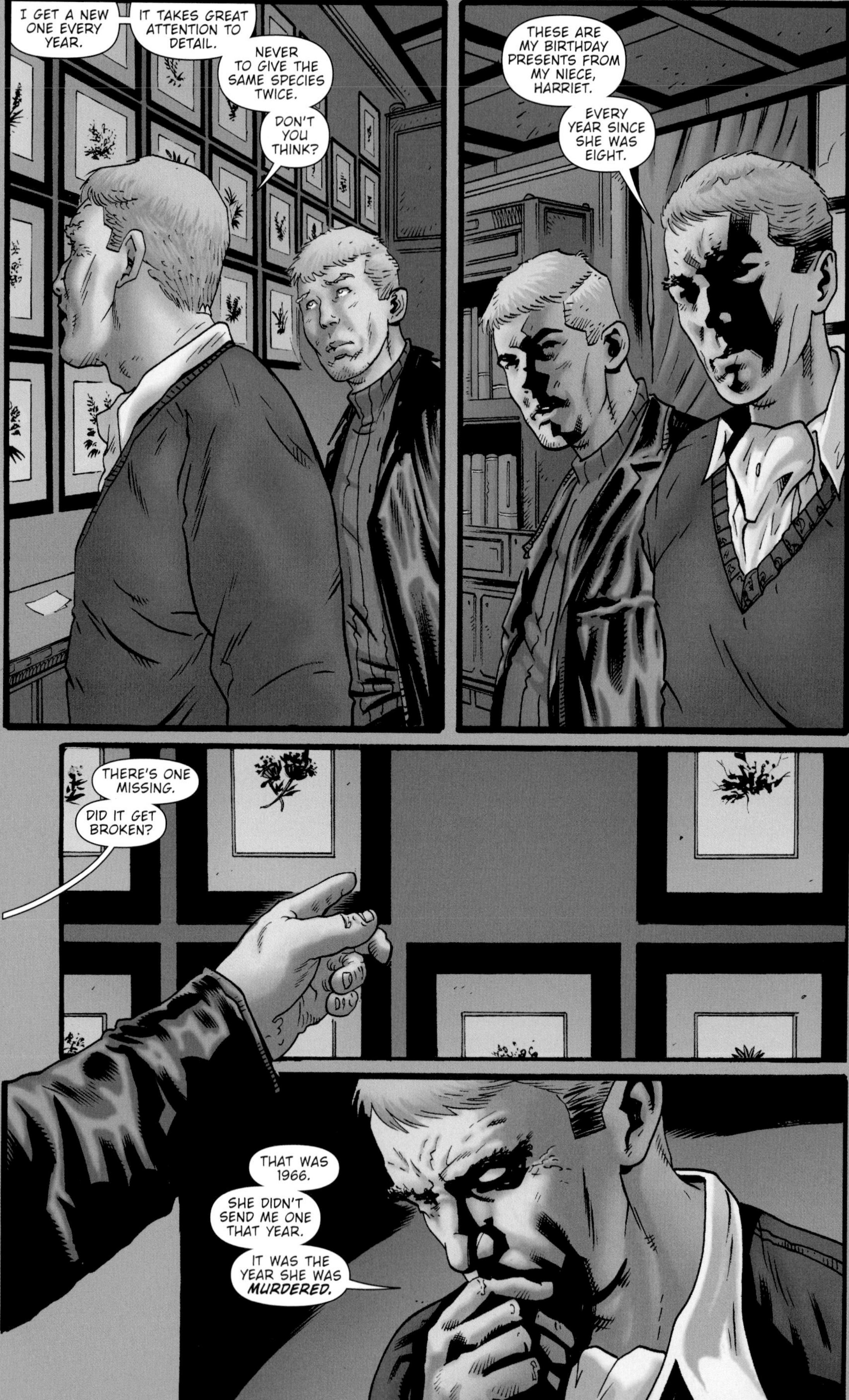
I GET A NEW ONE EVERY YEAR.
IT TAKES GREAT ATTENTION TO DETAIL.
NEVER TO GIVE THE SAME SPECIES TWICE.
DON'T YOU THINK?
THESE ARE MY BIRTHDAY PRESENTS FROM MY NIECE, HARRIET.
EVERY YEAR SINCE SHE WAS EIGHT.
THERE'S ONE MISSING.
DID IT GET BROKEN?
THAT WAS 1966.
SHE DIDN'T SEND ME ONE THAT YEAR.
IT WAS THE YEAR SHE WAS ***MURDERED.***

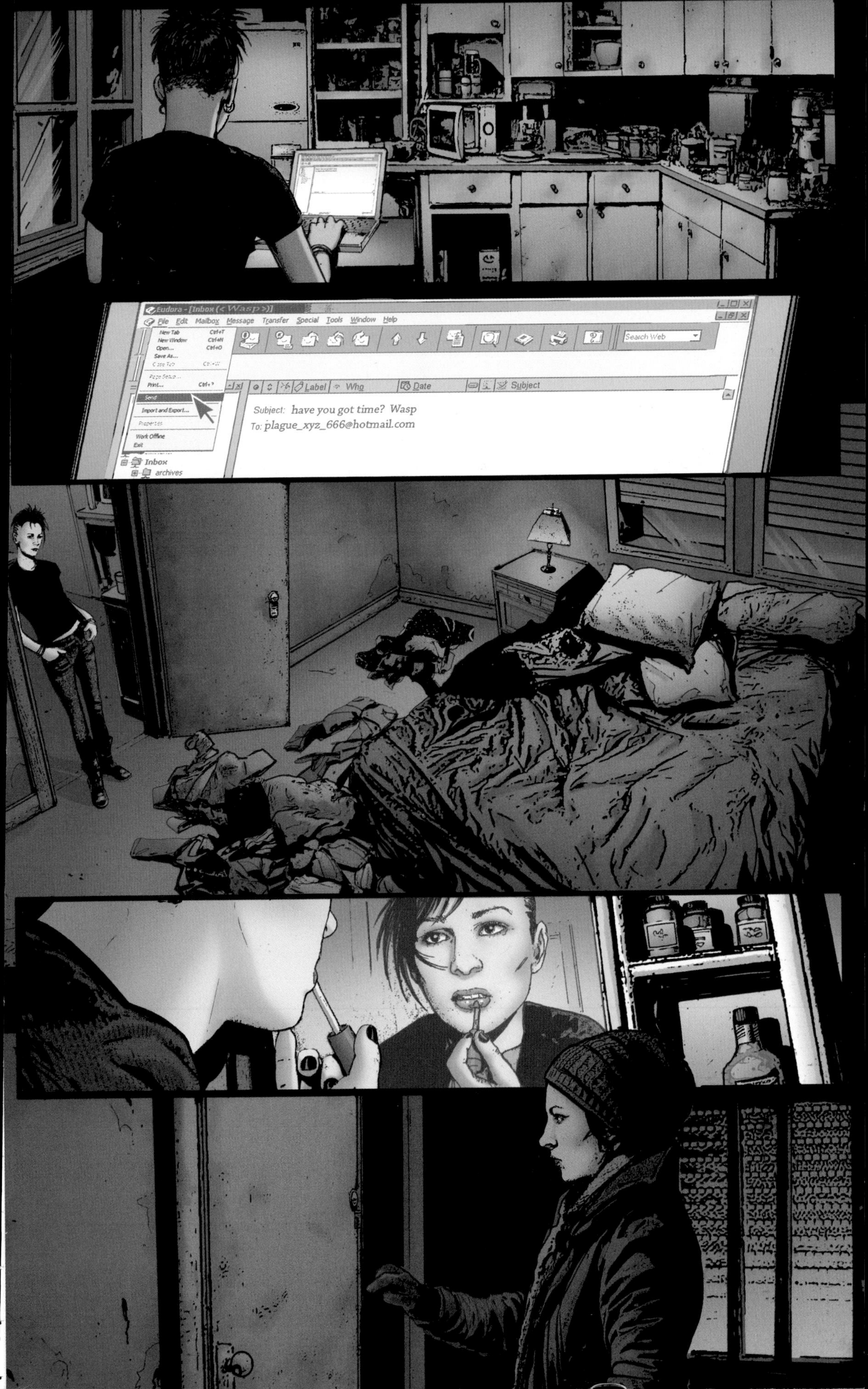
Eudora - [Inbox (< Wasp >)]
File Edit Mailbox Message Transfer Special Tools Window Help
New Tab Ctrl+T
New Window Ctrl+N
Open... Ctrl+O
Save As...
Print...
Send
Import and Export...
Work Offline
Exit
Search Web
Label Who Date Subject
Subject: have you got time? Wasp
To: plague_xyz_666@hotmail.com
Inbox
archives

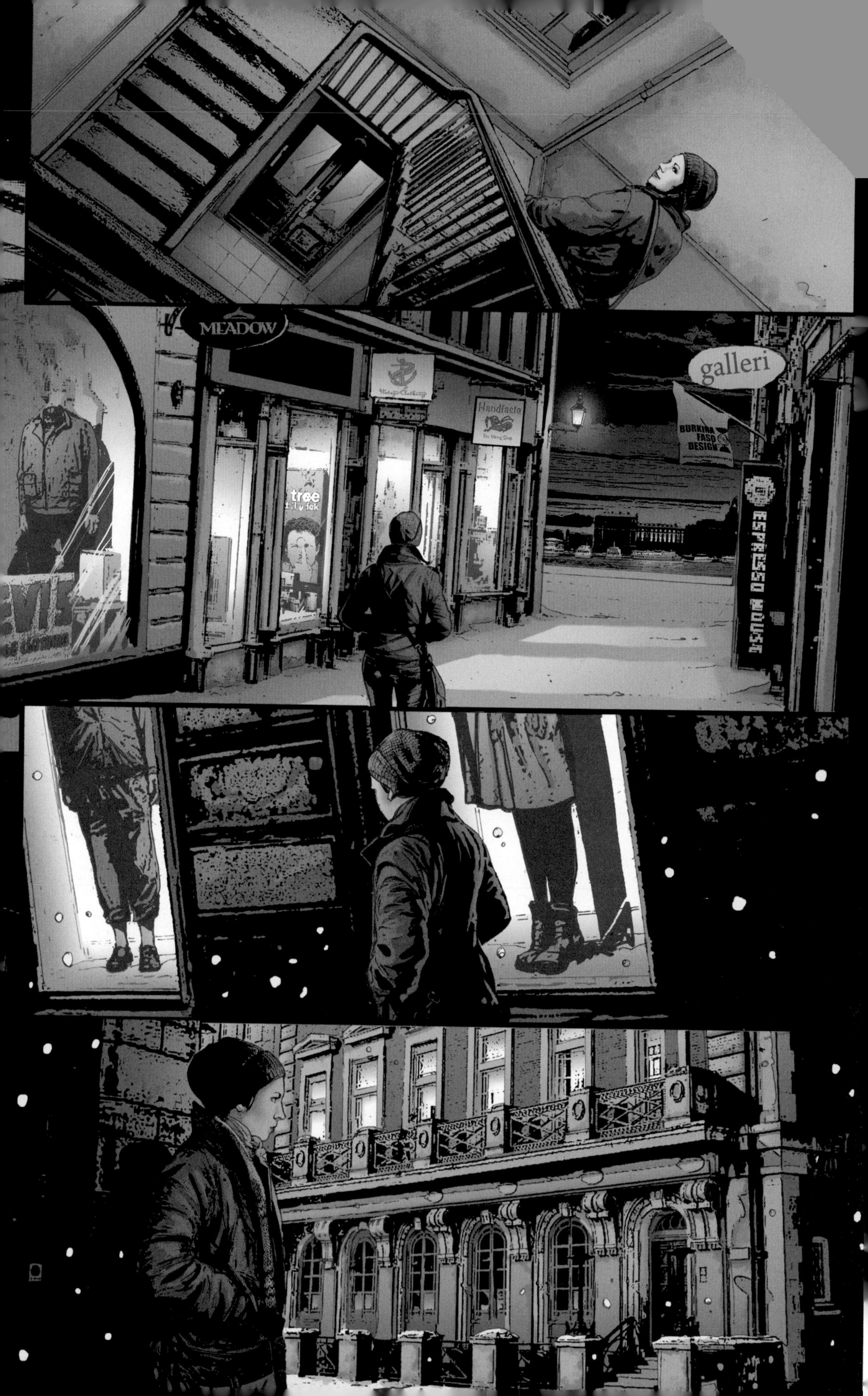
MEADOW
Handfaste
galleri
BURKINA FASO DESIGN

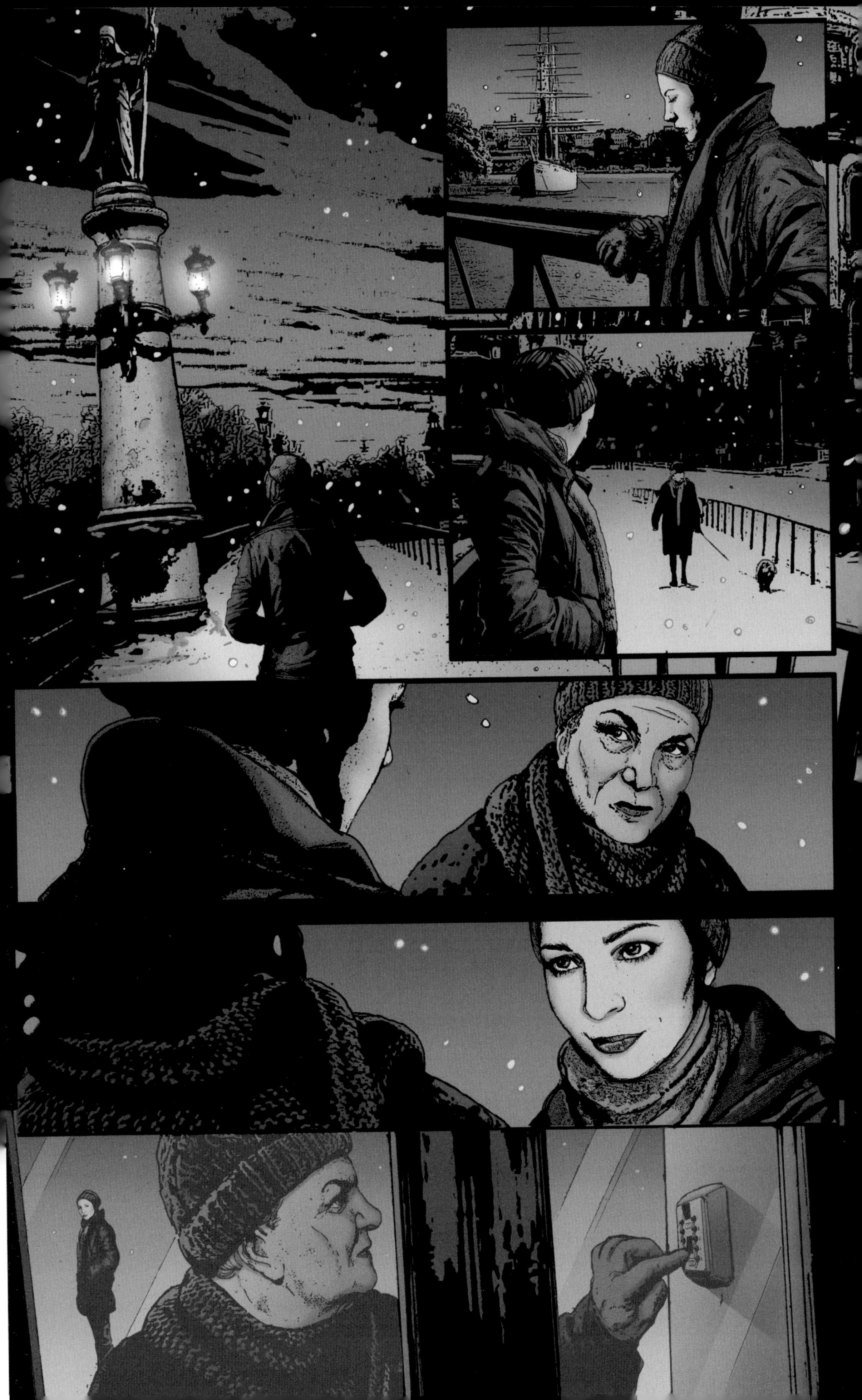

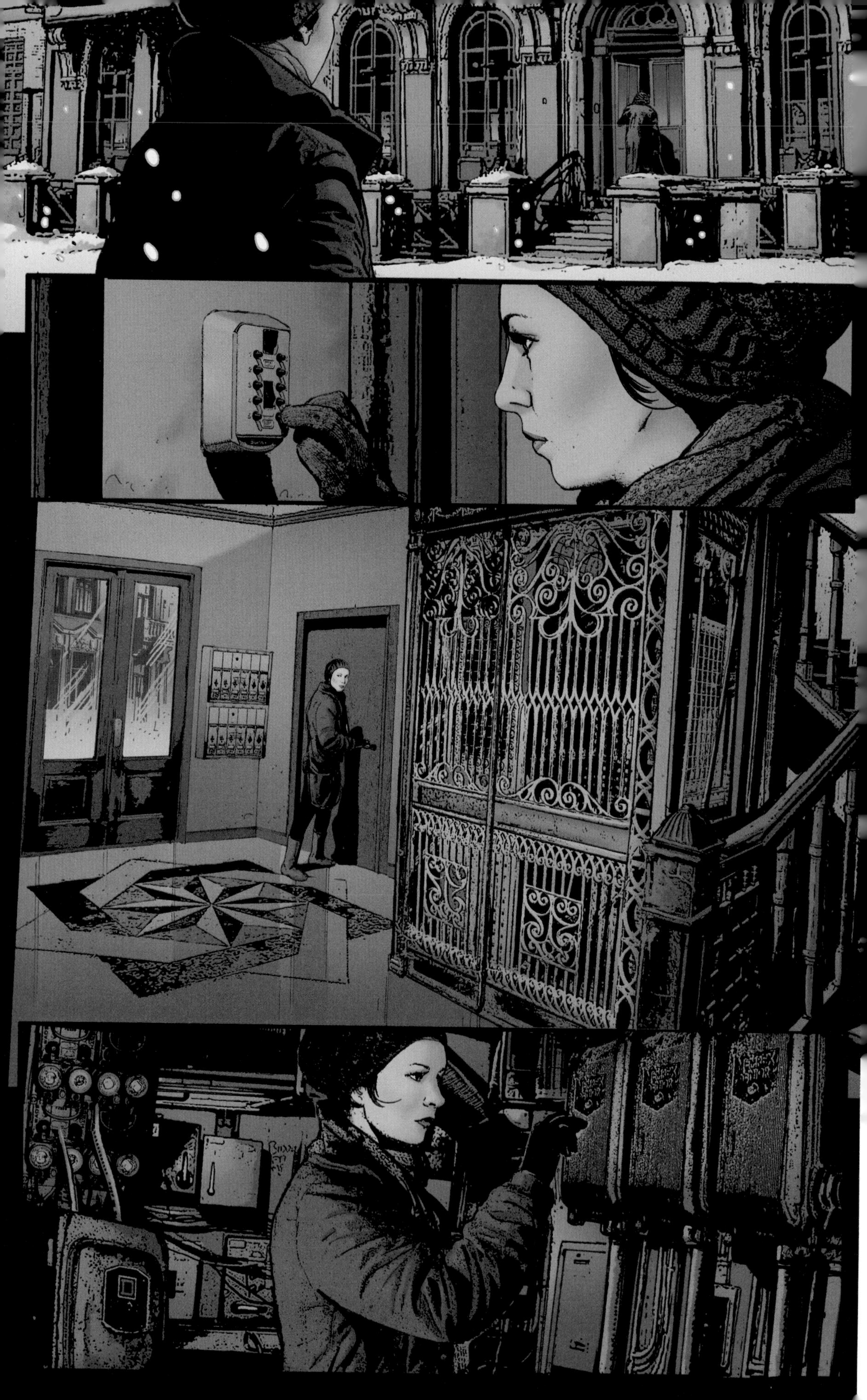

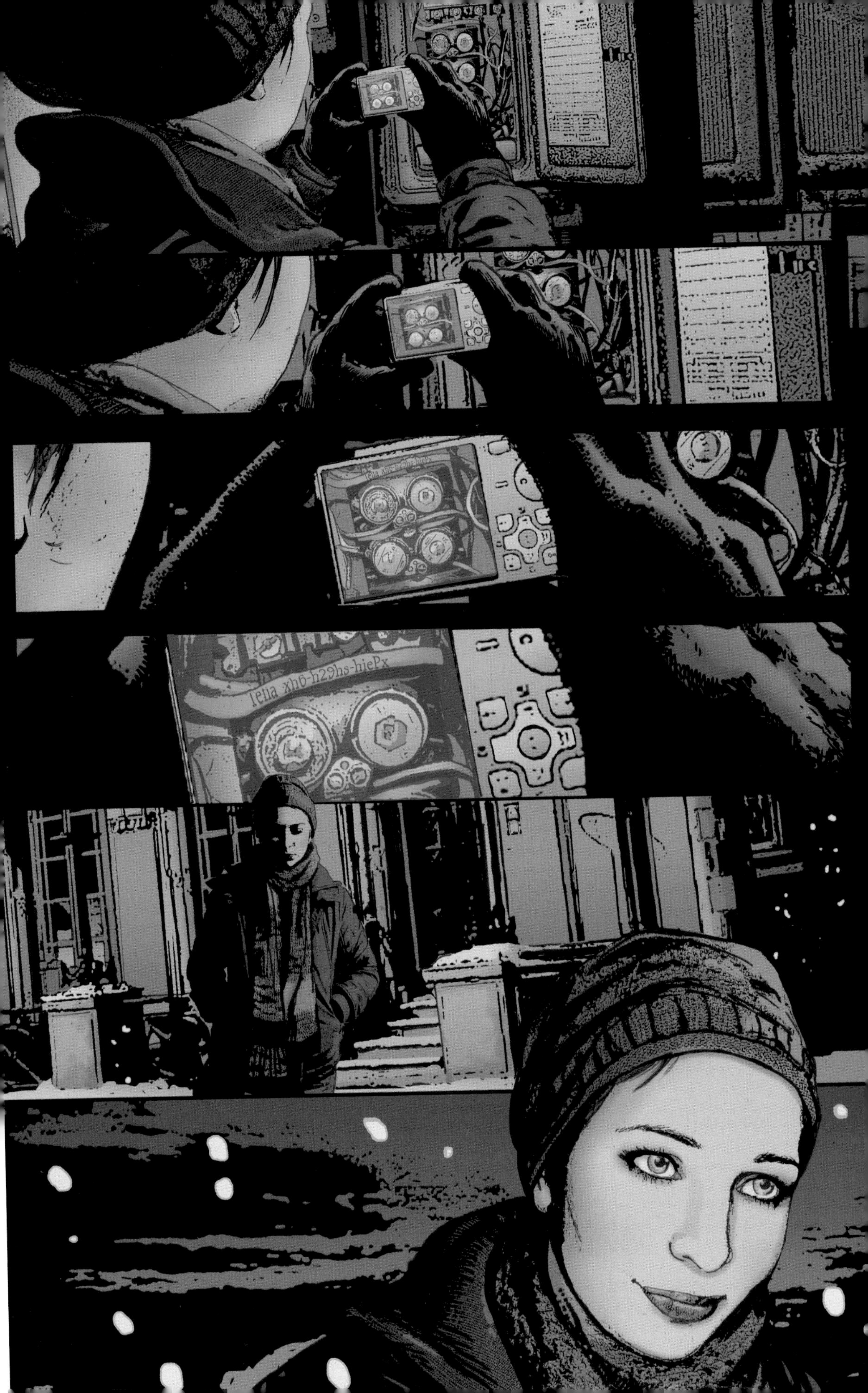
lella xh6-h29hs-hiePx

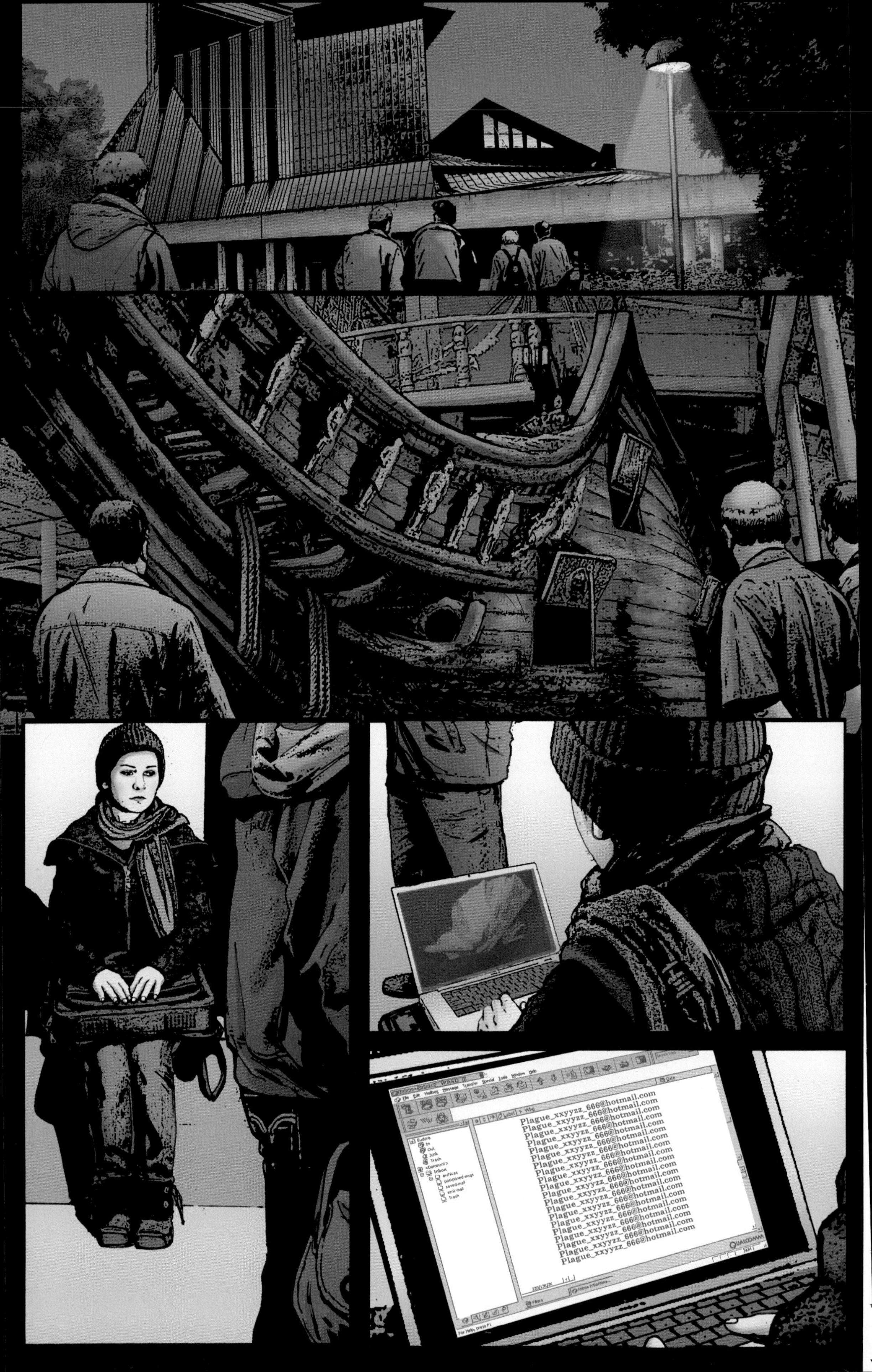

Plague_xxyyzz_666@hotmail.com
Plague_xxyyzz_666@hotmail.com
Plague_xxyyzz_666@hotmail.com
Plague_xxyyzz_666@hotmail.com
Plague_xxyyzz_666@hotmail.com
Plague_xxyyzz_666@hotmail.com
Plague_xxyyzz_666@hotmail.com
Plague_xxyyzz_666@hotmail.com
Plague_xxyyzz_666@hotmail.com
Plague_xxyyzz_666@hotmail.com
Plague_xxyyzz_666@hotmail.com
Plague_xxyyzz_666@hotmail.com
Plague_xxyyzz_666@hotmail.com
Plague_xxyyzz_666@hotmail.com
Plague_xxyyzz_666@hotmail.com
Plague_xxyyzz_666@hotmail.com
Plague_xxyyzz_666@hotmail.com
Plague_xxyyzz_666@hotmail.com

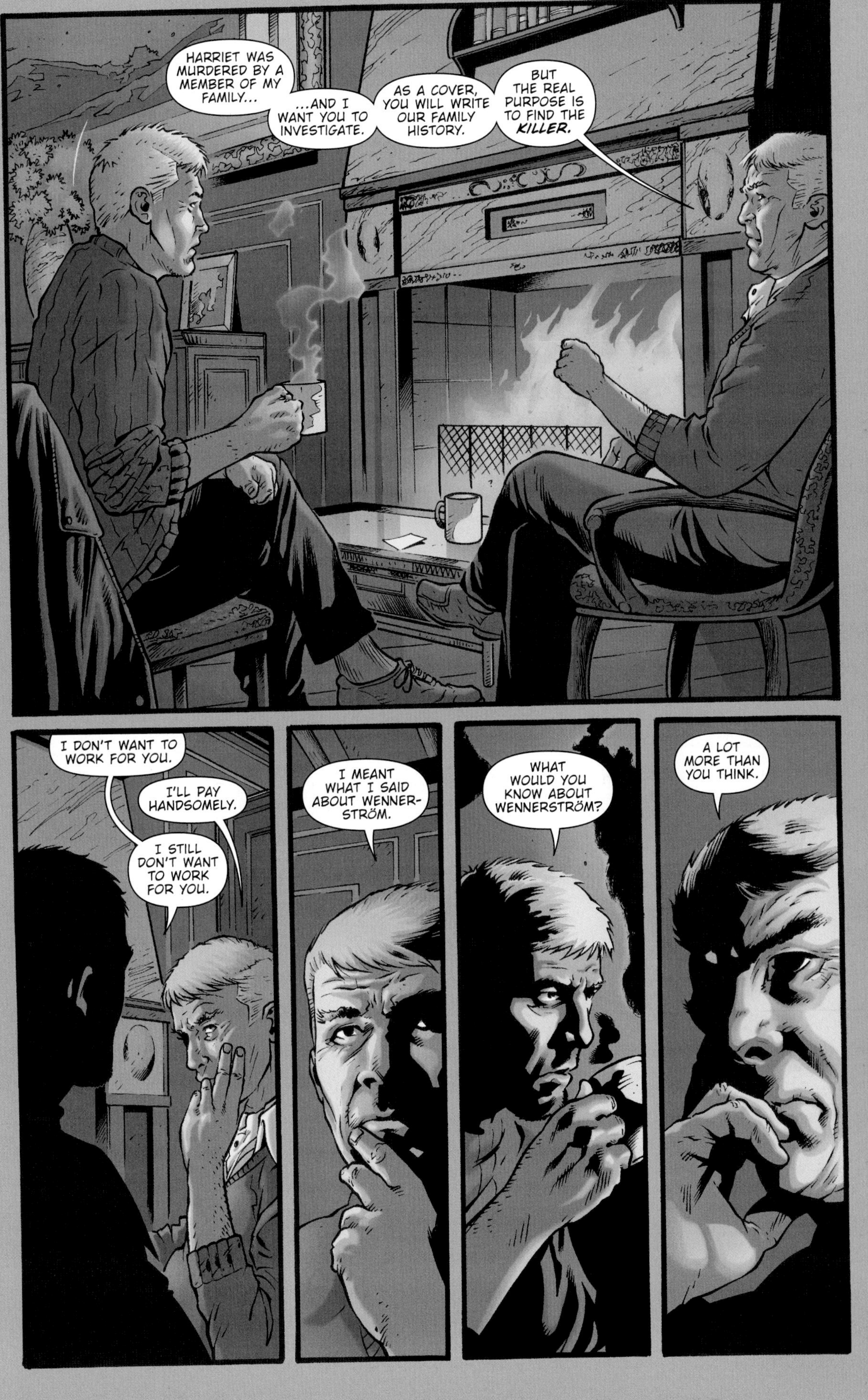
HARRIET WAS MURDERED BY A MEMBER OF MY FAMILY...
...AND I WANT YOU TO INVESTIGATE.
AS A COVER, YOU WILL WRITE OUR FAMILY HISTORY.
BUT THE REAL PURPOSE IS TO FIND THE *KILLER.*
I DON'T WANT TO WORK FOR YOU.
I'LL PAY HANDSOMELY.
I STILL DON'T WANT TO WORK FOR YOU.
I MEANT WHAT I SAID ABOUT WENNER-STRÖM.
WHAT WOULD YOU KNOW ABOUT WENNERSTRÖM?
A LOT MORE THAN YOU THINK.

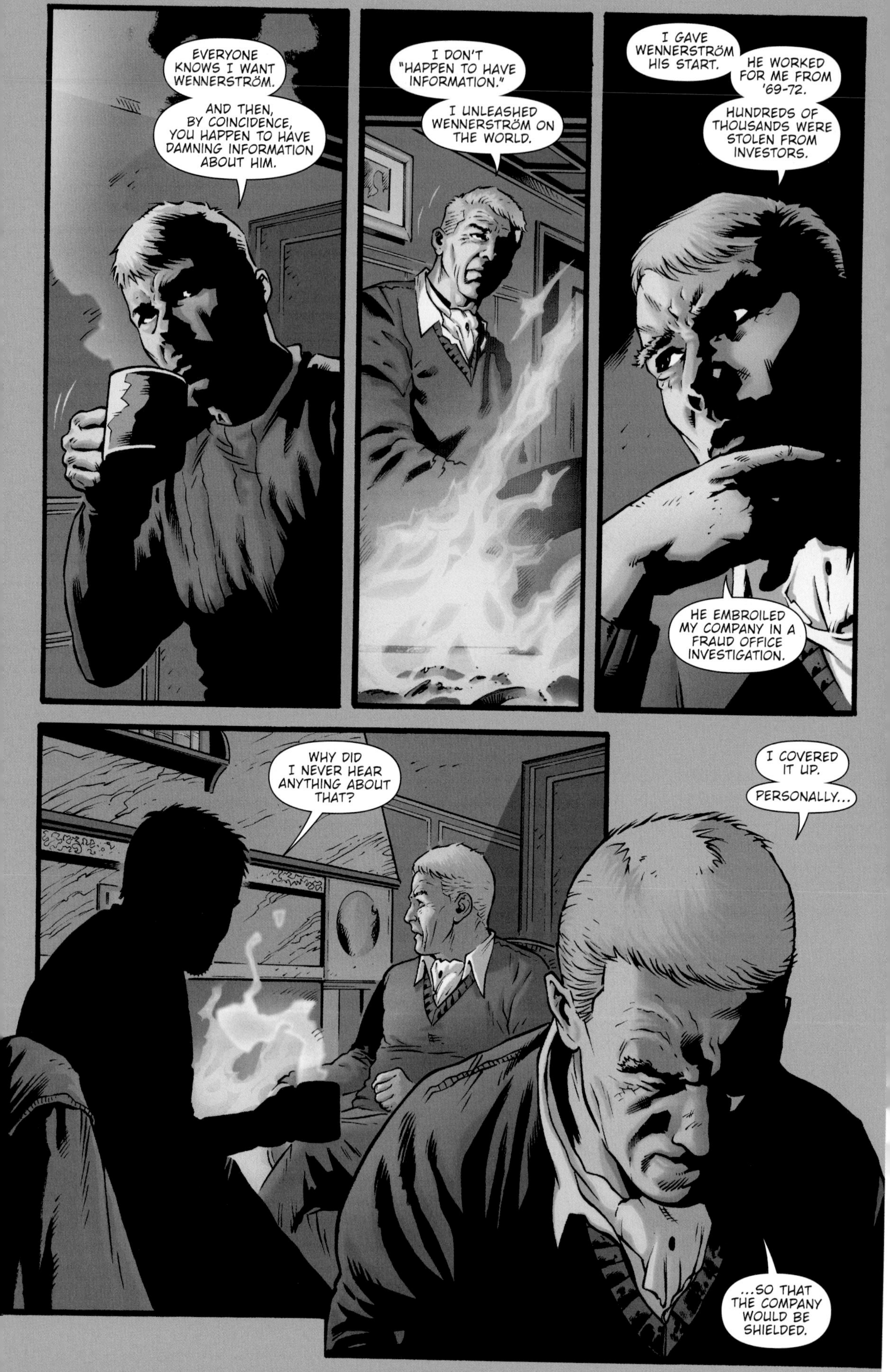
EVERYONE KNOWS I WANT WENNERSTRÖM.
AND THEN, BY COINCIDENCE, YOU HAPPEN TO HAVE DAMNING INFORMATION ABOUT HIM.
I DON'T "HAPPEN TO HAVE INFORMATION."
I UNLEASHED WENNERSTRÖM ON THE WORLD.
I GAVE WENNERSTRÖM HIS START.
HE WORKED FOR ME FROM '69-72.
HUNDREDS OF THOUSANDS WERE STOLEN FROM INVESTORS.
HE EMBROILED MY COMPANY IN A FRAUD OFFICE INVESTIGATION.
WHY DID I NEVER HEAR ANYTHING ABOUT THAT?
I COVERED IT UP.
PERSONALLY...
...SO THAT THE COMPANY WOULD BE SHIELDED.

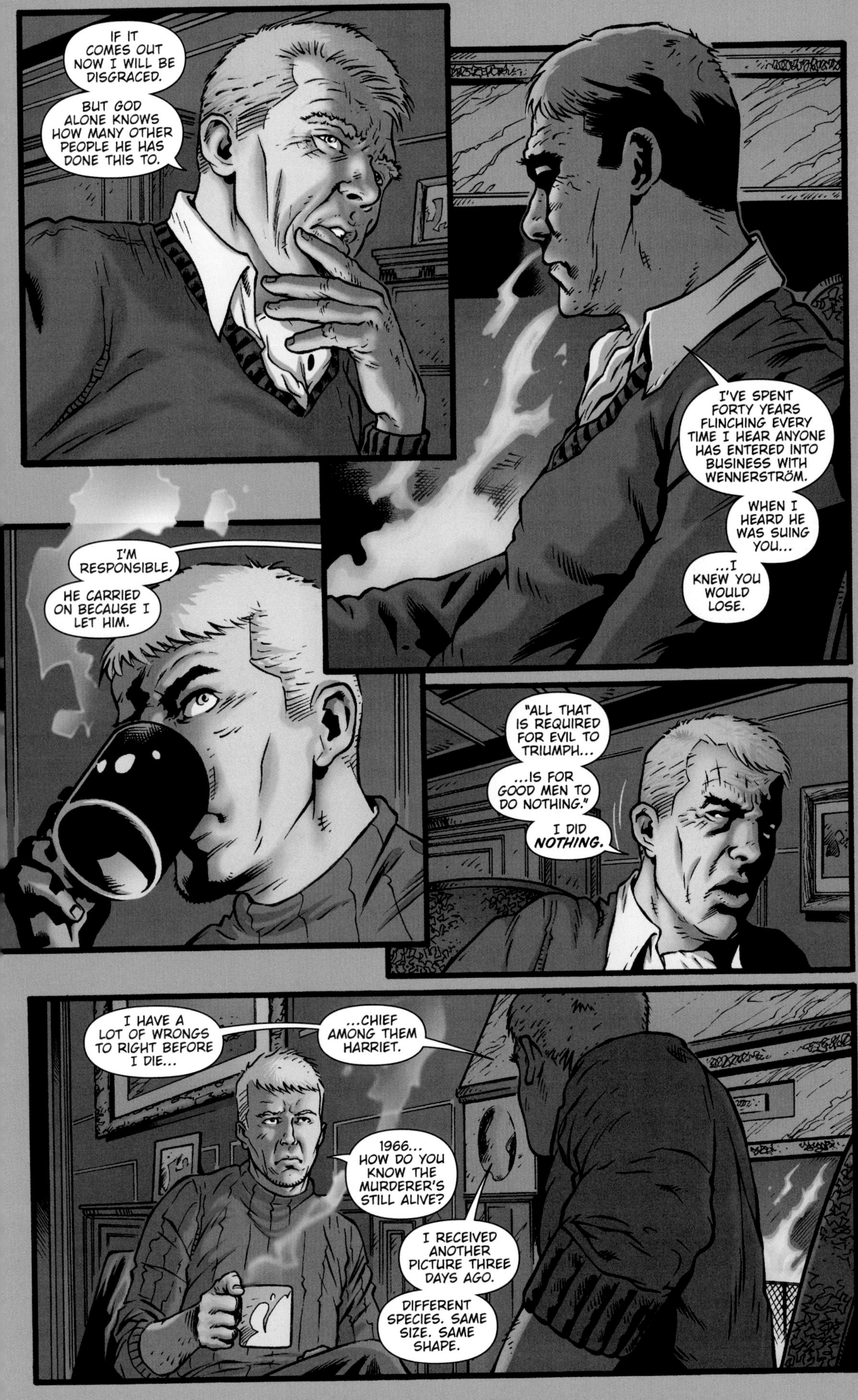

IF IT COMES OUT NOW I WILL BE DISGRACED.
BUT GOD ALONE KNOWS HOW MANY OTHER PEOPLE HE HAS DONE THIS TO.
I'VE SPENT FORTY YEARS FLINCHING EVERY TIME I HEAR ANYONE HAS ENTERED INTO BUSINESS WITH WENNERSTRÖM.
WHEN I HEARD HE WAS SUING YOU...
...I KNEW YOU WOULD LOSE.
I'M RESPONSIBLE.
HE CARRIED ON BECAUSE I LET HIM.
"ALL THAT IS REQUIRED FOR EVIL TO TRIUMPH...
...IS FOR GOOD MEN TO DO NOTHING."
I DID ***NOTHING.***
I HAVE A LOT OF WRONGS TO RIGHT BEFORE I DIE...
...CHIEF AMONG THEM HARRIET.
1966... HOW DO YOU KNOW THE MURDERER'S STILL ALIVE?
I RECEIVED ANOTHER PICTURE THREE DAYS AGO.
DIFFERENT SPECIES. SAME SIZE. SAME SHAPE.

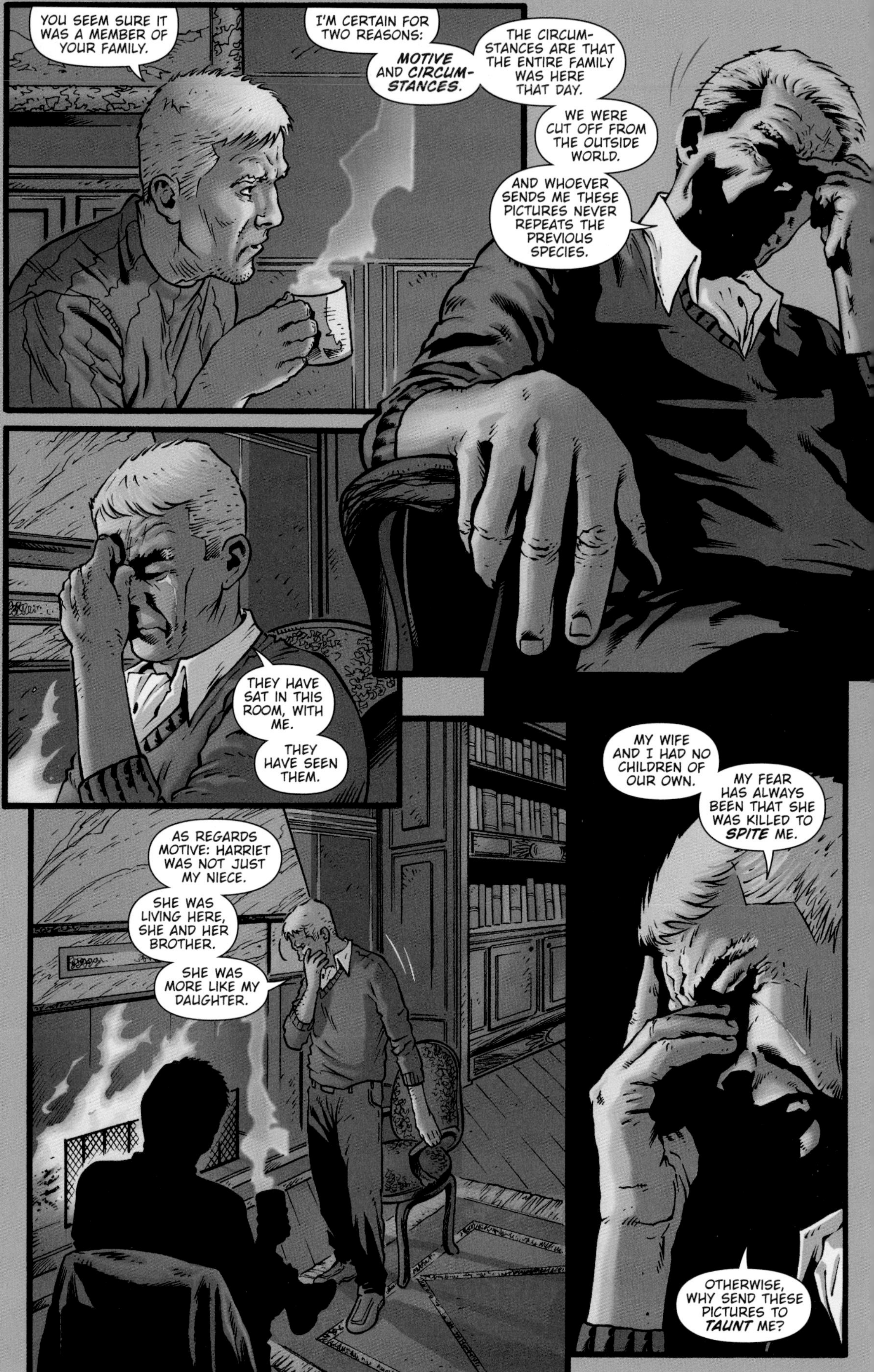
YOU SEEM SURE IT WAS A MEMBER OF YOUR FAMILY.
I'M CERTAIN FOR TWO REASONS: **MOTIVE** AND **CIRCUM-STANCES**.
THE CIRCUM-STANCES ARE THAT THE ENTIRE FAMILY WAS HERE THAT DAY.
WE WERE CUT OFF FROM THE OUTSIDE WORLD.
AND WHOEVER SENDS ME THESE PICTURES NEVER REPEATS THE PREVIOUS SPECIES.
THEY HAVE SAT IN THIS ROOM, WITH ME.
THEY HAVE SEEN THEM.
AS REGARDS MOTIVE: HARRIET WAS NOT JUST MY NIECE.
SHE WAS LIVING HERE, SHE AND HER BROTHER.
SHE WAS MORE LIKE MY DAUGHTER.
MY WIFE AND I HAD NO CHILDREN OF OUR OWN.
MY FEAR HAS ALWAYS BEEN THAT SHE WAS KILLED TO **SPITE** ME.
OTHERWISE, WHY SEND THESE PICTURES TO **TAUNT** ME?

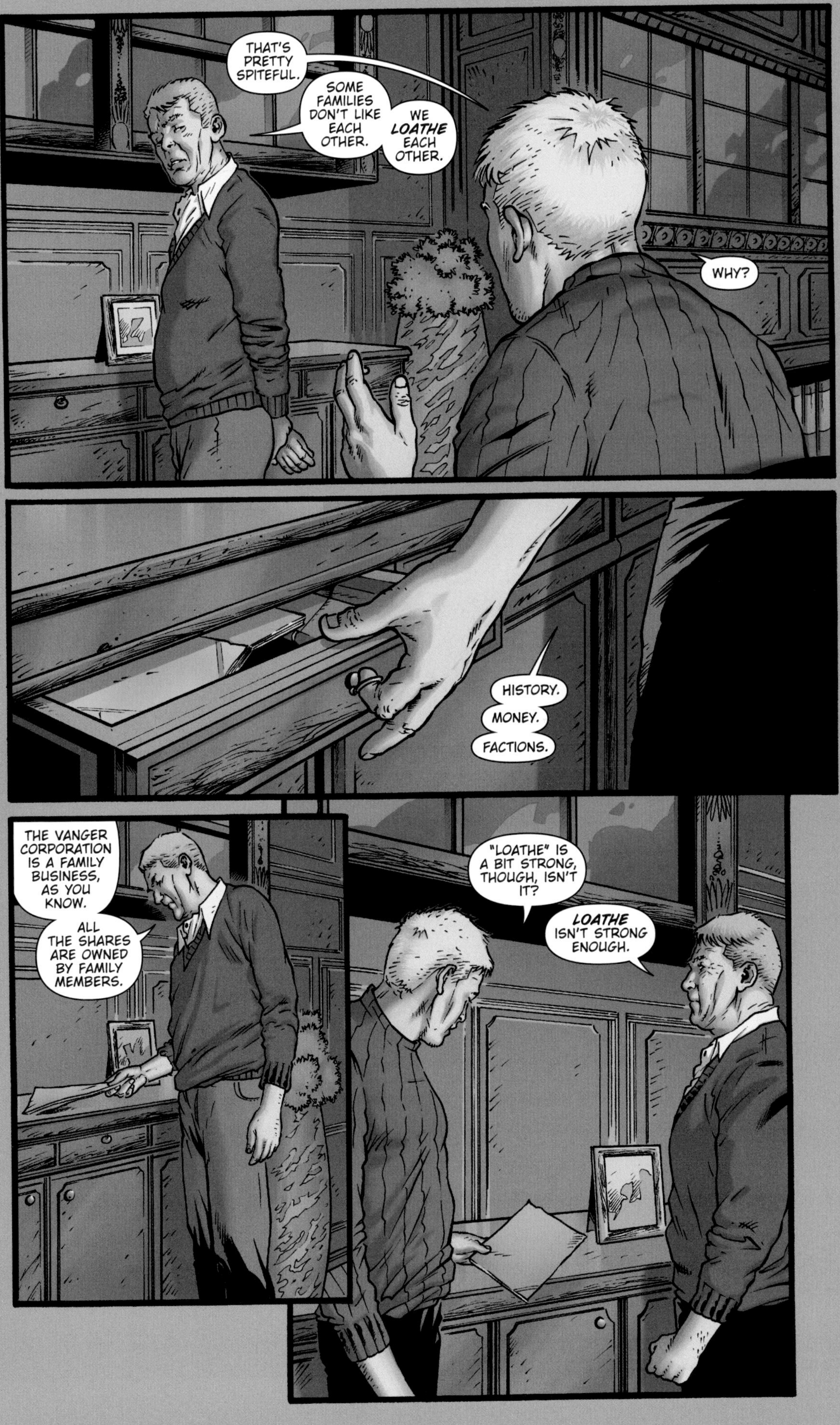
THAT'S PRETTY SPITEFUL.
SOME FAMILIES DON'T LIKE EACH OTHER.
WE *LOATHE* EACH OTHER.
WHY?
HISTORY.
MONEY.
FACTIONS.
THE VANGER CORPORATION IS A FAMILY BUSINESS, AS YOU KNOW.
ALL THE SHARES ARE OWNED BY FAMILY MEMBERS.
"LOATHE" IS A BIT STRONG, THOUGH, ISN'T IT?
LOATHE ISN'T STRONG ENOUGH.

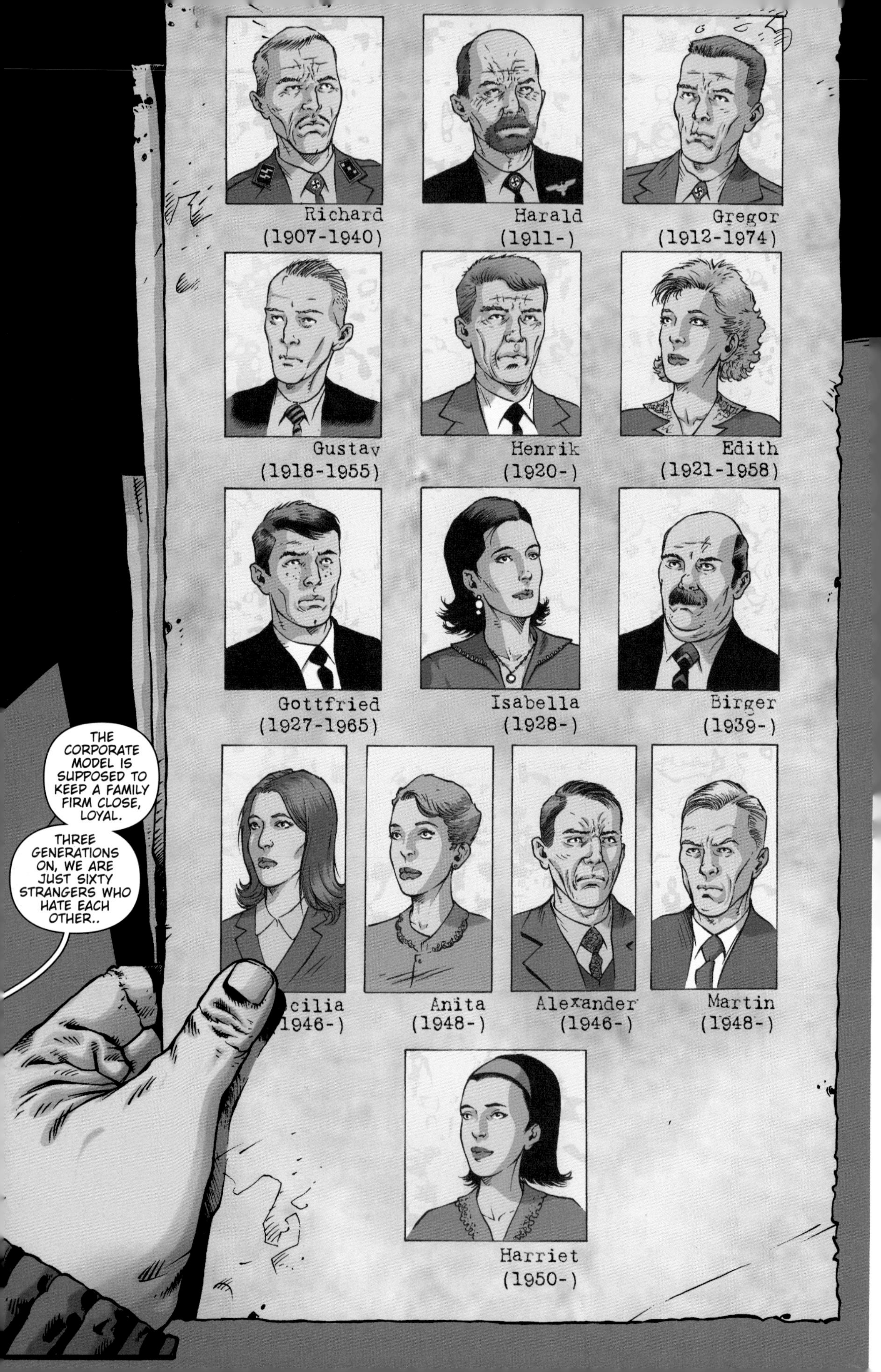
Richard
(1907-1940)
Harald
(1911-)
Gregor
(1912-1974)
Gustav
(1918-1955)
Henrik
(1920-)
Edith
(1921-1958)
Gottfried
(1927-1965)
Isabella
(1928-)
Birger
(1939-)
THE CORPORATE MODEL IS SUPPOSED TO KEEP A FAMILY FIRM CLOSE, LOYAL.
THREE GENERATIONS ON, WE ARE JUST SIXTY STRANGERS WHO HATE EACH OTHER..
1946-)
Anita
(1948-)
Alexander
(1946-)
Martin
(1948-)
Harriet
(1950-)

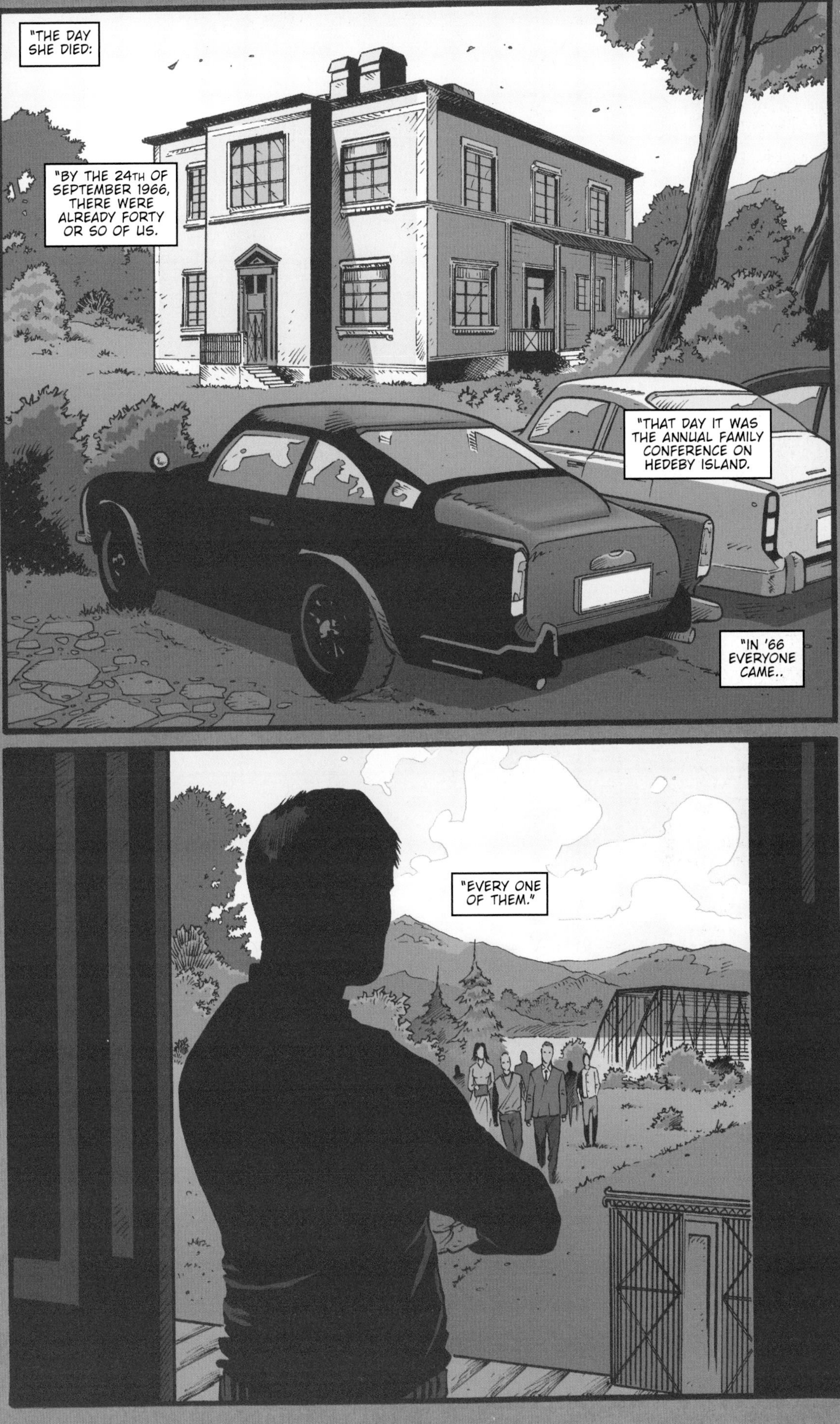
"THE DAY SHE DIED:
"BY THE 24TH OF SEPTEMBER 1966, THERE WERE ALREADY FORTY OR SO OF US.
"THAT DAY IT WAS THE ANNUAL FAMILY CONFERENCE ON HEDEBY ISLAND.
"IN '66 EVERYONE CAME..
"EVERY ONE OF THEM."

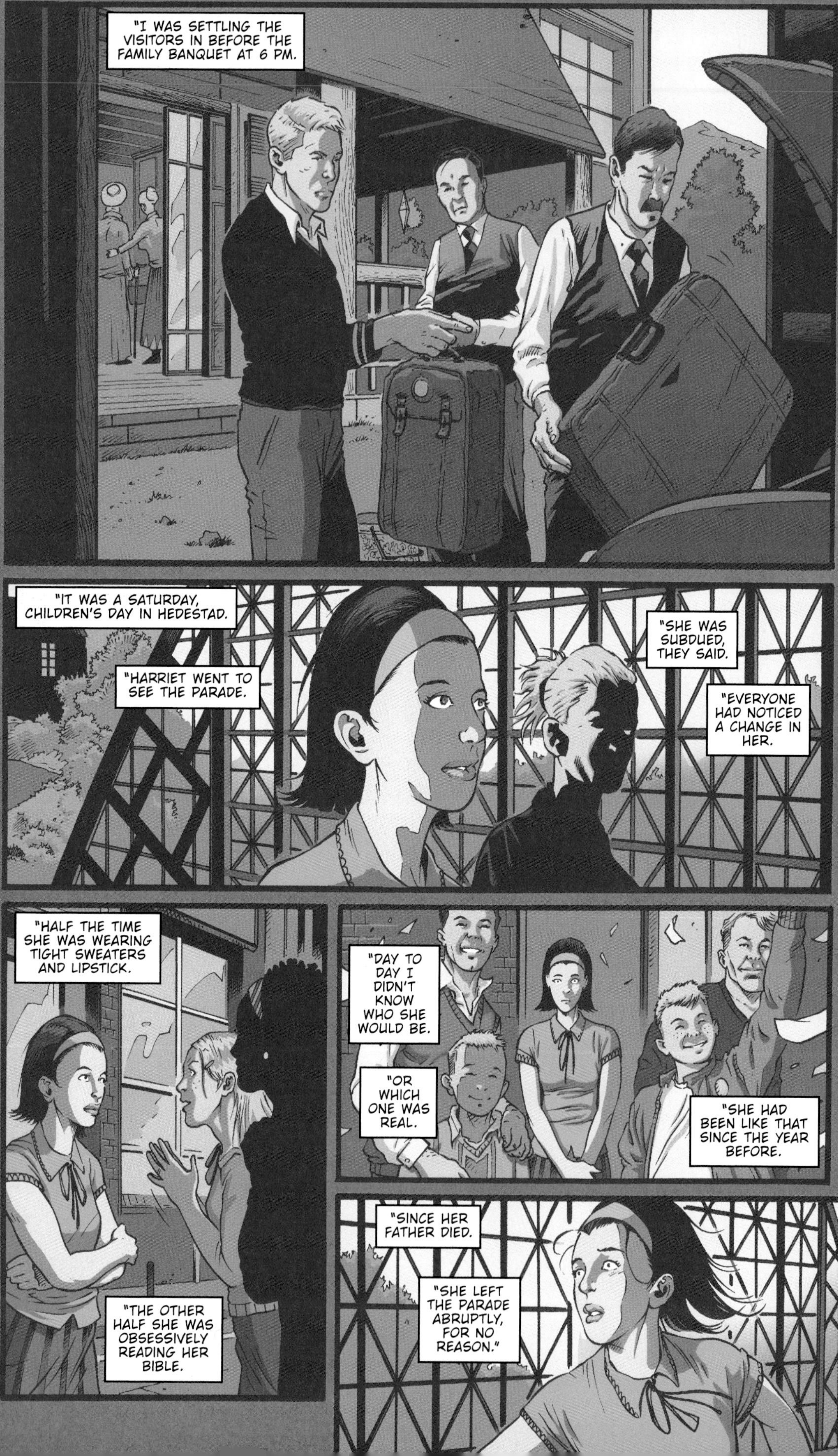
"I WAS SETTLING THE VISITORS IN BEFORE THE FAMILY BANQUET AT 6 PM.
"IT WAS A SATURDAY, CHILDREN'S DAY IN HEDESTAD.
"HARRIET WENT TO SEE THE PARADE.
"SHE WAS SUBDUED, THEY SAID.
"EVERYONE HAD NOTICED A CHANGE IN HER.
"HALF THE TIME SHE WAS WEARING TIGHT SWEATERS AND LIPSTICK.
"THE OTHER HALF SHE WAS OBSESSIVELY READING HER BIBLE.
"DAY TO DAY I DIDN'T KNOW WHO SHE WOULD BE.
"OR WHICH ONE WAS REAL.
"SHE HAD BEEN LIKE THAT SINCE THE YEAR BEFORE.
"SINCE HER FATHER DIED.
"SHE LEFT THE PARADE ABRUPTLY, FOR NO REASON."

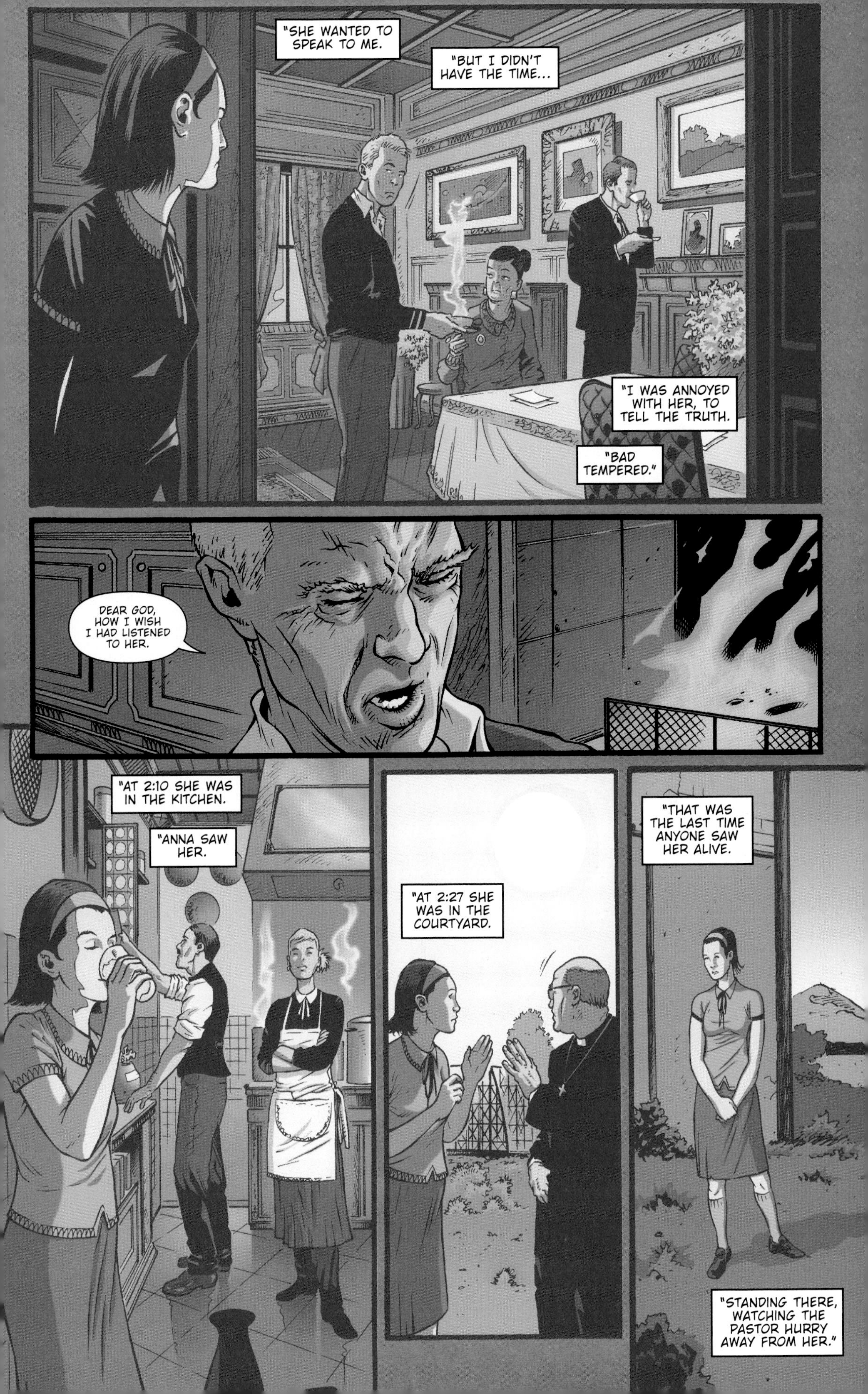
"SHE WANTED TO SPEAK TO ME.
"BUT I DIDN'T HAVE THE TIME...
"I WAS ANNOYED WITH HER, TO TELL THE TRUTH.
"BAD TEMPERED."
DEAR GOD, HOW I WISH I HAD LISTENED TO HER.
"AT 2:10 SHE WAS IN THE KITCHEN.
"ANNA SAW HER.
"AT 2:27 SHE WAS IN THE COURTYARD.
"THAT WAS THE LAST TIME ANYONE SAW HER ALIVE.
"STANDING THERE, WATCHING THE PASTOR HURRY AWAY FROM HER."

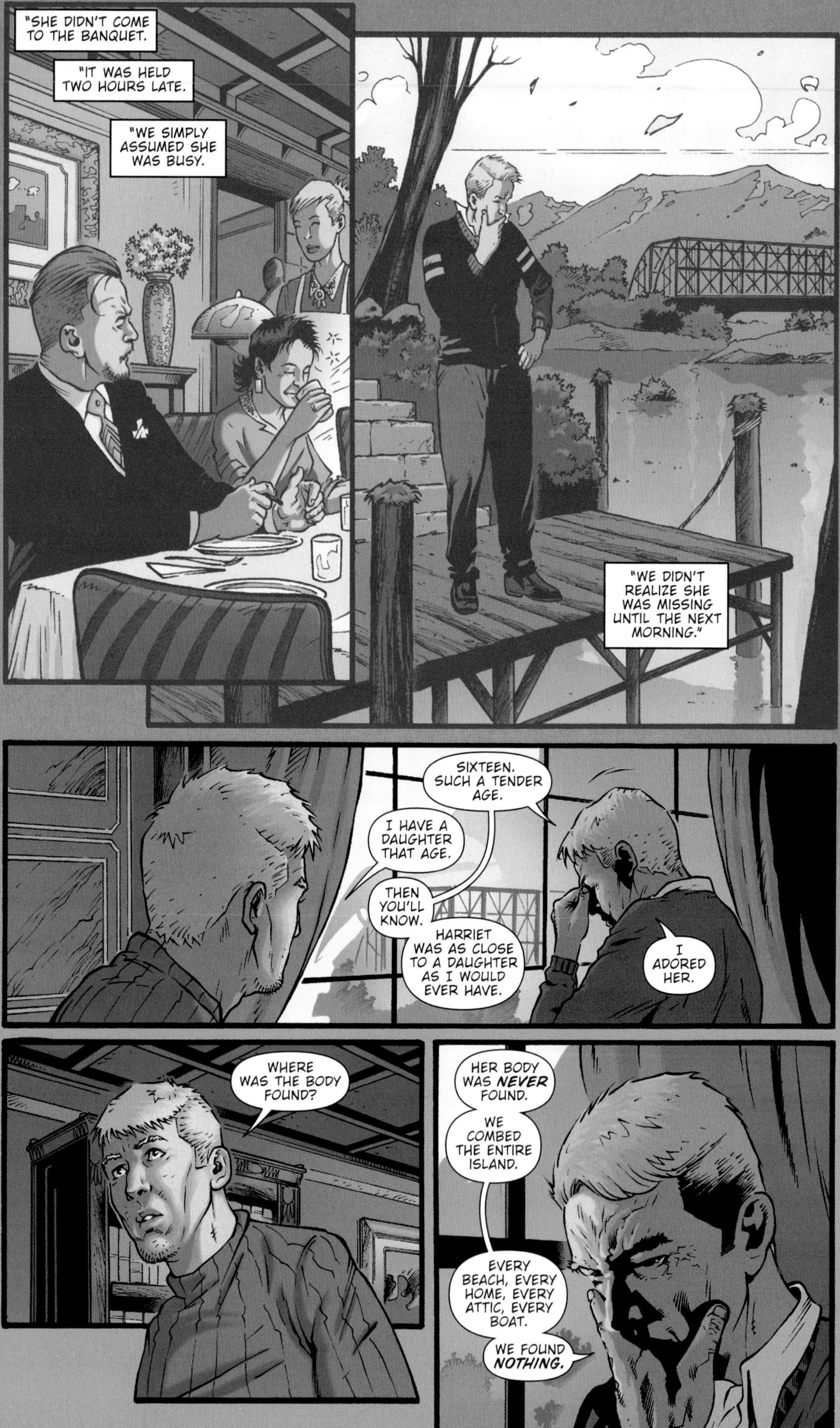
"SHE DIDN'T COME TO THE BANQUET.
"IT WAS HELD TWO HOURS LATE.
"WE SIMPLY ASSUMED SHE WAS BUSY.
"WE DIDN'T REALIZE SHE WAS MISSING UNTIL THE NEXT MORNING."
SIXTEEN. SUCH A TENDER AGE.
I HAVE A DAUGHTER THAT AGE.
THEN YOU'LL KNOW.
HARRIET WAS AS CLOSE TO A DAUGHTER AS I WOULD EVER HAVE.
I ADORED HER.
WHERE WAS THE BODY FOUND?
HER BODY WAS ***NEVER*** FOUND.
WE COMBED THE ENTIRE ISLAND.
EVERY BEACH, EVERY HOME, EVERY ATTIC, EVERY BOAT.
WE FOUND ***NOTHING.***

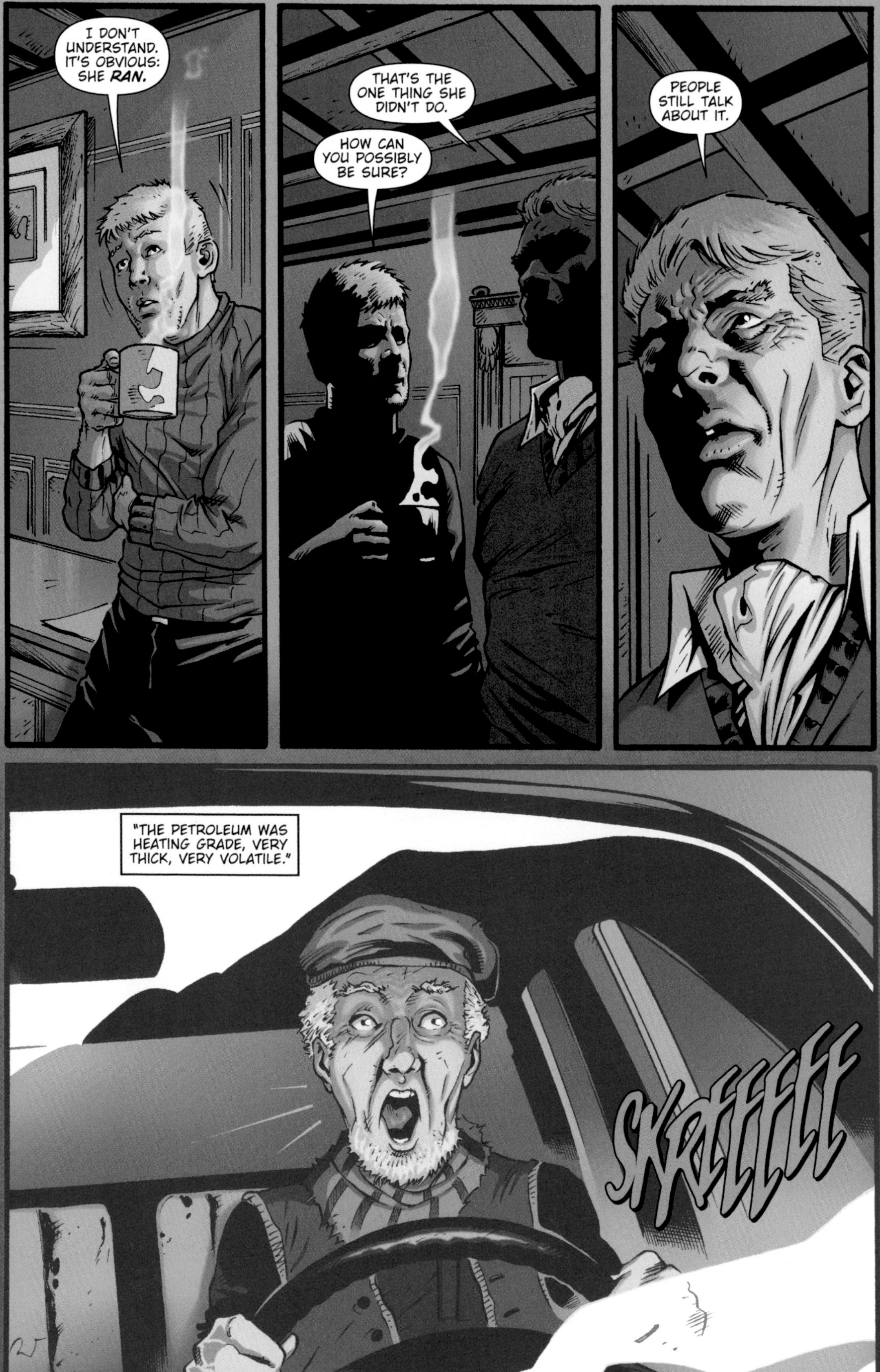
I DON'T UNDERSTAND. IT'S OBVIOUS: SHE RAN.
THAT'S THE ONE THING SHE DIDN'T DO.
HOW CAN YOU POSSIBLY BE SURE?
PEOPLE STILL TALK ABOUT IT.
"THE PETROLEUM WAS HEATING GRADE, VERY THICK, VERY VOLATILE."
SKREEEEE

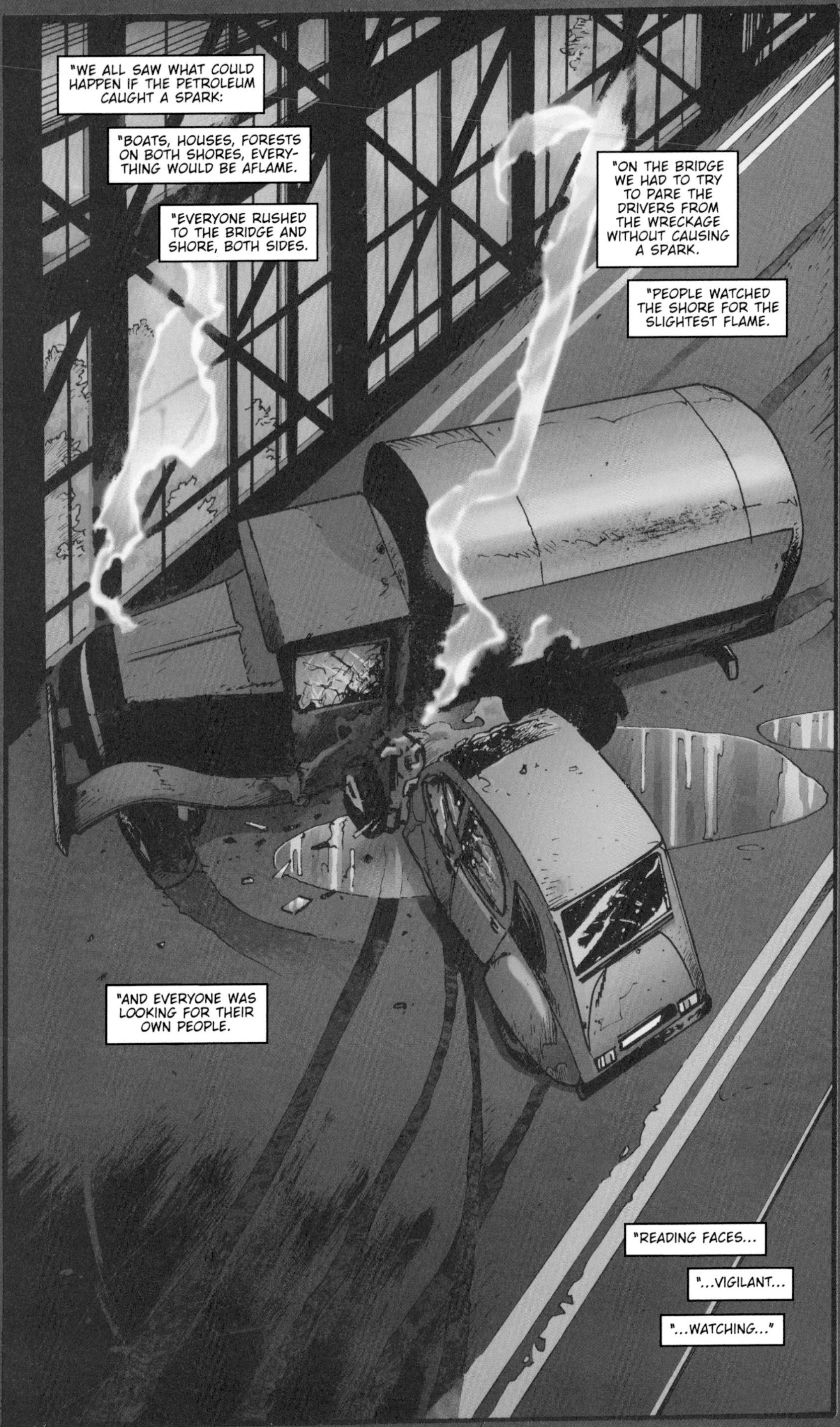
"WE ALL SAW WHAT COULD HAPPEN IF THE PETROLEUM CAUGHT A SPARK:
"BOATS, HOUSES, FORESTS ON BOTH SHORES, EVERYTHING WOULD BE AFLAME.
"EVERYONE RUSHED TO THE BRIDGE AND SHORE, BOTH SIDES.
"ON THE BRIDGE WE HAD TO TRY TO PARE THE DRIVERS FROM THE WRECKAGE WITHOUT CAUSING A SPARK.
"PEOPLE WATCHED THE SHORE FOR THE SLIGHTEST FLAME.
"AND EVERYONE WAS LOOKING FOR THEIR OWN PEOPLE.
"READING FACES...
"...VIGILANT...
"...WATCHING..."

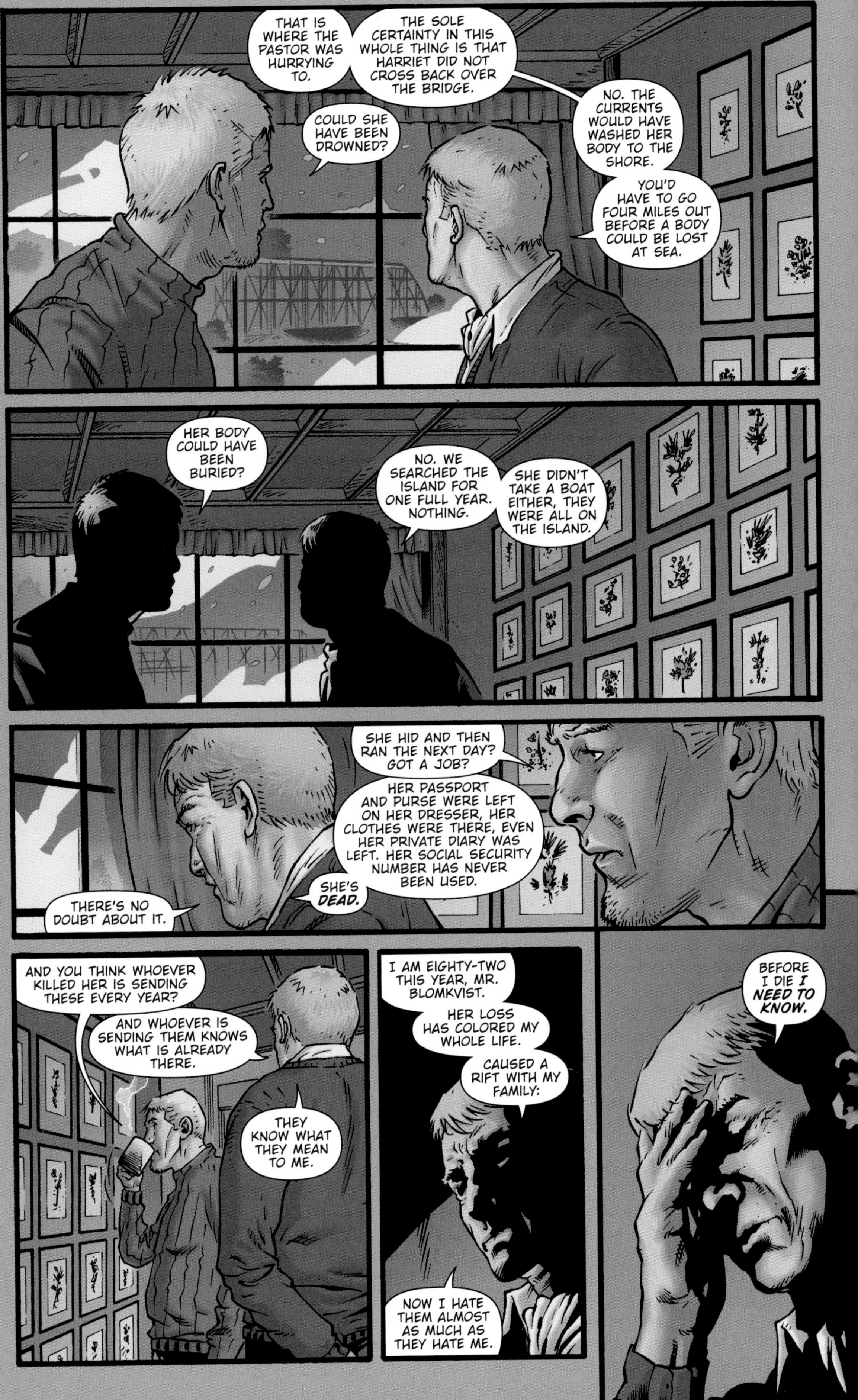
THAT IS WHERE THE PASTOR WAS HURRYING TO.
THE SOLE CERTAINTY IN THIS WHOLE THING IS THAT HARRIET DID NOT CROSS BACK OVER THE BRIDGE.
COULD SHE HAVE BEEN DROWNED?
NO. THE CURRENTS WOULD HAVE WASHED HER BODY TO THE SHORE.
YOU'D HAVE TO GO FOUR MILES OUT BEFORE A BODY COULD BE LOST AT SEA.
HER BODY COULD HAVE BEEN BURIED?
NO. WE SEARCHED THE ISLAND FOR ONE FULL YEAR. NOTHING.
SHE DIDN'T TAKE A BOAT EITHER, THEY WERE ALL ON THE ISLAND.
SHE HID AND THEN RAN THE NEXT DAY? GOT A JOB?
HER PASSPORT AND PURSE WERE LEFT ON HER DRESSER, HER CLOTHES WERE THERE, EVEN HER PRIVATE DIARY WAS LEFT. HER SOCIAL SECURITY NUMBER HAS NEVER BEEN USED.
SHE'S *DEAD.*
THERE'S NO DOUBT ABOUT IT.
AND YOU THINK WHOEVER KILLED HER IS SENDING THESE EVERY YEAR?
AND WHOEVER IS SENDING THEM KNOWS WHAT IS ALREADY THERE.
THEY KNOW WHAT THEY MEAN TO ME.
I AM EIGHTY-TWO THIS YEAR, MR. BLOMKVIST.
HER LOSS HAS COLORED MY WHOLE LIFE.
CAUSED A RIFT WITH MY FAMILY:
NOW I HATE THEM ALMOST AS MUCH AS THEY HATE ME.
BEFORE I DIE ***I NEED TO KNOW.***

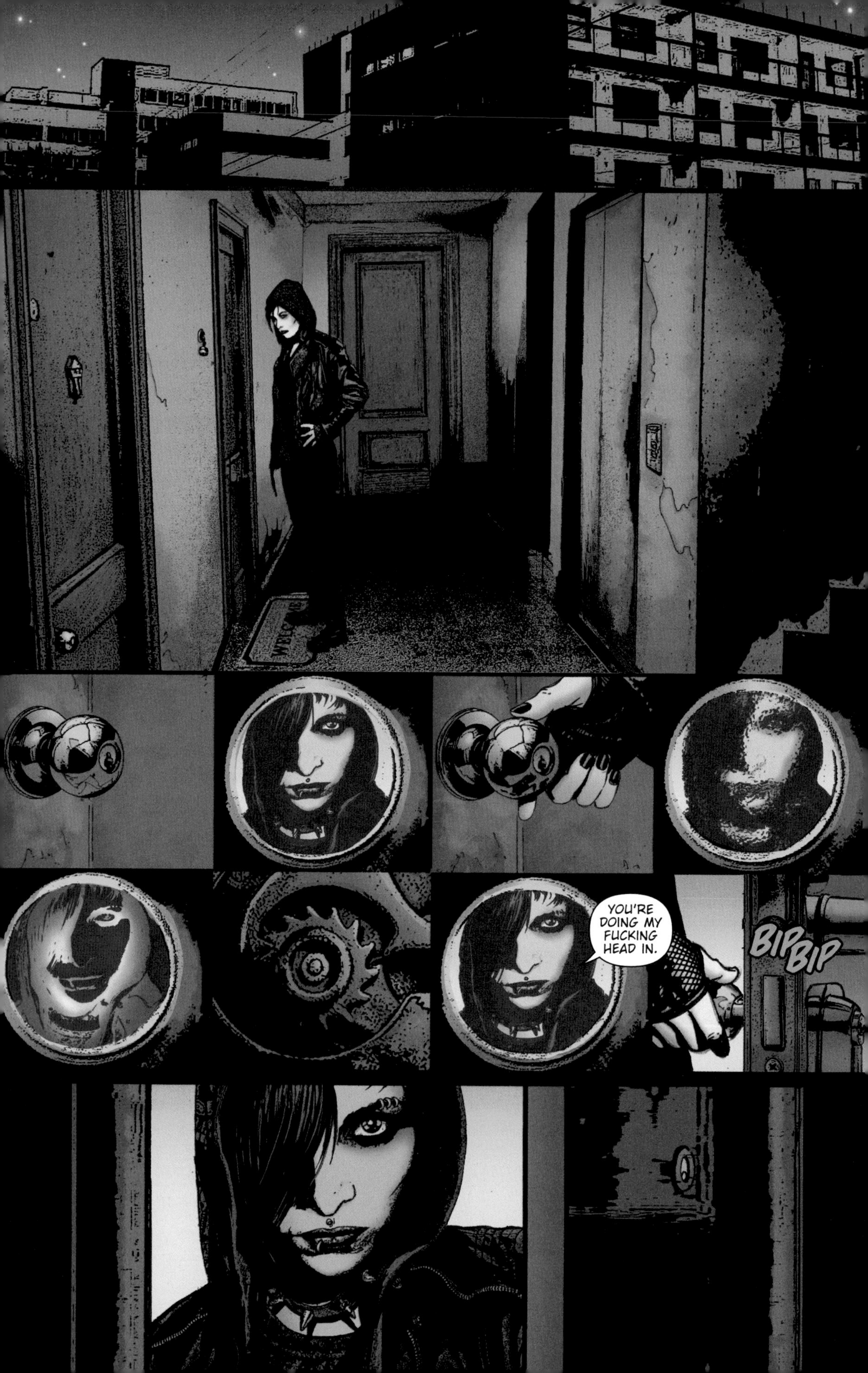
YOU'RE DOING MY FUCKING HEAD IN.
BIP BIP

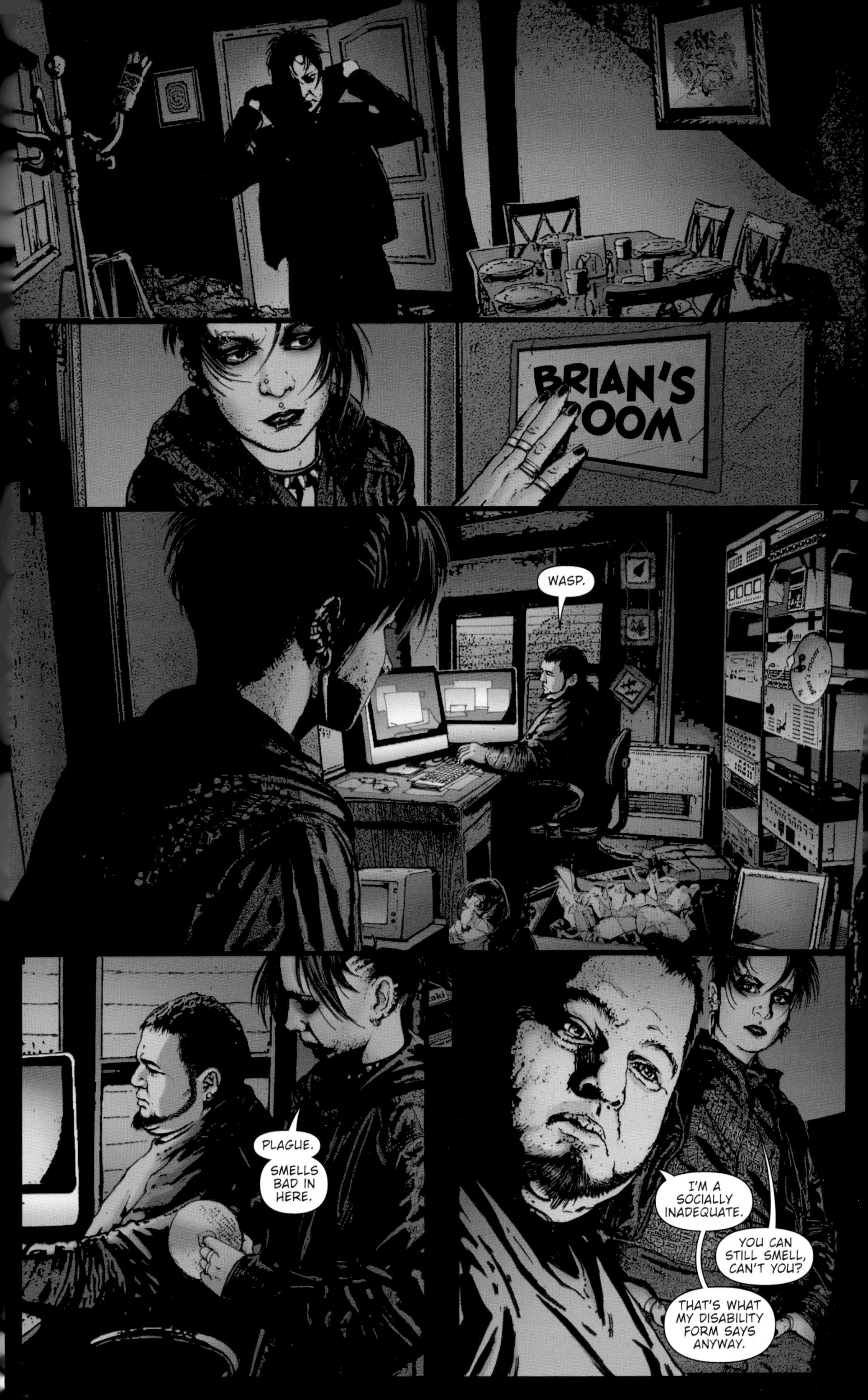
BRIAN'S ROOM
WASP.
PLAGUE.
SMELLS BAD IN HERE.
I'M A SOCIALLY INADEQUATE.
YOU CAN STILL SMELL, CAN'T YOU?
THAT'S WHAT MY DISABILITY FORM SAYS ANYWAY.

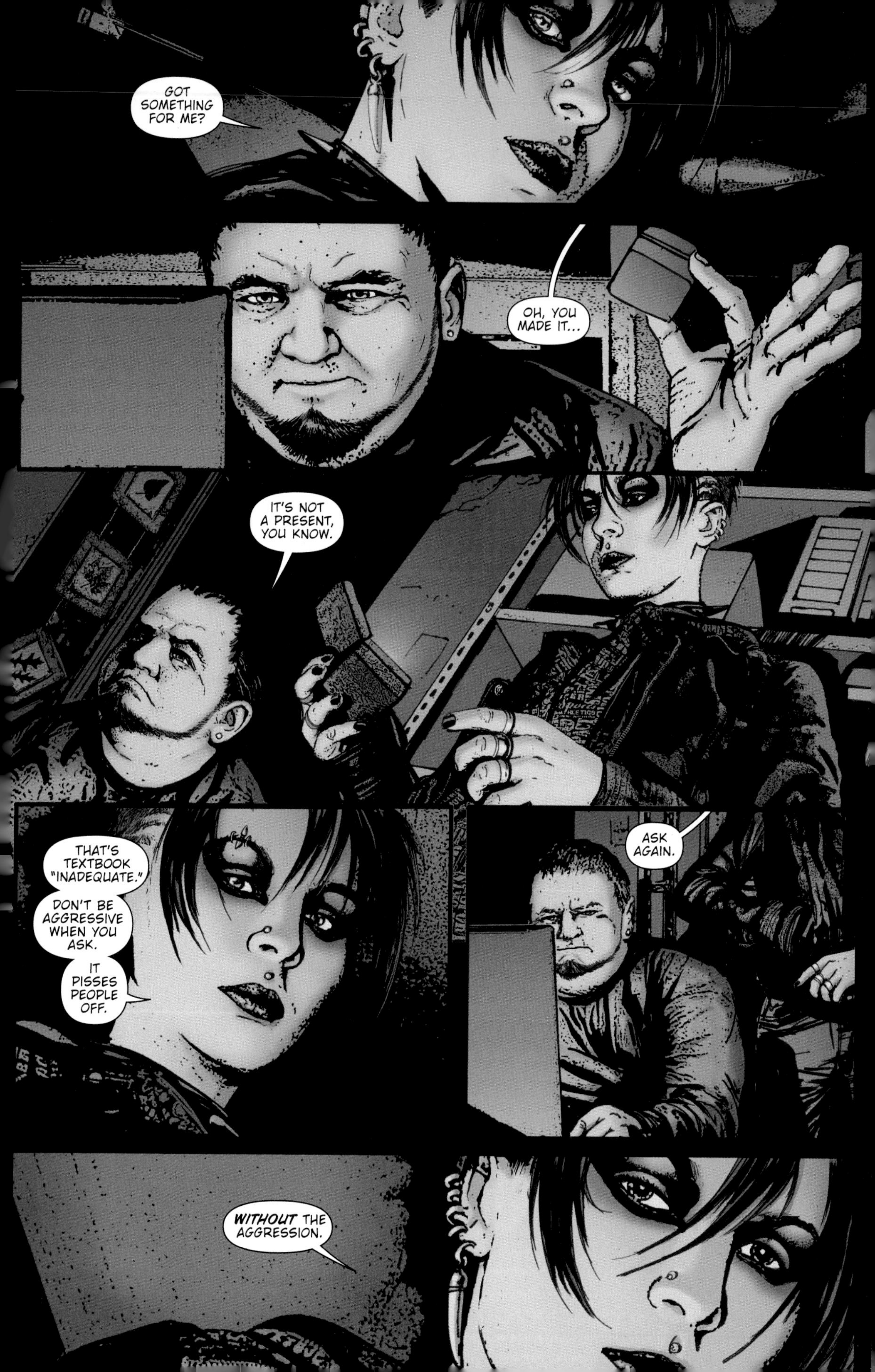
GOT SOMETHING FOR ME?
OH, YOU MADE IT...
IT'S NOT A PRESENT, YOU KNOW.
THAT'S TEXTBOOK "INADEQUATE."
DON'T BE AGGRESSIVE WHEN YOU ASK.
IT PISSES PEOPLE OFF.
ASK AGAIN.
WITHOUT THE AGGRESSION.

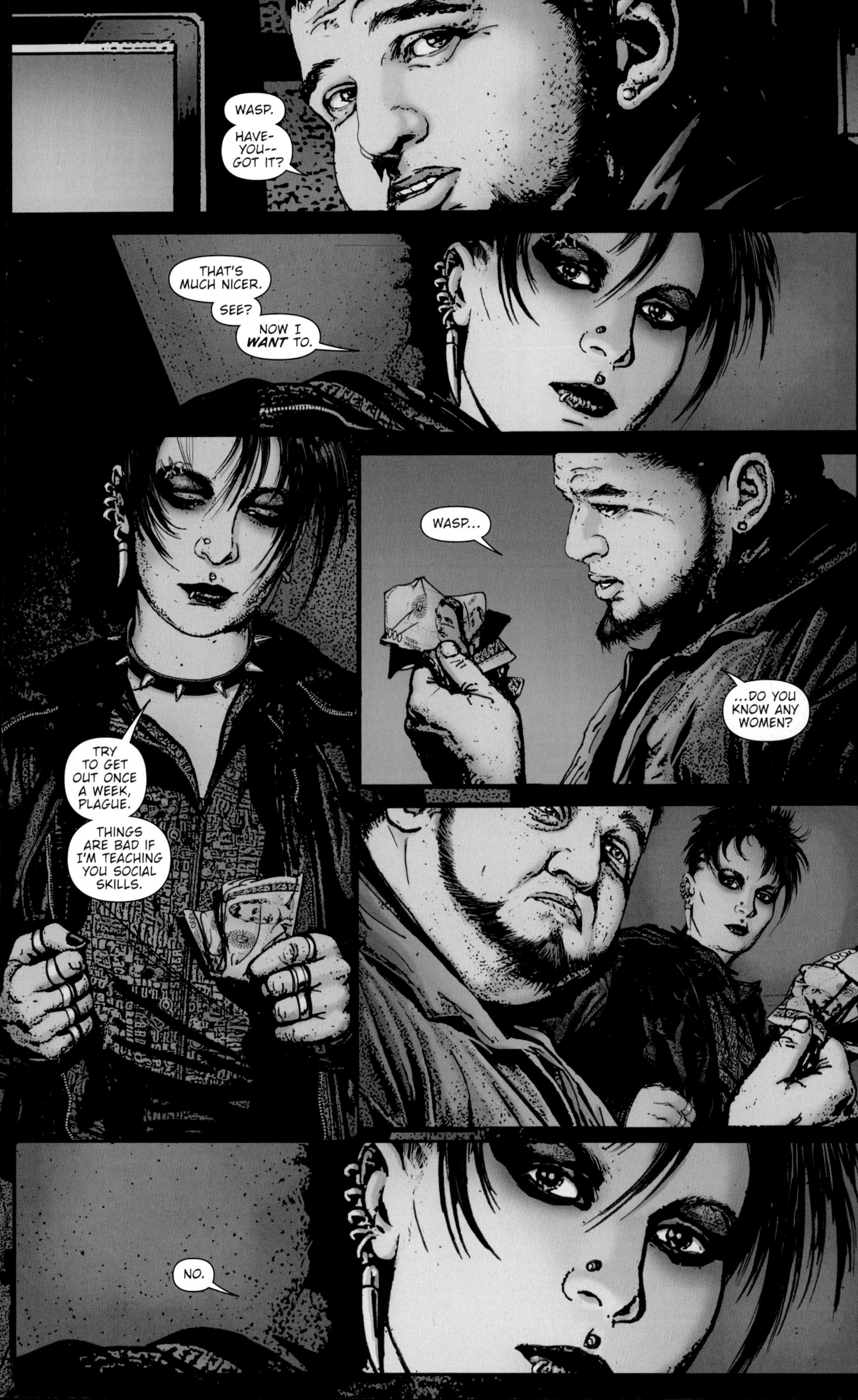
WASP.
HAVE-YOU--GOT IT?
THAT'S MUCH NICER.
SEE?
NOW I **WANT** TO.
TRY TO GET OUT ONCE A WEEK, PLAGUE.
THINGS ARE BAD IF I'M TEACHING YOU SOCIAL SKILLS.
WASP...
...DO YOU KNOW ANY WOMEN?
NO.

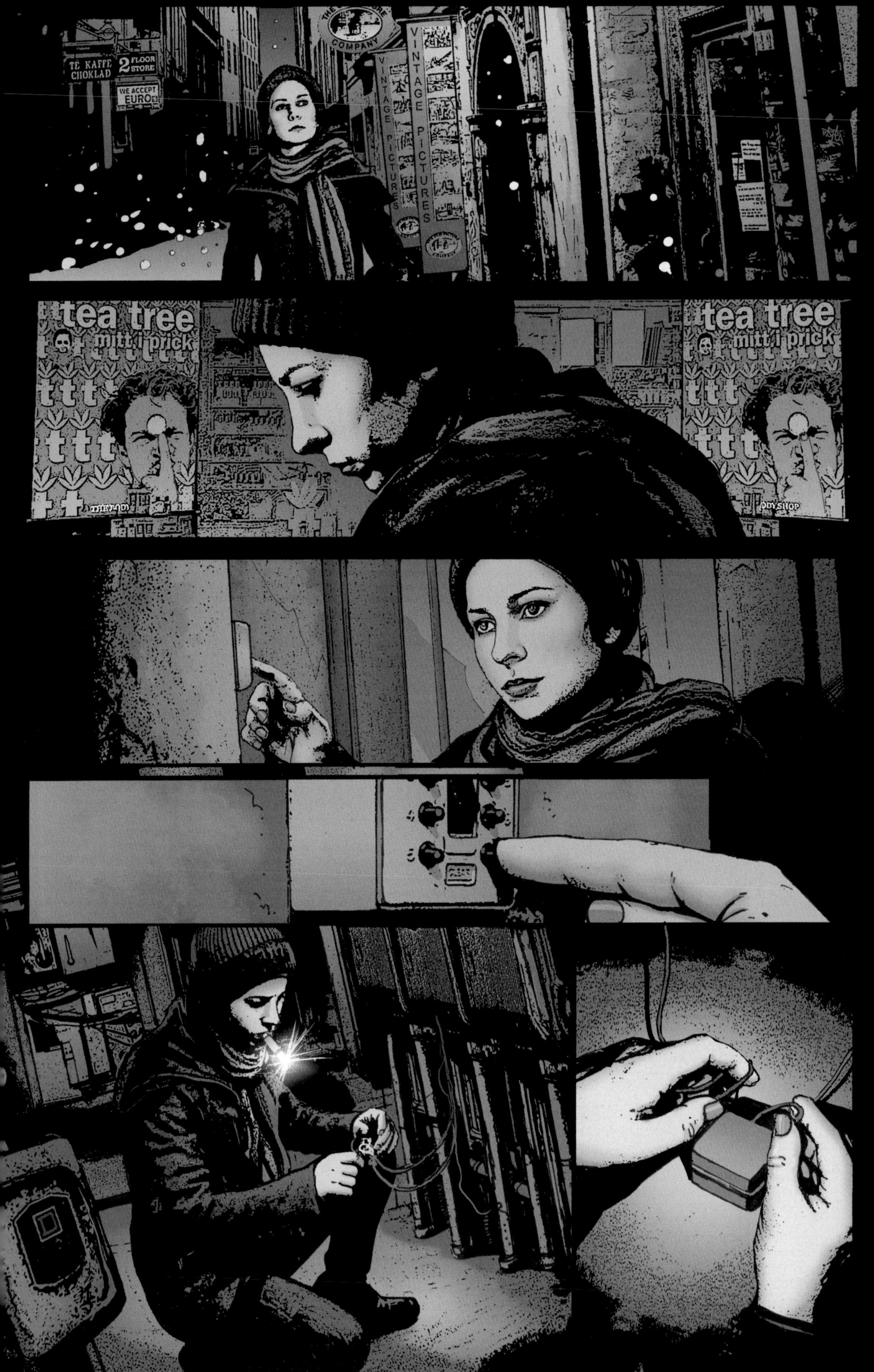
TE KAFFE
CHOKLAD
2 FLOOR
STORE
WE ACCEPT
EURO
COMPANY
VINTAGE PICTURES
VINTAGE PICTURES
tea tree
mitt i prick
tea tree
mitt i prick

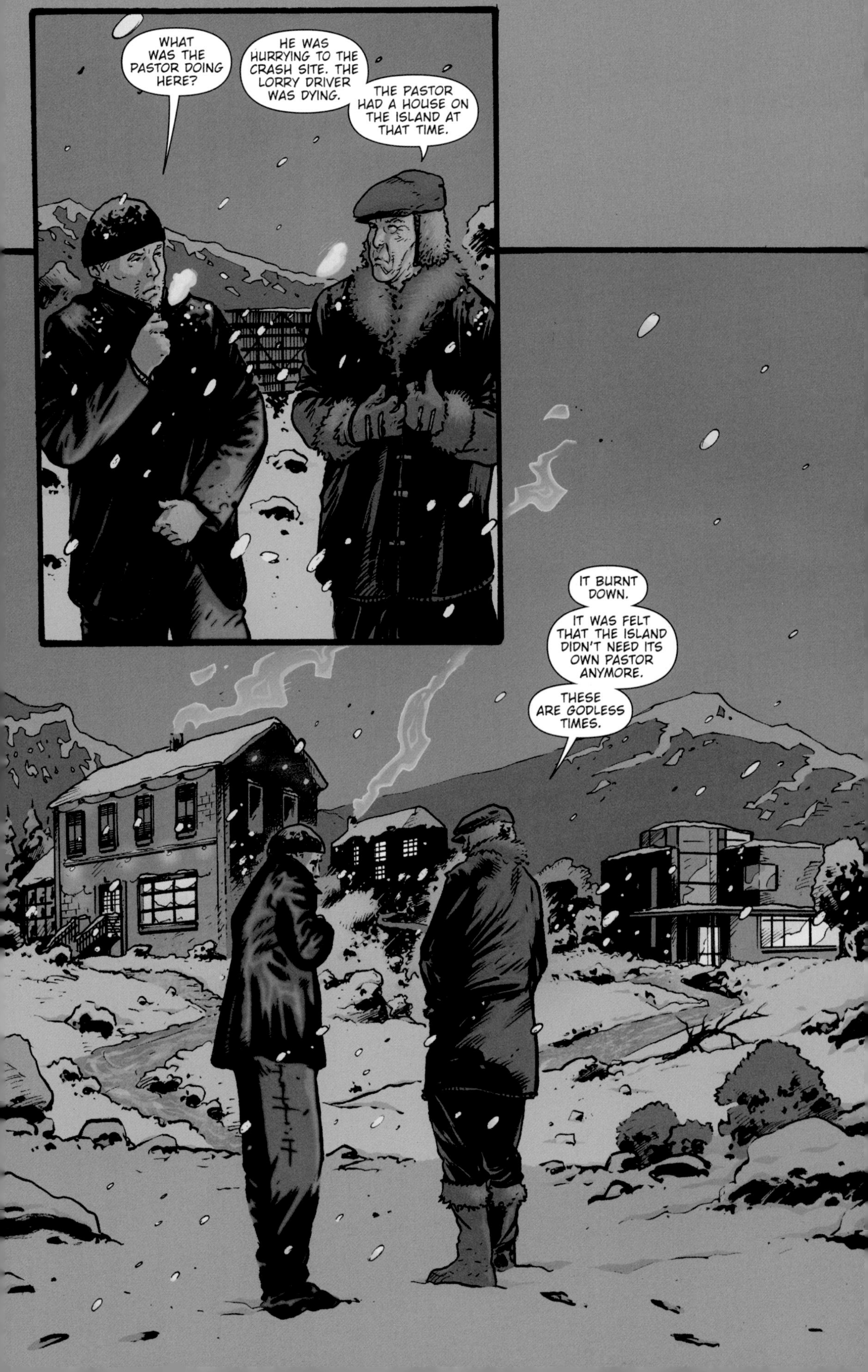
WHAT WAS THE PASTOR DOING HERE?
HE WAS HURRYING TO THE CRASH SITE. THE LORRY DRIVER WAS DYING.
THE PASTOR HAD A HOUSE ON THE ISLAND AT THAT TIME.
IT BURNT DOWN.
IT WAS FELT THAT THE ISLAND DIDN'T NEED ITS OWN PASTOR ANYMORE.
THESE ARE GODLESS TIMES.

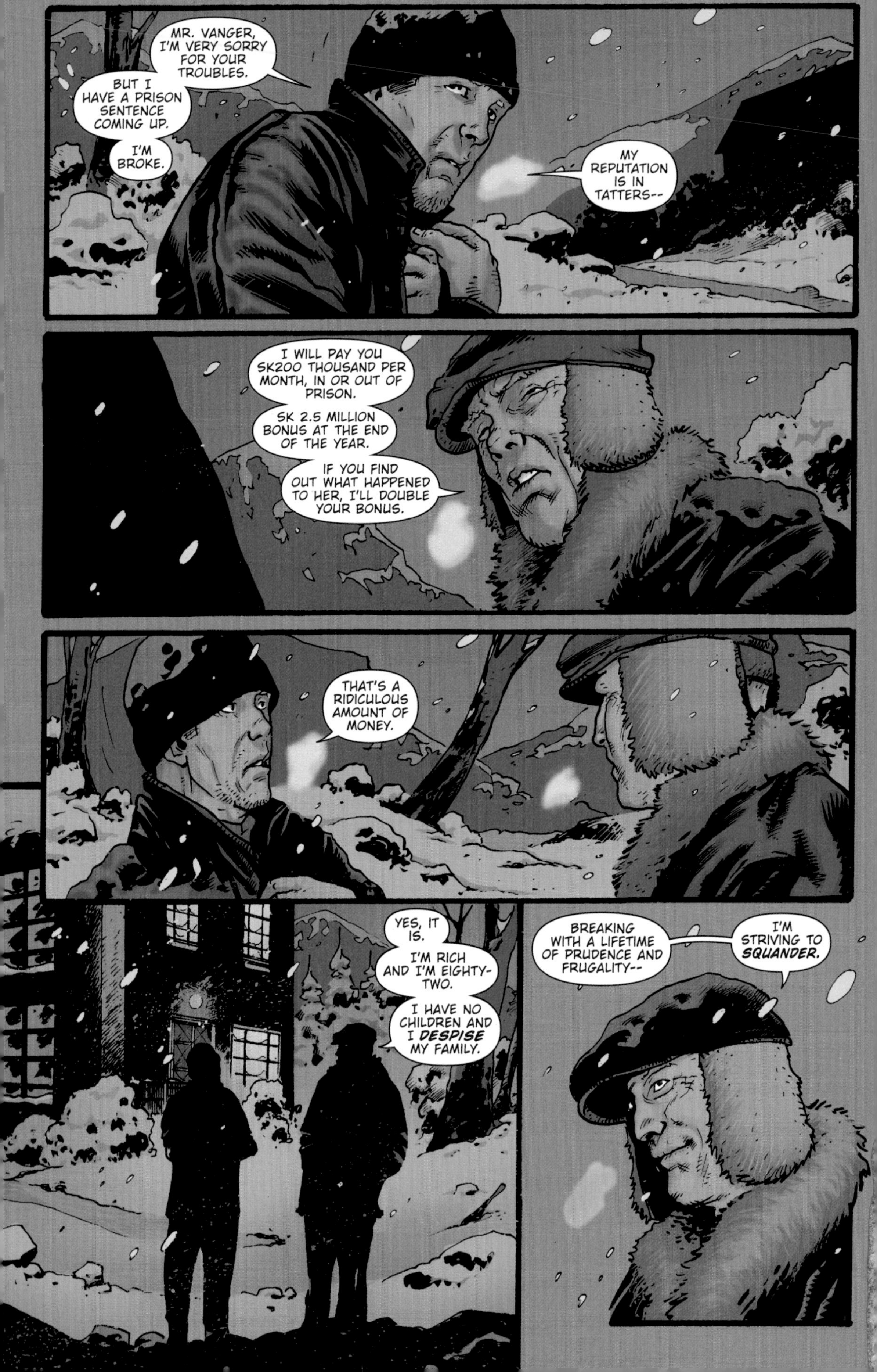
MR. VANGER, I'M VERY SORRY FOR YOUR TROUBLES.
BUT I HAVE A PRISON SENTENCE COMING UP.
I'M BROKE.
MY REPUTATION IS IN TATTERS--
I WILL PAY YOU SK200 THOUSAND PER MONTH, IN OR OUT OF PRISON.
SK 2.5 MILLION BONUS AT THE END OF THE YEAR.
IF YOU FIND OUT WHAT HAPPENED TO HER, I'LL DOUBLE YOUR BONUS.
THAT'S A RIDICULOUS AMOUNT OF MONEY.
YES, IT IS.
I'M RICH AND I'M EIGHTY-TWO.
I HAVE NO CHILDREN AND I *DESPISE* MY FAMILY.
BREAKING WITH A LIFETIME OF PRUDENCE AND FRUGALITY--
I'M STRIVING TO *SQUANDER.*

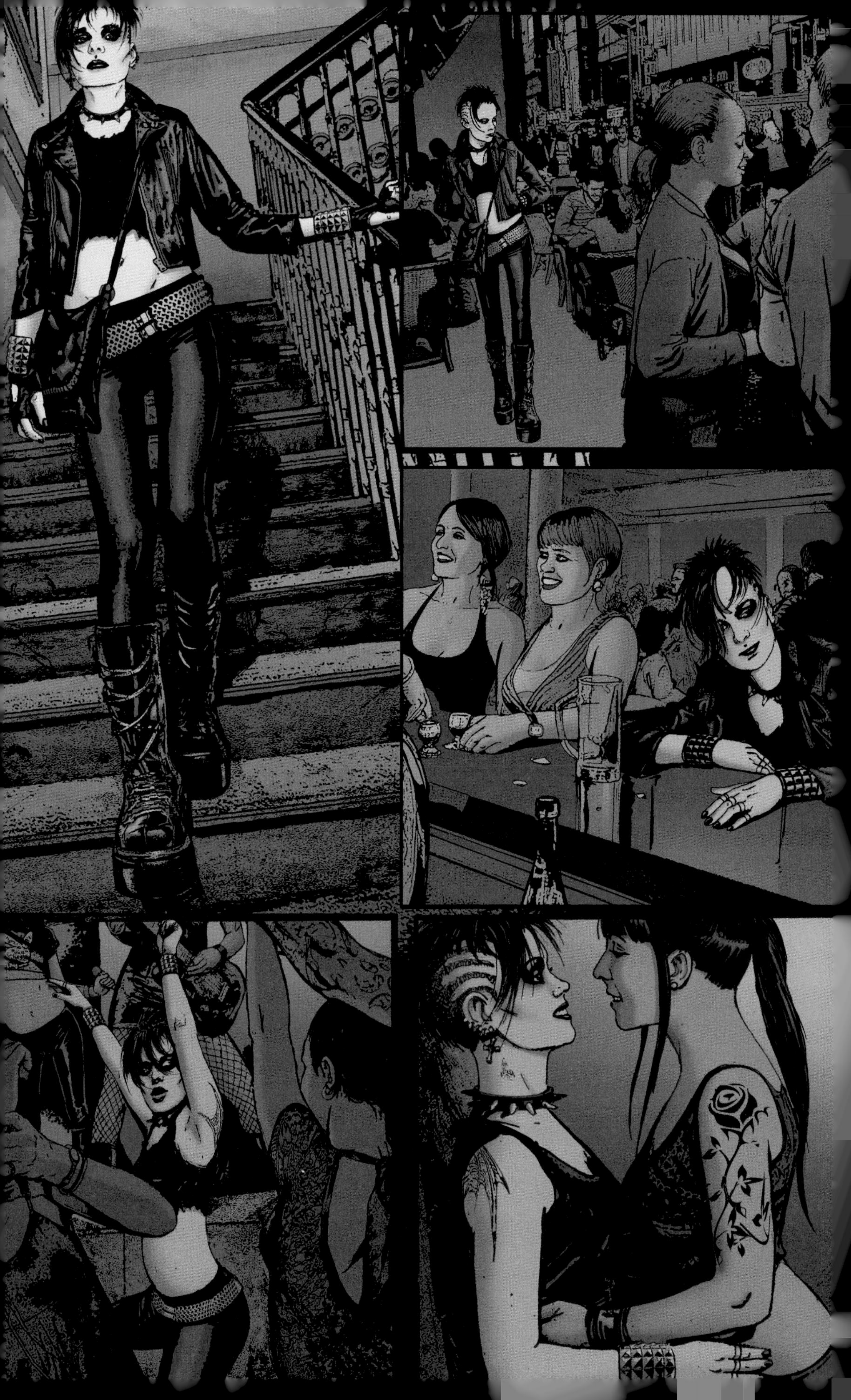

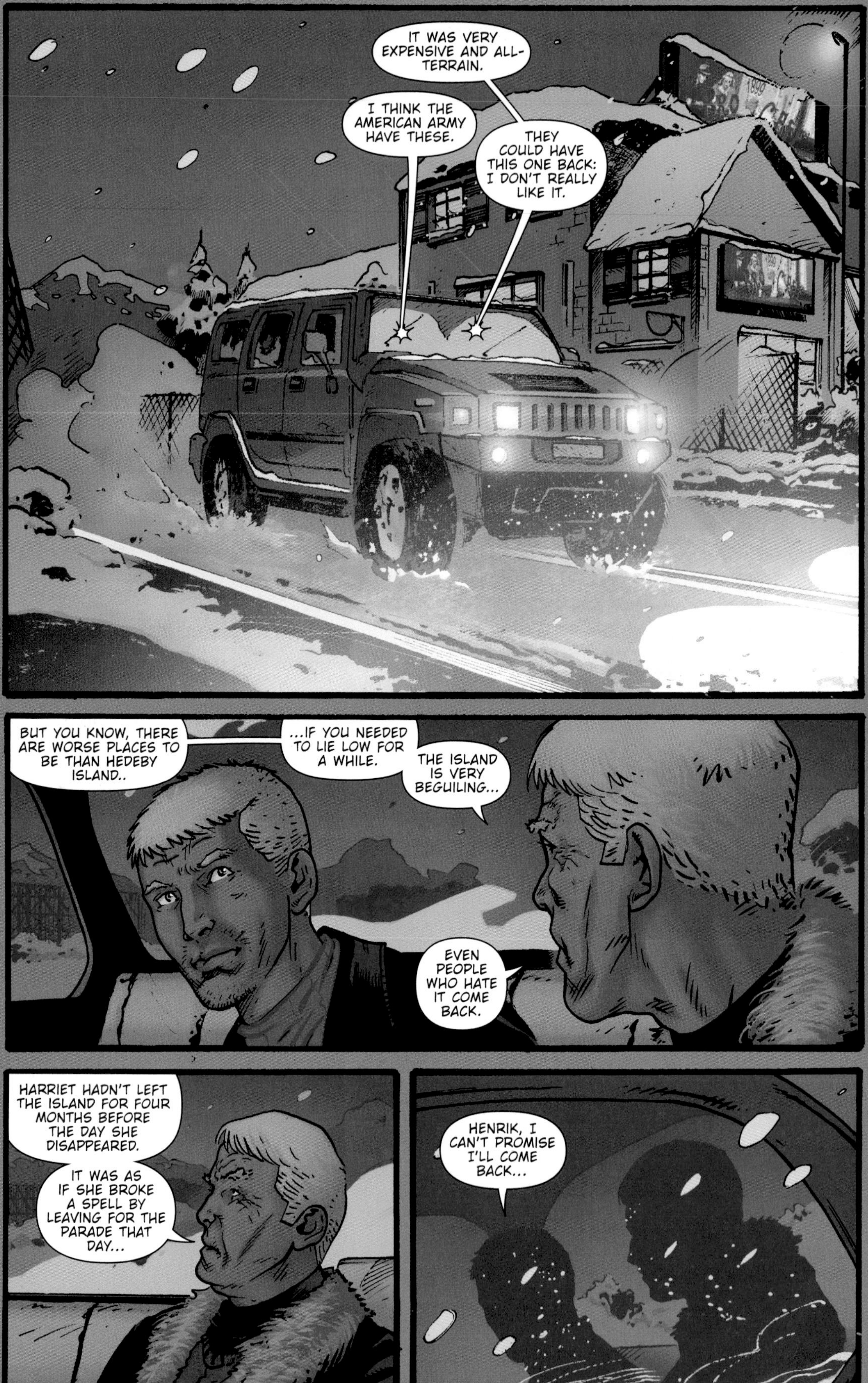
I THINK THE AMERICAN ARMY HAVE THESE.
IT WAS VERY EXPENSIVE AND ALL-TERRAIN.
THEY COULD HAVE THIS ONE BACK: I DON'T REALLY LIKE IT.
BUT YOU KNOW, THERE ARE WORSE PLACES TO BE THAN HEDEBY ISLAND..
...IF YOU NEEDED TO LIE LOW FOR A WHILE.
THE ISLAND IS VERY BEGUILING...
EVEN PEOPLE WHO HATE IT COME BACK.
HARRIET HADN'T LEFT THE ISLAND FOR FOUR MONTHS BEFORE THE DAY SHE DISAPPEARED.
IT WAS AS IF SHE BROKE A SPELL BY LEAVING FOR THE PARADE THAT DAY...
HENRIK, I CAN'T PROMISE I'LL COME BACK...

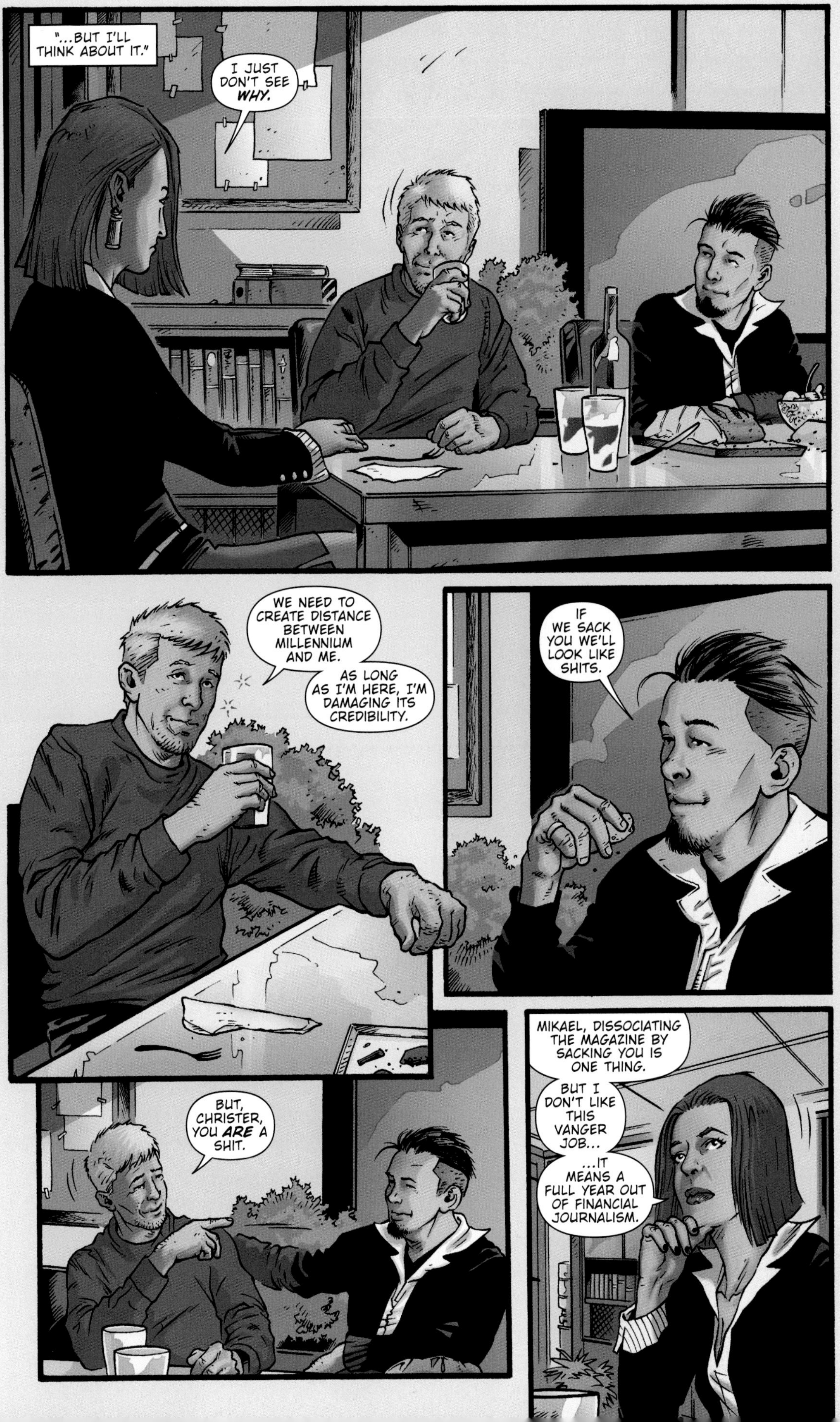
"...BUT I'LL THINK ABOUT IT."
I JUST DON'T SEE *WHY.*
WE NEED TO CREATE DISTANCE BETWEEN MILLENNIUM AND ME.
AS LONG AS I'M HERE, I'M DAMAGING ITS CREDIBILITY.
IF WE SACK YOU WE'LL LOOK LIKE SHITS.
BUT, CHRISTER, YOU *ARE* A SHIT.
MIKAEL, DISSOCIATING THE MAGAZINE BY SACKING YOU IS ONE THING.
BUT I DON'T LIKE THIS VANGER JOB...
...IT MEANS A FULL YEAR OUT OF FINANCIAL JOURNALISM.

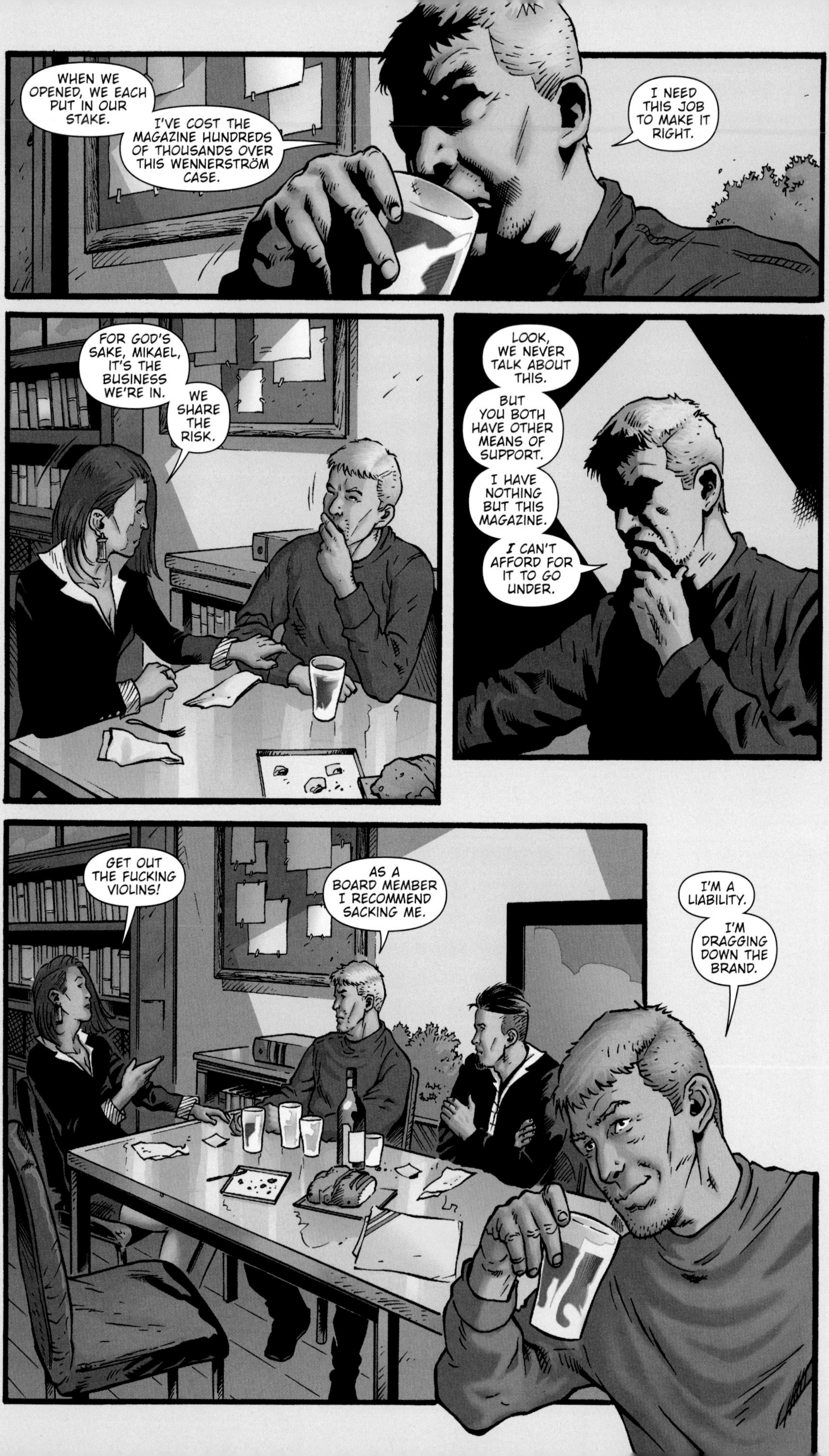

WHEN WE OPENED, WE EACH PUT IN OUR STAKE.
I'VE COST THE MAGAZINE HUNDREDS OF THOUSANDS OVER THIS WENNERSTRÖM CASE.
I NEED THIS JOB TO MAKE IT RIGHT.
FOR GOD'S SAKE, MIKAEL, IT'S THE BUSINESS WE'RE IN.
WE SHARE THE RISK.
LOOK, WE NEVER TALK ABOUT THIS.
BUT YOU BOTH HAVE OTHER MEANS OF SUPPORT.
I HAVE NOTHING BUT THIS MAGAZINE.
I CAN'T AFFORD FOR IT TO GO UNDER.
GET OUT THE FUCKING VIOLINS!
AS A BOARD MEMBER I RECOMMEND SACKING ME.
I'M A LIABILITY.
I'M DRAGGING DOWN THE BRAND.

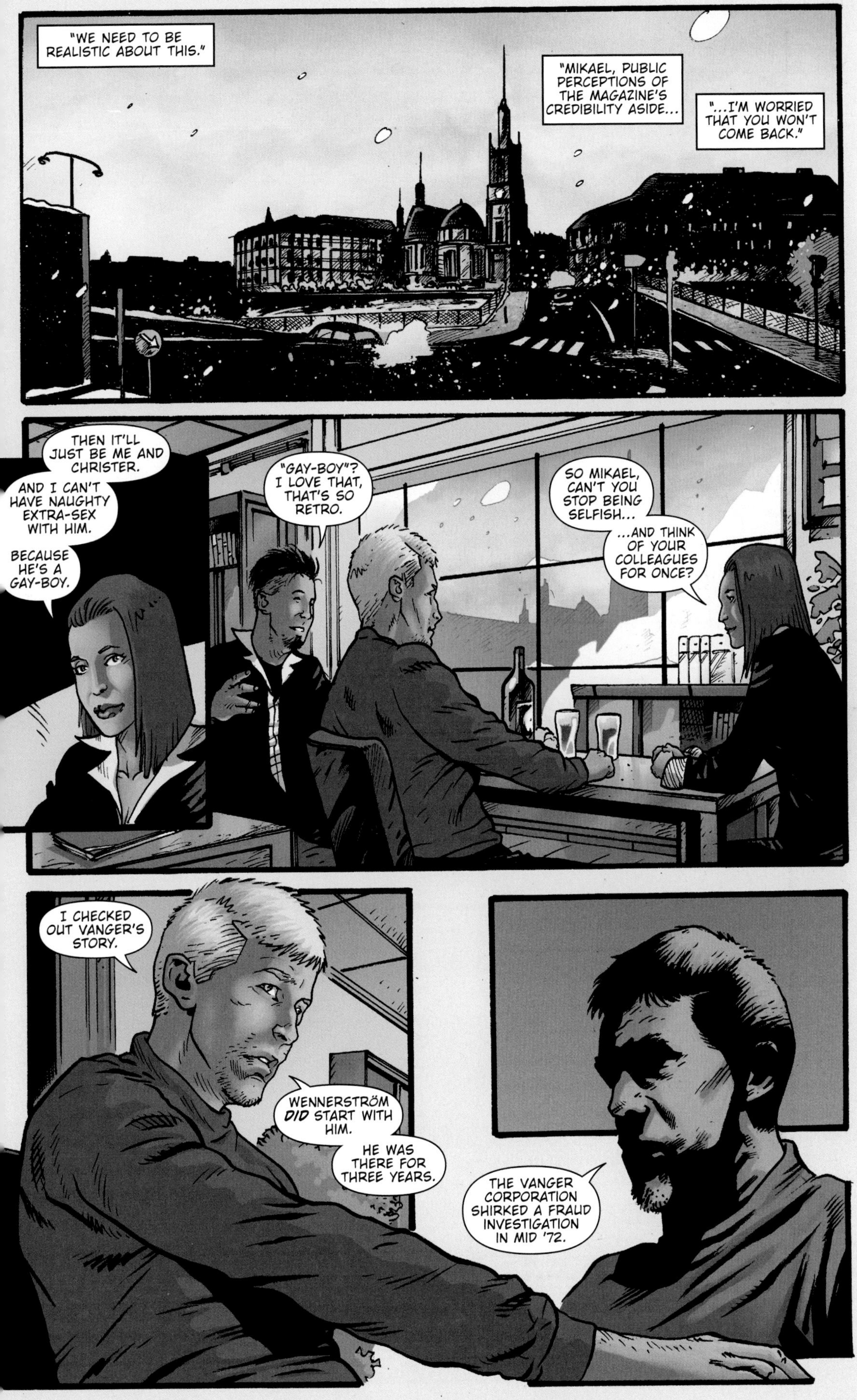
"WE NEED TO BE REALISTIC ABOUT THIS."
"MIKAEL, PUBLIC PERCEPTIONS OF THE MAGAZINE'S CREDIBILITY ASIDE...
"...I'M WORRIED THAT YOU WON'T COME BACK."
THEN IT'LL JUST BE ME AND CHRISTER.
AND I CAN'T HAVE NAUGHTY EXTRA-SEX WITH HIM.
BECAUSE HE'S A GAY-BOY.
"GAY-BOY"? I LOVE THAT, THAT'S SO RETRO.
SO MIKAEL, CAN'T YOU STOP BEING SELFISH...
...AND THINK OF YOUR COLLEAGUES FOR ONCE?
I CHECKED OUT VANGER'S STORY.
WENNERSTRÖM *DID* START WITH HIM.
HE WAS THERE FOR THREE YEARS.
THE VANGER CORPORATION SHIRKED A FRAUD INVESTIGATION IN MID '72.

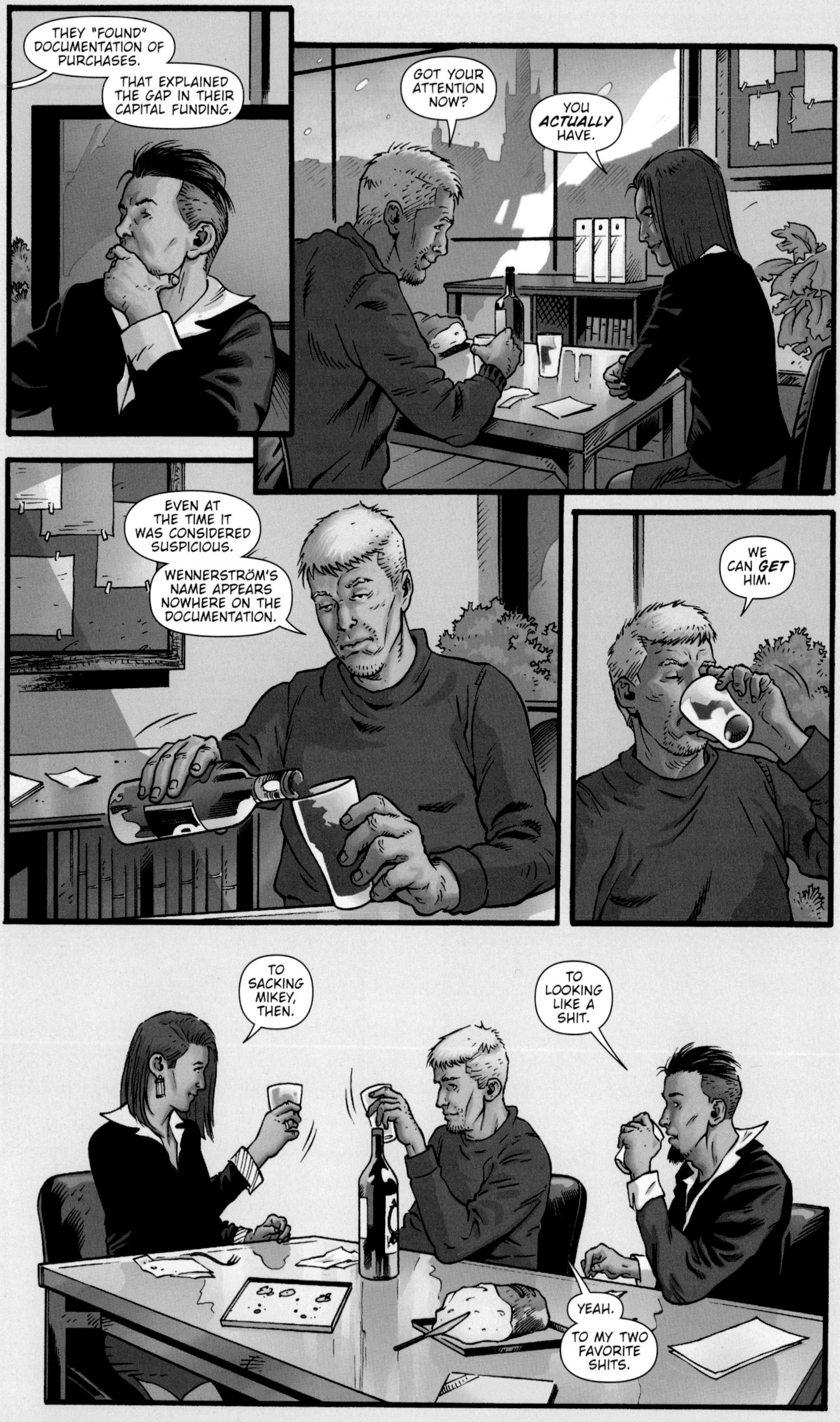
THEY "FOUND" DOCUMENTATION OF PURCHASES.
THAT EXPLAINED THE GAP IN THEIR CAPITAL FUNDING.
GOT YOUR ATTENTION NOW?
YOU ACTUALLY HAVE.
EVEN AT THE TIME IT WAS CONSIDERED SUSPICIOUS.
WENNERSTRÖM'S NAME APPEARS NOWHERE ON THE DOCUMENTATION.
WE CAN GET HIM.
TO SACKING MIKEY, THEN.
TO LOOKING LIKE A SHIT.
YEAH.
TO MY TWO FAVORITE SHITS.

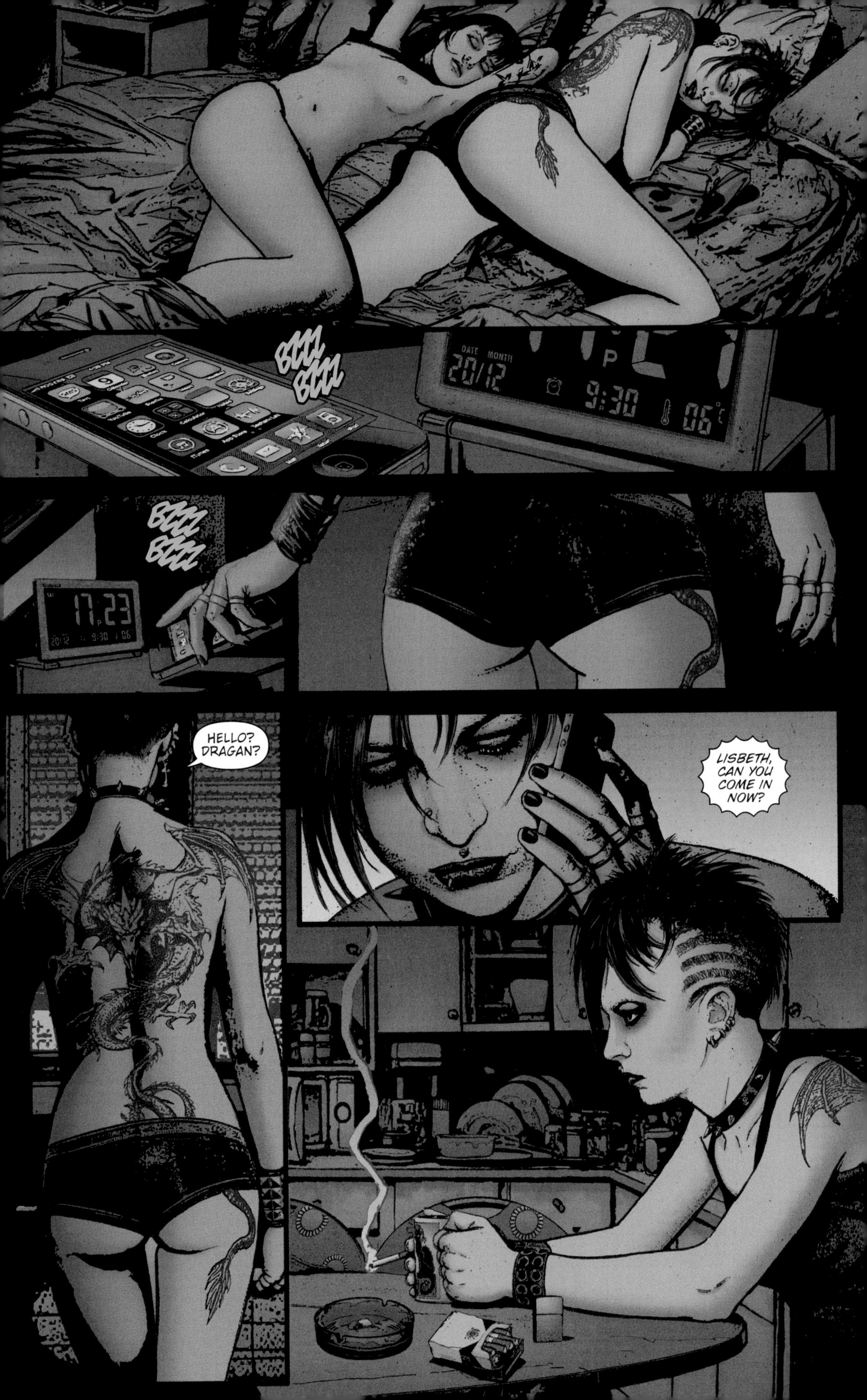
BZZZ BZZZ
BZZZ BZZZ
HELLO? DRAGAN?
LISBETH, CAN YOU COME IN NOW?

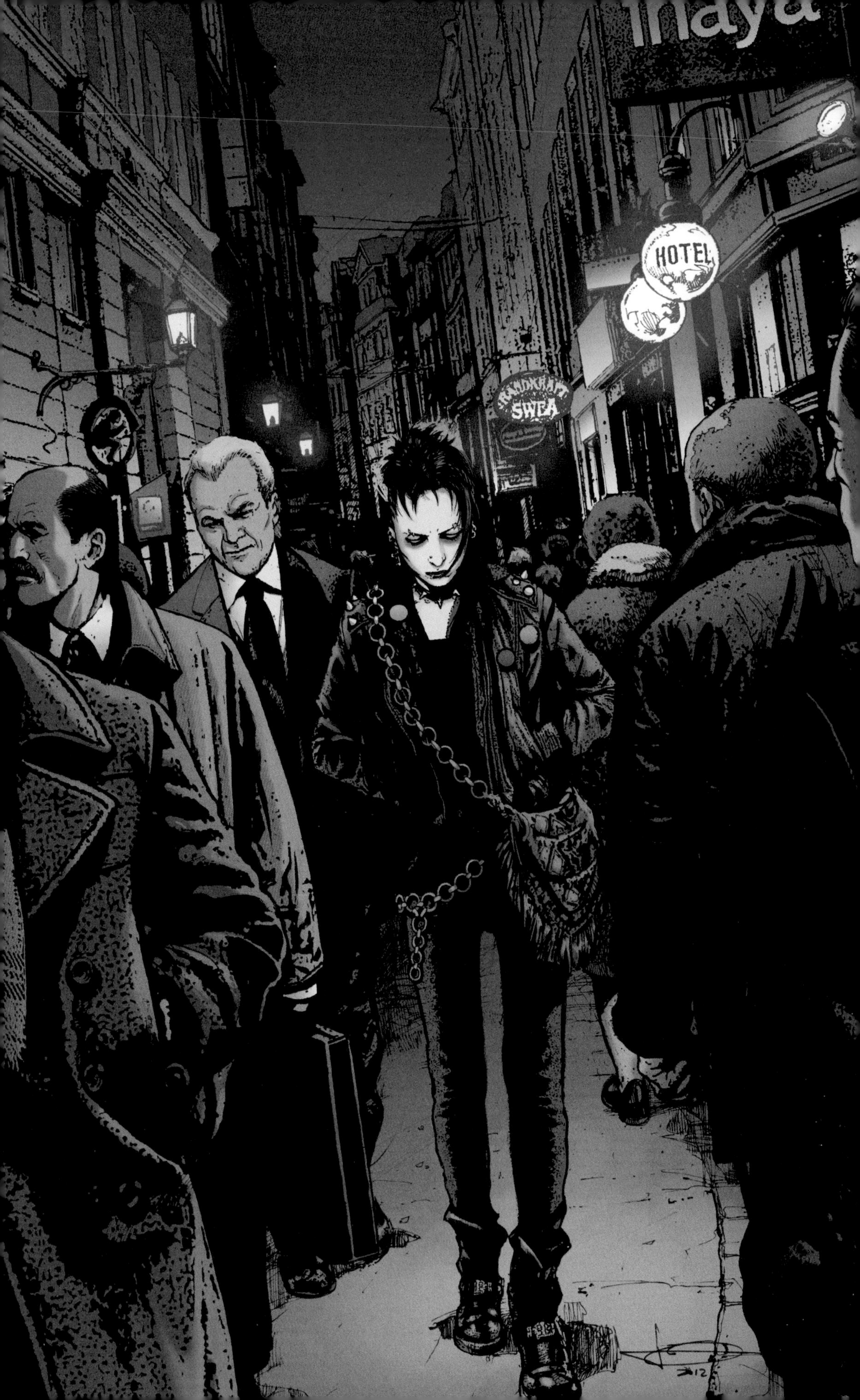
HOTEL
SWEA

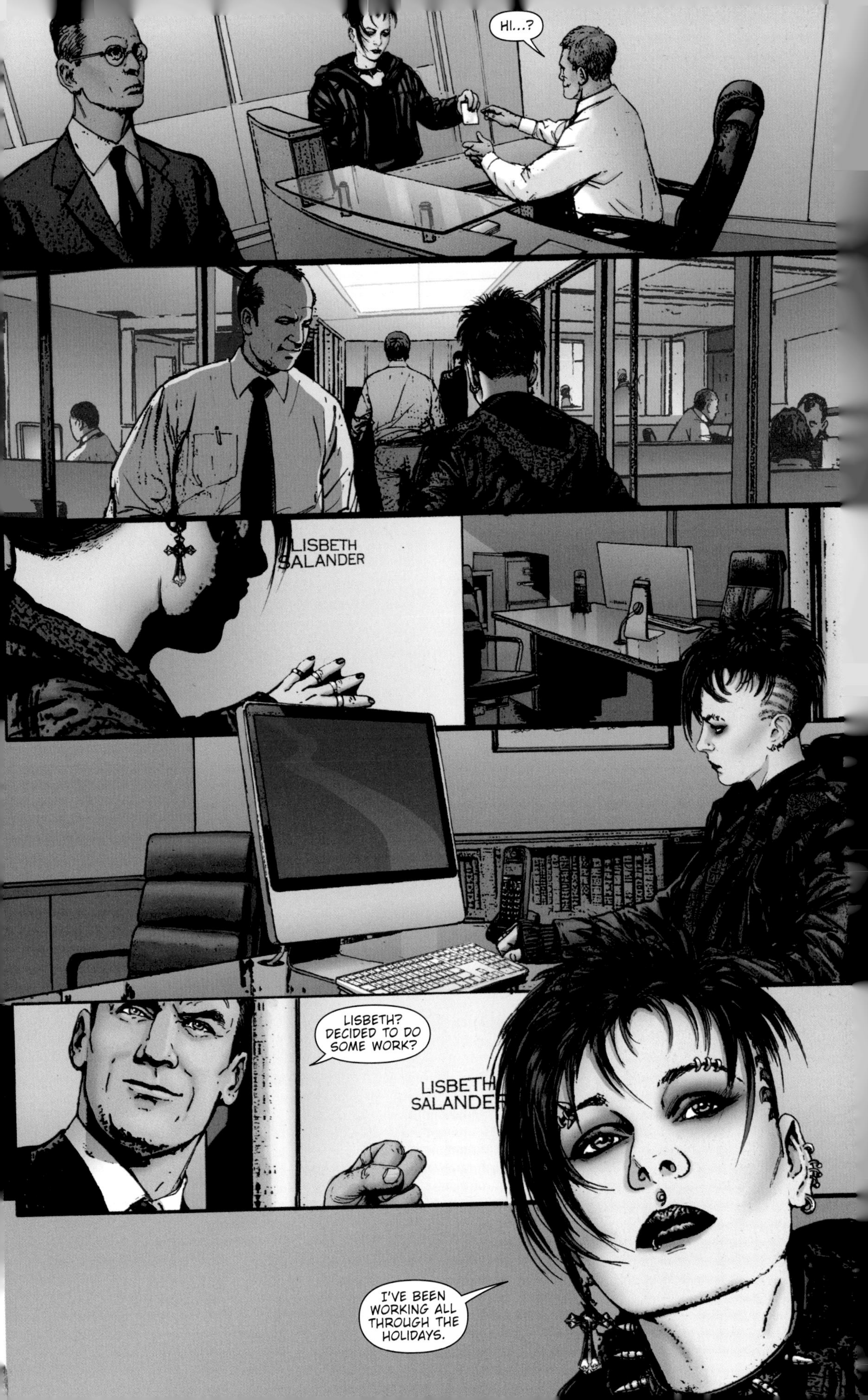
HI...?
LISBETH SALANDER
LISBETH? DECIDED TO DO SOME WORK?
LISBETH SALANDER
I'VE BEEN WORKING ALL THROUGH THE HOLIDAYS.

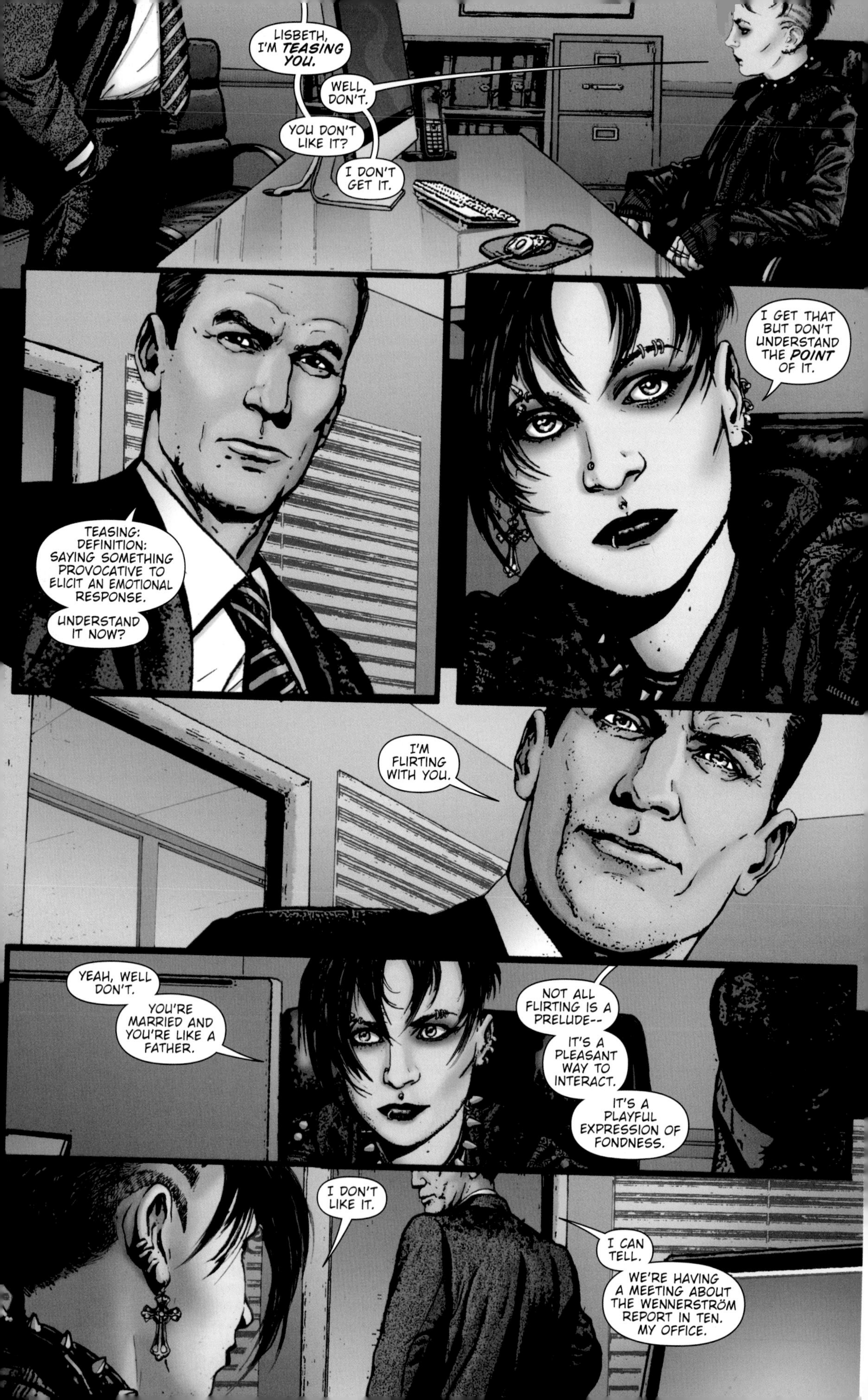
LISBETH, I'M *TEASING YOU.*
WELL, DON'T.
YOU DON'T LIKE IT?
I DON'T GET IT.
TEASING: DEFINITION: SAYING SOMETHING PROVOCATIVE TO ELICIT AN EMOTIONAL RESPONSE.
UNDERSTAND IT NOW?
I GET THAT BUT DON'T UNDERSTAND THE *POINT* OF IT.
I'M FLIRTING WITH YOU.
YEAH, WELL DON'T.
YOU'RE MARRIED AND YOU'RE LIKE A FATHER.
NOT ALL FLIRTING IS A PRELUDE--
IT'S A PLEASANT WAY TO INTERACT.
IT'S A PLAYFUL EXPRESSION OF FONDNESS.
I DON'T LIKE IT.
I CAN TELL.
WE'RE HAVING A MEETING ABOUT THE WENNERSTRÖM REPORT IN TEN. MY OFFICE.

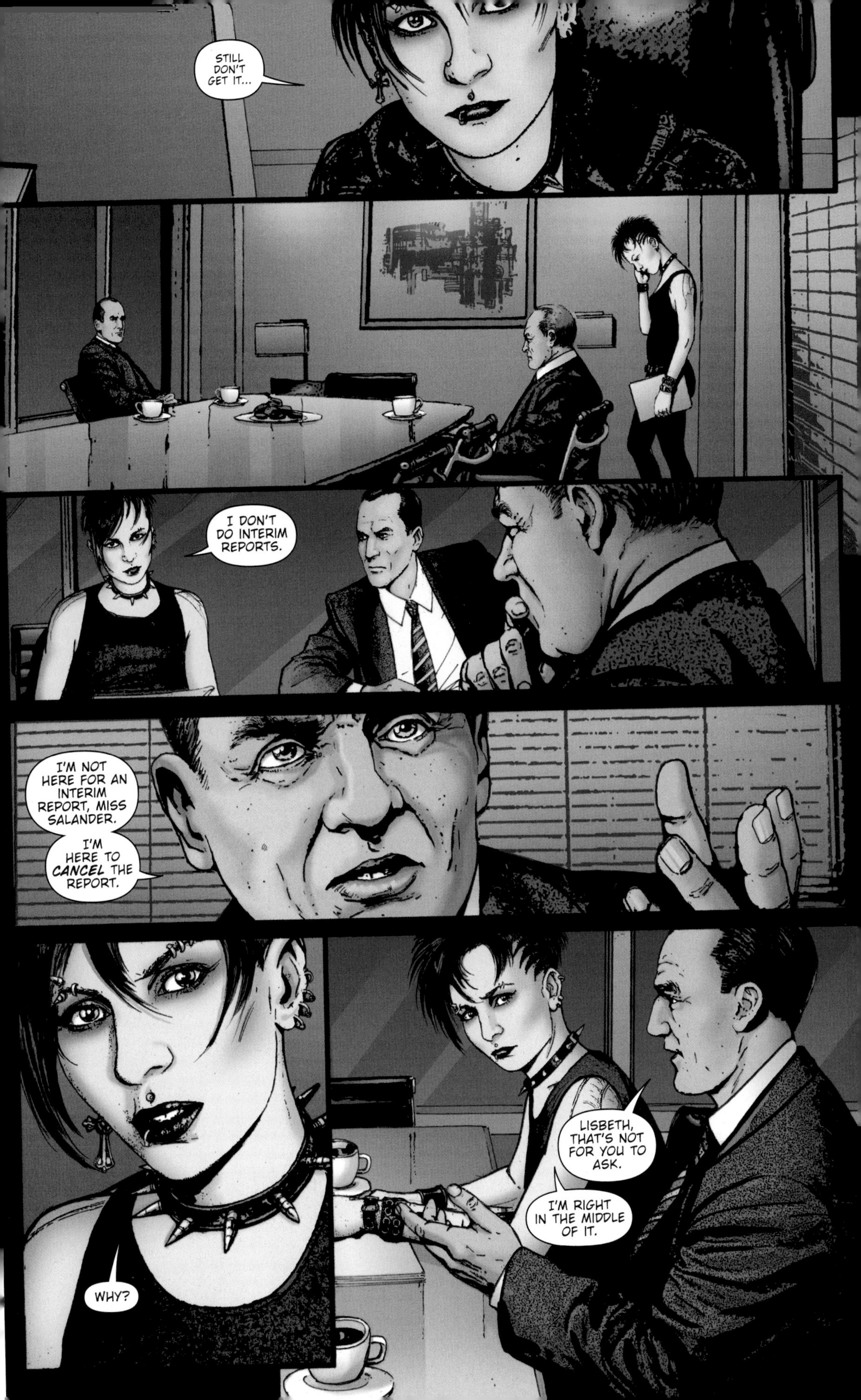
STILL DON'T GET IT...
I DON'T DO INTERIM REPORTS.
I'M NOT HERE FOR AN INTERIM REPORT, MISS SALANDER.
I'M HERE TO CANCEL THE REPORT.
WHY?
LISBETH, THAT'S NOT FOR YOU TO ASK.
I'M RIGHT IN THE MIDDLE OF IT.

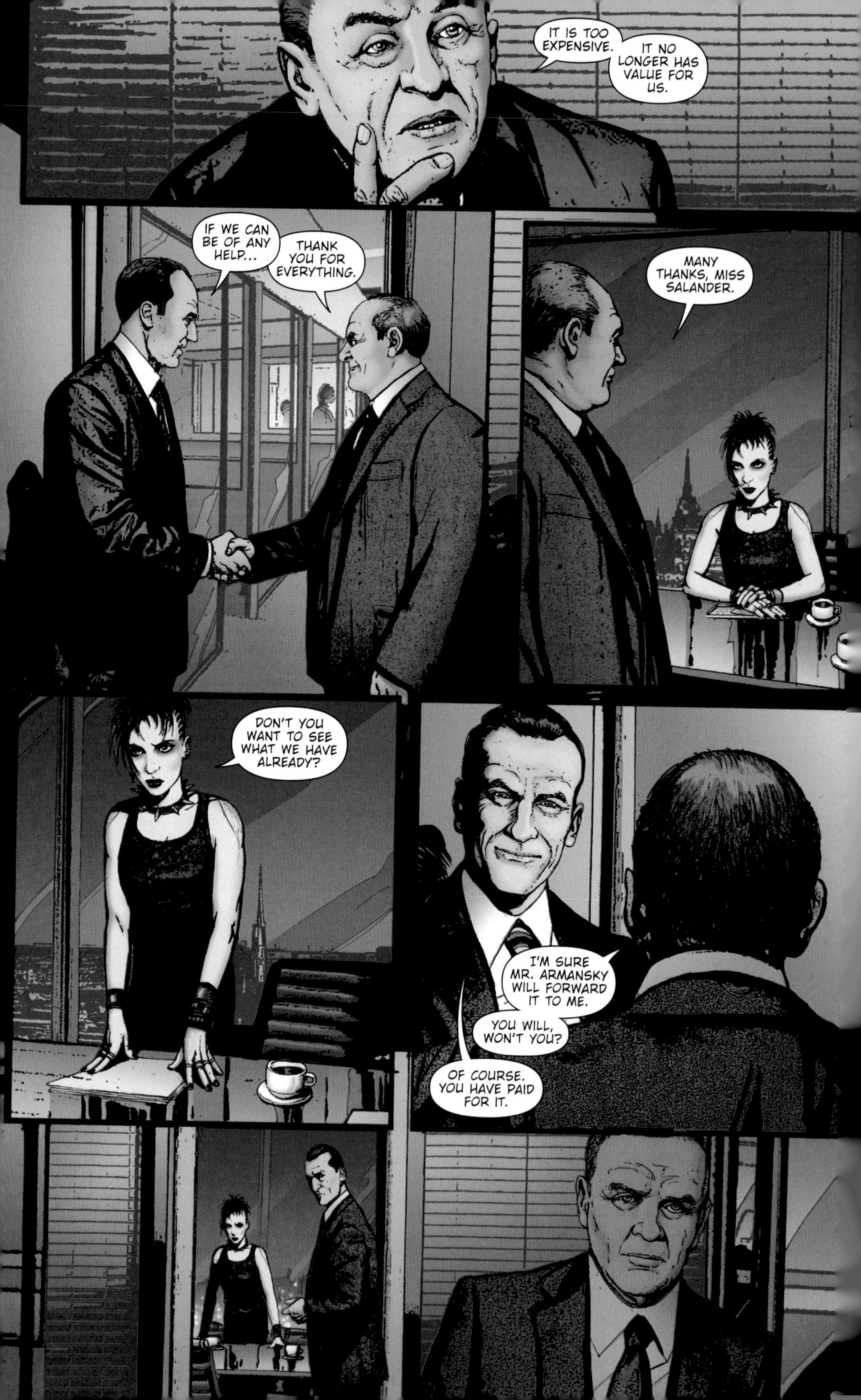
IT IS TOO EXPENSIVE.
IT NO LONGER HAS VALUE FOR US.
IF WE CAN BE OF ANY HELP...
THANK YOU FOR EVERYTHING.
MANY THANKS, MISS SALANDER.
DON'T YOU WANT TO SEE WHAT WE HAVE ALREADY?
I'M SURE MR. ARMANSKY WILL FORWARD IT TO ME.
YOU WILL, WON'T YOU?
OF COURSE. YOU HAVE PAID FOR IT.

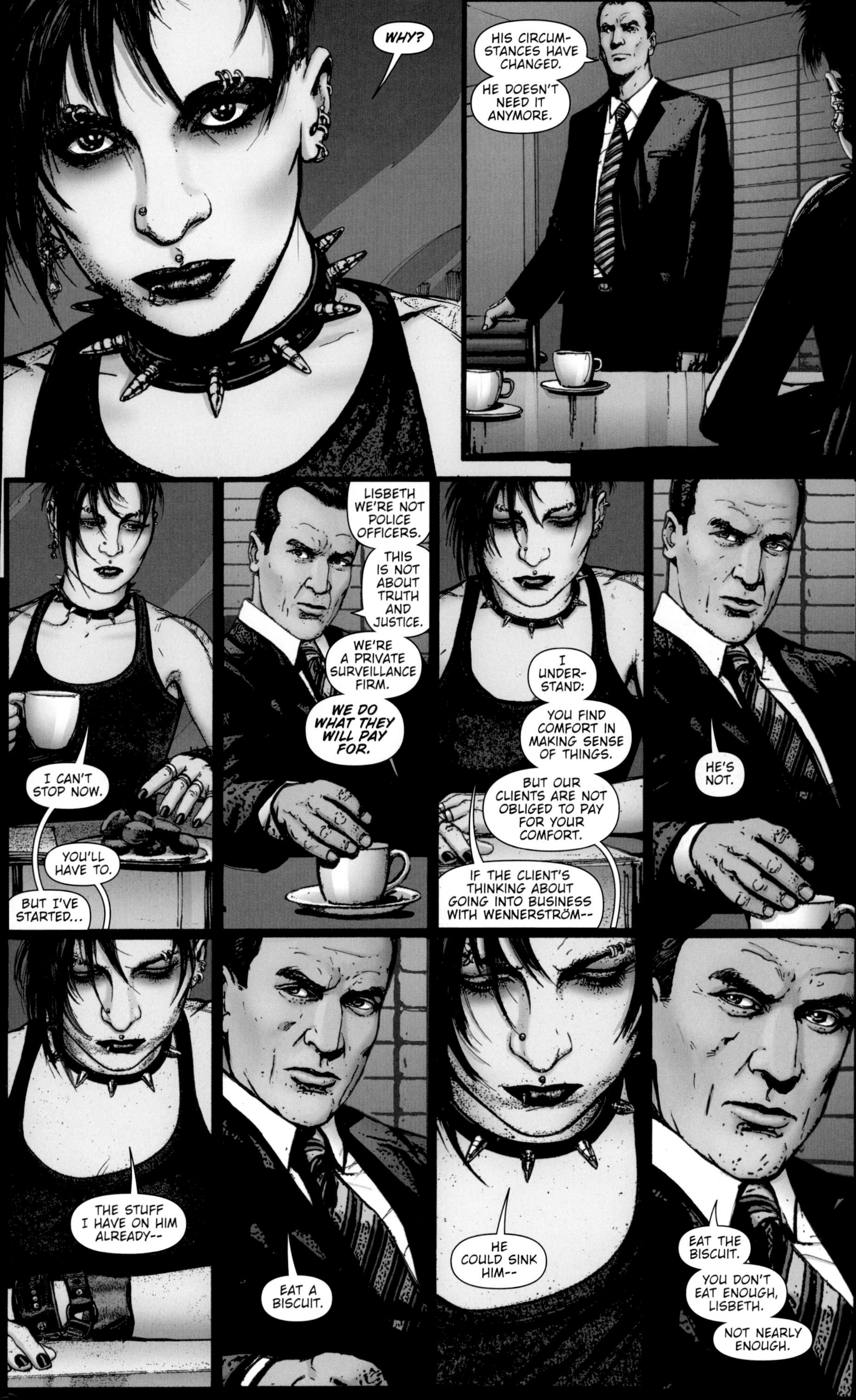
WHY?
HIS CIRCUMSTANCES HAVE CHANGED.
HE DOESN'T NEED IT ANYMORE.
I CAN'T STOP NOW.
YOU'LL HAVE TO.
BUT I'VE STARTED...
LISBETH WE'RE NOT POLICE OFFICERS.
THIS IS NOT ABOUT TRUTH AND JUSTICE.
WE'RE A PRIVATE SURVEILLANCE FIRM.
WE DO WHAT THEY WILL PAY FOR.
I UNDERSTAND:
YOU FIND COMFORT IN MAKING SENSE OF THINGS.
BUT OUR CLIENTS ARE NOT OBLIGED TO PAY FOR YOUR COMFORT.
IF THE CLIENT'S THINKING ABOUT GOING INTO BUSINESS WITH WENNERSTRÖM--
HE'S NOT.
THE STUFF I HAVE ON HIM ALREADY--
EAT A BISCUIT.
HE COULD SINK HIM--
EAT THE BISCUIT.
YOU DON'T EAT ENOUGH, LISBETH.
NOT NEARLY ENOUGH.

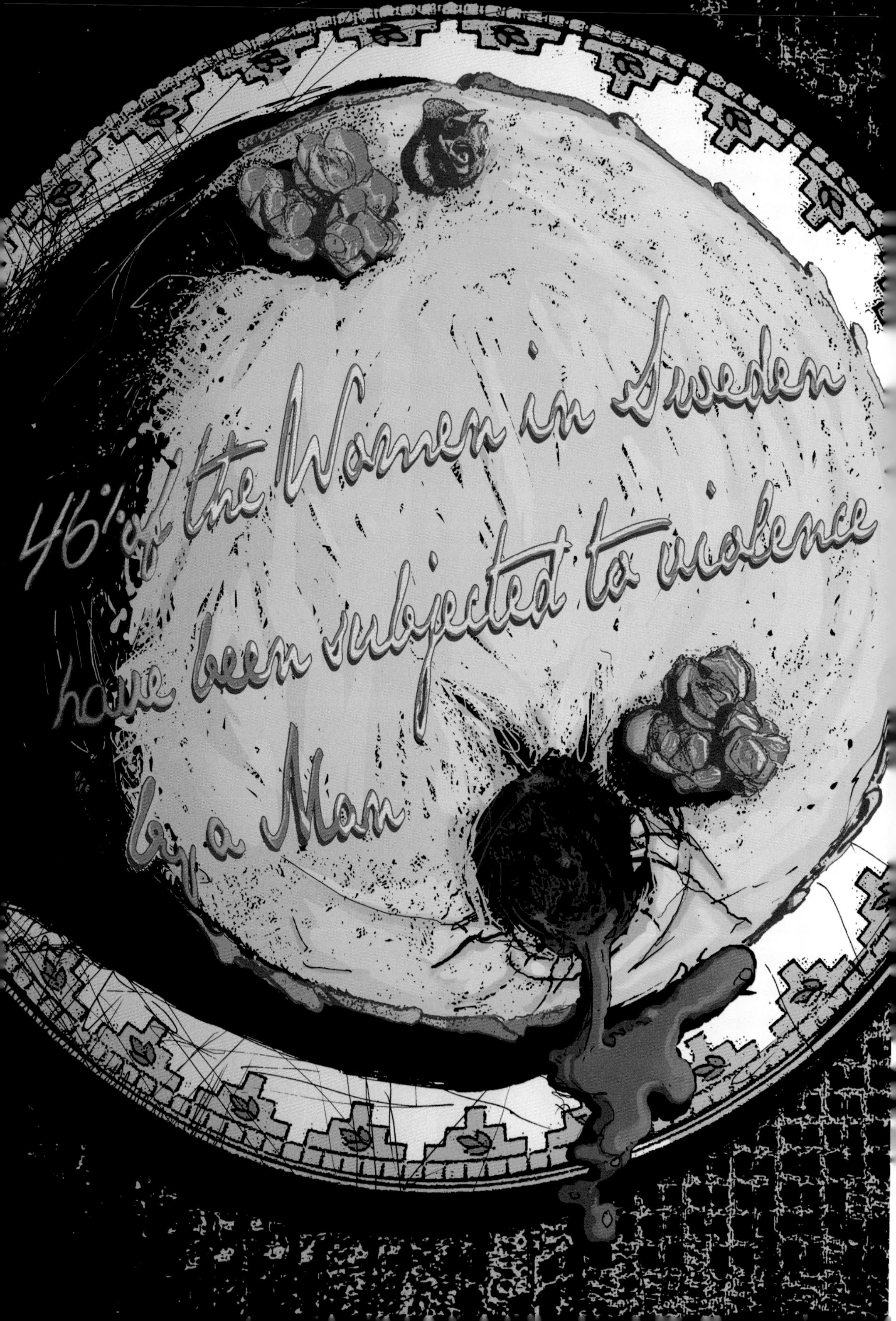
46% of the Women in Sweden
have been subjected to violence
by a Man

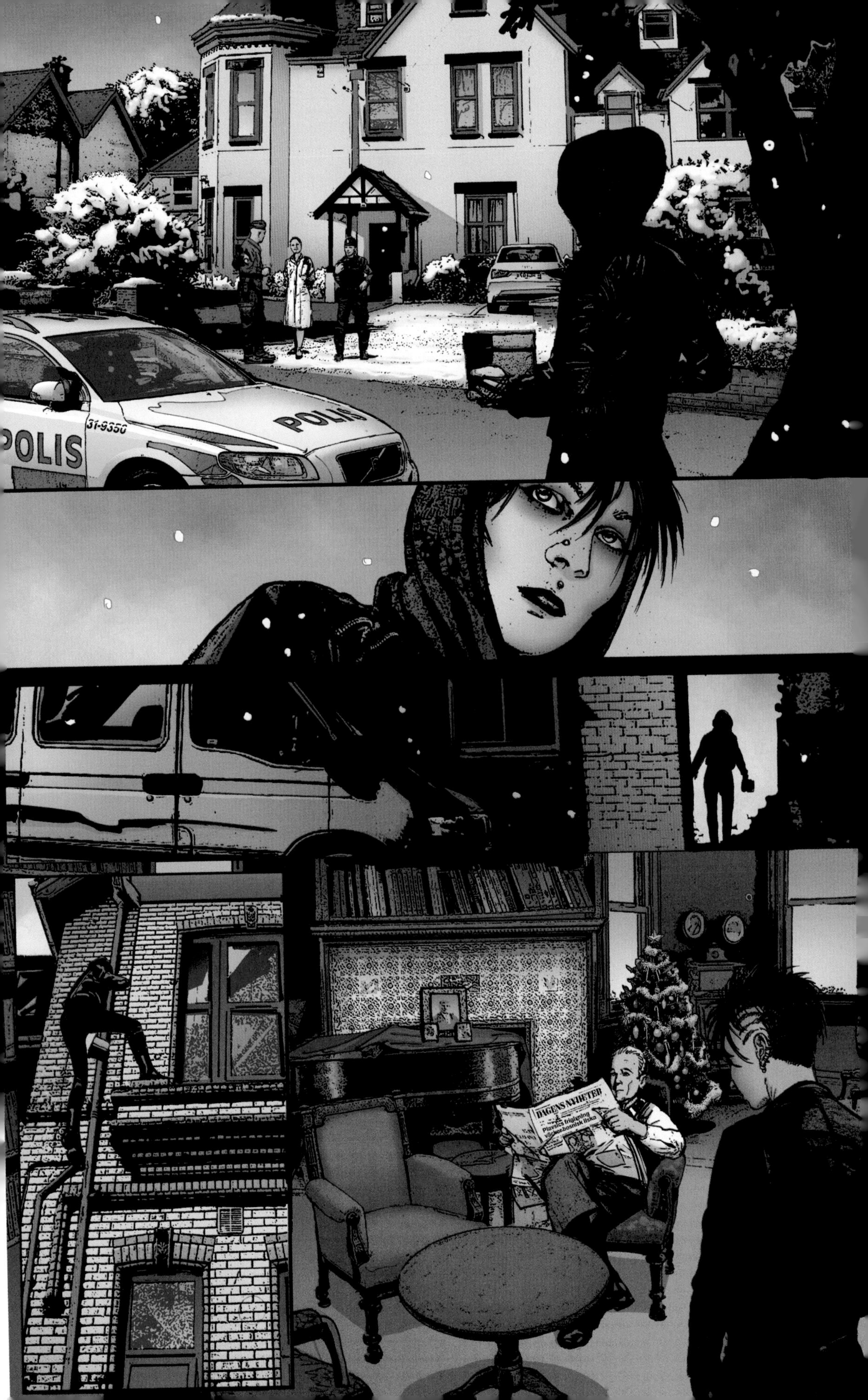
POLIS
31-9350
POLIS
DAGENS NYHETER
Plavsics frigivning
väcker bosnisk ilska

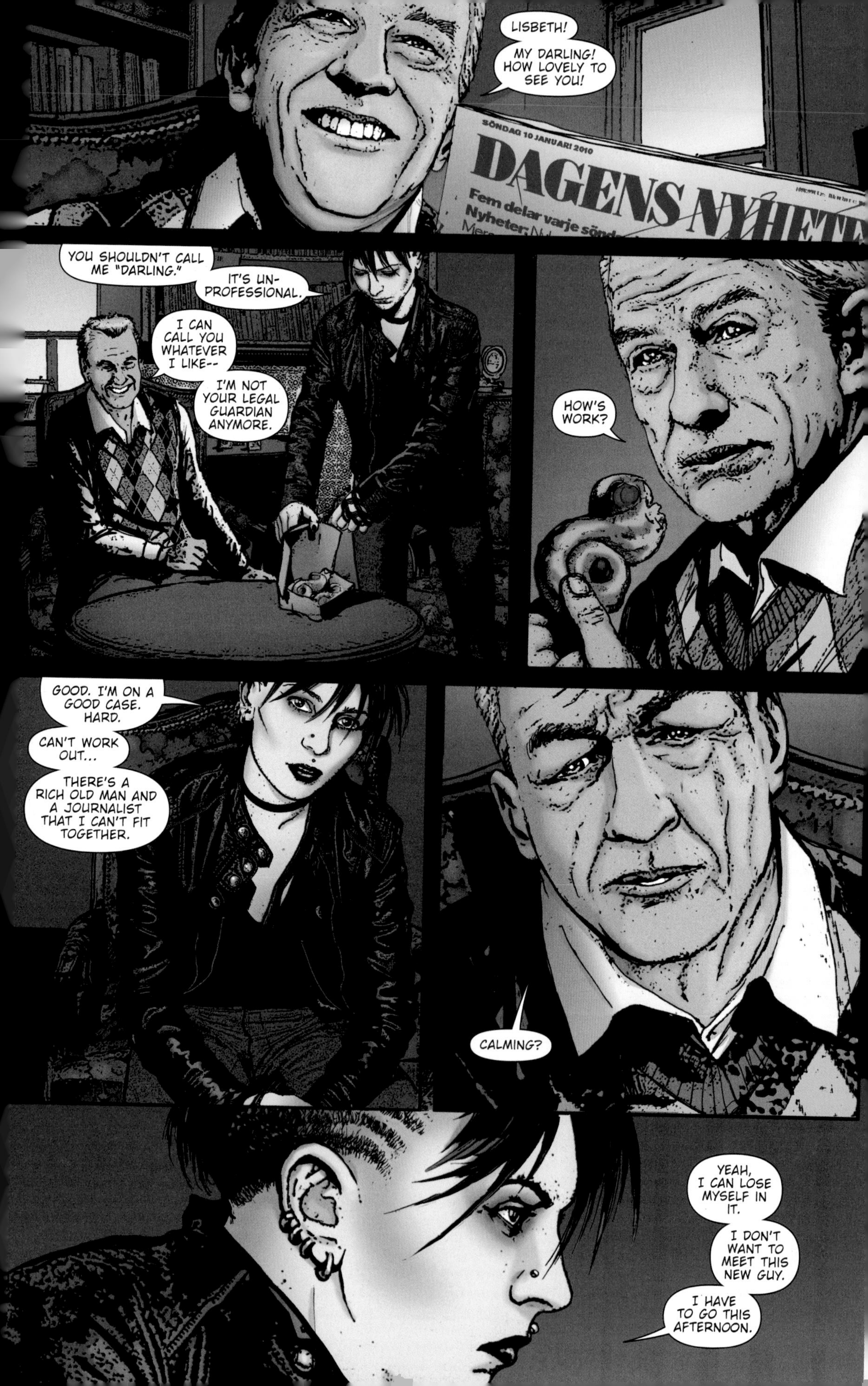
LISBETH!
MY DARLING! HOW LOVELY TO SEE YOU!
SÖNDAG 10 JANUARI 2010
DAGENS NYHETER
Fem delar varje sönd
YOU SHOULDN'T CALL ME "DARLING."
IT'S UN-PROFESSIONAL.
I CAN CALL YOU WHATEVER I LIKE--
I'M NOT YOUR LEGAL GUARDIAN ANYMORE.
HOW'S WORK?
GOOD. I'M ON A GOOD CASE. HARD.
CAN'T WORK OUT...
THERE'S A RICH OLD MAN AND A JOURNALIST THAT I CAN'T FIT TOGETHER.
CALMING?
YEAH, I CAN LOSE MYSELF IN IT.
I DON'T WANT TO MEET THIS NEW GUY.
I HAVE TO GO THIS AFTERNOON.

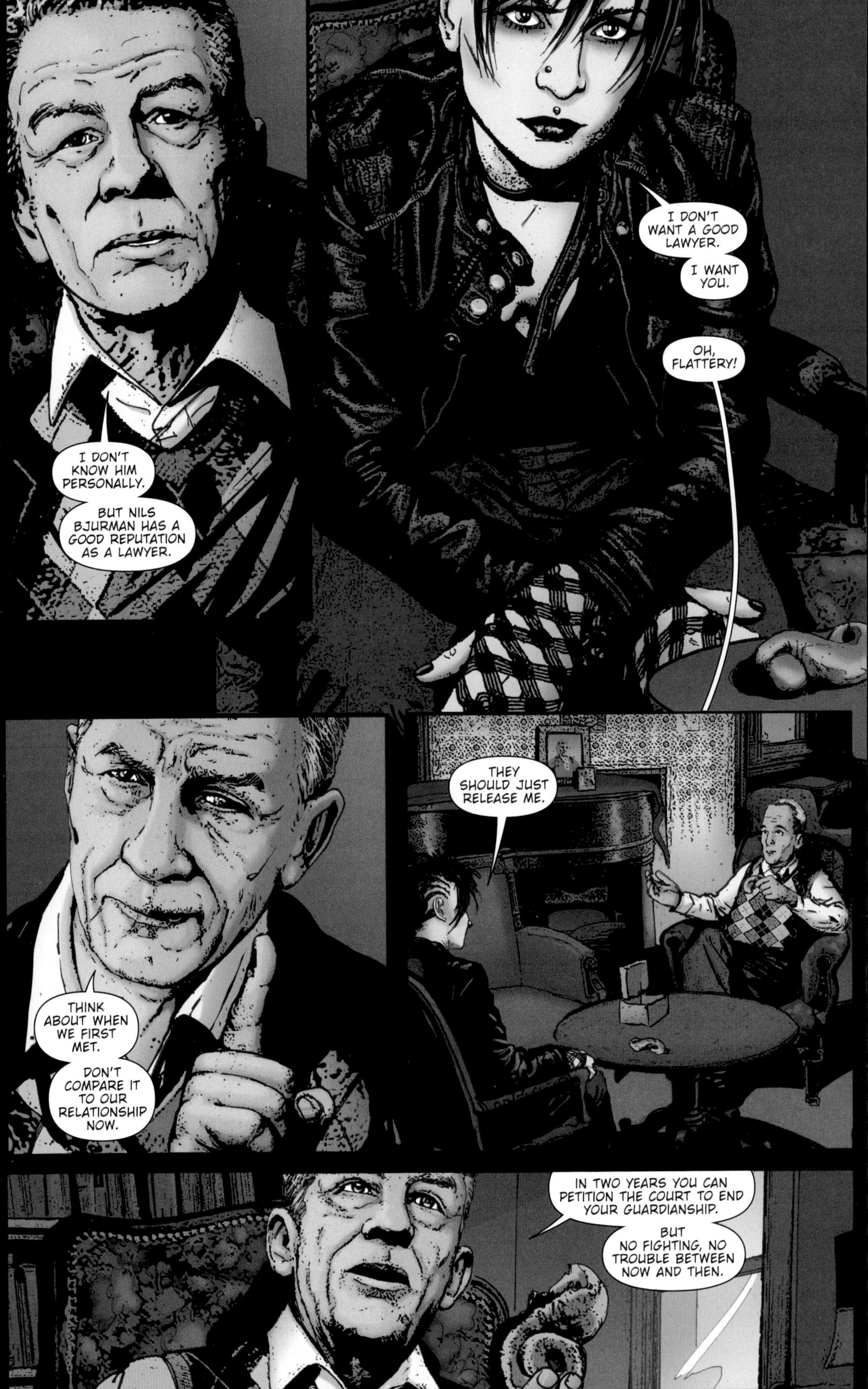
I DON'T WANT A GOOD LAWYER.
I WANT YOU.
OH, FLATTERY!
I DON'T KNOW HIM PERSONALLY.
BUT NILS BJURMAN HAS A GOOD REPUTATION AS A LAWYER.
THINK ABOUT WHEN WE FIRST MET.
DON'T COMPARE IT TO OUR RELATIONSHIP NOW.
THEY SHOULD JUST RELEASE ME.
IN TWO YEARS YOU CAN PETITION THE COURT TO END YOUR GUARDIANSHIP.
BUT NO FIGHTING, NO TROUBLE BETWEEN NOW AND THEN.

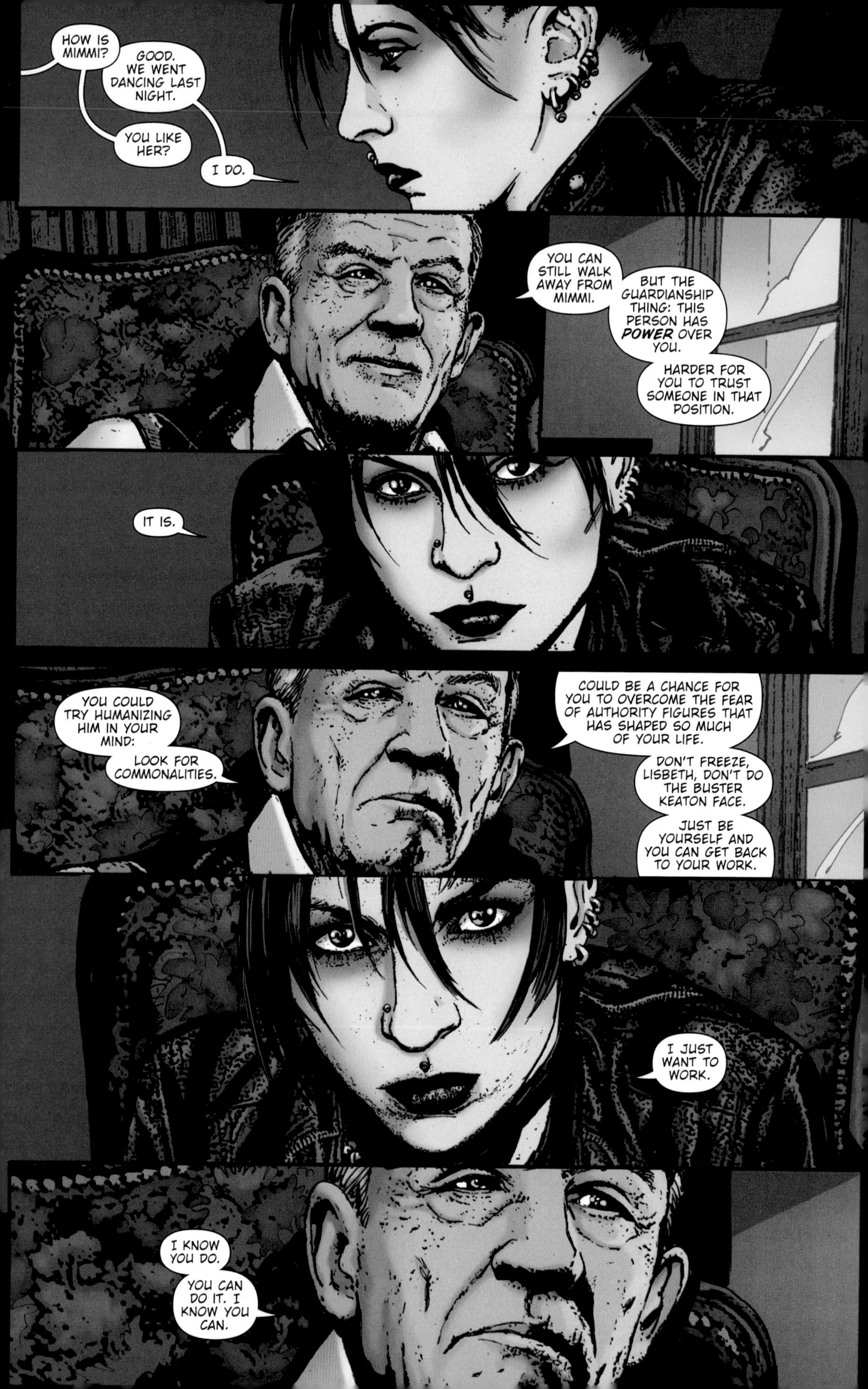
HOW IS MIMMI?
GOOD. WE WENT DANCING LAST NIGHT.
YOU LIKE HER?
I DO.
YOU CAN STILL WALK AWAY FROM MIMMI.
BUT THE GUARDIANSHIP THING: THIS PERSON HAS POWER OVER YOU.
HARDER FOR YOU TO TRUST SOMEONE IN THAT POSITION.
IT IS.
YOU COULD TRY HUMANIZING HIM IN YOUR MIND:
LOOK FOR COMMONALITIES.
COULD BE A CHANCE FOR YOU TO OVERCOME THE FEAR OF AUTHORITY FIGURES THAT HAS SHAPED SO MUCH OF YOUR LIFE.
DON'T FREEZE, LISBETH, DON'T DO THE BUSTER KEATON FACE.
JUST BE YOURSELF AND YOU CAN GET BACK TO YOUR WORK.
I JUST WANT TO WORK.
I KNOW YOU DO.
YOU CAN DO IT. I KNOW YOU CAN.

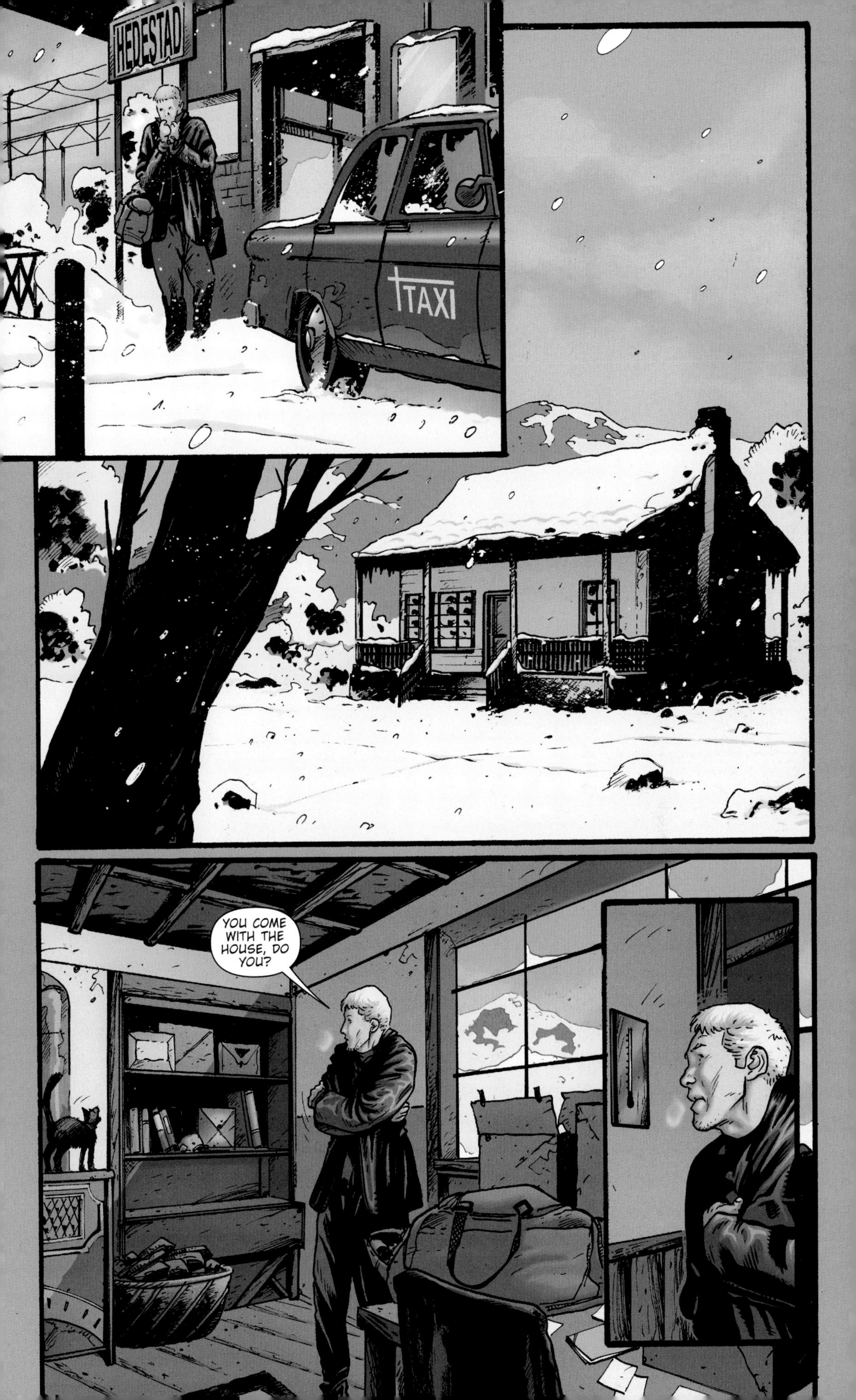
HEDESTAD
TAXI
YOU COME WITH THE HOUSE, DO YOU?

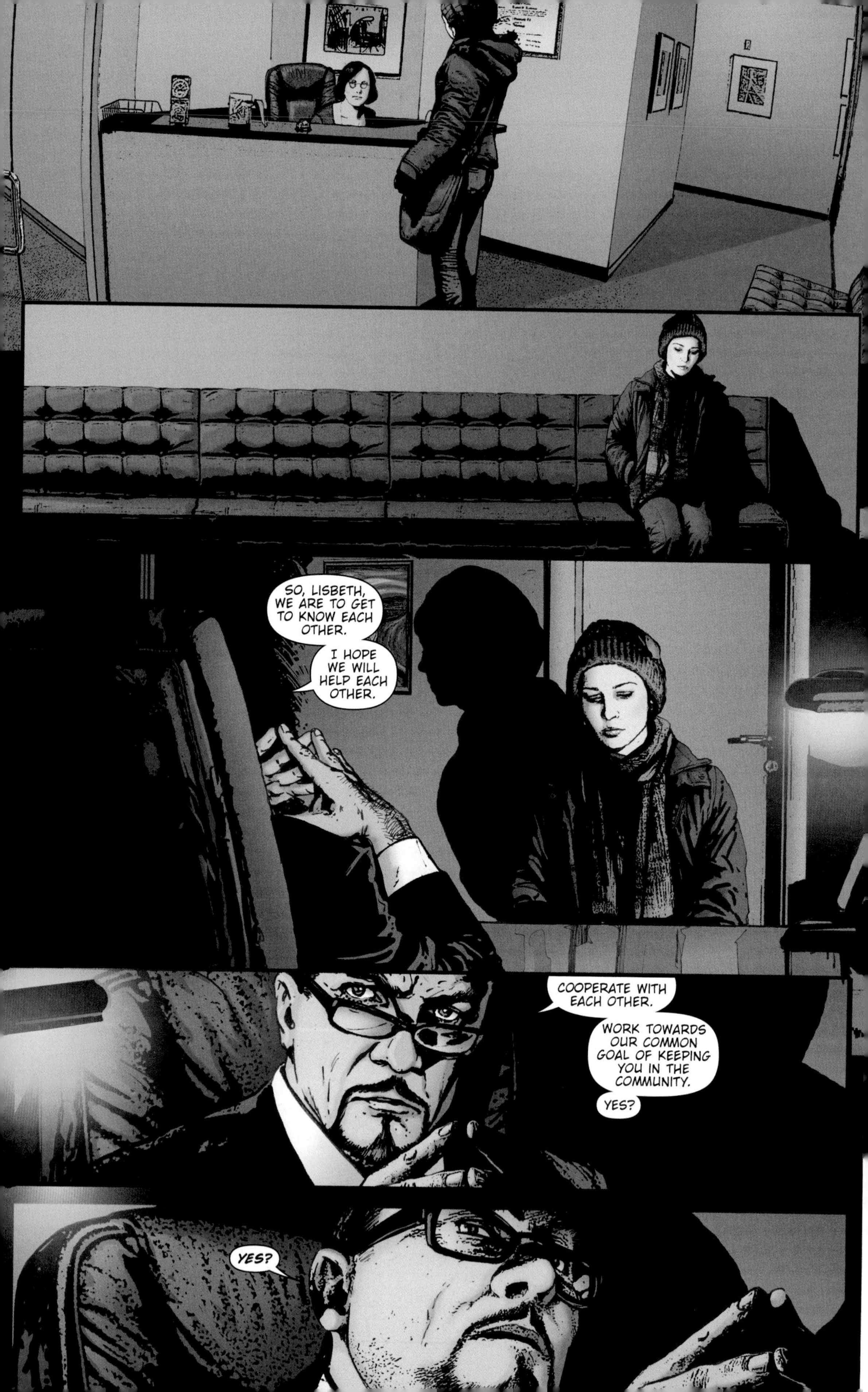
SO, LISBETH, WE ARE TO GET TO KNOW EACH OTHER.
I HOPE WE WILL HELP EACH OTHER.
COOPERATE WITH EACH OTHER.
WORK TOWARDS OUR COMMON GOAL OF KEEPING YOU IN THE COMMUNITY.
YES?
YES?

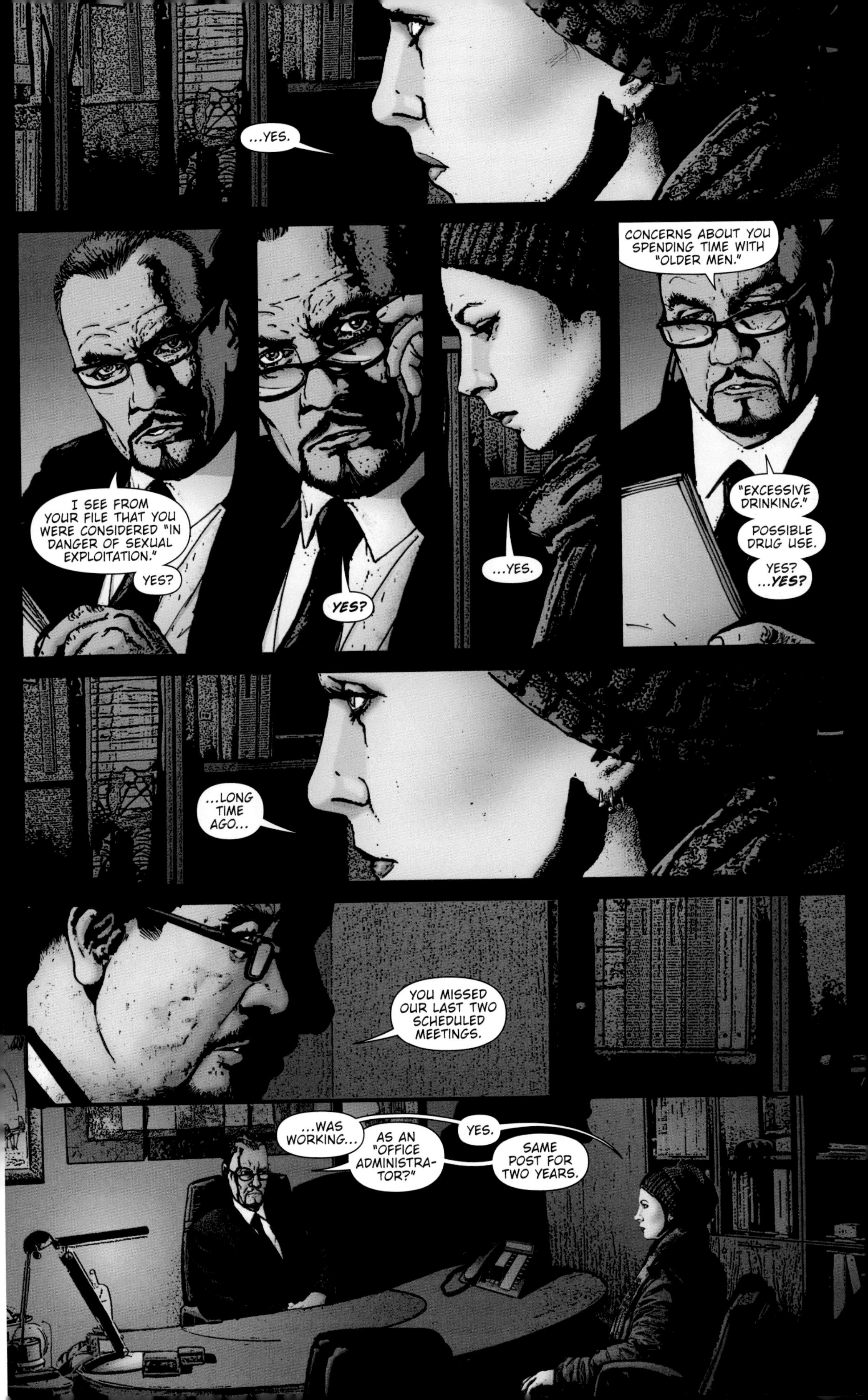
...YES.
I SEE FROM YOUR FILE THAT YOU WERE CONSIDERED "IN DANGER OF SEXUAL EXPLOITATION."
YES?
YES?
...YES.
CONCERNS ABOUT YOU SPENDING TIME WITH "OLDER MEN."
"EXCESSIVE DRINKING."
POSSIBLE DRUG USE.
YES? ...YES?
...LONG TIME AGO...
YOU MISSED OUR LAST TWO SCHEDULED MEETINGS.
...WAS WORKING...
AS AN "OFFICE ADMINISTRA-TOR?"
YES.
SAME POST FOR TWO YEARS.

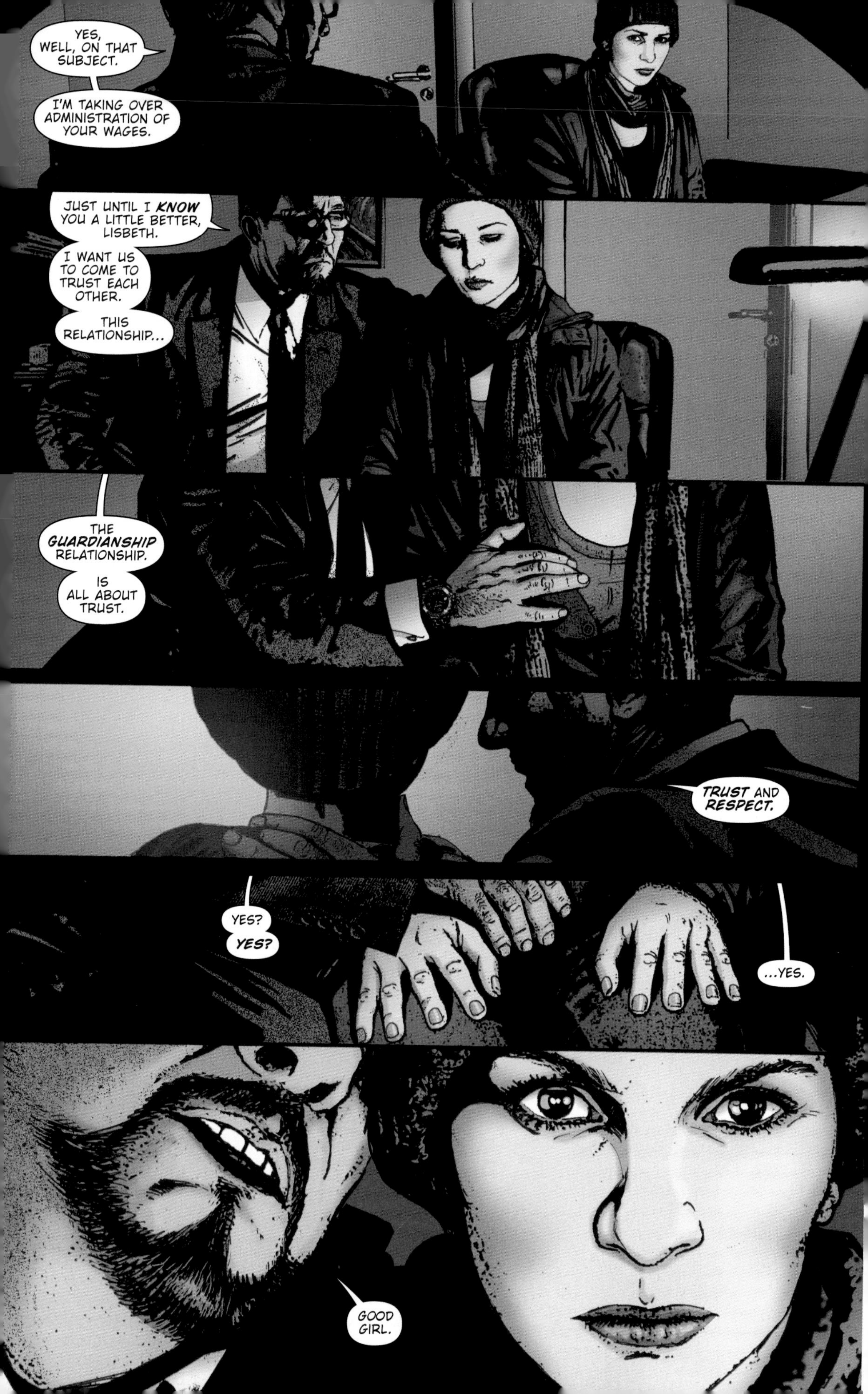
YES, WELL, ON THAT SUBJECT.
I'M TAKING OVER ADMINISTRATION OF YOUR WAGES.
JUST UNTIL I KNOW YOU A LITTLE BETTER, LISBETH.
I WANT US TO COME TO TRUST EACH OTHER.
THIS RELATIONSHIP...
THE GUARDIANSHIP RELATIONSHIP.
IS ALL ABOUT TRUST.
TRUST AND RESPECT.
YES?
YES?
...YES.
GOOD GIRL.

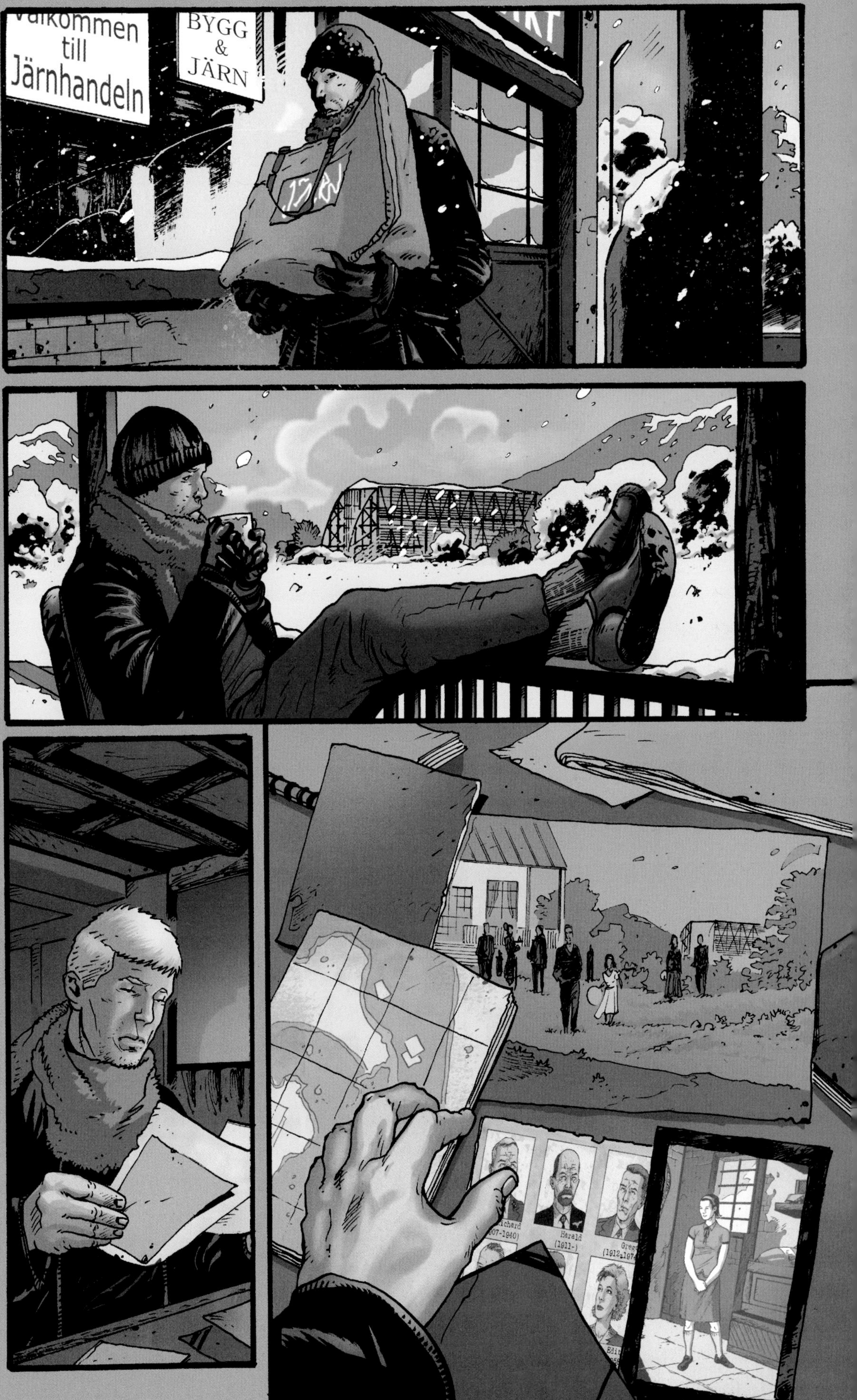
Välkommen till Järnhandeln
BYGG & JÄRN
Harald
(1911-)

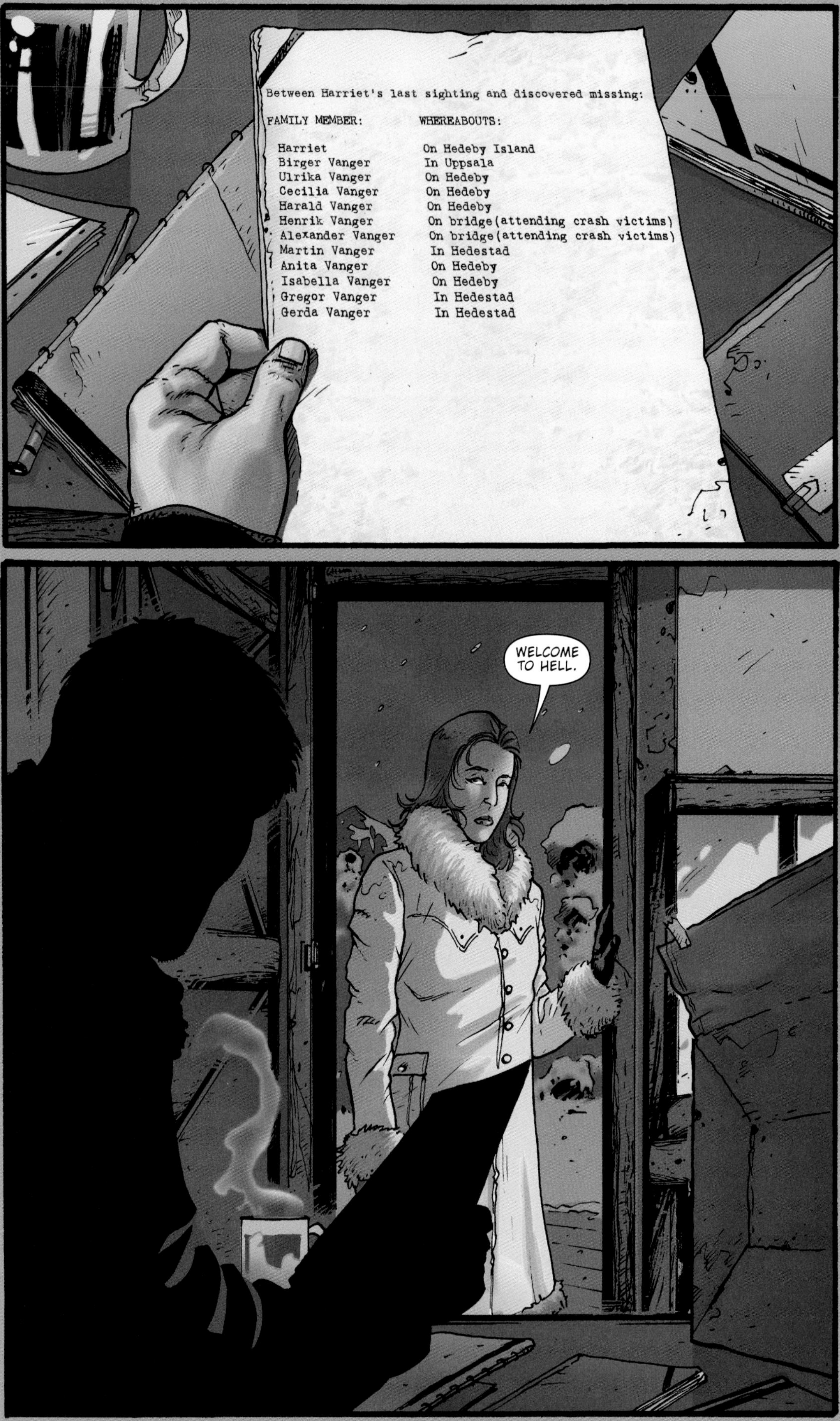
Between Harriet's last sighting and discovered missing:
FAMILY MEMBER: WHEREABOUTS:
Harriet On Hedeby Island
Birger Vanger In Uppsala
Ulrika Vanger On Hedeby
Cecilia Vanger On Hedeby
Harald Vanger On Hedeby
Henrik Vanger On bridge(attending crash victims)
Alexander Vanger On bridge(attending crash victims)
Martin Vanger In Hedestad
Anita Vanger On Hedeby
Isabella Vanger On Hedeby
Gregor Vanger In Hedestad
Gerda Vanger In Hedestad
WELCOME TO HELL.

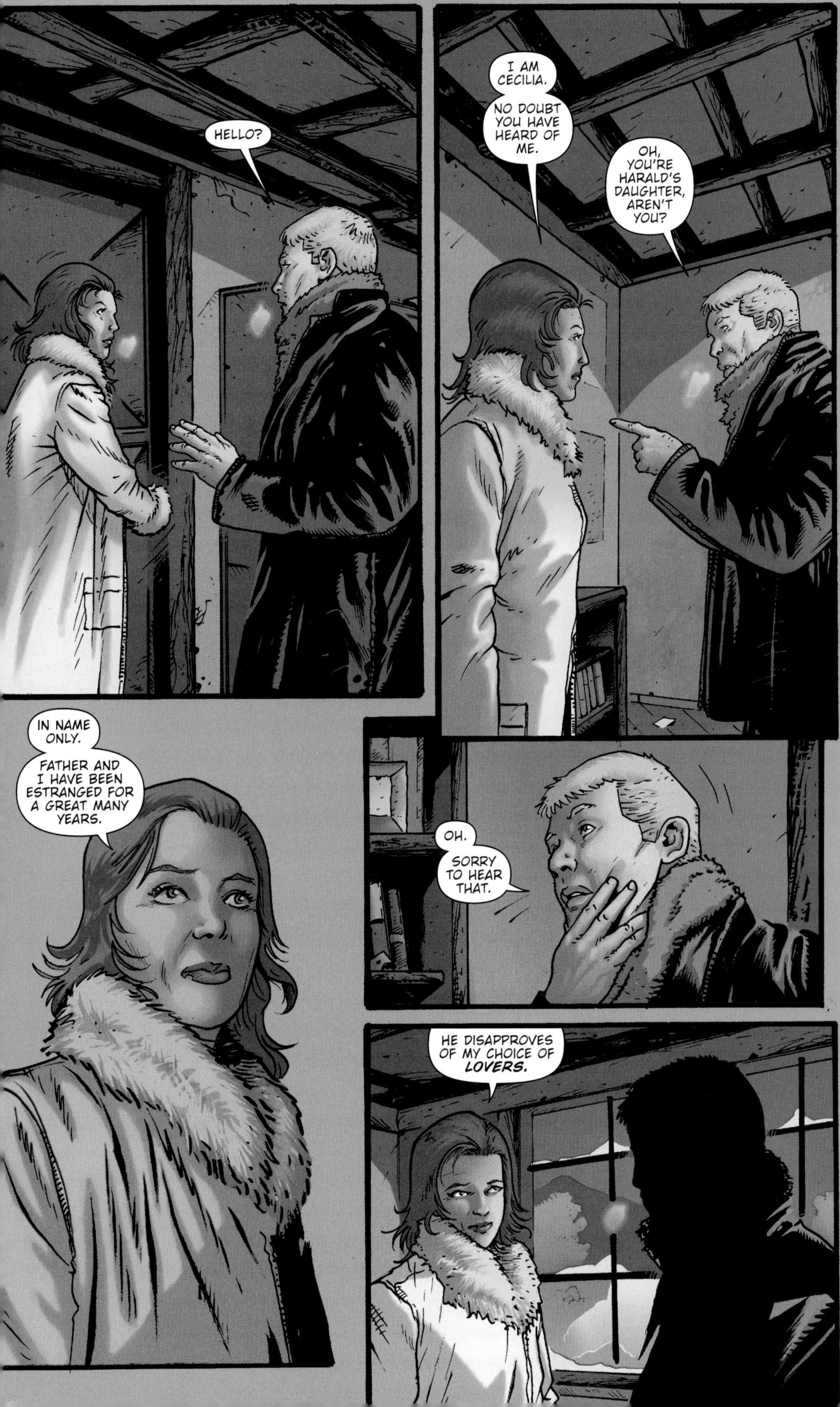
HELLO?
I AM CECILIA.
NO DOUBT YOU HAVE HEARD OF ME.
OH, YOU'RE HARALD'S DAUGHTER, AREN'T YOU?
IN NAME ONLY.
FATHER AND I HAVE BEEN ESTRANGED FOR A GREAT MANY YEARS.
OH.
SORRY TO HEAR THAT.
HE DISAPPROVES OF MY CHOICE OF *LOVERS.*

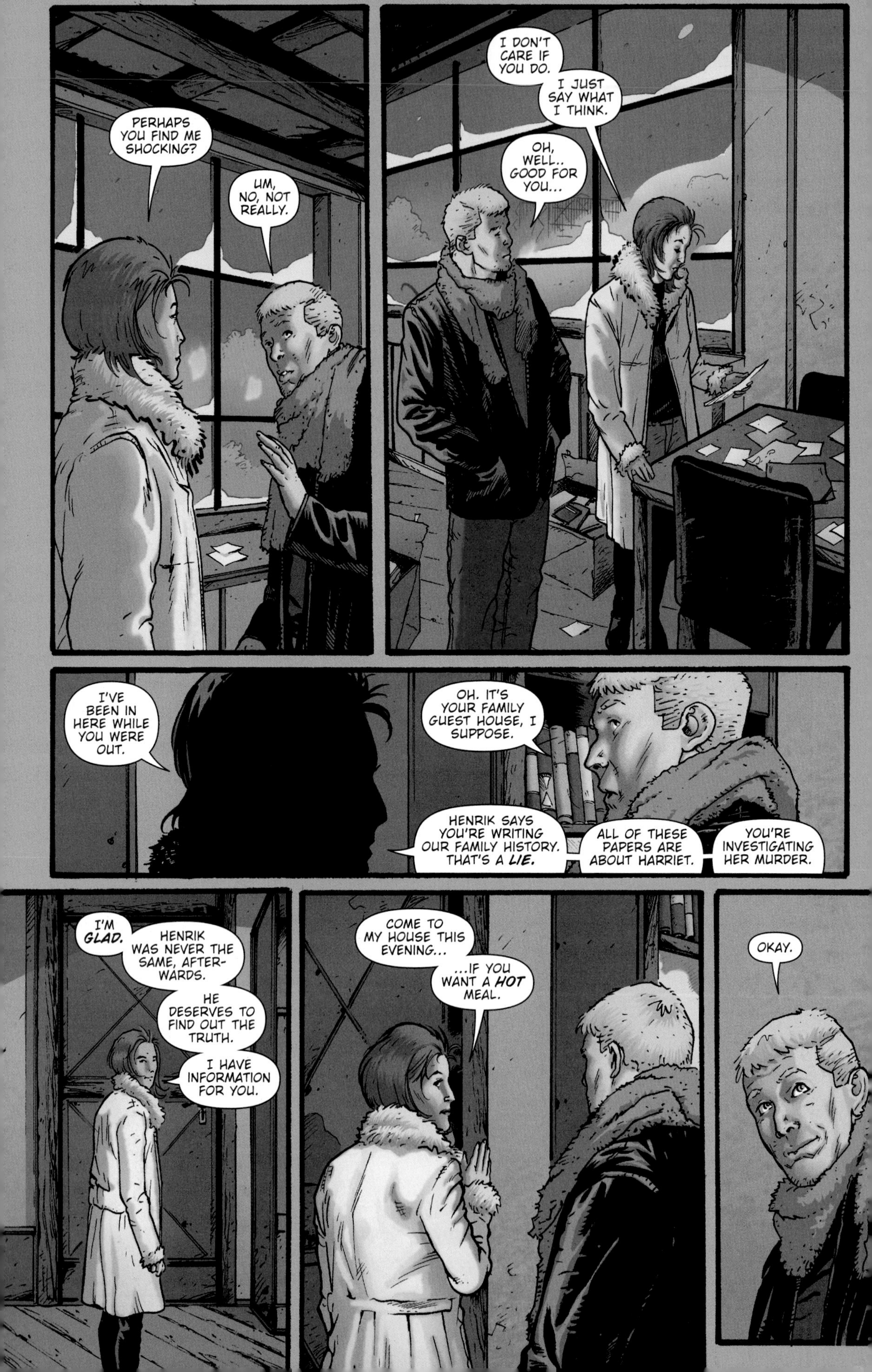
PERHAPS YOU FIND ME SHOCKING?
UM, NO, NOT REALLY.
I DON'T CARE IF YOU DO.
I JUST SAY WHAT I THINK.
OH, WELL.. GOOD FOR YOU...
I'VE BEEN IN HERE WHILE YOU WERE OUT.
OH. IT'S YOUR FAMILY GUEST HOUSE, I SUPPOSE.
HENRIK SAYS YOU'RE WRITING OUR FAMILY HISTORY. THAT'S A *LIE.*
ALL OF THESE PAPERS ARE ABOUT HARRIET.
YOU'RE INVESTIGATING HER MURDER.
I'M *GLAD.*
HENRIK WAS NEVER THE SAME, AFTER-WARDS.
HE DESERVES TO FIND OUT THE TRUTH.
I HAVE INFORMATION FOR YOU.
COME TO MY HOUSE THIS EVENING...
...IF YOU WANT A *HOT* MEAL.
OKAY.

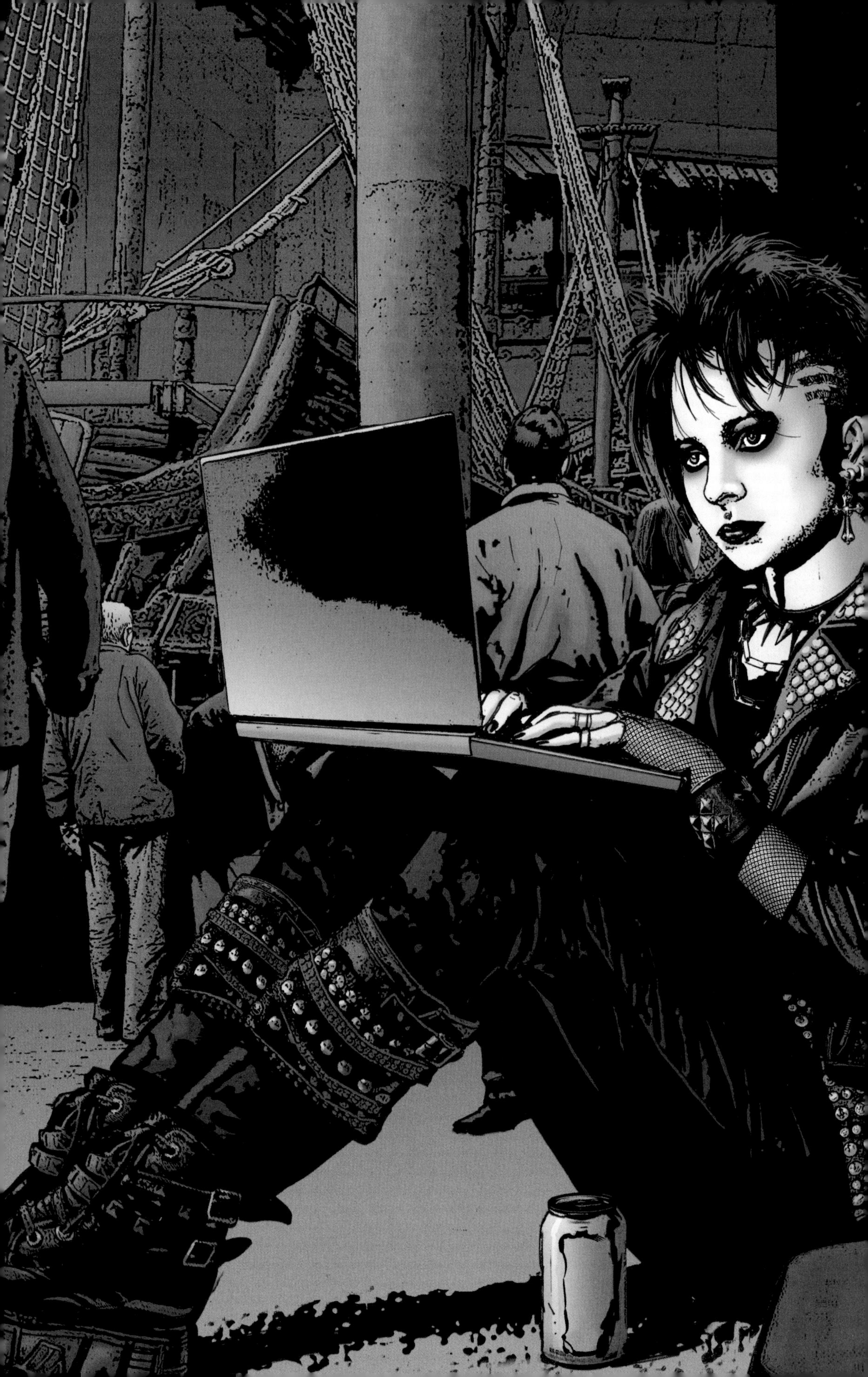

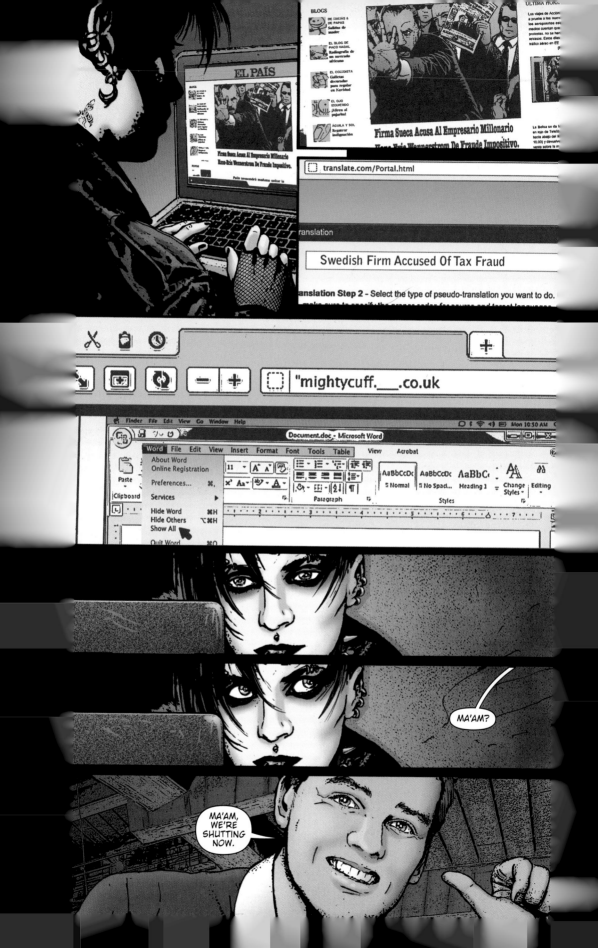

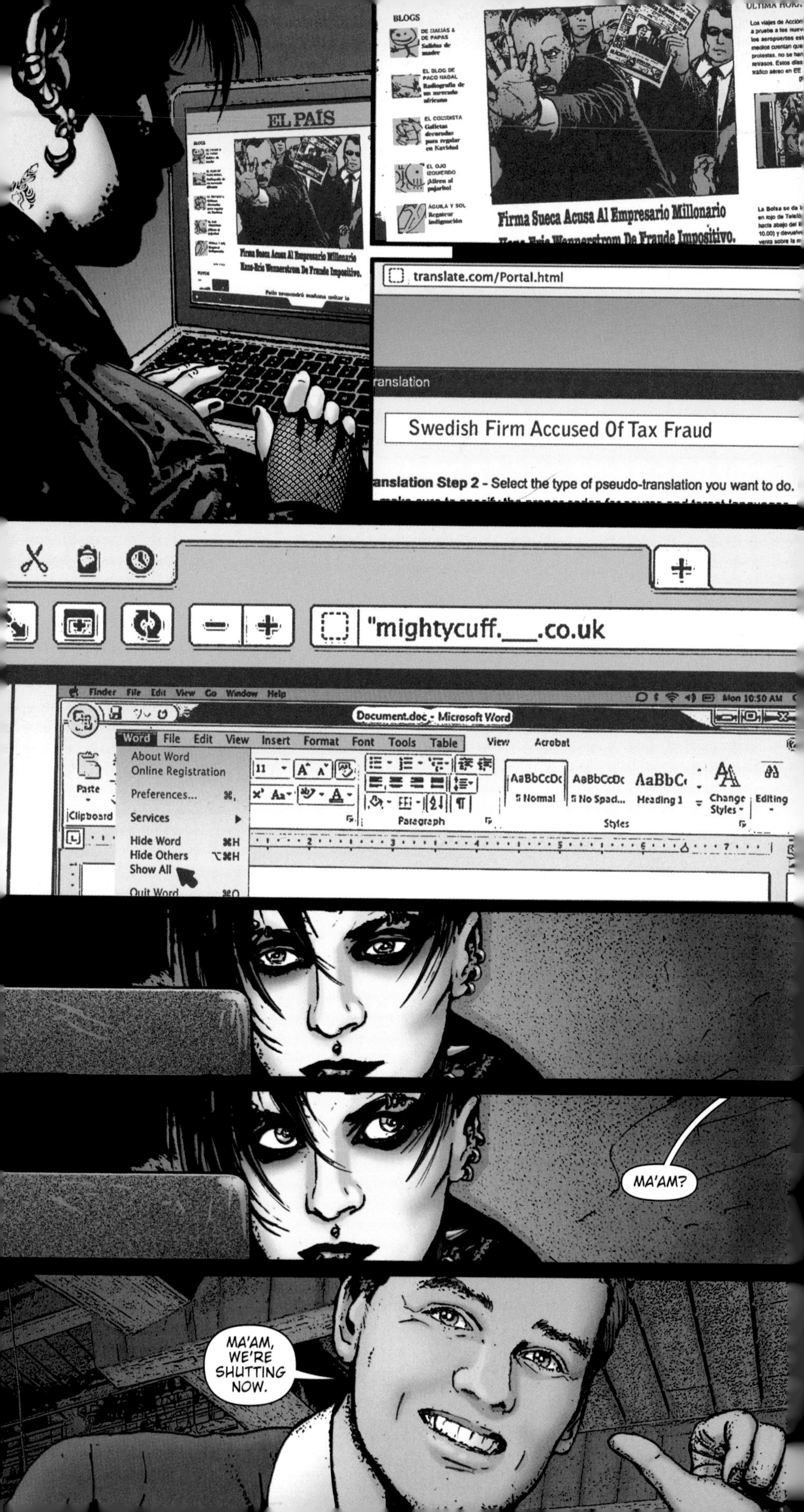
BLOGS
EL PAÍS
Firma Sueca Acusa Al Empresario Millonario
translate.com/Portal.html
ranslation
Swedish Firm Accused Of Tax Fraud
anslation Step 2 - Select the type of pseudo-translation you want to do.
"mightycuff.___.co.uk
Finder File Edit View Go Window Help
Document.doc - Microsoft Word
Word File Edit View Insert Format Font Tools Table
About Word
Online Registration
Preferences...
Services
Hide Word
Hide Others
Show All
MA'AM?
MA'AM, WE'RE SHUTTING NOW.

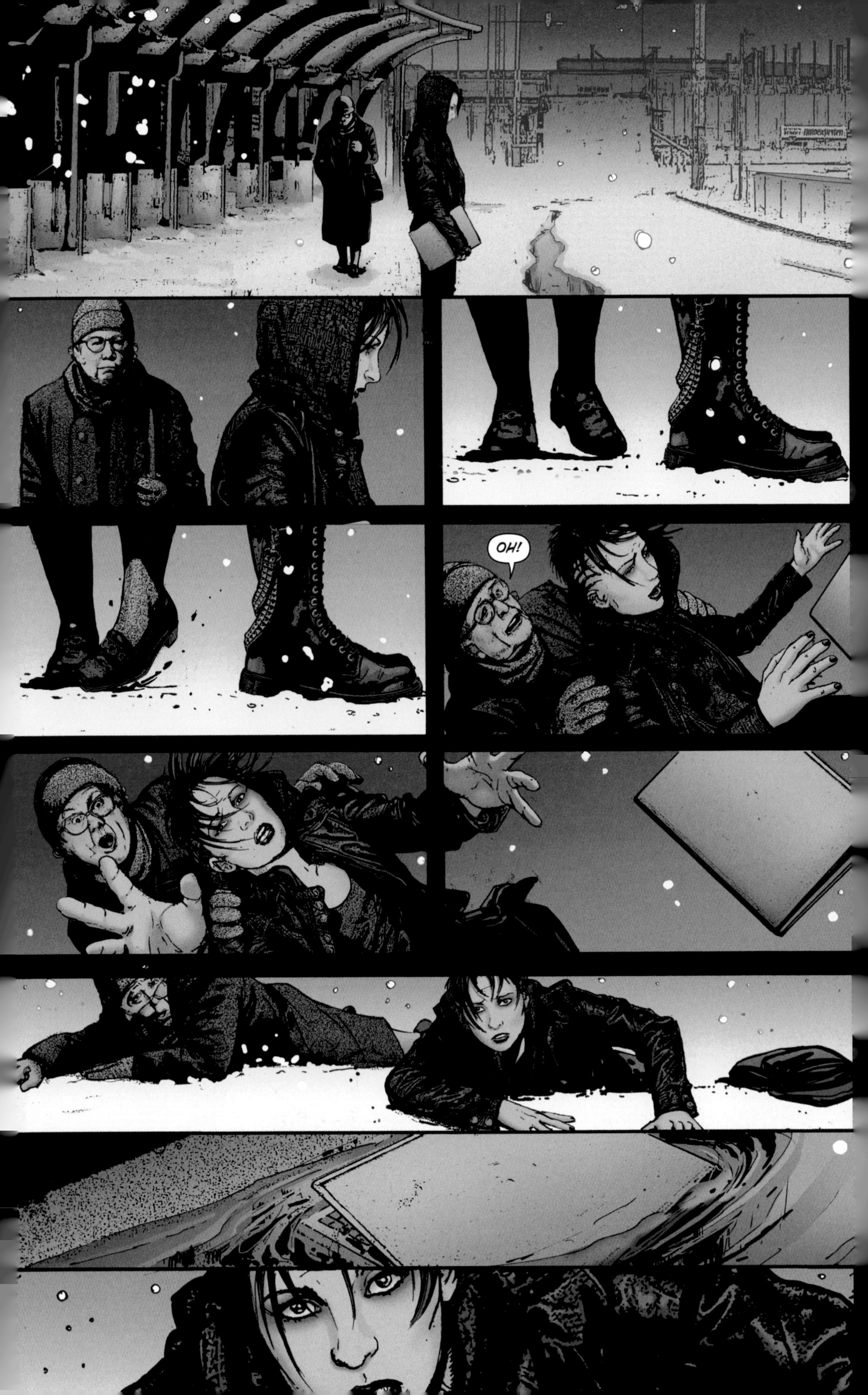
OH!

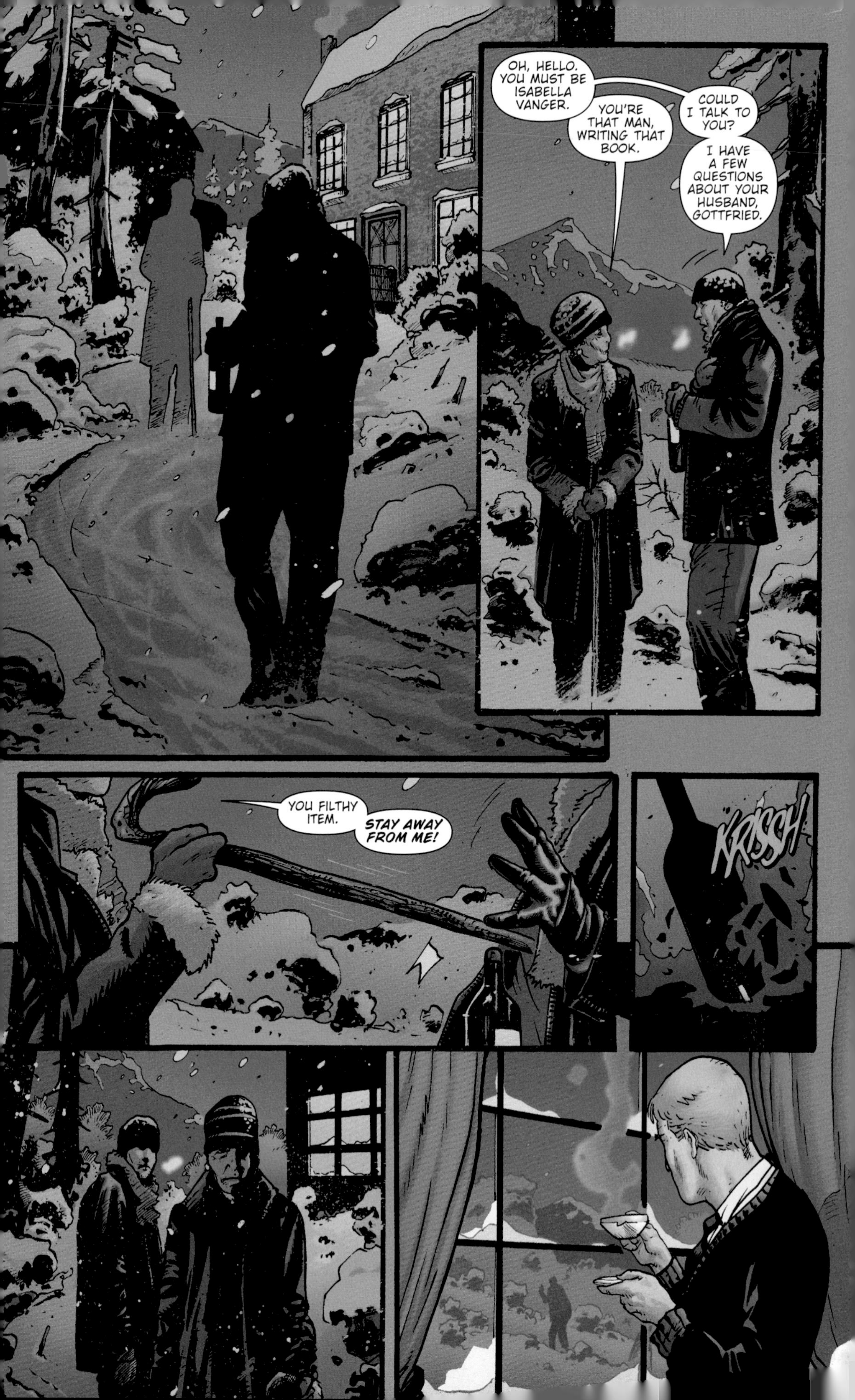
OH, HELLO. YOU MUST BE ISABELLA VANGER.
YOU'RE THAT MAN, WRITING THAT BOOK.
COULD I TALK TO YOU?
I HAVE A FEW QUESTIONS ABOUT YOUR HUSBAND, GOTTFRIED.
YOU FILTHY ITEM.
STAY AWAY FROM ME!
KRISSH

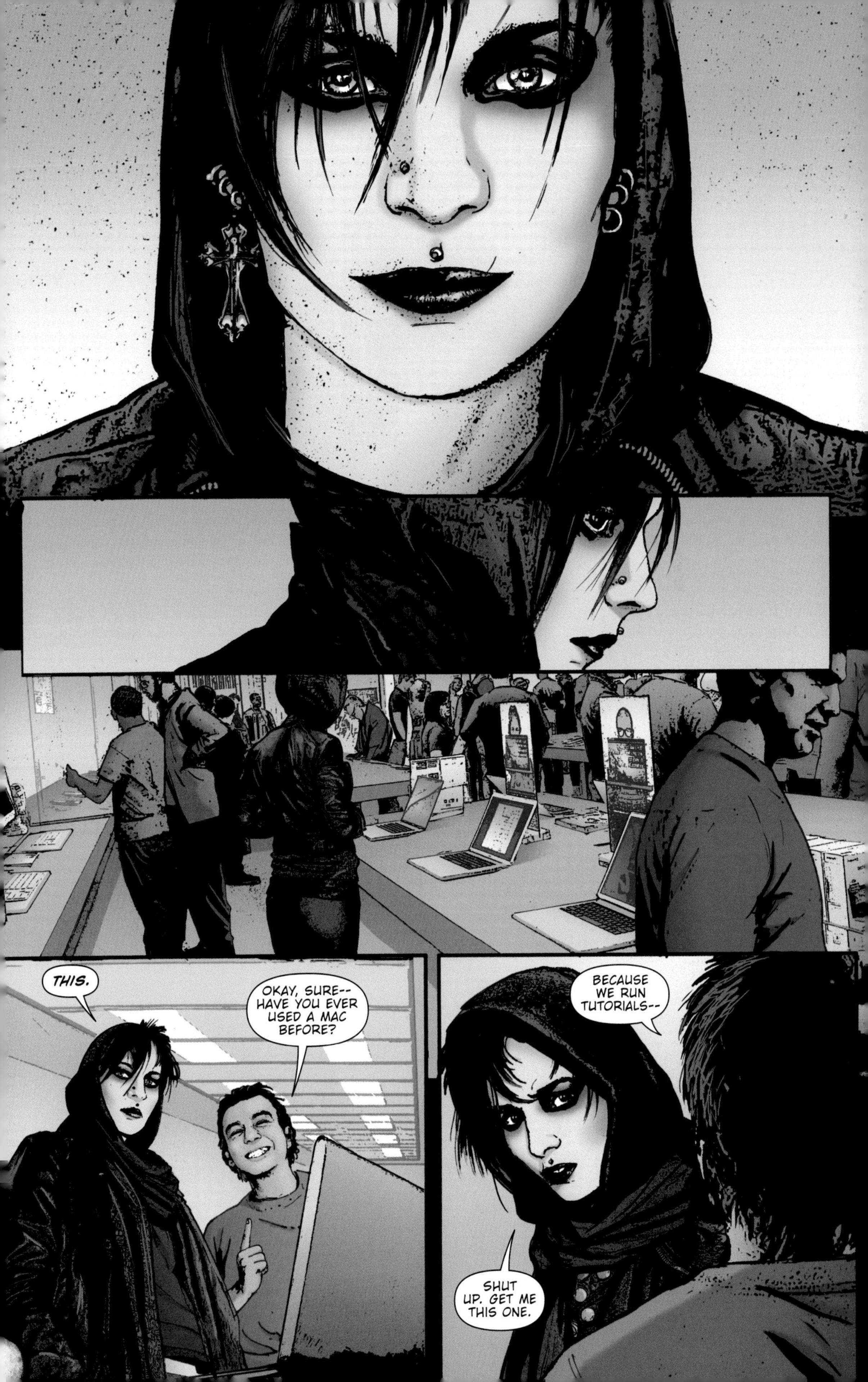
THIS.
OKAY, SURE-- HAVE YOU EVER USED A MAC BEFORE?
BECAUSE WE RUN TUTORIALS--
SHUT UP. GET ME THIS ONE.

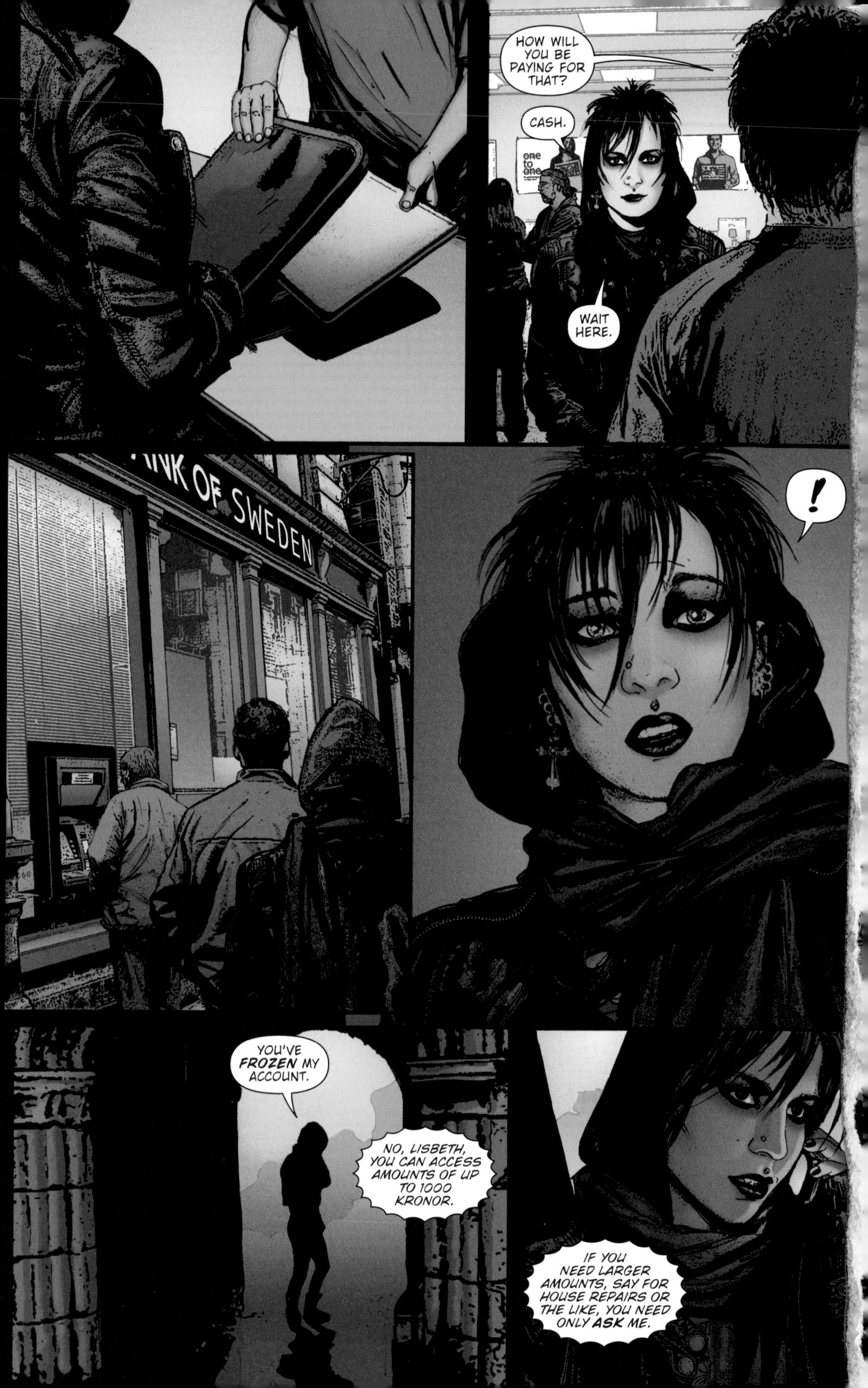
HOW WILL YOU BE PAYING FOR THAT?
CASH.
WAIT HERE.
...NK OF SWEDEN
!
YOU'VE FROZEN MY ACCOUNT.
NO, LISBETH, YOU CAN ACCESS AMOUNTS OF UP TO 1000 KRONOR.
IF YOU NEED LARGER AMOUNTS, SAY FOR HOUSE REPAIRS OR THE LIKE, YOU NEED ONLY ASK ME.

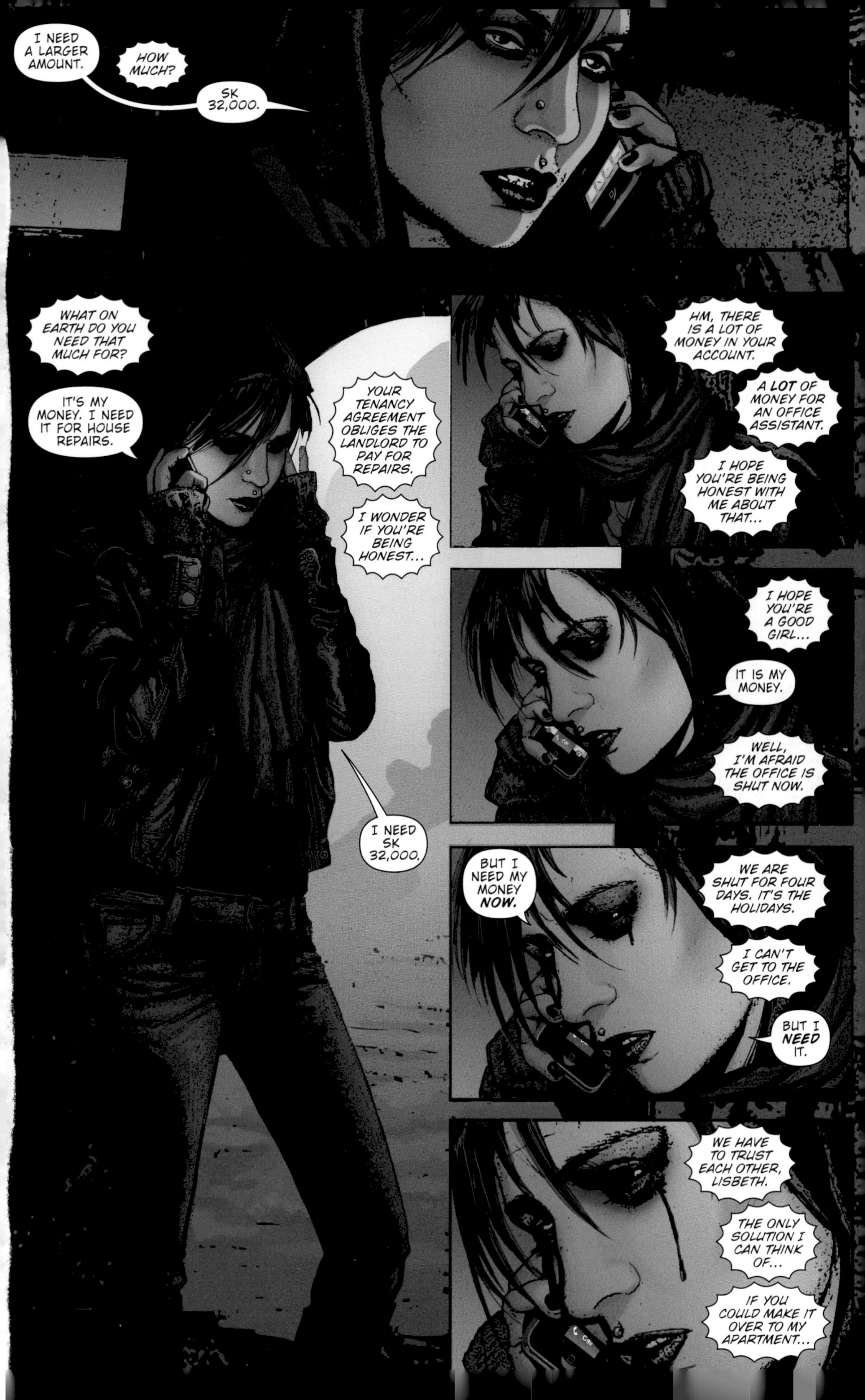
I NEED A LARGER AMOUNT.
HOW MUCH?
SK 32,000.
WHAT ON EARTH DO YOU NEED THAT MUCH FOR?
IT'S MY MONEY. I NEED IT FOR HOUSE REPAIRS.
YOUR TENANCY AGREEMENT OBLIGES THE LANDLORD TO PAY FOR REPAIRS.
I WONDER IF YOU'RE BEING HONEST...
I NEED SK 32,000.
HM, THERE IS A LOT OF MONEY IN YOUR ACCOUNT.
A LOT OF MONEY FOR AN OFFICE ASSISTANT.
I HOPE YOU'RE BEING HONEST WITH ME ABOUT THAT...
I HOPE YOU'RE A GOOD GIRL...
IT IS MY MONEY.
WELL, I'M AFRAID THE OFFICE IS SHUT NOW.
BUT I NEED MY MONEY NOW.
WE ARE SHUT FOR FOUR DAYS. IT'S THE HOLIDAYS.
I CAN'T GET TO THE OFFICE.
BUT I NEED IT.
WE HAVE TO TRUST EACH OTHER, LISBETH.
THE ONLY SOLUTION I CAN THINK OF...
IF YOU COULD MAKE IT OVER TO MY APARTMENT...

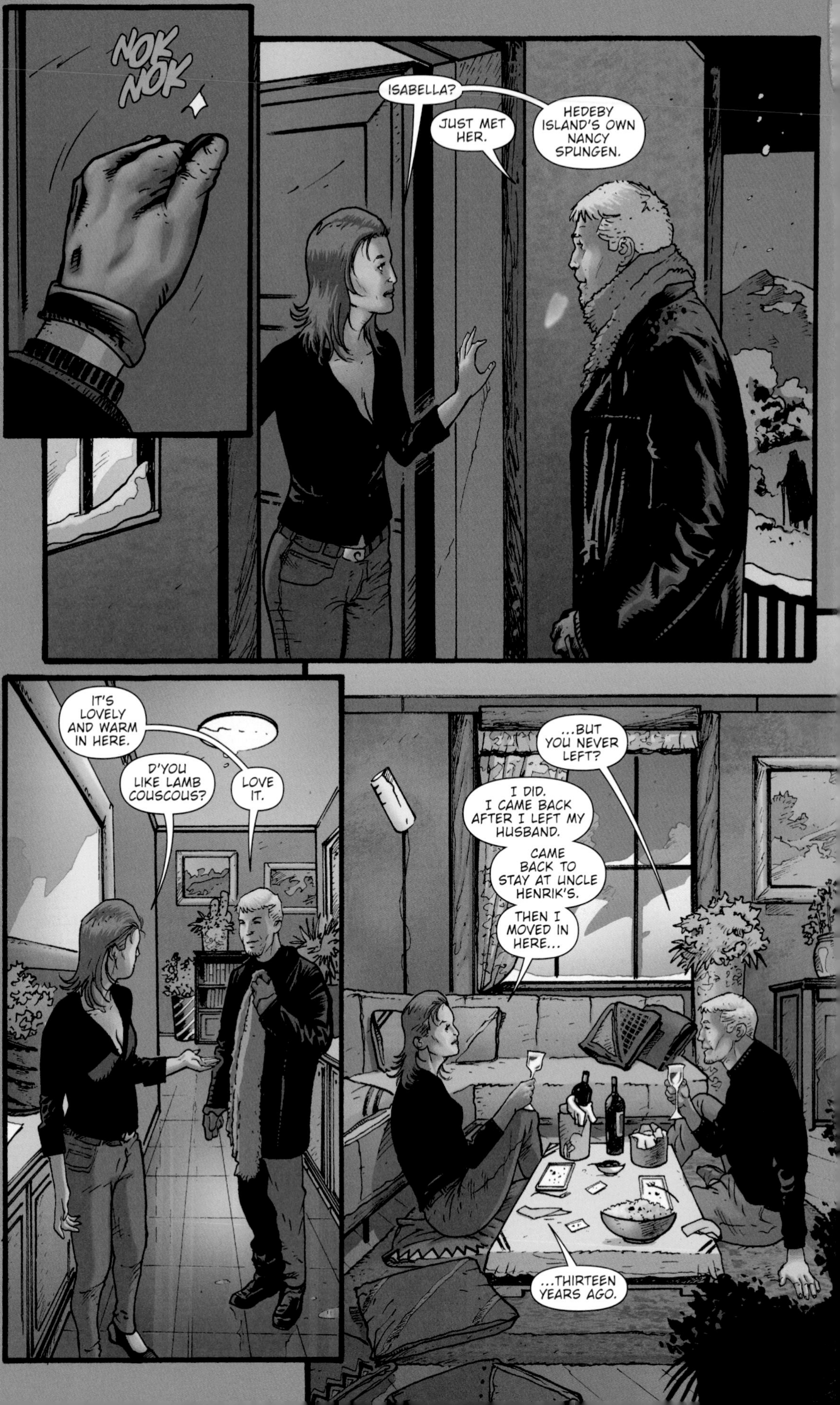
NOK NOK
ISABELLA?
JUST MET HER.
HEDEBY ISLAND'S OWN NANCY SPUNGEN.
IT'S LOVELY AND WARM IN HERE.
D'YOU LIKE LAMB COUSCOUS?
LOVE IT.
...BUT YOU NEVER LEFT?
I DID. I CAME BACK AFTER I LEFT MY HUSBAND.
CAME BACK TO STAY AT UNCLE HENRIK'S.
THEN I MOVED IN HERE...
...THIRTEEN YEARS AGO.

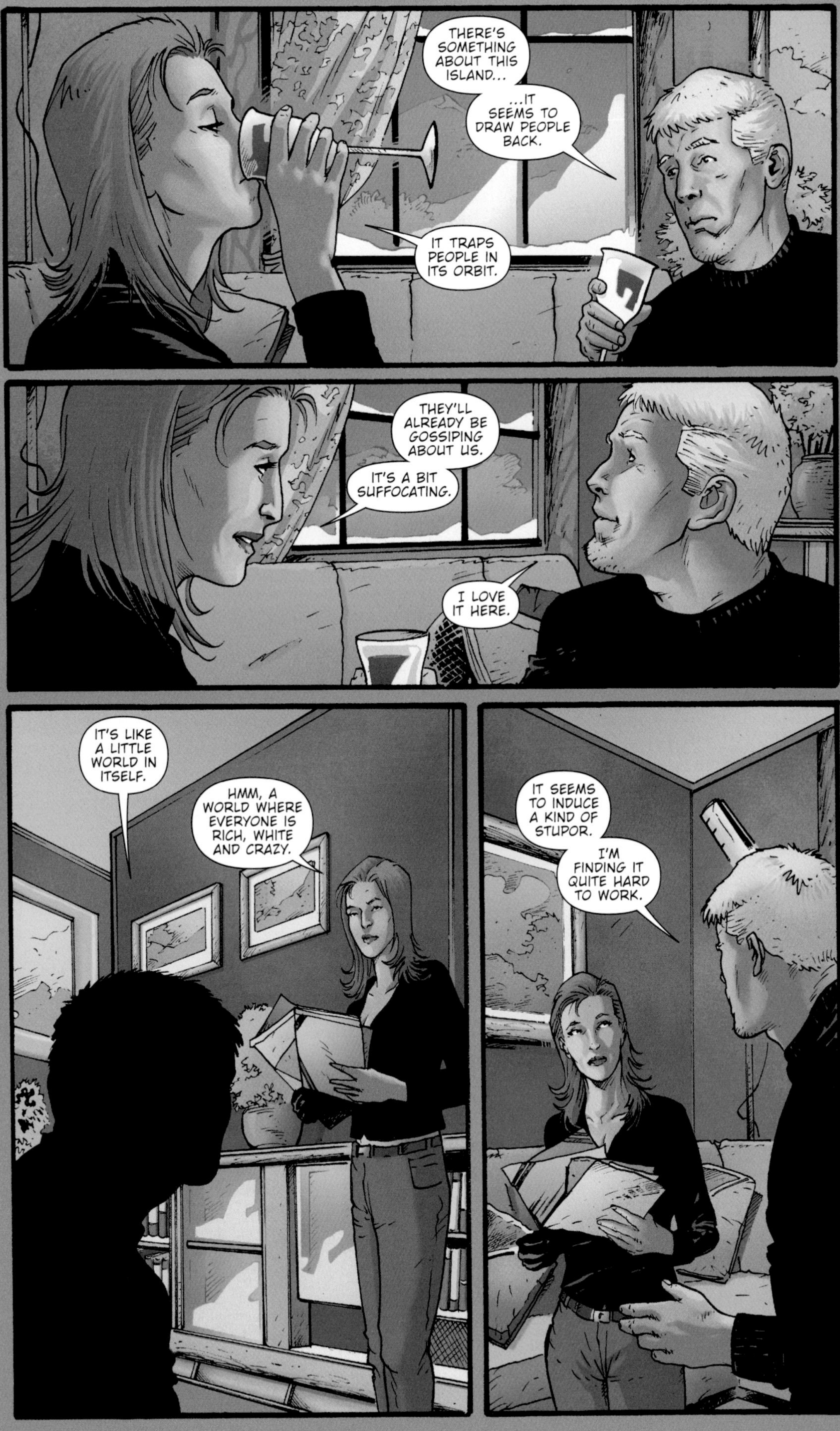
THERE'S SOMETHING ABOUT THIS ISLAND...
...IT SEEMS TO DRAW PEOPLE BACK.
IT TRAPS PEOPLE IN ITS ORBIT.
THEY'LL ALREADY BE GOSSIPING ABOUT US.
IT'S A BIT SUFFOCATING.
I LOVE IT HERE.
IT'S LIKE A LITTLE WORLD IN ITSELF.
HMM, A WORLD WHERE EVERYONE IS RICH, WHITE AND CRAZY.
IT SEEMS TO INDUCE A KIND OF STUPOR.
I'M FINDING IT QUITE HARD TO WORK.

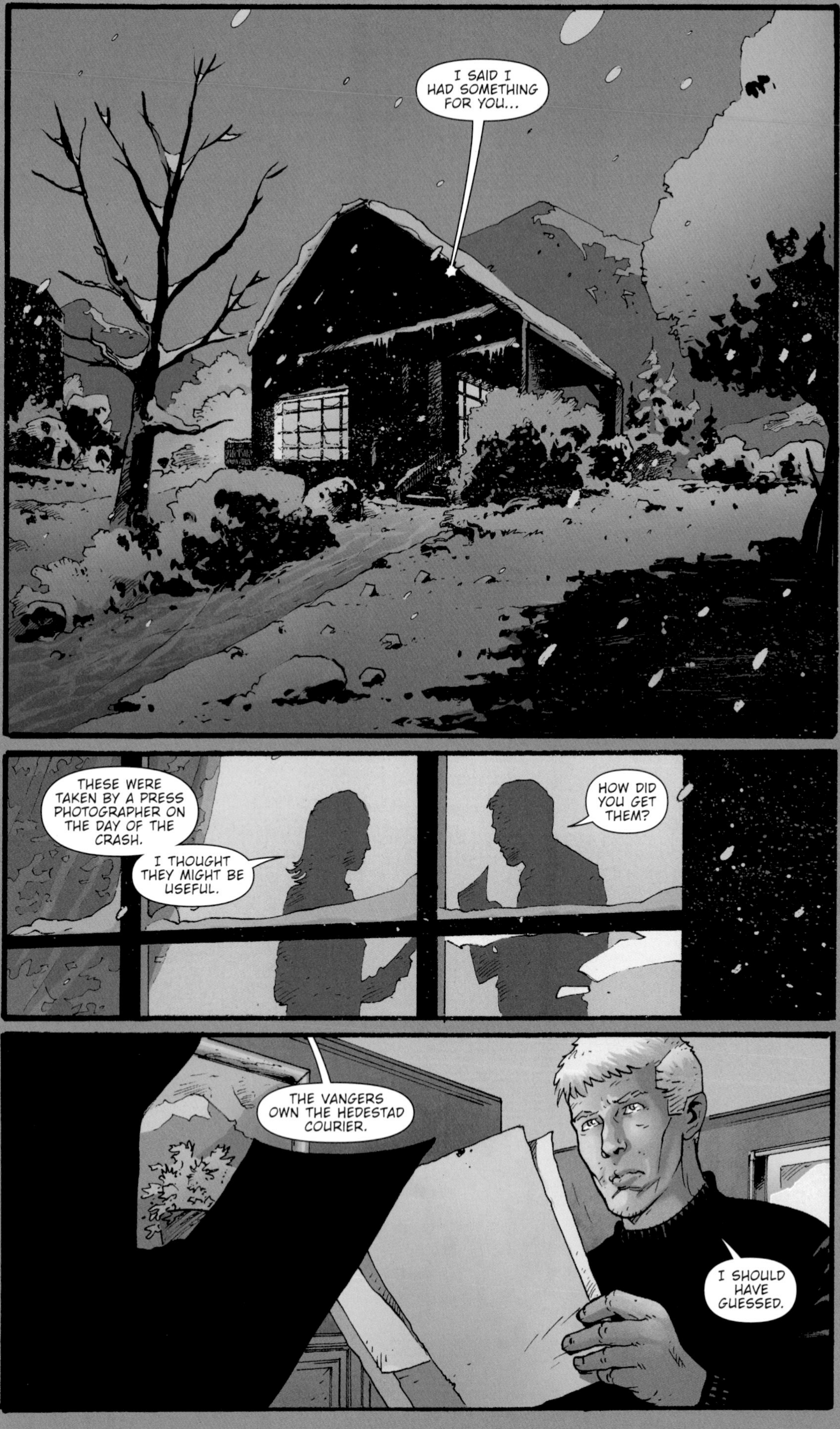
I SAID I HAD SOMETHING FOR YOU...
THESE WERE TAKEN BY A PRESS PHOTOGRAPHER ON THE DAY OF THE CRASH.
I THOUGHT THEY MIGHT BE USEFUL.
HOW DID YOU GET THEM?
THE VANGERS OWN THE HEDESTAD COURIER.
I SHOULD HAVE GUESSED.

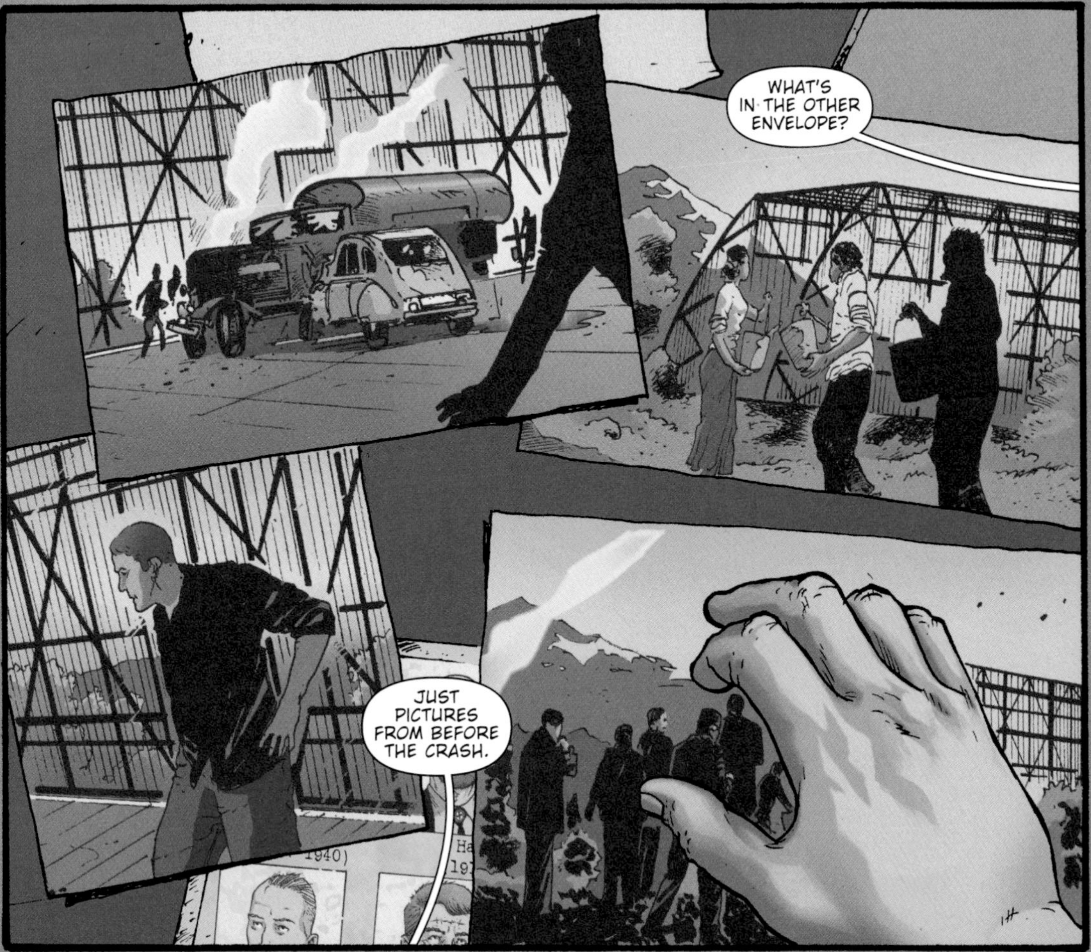
WHAT'S IN THE OTHER ENVELOPE?
JUST PICTURES FROM BEFORE THE CRASH.

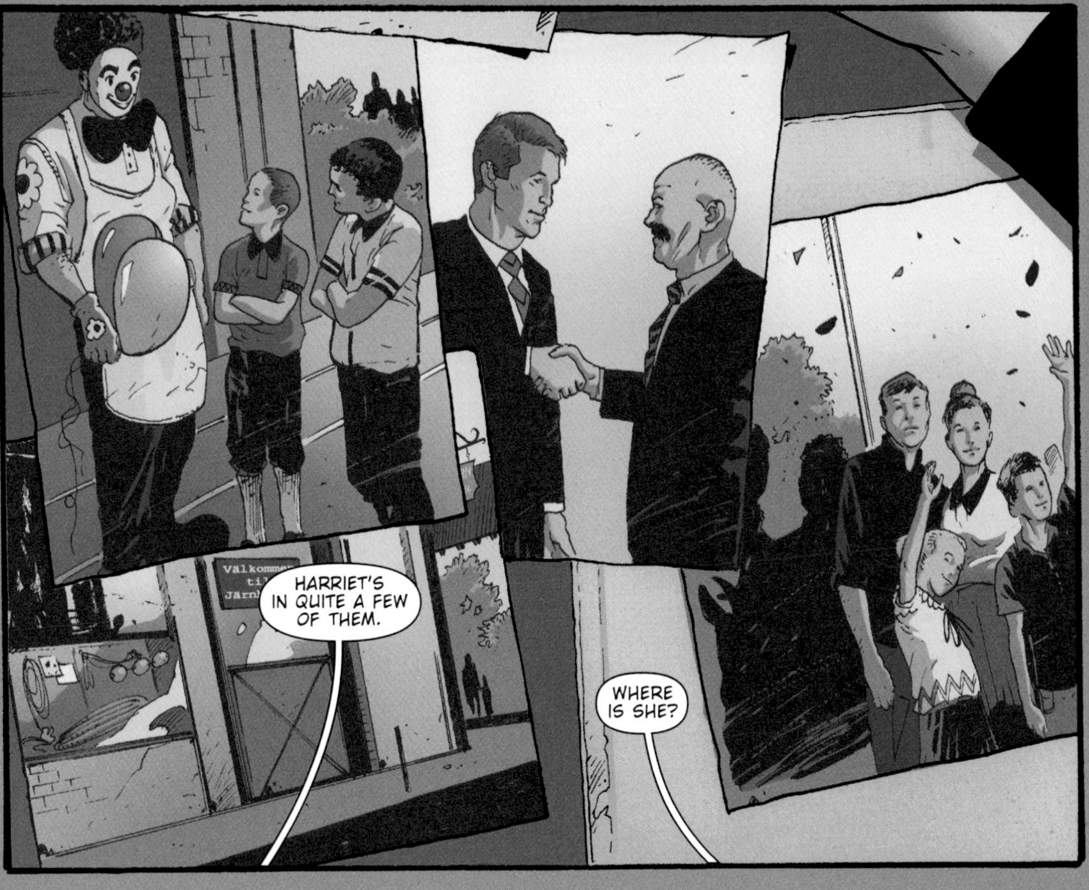
HARRIET'S IN QUITE A FEW OF THEM.
WHERE IS SHE?

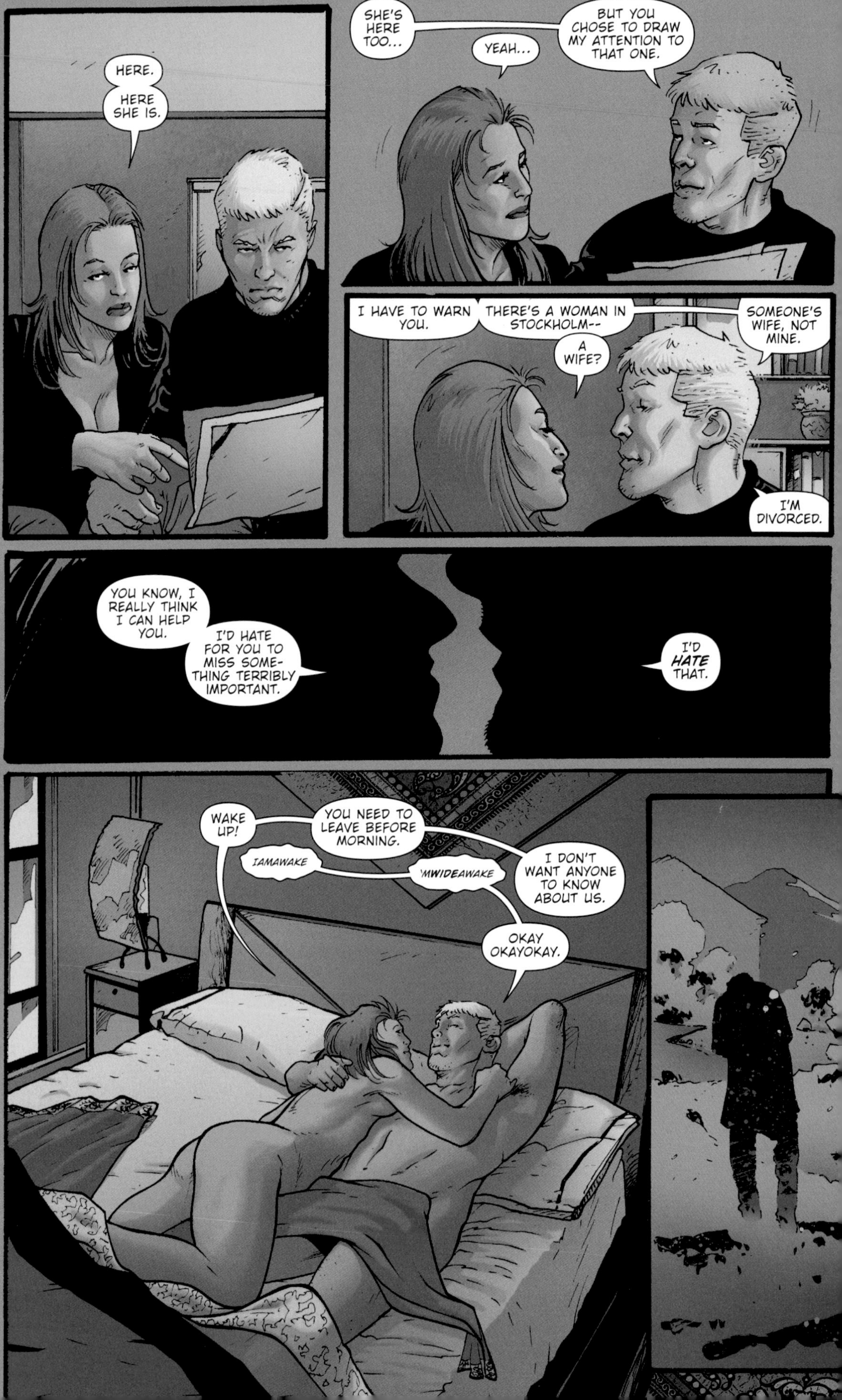
HERE.
HERE SHE IS.
SHE'S HERE TOO...
YEAH...
BUT YOU CHOSE TO DRAW MY ATTENTION TO THAT ONE.
I HAVE TO WARN YOU.
THERE'S A WOMAN IN STOCKHOLM--
A WIFE?
SOMEONE'S WIFE, NOT MINE.
I'M DIVORCED.
YOU KNOW, I REALLY THINK I CAN HELP YOU.
I'D HATE FOR YOU TO MISS SOME-THING TERRIBLY IMPORTANT.
I'D *HATE* THAT.
WAKE UP!
YOU NEED TO LEAVE BEFORE MORNING.
IAMAWAKE
'MWIDEAWAKE
I DON'T WANT ANYONE TO KNOW ABOUT US.
OKAY OKAYOKAY.

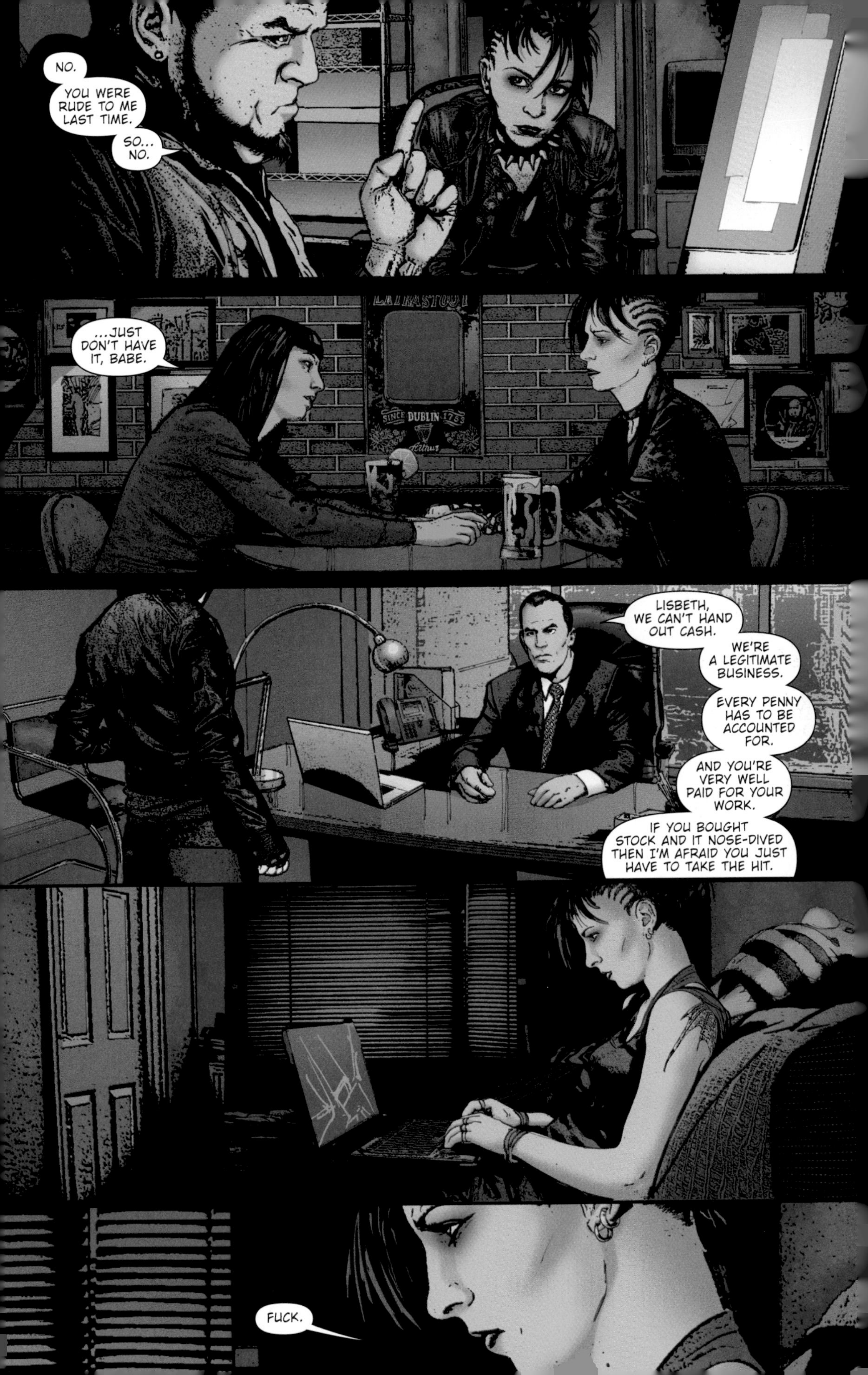
NO.
YOU WERE RUDE TO ME LAST TIME.
SO... NO.
...JUST DON'T HAVE IT, BABE.
SINCE DUBLIN 1759
LISBETH, WE CAN'T HAND OUT CASH.
WE'RE A LEGITIMATE BUSINESS.
EVERY PENNY HAS TO BE ACCOUNTED FOR.
AND YOU'RE VERY WELL PAID FOR YOUR WORK.
IF YOU BOUGHT STOCK AND IT NOSE-DIVED THEN I'M AFRAID YOU JUST HAVE TO TAKE THE HIT.
FUCK.

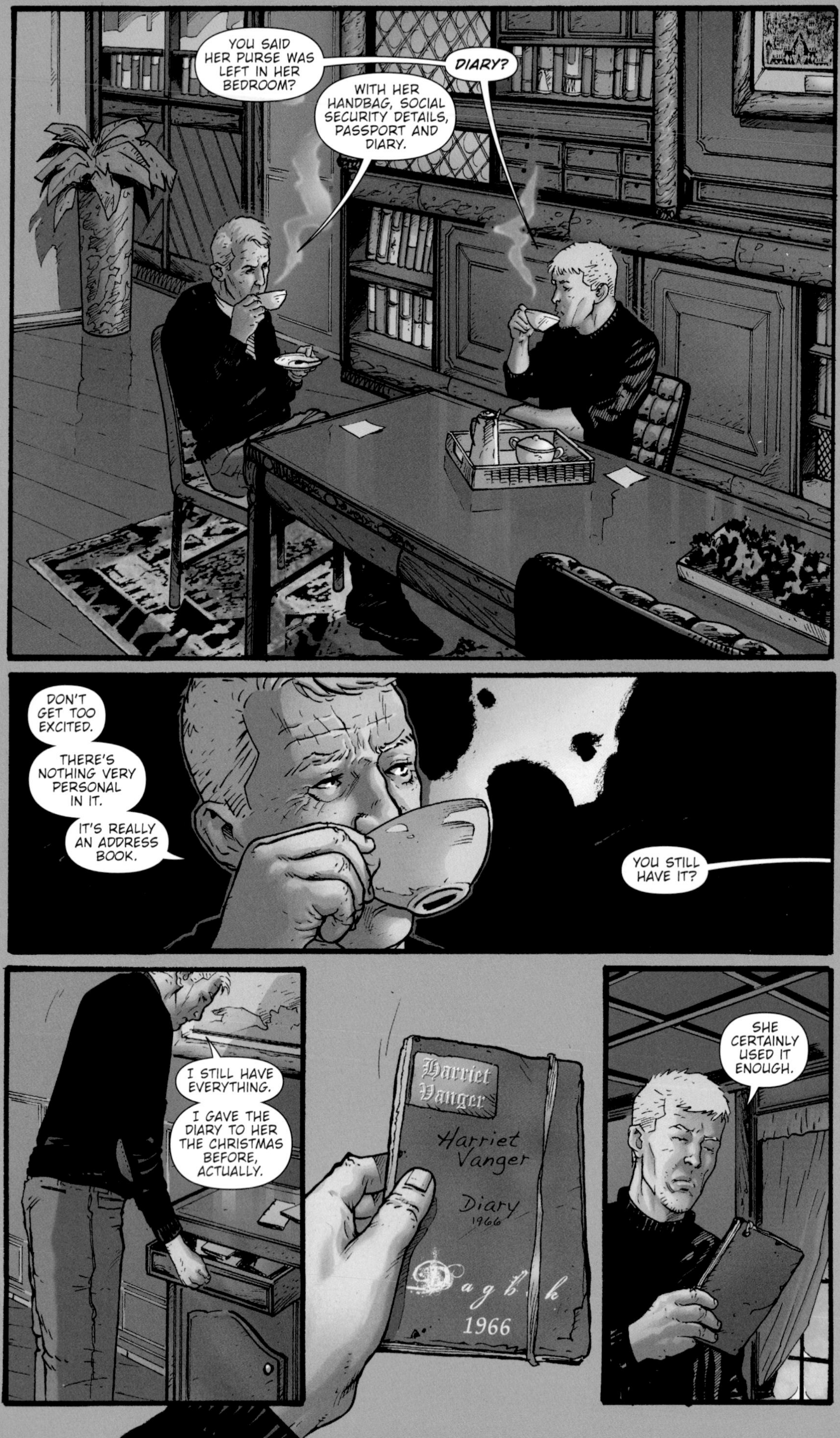
YOU SAID HER PURSE WAS LEFT IN HER BEDROOM?
WITH HER HANDBAG, SOCIAL SECURITY DETAILS, PASSPORT AND DIARY.
DIARY?
DON'T GET TOO EXCITED.
THERE'S NOTHING VERY PERSONAL IN IT.
IT'S REALLY AN ADDRESS BOOK.
YOU STILL HAVE IT?
I STILL HAVE EVERYTHING.
I GAVE THE DIARY TO HER THE CHRISTMAS BEFORE, ACTUALLY.
Harriet Vanger
Harriet Vanger
Diary
1966
1966
SHE CERTAINLY USED IT ENOUGH.

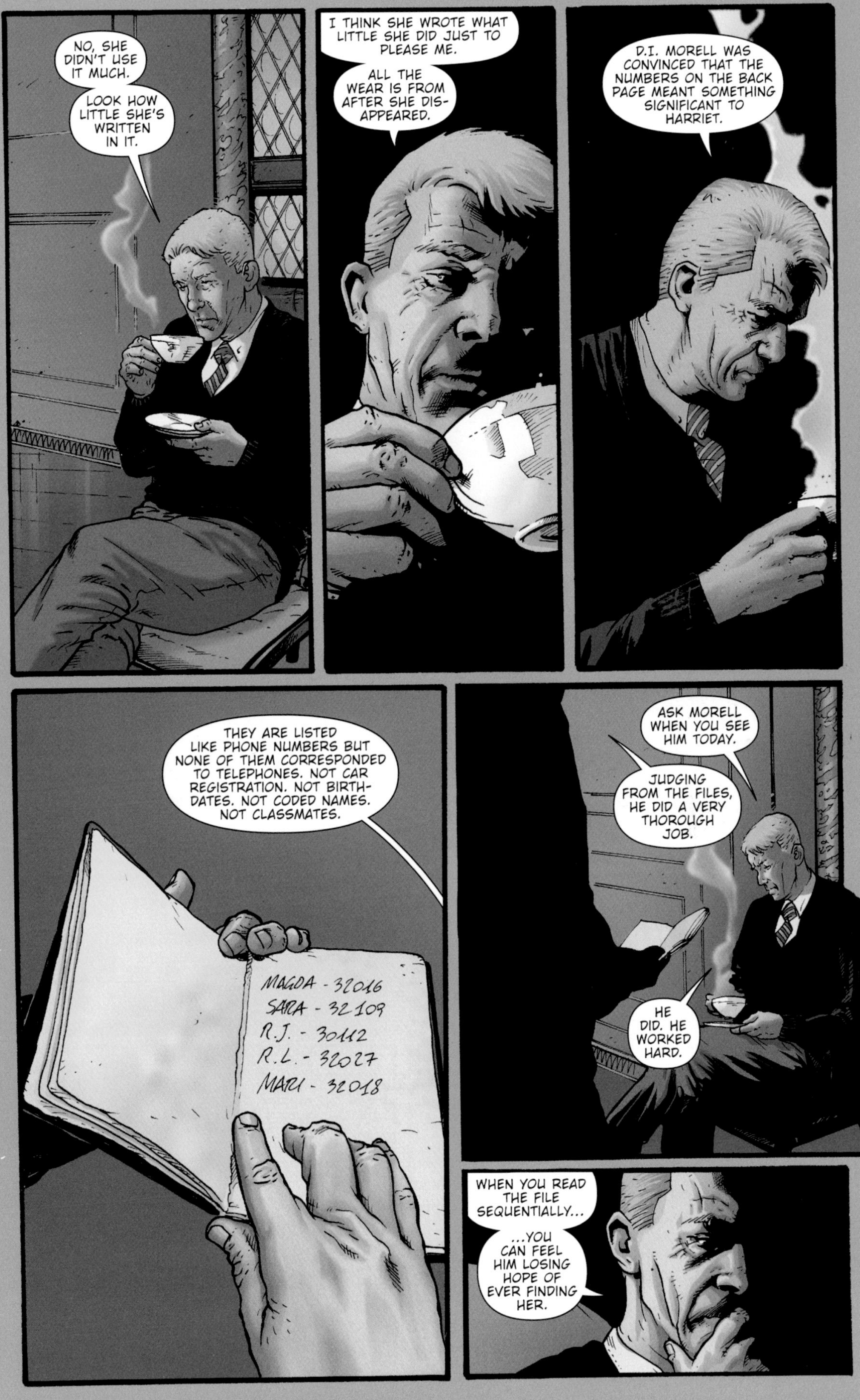
NO, SHE DIDN'T USE IT MUCH.
LOOK HOW LITTLE SHE'S WRITTEN IN IT.
I THINK SHE WROTE WHAT LITTLE SHE DID JUST TO PLEASE ME.
ALL THE WEAR IS FROM AFTER SHE DISAPPEARED.
D.I. MORELL WAS CONVINCED THAT THE NUMBERS ON THE BACK PAGE MEANT SOMETHING SIGNIFICANT TO HARRIET.
THEY ARE LISTED LIKE PHONE NUMBERS BUT NONE OF THEM CORRESPONDED TO TELEPHONES. NOT CAR REGISTRATION. NOT BIRTHDATES. NOT CODED NAMES. NOT CLASSMATES.
MAGDA - 32016
SARA - 32109
R.J. - 30112
R.L. - 32027
MARI - 32018
ASK MORELL WHEN YOU SEE HIM TODAY.
JUDGING FROM THE FILES, HE DID A VERY THOROUGH JOB.
HE DID. HE WORKED HARD.
WHEN YOU READ THE FILE SEQUENTIALLY...
...YOU CAN FEEL HIM LOSING HOPE OF EVER FINDING HER.

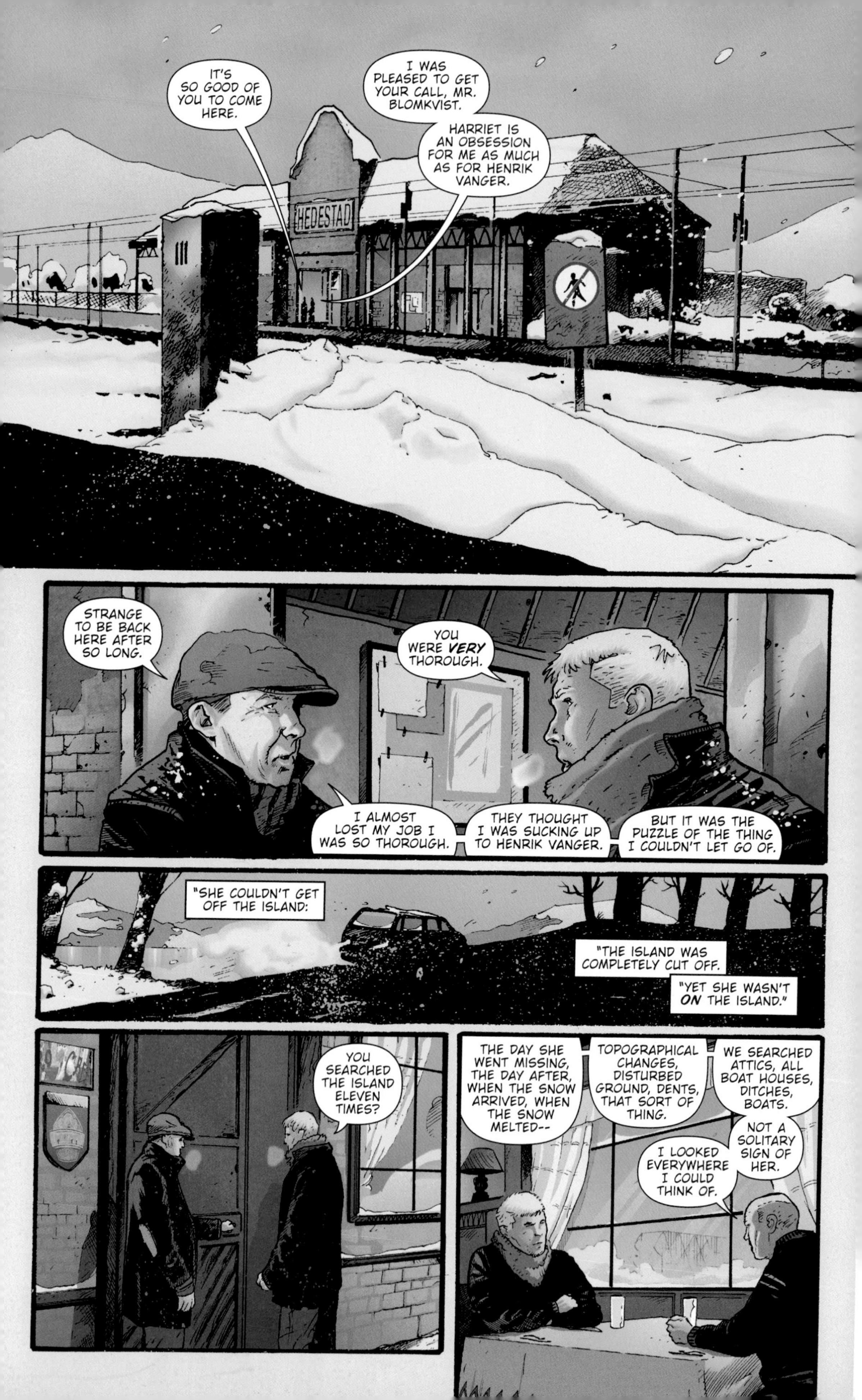

IT'S SO GOOD OF YOU TO COME HERE.
I WAS PLEASED TO GET YOUR CALL, MR. BLOMKVIST.
HARRIET IS AN OBSESSION FOR ME AS MUCH AS FOR HENRIK VANGER.
HEDESTAD
STRANGE TO BE BACK HERE AFTER SO LONG.
YOU WERE **VERY** THOROUGH.
I ALMOST LOST MY JOB I WAS SO THOROUGH.
THEY THOUGHT I WAS SUCKING UP TO HENRIK VANGER.
BUT IT WAS THE PUZZLE OF THE THING I COULDN'T LET GO OF.
"SHE COULDN'T GET OFF THE ISLAND:
"THE ISLAND WAS COMPLETELY CUT OFF.
"YET SHE WASN'T **ON** THE ISLAND."
YOU SEARCHED THE ISLAND ELEVEN TIMES?
THE DAY SHE WENT MISSING, THE DAY AFTER, WHEN THE SNOW ARRIVED, WHEN THE SNOW MELTED--
TOPOGRAPHICAL CHANGES, DISTURBED GROUND, DENTS, THAT SORT OF THING.
WE SEARCHED ATTICS, ALL BOAT HOUSES, DITCHES, BOATS.
NOT A SOLITARY SIGN OF HER.
I LOOKED EVERYWHERE I COULD THINK OF.

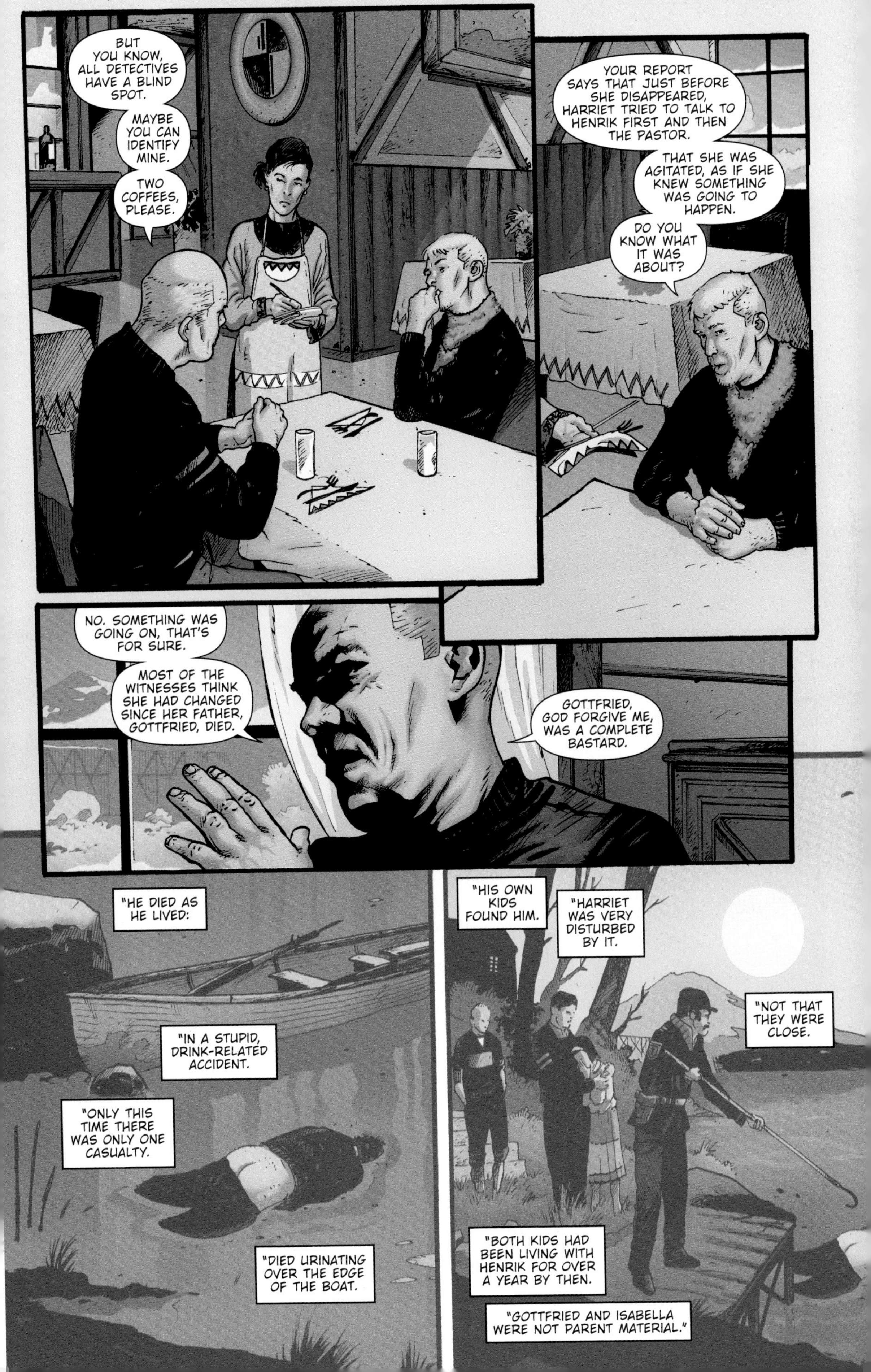
BUT YOU KNOW, ALL DETECTIVES HAVE A BLIND SPOT.
MAYBE YOU CAN IDENTIFY MINE.
TWO COFFEES, PLEASE.
YOUR REPORT SAYS THAT JUST BEFORE SHE DISAPPEARED, HARRIET TRIED TO TALK TO HENRIK FIRST AND THEN THE PASTOR.
THAT SHE WAS AGITATED, AS IF SHE KNEW SOMETHING WAS GOING TO HAPPEN.
DO YOU KNOW WHAT IT WAS ABOUT?
NO. SOMETHING WAS GOING ON, THAT'S FOR SURE.
MOST OF THE WITNESSES THINK SHE HAD CHANGED SINCE HER FATHER, GOTTFRIED, DIED.
GOTTFRIED, GOD FORGIVE ME, WAS A COMPLETE BASTARD.
"HE DIED AS HE LIVED:
"IN A STUPID, DRINK-RELATED ACCIDENT.
"ONLY THIS TIME THERE WAS ONLY ONE CASUALTY.
"DIED URINATING OVER THE EDGE OF THE BOAT.
"HIS OWN KIDS FOUND HIM.
"HARRIET WAS VERY DISTURBED BY IT.
"NOT THAT THEY WERE CLOSE.
"BOTH KIDS HAD BEEN LIVING WITH HENRIK FOR OVER A YEAR BY THEN.
"GOTTFRIED AND ISABELLA WERE NOT PARENT MATERIAL."

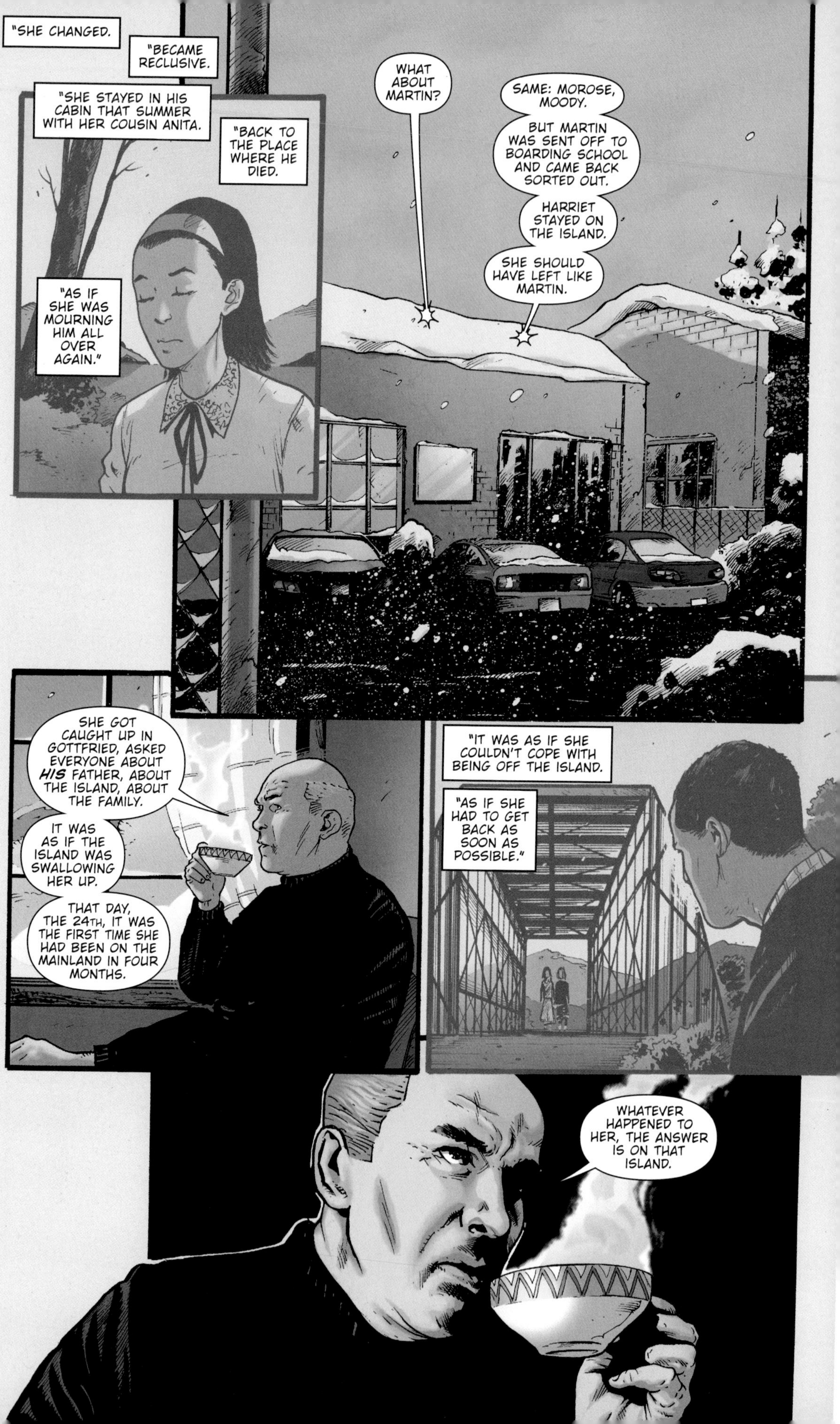
"SHE CHANGED.
"BECAME RECLUSIVE.
"SHE STAYED IN HIS CABIN THAT SUMMER WITH HER COUSIN ANITA.
"BACK TO THE PLACE WHERE HE DIED.
"AS IF SHE WAS MOURNING HIM ALL OVER AGAIN."
WHAT ABOUT MARTIN?
SAME: MOROSE, MOODY.
BUT MARTIN WAS SENT OFF TO BOARDING SCHOOL AND CAME BACK SORTED OUT.
HARRIET STAYED ON THE ISLAND.
SHE SHOULD HAVE LEFT LIKE MARTIN.
SHE GOT CAUGHT UP IN GOTTFRIED, ASKED EVERYONE ABOUT HIS FATHER, ABOUT THE ISLAND, ABOUT THE FAMILY.
IT WAS AS IF THE ISLAND WAS SWALLOWING HER UP.
THAT DAY, THE 24TH, IT WAS THE FIRST TIME SHE HAD BEEN ON THE MAINLAND IN FOUR MONTHS.
"IT WAS AS IF SHE COULDN'T COPE WITH BEING OFF THE ISLAND.
"AS IF SHE HAD TO GET BACK AS SOON AS POSSIBLE."
WHATEVER HAPPENED TO HER, THE ANSWER IS ON THAT ISLAND.

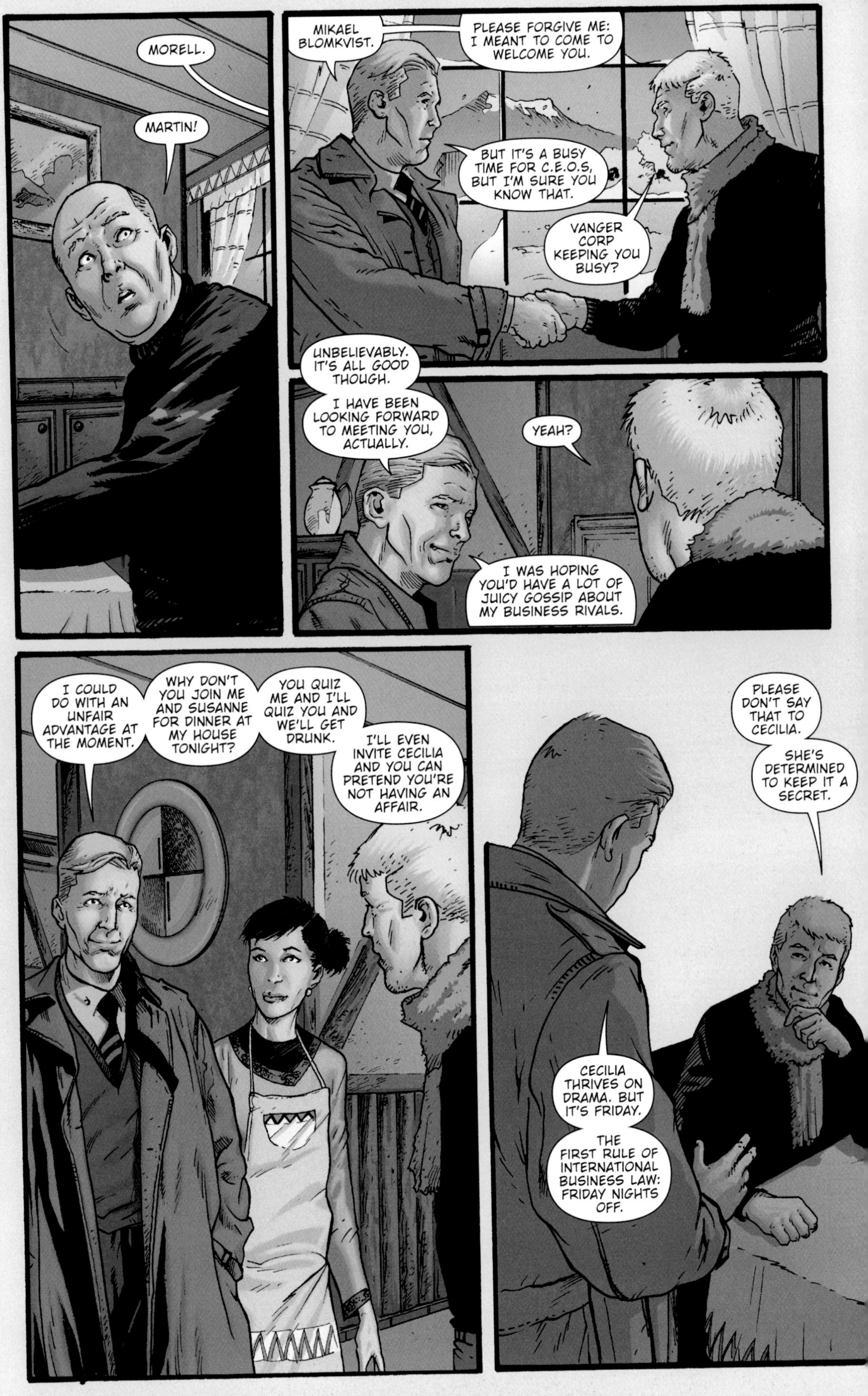
MORELL.
MARTIN!
MIKAEL BLOMKVIST.
PLEASE FORGIVE ME: I MEANT TO COME TO WELCOME YOU.
BUT IT'S A BUSY TIME FOR C.E.O.S, BUT I'M SURE YOU KNOW THAT.
VANGER CORP KEEPING YOU BUSY?
UNBELIEVABLY. IT'S ALL GOOD THOUGH.
I HAVE BEEN LOOKING FORWARD TO MEETING YOU, ACTUALLY.
YEAH?
I WAS HOPING YOU'D HAVE A LOT OF JUICY GOSSIP ABOUT MY BUSINESS RIVALS.
I COULD DO WITH AN UNFAIR ADVANTAGE AT THE MOMENT.
WHY DON'T YOU JOIN ME AND SUSANNE FOR DINNER AT MY HOUSE TONIGHT?
YOU QUIZ ME AND I'LL QUIZ YOU AND WE'LL GET DRUNK.
I'LL EVEN INVITE CECILIA AND YOU CAN PRETEND YOU'RE NOT HAVING AN AFFAIR.
PLEASE DON'T SAY THAT TO CECILIA.
SHE'S DETERMINED TO KEEP IT A SECRET.
CECILIA THRIVES ON DRAMA. BUT IT'S FRIDAY.
THE FIRST RULE OF INTERNATIONAL BUSINESS LAW: FRIDAY NIGHTS OFF.

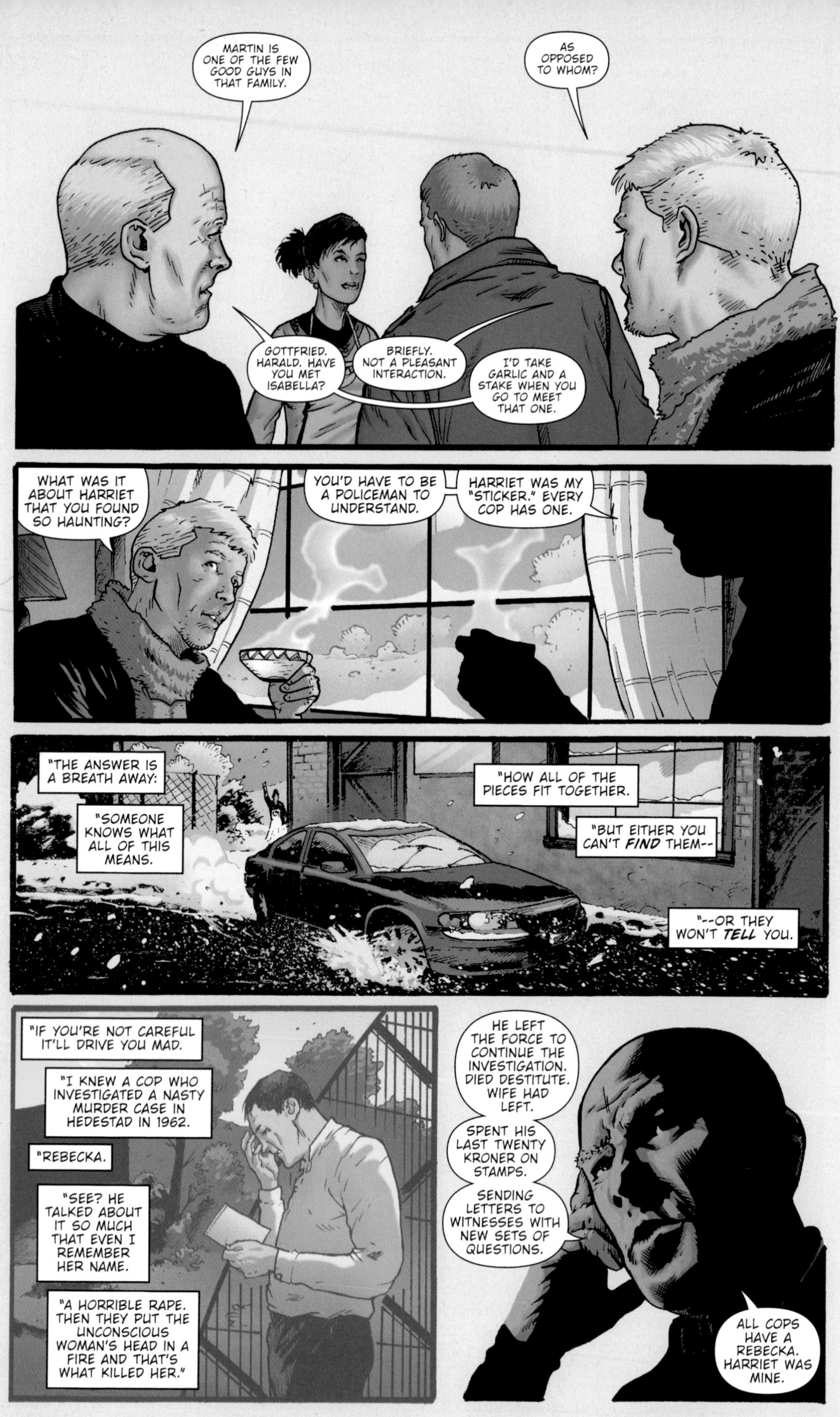
MARTIN IS ONE OF THE FEW GOOD GUYS IN THAT FAMILY.
AS OPPOSED TO WHOM?
GOTTFRIED. HARALD. HAVE YOU MET ISABELLA?
BRIEFLY. NOT A PLEASANT INTERACTION.
I'D TAKE GARLIC AND A STAKE WHEN YOU GO TO MEET THAT ONE.
WHAT WAS IT ABOUT HARRIET THAT YOU FOUND SO HAUNTING?
YOU'D HAVE TO BE A POLICEMAN TO UNDERSTAND.
HARRIET WAS MY "STICKER." EVERY COP HAS ONE.
"THE ANSWER IS A BREATH AWAY:
"SOMEONE KNOWS WHAT ALL OF THIS MEANS.
"HOW ALL OF THE PIECES FIT TOGETHER.
"BUT EITHER YOU CAN'T *FIND* THEM--
"--OR THEY WON'T *TELL* YOU.
"IF YOU'RE NOT CAREFUL IT'LL DRIVE YOU MAD.
"I KNEW A COP WHO INVESTIGATED A NASTY MURDER CASE IN HEDESTAD IN 1962.
"REBECKA.
"SEE? HE TALKED ABOUT IT SO MUCH THAT EVEN I REMEMBER HER NAME.
"A HORRIBLE RAPE. THEN THEY PUT THE UNCONSCIOUS WOMAN'S HEAD IN A FIRE AND THAT'S WHAT KILLED HER."
HE LEFT THE FORCE TO CONTINUE THE INVESTIGATION. DIED DESTITUTE. WIFE HAD LEFT.
SPENT HIS LAST TWENTY KRONER ON STAMPS.
SENDING LETTERS TO WITNESSES WITH NEW SETS OF QUESTIONS.
ALL COPS HAVE A REBECKA. HARRIET WAS MINE.

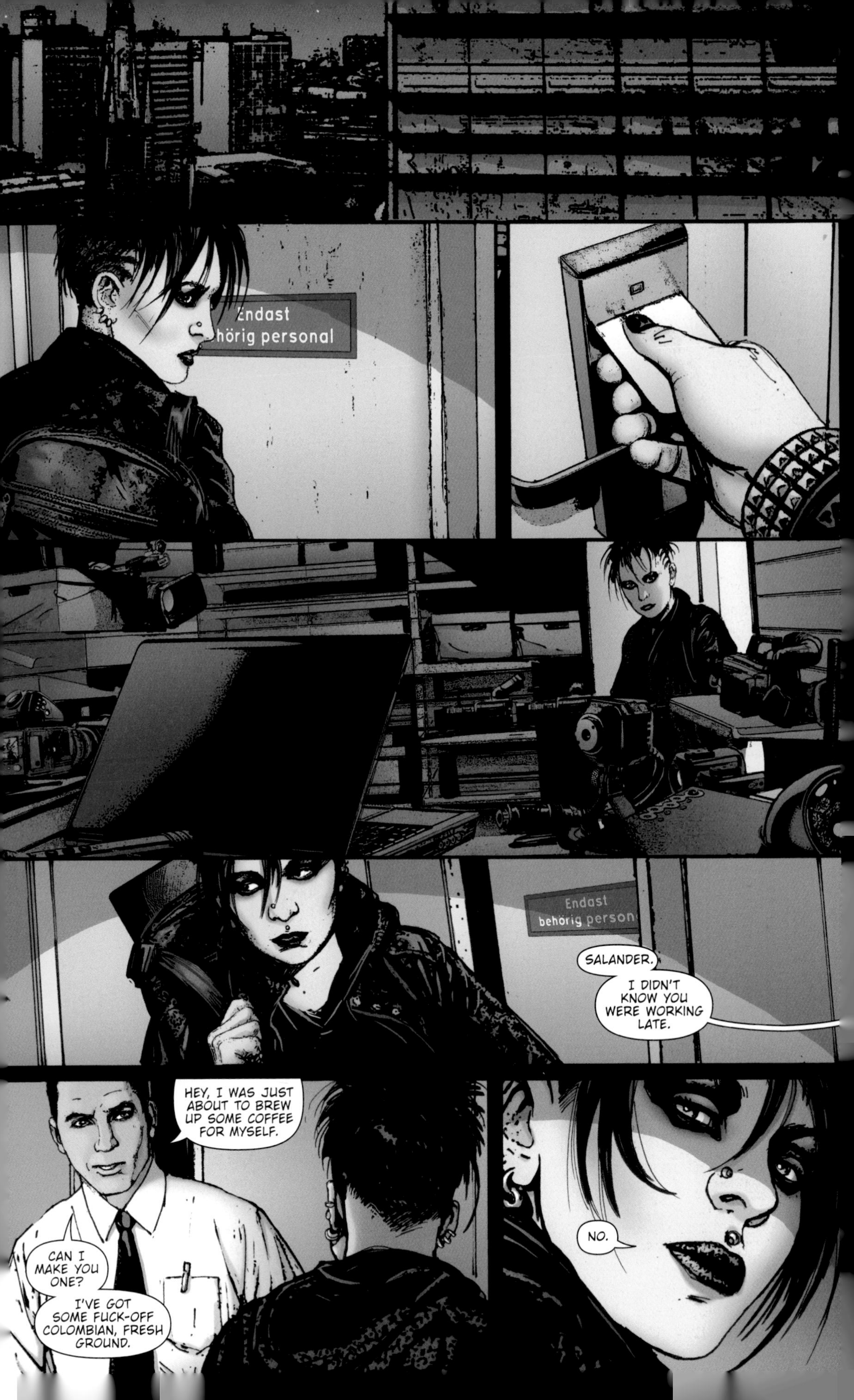
Endast
behörig personal
Endast
behörig person
SALANDER.
I DIDN'T KNOW YOU WERE WORKING LATE.
HEY, I WAS JUST ABOUT TO BREW UP SOME COFFEE FOR MYSELF.
CAN I MAKE YOU ONE?
I'VE GOT SOME FUCK-OFF COLOMBIAN, FRESH GROUND.
NO.

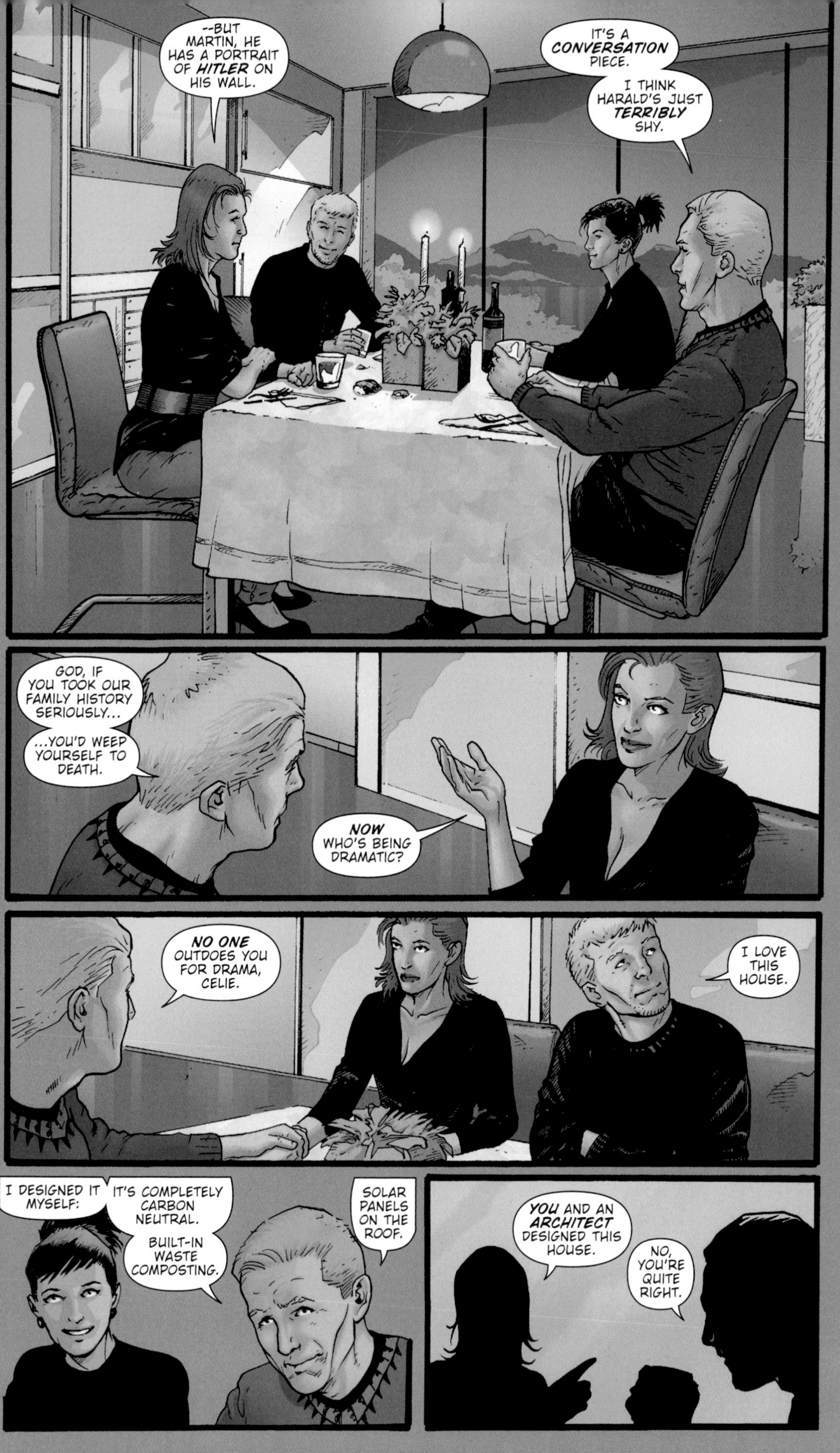
--BUT MARTIN, HE HAS A PORTRAIT OF HITLER ON HIS WALL.
IT'S A CONVERSATION PIECE.
I THINK HARALD'S JUST TERRIBLY SHY.
GOD, IF YOU TOOK OUR FAMILY HISTORY SERIOUSLY...
...YOU'D WEEP YOURSELF TO DEATH.
NOW WHO'S BEING DRAMATIC?
NO ONE OUTDOES YOU FOR DRAMA, CELIE.
I LOVE THIS HOUSE.
I DESIGNED IT MYSELF:
IT'S COMPLETELY CARBON NEUTRAL.
BUILT-IN WASTE COMPOSTING.
SOLAR PANELS ON THE ROOF.
YOU AND AN ARCHITECT DESIGNED THIS HOUSE.
NO, YOU'RE QUITE RIGHT.

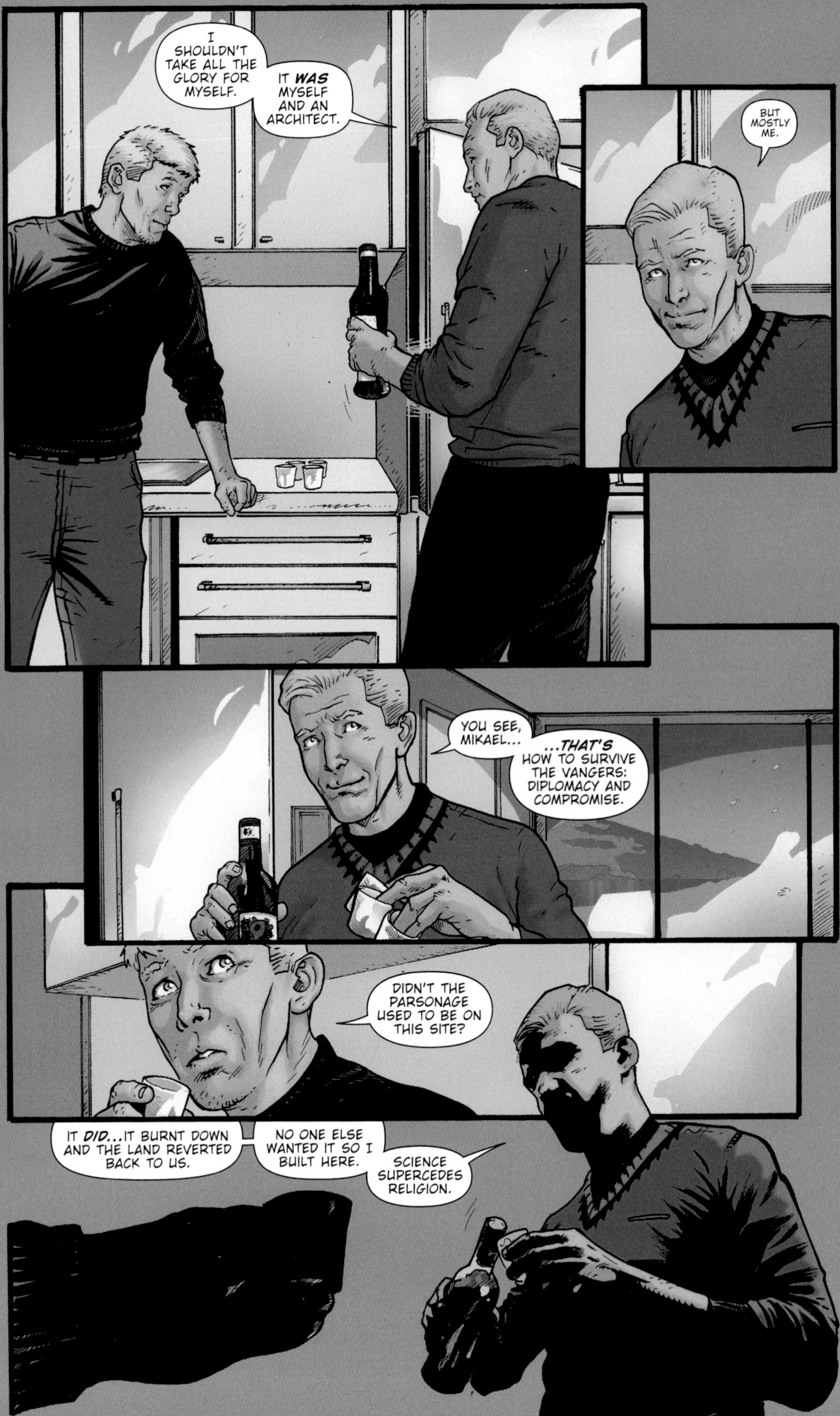
I SHOULDN'T TAKE ALL THE GLORY FOR MYSELF.
IT WAS MYSELF AND AN ARCHITECT.
BUT MOSTLY ME.
YOU SEE, MIKAEL...
...THAT'S HOW TO SURVIVE THE VANGERS: DIPLOMACY AND COMPROMISE.
DIDN'T THE PARSONAGE USED TO BE ON THIS SITE?
IT DID...IT BURNT DOWN AND THE LAND REVERTED BACK TO US.
NO ONE ELSE WANTED IT SO I BUILT HERE.
SCIENCE SUPERCEDES RELIGION.

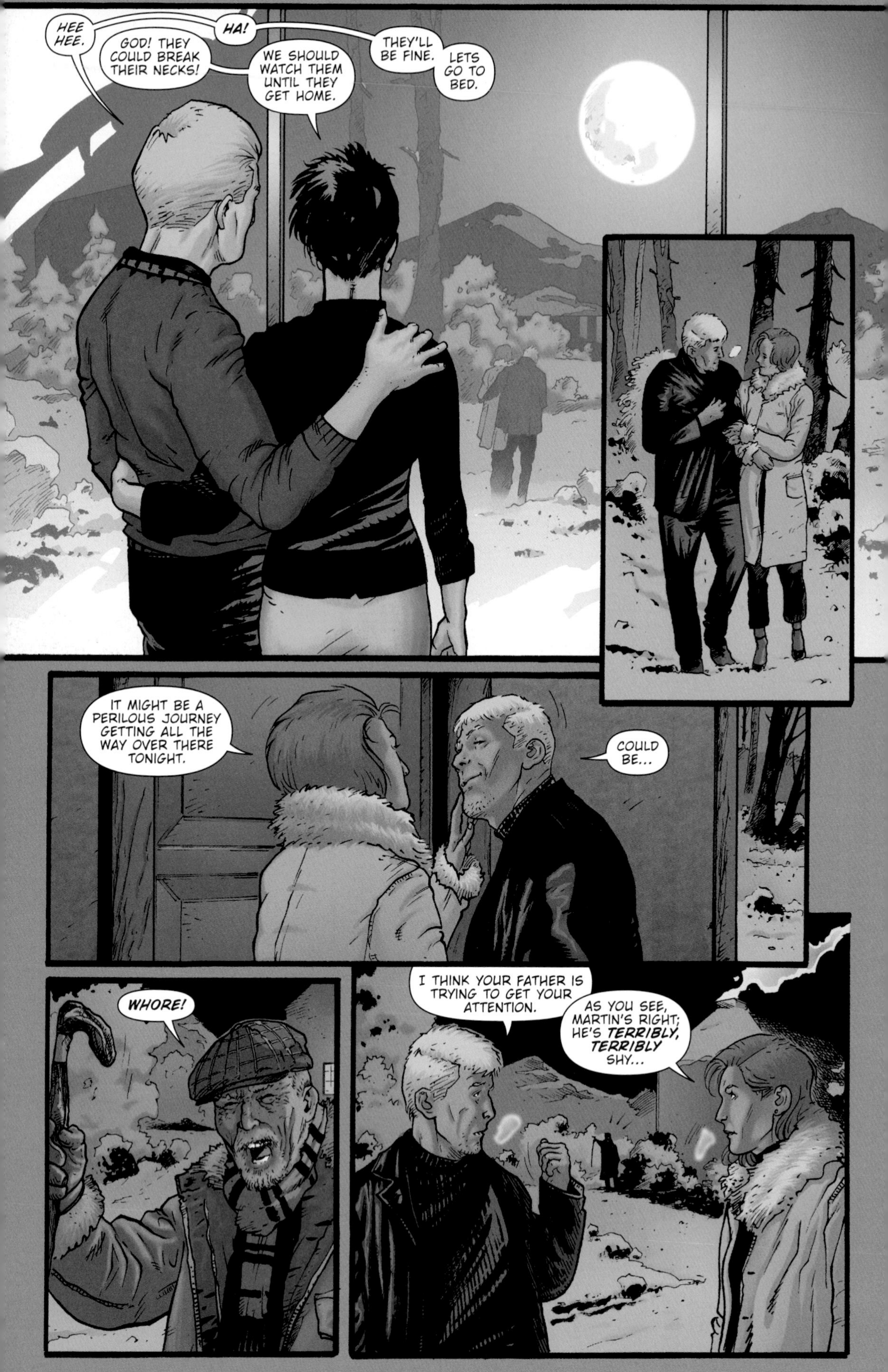
HEE HEE.
GOD! THEY COULD BREAK THEIR NECKS!
HA!
WE SHOULD WATCH THEM UNTIL THEY GET HOME.
THEY'LL BE FINE.
LETS GO TO BED.
IT MIGHT BE A PERILOUS JOURNEY GETTING ALL THE WAY OVER THERE TONIGHT.
COULD BE...
WHORE!
I THINK YOUR FATHER IS TRYING TO GET YOUR ATTENTION.
AS YOU SEE, MARTIN'S RIGHT; HE'S TERRIBLY, TERRIBLY SHY...

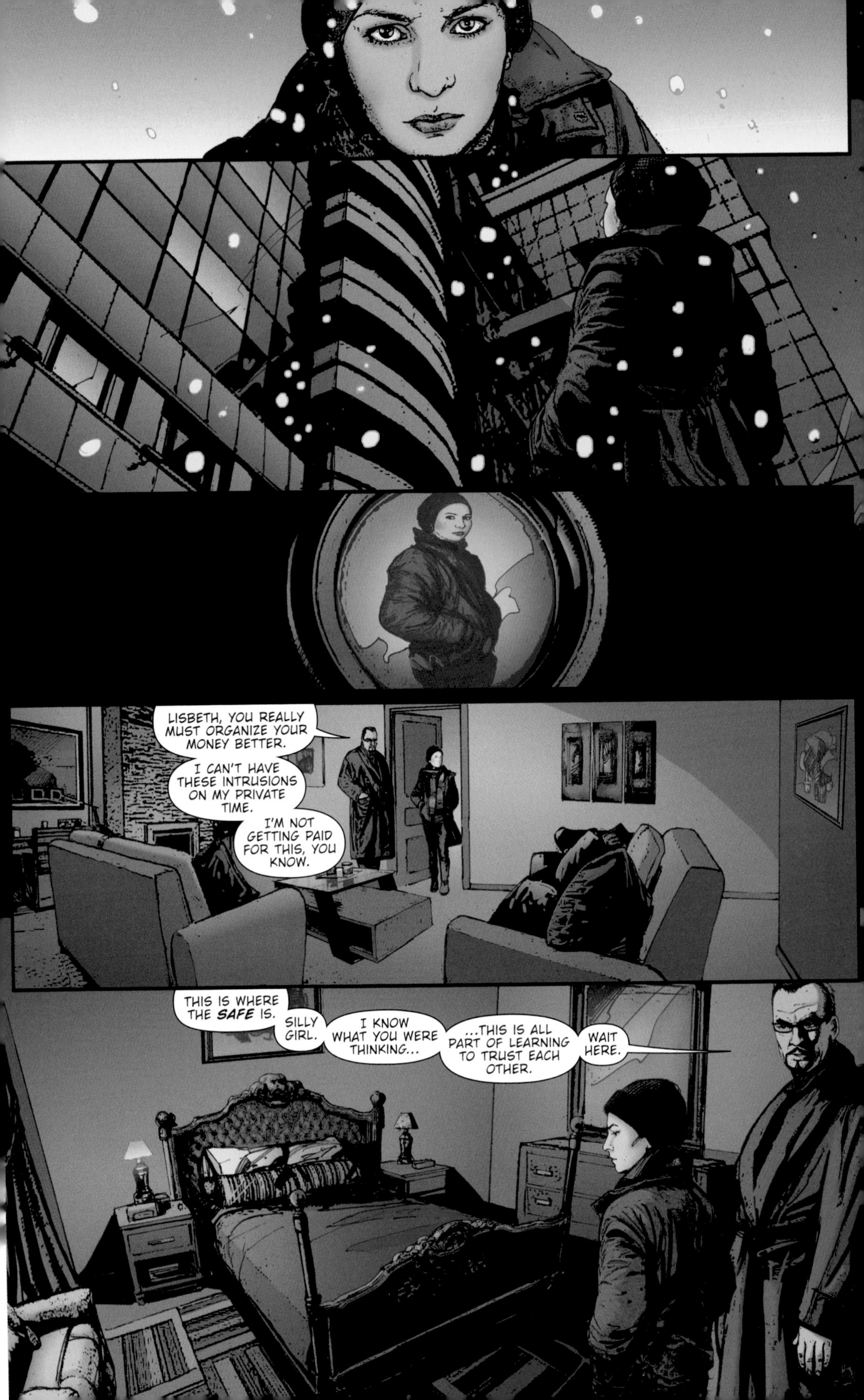
LISBETH, YOU REALLY MUST ORGANIZE YOUR MONEY BETTER.
I CAN'T HAVE THESE INTRUSIONS ON MY PRIVATE TIME.
I'M NOT GETTING PAID FOR THIS, YOU KNOW.
THIS IS WHERE THE SAFE IS.
SILLY GIRL.
I KNOW WHAT YOU WERE THINKING...
...THIS IS ALL PART OF LEARNING TO TRUST EACH OTHER.
WAIT HERE.

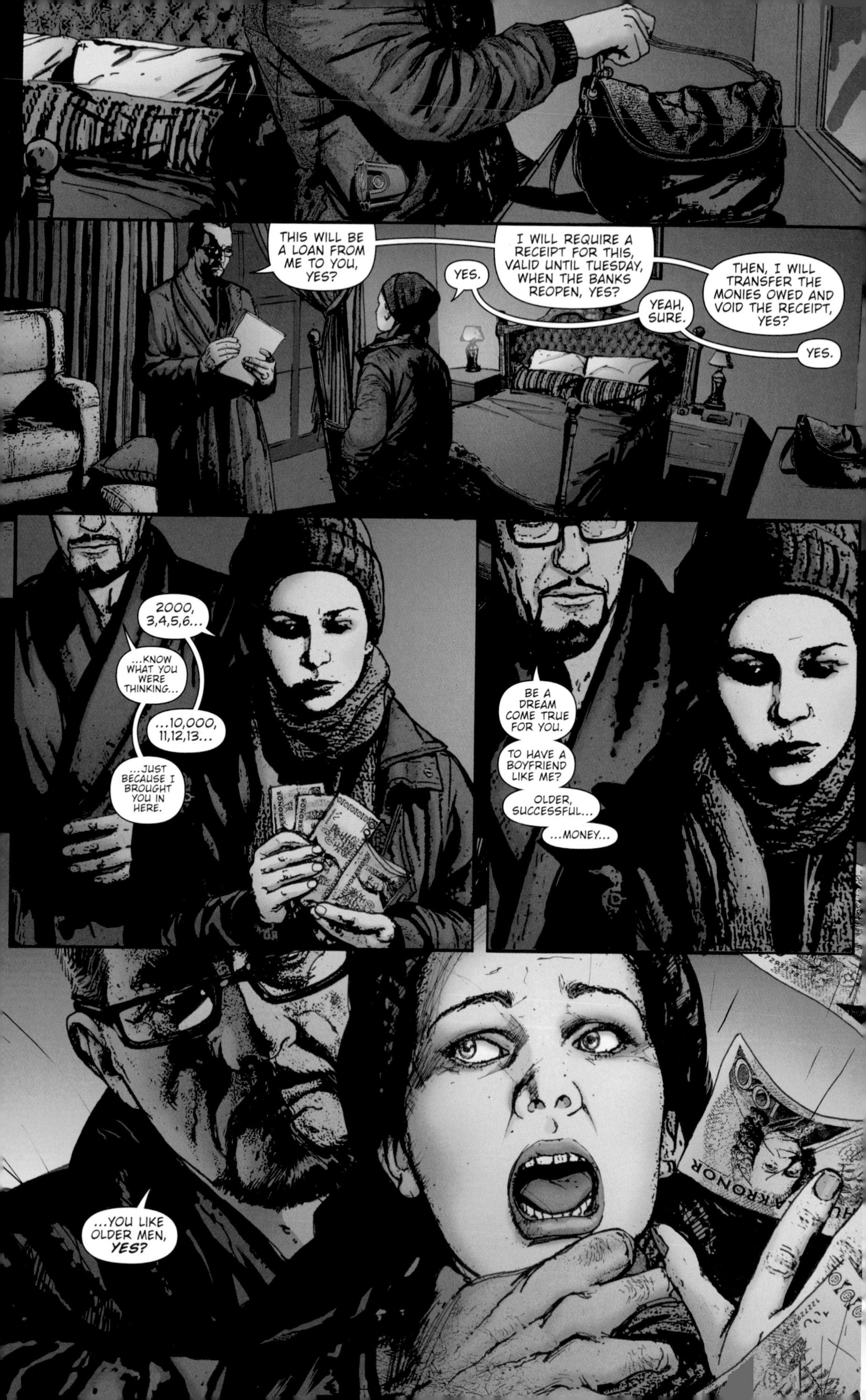
THIS WILL BE A LOAN FROM ME TO YOU, YES?
YES.
I WILL REQUIRE A RECEIPT FOR THIS, VALID UNTIL TUESDAY, WHEN THE BANKS REOPEN, YES?
YEAH, SURE.
THEN, I WILL TRANSFER THE MONIES OWED AND VOID THE RECEIPT, YES?
YES.
2000, 3,4,5,6...
...KNOW WHAT YOU WERE THINKING...
...10,000, 11,12,13...
...JUST BECAUSE I BROUGHT YOU IN HERE.
BE A DREAM COME TRUE FOR YOU.
TO HAVE A BOYFRIEND LIKE ME?
OLDER, SUCCESSFUL...
...MONEY...
...YOU LIKE OLDER MEN, *YES?*

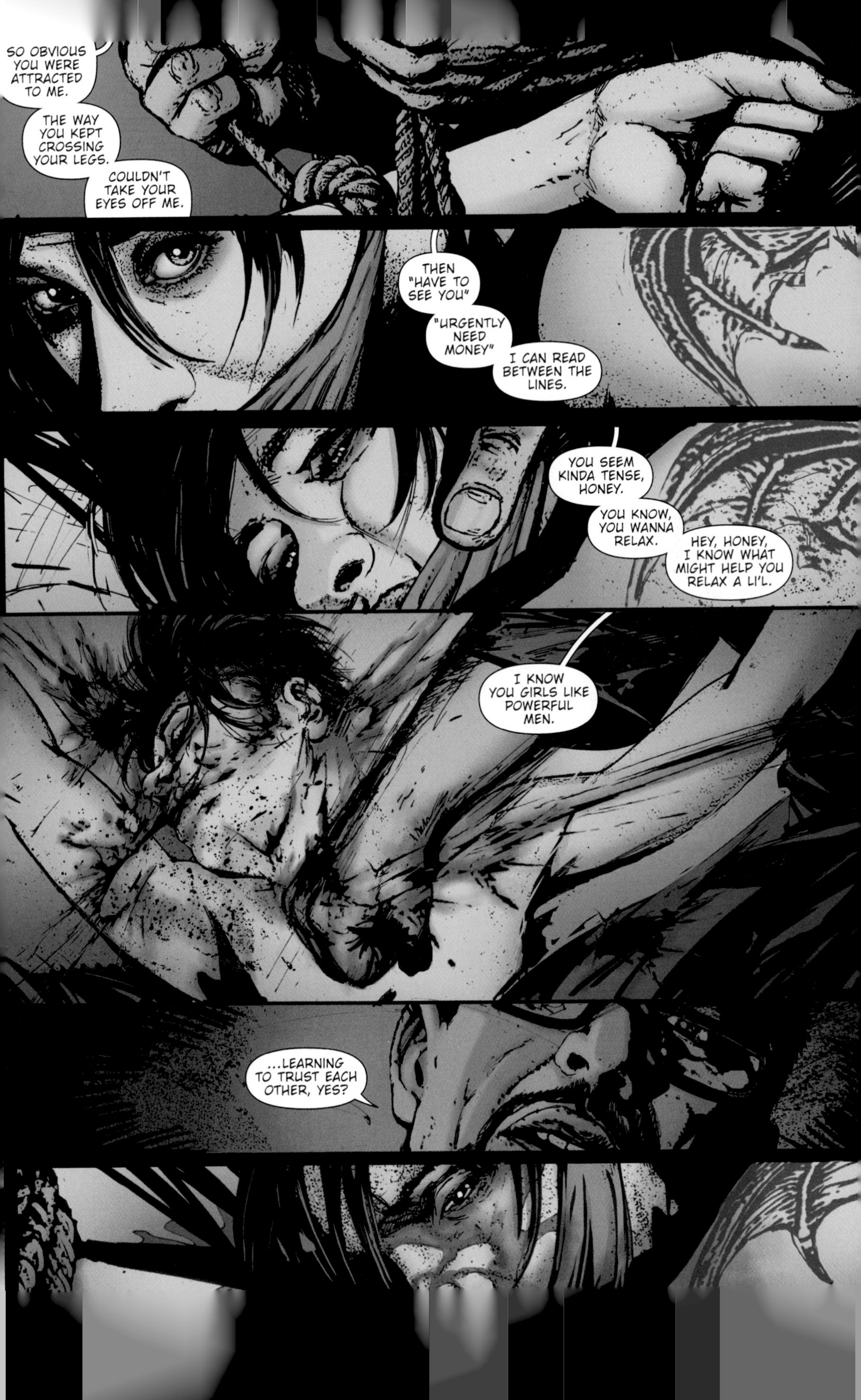
SO OBVIOUS YOU WERE ATTRACTED TO ME.
THE WAY YOU KEPT CROSSING YOUR LEGS.
COULDN'T TAKE YOUR EYES OFF ME.
THEN "HAVE TO SEE YOU"
"URGENTLY NEED MONEY"
I CAN READ BETWEEN THE LINES.
YOU SEEM KINDA TENSE, HONEY.
YOU KNOW, YOU WANNA RELAX.
HEY, HONEY, I KNOW WHAT MIGHT HELP YOU RELAX A LI'L.
I KNOW YOU GIRLS LIKE POWERFUL MEN.
...LEARNING TO TRUST EACH OTHER, YES?

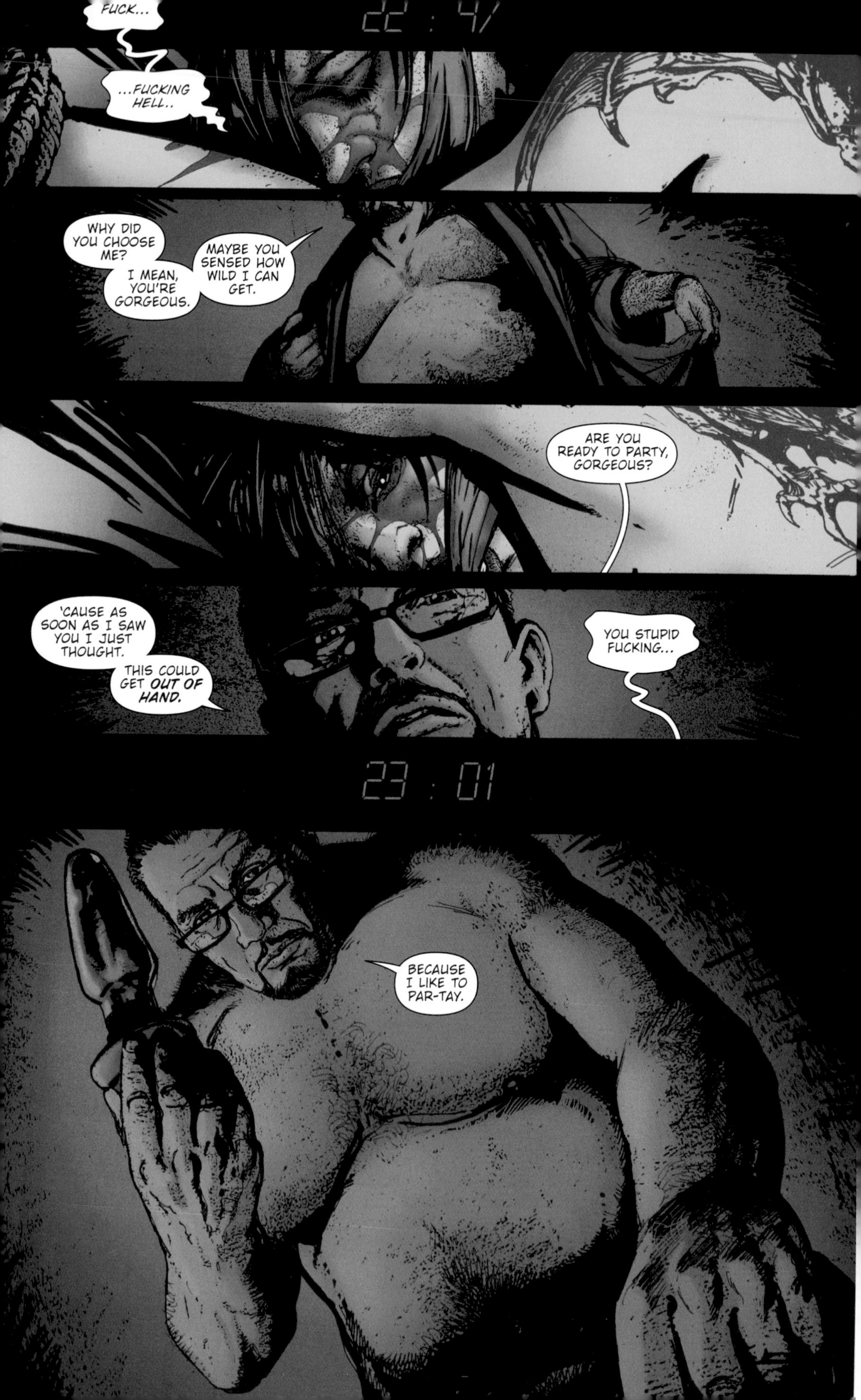
FUCK...
22 : 47
...FUCKING HELL...
WHY DID YOU CHOOSE ME?
I MEAN, YOU'RE GORGEOUS.
MAYBE YOU SENSED HOW WILD I CAN GET.
ARE YOU READY TO PARTY, GORGEOUS?
'CAUSE AS SOON AS I SAW YOU I JUST THOUGHT.
THIS COULD GET ***OUT OF HAND.***
YOU STUPID FUCKING...
23 : 01
BECAUSE I LIKE TO PAR-TAY.

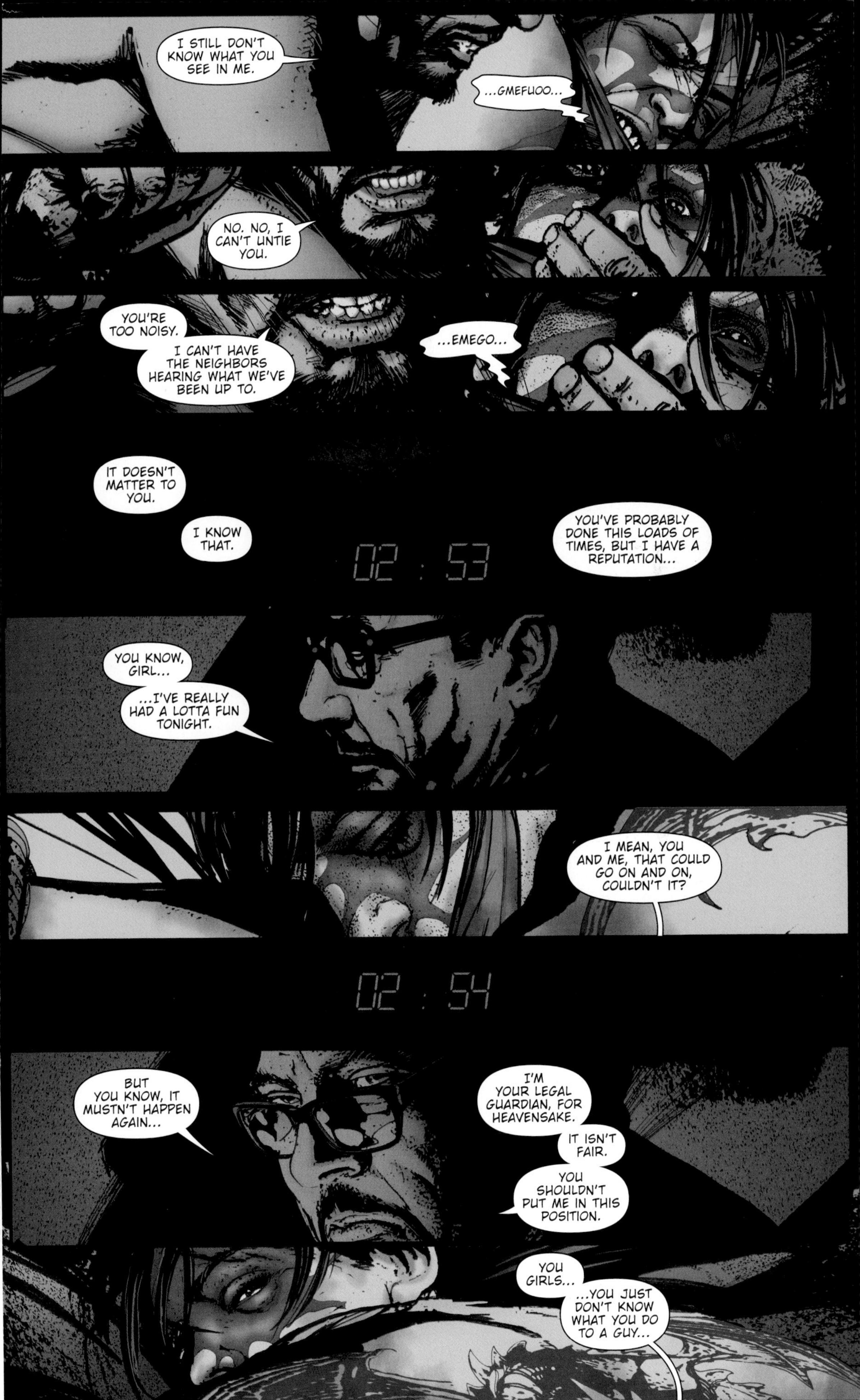
I STILL DON'T KNOW WHAT YOU SEE IN ME.
...GMEFUOO...
NO. NO, I CAN'T UNTIE YOU.
YOU'RE TOO NOISY.
I CAN'T HAVE THE NEIGHBORS HEARING WHAT WE'VE BEEN UP TO.
...EMEGO...
IT DOESN'T MATTER TO YOU.
I KNOW THAT.
YOU'VE PROBABLY DONE THIS LOADS OF TIMES, BUT I HAVE A REPUTATION...
02 : 53
YOU KNOW, GIRL...
...I'VE REALLY HAD A LOTTA FUN TONIGHT.
I MEAN, YOU AND ME, THAT COULD GO ON AND ON, COULDN'T IT?
02 : 54
BUT YOU KNOW, IT MUSTN'T HAPPEN AGAIN...
I'M YOUR LEGAL GUARDIAN, FOR HEAVENSAKE.
IT ISN'T FAIR.
YOU SHOULDN'T PUT ME IN THIS POSITION.
YOU GIRLS...
...YOU JUST DON'T KNOW WHAT YOU DO TO A GUY...

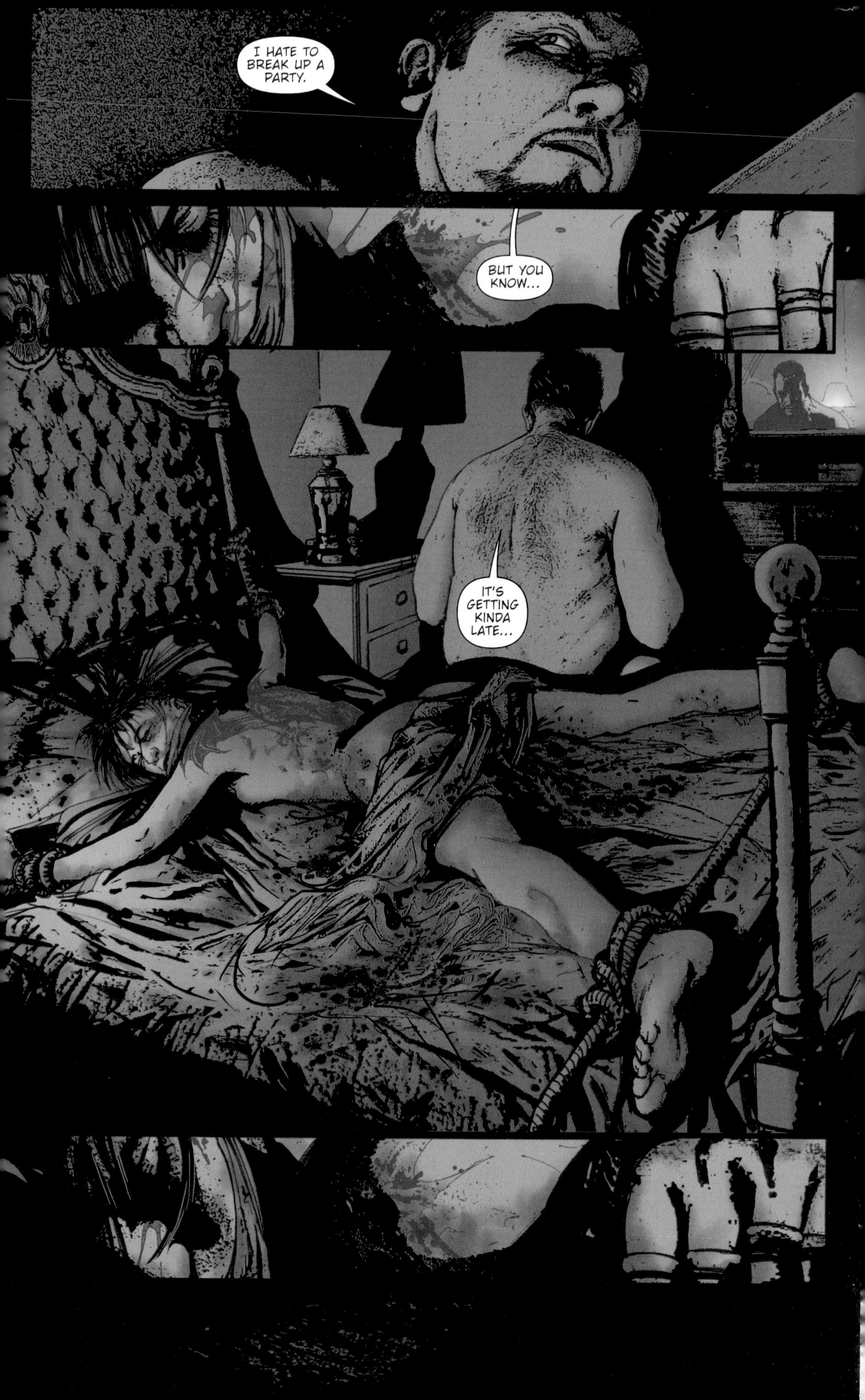
I HATE TO BREAK UP A PARTY.
BUT YOU KNOW...
IT'S GETTING KINDA LATE...

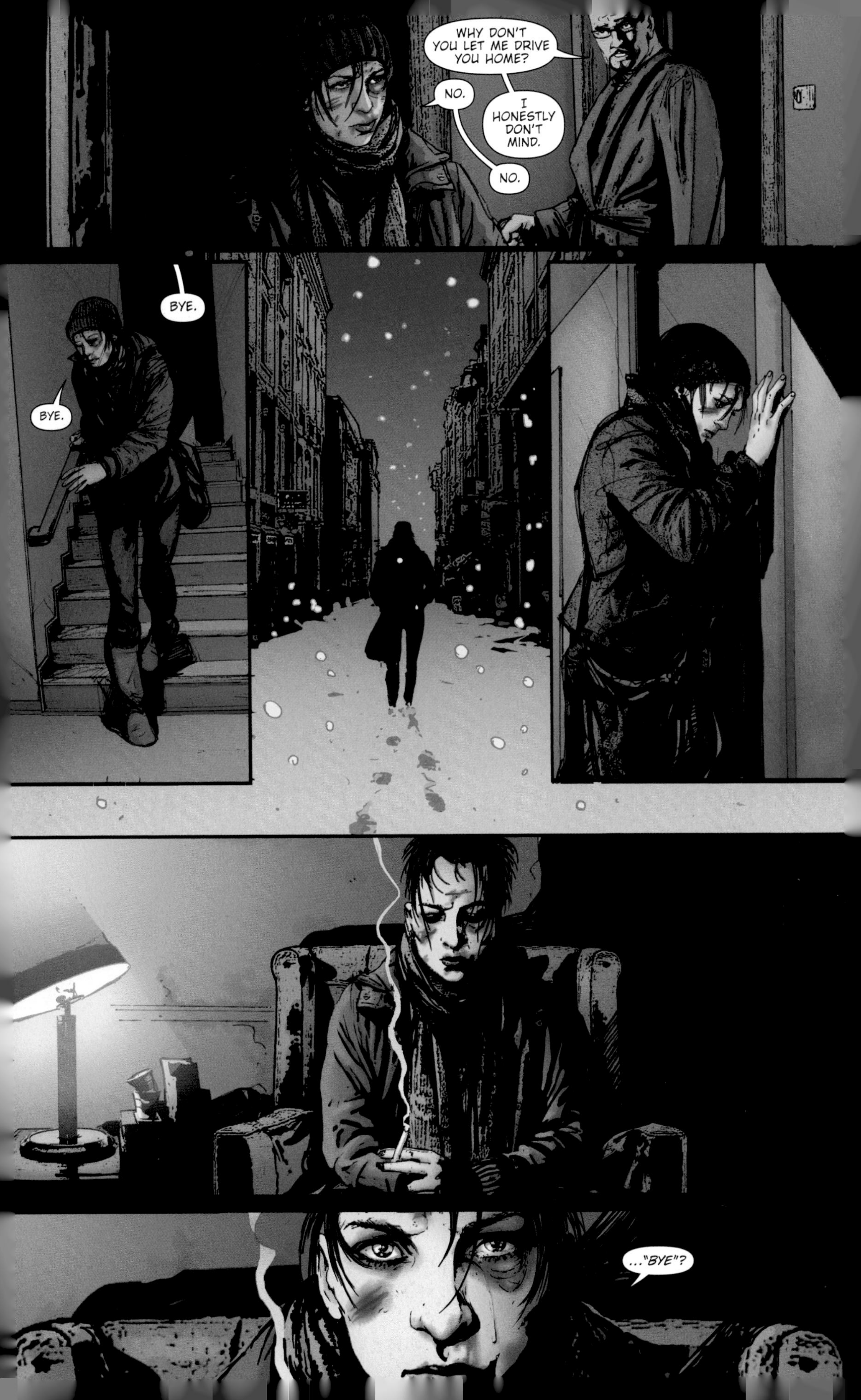
WHY DON'T YOU LET ME DRIVE YOU HOME?
NO.
I HONESTLY DON'T MIND.
NO.
BYE.
BYE.
..."BYE"?

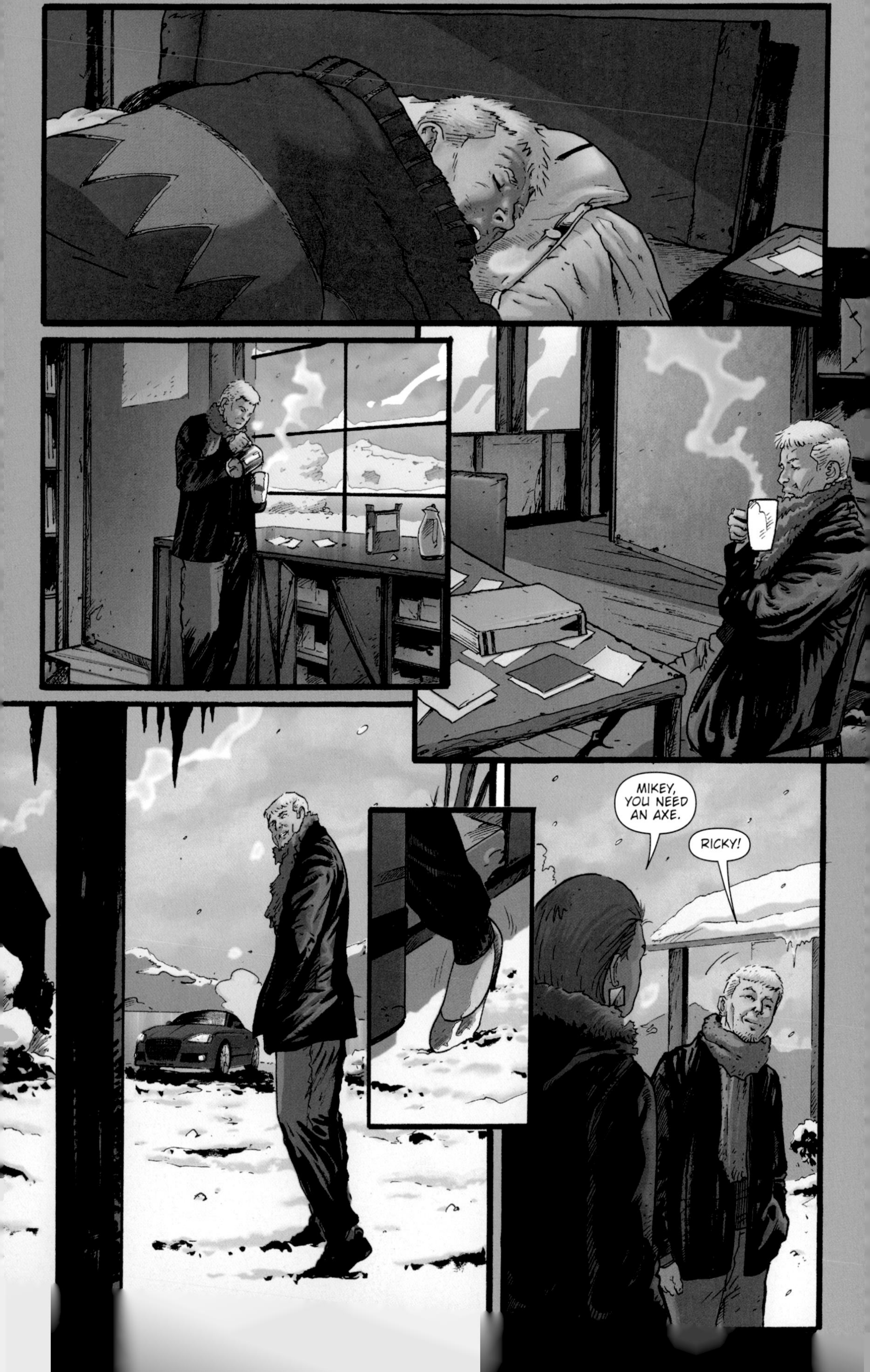
MIKEY, YOU NEED AN AXE.
RICKY!

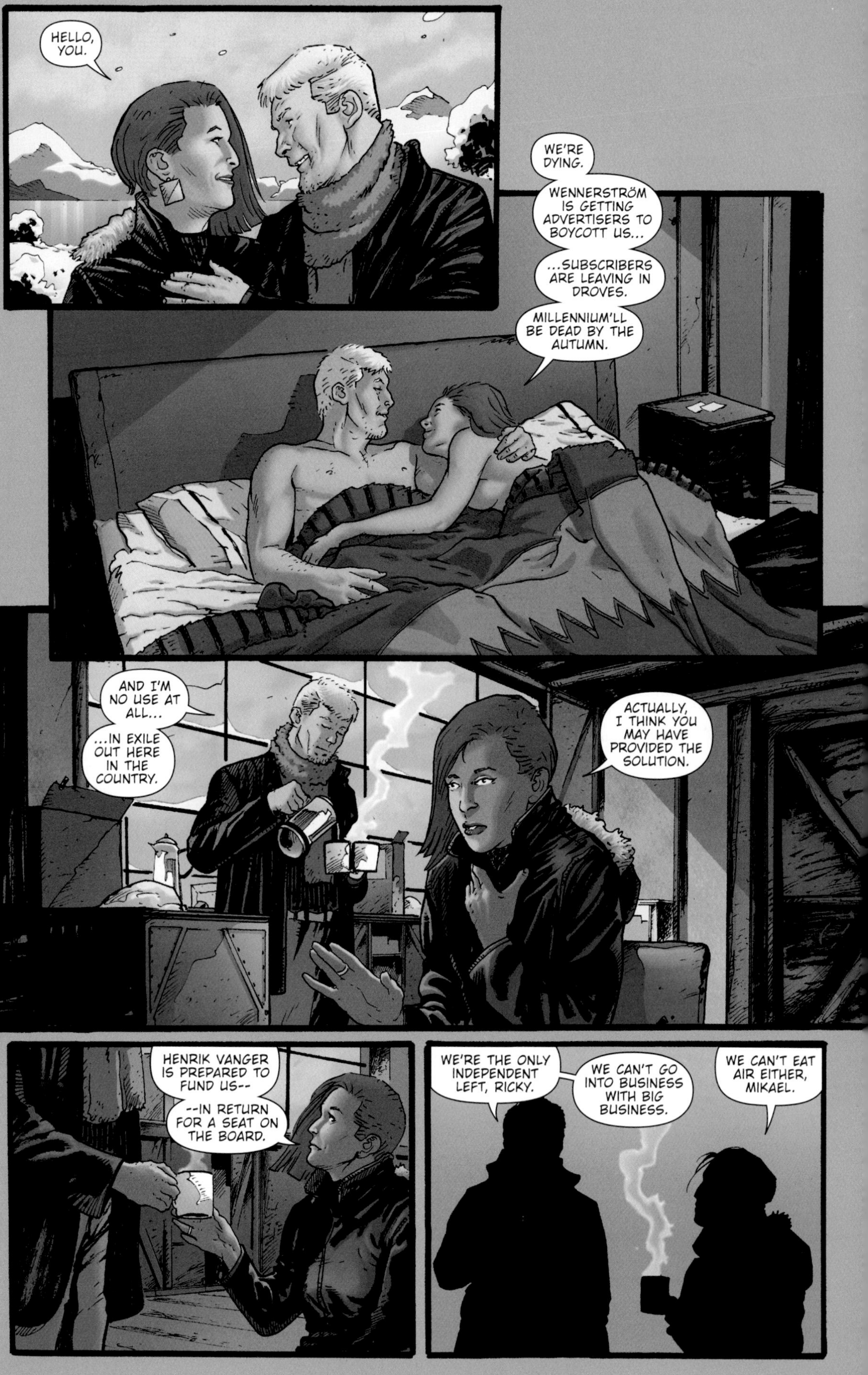

HELLO, YOU.
WE'RE DYING.
WENNERSTRÖM IS GETTING ADVERTISERS TO BOYCOTT US...
...SUBSCRIBERS ARE LEAVING IN DROVES.
MILLENNIUM'LL BE DEAD BY THE AUTUMN.
AND I'M NO USE AT ALL...
...IN EXILE OUT HERE IN THE COUNTRY.
ACTUALLY, I THINK YOU MAY HAVE PROVIDED THE SOLUTION.
HENRIK VANGER IS PREPARED TO FUND US--
--IN RETURN FOR A SEAT ON THE BOARD.
WE'RE THE ONLY INDEPENDENT LEFT, RICKY.
WE CAN'T GO INTO BUSINESS WITH BIG BUSINESS.
WE CAN'T EAT AIR EITHER, MIKAEL.

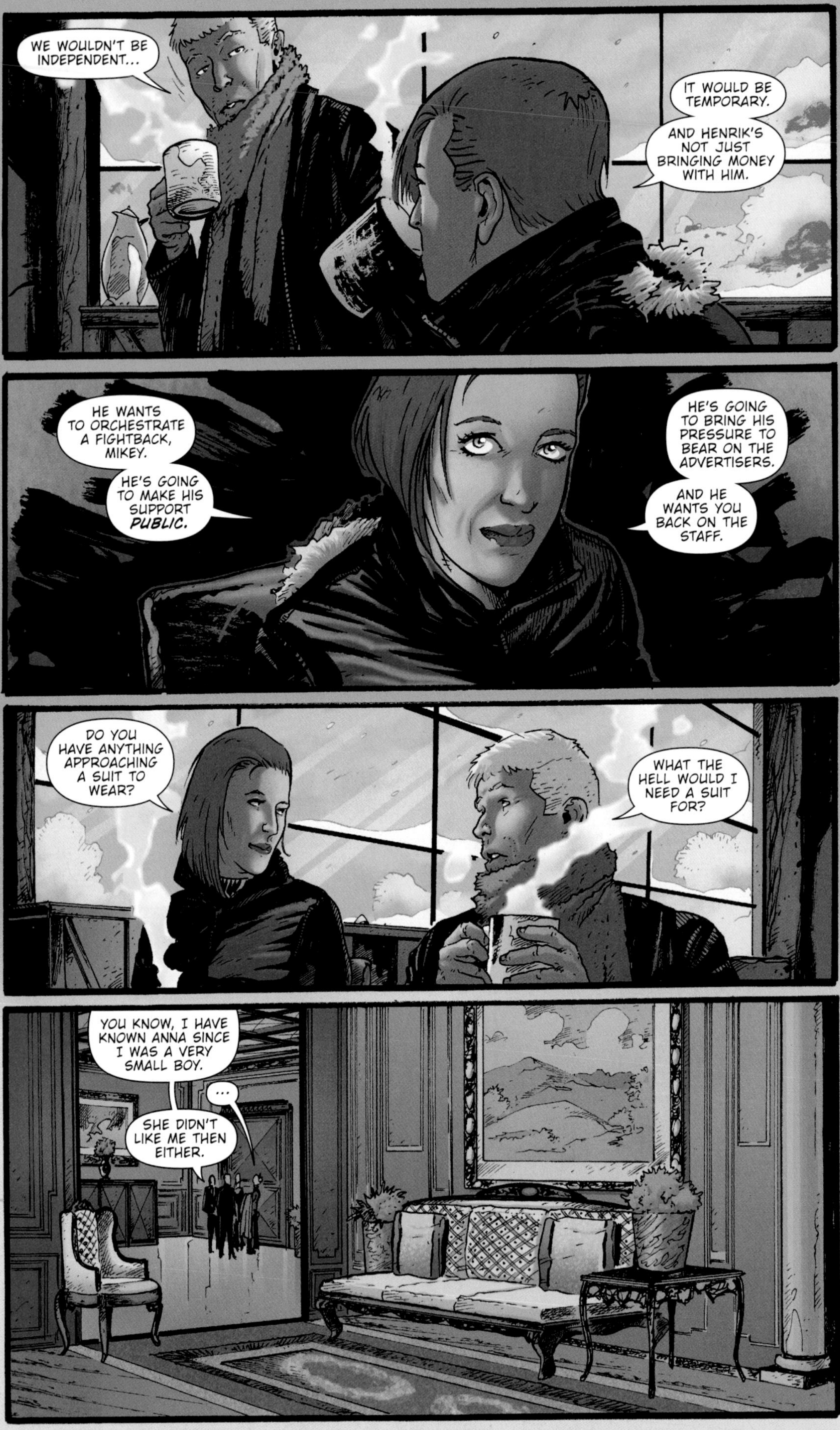
WE WOULDN'T BE INDEPENDENT...
IT WOULD BE TEMPORARY.
AND HENRIK'S NOT JUST BRINGING MONEY WITH HIM.
HE WANTS TO ORCHESTRATE A FIGHTBACK, MIKEY.
HE'S GOING TO MAKE HIS SUPPORT *PUBLIC.*
HE'S GOING TO BRING HIS PRESSURE TO BEAR ON THE ADVERTISERS.
AND HE WANTS YOU BACK ON THE STAFF.
DO YOU HAVE ANYTHING APPROACHING A SUIT TO WEAR?
WHAT THE HELL WOULD I NEED A SUIT FOR?
YOU KNOW, I HAVE KNOWN ANNA SINCE I WAS A VERY SMALL BOY.
...
SHE DIDN'T LIKE ME THEN EITHER.

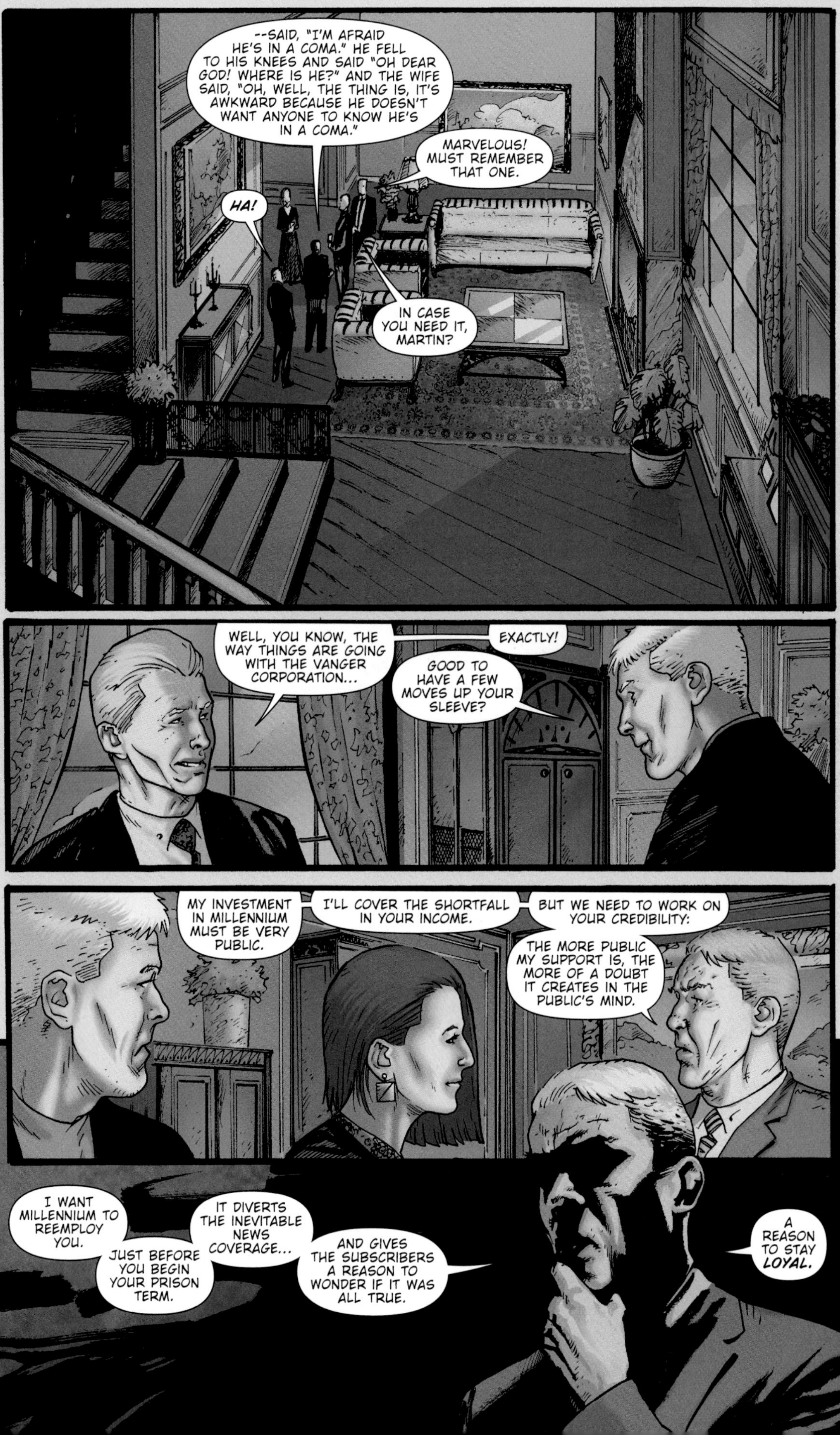
--SAID, "I'M AFRAID HE'S IN A COMA." HE FELL TO HIS KNEES AND SAID "OH DEAR GOD! WHERE IS HE?" AND THE WIFE SAID, "OH, WELL, THE THING IS, IT'S AWKWARD BECAUSE HE DOESN'T WANT ANYONE TO KNOW HE'S IN A COMA."
HA!
MARVELOUS! MUST REMEMBER THAT ONE.
IN CASE YOU NEED IT, MARTIN?
WELL, YOU KNOW, THE WAY THINGS ARE GOING WITH THE VANGER CORPORATION...
EXACTLY!
GOOD TO HAVE A FEW MOVES UP YOUR SLEEVE?
MY INVESTMENT IN MILLENNIUM MUST BE VERY PUBLIC.
I'LL COVER THE SHORTFALL IN YOUR INCOME.
BUT WE NEED TO WORK ON YOUR CREDIBILITY:
THE MORE PUBLIC MY SUPPORT IS, THE MORE OF A DOUBT IT CREATES IN THE PUBLIC'S MIND.
I WANT MILLENNIUM TO REEMPLOY YOU.
JUST BEFORE YOU BEGIN YOUR PRISON TERM.
IT DIVERTS THE INEVITABLE NEWS COVERAGE...
AND GIVES THE SUBSCRIBERS A REASON TO WONDER IF IT WAS ALL TRUE.
A REASON TO STAY *LOYAL.*

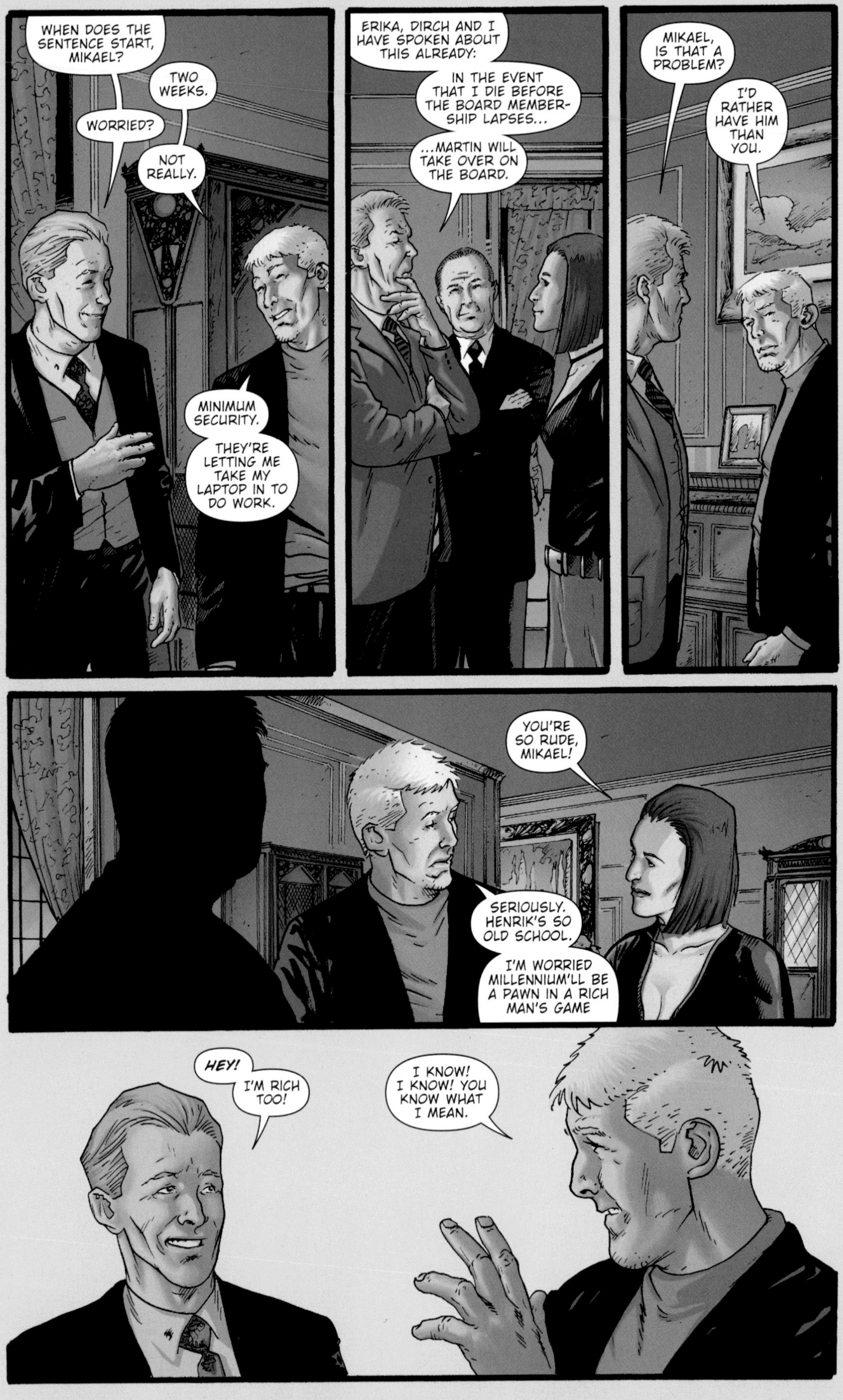

WHEN DOES THE SENTENCE START, MIKAEL?
TWO WEEKS.
WORRIED?
NOT REALLY.
MINIMUM SECURITY.
THEY'RE LETTING ME TAKE MY LAPTOP IN TO DO WORK.
ERIKA, DIRCH AND I HAVE SPOKEN ABOUT THIS ALREADY:
IN THE EVENT THAT I DIE BEFORE THE BOARD MEMBERSHIP LAPSES...
...MARTIN WILL TAKE OVER ON THE BOARD.
MIKAEL, IS THAT A PROBLEM?
I'D RATHER HAVE HIM THAN YOU.
YOU'RE SO RUDE, MIKAEL!
SERIOUSLY. HENRIK'S SO OLD SCHOOL.
I'M WORRIED MILLENNIUM'LL BE A PAWN IN A RICH MAN'S GAME
HEY!
I'M RICH TOO!
I KNOW! I KNOW! YOU KNOW WHAT I MEAN.

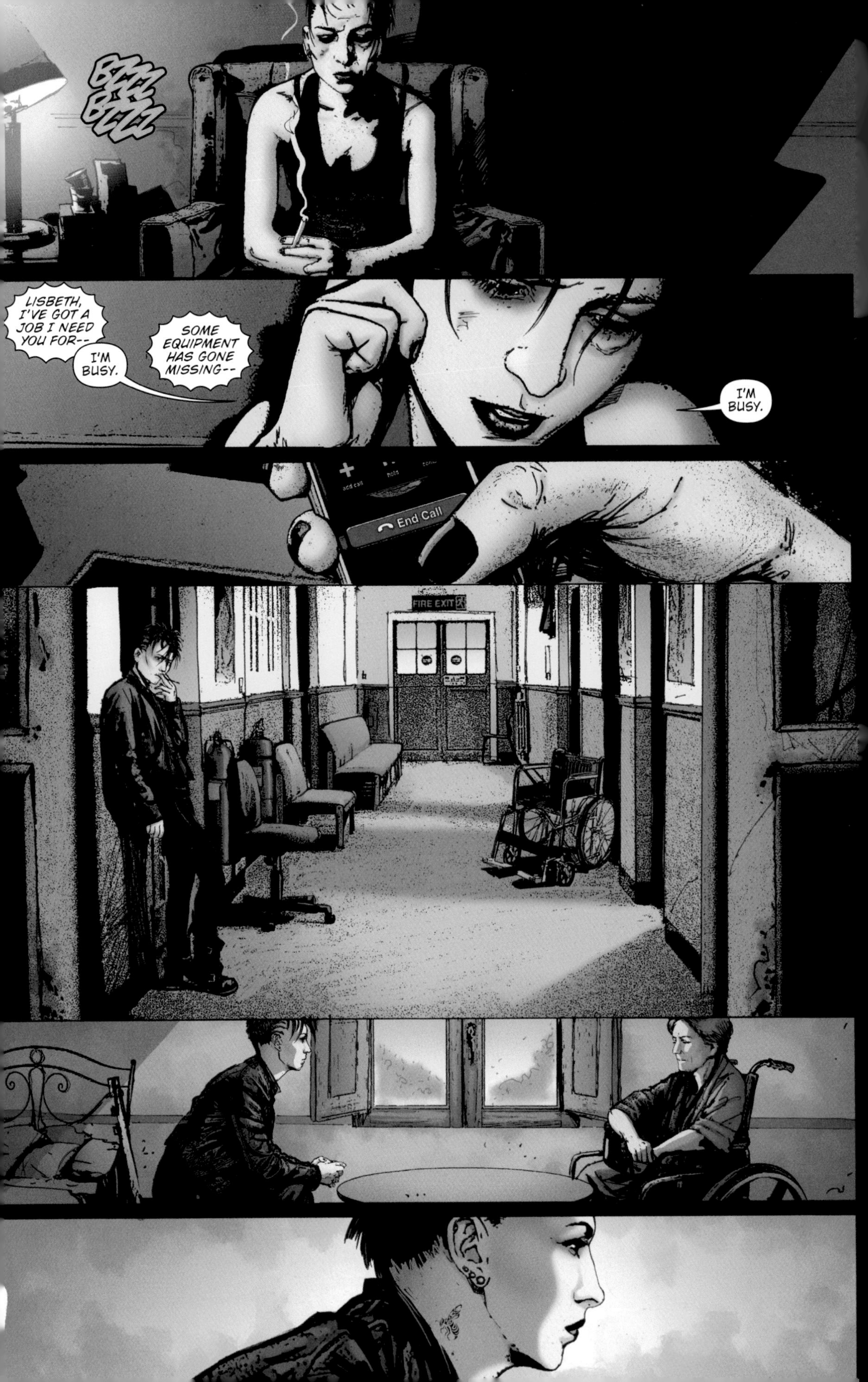
BZZZ BZZZ
LISBETH, I'VE GOT A JOB I NEED YOU FOR--
I'M BUSY.
SOME EQUIPMENT HAS GONE MISSING--
I'M BUSY.
add call
hold
End Call
FIRE EXIT

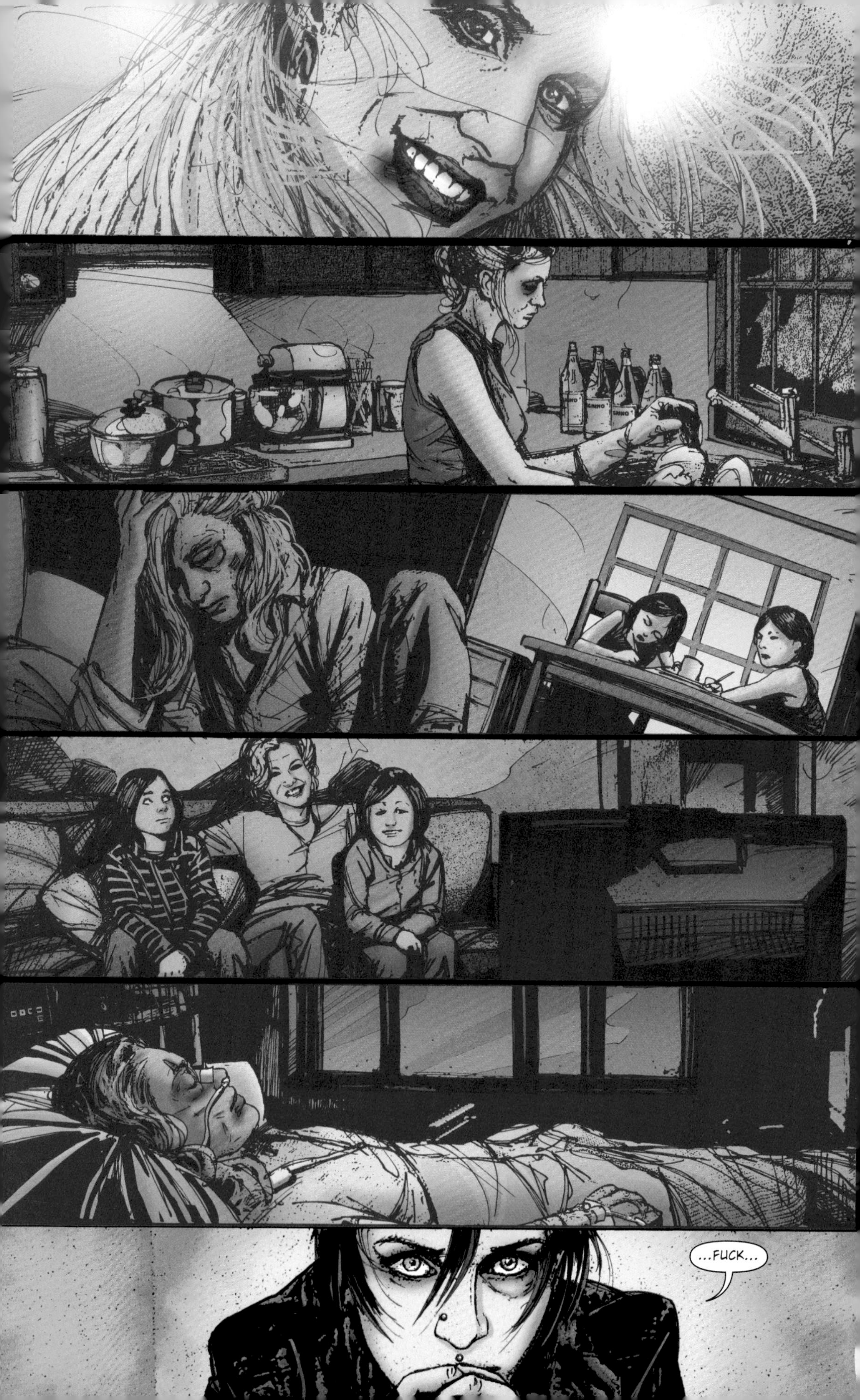
...FUCK...

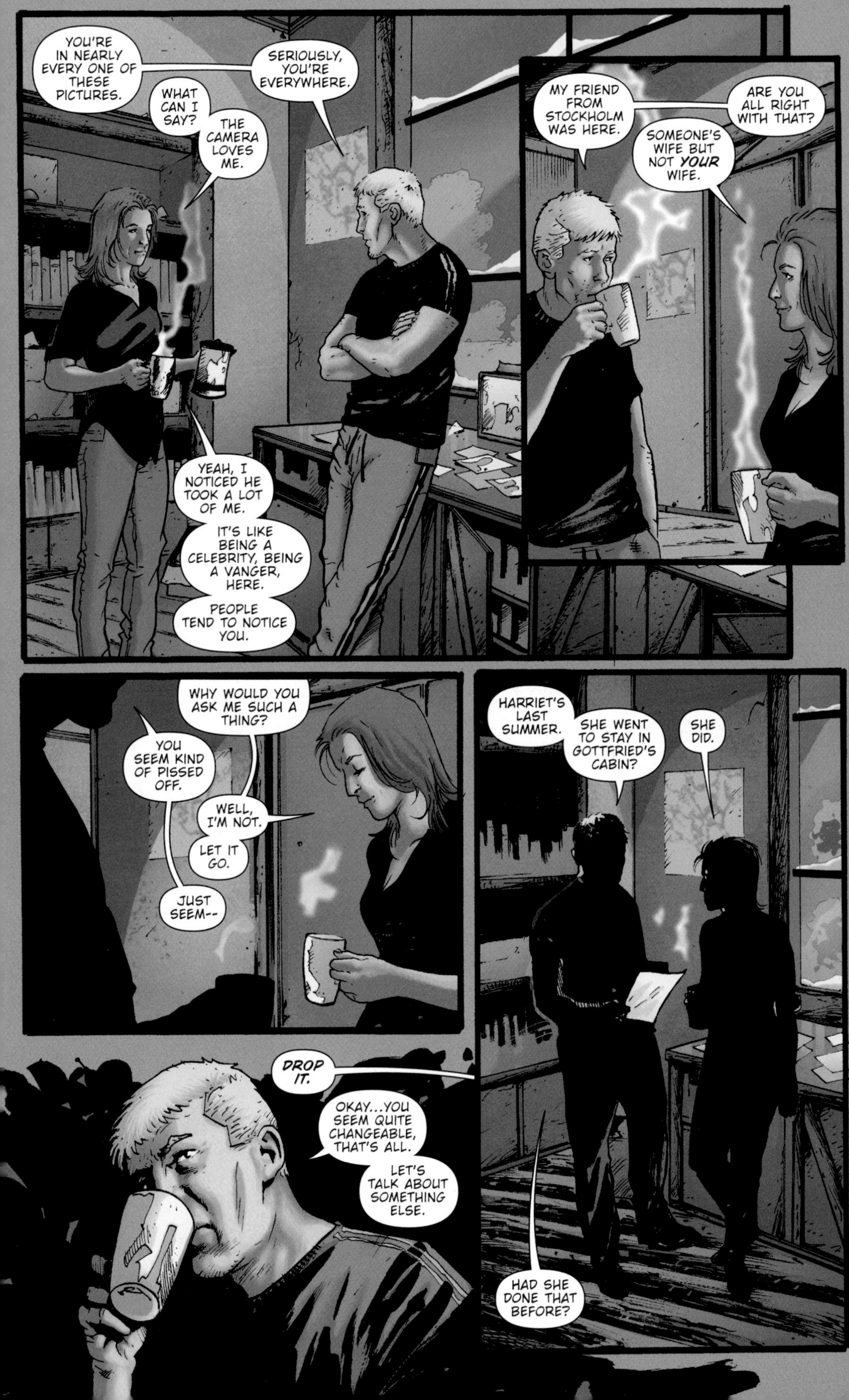
YOU'RE IN NEARLY EVERY ONE OF THESE PICTURES.
SERIOUSLY, YOU'RE EVERYWHERE.
WHAT CAN I SAY?
THE CAMERA LOVES ME.
YEAH, I NOTICED HE TOOK A LOT OF ME.
IT'S LIKE BEING A CELEBRITY, BEING A VANGER, HERE.
PEOPLE TEND TO NOTICE YOU.
MY FRIEND FROM STOCKHOLM WAS HERE.
ARE YOU ALL RIGHT WITH THAT?
SOMEONE'S WIFE BUT NOT *YOUR* WIFE.
WHY WOULD YOU ASK ME SUCH A THING?
YOU SEEM KIND OF PISSED OFF.
WELL, I'M NOT.
LET IT GO.
JUST SEEM--
DROP IT.
OKAY...YOU SEEM QUITE CHANGEABLE, THAT'S ALL.
LET'S TALK ABOUT SOMETHING ELSE.
HARRIET'S LAST SUMMER.
SHE WENT TO STAY IN GOTTFRIED'S CABIN?
SHE DID.
HAD SHE DONE THAT BEFORE?

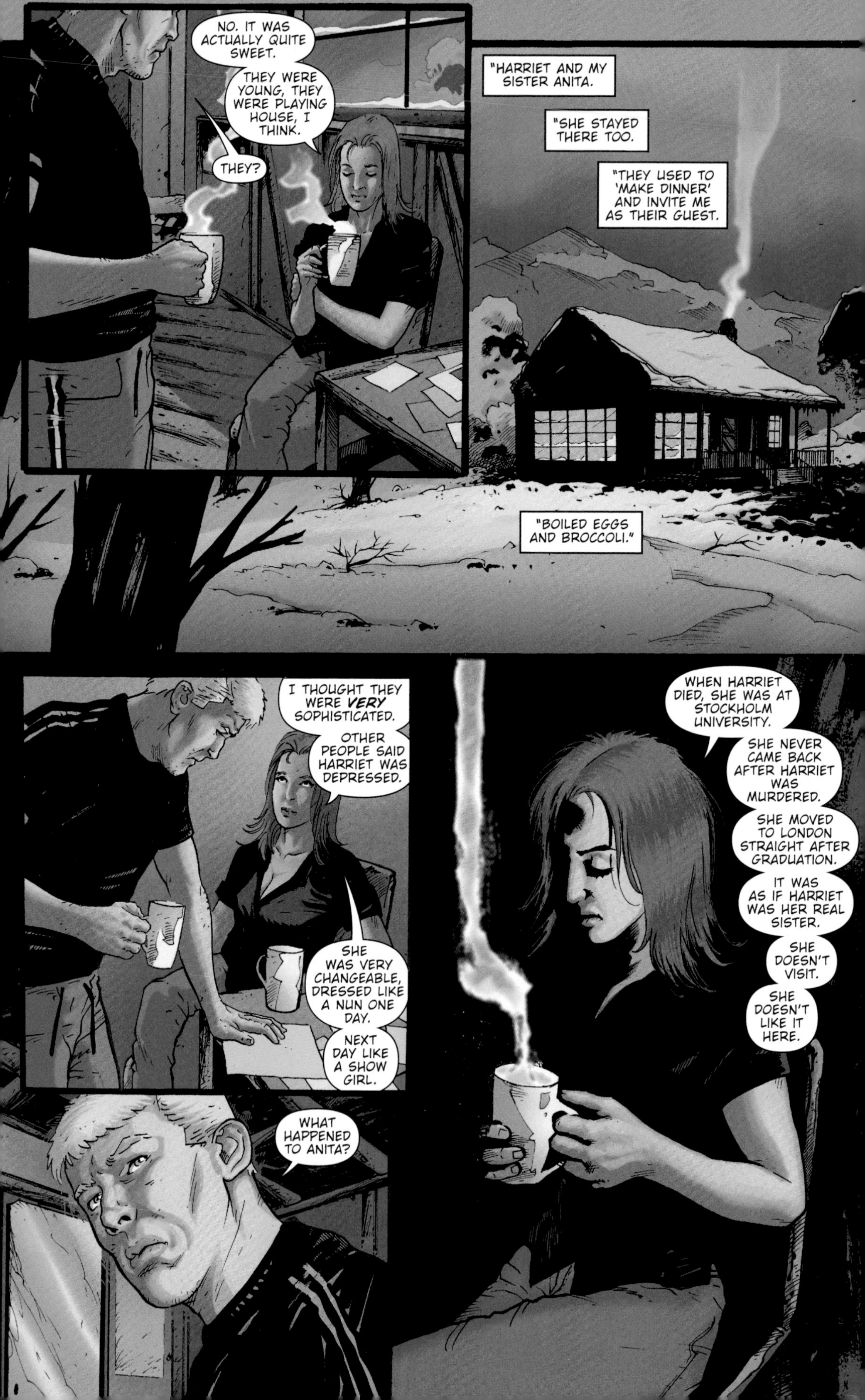

NO. IT WAS ACTUALLY QUITE SWEET.
THEY WERE YOUNG, THEY WERE PLAYING HOUSE, I THINK.
THEY?
"HARRIET AND MY SISTER ANITA.
"SHE STAYED THERE TOO.
"THEY USED TO 'MAKE DINNER' AND INVITE ME AS THEIR GUEST.
"BOILED EGGS AND BROCCOLI."
I THOUGHT THEY WERE VERY SOPHISTICATED.
OTHER PEOPLE SAID HARRIET WAS DEPRESSED.
SHE WAS VERY CHANGEABLE, DRESSED LIKE A NUN ONE DAY.
NEXT DAY LIKE A SHOW GIRL.
WHAT HAPPENED TO ANITA?
WHEN HARRIET DIED, SHE WAS AT STOCKHOLM UNIVERSITY.
SHE NEVER CAME BACK AFTER HARRIET WAS MURDERED.
SHE MOVED TO LONDON STRAIGHT AFTER GRADUATION.
IT WAS AS IF HARRIET WAS HER REAL SISTER.
SHE DOESN'T VISIT.
SHE DOESN'T LIKE IT HERE.

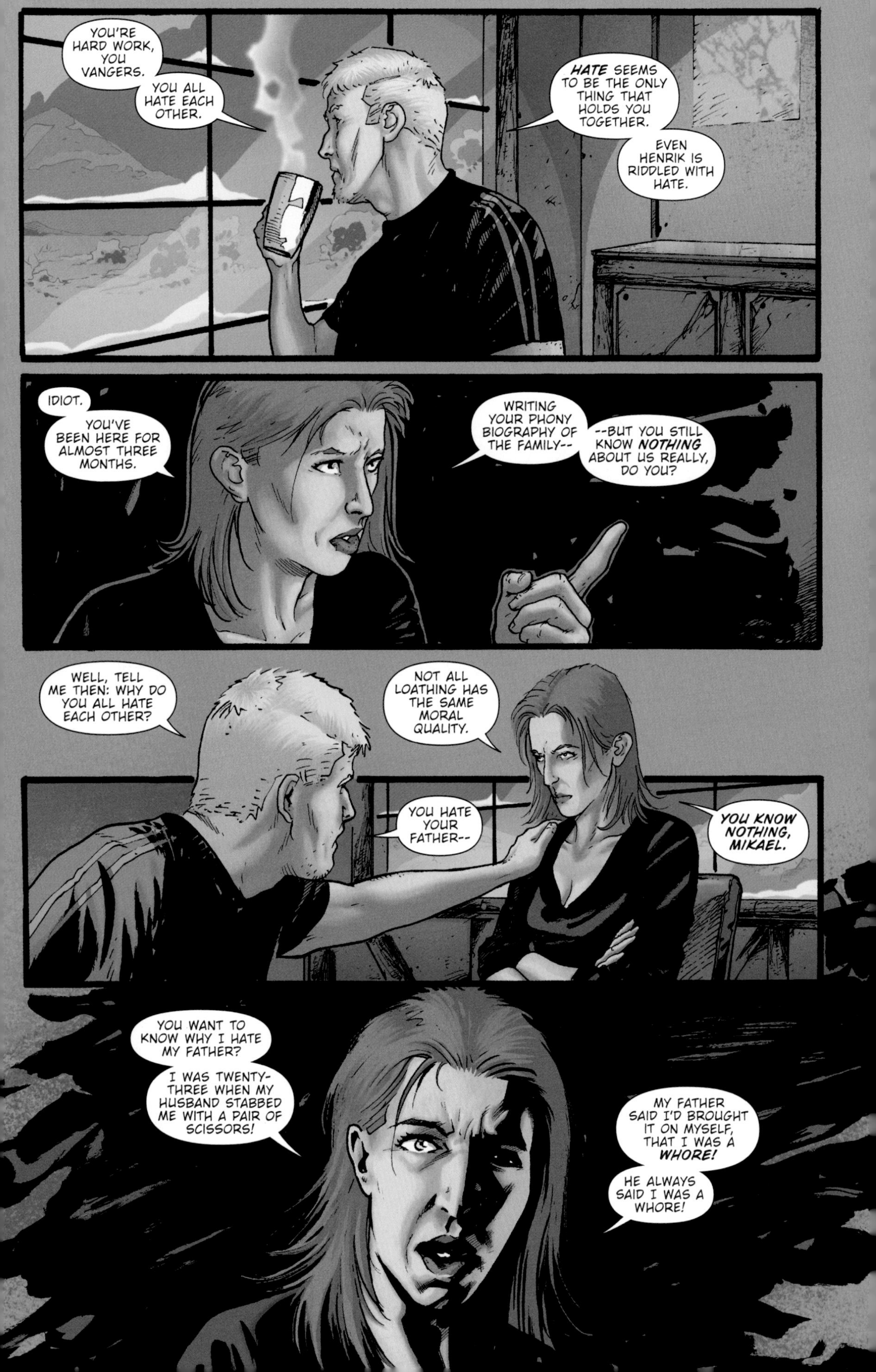

YOU'RE HARD WORK, YOU VANGERS.
YOU ALL HATE EACH OTHER.
HATE SEEMS TO BE THE ONLY THING THAT HOLDS YOU TOGETHER.
EVEN HENRIK IS RIDDLED WITH HATE.
IDIOT.
YOU'VE BEEN HERE FOR ALMOST THREE MONTHS.
WRITING YOUR PHONY BIOGRAPHY OF THE FAMILY--
--BUT YOU STILL KNOW NOTHING ABOUT US REALLY, DO YOU?
WELL, TELL ME THEN: WHY DO YOU ALL HATE EACH OTHER?
NOT ALL LOATHING HAS THE SAME MORAL QUALITY.
YOU HATE YOUR FATHER--
YOU KNOW NOTHING, MIKAEL.
YOU WANT TO KNOW WHY I HATE MY FATHER?
I WAS TWENTY-THREE WHEN MY HUSBAND STABBED ME WITH A PAIR OF SCISSORS!
MY FATHER SAID I'D BROUGHT IT ON MYSELF, THAT I WAS A WHORE!
HE ALWAYS SAID I WAS A WHORE!

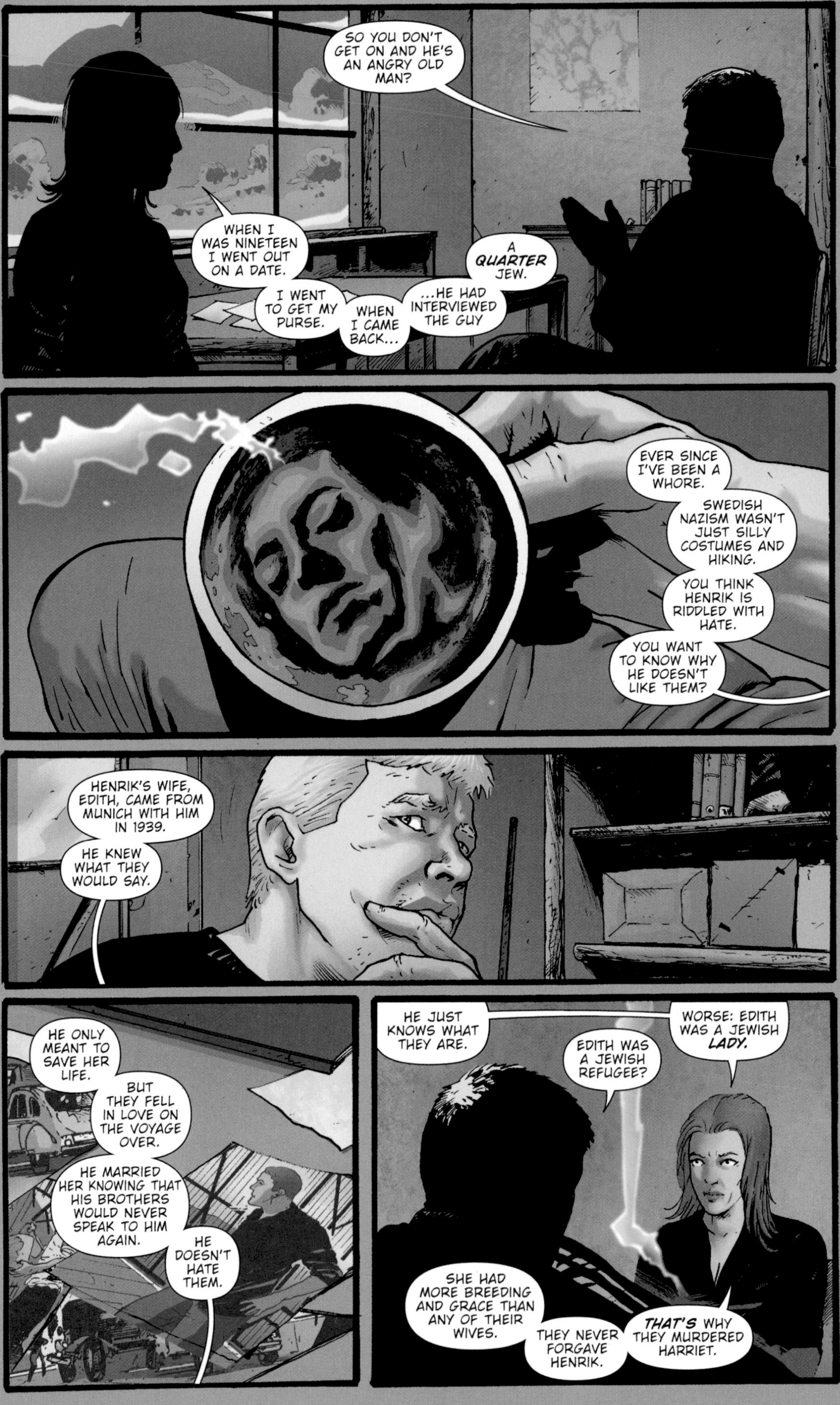
SO YOU DON'T GET ON AND HE'S AN ANGRY OLD MAN?
WHEN I WAS NINETEEN I WENT OUT ON A DATE.
I WENT TO GET MY PURSE.
WHEN I CAME BACK...
...HE HAD INTERVIEWED THE GUY
A QUARTER JEW.
EVER SINCE I'VE BEEN A WHORE.
SWEDISH NAZISM WASN'T JUST SILLY COSTUMES AND HIKING.
YOU THINK HENRIK IS RIDDLED WITH HATE.
YOU WANT TO KNOW WHY HE DOESN'T LIKE THEM?
HENRIK'S WIFE, EDITH, CAME FROM MUNICH WITH HIM IN 1939.
HE KNEW WHAT THEY WOULD SAY.
HE ONLY MEANT TO SAVE HER LIFE.
BUT THEY FELL IN LOVE ON THE VOYAGE OVER.
HE MARRIED HER KNOWING THAT HIS BROTHERS WOULD NEVER SPEAK TO HIM AGAIN.
HE DOESN'T HATE THEM.
HE JUST KNOWS WHAT THEY ARE.
EDITH WAS A JEWISH REFUGEE?
WORSE: EDITH WAS A JEWISH LADY.
SHE HAD MORE BREEDING AND GRACE THAN ANY OF THEIR WIVES.
THEY NEVER FORGAVE HENRIK.
THAT'S WHY THEY MURDERED HARRIET.

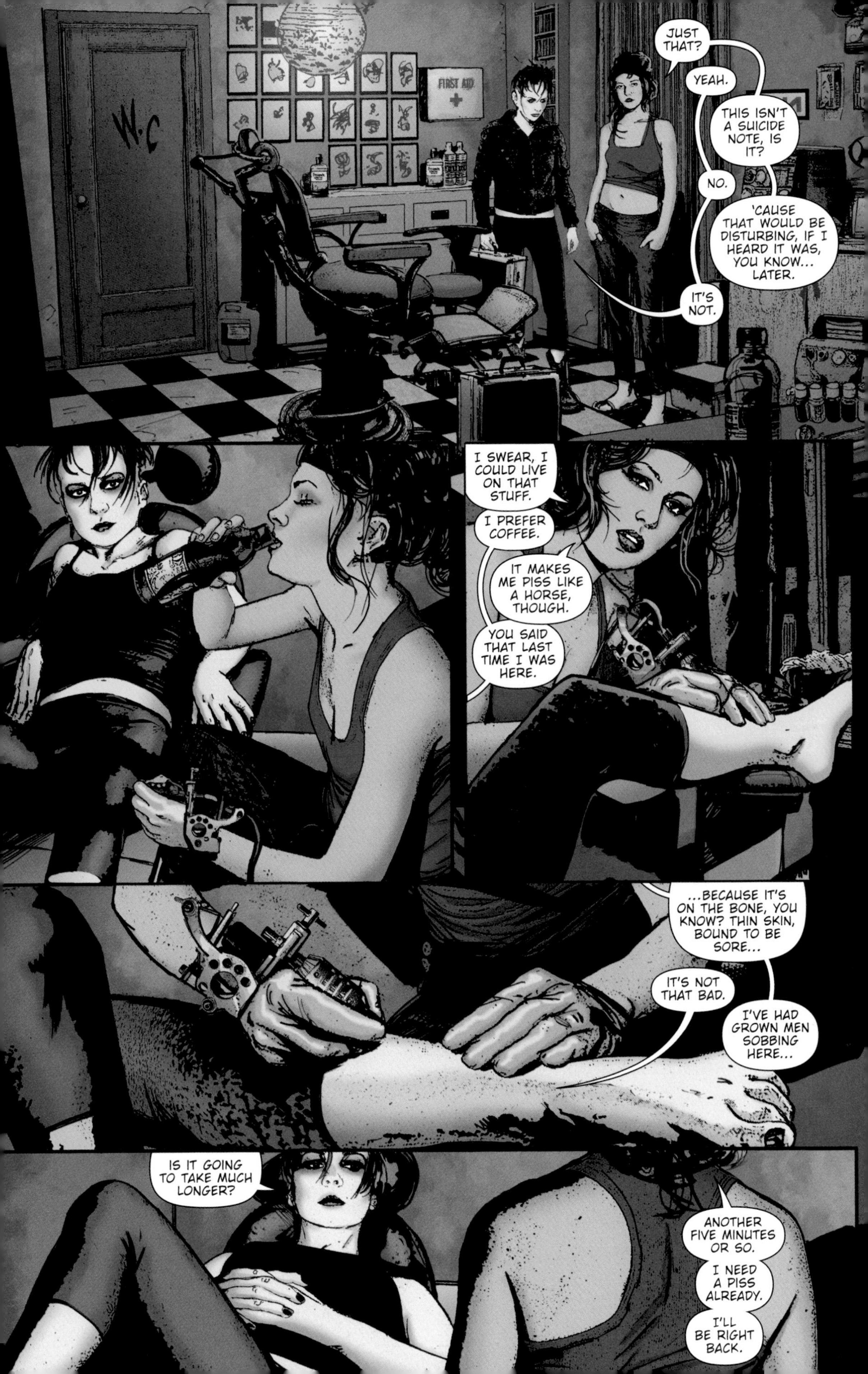
JUST THAT?
YEAH.
THIS ISN'T A SUICIDE NOTE, IS IT?
NO.
'CAUSE THAT WOULD BE DISTURBING, IF I HEARD IT WAS, YOU KNOW... LATER.
IT'S NOT.
I SWEAR, I COULD LIVE ON THAT STUFF.
I PREFER COFFEE.
IT MAKES ME PISS LIKE A HORSE, THOUGH.
YOU SAID THAT LAST TIME I WAS HERE.
...BECAUSE IT'S ON THE BONE, YOU KNOW? THIN SKIN, BOUND TO BE SORE...
IT'S NOT THAT BAD.
I'VE HAD GROWN MEN SOBBING HERE...
IS IT GOING TO TAKE MUCH LONGER?
ANOTHER FIVE MINUTES OR SO.
I NEED A PISS ALREADY.
I'LL BE RIGHT BACK.

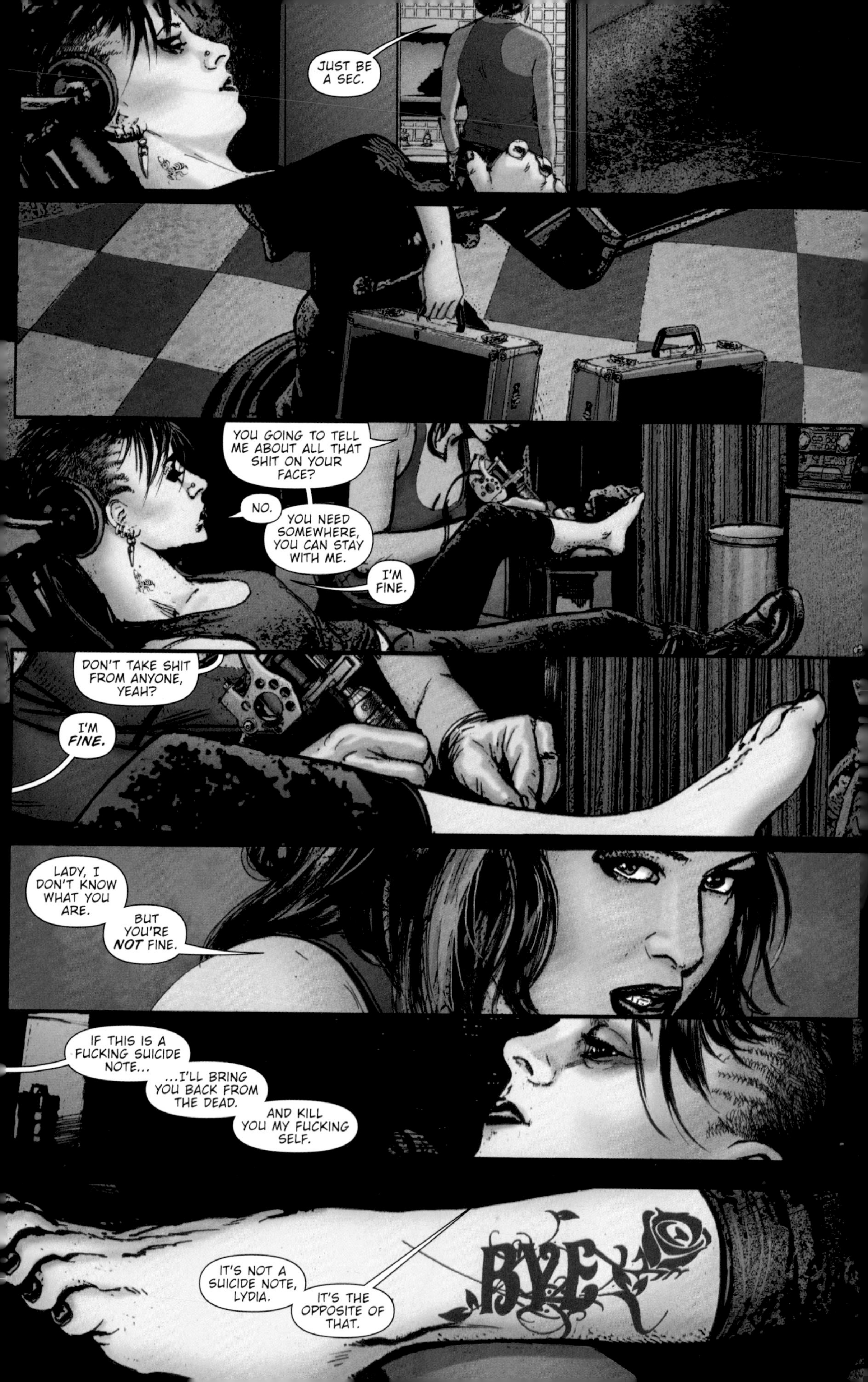
JUST BE A SEC.
YOU GOING TO TELL ME ABOUT ALL THAT SHIT ON YOUR FACE?
NO.
YOU NEED SOMEWHERE, YOU CAN STAY WITH ME.
I'M FINE.
DON'T TAKE SHIT FROM ANYONE, YEAH?
I'M *FINE.*
LADY, I DON'T KNOW WHAT YOU ARE.
BUT YOU'RE ***NOT*** FINE.
IF THIS IS A FUCKING SUICIDE NOTE...
...I'LL BRING YOU BACK FROM THE DEAD.
AND KILL YOU MY FUCKING SELF.
BYE
IT'S NOT A SUICIDE NOTE, LYDIA.
IT'S THE OPPOSITE OF THAT.

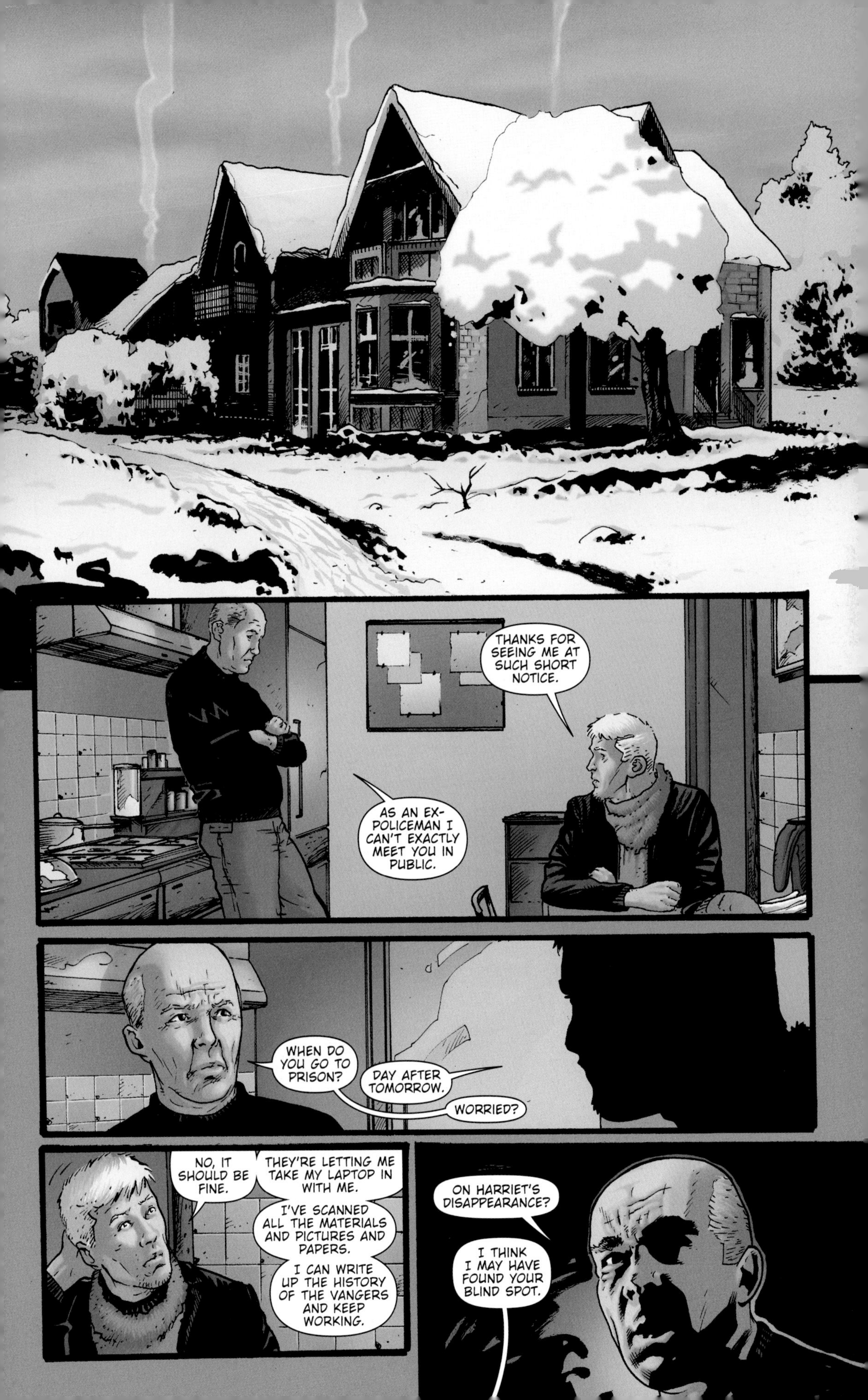
THANKS FOR SEEING ME AT SUCH SHORT NOTICE.
AS AN EX-POLICEMAN I CAN'T EXACTLY MEET YOU IN PUBLIC.
WHEN DO YOU GO TO PRISON?
DAY AFTER TOMORROW.
WORRIED?
NO, IT SHOULD BE FINE.
THEY'RE LETTING ME TAKE MY LAPTOP IN WITH ME.
I'VE SCANNED ALL THE MATERIALS AND PICTURES AND PAPERS.
I CAN WRITE UP THE HISTORY OF THE VANGERS AND KEEP WORKING.
ON HARRIET'S DISAPPEARANCE?
I THINK I MAY HAVE FOUND YOUR BLIND SPOT.

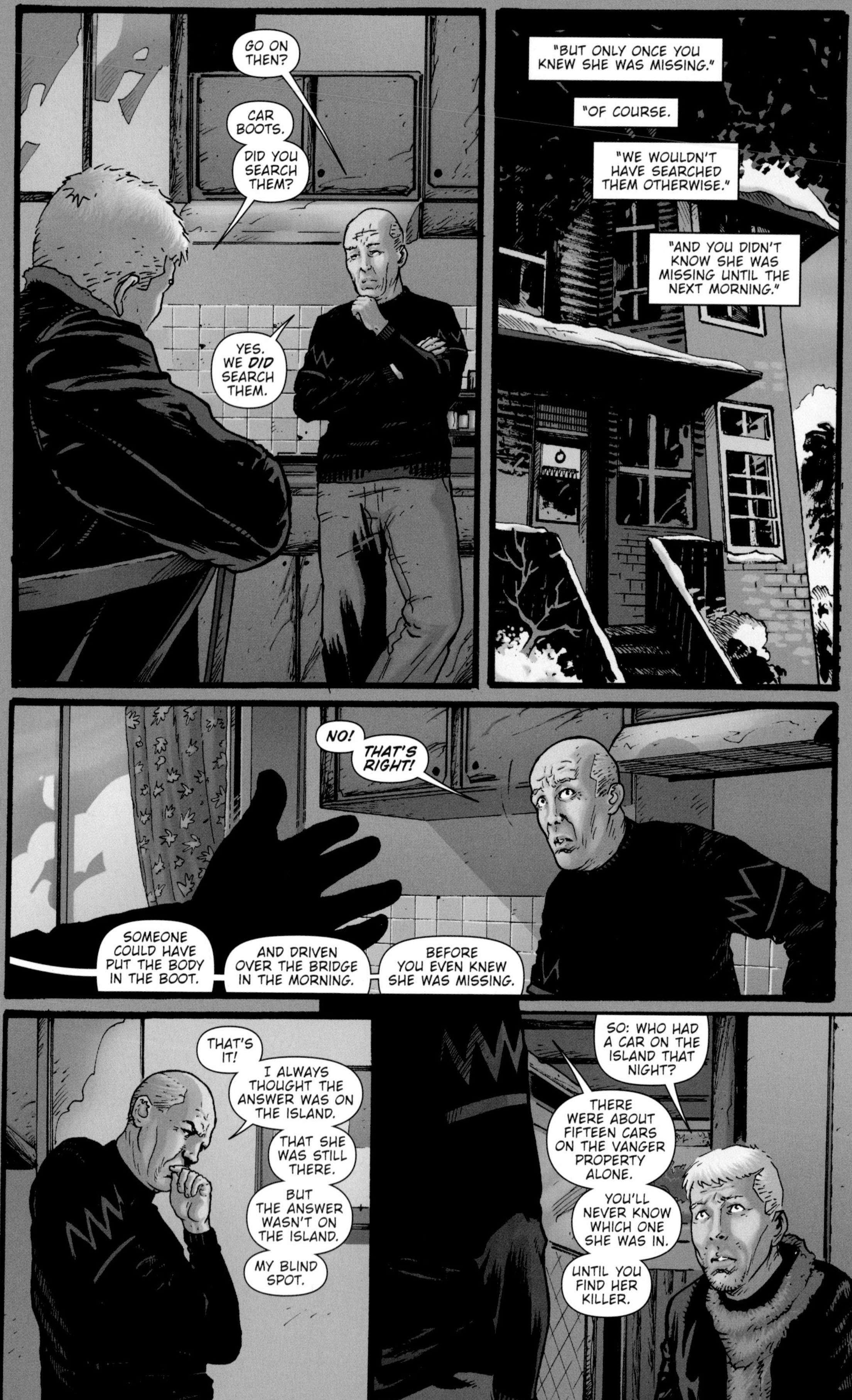
GO ON THEN?
CAR BOOTS.
DID YOU SEARCH THEM?
YES. WE *DID* SEARCH THEM.
"BUT ONLY ONCE YOU KNEW SHE WAS MISSING."
"OF COURSE.
"WE WOULDN'T HAVE SEARCHED THEM OTHERWISE."
"AND YOU DIDN'T KNOW SHE WAS MISSING UNTIL THE NEXT MORNING."
SOMEONE COULD HAVE PUT THE BODY IN THE BOOT.
AND DRIVEN OVER THE BRIDGE IN THE MORNING.
BEFORE YOU EVEN KNEW SHE WAS MISSING.
NO! THAT'S RIGHT!
THAT'S IT!
I ALWAYS THOUGHT THE ANSWER WAS ON THE ISLAND.
THAT SHE WAS STILL THERE.
BUT THE ANSWER WASN'T ON THE ISLAND.
MY BLIND SPOT.
SO: WHO HAD A CAR ON THE ISLAND THAT NIGHT?
THERE WERE ABOUT FIFTEEN CARS ON THE VANGER PROPERTY ALONE.
YOU'LL NEVER KNOW WHICH ONE SHE WAS IN.
UNTIL YOU FIND HER KILLER.

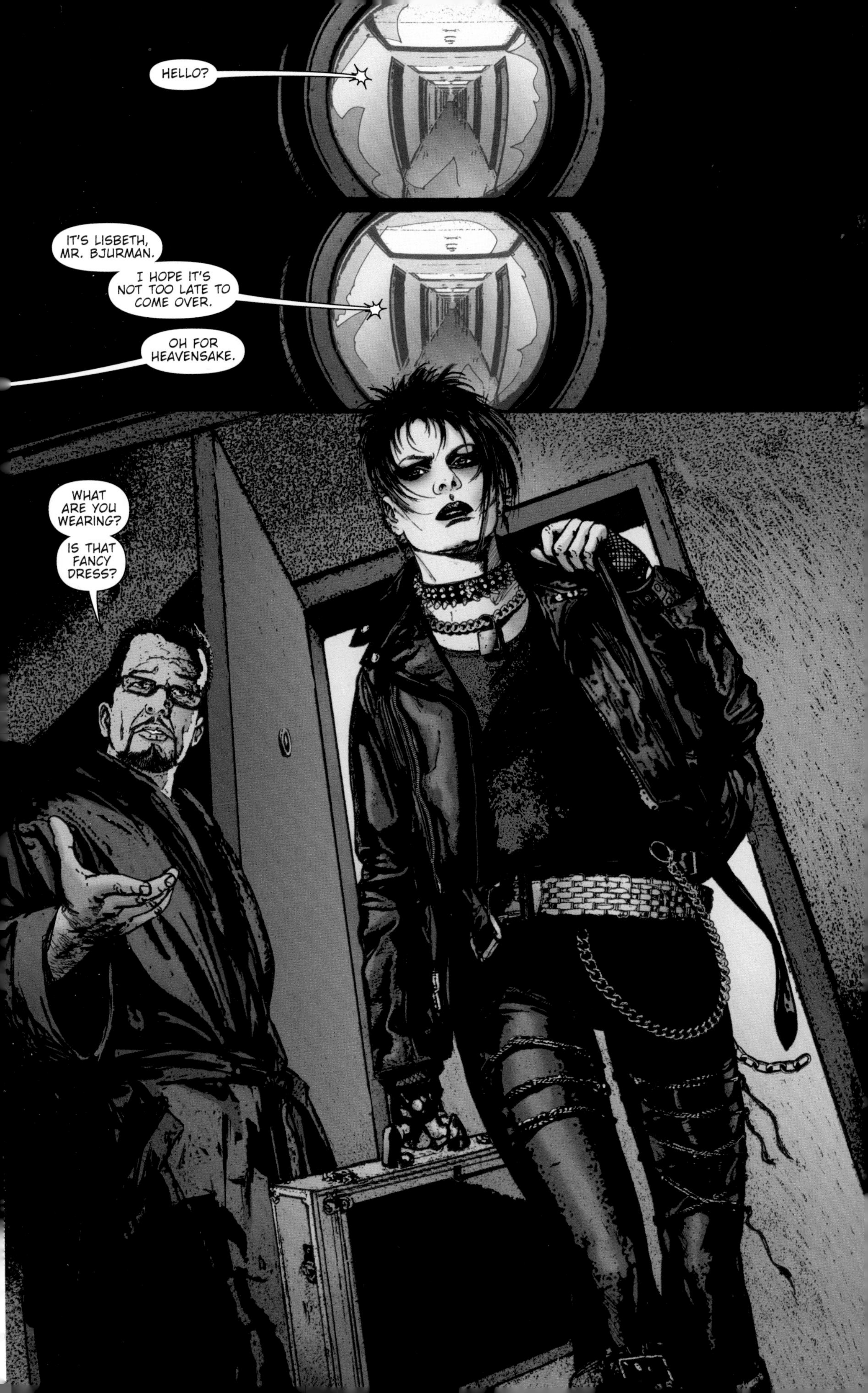
HELLO?
IT'S LISBETH, MR. BJURMAN.
I HOPE IT'S NOT TOO LATE TO COME OVER.
OH FOR HEAVENSAKE.
WHAT ARE YOU WEARING?
IS THAT FANCY DRESS?

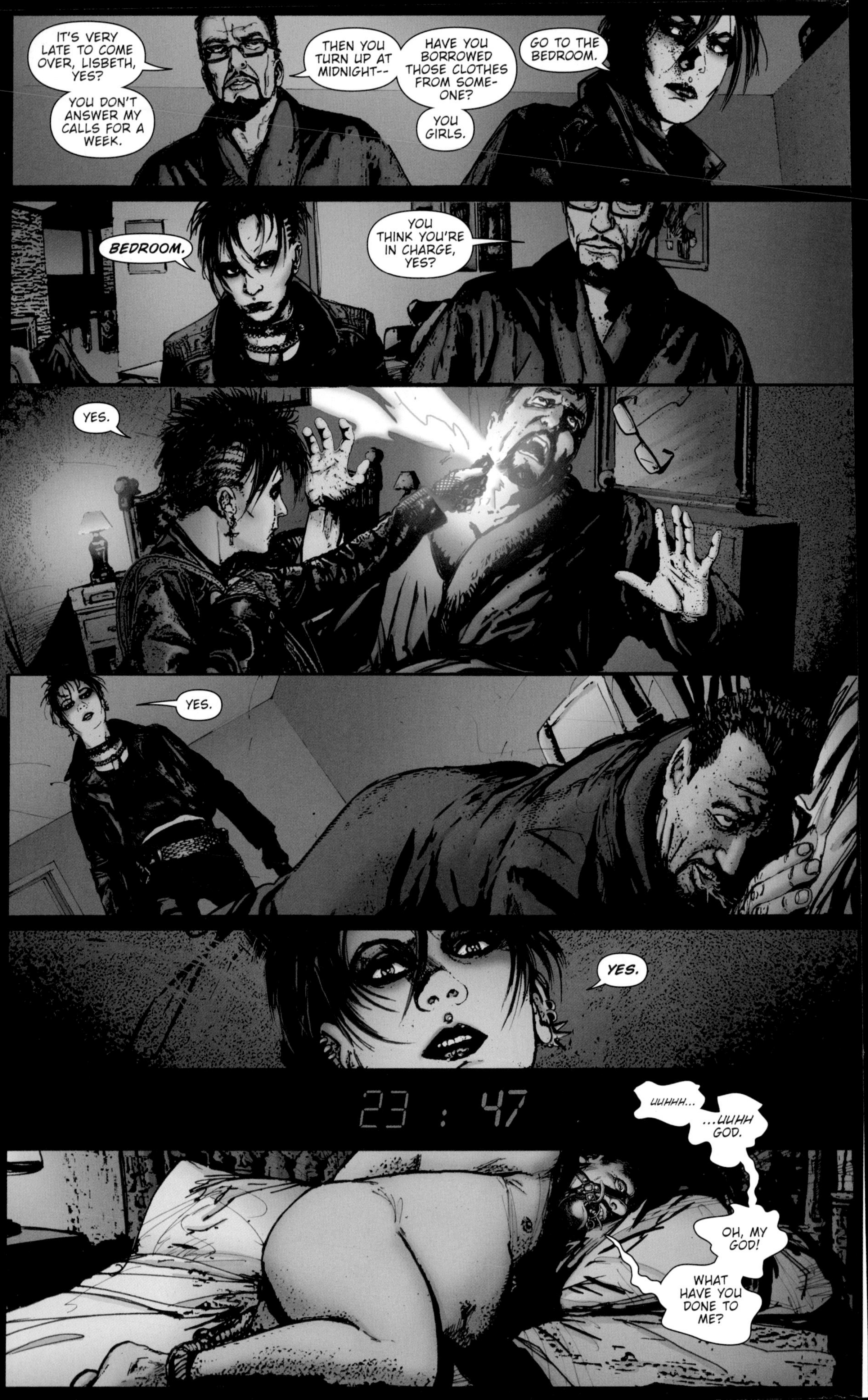
IT'S VERY LATE TO COME OVER, LISBETH, YES?
YOU DON'T ANSWER MY CALLS FOR A WEEK.
THEN YOU TURN UP AT MIDNIGHT--
HAVE YOU BORROWED THOSE CLOTHES FROM SOME-ONE?
YOU GIRLS.
GO TO THE BEDROOM.
BEDROOM.
YOU THINK YOU'RE IN CHARGE, YES?
YES.
YES.
YES.
23 : 47
UUHHH...
...UUHH GOD.
OH, MY GOD!
WHAT HAVE YOU DONE TO ME?

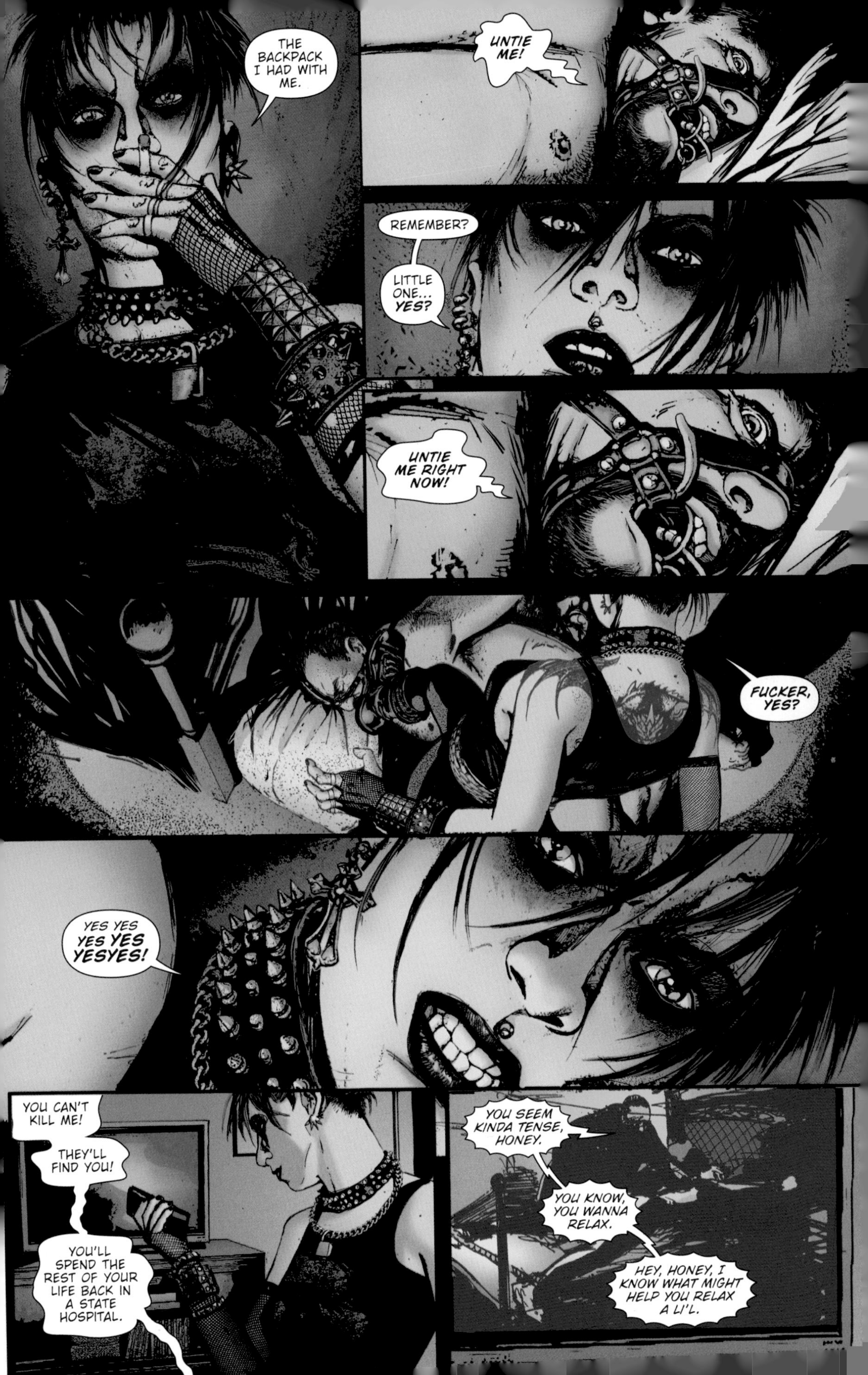
THE BACKPACK I HAD WITH ME.
UNTIE ME!
REMEMBER?
LITTLE ONE... YES?
UNTIE ME RIGHT NOW!
FUCKER, YES?
YES YES YES YES YESYES!
YOU CAN'T KILL ME!
THEY'LL FIND YOU!
YOU'LL SPEND THE REST OF YOUR LIFE BACK IN A STATE HOSPITAL.
YOU SEEM KINDA TENSE, HONEY.
YOU KNOW, YOU WANNA RELAX.
HEY, HONEY, I KNOW WHAT MIGHT HELP YOU RELAX A LI'L.

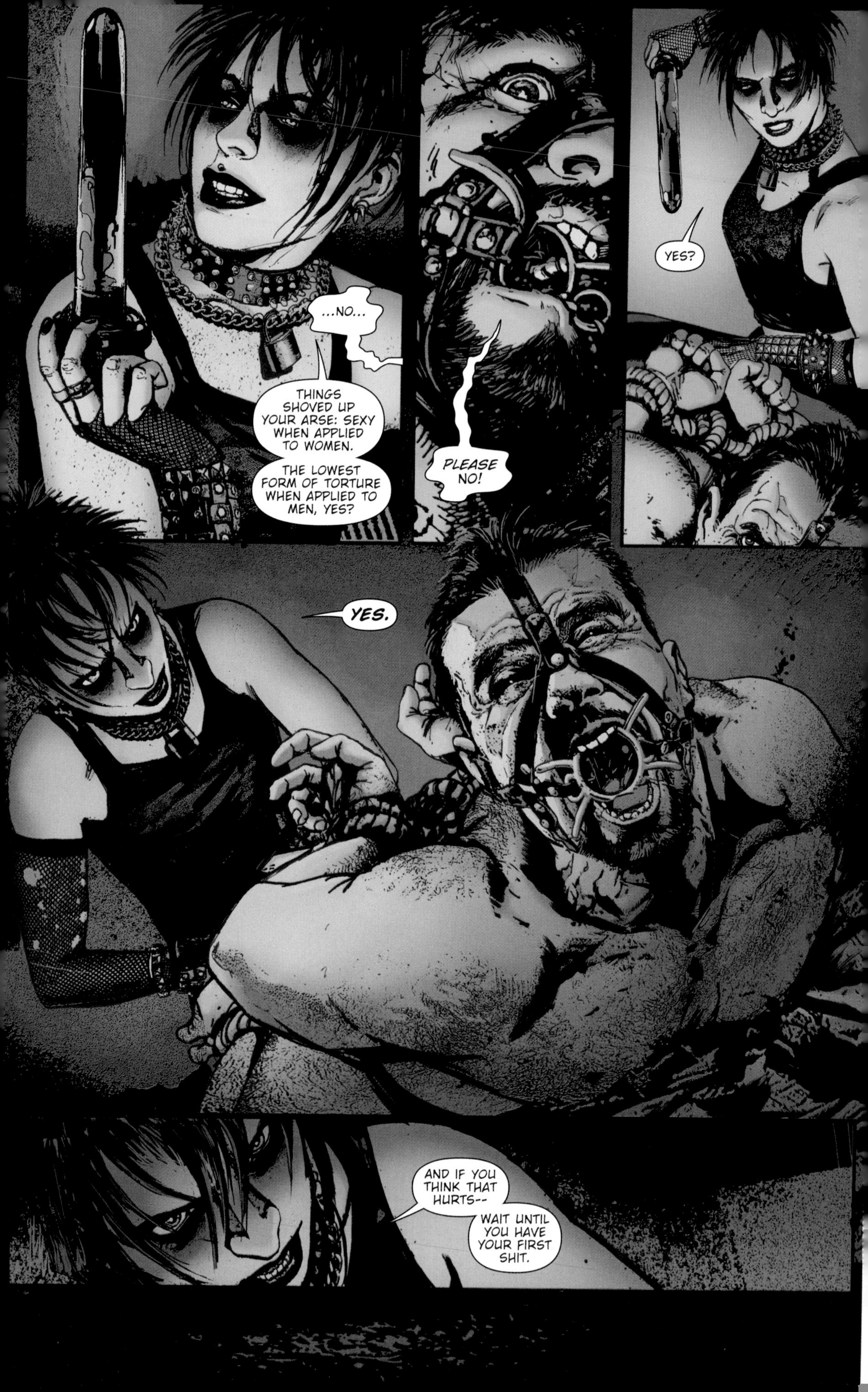
...NO...
THINGS SHOVED UP YOUR ARSE: SEXY WHEN APPLIED TO WOMEN.
THE LOWEST FORM OF TORTURE WHEN APPLIED TO MEN, YES?
PLEASE NO!
YES?
YES.
AND IF YOU THINK THAT HURTS--
WAIT UNTIL YOU HAVE YOUR FIRST SHIT.

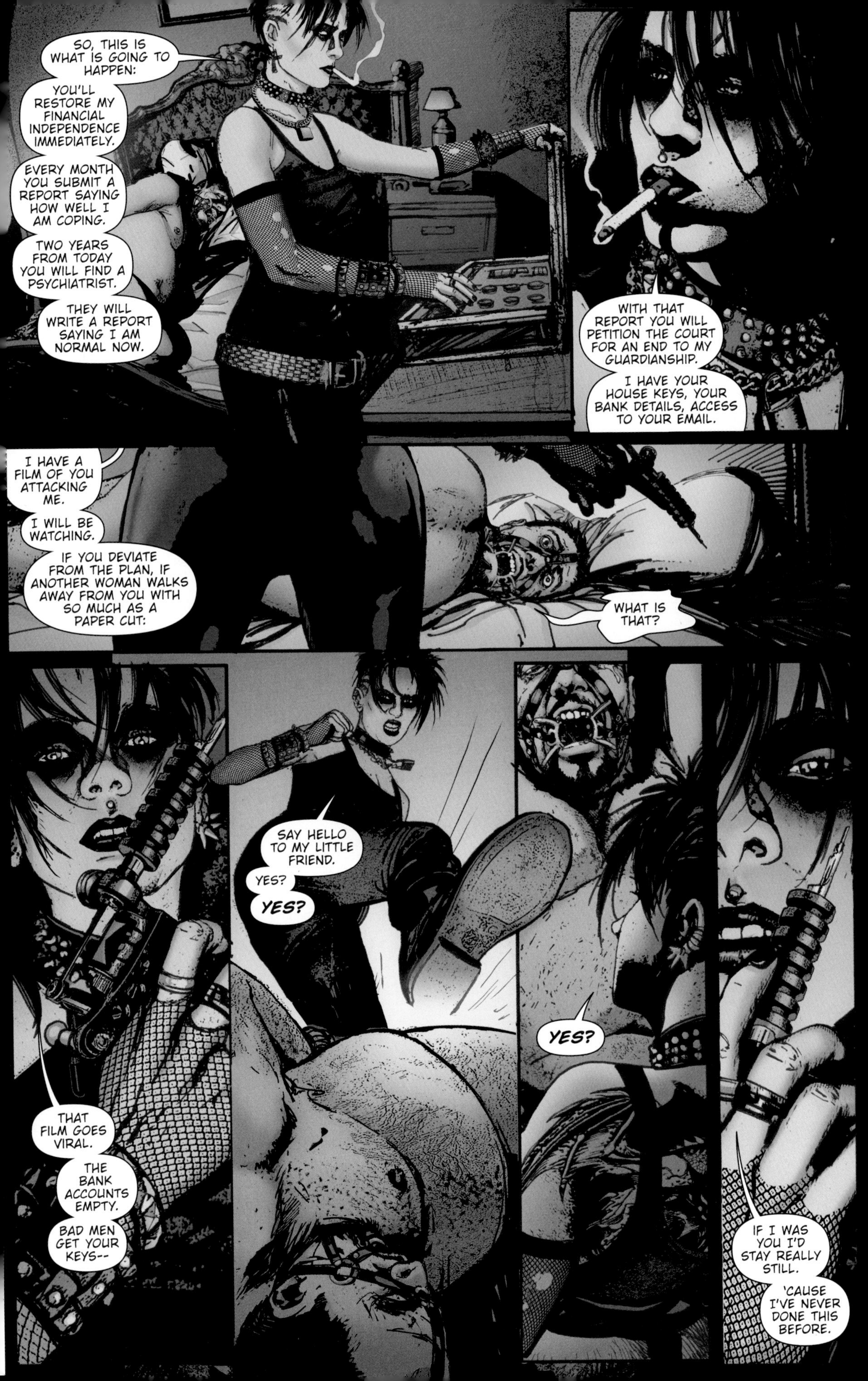
SO, THIS IS WHAT IS GOING TO HAPPEN:
YOU'LL RESTORE MY FINANCIAL INDEPENDENCE IMMEDIATELY.
EVERY MONTH YOU SUBMIT A REPORT SAYING HOW WELL I AM COPING.
TWO YEARS FROM TODAY YOU WILL FIND A PSYCHIATRIST.
THEY WILL WRITE A REPORT SAYING I AM NORMAL NOW.
WITH THAT REPORT YOU WILL PETITION THE COURT FOR AN END TO MY GUARDIANSHIP.
I HAVE YOUR HOUSE KEYS, YOUR BANK DETAILS, ACCESS TO YOUR EMAIL.
I HAVE A FILM OF YOU ATTACKING ME.
I WILL BE WATCHING.
IF YOU DEVIATE FROM THE PLAN, IF ANOTHER WOMAN WALKS AWAY FROM YOU WITH SO MUCH AS A PAPER CUT:
WHAT IS THAT?
THAT FILM GOES VIRAL.
THE BANK ACCOUNTS EMPTY.
BAD MEN GET YOUR KEYS--
SAY HELLO TO MY LITTLE FRIEND.
YES?
YES?
YES?
IF I WAS YOU I'D STAY REALLY STILL.
'CAUSE I'VE NEVER DONE THIS BEFORE.

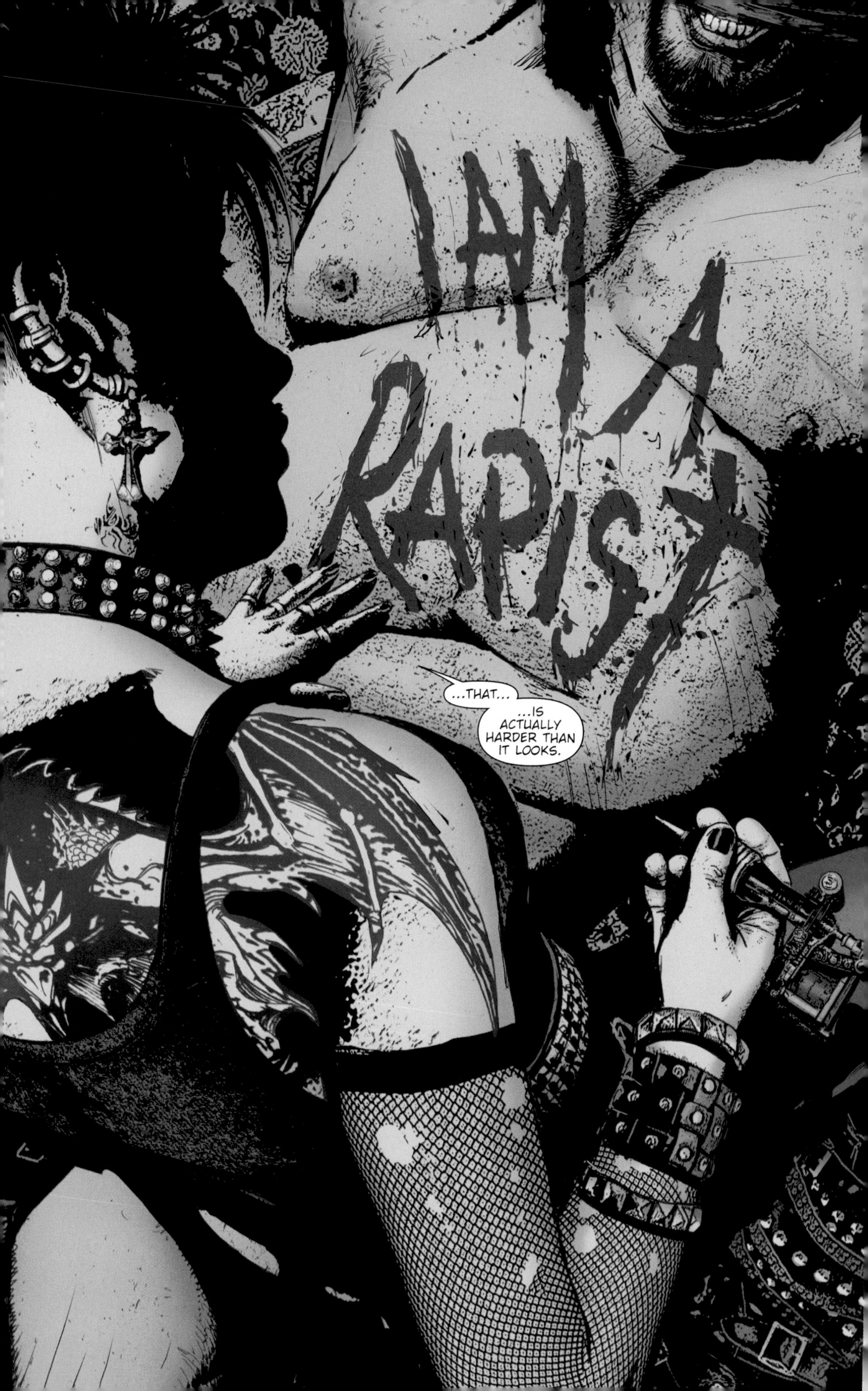
I AM A RAPIST
...THAT...
...IS ACTUALLY HARDER THAN IT LOOKS.

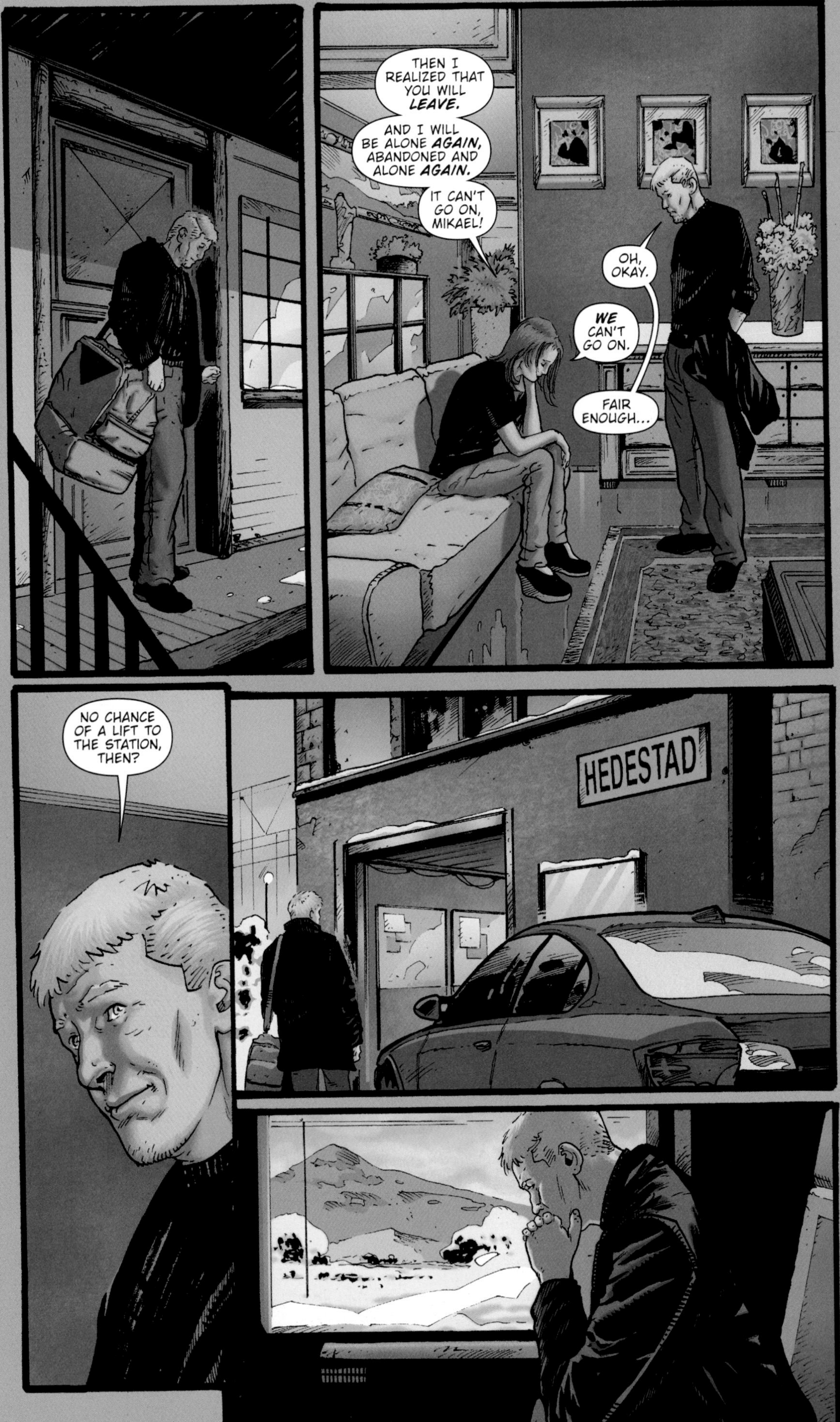
THEN I REALIZED THAT YOU WILL LEAVE.
AND I WILL BE ALONE AGAIN, ABANDONED AND ALONE AGAIN.
IT CAN'T GO ON, MIKAEL!
OH, OKAY.
WE CAN'T GO ON.
FAIR ENOUGH...
NO CHANCE OF A LIFT TO THE STATION, THEN?
HEDESTAD

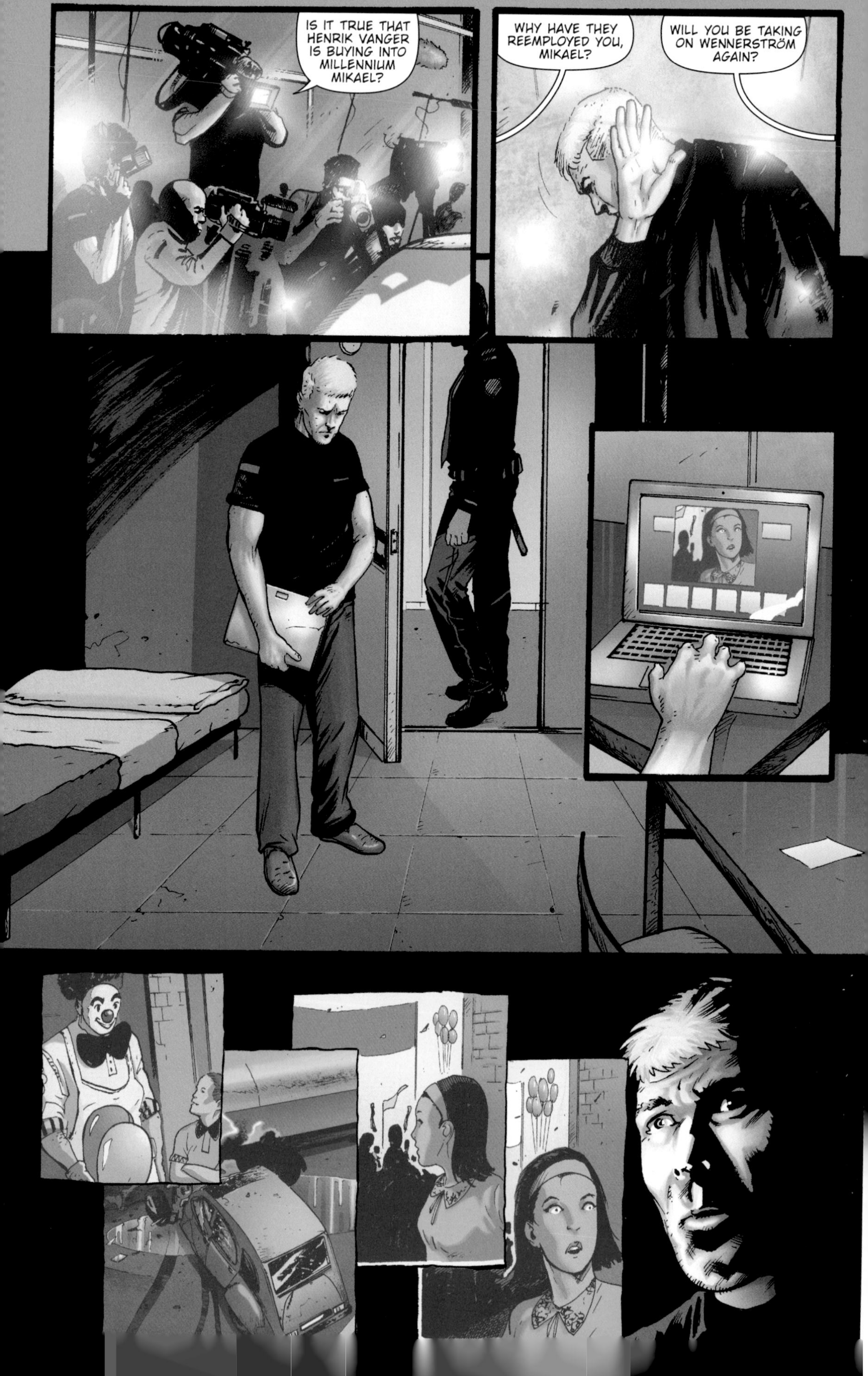
IS IT TRUE THAT HENRIK VANGER IS BUYING INTO MILLENNIUM MIKAEL?
WHY HAVE THEY REEMPLOYED YOU, MIKAEL?
WILL YOU BE TAKING ON WENNERSTRÖM AGAIN?

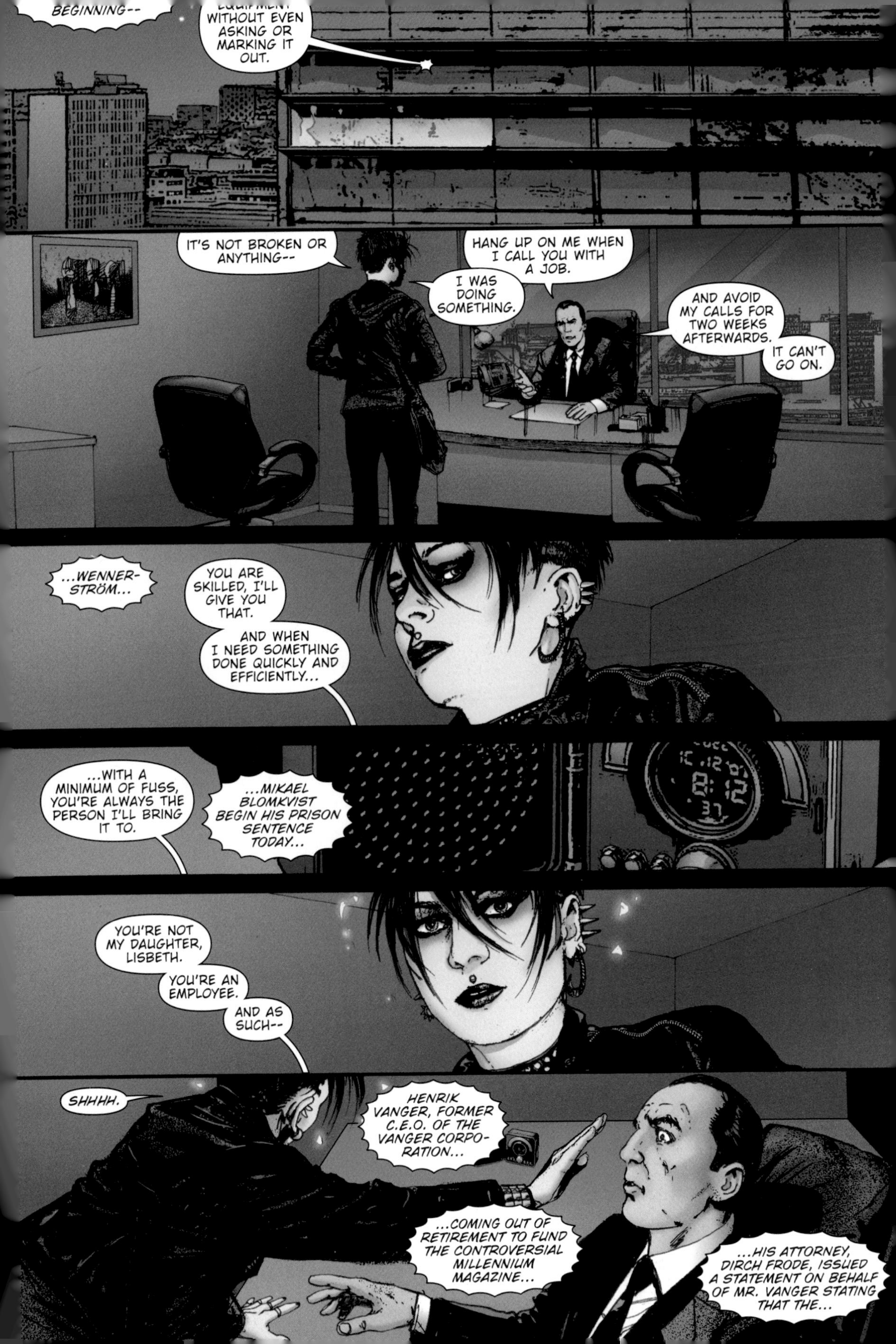
BEGINNING--
WITHOUT EVEN ASKING OR MARKING IT OUT.
IT'S NOT BROKEN OR ANYTHING--
HANG UP ON ME WHEN I CALL YOU WITH A JOB.
I WAS DOING SOMETHING.
AND AVOID MY CALLS FOR TWO WEEKS AFTERWARDS.
IT CAN'T GO ON.
...WENNER-STRÖM...
YOU ARE SKILLED, I'LL GIVE YOU THAT.
AND WHEN I NEED SOMETHING DONE QUICKLY AND EFFICIENTLY...
...WITH A MINIMUM OF FUSS, YOU'RE ALWAYS THE PERSON I'LL BRING IT TO.
...MIKAEL BLOMKVIST BEGIN HIS PRISON SENTENCE TODAY...
YOU'RE NOT MY DAUGHTER, LISBETH.
YOU'RE AN EMPLOYEE.
AND AS SUCH--
SHHHH.
HENRIK VANGER, FORMER C.E.O. OF THE VANGER CORPO-RATION...
...COMING OUT OF RETIREMENT TO FUND THE CONTROVERSIAL MILLENNIUM MAGAZINE...
...HIS ATTORNEY, DIRCH FRODE, ISSUED A STATEMENT ON BEHALF OF MR. VANGER STATING THAT THE...

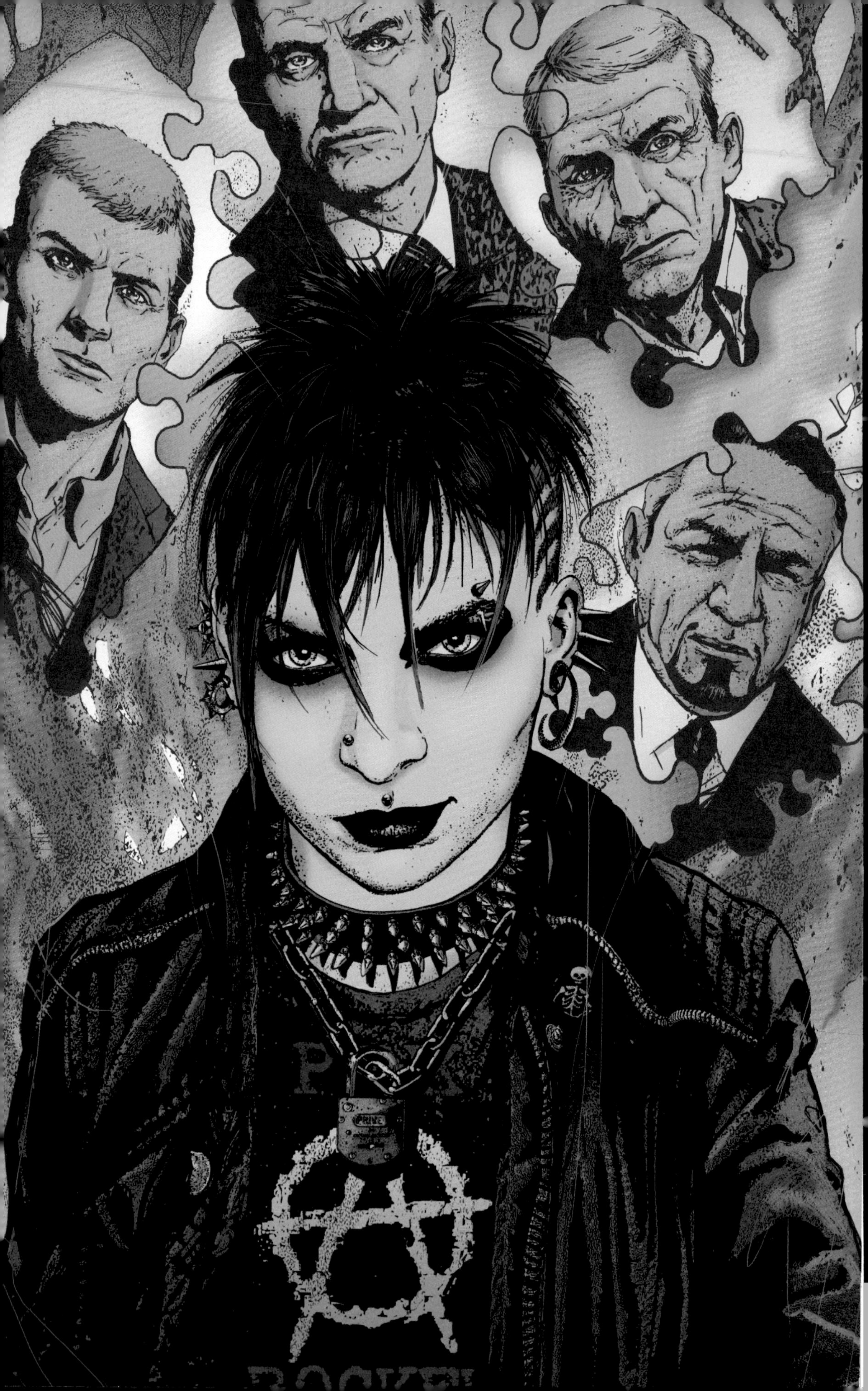

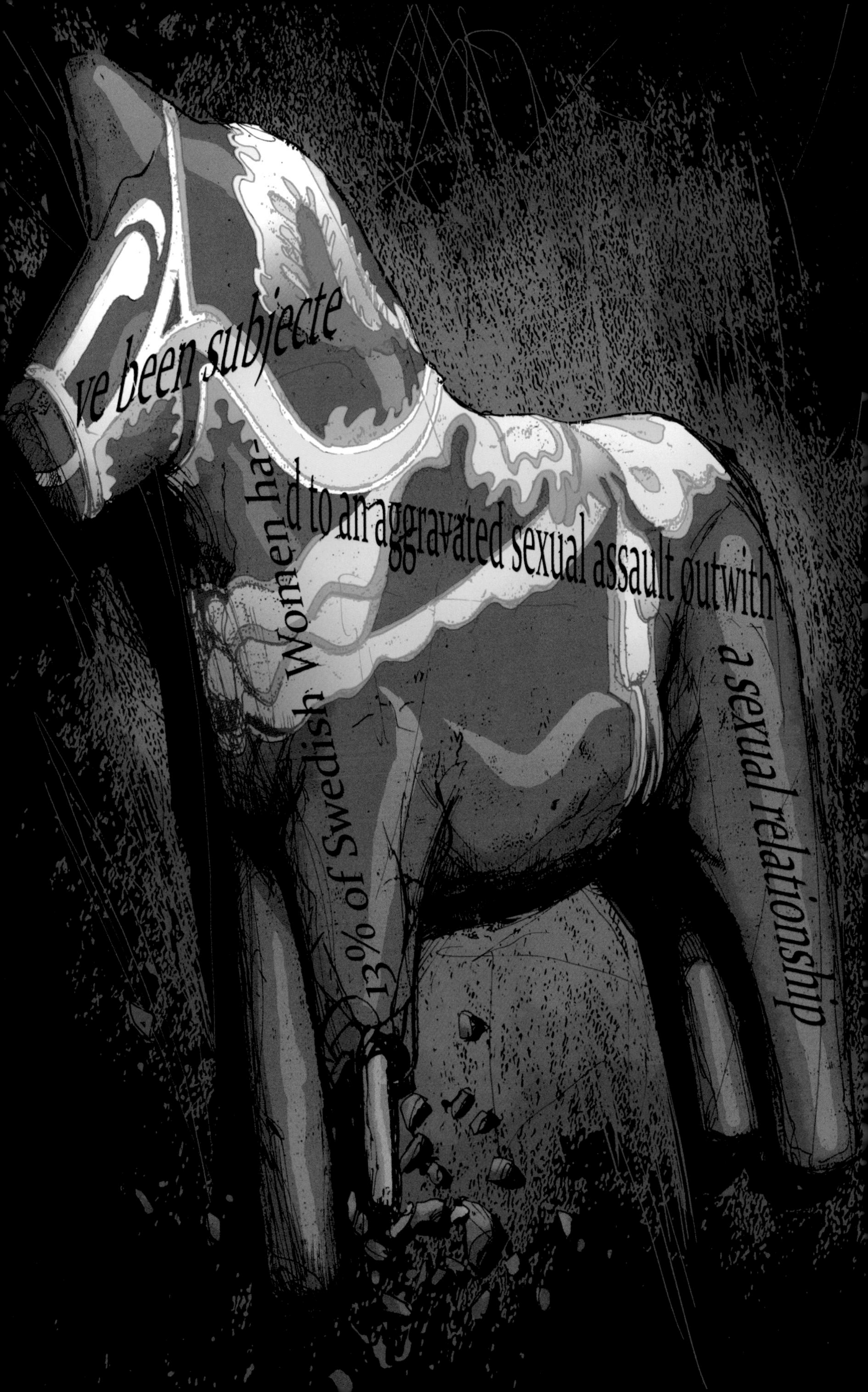
13% of Swedish Women ha-
ve been subjecte
d to an aggravated sexual assault outwith
a sexual relationship

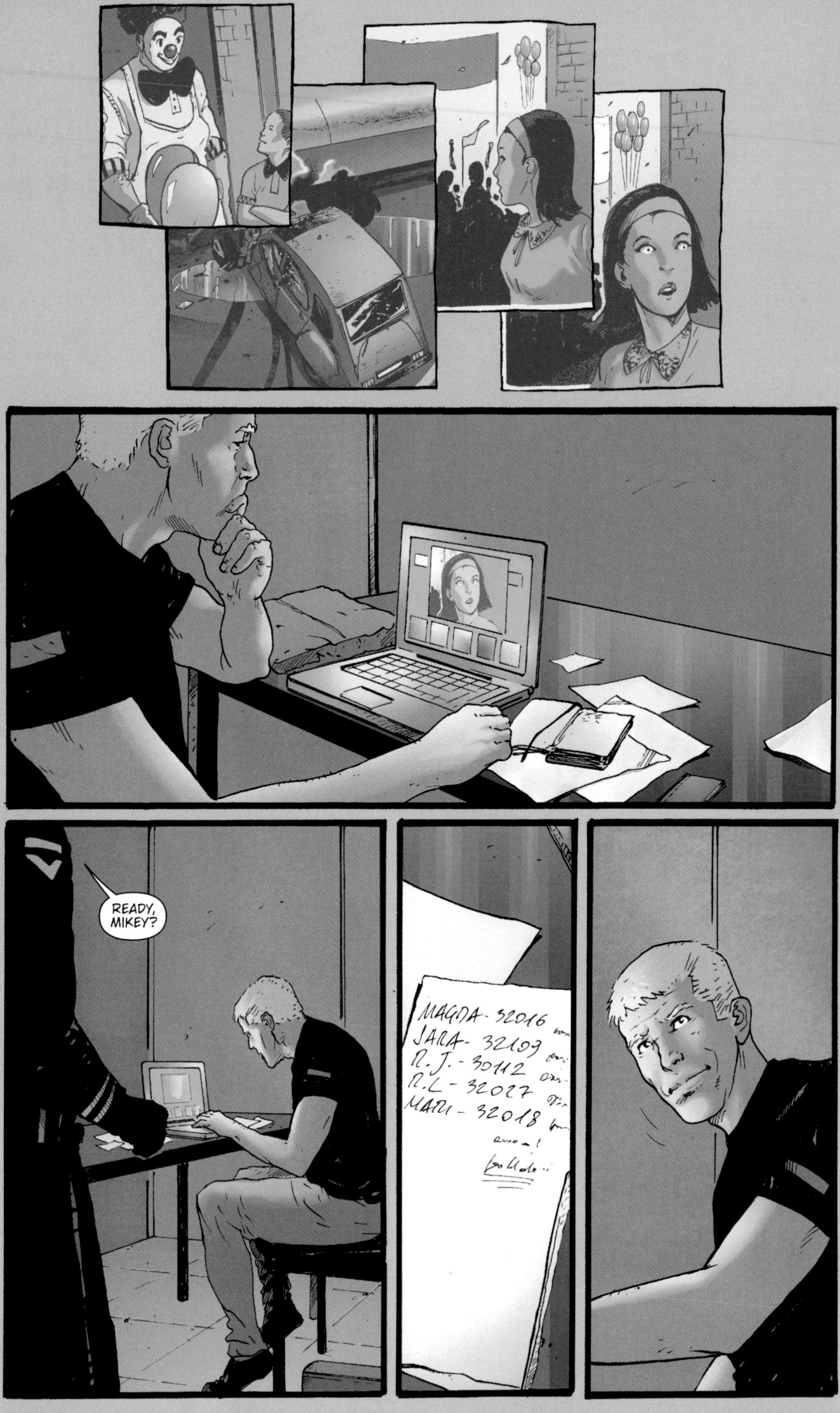
READY, MIKEY?
MAGDA - 32016
SARA - 32109
R.J. - 30112
R.L - 32027
MARI - 32018

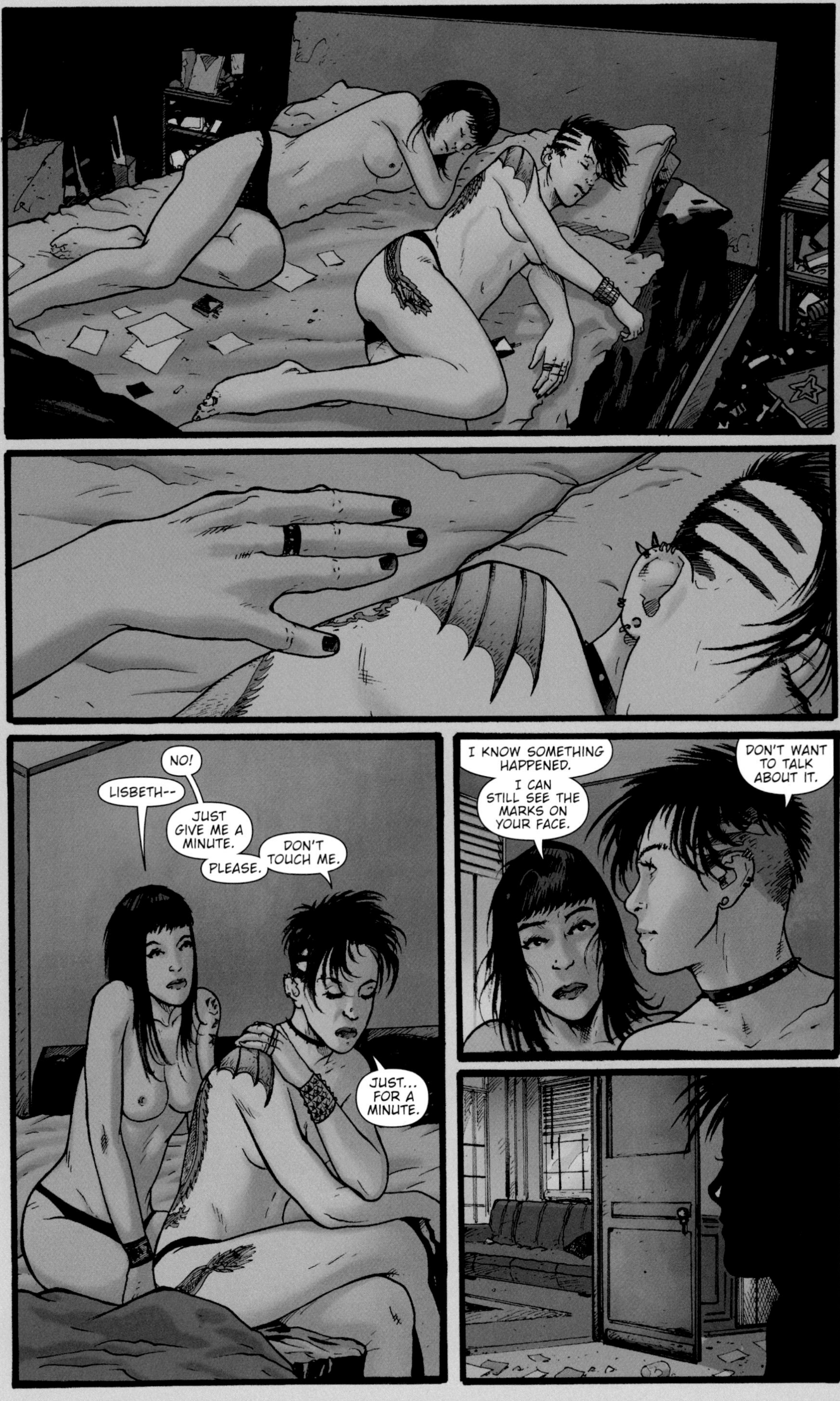

NO!
LISBETH--
JUST GIVE ME A MINUTE.
PLEASE.
DON'T TOUCH ME.
JUST... FOR A MINUTE.
I KNOW SOMETHING HAPPENED.
I CAN STILL SEE THE MARKS ON YOUR FACE.
DON'T WANT TO TALK ABOUT IT.

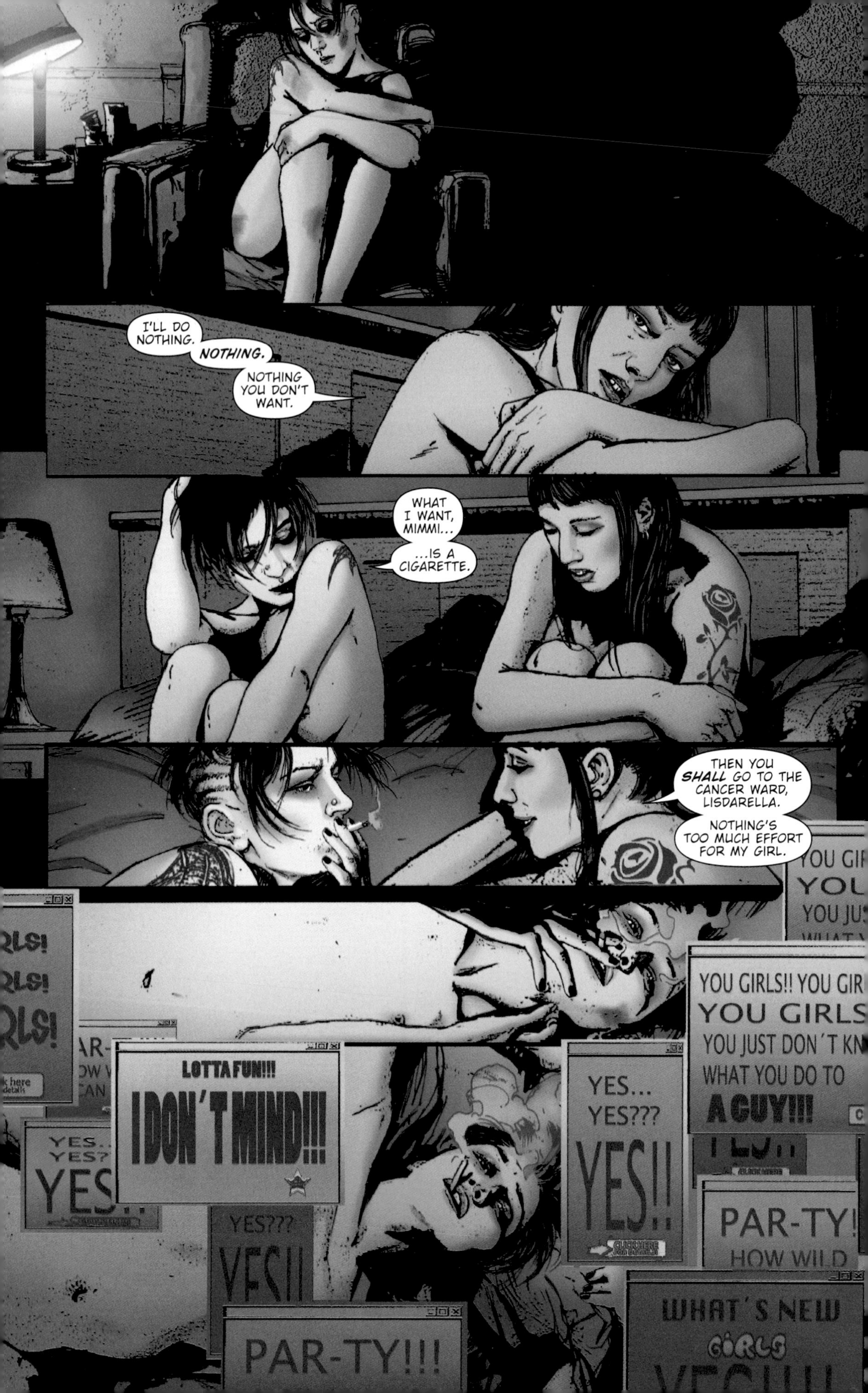

I'LL DO NOTHING.
NOTHING.
NOTHING YOU DON'T WANT.
WHAT I WANT, MIMMI...
...IS A CIGARETTE.
THEN YOU SHALL GO TO THE CANCER WARD, LISDARELLA.
NOTHING'S TOO MUCH EFFORT FOR MY GIRL.
YOU GIRLS!! YOU GIR
YOU GIRLS
YOU JUST DON'T KN
WHAT YOU DO TO
A GUY!!!
LOTTA FUN!!!
I DON'T MIND!!!
YES...
YES???
YES!!
YES???
PAR-TY!
HOW WILD
PAR-TY!!!
WHAT'S NEW
GIRLS

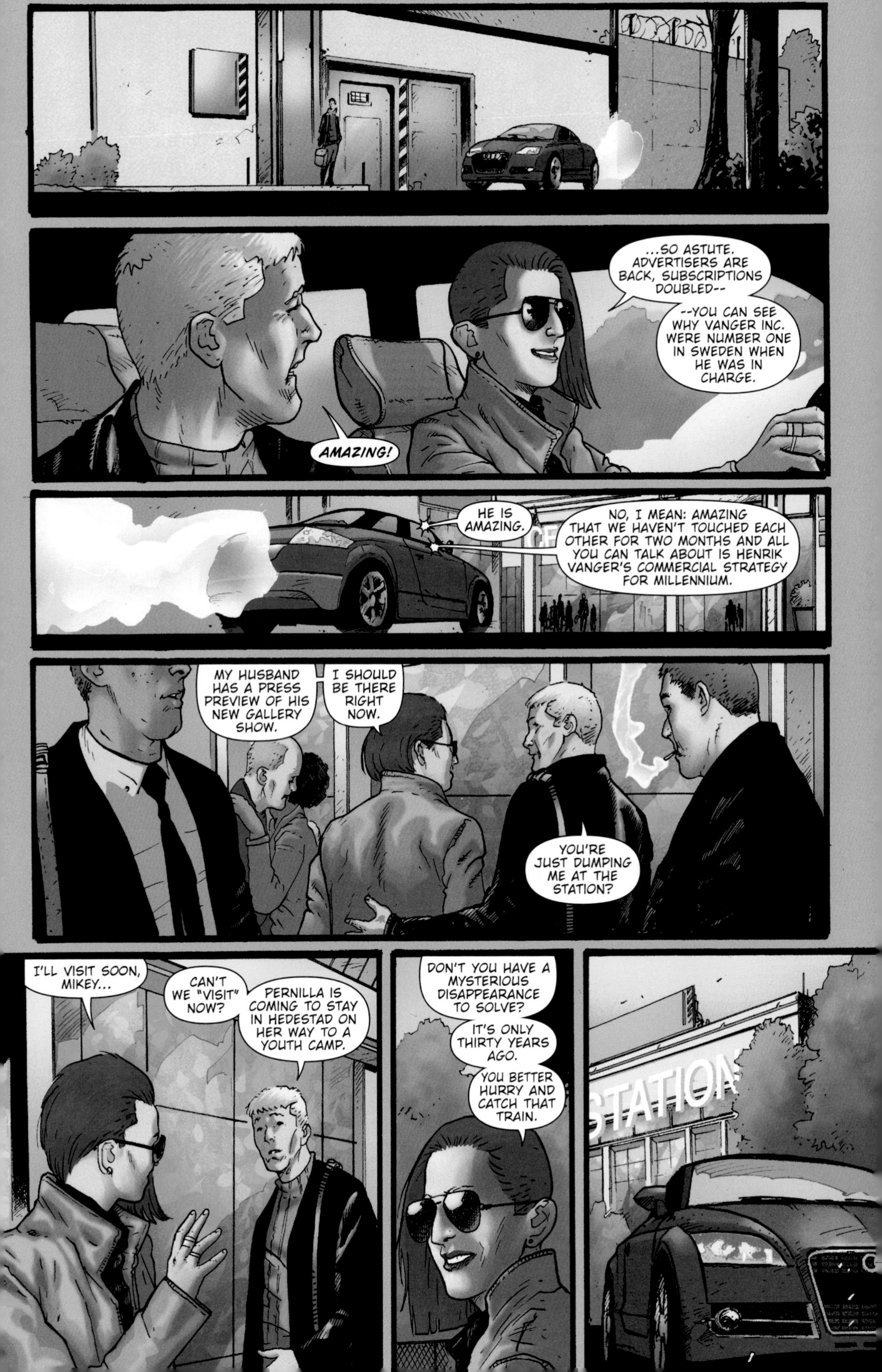
...SO ASTUTE. ADVERTISERS ARE BACK, SUBSCRIPTIONS DOUBLED--
--YOU CAN SEE WHY VANGER INC. WERE NUMBER ONE IN SWEDEN WHEN HE WAS IN CHARGE.
AMAZING!
HE IS AMAZING.
NO, I MEAN: AMAZING THAT WE HAVEN'T TOUCHED EACH OTHER FOR TWO MONTHS AND ALL YOU CAN TALK ABOUT IS HENRIK VANGER'S COMMERCIAL STRATEGY FOR MILLENNIUM.
MY HUSBAND HAS A PRESS PREVIEW OF HIS NEW GALLERY SHOW.
I SHOULD BE THERE RIGHT NOW.
YOU'RE JUST DUMPING ME AT THE STATION?
I'LL VISIT SOON, MIKEY...
CAN'T WE "VISIT" NOW?
PERNILLA IS COMING TO STAY IN HEDESTAD ON HER WAY TO A YOUTH CAMP.
DON'T YOU HAVE A MYSTERIOUS DISAPPEARANCE TO SOLVE?
IT'S ONLY THIRTY YEARS AGO.
YOU BETTER HURRY AND CATCH THAT TRAIN.
STATION

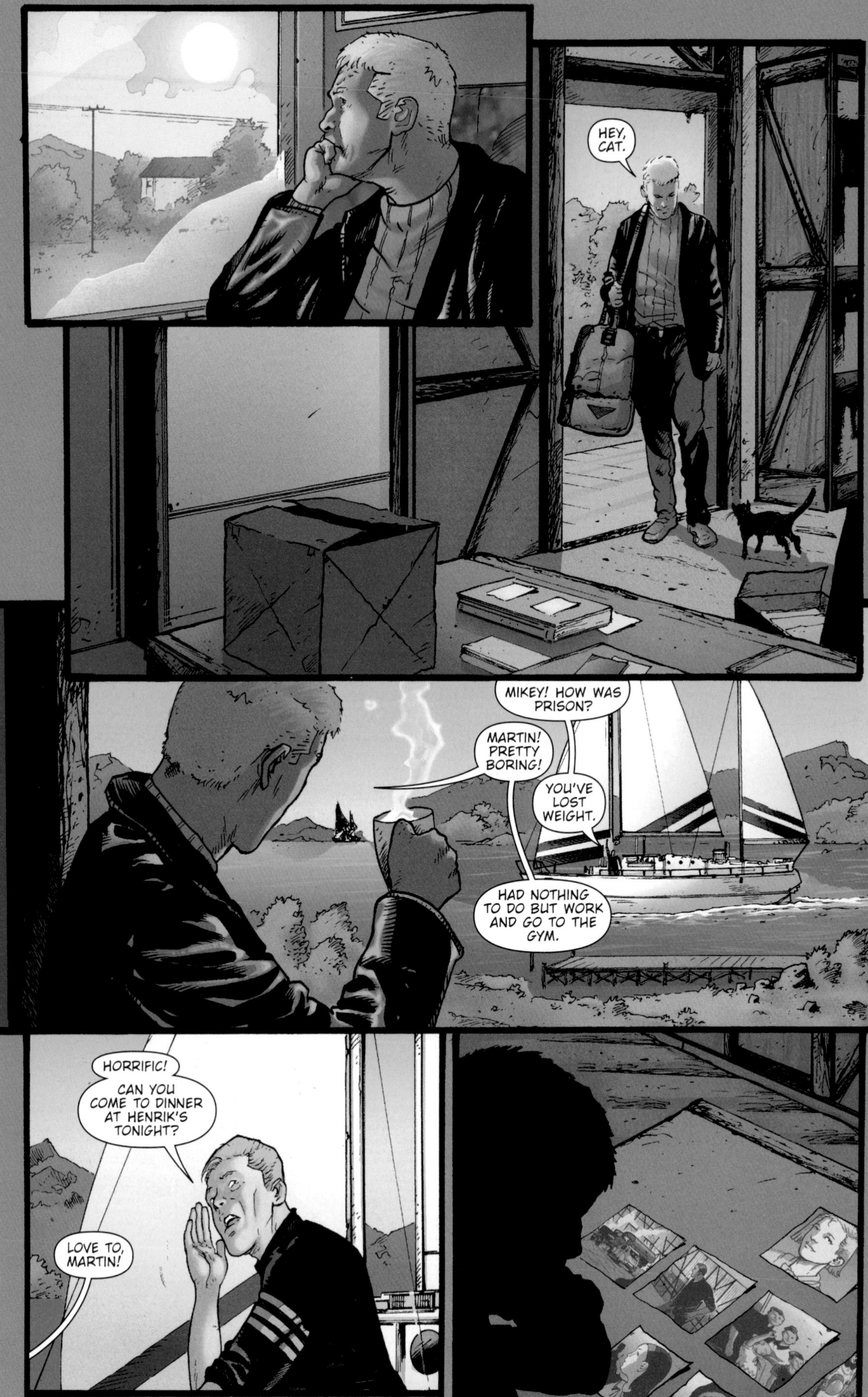
HEY, CAT.
MIKEY! HOW WAS PRISON?
MARTIN! PRETTY BORING!
YOU'VE LOST WEIGHT.
HAD NOTHING TO DO BUT WORK AND GO TO THE GYM.
HORRIFIC!
CAN YOU COME TO DINNER AT HENRIK'S TONIGHT?
LOVE TO, MARTIN!

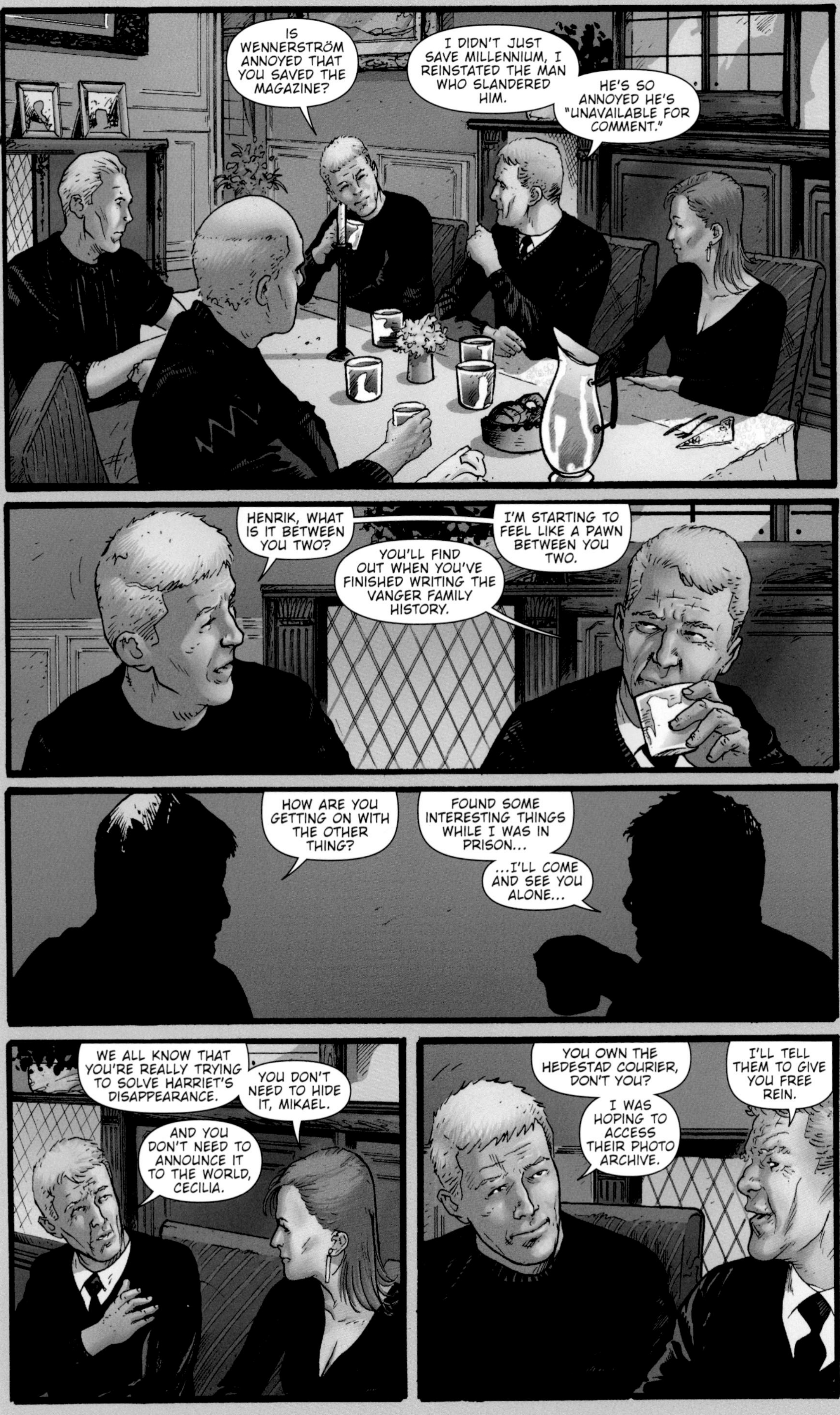
IS WENNERSTRÖM ANNOYED THAT YOU SAVED THE MAGAZINE?
I DIDN'T JUST SAVE MILLENNIUM, I REINSTATED THE MAN WHO SLANDERED HIM.
HE'S SO ANNOYED HE'S "UNAVAILABLE FOR COMMENT."
HENRIK, WHAT IS IT BETWEEN YOU TWO?
I'M STARTING TO FEEL LIKE A PAWN BETWEEN YOU TWO.
YOU'LL FIND OUT WHEN YOU'VE FINISHED WRITING THE VANGER FAMILY HISTORY.
HOW ARE YOU GETTING ON WITH THE OTHER THING?
FOUND SOME INTERESTING THINGS WHILE I WAS IN PRISON...
...I'LL COME AND SEE YOU ALONE...
WE ALL KNOW THAT YOU'RE REALLY TRYING TO SOLVE HARRIET'S DISAPPEARANCE.
YOU DON'T NEED TO HIDE IT, MIKAEL.
AND YOU DON'T NEED TO ANNOUNCE IT TO THE WORLD, CECILIA.
YOU OWN THE HEDESTAD COURIER, DON'T YOU?
I WAS HOPING TO ACCESS THEIR PHOTO ARCHIVE.
I'LL TELL THEM TO GIVE YOU FREE REIN.

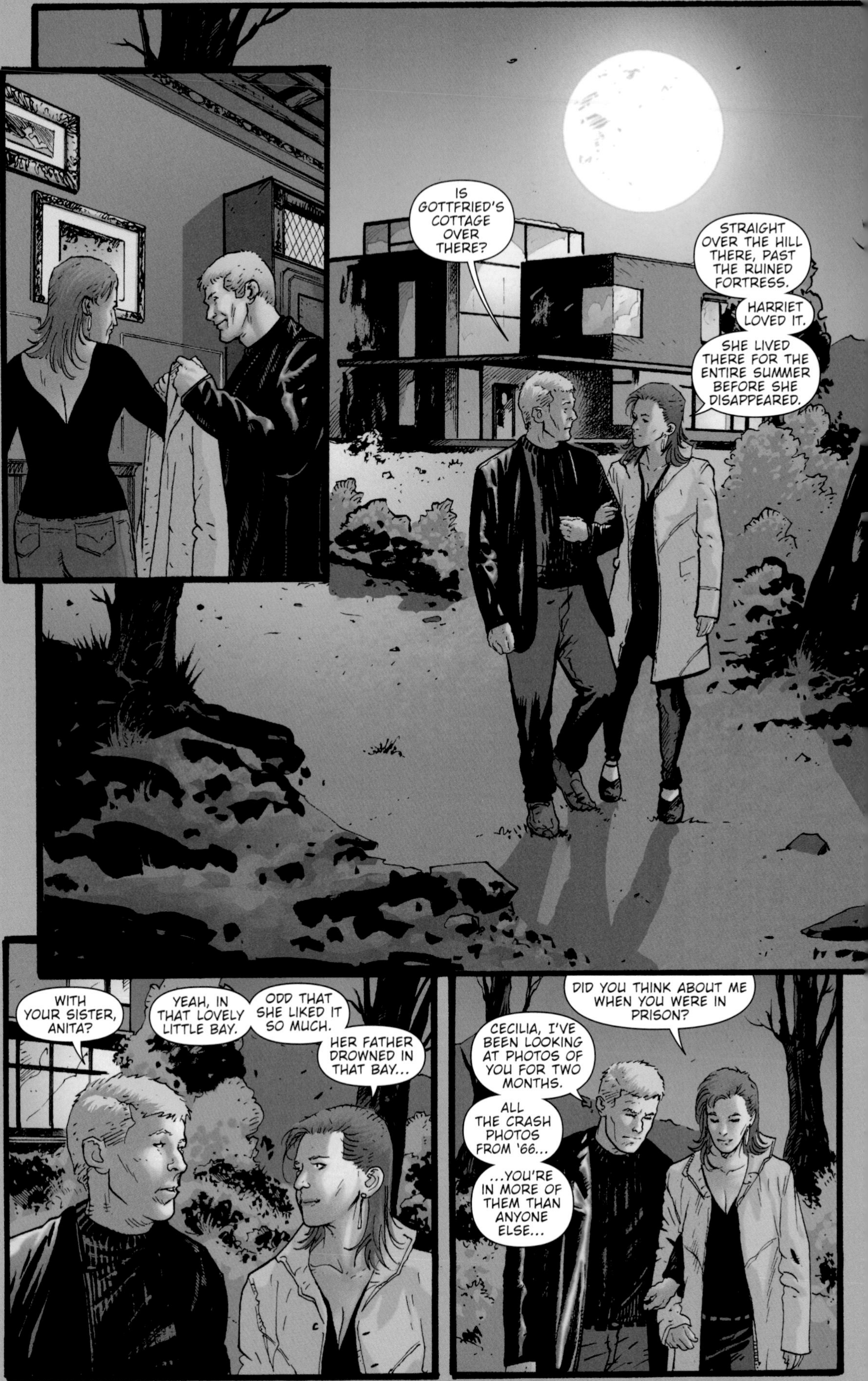
IS GOTTFRIED'S COTTAGE OVER THERE?
STRAIGHT OVER THE HILL THERE, PAST THE RUINED FORTRESS.
HARRIET LOVED IT.
SHE LIVED THERE FOR THE ENTIRE SUMMER BEFORE SHE DISAPPEARED.
WITH YOUR SISTER, ANITA?
YEAH, IN THAT LOVELY LITTLE BAY.
ODD THAT SHE LIKED IT SO MUCH.
HER FATHER DROWNED IN THAT BAY...
DID YOU THINK ABOUT ME WHEN YOU WERE IN PRISON?
CECILIA, I'VE BEEN LOOKING AT PHOTOS OF YOU FOR TWO MONTHS.
ALL THE CRASH PHOTOS FROM '66...
...YOU'RE IN MORE OF THEM THAN ANYONE ELSE...

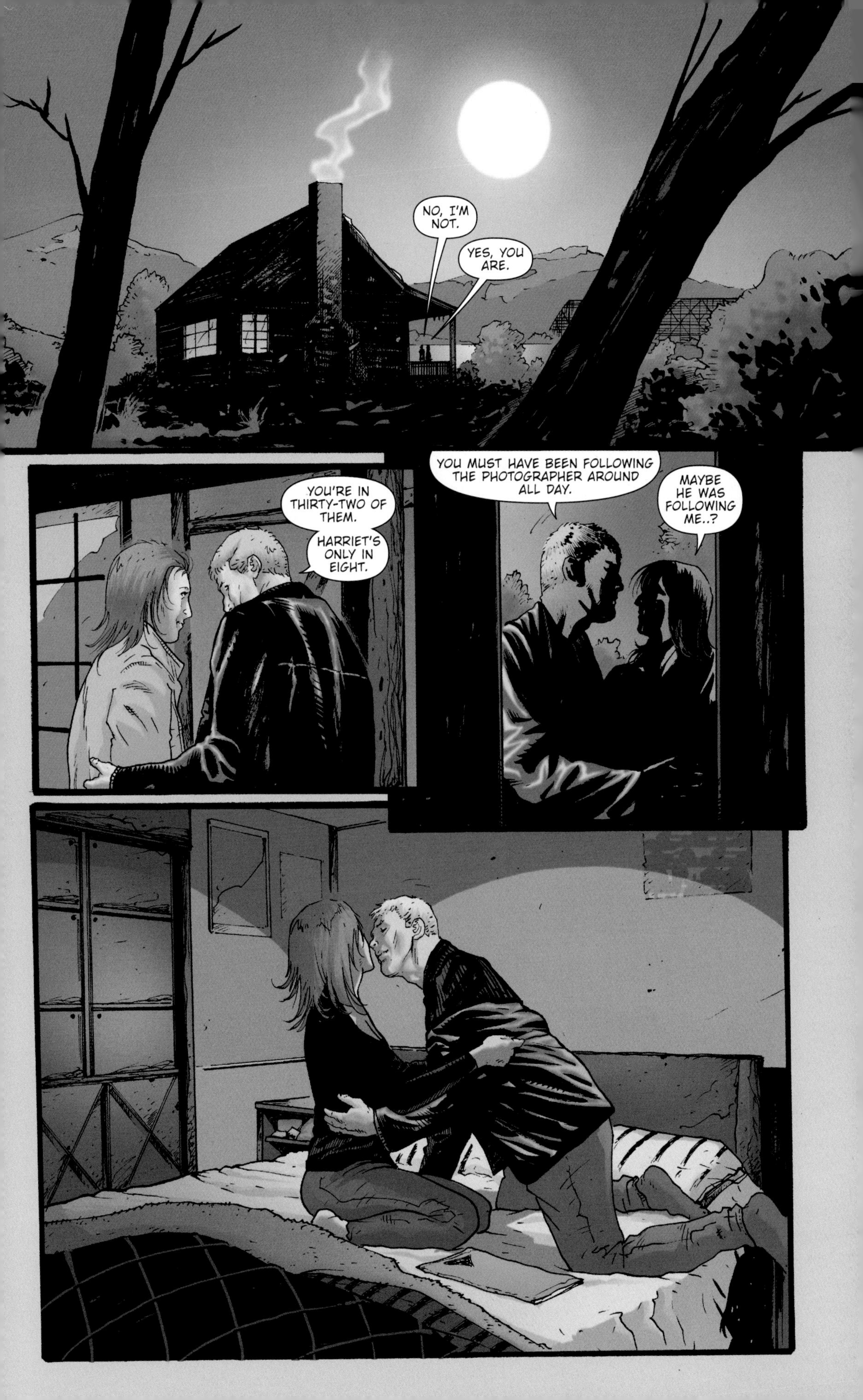
NO, I'M NOT.
YES, YOU ARE.
YOU'RE IN THIRTY-TWO OF THEM.
HARRIET'S ONLY IN EIGHT.
YOU MUST HAVE BEEN FOLLOWING THE PHOTOGRAPHER AROUND ALL DAY.
MAYBE HE WAS FOLLOWING ME..?

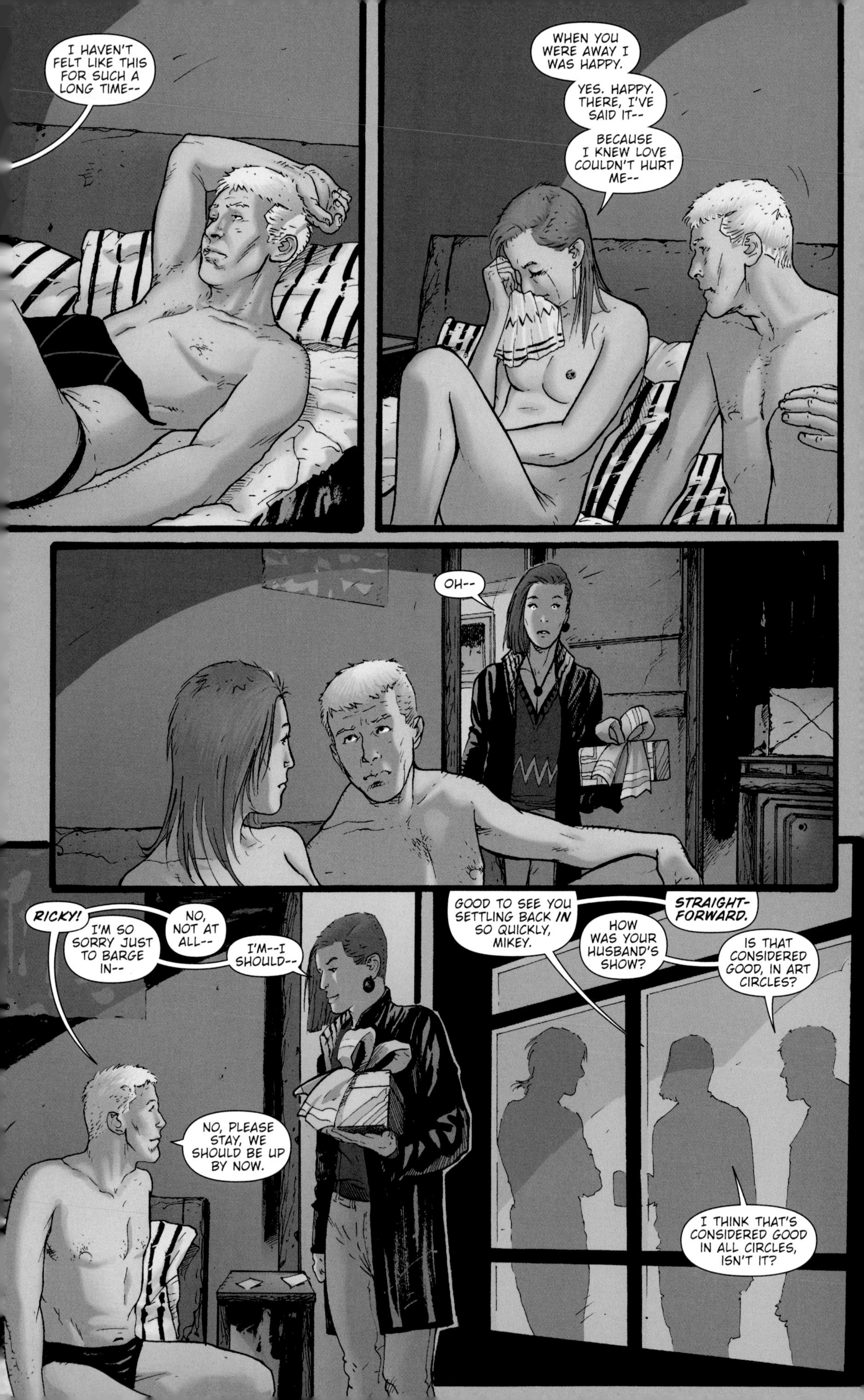
I HAVEN'T FELT LIKE THIS FOR SUCH A LONG TIME--
WHEN YOU WERE AWAY I WAS HAPPY.
YES. HAPPY. THERE, I'VE SAID IT--
BECAUSE I KNEW LOVE COULDN'T HURT ME--
OH--
RICKY!
I'M SO SORRY JUST TO BARGE IN--
NO, NOT AT ALL--
I'M--I SHOULD--
NO, PLEASE STAY, WE SHOULD BE UP BY NOW.
GOOD TO SEE YOU SETTLING BACK IN SO QUICKLY, MIKEY.
STRAIGHT-FORWARD.
HOW WAS YOUR HUSBAND'S SHOW?
IS THAT CONSIDERED GOOD, IN ART CIRCLES?
I THINK THAT'S CONSIDERED GOOD IN ALL CIRCLES, ISN'T IT?

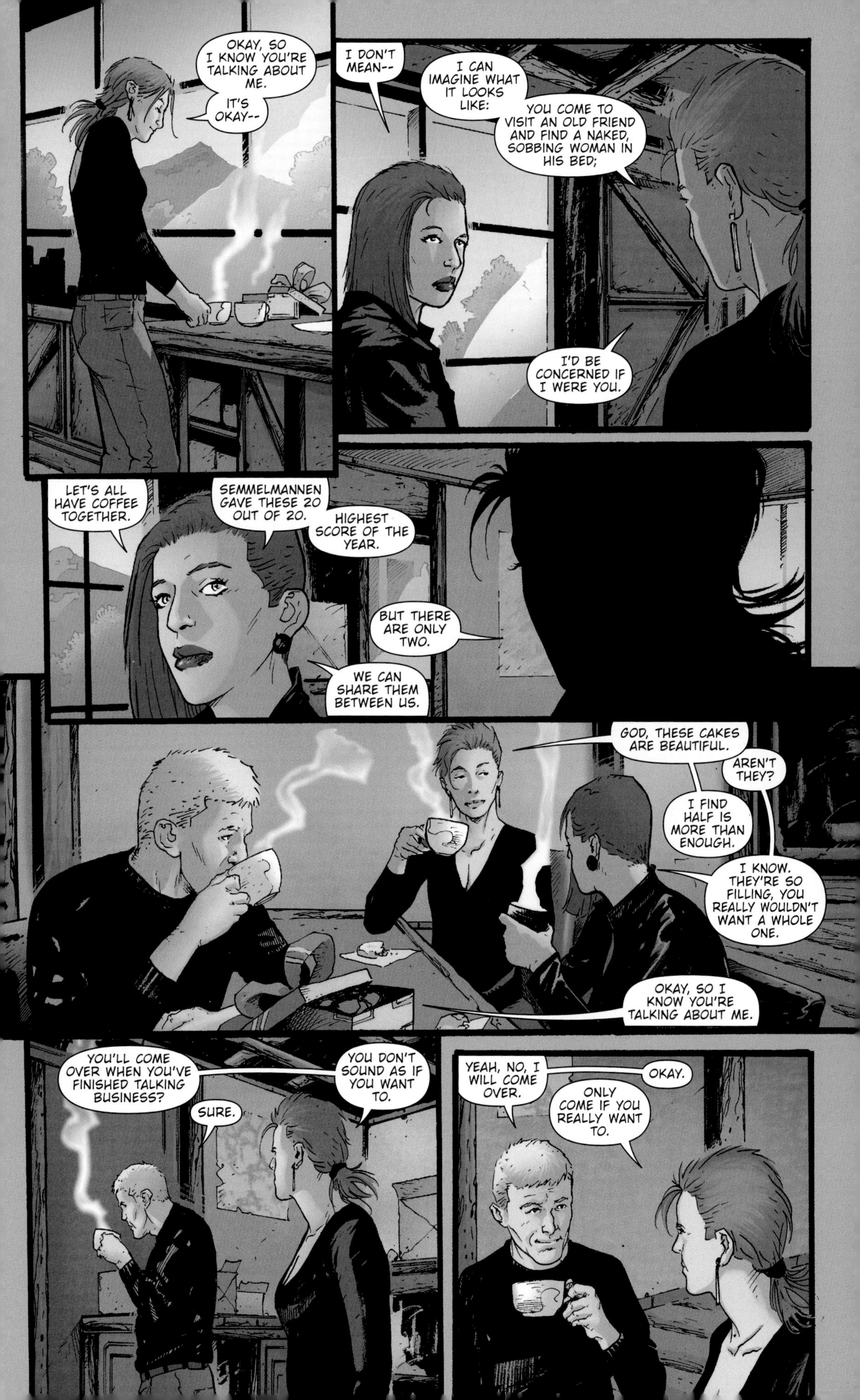
OKAY, SO I KNOW YOU'RE TALKING ABOUT ME.
IT'S OKAY--
I DON'T MEAN--
I CAN IMAGINE WHAT IT LOOKS LIKE:
YOU COME TO VISIT AN OLD FRIEND AND FIND A NAKED, SOBBING WOMAN IN HIS BED;
I'D BE CONCERNED IF I WERE YOU.
LET'S ALL HAVE COFFEE TOGETHER.
SEMMELMANNEN GAVE THESE 20 OUT OF 20.
HIGHEST SCORE OF THE YEAR.
BUT THERE ARE ONLY TWO.
WE CAN SHARE THEM BETWEEN US.
GOD, THESE CAKES ARE BEAUTIFUL.
AREN'T THEY?
I FIND HALF IS MORE THAN ENOUGH.
I KNOW. THEY'RE SO FILLING, YOU REALLY WOULDN'T WANT A WHOLE ONE.
OKAY, SO I KNOW YOU'RE TALKING ABOUT ME.
YOU'LL COME OVER WHEN YOU'VE FINISHED TALKING BUSINESS?
SURE.
YOU DON'T SOUND AS IF YOU WANT TO.
YEAH, NO, I WILL COME OVER.
OKAY.
ONLY COME IF YOU REALLY WANT TO.

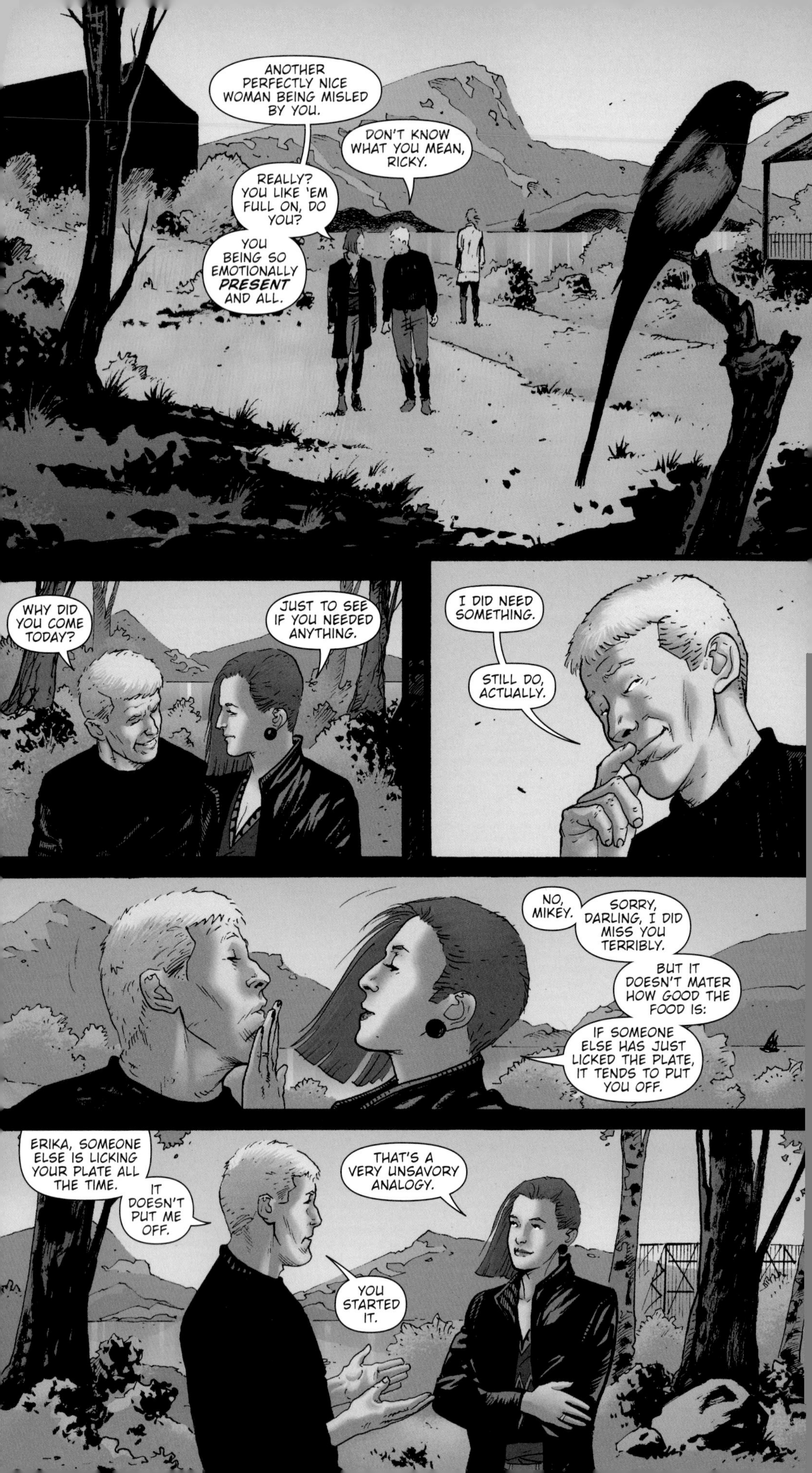
ANOTHER PERFECTLY NICE WOMAN BEING MISLED BY YOU.
DON'T KNOW WHAT YOU MEAN, RICKY.
REALLY? YOU LIKE 'EM FULL ON, DO YOU?
YOU BEING SO EMOTIONALLY *PRESENT* AND ALL.
WHY DID YOU COME TODAY?
JUST TO SEE IF YOU NEEDED ANYTHING.
I DID NEED SOMETHING.
STILL DO, ACTUALLY.
NO, MIKEY.
SORRY, DARLING, I DID MISS YOU TERRIBLY.
BUT IT DOESN'T MATER HOW GOOD THE FOOD IS:
IF SOMEONE ELSE HAS JUST LICKED THE PLATE, IT TENDS TO PUT YOU OFF.
ERIKA, SOMEONE ELSE IS LICKING YOUR PLATE ALL THE TIME.
IT DOESN'T PUT ME OFF.
THAT'S A VERY UNSAVORY ANALOGY.
YOU STARTED IT.

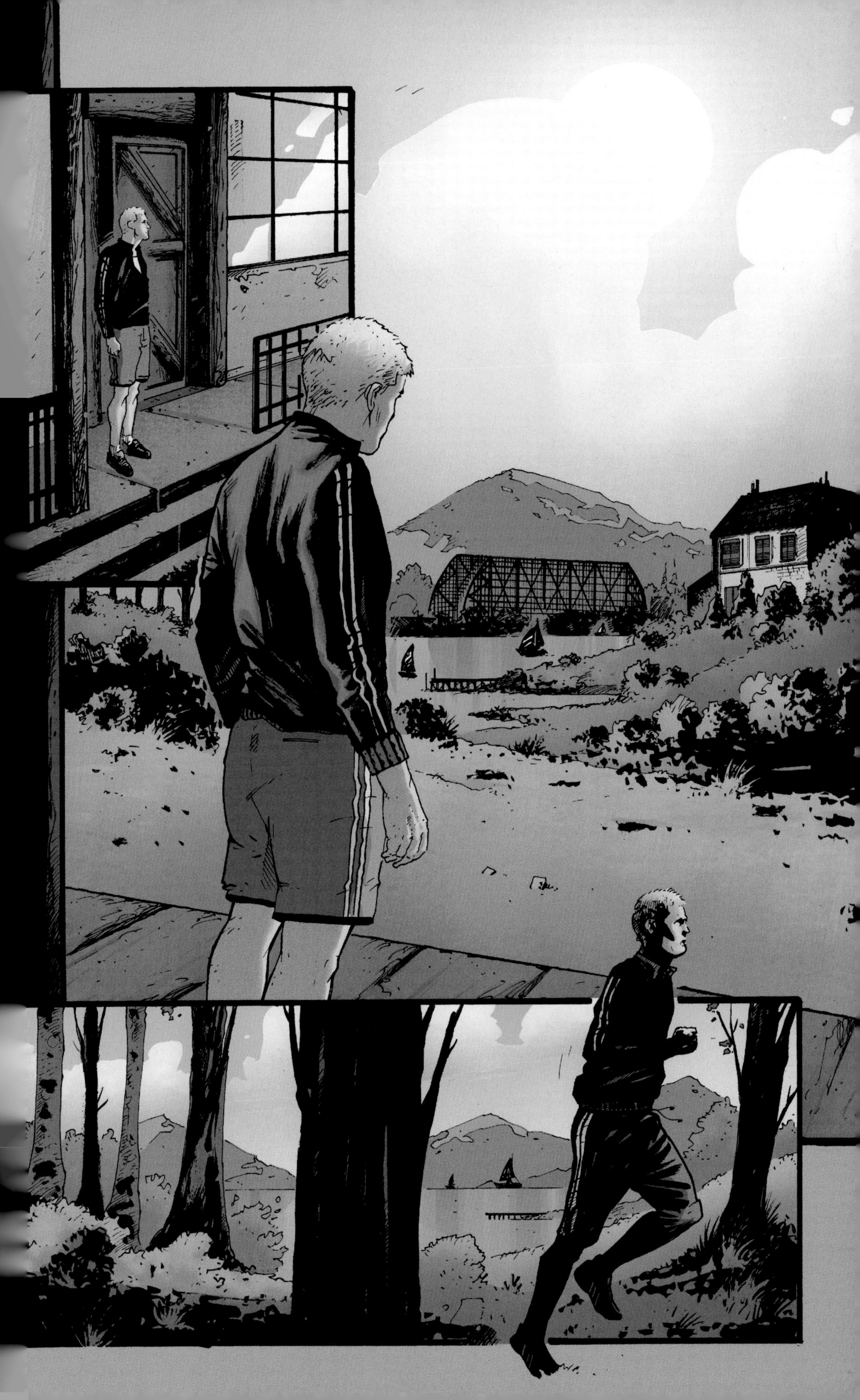

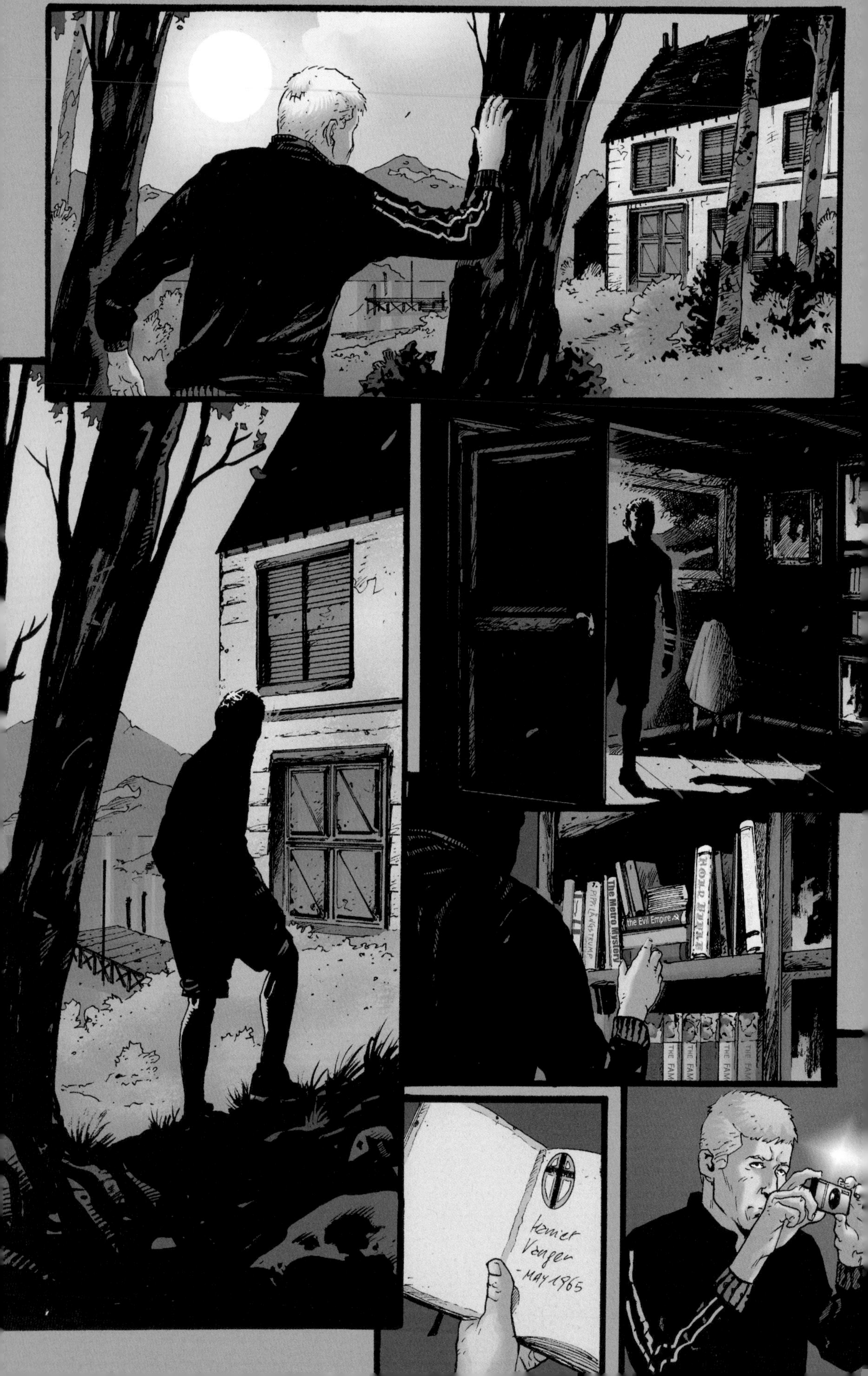

PIPPI LÅNGSTRUMP
The Metro Mystery
the Evil Empire
HOLY BIBLE
THE FAM
THE FAM
THE FAM
THE FAM
Harriet Vanger - May 1965

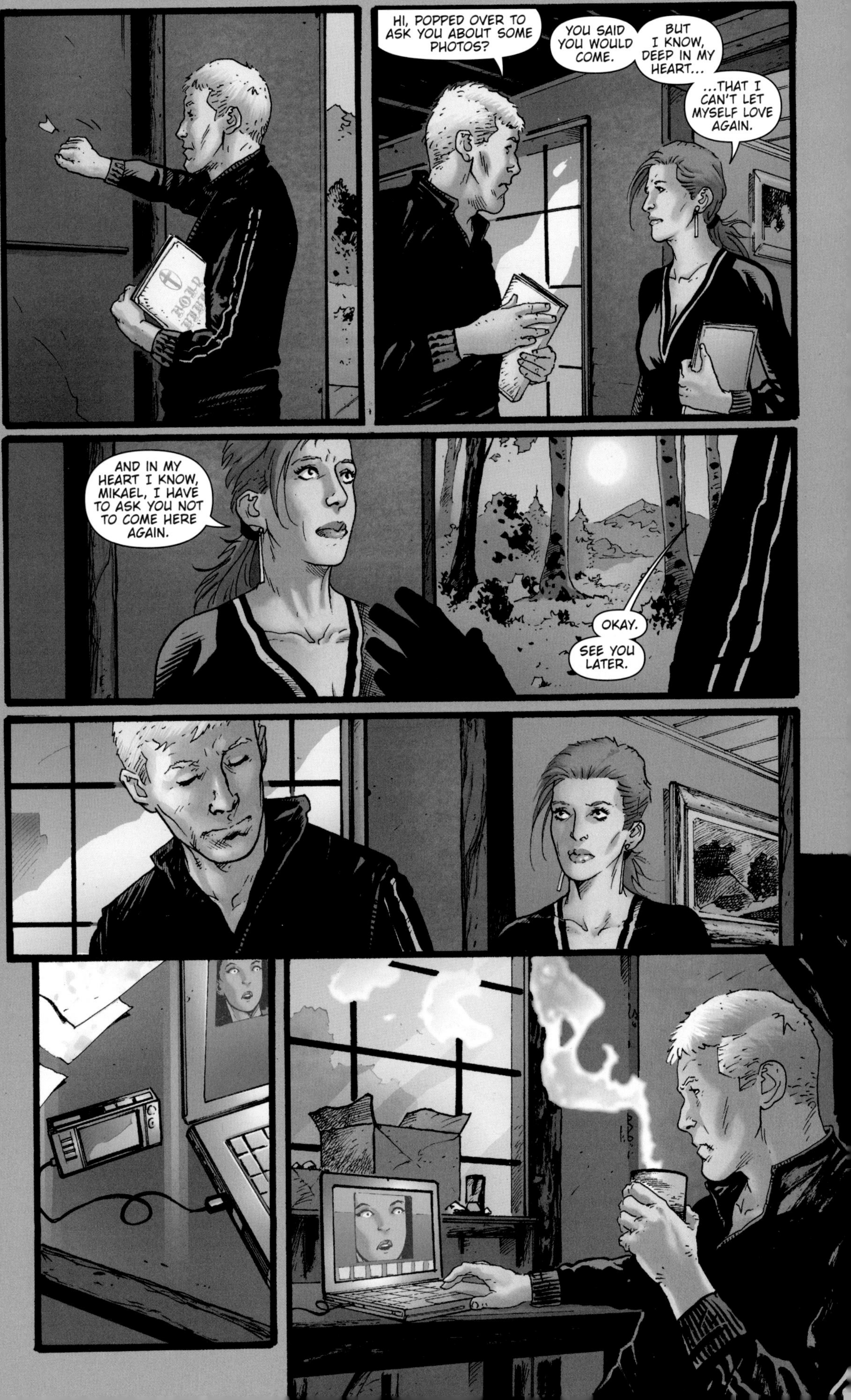
HI, POPPED OVER TO ASK YOU ABOUT SOME PHOTOS?
YOU SAID YOU WOULD COME.
BUT I KNOW, DEEP IN MY HEART...
...THAT I CAN'T LET MYSELF LOVE AGAIN.
AND IN MY HEART I KNOW, MIKAEL, I HAVE TO ASK YOU NOT TO COME HERE AGAIN.
OKAY.
SEE YOU LATER.

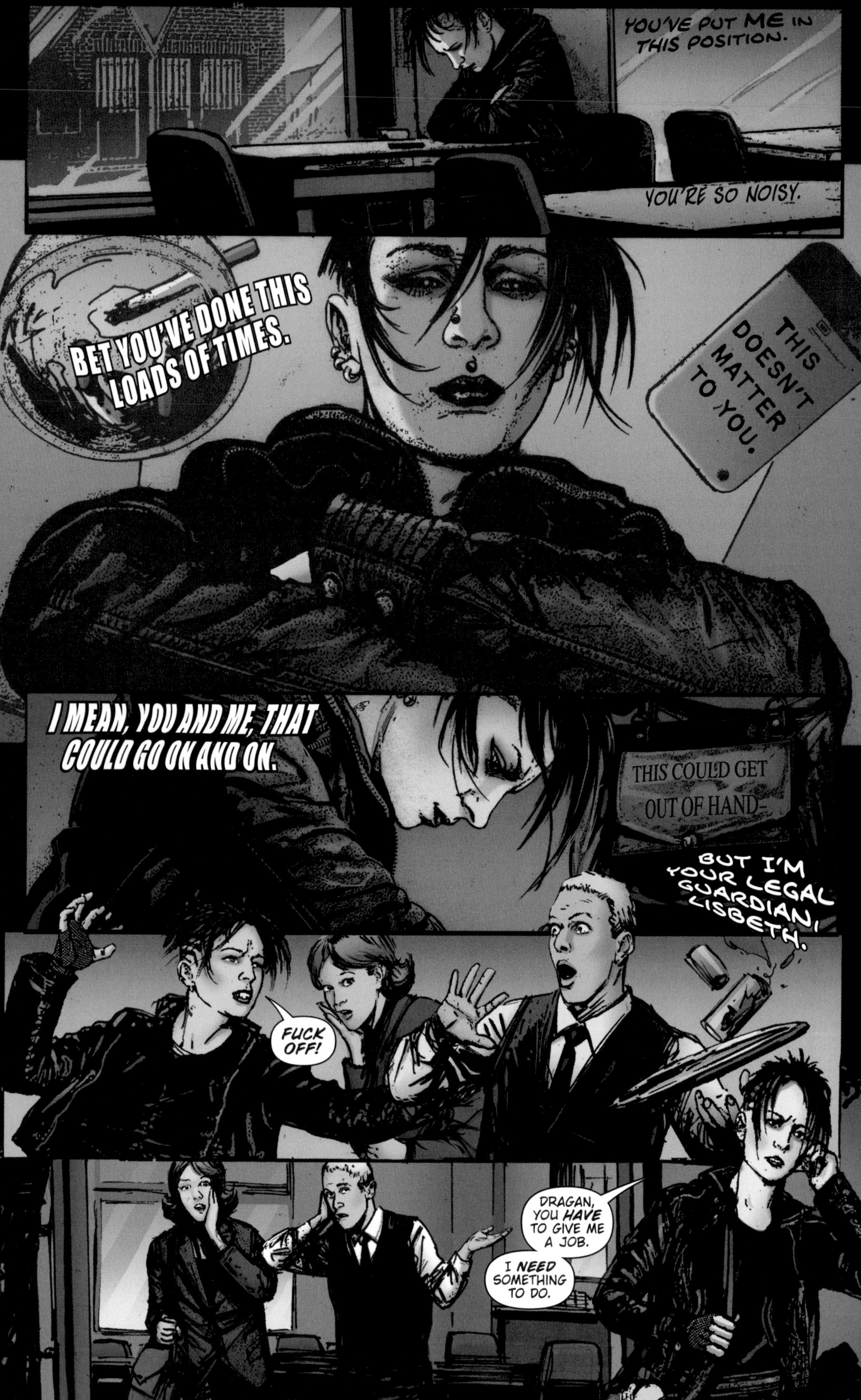

YOU'VE PUT ME IN THIS POSITION.
YOU'RE SO NOISY.
BET YOU'VE DONE THIS LOADS OF TIMES.
THIS DOESN'T MATTER TO YOU.
I MEAN, YOU AND ME, THAT COULD GO ON AND ON.
THIS COULD GET OUT OF HAND-
BUT I'M YOUR LEGAL GUARDIAN, LISBETH.
FUCK OFF!
DRAGAN, YOU HAVE TO GIVE ME A JOB.
I NEED SOMETHING TO DO.

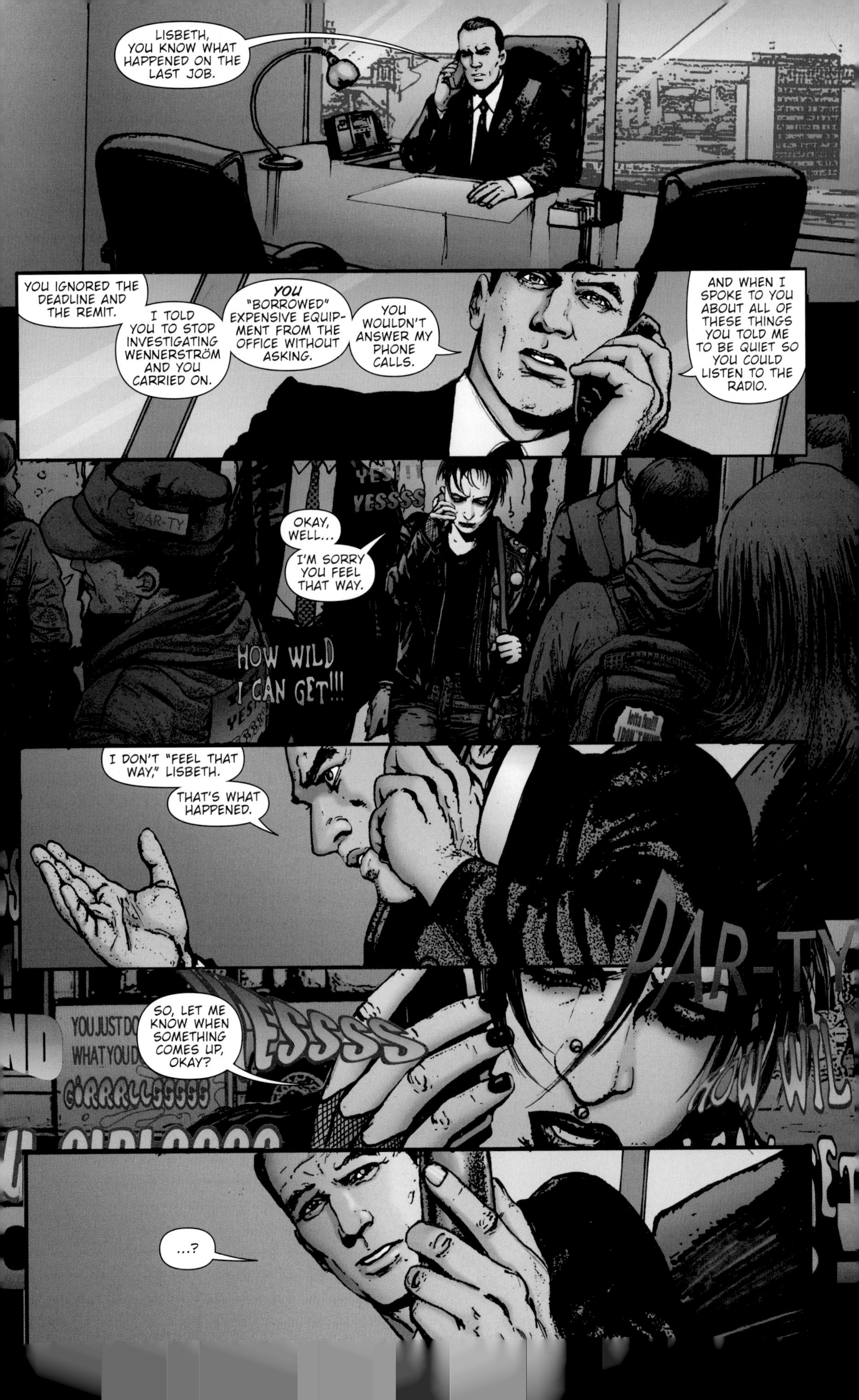
LISBETH, YOU KNOW WHAT HAPPENED ON THE LAST JOB.
YOU IGNORED THE DEADLINE AND THE REMIT.
I TOLD YOU TO STOP INVESTIGATING WENNERSTRÖM AND YOU CARRIED ON.
YOU "BORROWED" EXPENSIVE EQUIPMENT FROM THE OFFICE WITHOUT ASKING.
YOU WOULDN'T ANSWER MY PHONE CALLS.
AND WHEN I SPOKE TO YOU ABOUT ALL OF THESE THINGS YOU TOLD ME TO BE QUIET SO YOU COULD LISTEN TO THE RADIO.
YESSSS
OKAY, WELL...
I'M SORRY YOU FEEL THAT WAY.
HOW WILD I CAN GET!!!
I DON'T "FEEL THAT WAY," LISBETH.
THAT'S WHAT HAPPENED.
PAR-TY
SO, LET ME KNOW WHEN SOMETHING COMES UP, OKAY?
...?

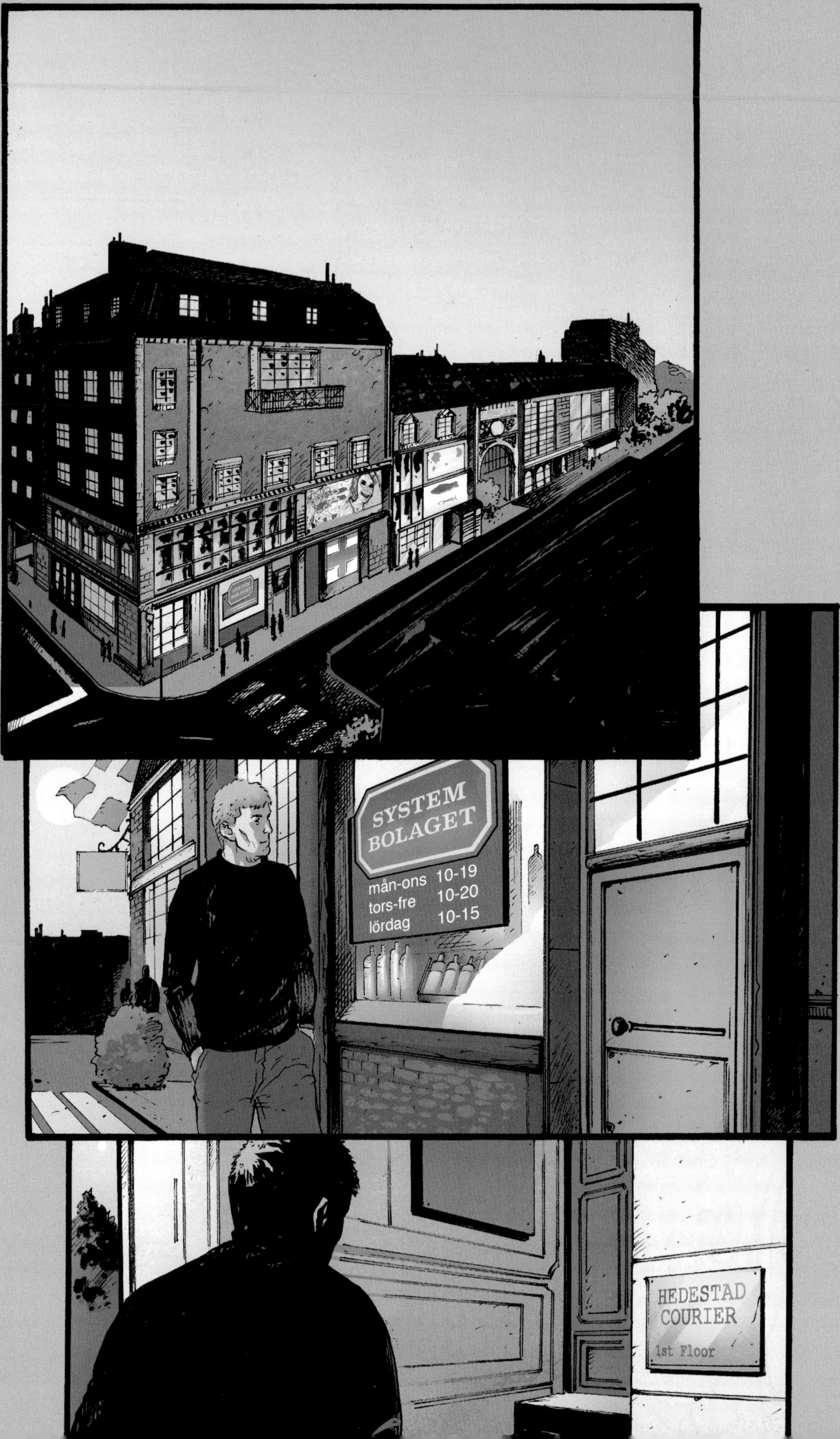
SYSTEM BOLAGET
mån-ons 10-19
tors-fre 10-20
lördag 10-15
HEDESTAD COURIER
1st Floor

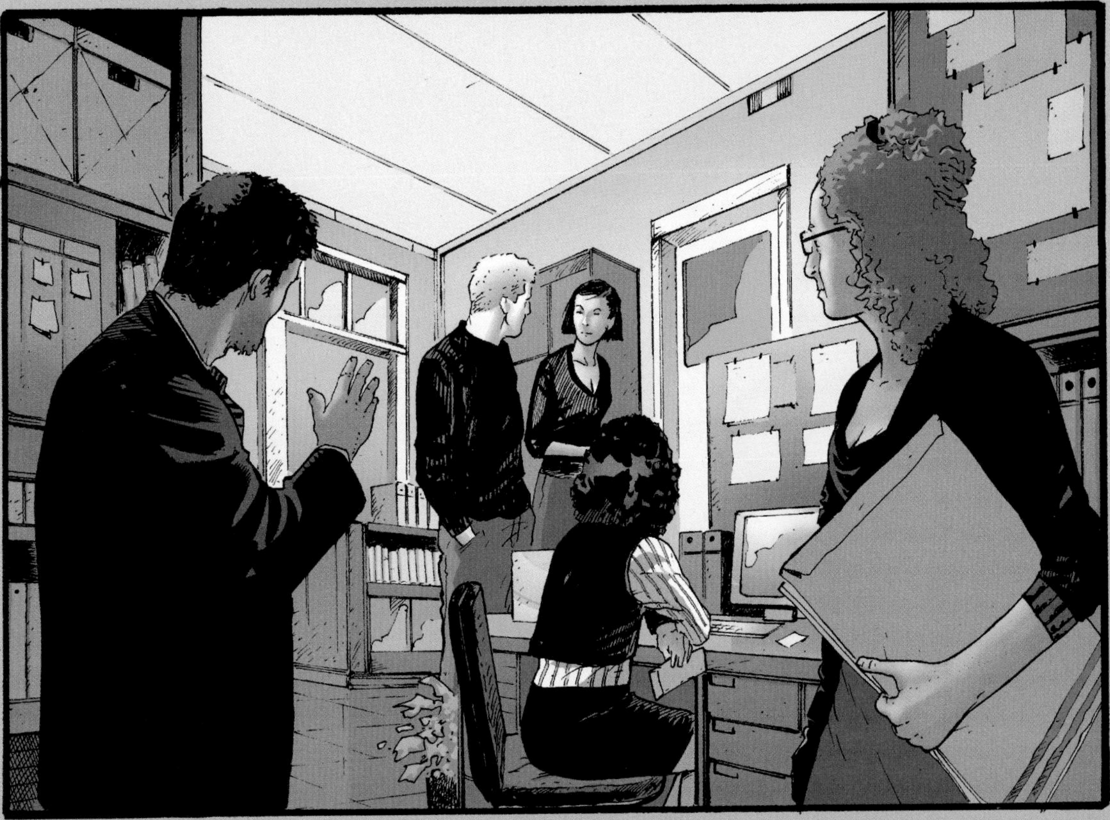

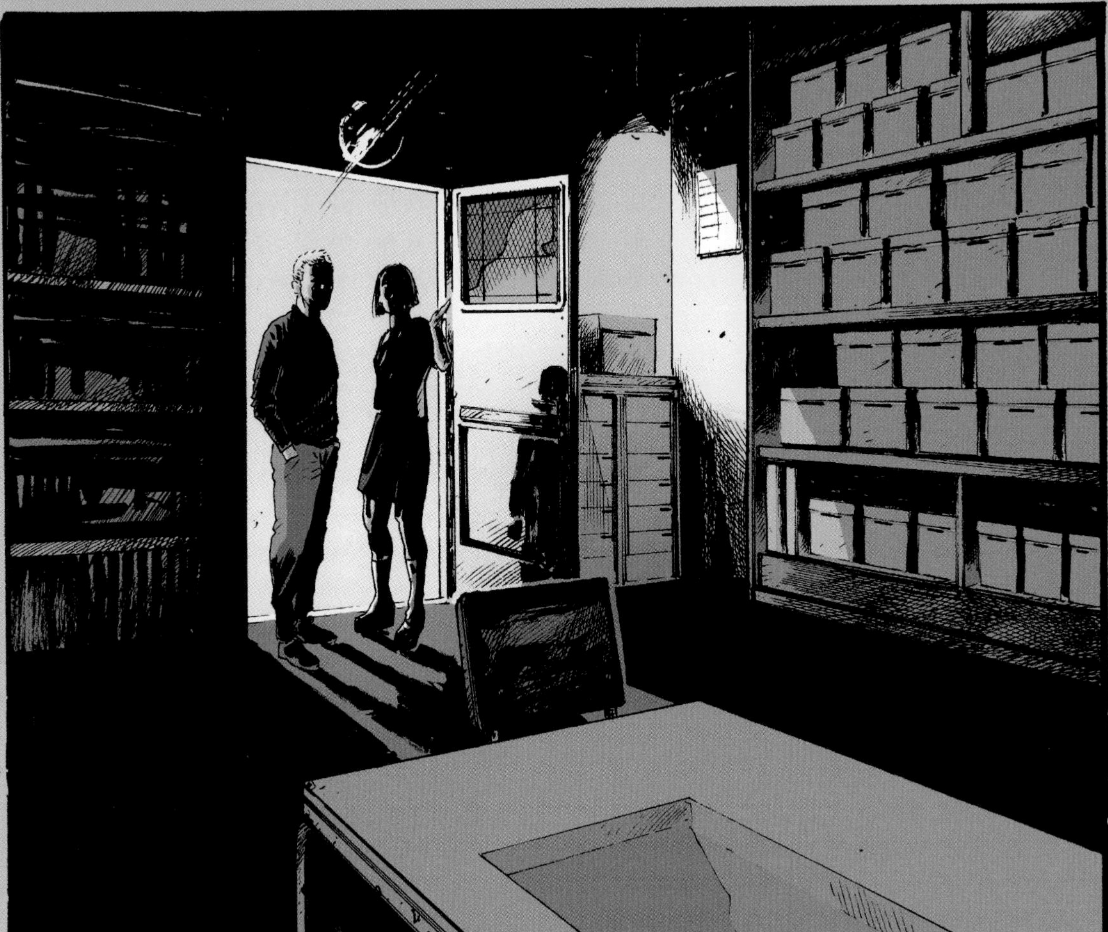

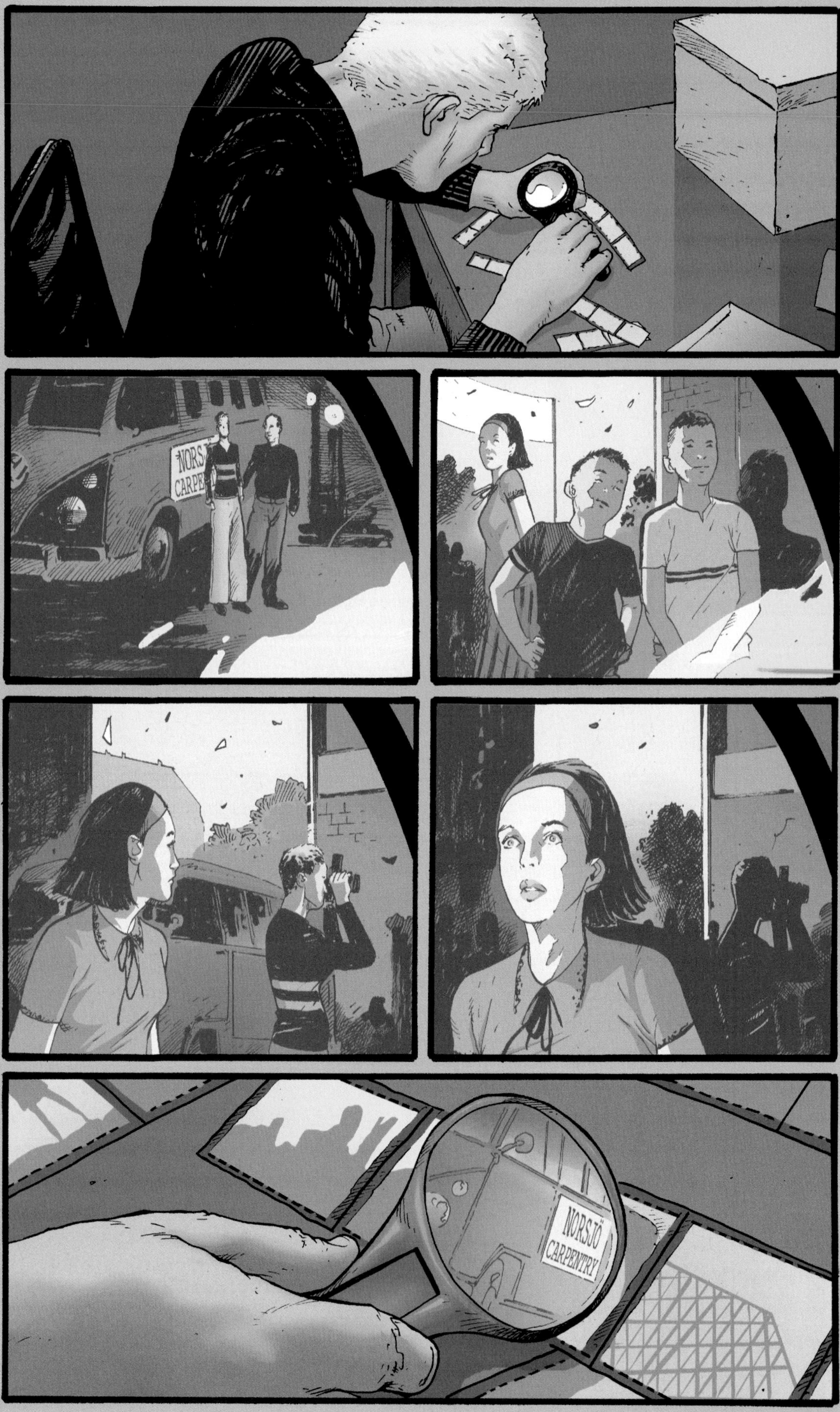
NORSJÖ
CARPENTRY

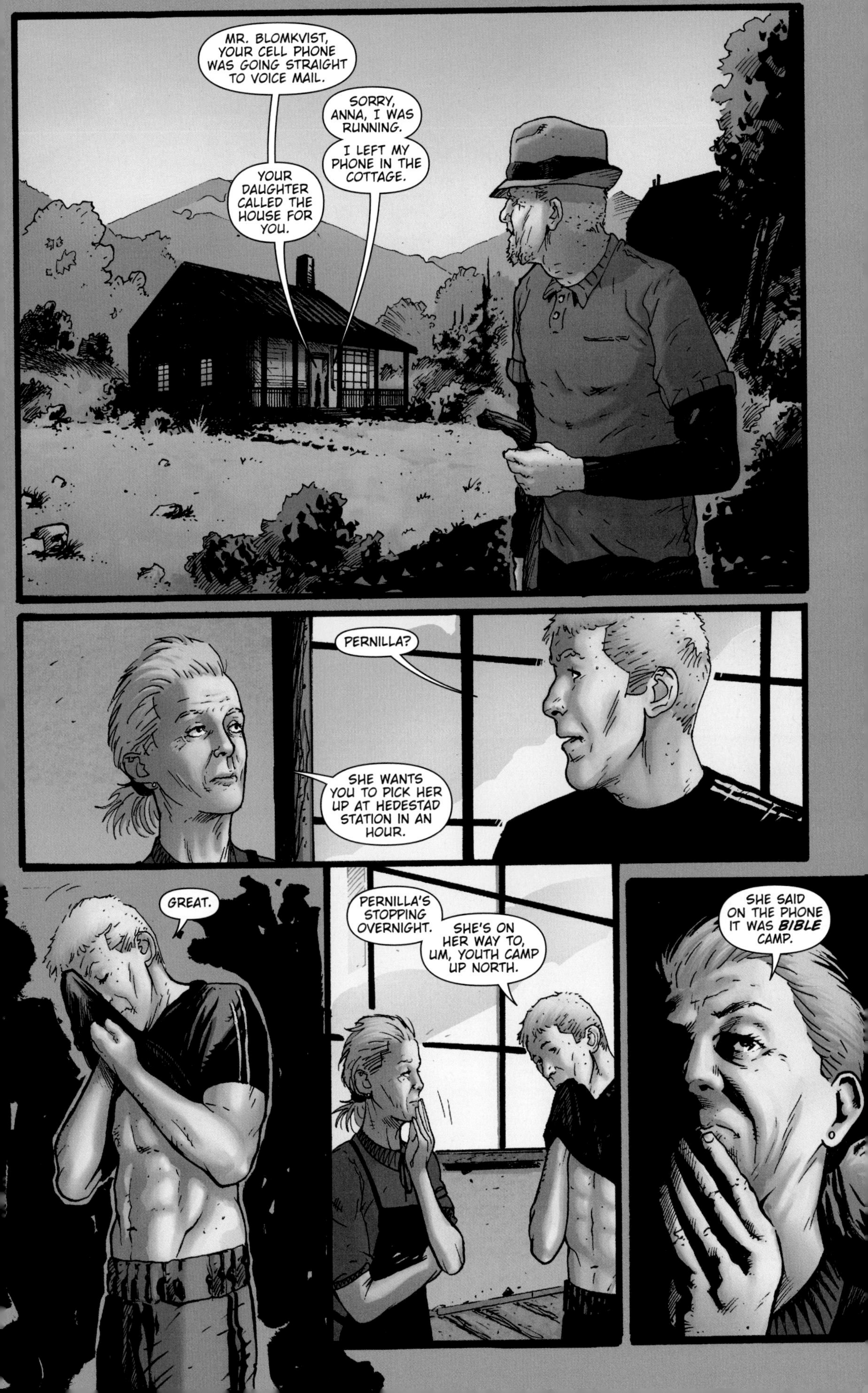
MR. BLOMKVIST, YOUR CELL PHONE WAS GOING STRAIGHT TO VOICE MAIL.
YOUR DAUGHTER CALLED THE HOUSE FOR YOU.
SORRY, ANNA, I WAS RUNNING.
I LEFT MY PHONE IN THE COTTAGE.
PERNILLA?
SHE WANTS YOU TO PICK HER UP AT HEDESTAD STATION IN AN HOUR.
GREAT.
PERNILLA'S STOPPING OVERNIGHT.
SHE'S ON HER WAY TO, UM, YOUTH CAMP UP NORTH.
SHE SAID ON THE PHONE IT WAS *BIBLE* CAMP.

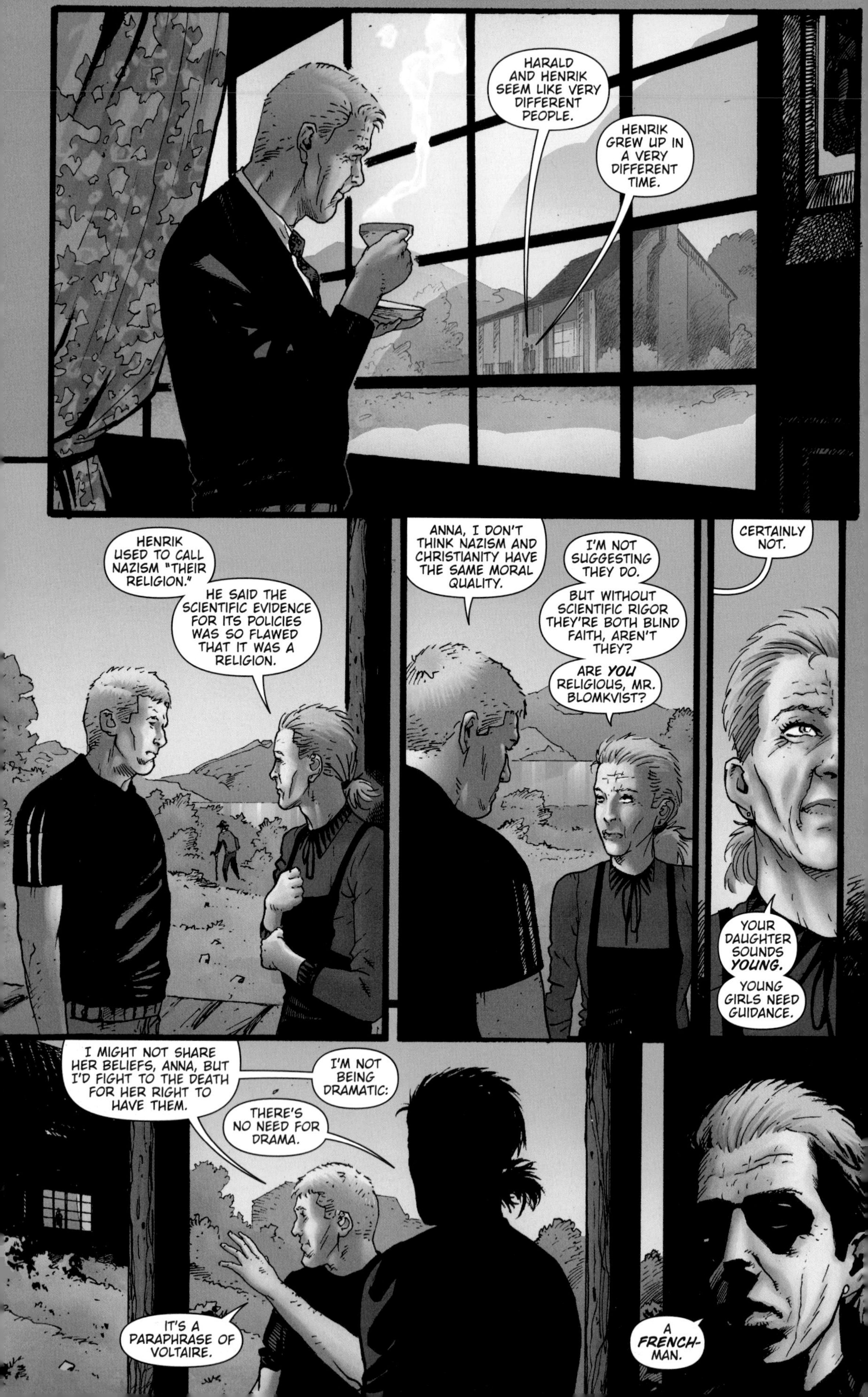
HARALD AND HENRIK SEEM LIKE VERY DIFFERENT PEOPLE.
HENRIK GREW UP IN A VERY DIFFERENT TIME.
HENRIK USED TO CALL NAZISM "THEIR RELIGION."
HE SAID THE SCIENTIFIC EVIDENCE FOR ITS POLICIES WAS SO FLAWED THAT IT WAS A RELIGION.
ANNA, I DON'T THINK NAZISM AND CHRISTIANITY HAVE THE SAME MORAL QUALITY.
I'M NOT SUGGESTING THEY DO.
BUT WITHOUT SCIENTIFIC RIGOR THEY'RE BOTH BLIND FAITH, AREN'T THEY?
ARE *YOU* RELIGIOUS, MR. BLOMKVIST?
CERTAINLY NOT.
YOUR DAUGHTER SOUNDS **YOUNG.**
YOUNG GIRLS NEED GUIDANCE.
I MIGHT NOT SHARE HER BELIEFS, ANNA, BUT I'D FIGHT TO THE DEATH FOR HER RIGHT TO HAVE THEM.
I'M NOT BEING DRAMATIC:
THERE'S NO NEED FOR DRAMA.
IT'S A PARAPHRASE OF VOLTAIRE.
A **FRENCH-** MAN.

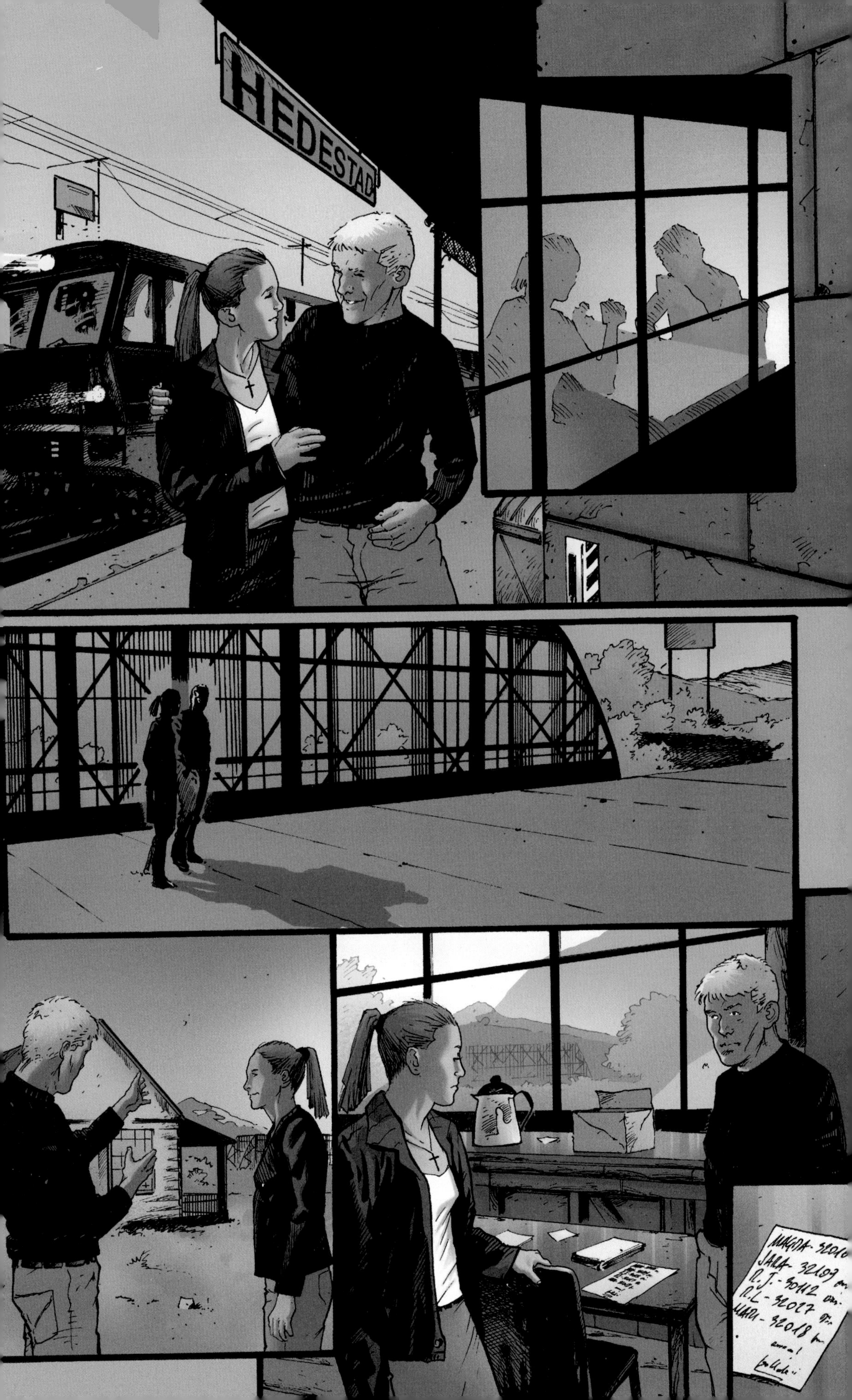
HEDESTAD
MAGDA - 32016
SARA - 32109
R.J. - 30112
R.L. - 32027
MARI - 32018

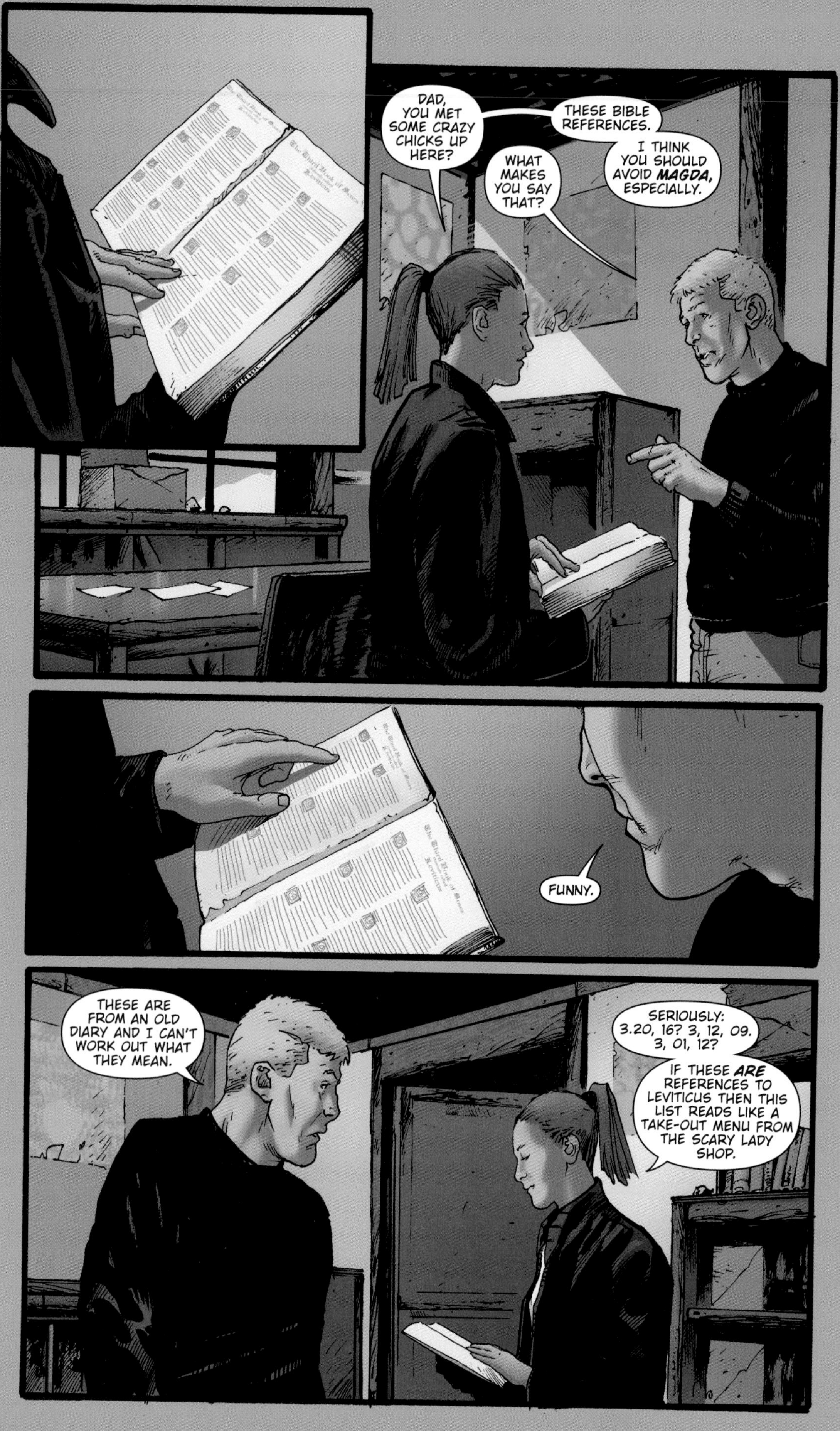
DAD, YOU MET SOME CRAZY CHICKS UP HERE?
THESE BIBLE REFERENCES.
I THINK YOU SHOULD AVOID MAGDA, ESPECIALLY.
WHAT MAKES YOU SAY THAT?
FUNNY.
THESE ARE FROM AN OLD DIARY AND I CAN'T WORK OUT WHAT THEY MEAN.
SERIOUSLY: 3.20, 16? 3, 12, 09. 3, 01, 12?
IF THESE ARE REFERENCES TO LEVITICUS THEN THIS LIST READS LIKE A TAKE-OUT MENU FROM THE SCARY LADY SHOP.

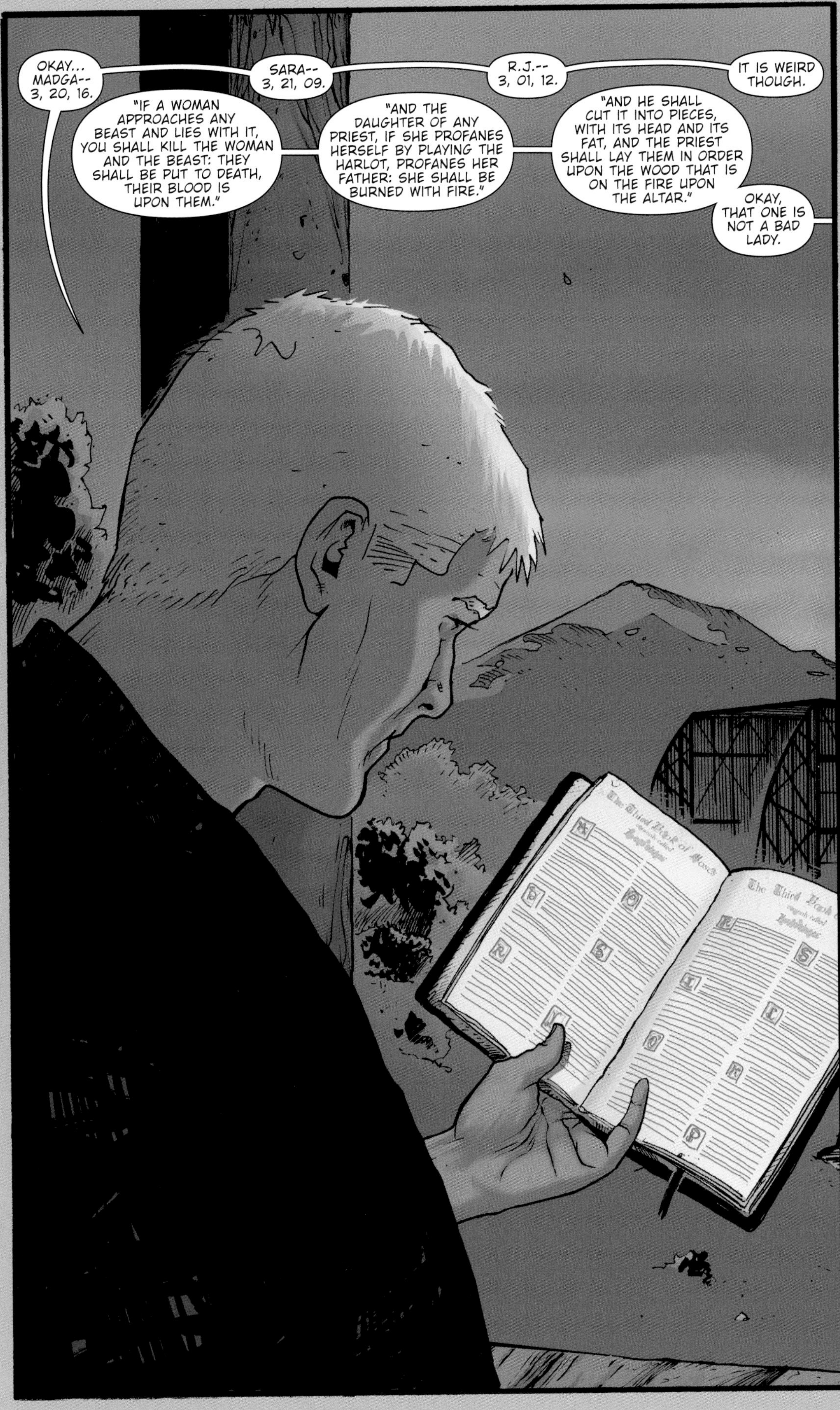
OKAY... MADGA-- 3, 20, 16.
"IF A WOMAN APPROACHES ANY BEAST AND LIES WITH IT, YOU SHALL KILL THE WOMAN AND THE BEAST: THEY SHALL BE PUT TO DEATH, THEIR BLOOD IS UPON THEM."
SARA-- 3, 21, 09.
"AND THE DAUGHTER OF ANY PRIEST, IF SHE PROFANES HERSELF BY PLAYING THE HARLOT, PROFANES HER FATHER: SHE SHALL BE BURNED WITH FIRE."
R.J.-- 3, 01, 12.
"AND HE SHALL CUT IT INTO PIECES, WITH ITS HEAD AND ITS FAT, AND THE PRIEST SHALL LAY THEM IN ORDER UPON THE WOOD THAT IS ON THE FIRE UPON THE ALTAR."
OKAY, THAT ONE IS NOT A BAD LADY.
IT IS WEIRD THOUGH.

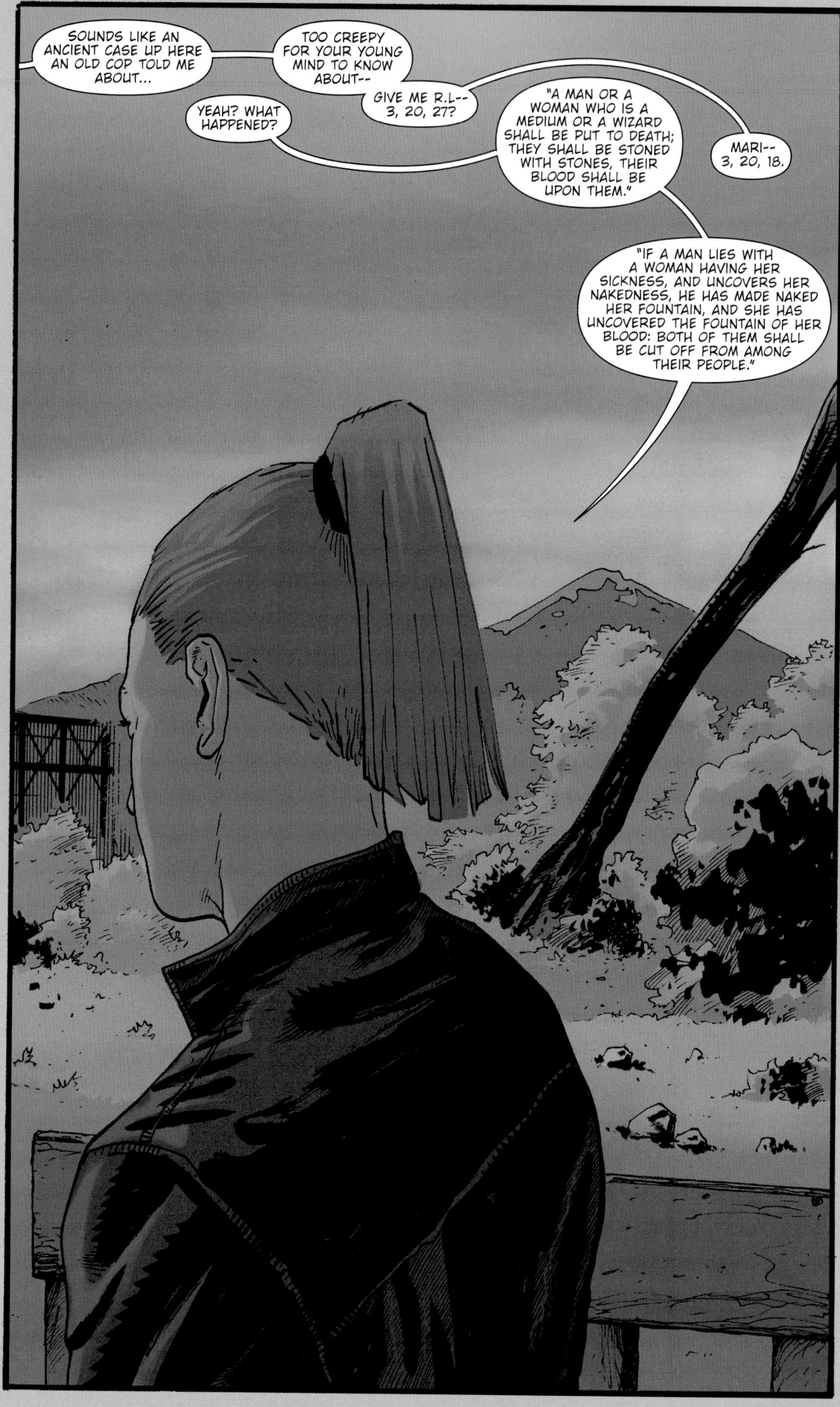
SOUNDS LIKE AN ANCIENT CASE UP HERE AN OLD COP TOLD ME ABOUT...
TOO CREEPY FOR YOUR YOUNG MIND TO KNOW ABOUT--
YEAH? WHAT HAPPENED?
GIVE ME R.L-- 3, 20, 27?
"A MAN OR A WOMAN WHO IS A MEDIUM OR A WIZARD SHALL BE PUT TO DEATH; THEY SHALL BE STONED WITH STONES, THEIR BLOOD SHALL BE UPON THEM."
MARI-- 3, 20, 18.
"IF A MAN LIES WITH A WOMAN HAVING HER SICKNESS, AND UNCOVERS HER NAKEDNESS, HE HAS MADE NAKED HER FOUNTAIN, AND SHE HAS UNCOVERED THE FOUNTAIN OF HER BLOOD: BOTH OF THEM SHALL BE CUT OFF FROM AMONG THEIR PEOPLE."

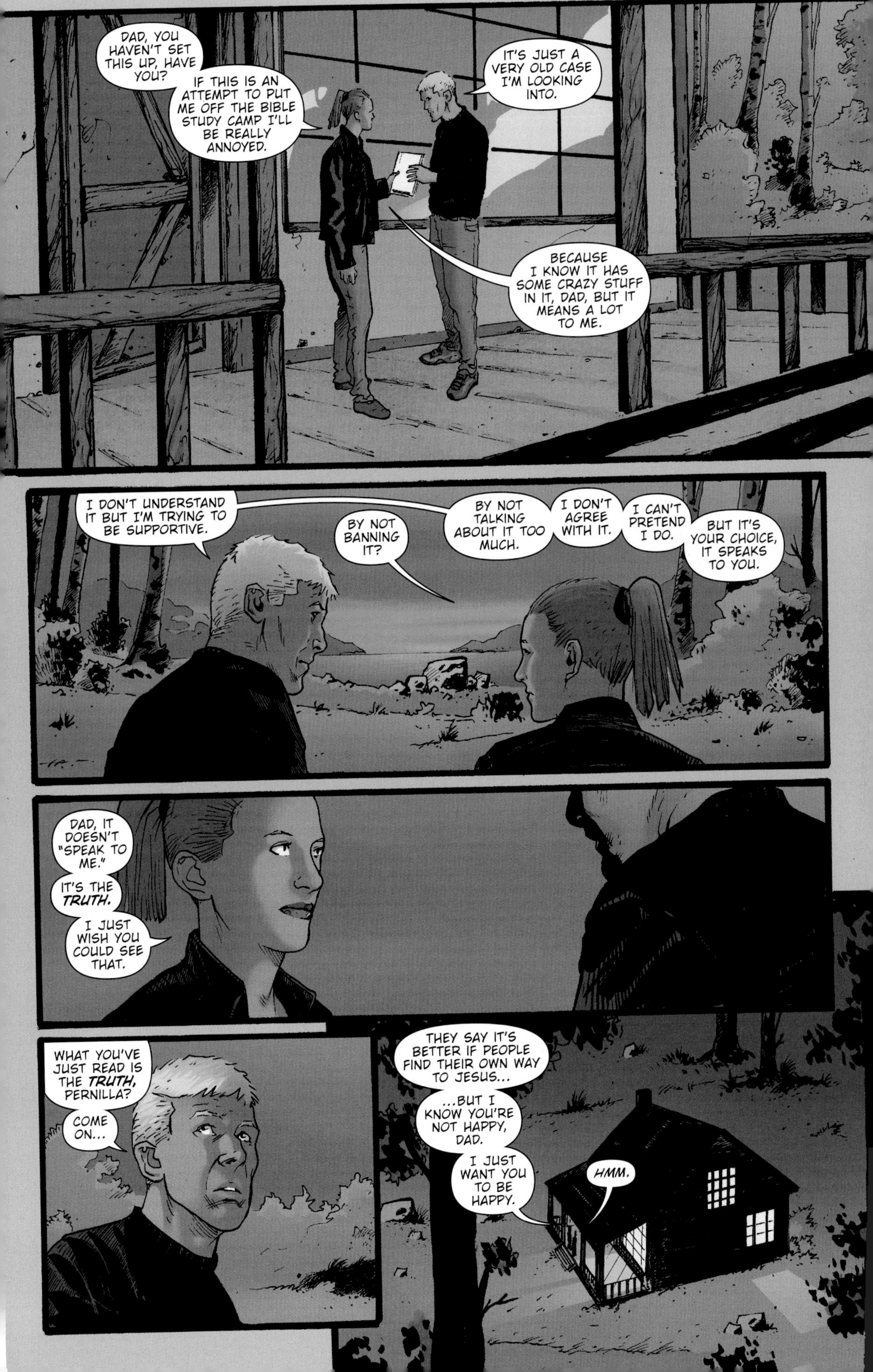
DAD, YOU HAVEN'T SET THIS UP, HAVE YOU?
IF THIS IS AN ATTEMPT TO PUT ME OFF THE BIBLE STUDY CAMP I'LL BE REALLY ANNOYED.
IT'S JUST A VERY OLD CASE I'M LOOKING INTO.
BECAUSE I KNOW IT HAS SOME CRAZY STUFF IN IT, DAD, BUT IT MEANS A LOT TO ME.
I DON'T UNDERSTAND IT BUT I'M TRYING TO BE SUPPORTIVE.
BY NOT BANNING IT?
BY NOT TALKING ABOUT IT TOO MUCH.
I DON'T AGREE WITH IT.
I CAN'T PRETEND I DO.
BUT IT'S YOUR CHOICE, IT SPEAKS TO YOU.
DAD, IT DOESN'T "SPEAK TO ME."
IT'S THE TRUTH.
I JUST WISH YOU COULD SEE THAT.
WHAT YOU'VE JUST READ IS THE TRUTH, PERNILLA?
COME ON...
THEY SAY IT'S BETTER IF PEOPLE FIND THEIR OWN WAY TO JESUS...
...BUT I KNOW YOU'RE NOT HAPPY, DAD.
I JUST WANT YOU TO BE HAPPY.
HMM.

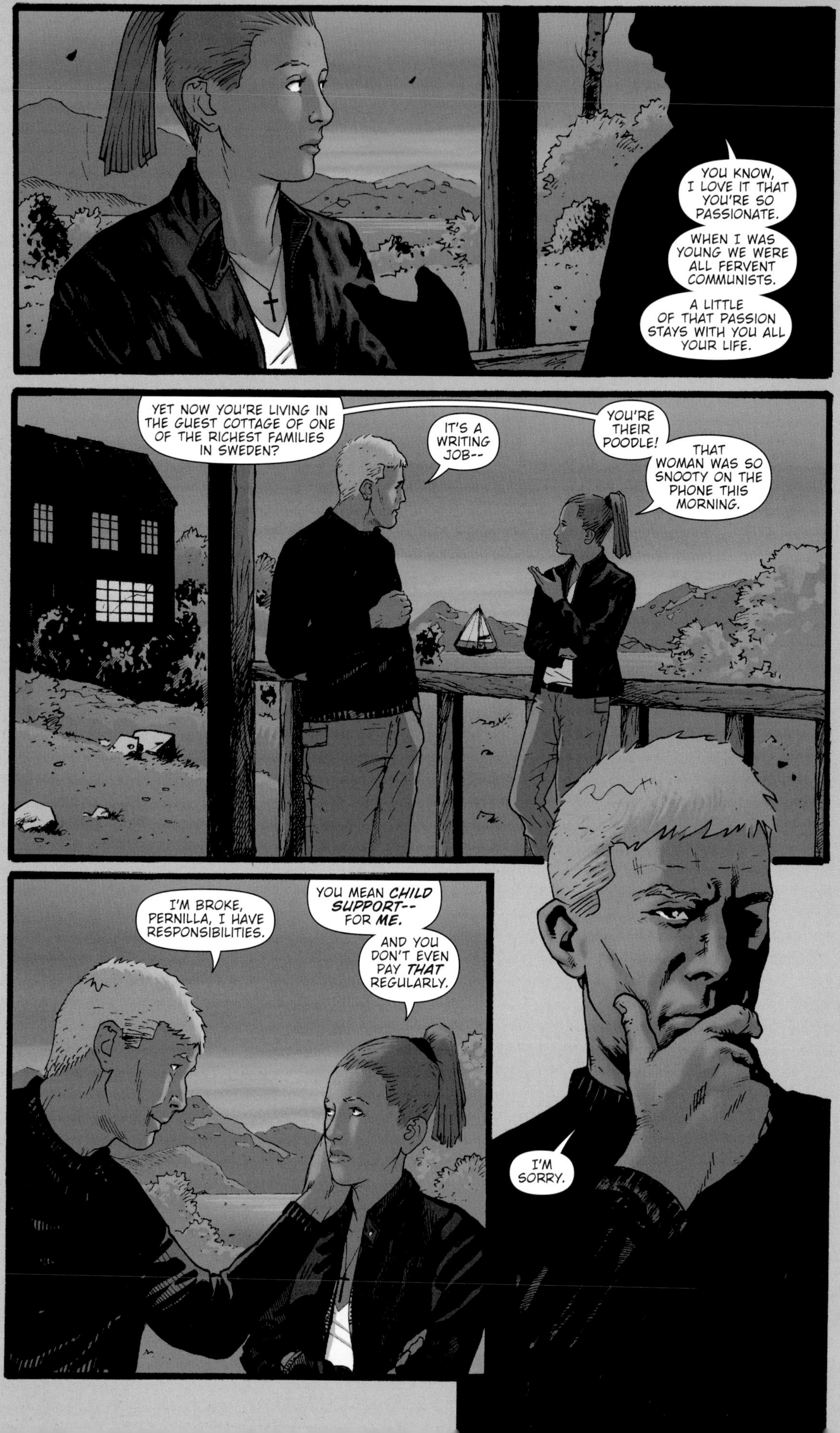
YOU KNOW, I LOVE IT THAT YOU'RE SO PASSIONATE.
WHEN I WAS YOUNG WE WERE ALL FERVENT COMMUNISTS.
A LITTLE OF THAT PASSION STAYS WITH YOU ALL YOUR LIFE.
YET NOW YOU'RE LIVING IN THE GUEST COTTAGE OF ONE OF THE RICHEST FAMILIES IN SWEDEN?
IT'S A WRITING JOB--
YOU'RE THEIR POODLE!
THAT WOMAN WAS SO SNOOTY ON THE PHONE THIS MORNING.
I'M BROKE, PERNILLA, I HAVE RESPONSIBILITIES.
YOU MEAN CHILD SUPPORT-- FOR ME.
AND YOU DON'T EVEN PAY THAT REGULARLY.
I'M SORRY.

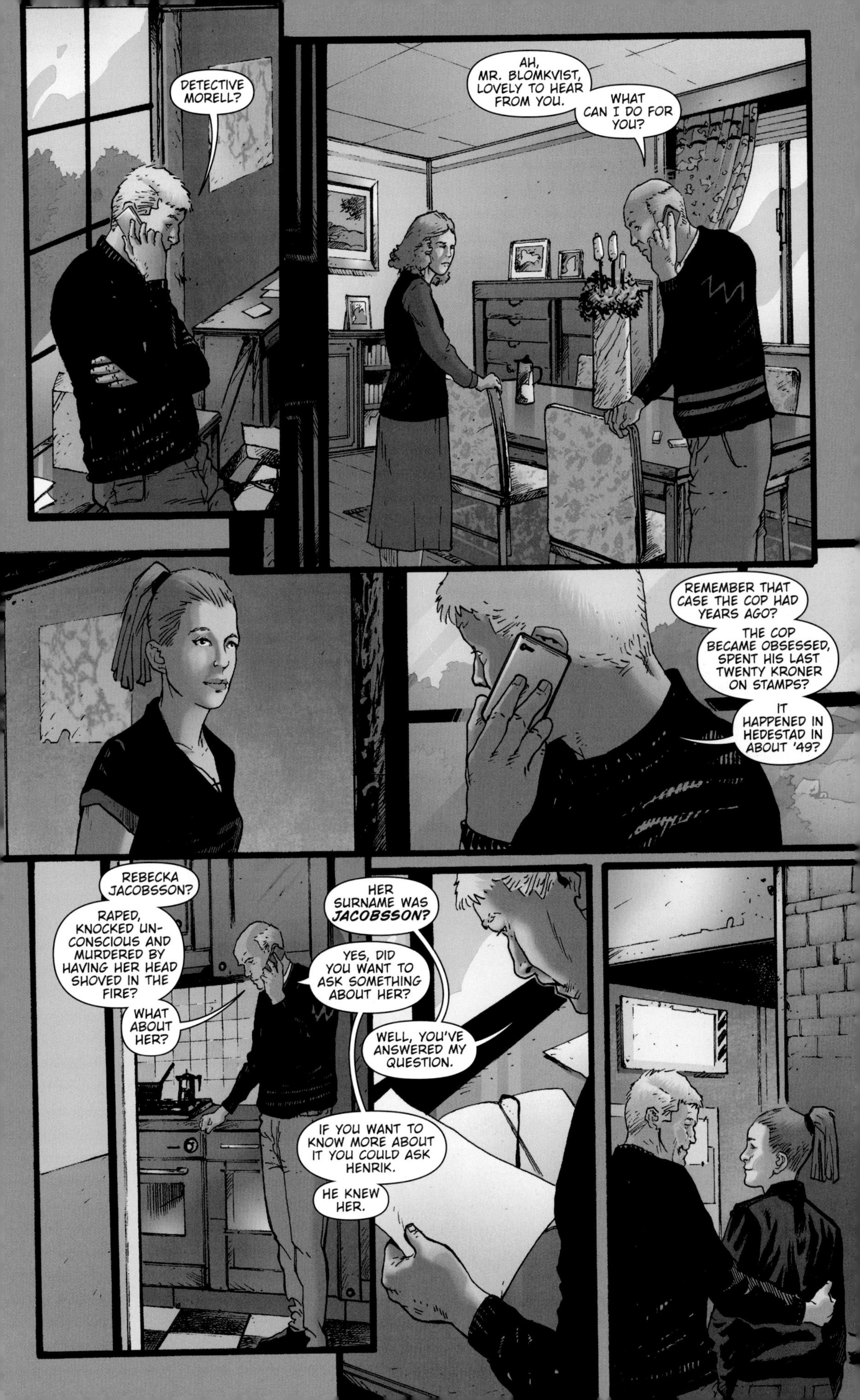
DETECTIVE MORELL?
AH, MR. BLOMKVIST, LOVELY TO HEAR FROM YOU.
WHAT CAN I DO FOR YOU?
REMEMBER THAT CASE THE COP HAD YEARS AGO?
THE COP BECAME OBSESSED, SPENT HIS LAST TWENTY KRONER ON STAMPS?
IT HAPPENED IN HEDESTAD IN ABOUT '49?
REBECKA JACOBSSON?
RAPED, KNOCKED UN-CONSCIOUS AND MURDERED BY HAVING HER HEAD SHOVED IN THE FIRE?
WHAT ABOUT HER?
HER SURNAME WAS *JACOBSSON?*
YES, DID YOU WANT TO ASK SOMETHING ABOUT HER?
WELL, YOU'VE ANSWERED MY QUESTION.
IF YOU WANT TO KNOW MORE ABOUT IT YOU COULD ASK HENRIK.
HE KNEW HER.

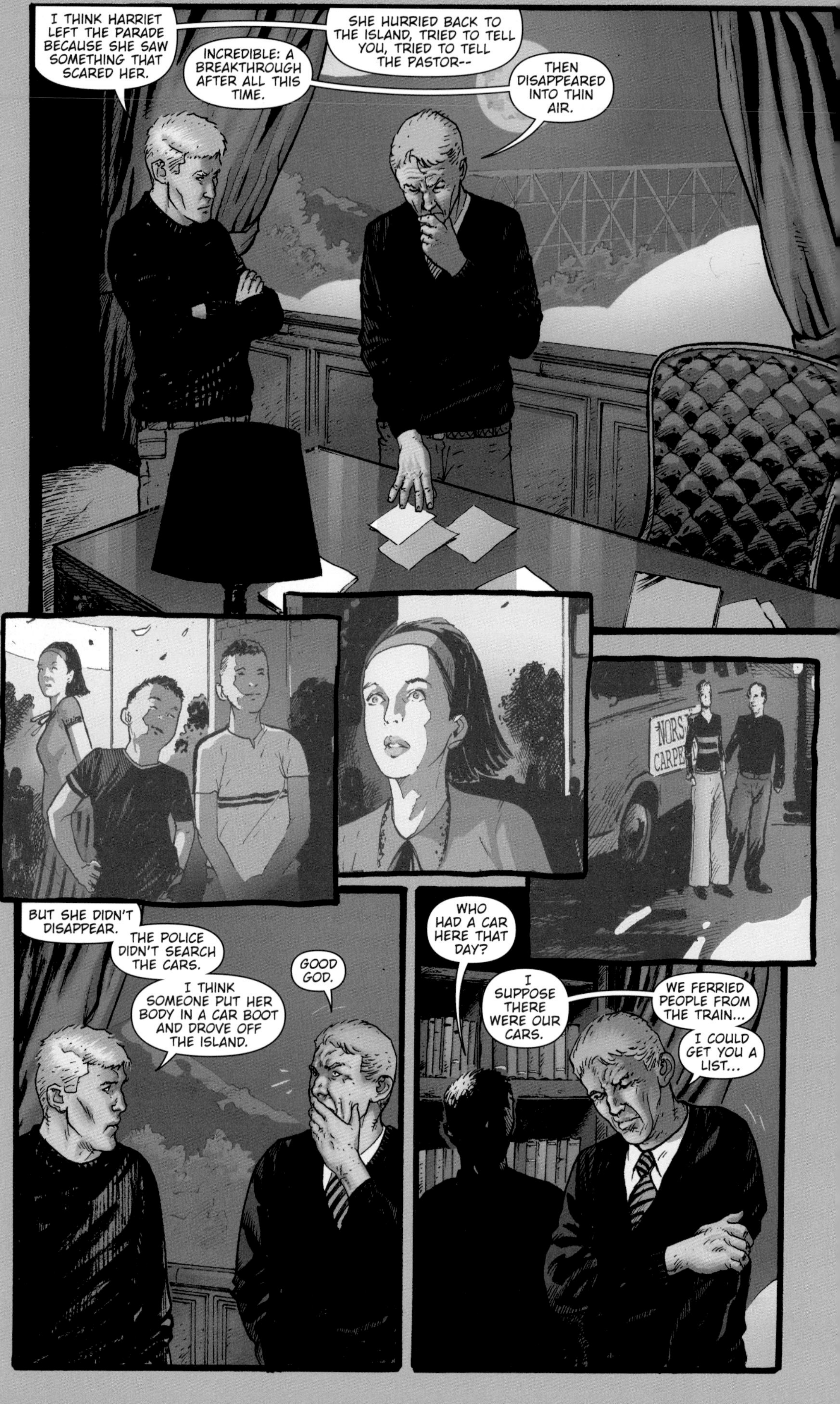
I THINK HARRIET LEFT THE PARADE BECAUSE SHE SAW SOMETHING THAT SCARED HER.
SHE HURRIED BACK TO THE ISLAND, TRIED TO TELL YOU, TRIED TO TELL THE PASTOR--
INCREDIBLE: A BREAKTHROUGH AFTER ALL THIS TIME.
THEN DISAPPEARED INTO THIN AIR.
BUT SHE DIDN'T DISAPPEAR.
THE POLICE DIDN'T SEARCH THE CARS.
I THINK SOMEONE PUT HER BODY IN A CAR BOOT AND DROVE OFF THE ISLAND.
GOOD GOD.
WHO HAD A CAR HERE THAT DAY?
I SUPPOSE THERE WERE OUR CARS.
WE FERRIED PEOPLE FROM THE TRAIN...
I COULD GET YOU A LIST...

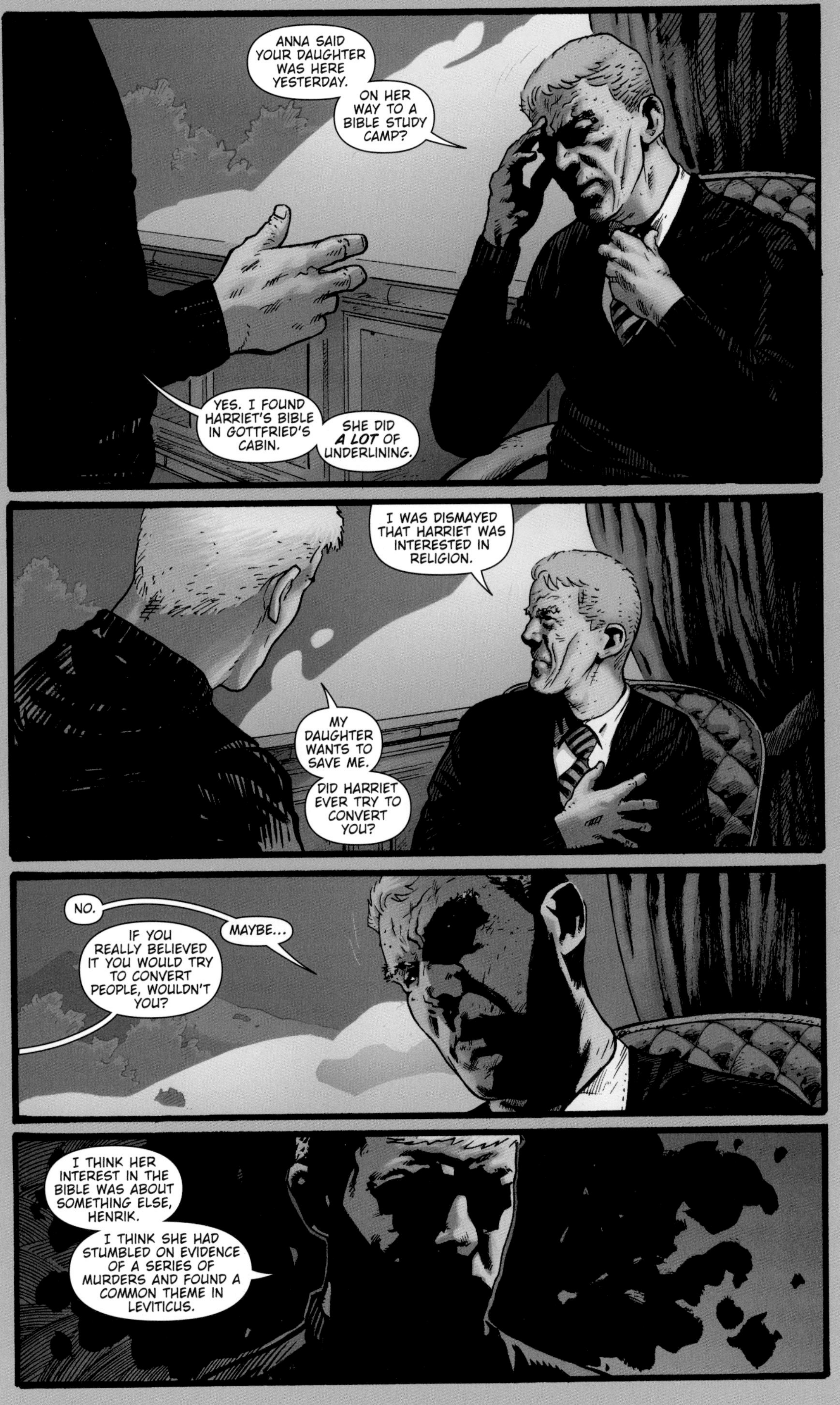

ANNA SAID YOUR DAUGHTER WAS HERE YESTERDAY.
ON HER WAY TO A BIBLE STUDY CAMP?
YES. I FOUND HARRIET'S BIBLE IN GOTTFRIED'S CABIN.
SHE DID *A LOT* OF UNDERLINING.
I WAS DISMAYED THAT HARRIET WAS INTERESTED IN RELIGION.
MY DAUGHTER WANTS TO SAVE ME.
DID HARRIET EVER TRY TO CONVERT YOU?
NO.
MAYBE...
IF YOU REALLY BELIEVED IT YOU WOULD TRY TO CONVERT PEOPLE, WOULDN'T YOU?
I THINK HER INTEREST IN THE BIBLE WAS ABOUT SOMETHING ELSE, HENRIK.
I THINK SHE HAD STUMBLED ON EVIDENCE OF A SERIES OF MURDERS AND FOUND A COMMON THEME IN LEVITICUS.

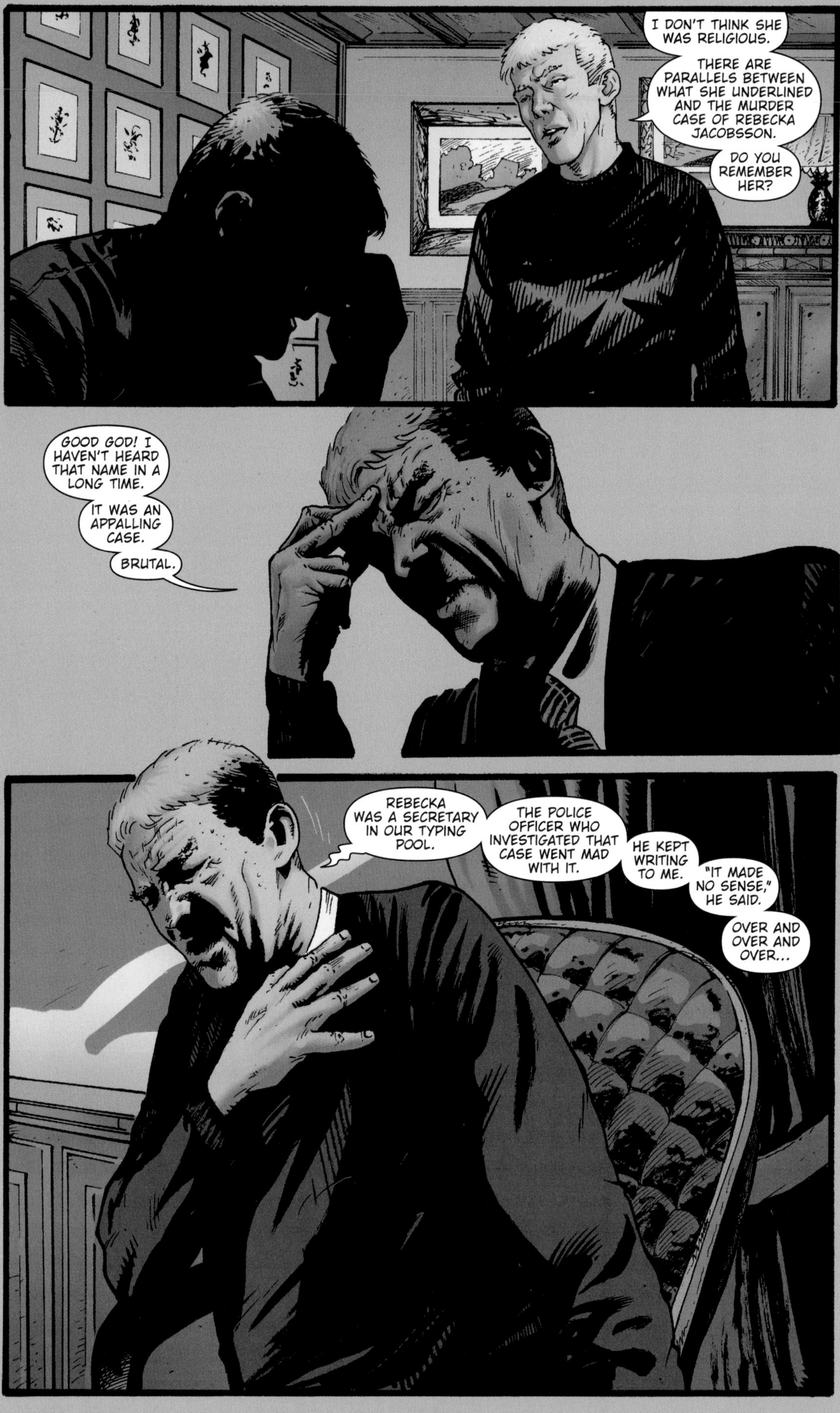
I DON'T THINK SHE WAS RELIGIOUS.
THERE ARE PARALLELS BETWEEN WHAT SHE UNDERLINED AND THE MURDER CASE OF REBECKA JACOBSSON.
DO YOU REMEMBER HER?
GOOD GOD! I HAVEN'T HEARD THAT NAME IN A LONG TIME.
IT WAS AN APPALLING CASE.
BRUTAL.
REBECKA WAS A SECRETARY IN OUR TYPING POOL.
THE POLICE OFFICER WHO INVESTIGATED THAT CASE WENT MAD WITH IT.
HE KEPT WRITING TO ME.
"IT MADE NO SENSE," HE SAID.
OVER AND OVER AND OVER...

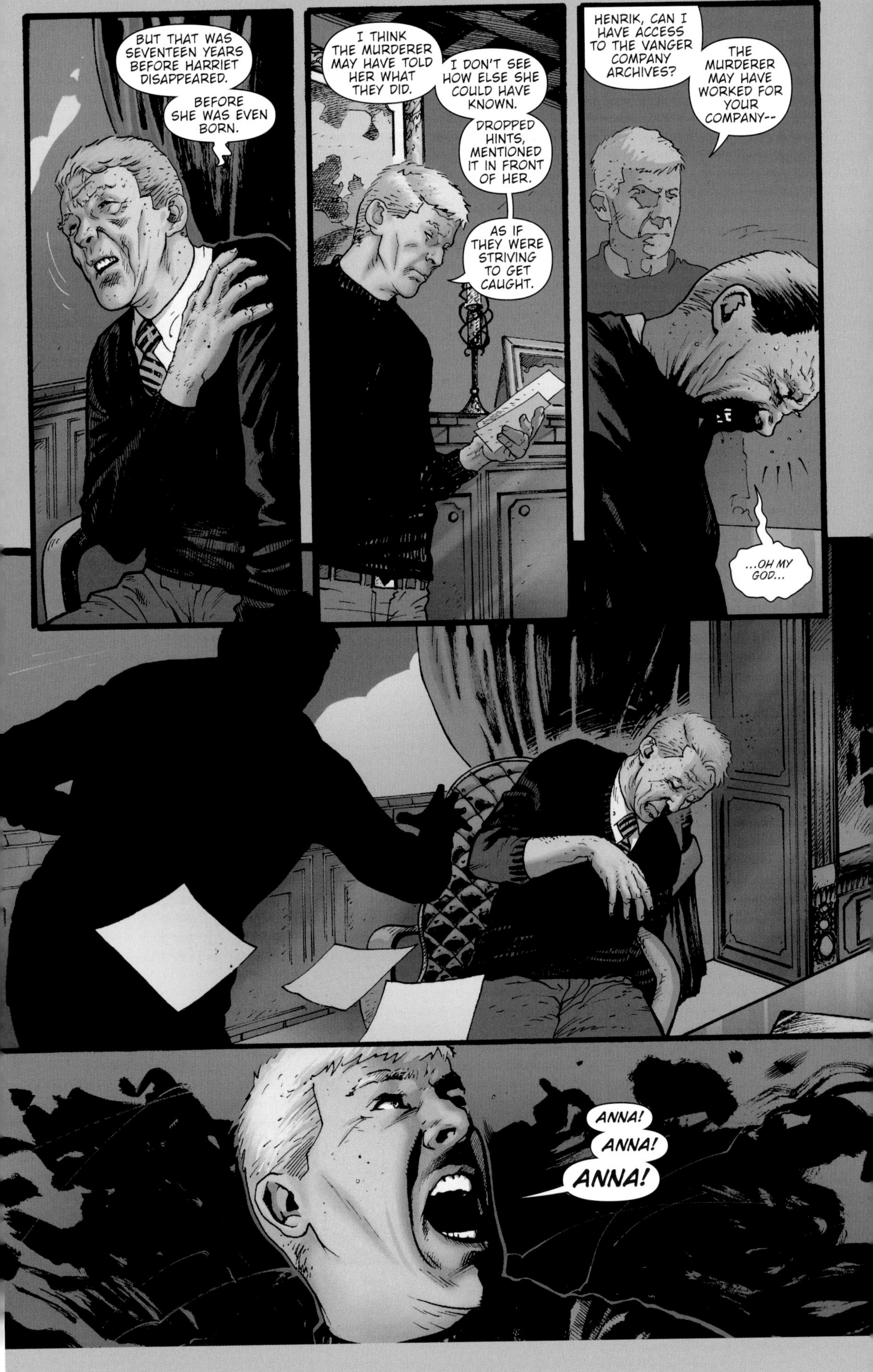
BUT THAT WAS SEVENTEEN YEARS BEFORE HARRIET DISAPPEARED.
BEFORE SHE WAS EVEN BORN.
I THINK THE MURDERER MAY HAVE TOLD HER WHAT THEY DID.
I DON'T SEE HOW ELSE SHE COULD HAVE KNOWN.
DROPPED HINTS, MENTIONED IT IN FRONT OF HER.
AS IF THEY WERE STRIVING TO GET CAUGHT.
HENRIK, CAN I HAVE ACCESS TO THE VANGER COMPANY ARCHIVES?
THE MURDERER MAY HAVE WORKED FOR YOUR COMPANY--
...OH MY GOD...
ANNA!
ANNA!
ANNA!

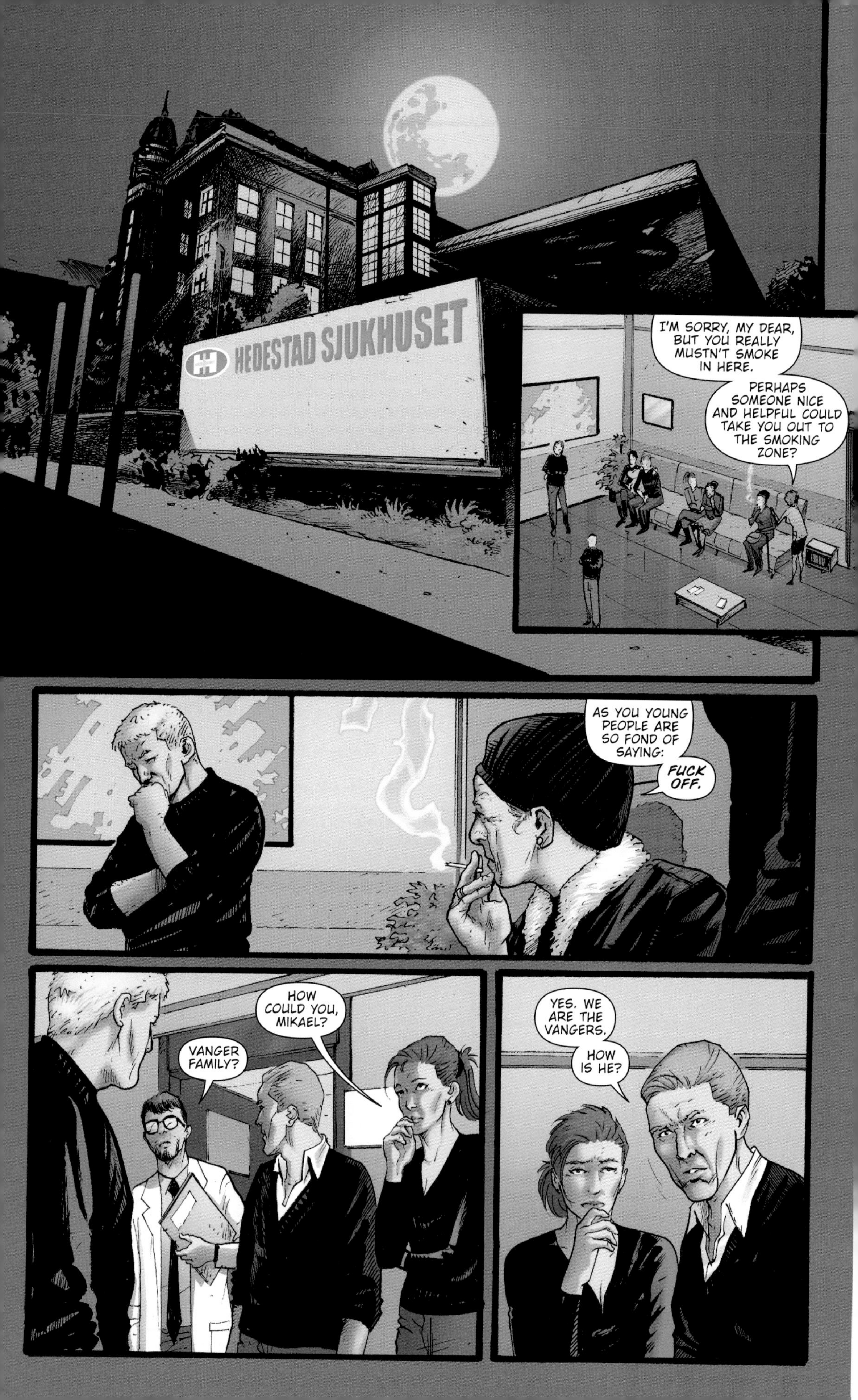
HEDESTAD SJUKHUSET
I'M SORRY, MY DEAR, BUT YOU REALLY MUSTN'T SMOKE IN HERE.
PERHAPS SOMEONE NICE AND HELPFUL COULD TAKE YOU OUT TO THE SMOKING ZONE?
AS YOU YOUNG PEOPLE ARE SO FOND OF SAYING:
FUCK OFF.
VANGER FAMILY?
HOW COULD YOU, MIKAEL?
YES. WE ARE THE VANGERS.
HOW IS HE?

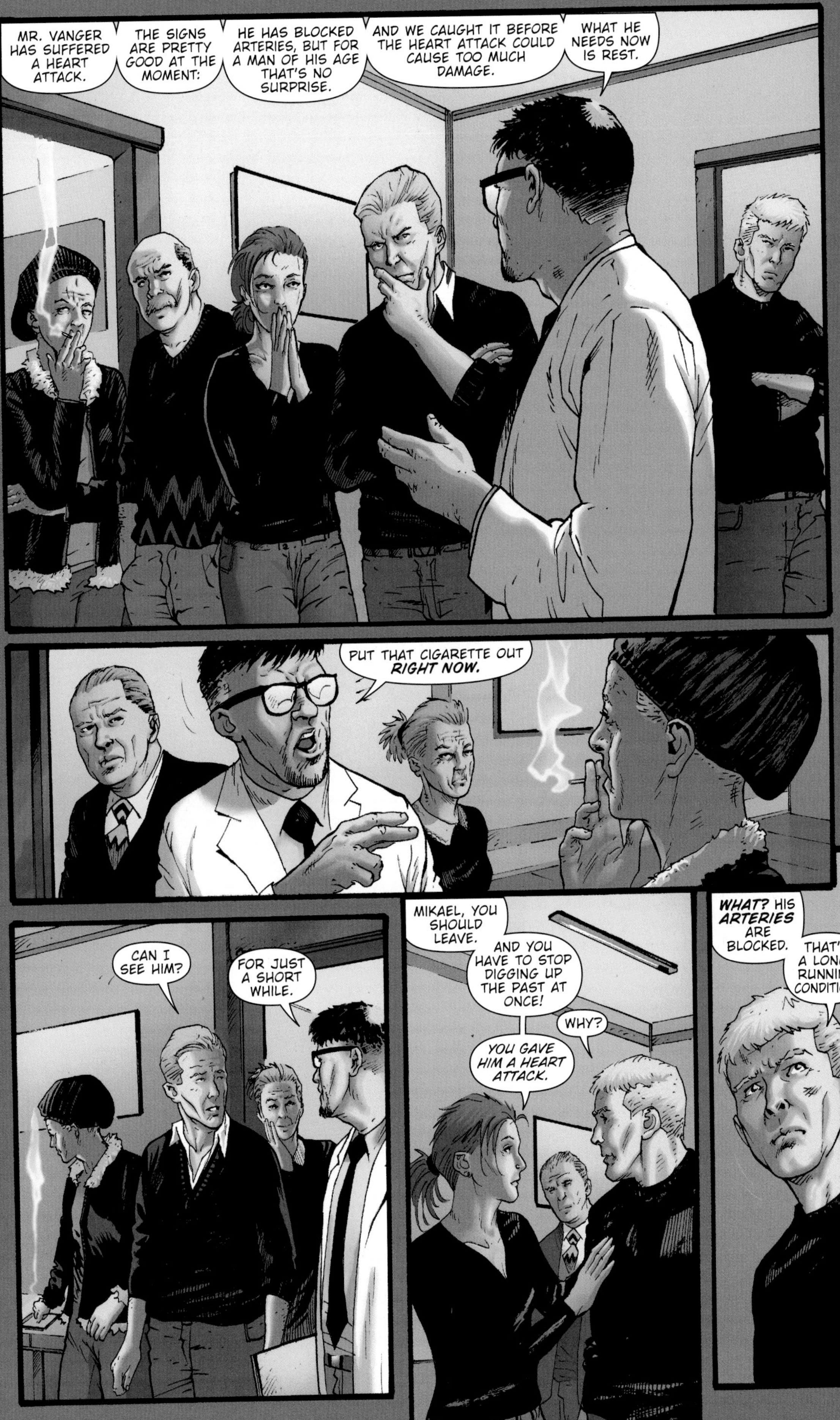
MR. VANGER HAS SUFFERED A HEART ATTACK.
THE SIGNS ARE PRETTY GOOD AT THE MOMENT:
HE HAS BLOCKED ARTERIES, BUT FOR A MAN OF HIS AGE THAT'S NO SURPRISE.
AND WE CAUGHT IT BEFORE THE HEART ATTACK COULD CAUSE TOO MUCH DAMAGE.
WHAT HE NEEDS NOW IS REST.
PUT THAT CIGARETTE OUT *RIGHT NOW.*
CAN I SEE HIM?
FOR JUST A SHORT WHILE.
MIKAEL, YOU SHOULD LEAVE.
AND YOU HAVE TO STOP DIGGING UP THE PAST AT ONCE!
WHY?
YOU GAVE HIM A HEART ATTACK.
WHAT? HIS *ARTERIES* ARE BLOCKED.
THAT'S A LONG-RUNNING CONDITION.

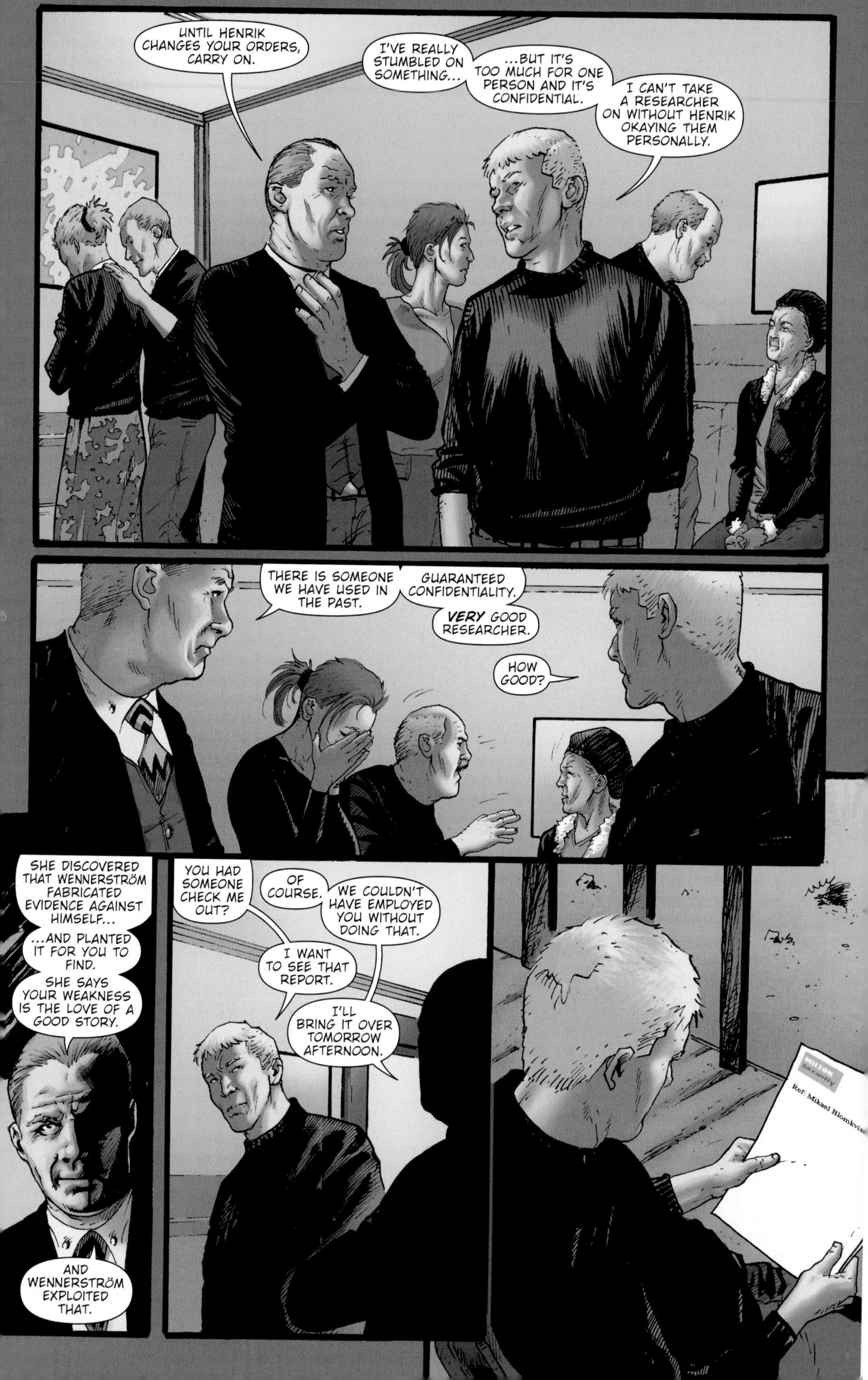
UNTIL HENRIK CHANGES YOUR ORDERS, CARRY ON.
I'VE REALLY STUMBLED ON SOMETHING...
...BUT IT'S TOO MUCH FOR ONE PERSON AND IT'S CONFIDENTIAL.
I CAN'T TAKE A RESEARCHER ON WITHOUT HENRIK OKAYING THEM PERSONALLY.
THERE IS SOMEONE WE HAVE USED IN THE PAST.
GUARANTEED CONFIDENTIALITY.
VERY GOOD RESEARCHER.
HOW GOOD?
SHE DISCOVERED THAT WENNERSTRÖM FABRICATED EVIDENCE AGAINST HIMSELF...
...AND PLANTED IT FOR YOU TO FIND.
SHE SAYS YOUR WEAKNESS IS THE LOVE OF A GOOD STORY.
AND WENNERSTRÖM EXPLOITED THAT.
YOU HAD SOMEONE CHECK ME OUT?
OF COURSE.
WE COULDN'T HAVE EMPLOYED YOU WITHOUT DOING THAT.
I WANT TO SEE THAT REPORT.
I'LL BRING IT OVER TOMORROW AFTERNOON.
MILTON Security
Ref: Mikael Blomkvis

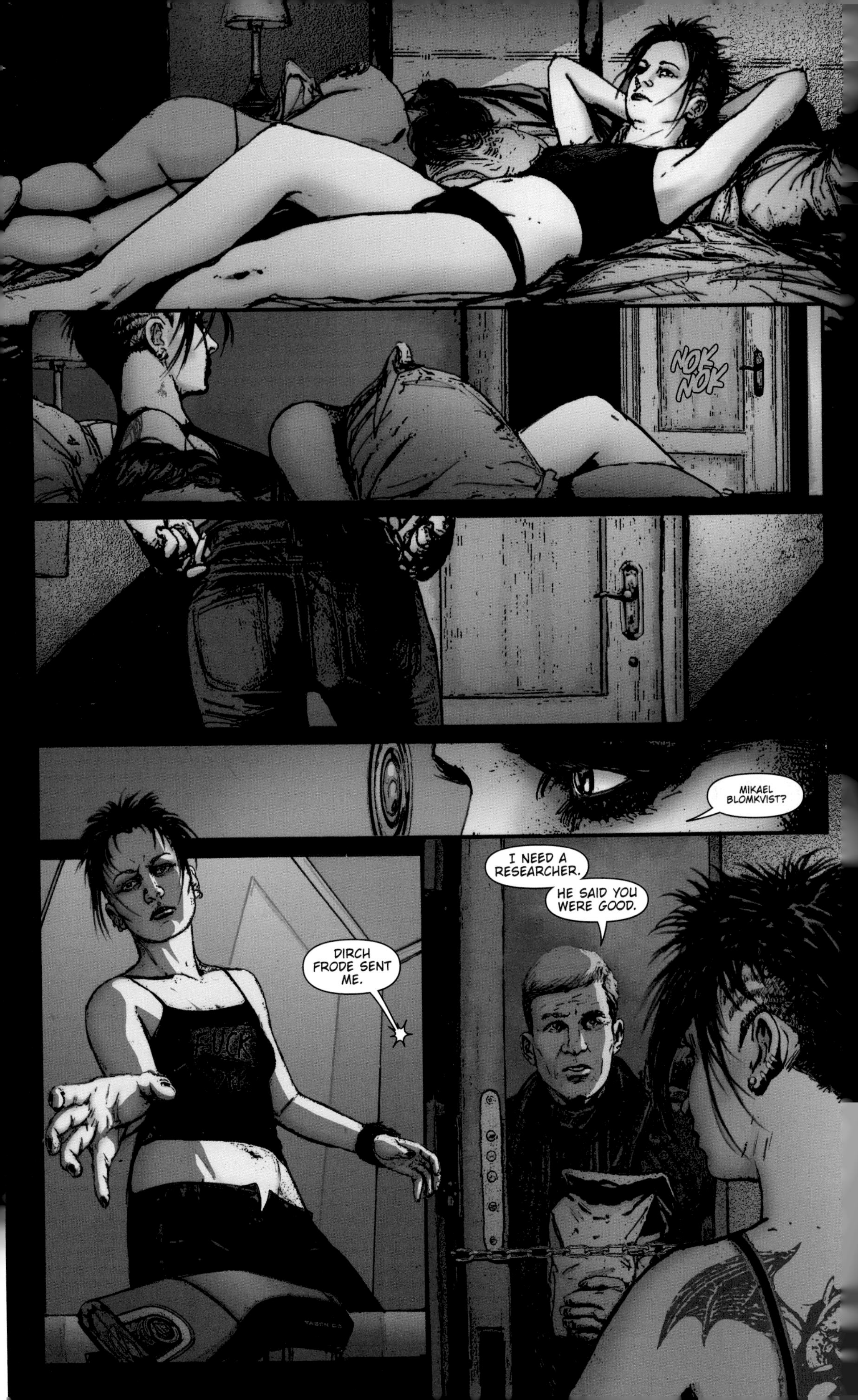
NOK NOK
MIKAEL BLOMKVIST?
DIRCH FRODE SENT ME.
I NEED A RESEARCHER.
HE SAID YOU WERE GOOD.

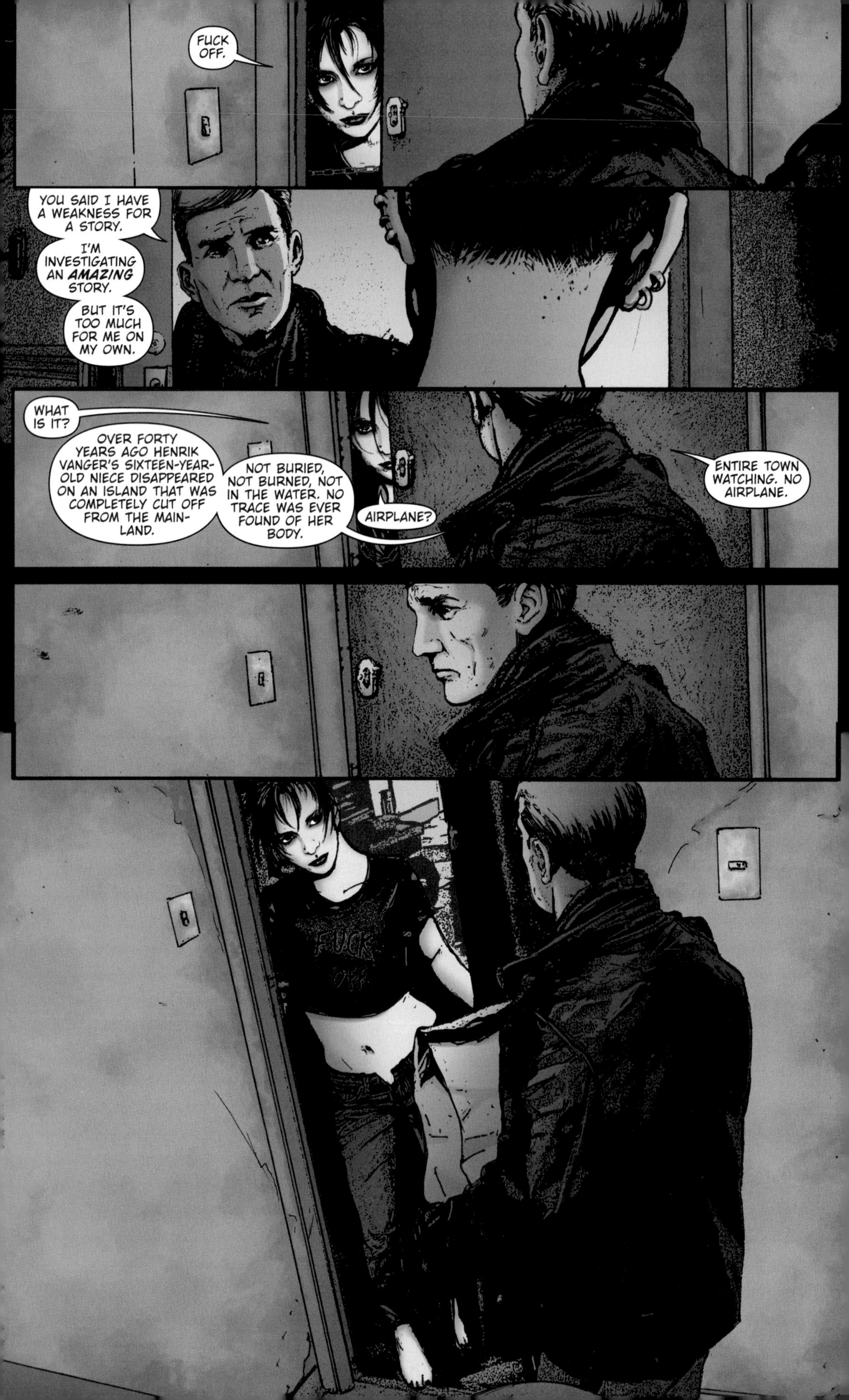
FUCK OFF.
YOU SAID I HAVE A WEAKNESS FOR A STORY.
I'M INVESTIGATING AN *AMAZING* STORY.
BUT IT'S TOO MUCH FOR ME ON MY OWN.
WHAT IS IT?
OVER FORTY YEARS AGO HENRIK VANGER'S SIXTEEN-YEAR-OLD NIECE DISAPPEARED ON AN ISLAND THAT WAS COMPLETELY CUT OFF FROM THE MAIN-LAND.
NOT BURIED, NOT BURNED, NOT IN THE WATER. NO TRACE WAS EVER FOUND OF HER BODY.
AIRPLANE?
ENTIRE TOWN WATCHING. NO AIRPLANE.
FUCK OFF

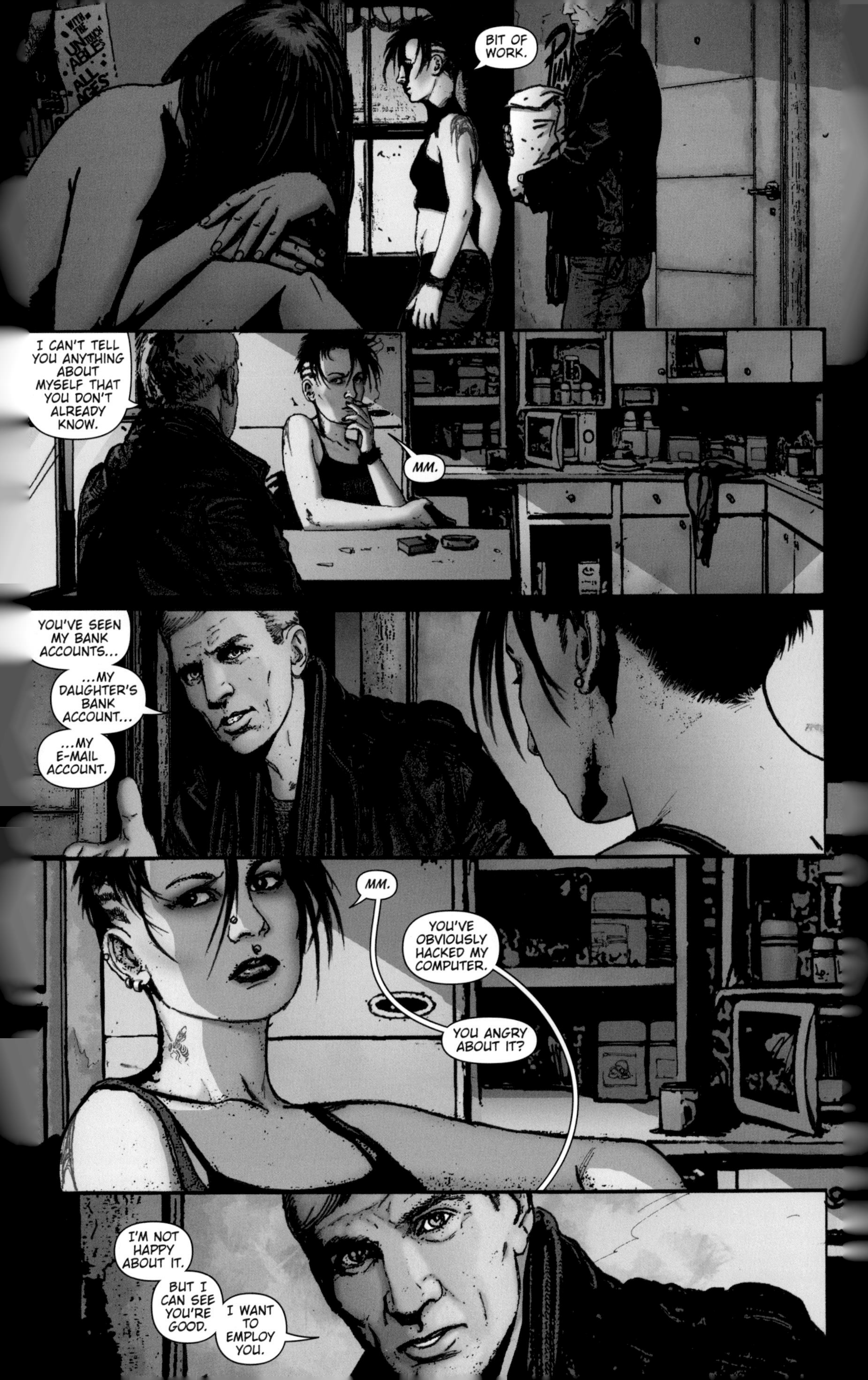
WITH THE UNTOUCHABLES ALL AGES
BIT OF WORK.
I CAN'T TELL YOU ANYTHING ABOUT MYSELF THAT YOU DON'T ALREADY KNOW.
MM.
YOU'VE SEEN MY BANK ACCOUNTS...
...MY DAUGHTER'S BANK ACCOUNT...
...MY E-MAIL ACCOUNT.
MM.
YOU'VE OBVIOUSLY HACKED MY COMPUTER.
YOU ANGRY ABOUT IT?
I'M NOT HAPPY ABOUT IT.
BUT I CAN SEE YOU'RE GOOD.
I WANT TO EMPLOY YOU.

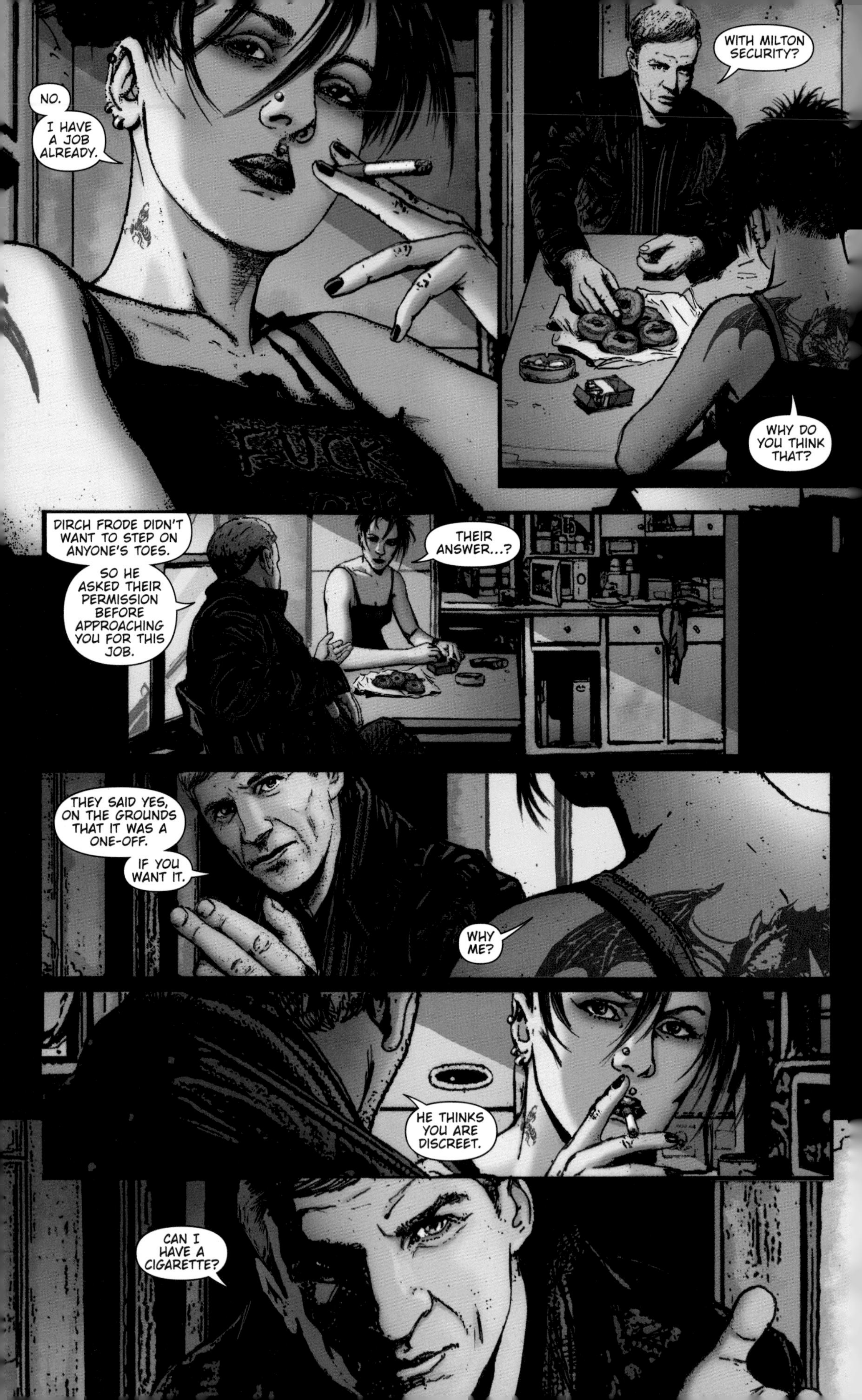
NO.
I HAVE A JOB ALREADY.
FUCK
WITH MILTON SECURITY?
WHY DO YOU THINK THAT?
DIRCH FRODE DIDN'T WANT TO STEP ON ANYONE'S TOES.
SO HE ASKED THEIR PERMISSION BEFORE APPROACHING YOU FOR THIS JOB.
THEIR ANSWER...?
THEY SAID YES, ON THE GROUNDS THAT IT WAS A ONE-OFF.
IF YOU WANT IT.
WHY ME?
HE THINKS YOU ARE DISCREET.
CAN I HAVE A CIGARETTE?

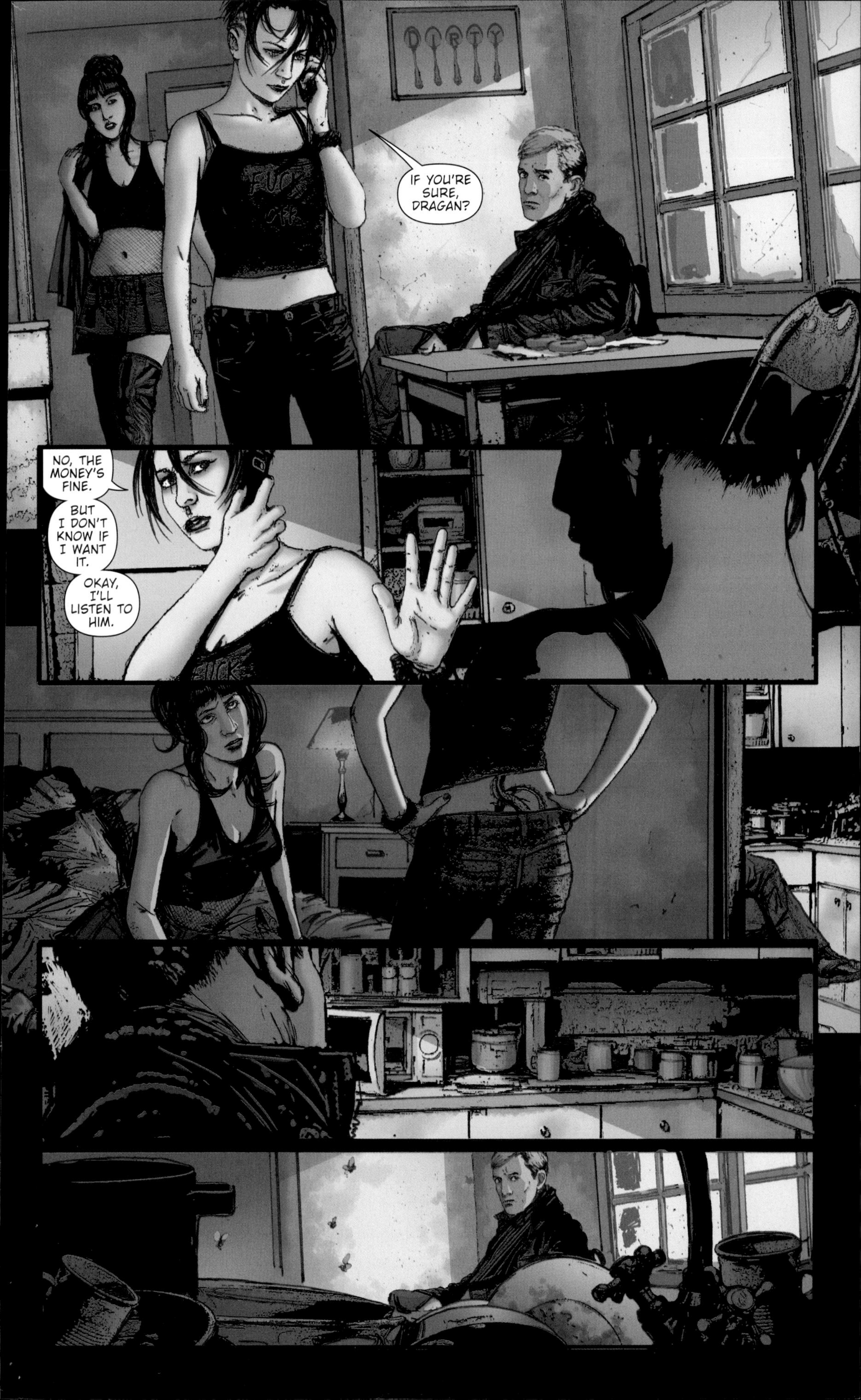
DIRTY
IF YOU'RE SURE, DRAGAN?
NO, THE MONEY'S FINE.
BUT I DON'T KNOW IF I WANT IT.
OKAY, I'LL LISTEN TO HIM.

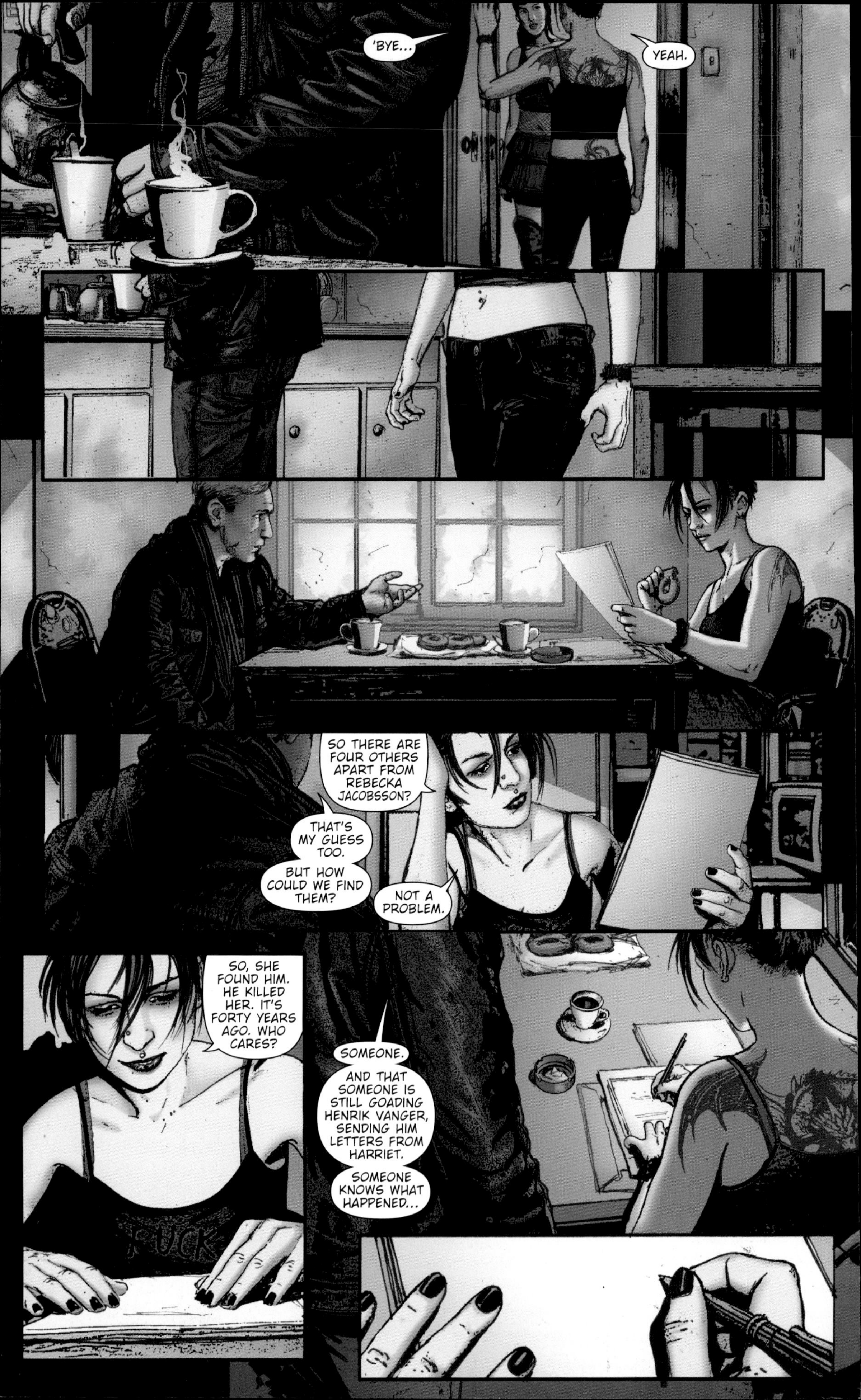
'BYE...
YEAH.
SO THERE ARE FOUR OTHERS APART FROM REBECKA JACOBSSON?
THAT'S MY GUESS TOO.
BUT HOW COULD WE FIND THEM?
NOT A PROBLEM.
SO, SHE FOUND HIM. HE KILLED HER. IT'S FORTY YEARS AGO. WHO CARES?
SOMEONE.
AND THAT SOMEONE IS STILL GOADING HENRIK VANGER, SENDING HIM LETTERS FROM HARRIET.
SOMEONE KNOWS WHAT HAPPENED...

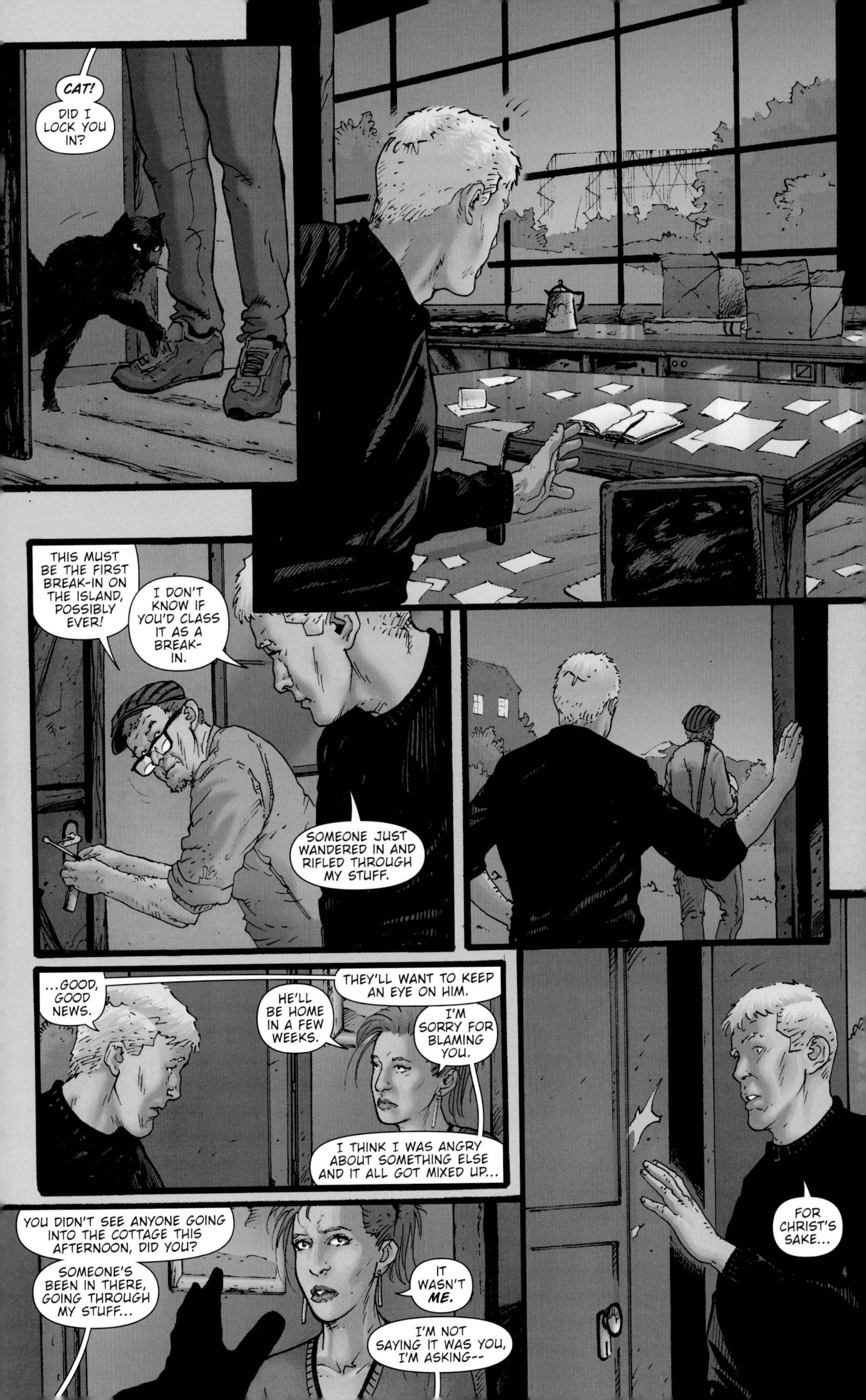
CAT!
DID I LOCK YOU IN?
THIS MUST BE THE FIRST BREAK-IN ON THE ISLAND, POSSIBLY EVER!
I DON'T KNOW IF YOU'D CLASS IT AS A BREAK-IN.
SOMEONE JUST WANDERED IN AND RIFLED THROUGH MY STUFF.
...GOOD, GOOD NEWS.
THEY'LL WANT TO KEEP AN EYE ON HIM.
HE'LL BE HOME IN A FEW WEEKS.
I'M SORRY FOR BLAMING YOU.
I THINK I WAS ANGRY ABOUT SOMETHING ELSE AND IT ALL GOT MIXED UP...
FOR CHRIST'S SAKE...
YOU DIDN'T SEE ANYONE GOING INTO THE COTTAGE THIS AFTERNOON, DID YOU?
SOMEONE'S BEEN IN THERE, GOING THROUGH MY STUFF...
IT WASN'T ME.
I'M NOT SAYING IT WAS YOU, I'M ASKING--

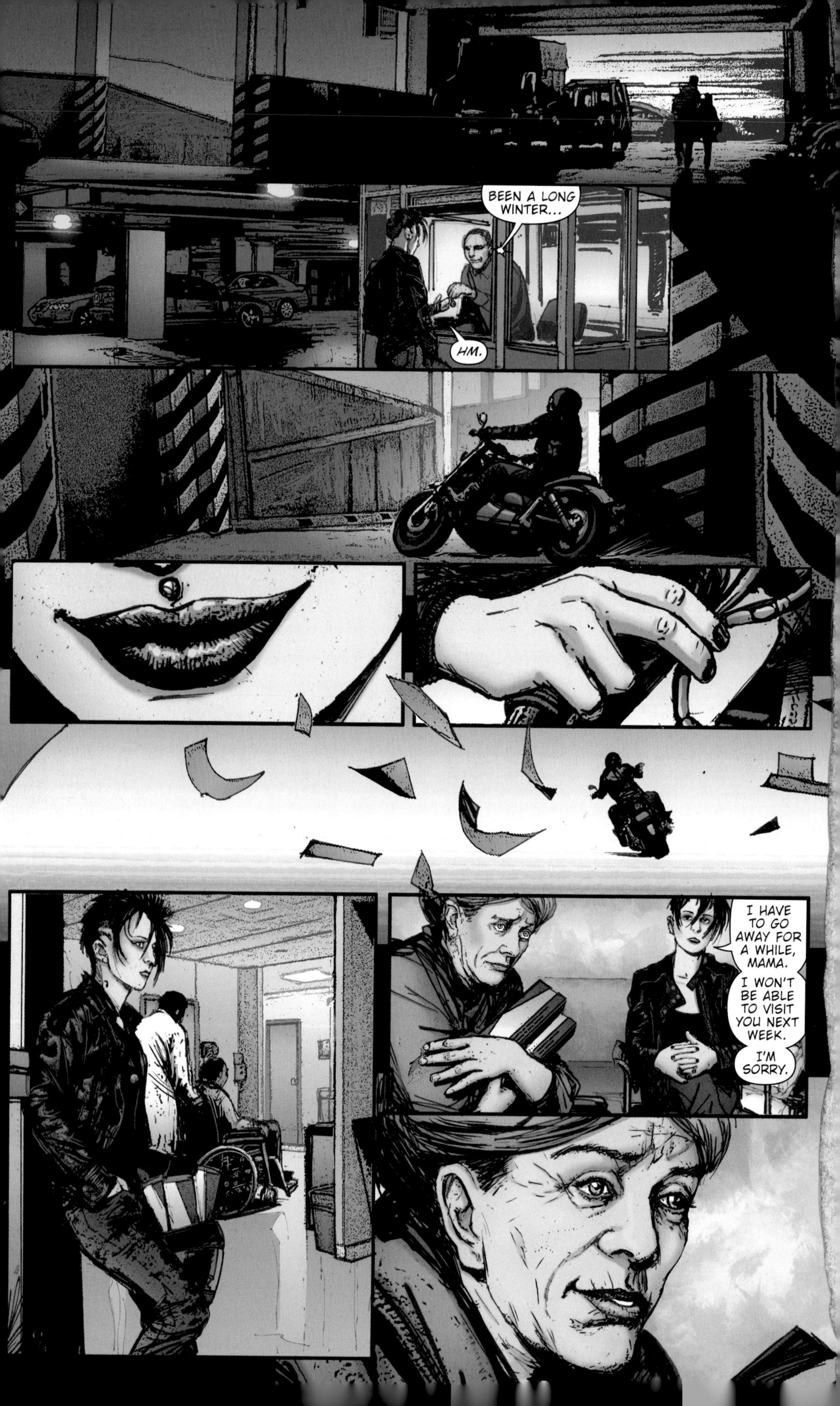
BEEN A LONG WINTER...
HM.
I HAVE TO GO AWAY FOR A WHILE, MAMA.
I WON'T BE ABLE TO VISIT YOU NEXT WEEK.
I'M SORRY.

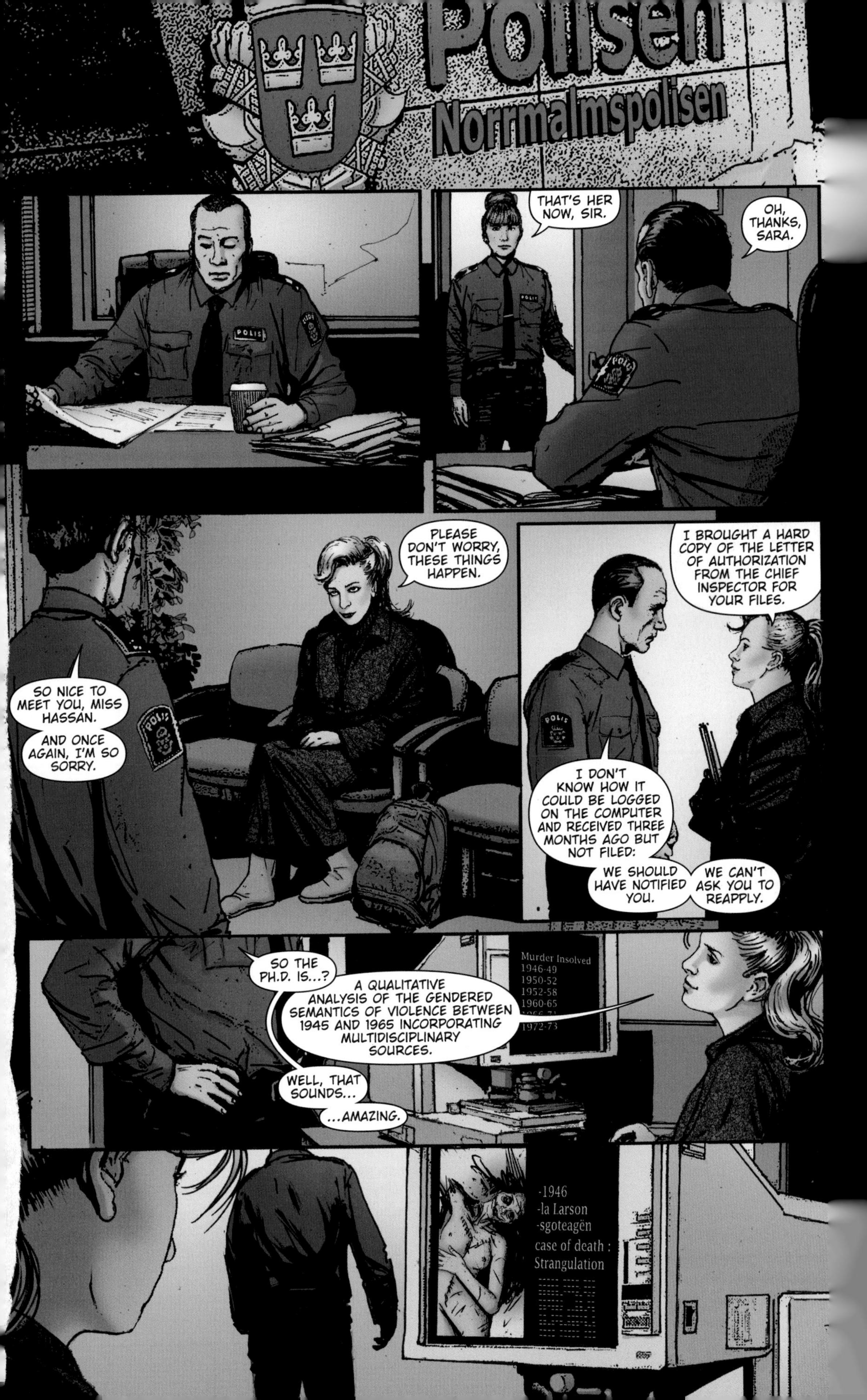
Polisen
Norrmalmspolisen
POLIS
THAT'S HER NOW, SIR.
OH, THANKS, SARA.
PLEASE DON'T WORRY, THESE THINGS HAPPEN.
SO NICE TO MEET YOU, MISS HASSAN.
AND ONCE AGAIN, I'M SO SORRY.
I BROUGHT A HARD COPY OF THE LETTER OF AUTHORIZATION FROM THE CHIEF INSPECTOR FOR YOUR FILES.
I DON'T KNOW HOW IT COULD BE LOGGED ON THE COMPUTER AND RECEIVED THREE MONTHS AGO BUT NOT FILED:
WE SHOULD HAVE NOTIFIED YOU.
WE CAN'T ASK YOU TO REAPPLY.
Murder Insolved
1946-49
1950-52
1952-58
1960-65
1972-73
SO THE PH.D. IS...?
A QUALITATIVE ANALYSIS OF THE GENDERED SEMANTICS OF VIOLENCE BETWEEN 1945 AND 1965 INCORPORATING MULTIDISCIPLINARY SOURCES.
WELL, THAT SOUNDS...
...AMAZING.
-1946
-la Larson
-sgoteagën
case of death :
Strangulation

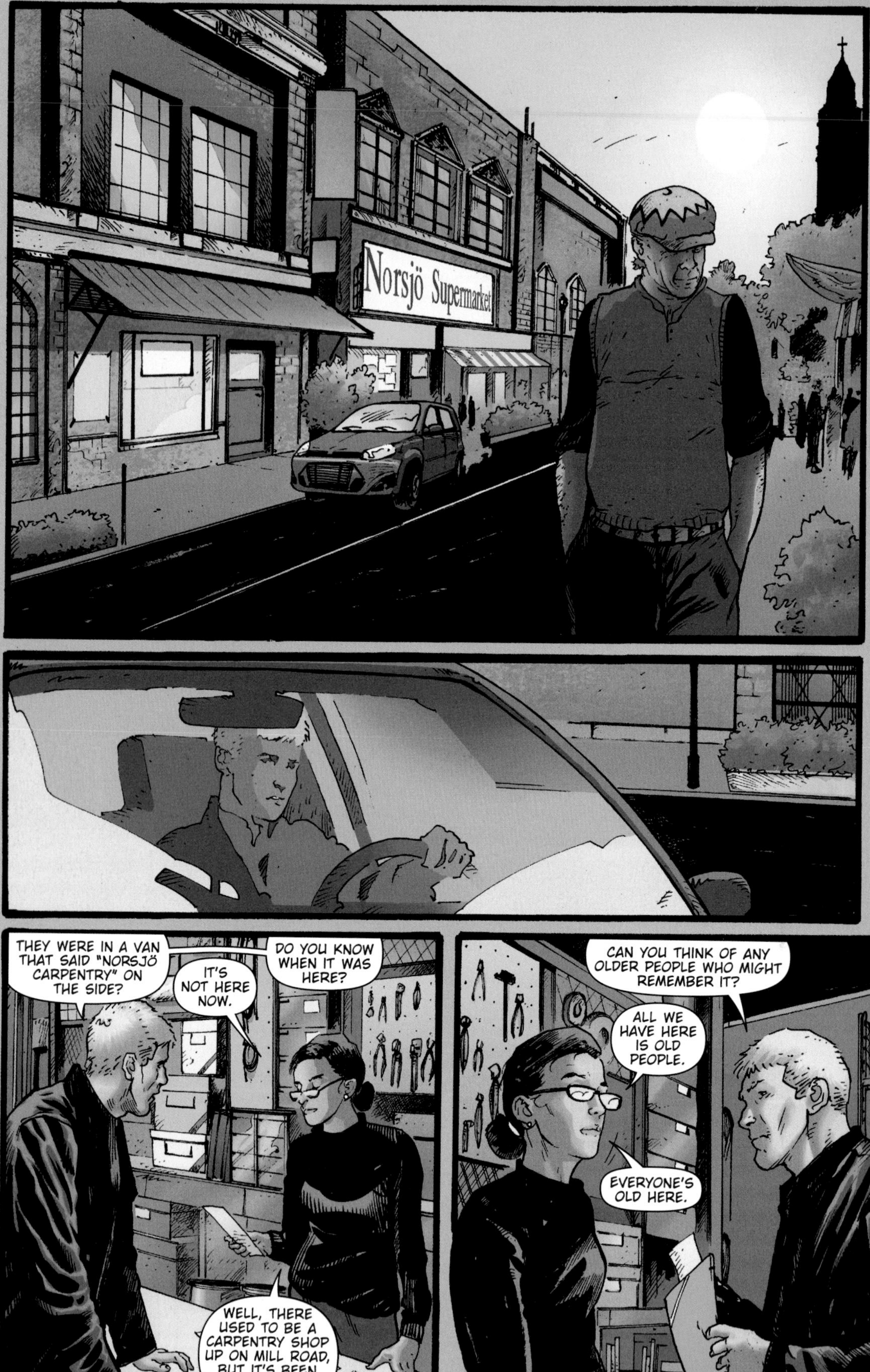
Norsjö Supermarket
THEY WERE IN A VAN THAT SAID "NORSJÖ CARPENTRY" ON THE SIDE?
IT'S NOT HERE NOW.
DO YOU KNOW WHEN IT WAS HERE?
WELL, THERE USED TO BE A CARPENTRY SHOP UP ON MILL ROAD, BUT IT'S BEEN SHUT A LONG TIME.
CAN YOU THINK OF ANY OLDER PEOPLE WHO MIGHT REMEMBER IT?
ALL WE HAVE HERE IS OLD PEOPLE.
EVERYONE'S OLD HERE.

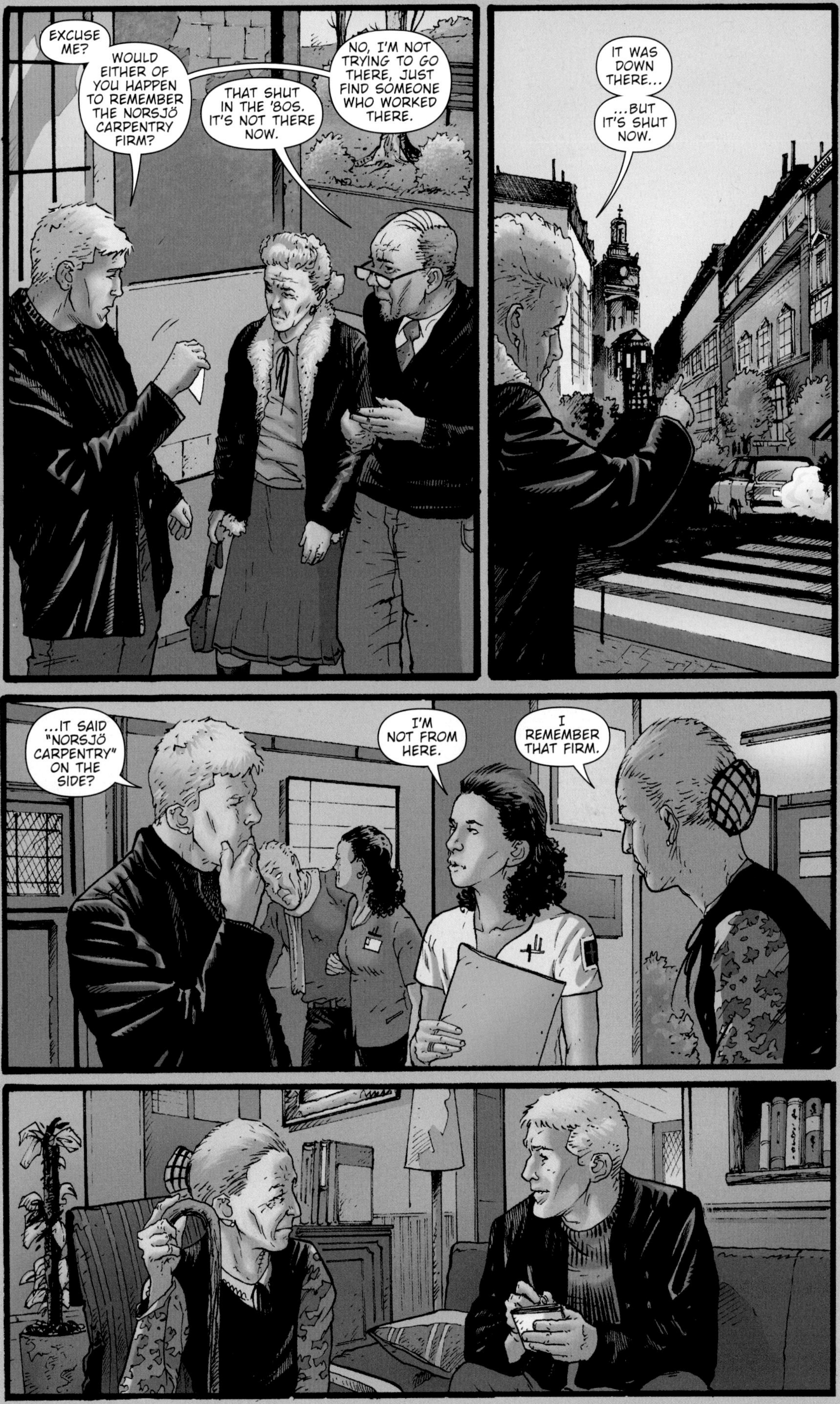
EXCUSE ME?
WOULD EITHER OF YOU HAPPEN TO REMEMBER THE NORSJÖ CARPENTRY FIRM?
THAT SHUT IN THE '80S. IT'S NOT THERE NOW.
NO, I'M NOT TRYING TO GO THERE, JUST FIND SOMEONE WHO WORKED THERE.
IT WAS DOWN THERE...
...BUT IT'S SHUT NOW.
...IT SAID "NORSJÖ CARPENTRY" ON THE SIDE?
I'M NOT FROM HERE.
I REMEMBER THAT FIRM.

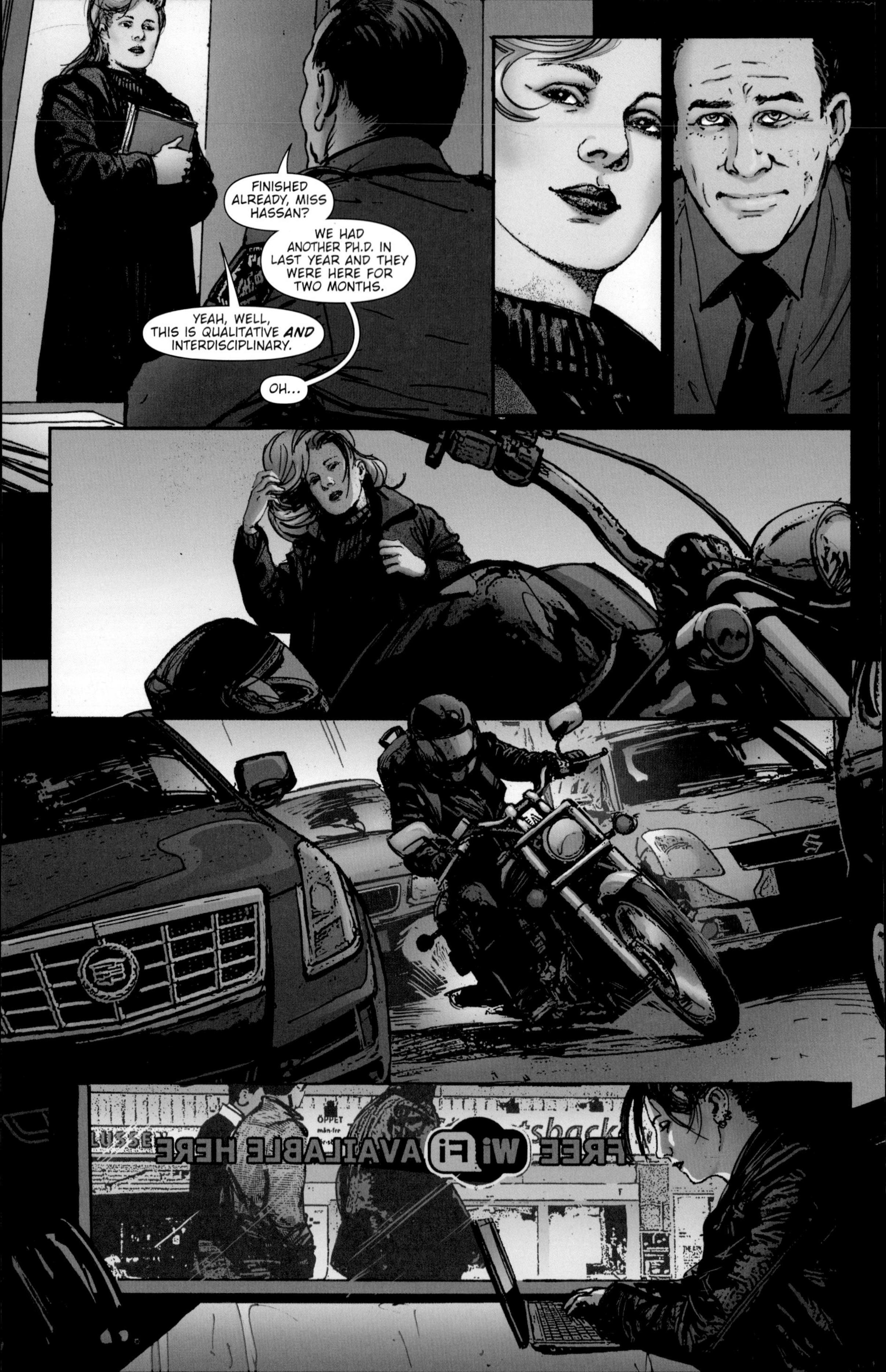

FINISHED ALREADY, MISS HASSAN?
WE HAD ANOTHER PH.D. IN LAST YEAR AND THEY WERE HERE FOR TWO MONTHS.
YEAH, WELL, THIS IS QUALITATIVE ***AND*** INTERDISCIPLINARY.
OH...
FREE WiFi AVAILABLE HERE
ÖPPET

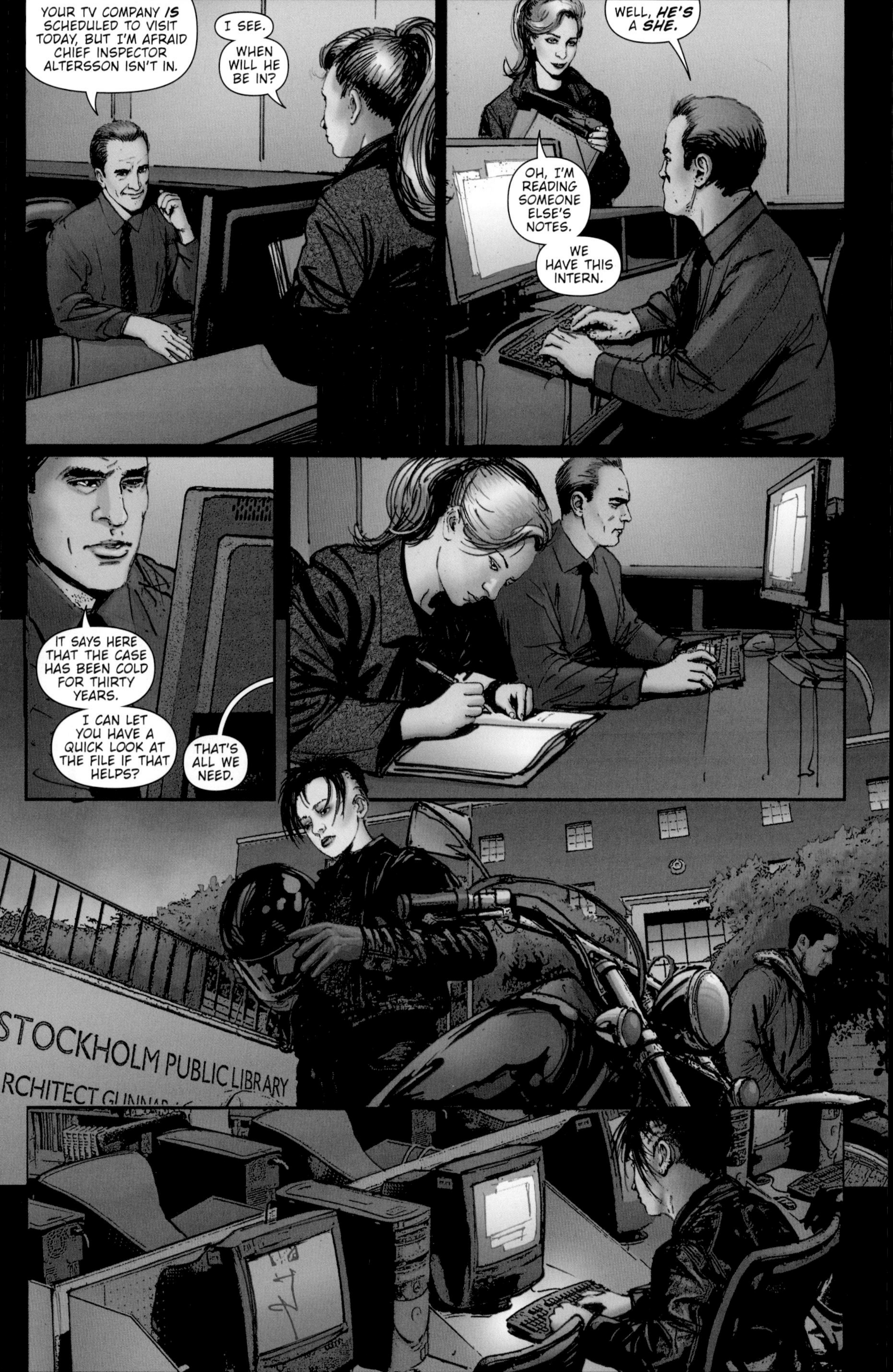
YOUR TV COMPANY IS SCHEDULED TO VISIT TODAY, BUT I'M AFRAID CHIEF INSPECTOR ALTERSSON ISN'T IN.
I SEE.
WHEN WILL HE BE IN?
WELL, HE'S A SHE.
OH, I'M READING SOMEONE ELSE'S NOTES.
WE HAVE THIS INTERN.
IT SAYS HERE THAT THE CASE HAS BEEN COLD FOR THIRTY YEARS.
I CAN LET YOU HAVE A QUICK LOOK AT THE FILE IF THAT HELPS?
THAT'S ALL WE NEED.
STOCKHOLM PUBLIC LIBRARY
RCHITECT GUNNAR

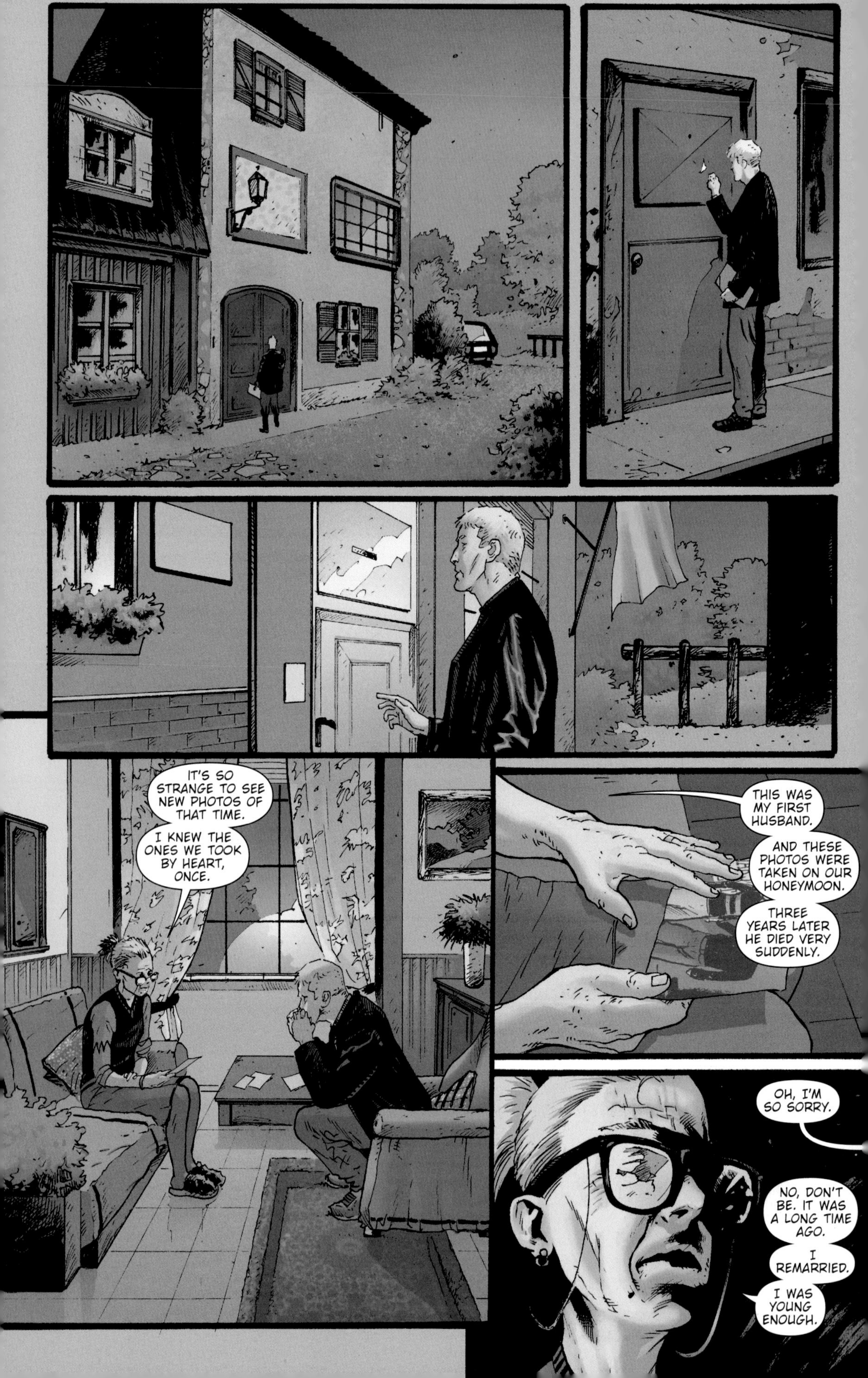
IT'S SO STRANGE TO SEE NEW PHOTOS OF THAT TIME.
I KNEW THE ONES WE TOOK BY HEART, ONCE.
THIS WAS MY FIRST HUSBAND.
AND THESE PHOTOS WERE TAKEN ON OUR HONEYMOON.
THREE YEARS LATER HE DIED VERY SUDDENLY.
OH, I'M SO SORRY.
NO, DON'T BE. IT WAS A LONG TIME AGO.
I REMARRIED.
I WAS YOUNG ENOUGH.

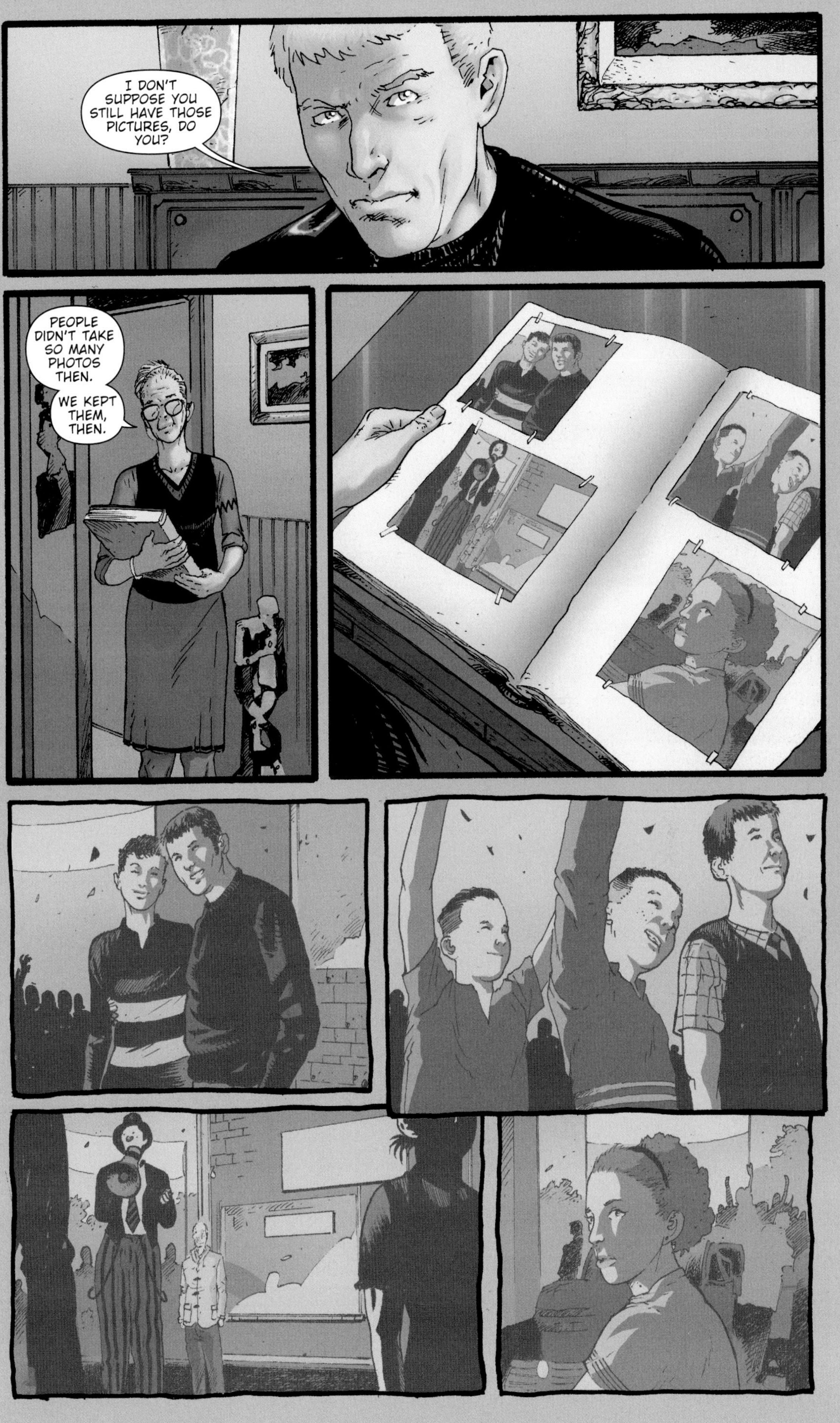
I DON'T SUPPOSE YOU STILL HAVE THOSE PICTURES, DO YOU?
PEOPLE DIDN'T TAKE SO MANY PHOTOS THEN.
WE KEPT THEM, THEN.

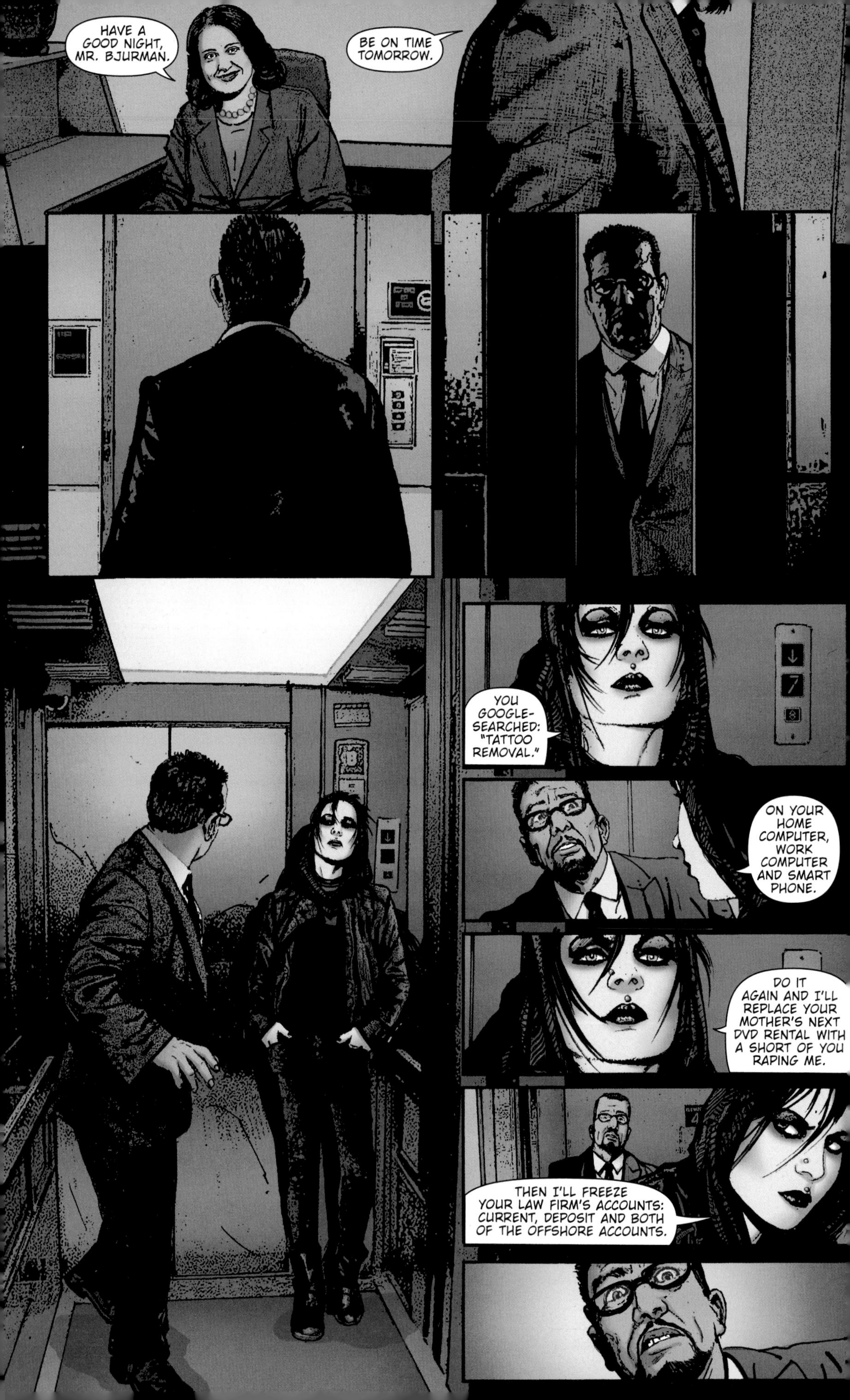
HAVE A GOOD NIGHT, MR. BJURMAN.
BE ON TIME TOMORROW.
YOU GOOGLE-SEARCHED: "TATTOO REMOVAL."
ON YOUR HOME COMPUTER, WORK COMPUTER AND SMART PHONE.
DO IT AGAIN AND I'LL REPLACE YOUR MOTHER'S NEXT DVD RENTAL WITH A SHORT OF YOU RAPING ME.
THEN I'LL FREEZE YOUR LAW FIRM'S ACCOUNTS: CURRENT, DEPOSIT AND BOTH OF THE OFFSHORE ACCOUNTS.

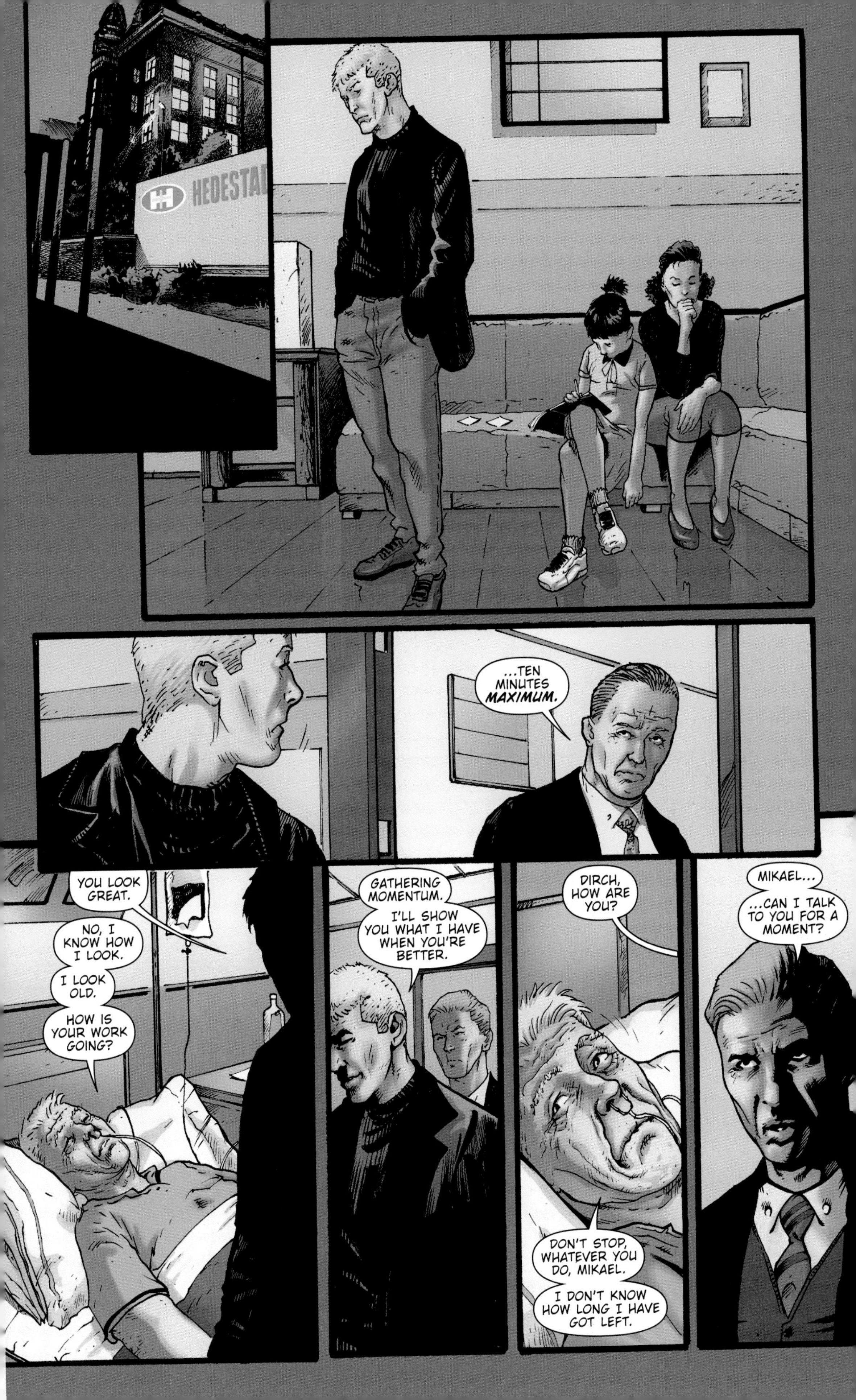
HEDESTAD
...TEN MINUTES MAXIMUM.
YOU LOOK GREAT.
NO, I KNOW HOW I LOOK.
I LOOK OLD.
HOW IS YOUR WORK GOING?
GATHERING MOMENTUM.
I'LL SHOW YOU WHAT I HAVE WHEN YOU'RE BETTER.
DIRCH, HOW ARE YOU?
DON'T STOP, WHATEVER YOU DO, MIKAEL.
I DON'T KNOW HOW LONG I HAVE GOT LEFT.
MIKAEL...
...CAN I TALK TO YOU FOR A MOMENT?

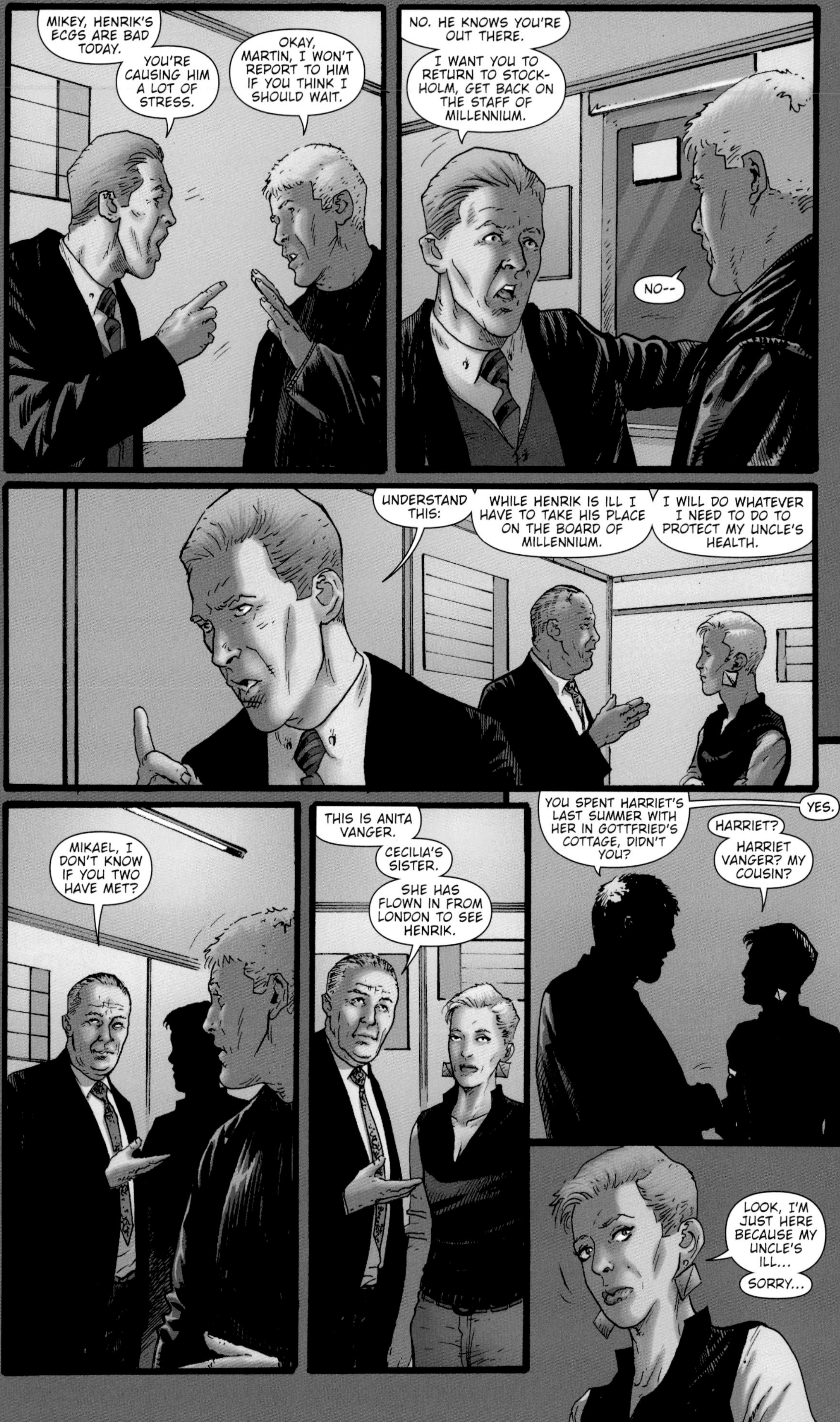
MIKEY, HENRIK'S ECGS ARE BAD TODAY.
YOU'RE CAUSING HIM A LOT OF STRESS.
OKAY, MARTIN, I WON'T REPORT TO HIM IF YOU THINK I SHOULD WAIT.
NO. HE KNOWS YOU'RE OUT THERE.
I WANT YOU TO RETURN TO STOCK-HOLM, GET BACK ON THE STAFF OF MILLENNIUM.
NO--
UNDERSTAND THIS:
WHILE HENRIK IS ILL I HAVE TO TAKE HIS PLACE ON THE BOARD OF MILLENNIUM.
I WILL DO WHATEVER I NEED TO DO TO PROTECT MY UNCLE'S HEALTH.
MIKAEL, I DON'T KNOW IF YOU TWO HAVE MET?
THIS IS ANITA VANGER.
CECILIA'S SISTER.
SHE HAS FLOWN IN FROM LONDON TO SEE HENRIK.
YOU SPENT HARRIET'S LAST SUMMER WITH HER IN GOTTFRIED'S COTTAGE, DIDN'T YOU?
YES.
HARRIET?
HARRIET VANGER? MY COUSIN?
LOOK, I'M JUST HERE BECAUSE MY UNCLE'S ILL...
SORRY...

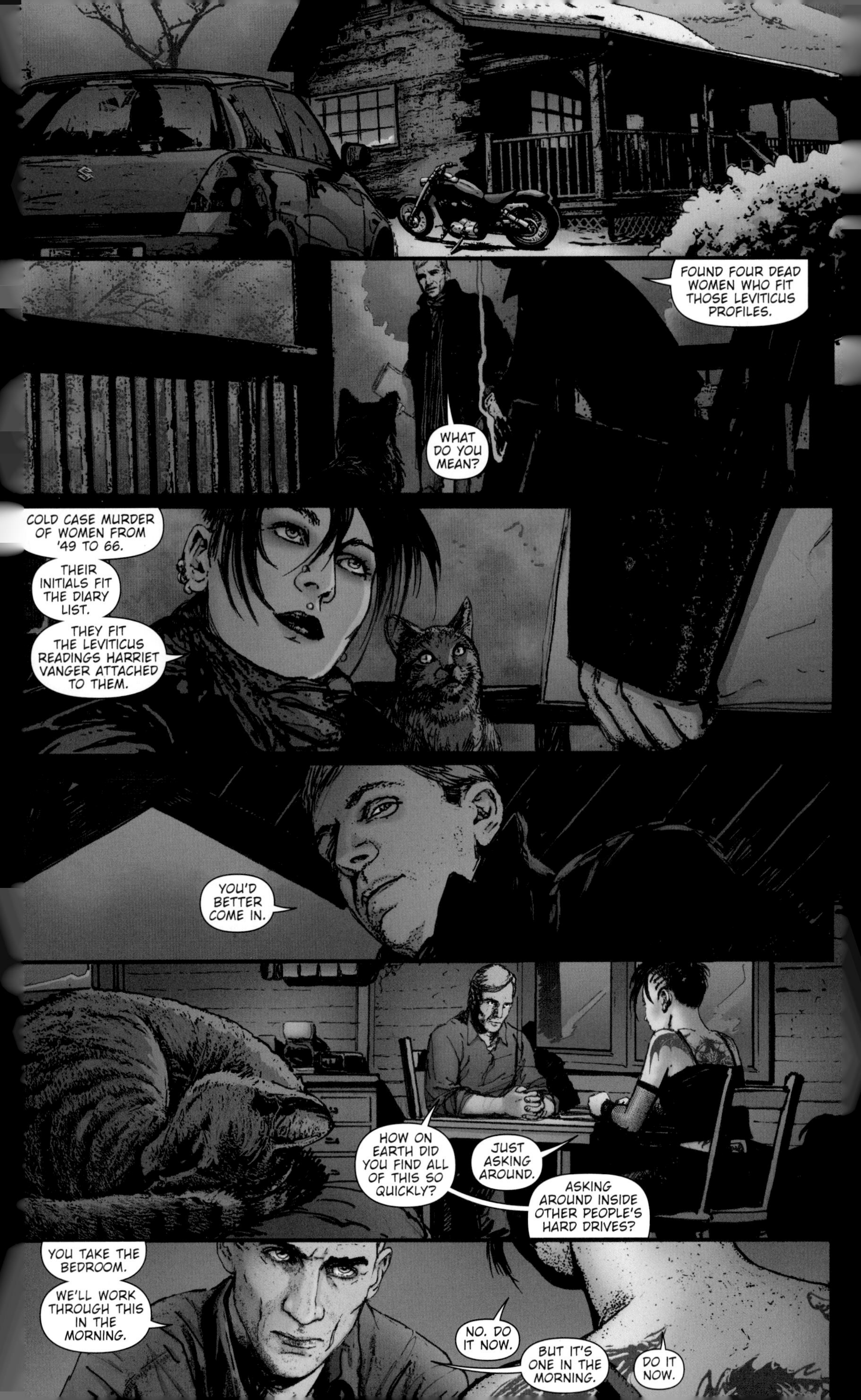
FOUND FOUR DEAD WOMEN WHO FIT THOSE LEVITICUS PROFILES.
WHAT DO YOU MEAN?
COLD CASE MURDER OF WOMEN FROM '49 TO 66.
THEIR INITIALS FIT THE DIARY LIST.
THEY FIT THE LEVITICUS READINGS HARRIET VANGER ATTACHED TO THEM.
YOU'D BETTER COME IN.
HOW ON EARTH DID YOU FIND ALL OF THIS SO QUICKLY?
JUST ASKING AROUND.
ASKING AROUND INSIDE OTHER PEOPLE'S HARD DRIVES?
YOU TAKE THE BEDROOM.
WE'LL WORK THROUGH THIS IN THE MORNING.
NO. DO IT NOW.
BUT IT'S ONE IN THE MORNING.
DO IT NOW.

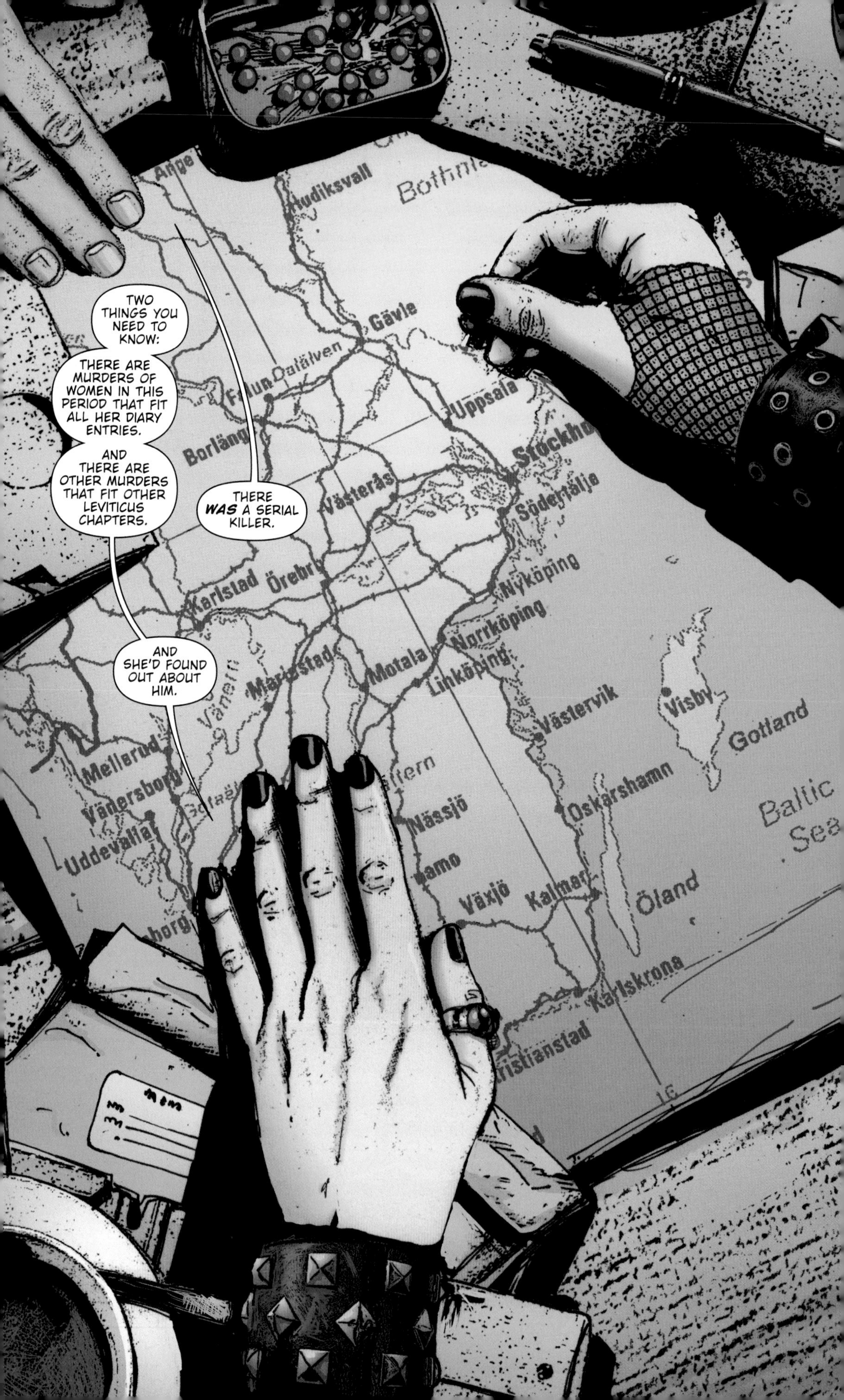

TWO THINGS YOU NEED TO KNOW:
THERE ARE MURDERS OF WOMEN IN THIS PERIOD THAT FIT ALL HER DIARY ENTRIES.
AND THERE ARE OTHER MURDERS THAT FIT OTHER LEVITICUS CHAPTERS.
THERE *WAS* A SERIAL KILLER.
AND SHE'D FOUND OUT ABOUT HIM.
Hudiksvall
Gävle
Dalälven
Falun
Uppsala
Borläng
Västerås
Södertälje
Karlstad
Örebro
Nyköping
Norrköping
Mariestad
Motala
Linköping
Västervik
Visby
Gotland
Mellerud
Vänersborg
Uddevalla
Nässjö
Oskarshamn
Baltic Sea
Växjö
Kalmar
Öland
Karlskrona

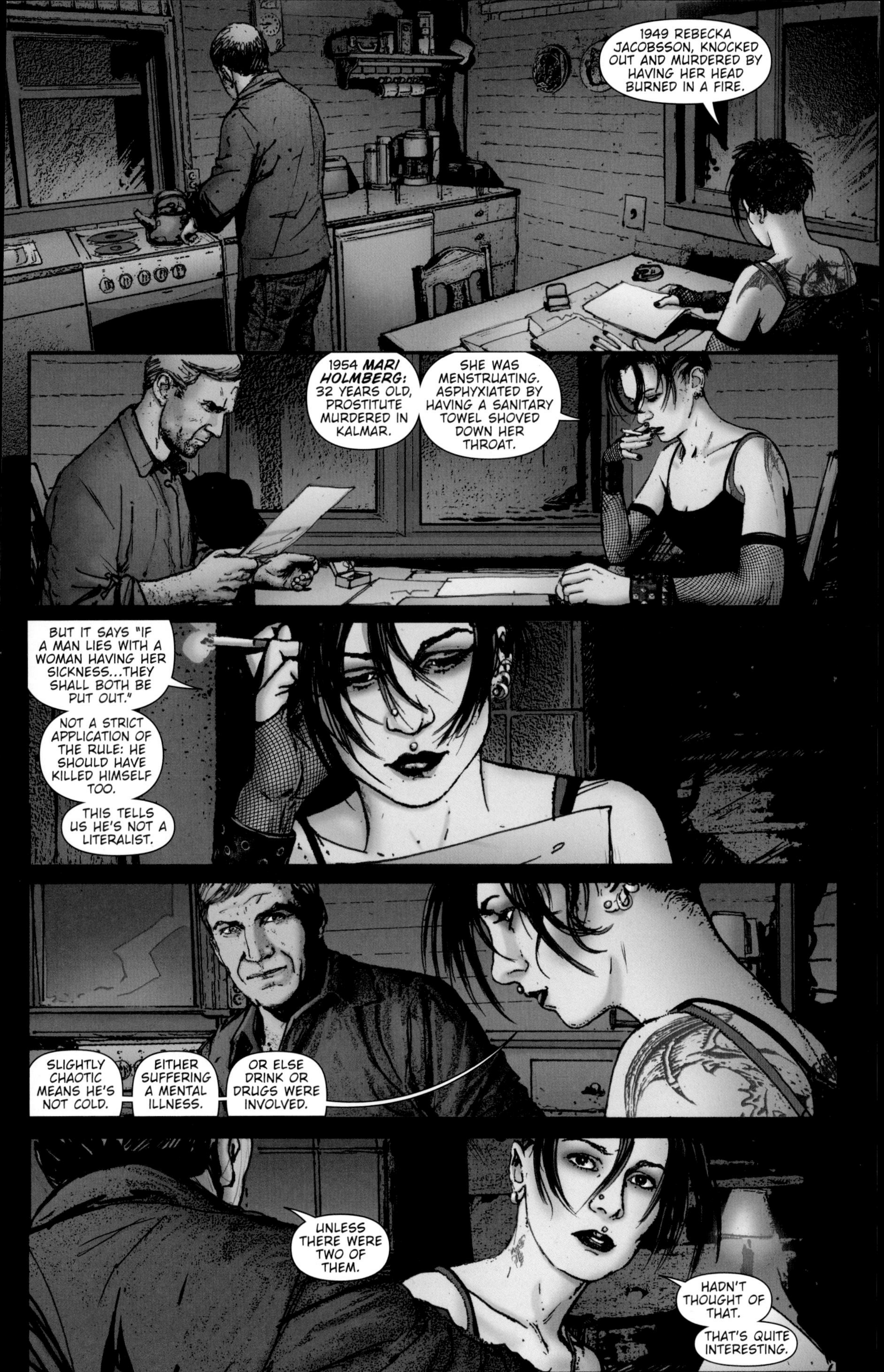
1949 REBECKA JACOBSSON, KNOCKED OUT AND MURDERED BY HAVING HER HEAD BURNED IN A FIRE.
1954 **MARI HOLMBERG:** 32 YEARS OLD, PROSTITUTE MURDERED IN KALMAR.
SHE WAS MENSTRUATING. ASPHYXIATED BY HAVING A SANITARY TOWEL SHOVED DOWN HER THROAT.
BUT IT SAYS "IF A MAN LIES WITH A WOMAN HAVING HER SICKNESS...THEY SHALL BOTH BE PUT OUT."
NOT A STRICT APPLICATION OF THE RULE: HE SHOULD HAVE KILLED HIMSELF TOO.
THIS TELLS US HE'S NOT A LITERALIST.
SLIGHTLY CHAOTIC MEANS HE'S NOT COLD.
EITHER SUFFERING A MENTAL ILLNESS.
OR ELSE DRINK OR DRUGS WERE INVOLVED.
UNLESS THERE WERE TWO OF THEM.
HADN'T THOUGHT OF THAT.
THAT'S QUITE INTERESTING.

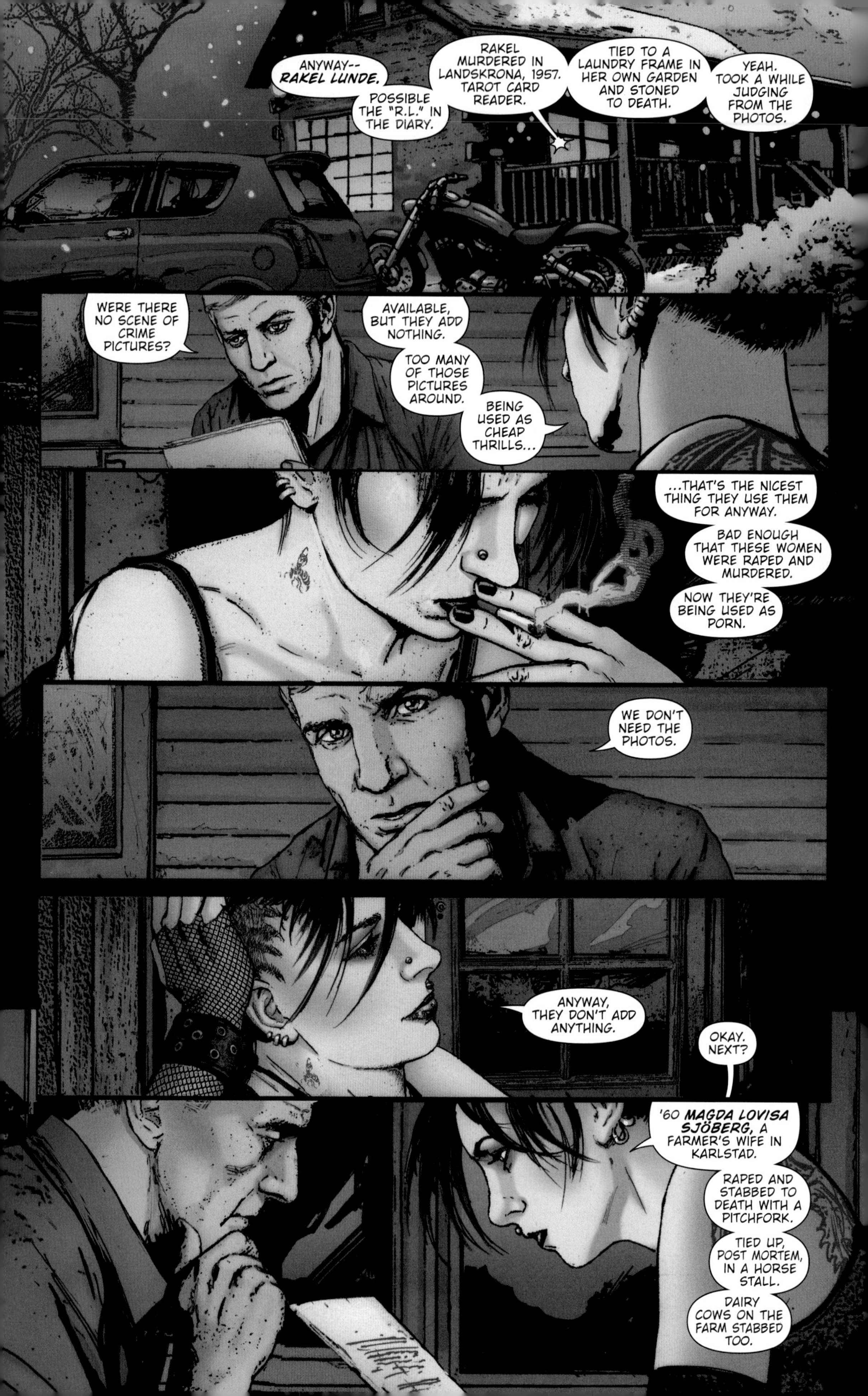
ANYWAY-- RAKEL LUNDE.
POSSIBLE THE "R.L." IN THE DIARY.
RAKEL MURDERED IN LANDSKRONA, 1957. TAROT CARD READER.
TIED TO A LAUNDRY FRAME IN HER OWN GARDEN AND STONED TO DEATH.
YEAH. TOOK A WHILE JUDGING FROM THE PHOTOS.
WERE THERE NO SCENE OF CRIME PICTURES?
AVAILABLE, BUT THEY ADD NOTHING.
TOO MANY OF THOSE PICTURES AROUND.
BEING USED AS CHEAP THRILLS...
...THAT'S THE NICEST THING THEY USE THEM FOR ANYWAY.
BAD ENOUGH THAT THESE WOMEN WERE RAPED AND MURDERED.
NOW THEY'RE BEING USED AS PORN.
WE DON'T NEED THE PHOTOS.
ANYWAY, THEY DON'T ADD ANYTHING.
OKAY. NEXT?
'60 MAGDA LOVISA SJÖBERG, A FARMER'S WIFE IN KARLSTAD.
RAPED AND STABBED TO DEATH WITH A PITCHFORK.
TIED UP, POST MORTEM, IN A HORSE STALL.
DAIRY COWS ON THE FARM STABBED TOO.

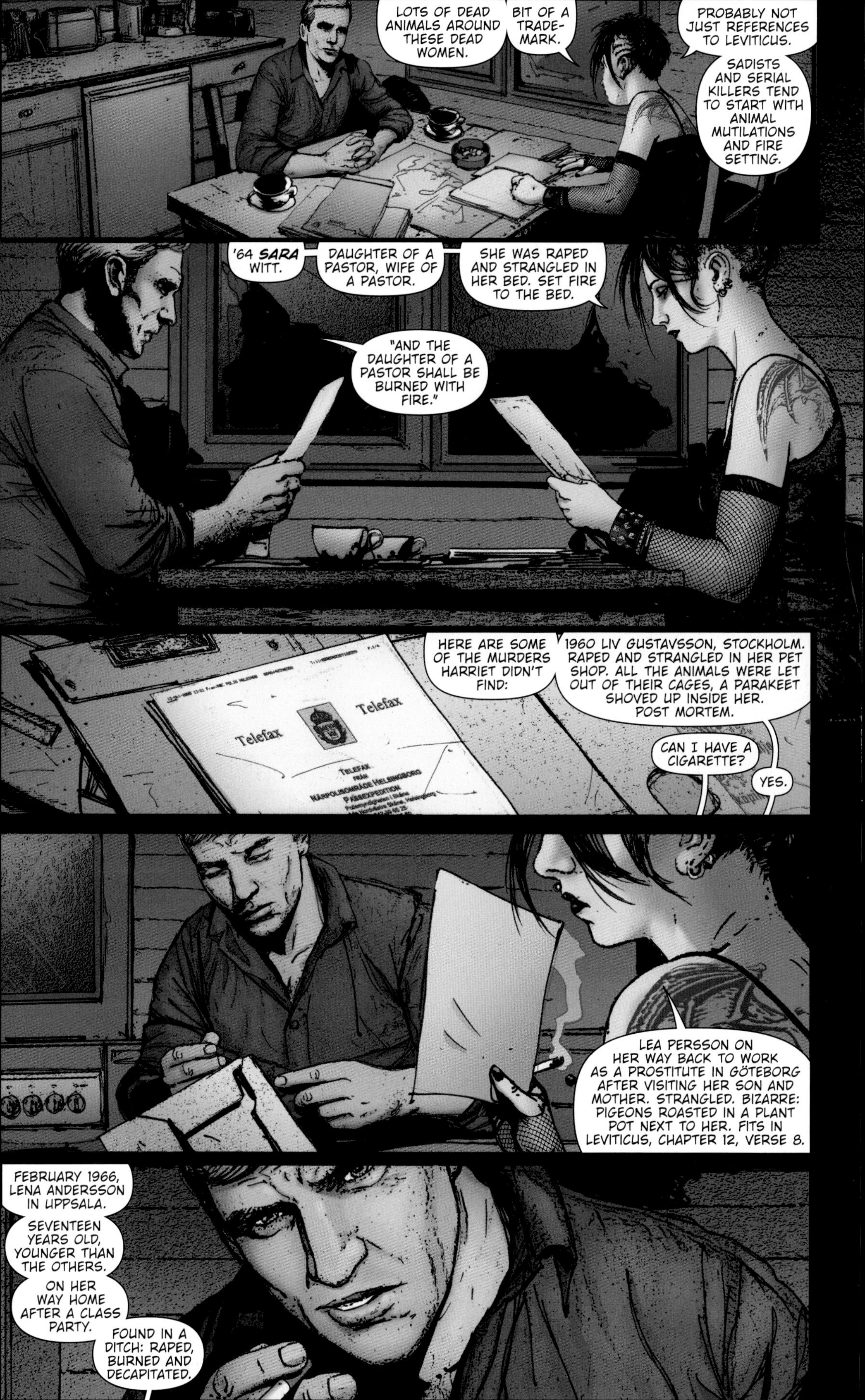
LOTS OF DEAD ANIMALS AROUND THESE DEAD WOMEN.
BIT OF A TRADE-MARK.
PROBABLY NOT JUST REFERENCES TO LEVITICUS.
SADISTS AND SERIAL KILLERS TEND TO START WITH ANIMAL MUTILATIONS AND FIRE SETTING.
'64 **SARA** WITT.
DAUGHTER OF A PASTOR, WIFE OF A PASTOR.
SHE WAS RAPED AND STRANGLED IN HER BED. SET FIRE TO THE BED.
"AND THE DAUGHTER OF A PASTOR SHALL BE BURNED WITH FIRE."
HERE ARE SOME OF THE MURDERS HARRIET DIDN'T FIND:
1960 LIV GUSTAVSSON, STOCKHOLM. RAPED AND STRANGLED IN HER PET SHOP. ALL THE ANIMALS WERE LET OUT OF THEIR CAGES, A PARAKEET SHOVED UP INSIDE HER. POST MORTEM.
CAN I HAVE A CIGARETTE?
YES.
LEA PERSSON ON HER WAY BACK TO WORK AS A PROSTITUTE IN GÖTEBORG AFTER VISITING HER SON AND MOTHER. STRANGLED. BIZARRE: PIGEONS ROASTED IN A PLANT POT NEXT TO HER. FITS IN LEVITICUS, CHAPTER 12, VERSE 8.
FEBRUARY 1966, LENA ANDERSSON IN UPPSALA.
SEVENTEEN YEARS OLD, YOUNGER THAN THE OTHERS.
ON HER WAY HOME AFTER A CLASS PARTY.
FOUND IN A DITCH: RAPED, BURNED AND DECAPITATED.

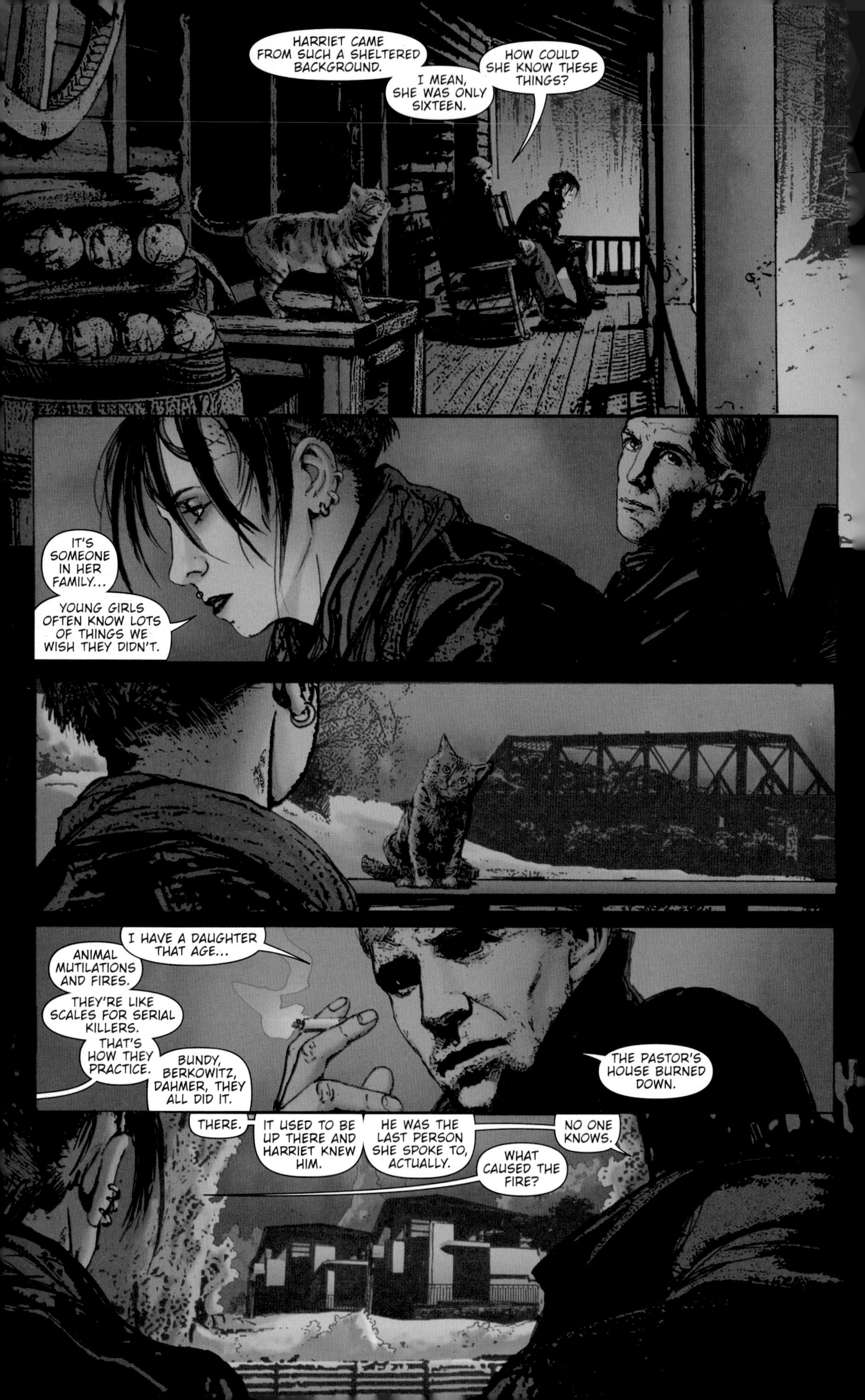
HARRIET CAME FROM SUCH A SHELTERED BACKGROUND.
I MEAN, SHE WAS ONLY SIXTEEN.
HOW COULD SHE KNOW THESE THINGS?
IT'S SOMEONE IN HER FAMILY...
YOUNG GIRLS OFTEN KNOW LOTS OF THINGS WE WISH THEY DIDN'T.
I HAVE A DAUGHTER THAT AGE...
ANIMAL MUTILATIONS AND FIRES.
THEY'RE LIKE SCALES FOR SERIAL KILLERS.
THAT'S HOW THEY PRACTICE.
BUNDY, BERKOWITZ, DAHMER, THEY ALL DID IT.
THE PASTOR'S HOUSE BURNED DOWN.
THERE.
IT USED TO BE UP THERE AND HARRIET KNEW HIM.
HE WAS THE LAST PERSON SHE SPOKE TO, ACTUALLY.
NO ONE KNOWS.
WHAT CAUSED THE FIRE?

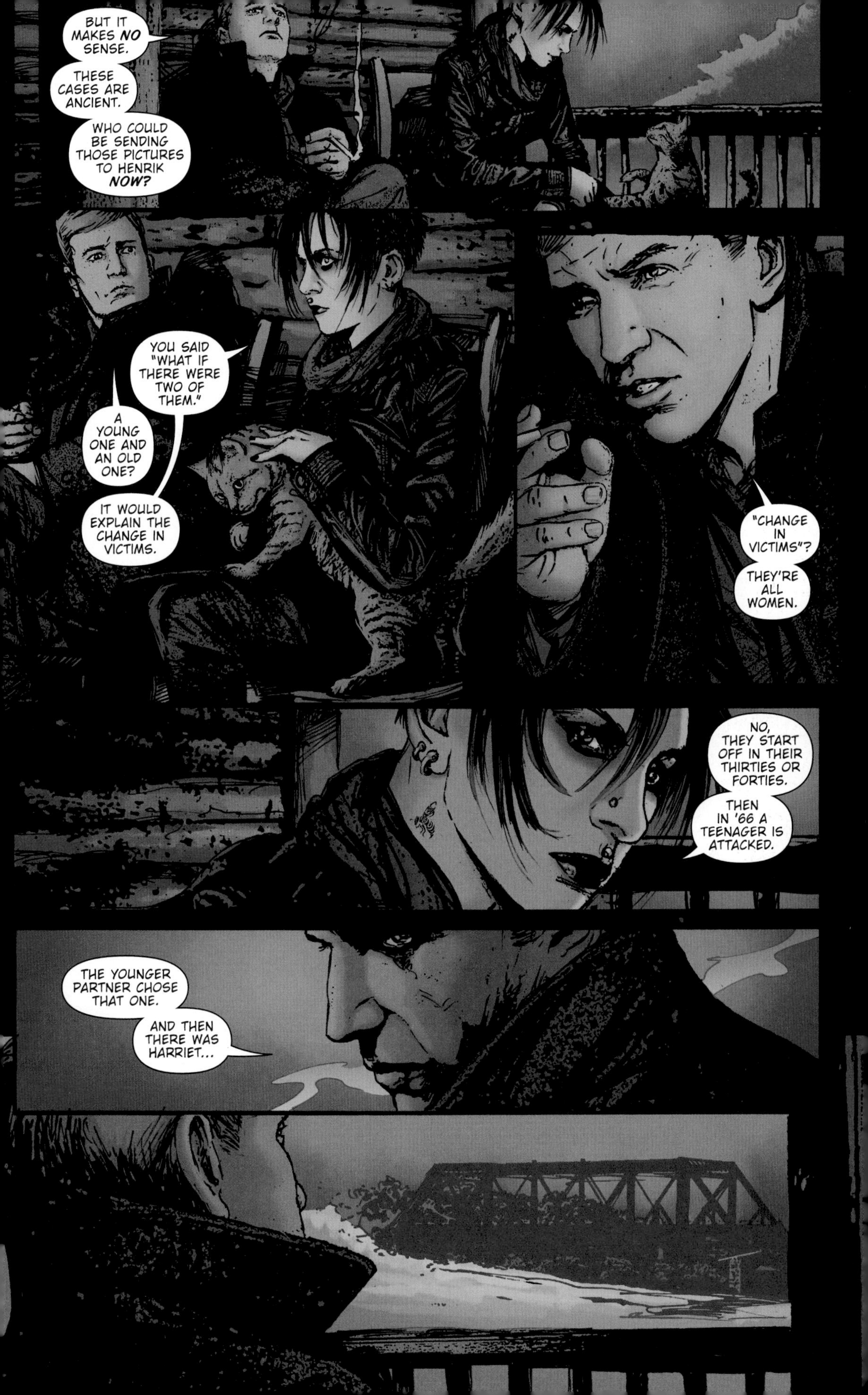
BUT IT MAKES NO SENSE.
THESE CASES ARE ANCIENT.
WHO COULD BE SENDING THOSE PICTURES TO HENRIK NOW?
YOU SAID "WHAT IF THERE WERE TWO OF THEM."
A YOUNG ONE AND AN OLD ONE?
IT WOULD EXPLAIN THE CHANGE IN VICTIMS.
"CHANGE IN VICTIMS"?
THEY'RE ALL WOMEN.
NO, THEY START OFF IN THEIR THIRTIES OR FORTIES.
THEN IN '66 A TEENAGER IS ATTACKED.
THE YOUNGER PARTNER CHOSE THAT ONE.
AND THEN THERE WAS HARRIET...

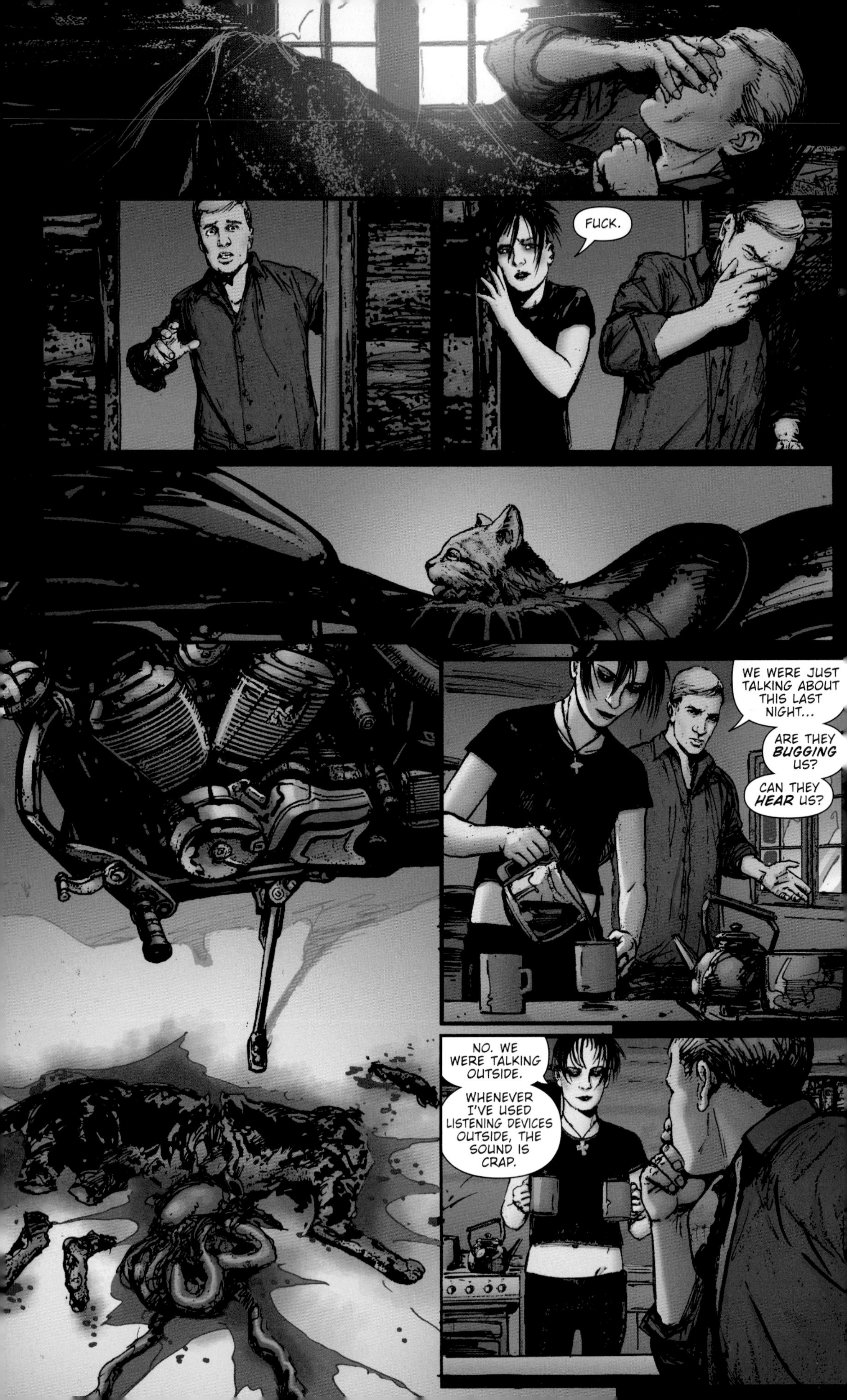
FUCK.
WE WERE JUST TALKING ABOUT THIS LAST NIGHT...
ARE THEY BUGGING US?
CAN THEY HEAR US?
NO. WE WERE TALKING OUTSIDE.
WHENEVER I'VE USED LISTENING DEVICES OUTSIDE, THE SOUND IS CRAP.

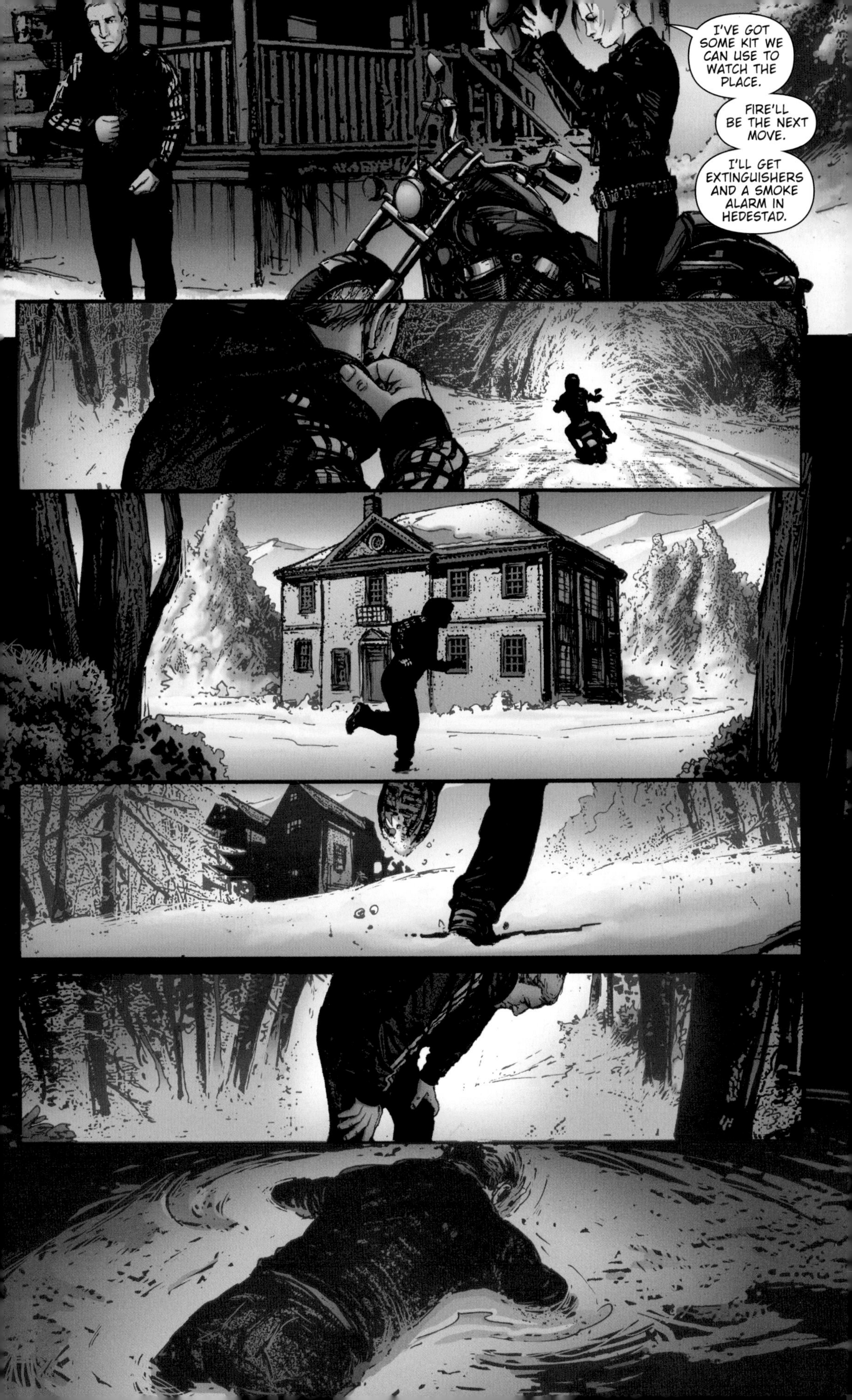
I'VE GOT SOME KIT WE CAN USE TO WATCH THE PLACE.
FIRE'LL BE THE NEXT MOVE.
I'LL GET EXTINGUISHERS AND A SMOKE ALARM IN HEDESTAD.

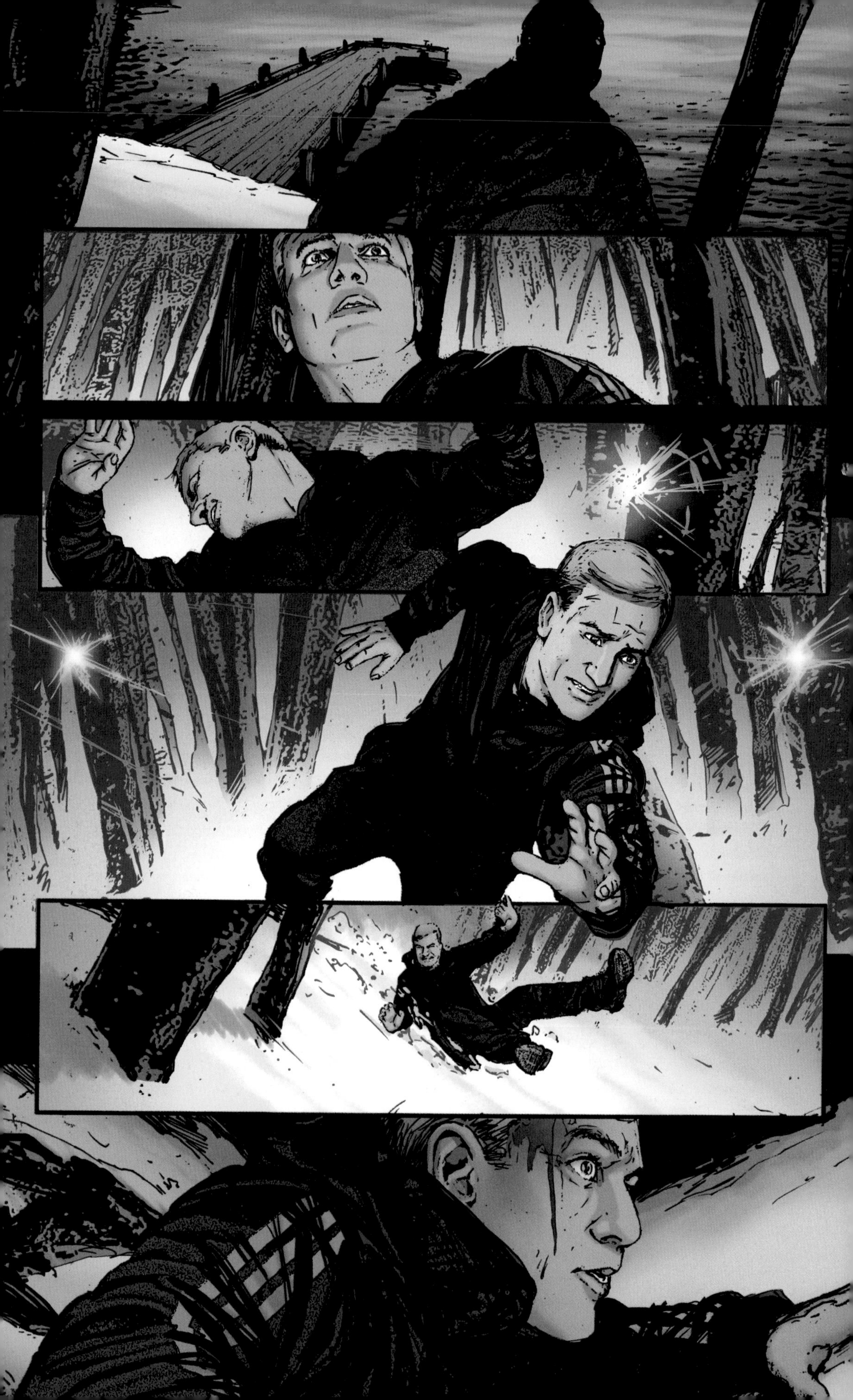

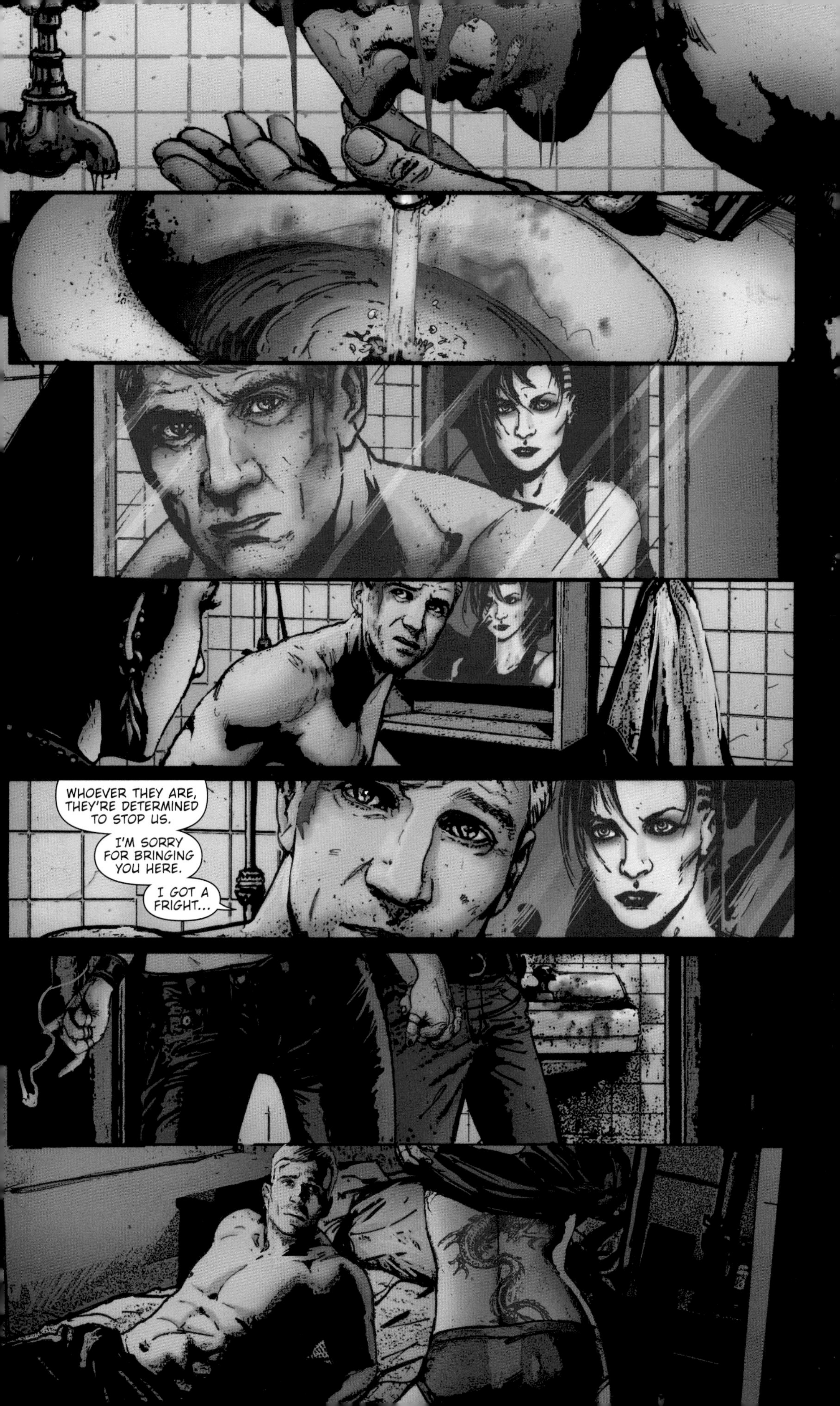
WHOEVER THEY ARE, THEY'RE DETERMINED TO STOP US.
I'M SORRY FOR BRINGING YOU HERE.
I GOT A FRIGHT...

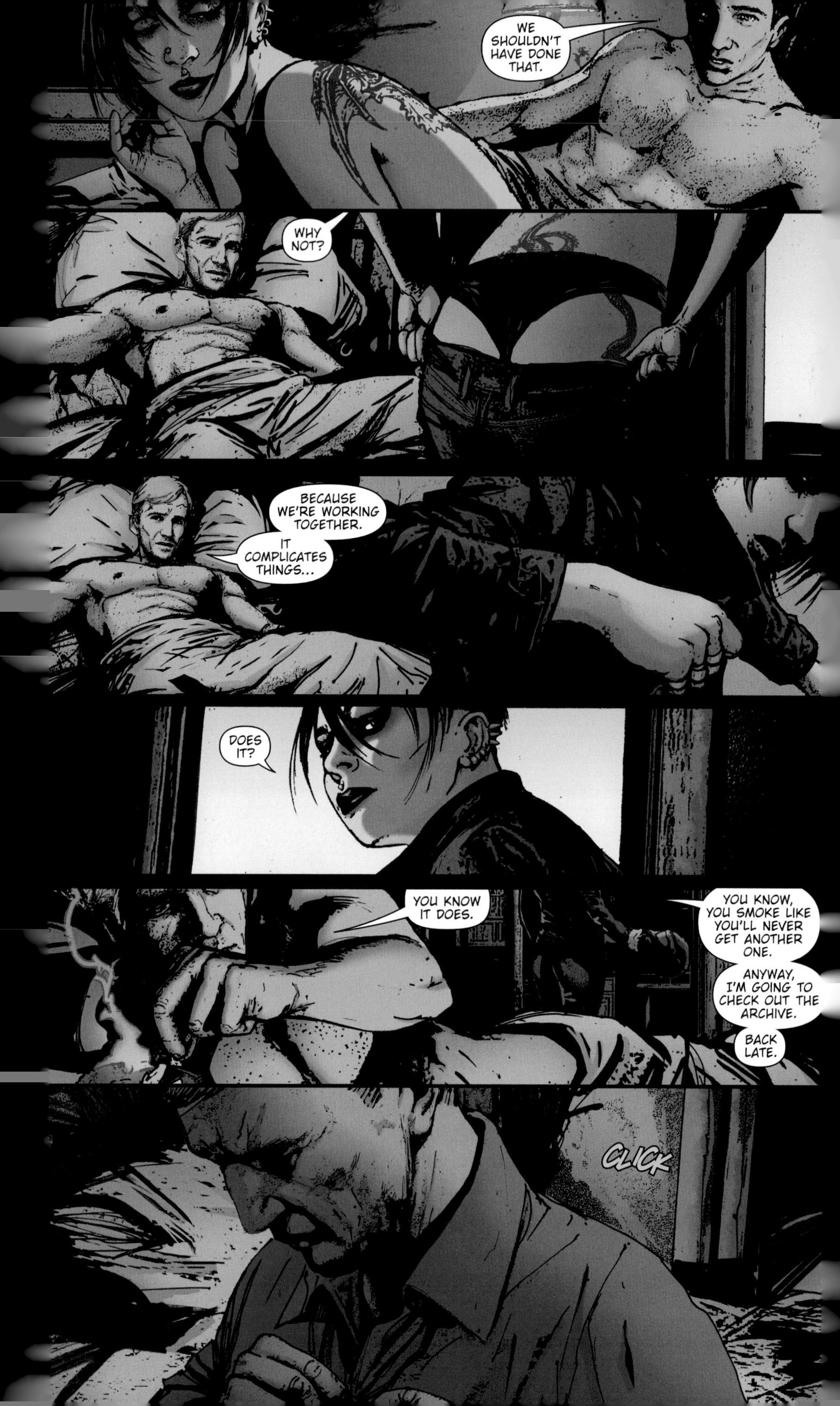
WE SHOULDN'T HAVE DONE THAT.
WHY NOT?
BECAUSE WE'RE WORKING TOGETHER.
IT COMPLICATES THINGS...
DOES IT?
YOU KNOW IT DOES.
YOU KNOW, YOU SMOKE LIKE YOU'LL NEVER GET ANOTHER ONE.
ANYWAY, I'M GOING TO CHECK OUT THE ARCHIVE.
BACK LATE.
CLICK

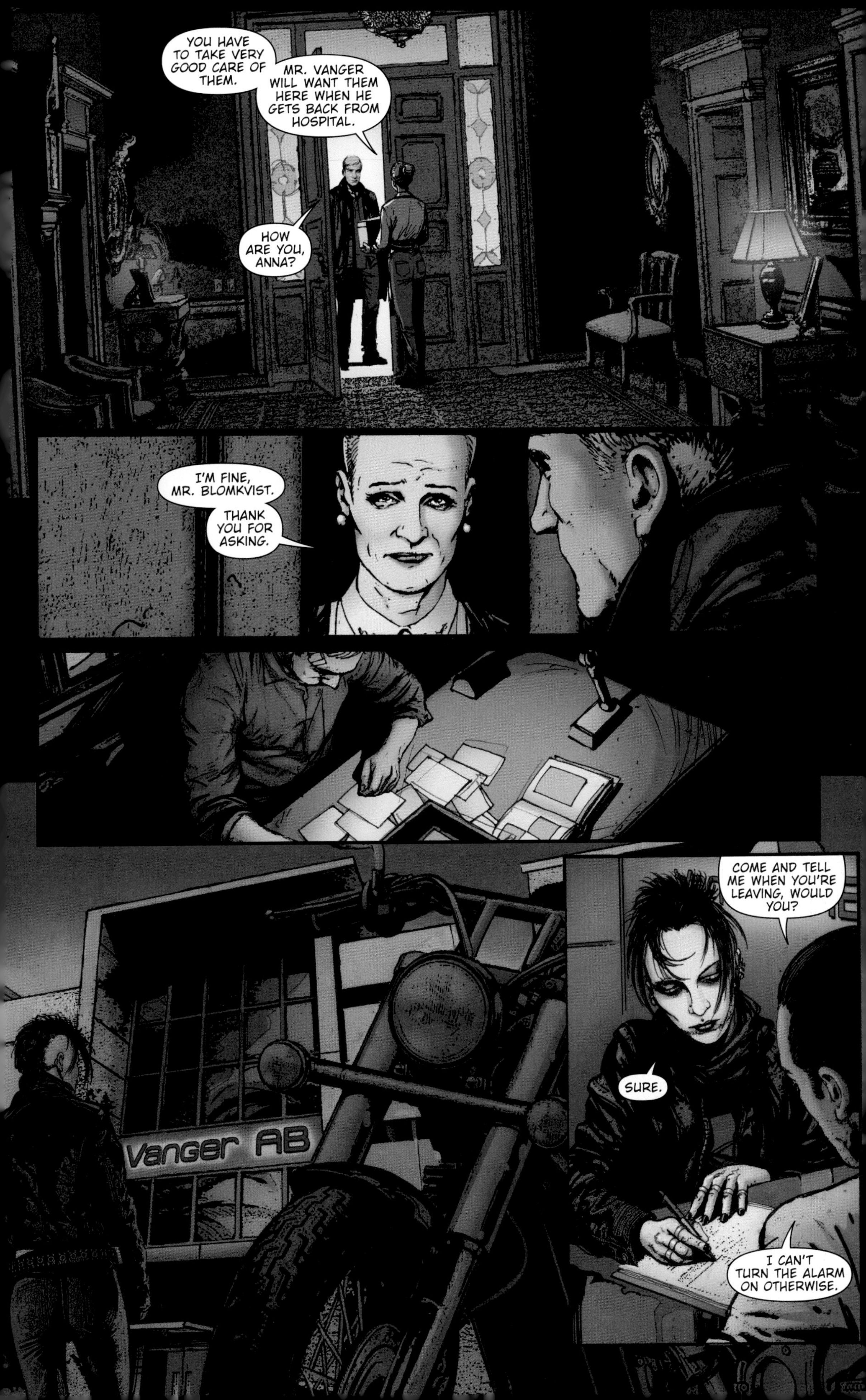
YOU HAVE TO TAKE VERY GOOD CARE OF THEM.
MR. VANGER WILL WANT THEM HERE WHEN HE GETS BACK FROM HOSPITAL.
HOW ARE YOU, ANNA?
I'M FINE, MR. BLOMKVIST.
THANK YOU FOR ASKING.
Vanger AB
COME AND TELL ME WHEN YOU'RE LEAVING, WOULD YOU?
SURE.
I CAN'T TURN THE ALARM ON OTHERWISE.

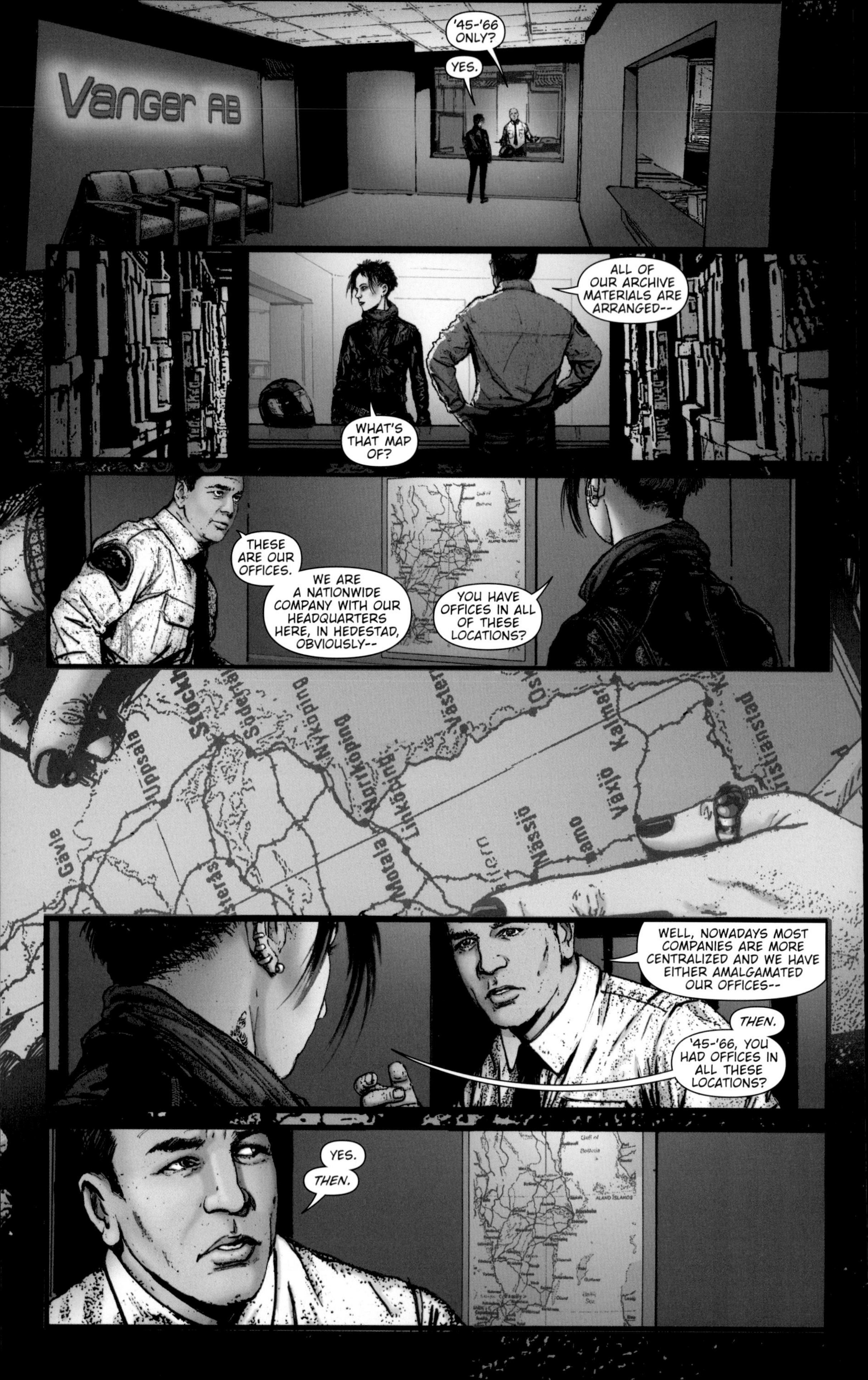

Vanger AB
'45-'66 ONLY?
YES.
ALL OF OUR ARCHIVE MATERIALS ARE ARRANGED--
WHAT'S THAT MAP OF?
THESE ARE OUR OFFICES.
WE ARE A NATIONWIDE COMPANY WITH OUR HEADQUARTERS HERE, IN HEDESTAD, OBVIOUSLY--
YOU HAVE OFFICES IN ALL OF THESE LOCATIONS?
Uppsala
Gävle
Nyköping
Norrköping
Linköping
Motala
Nässjö
Växjö
Kalmar
WELL, NOWADAYS MOST COMPANIES ARE MORE CENTRALIZED AND WE HAVE EITHER AMALGAMATED OUR OFFICES--
THEN.
'45-'66, YOU HAD OFFICES IN ALL THESE LOCATIONS?
YES.
THEN.

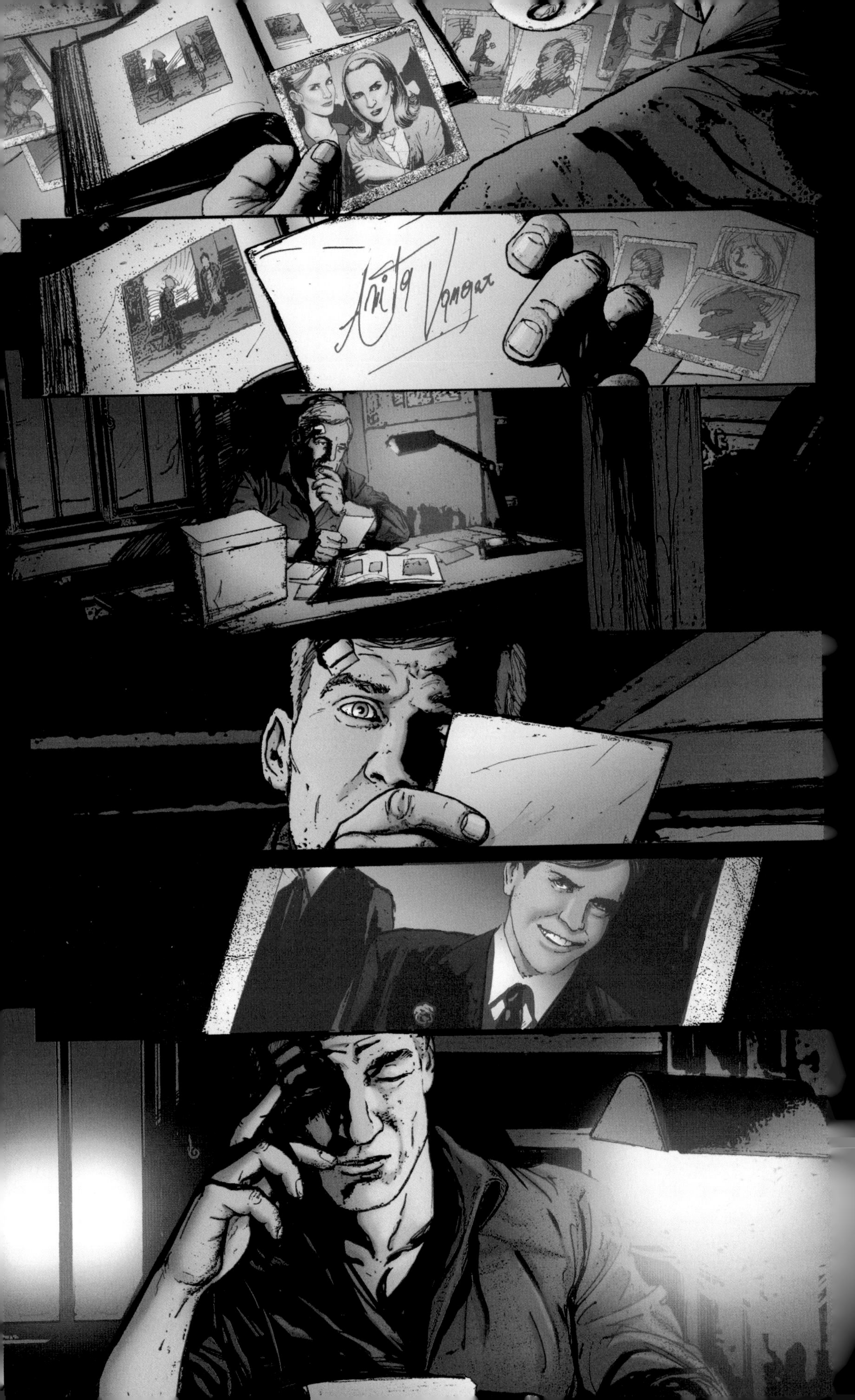
Anita Vangar

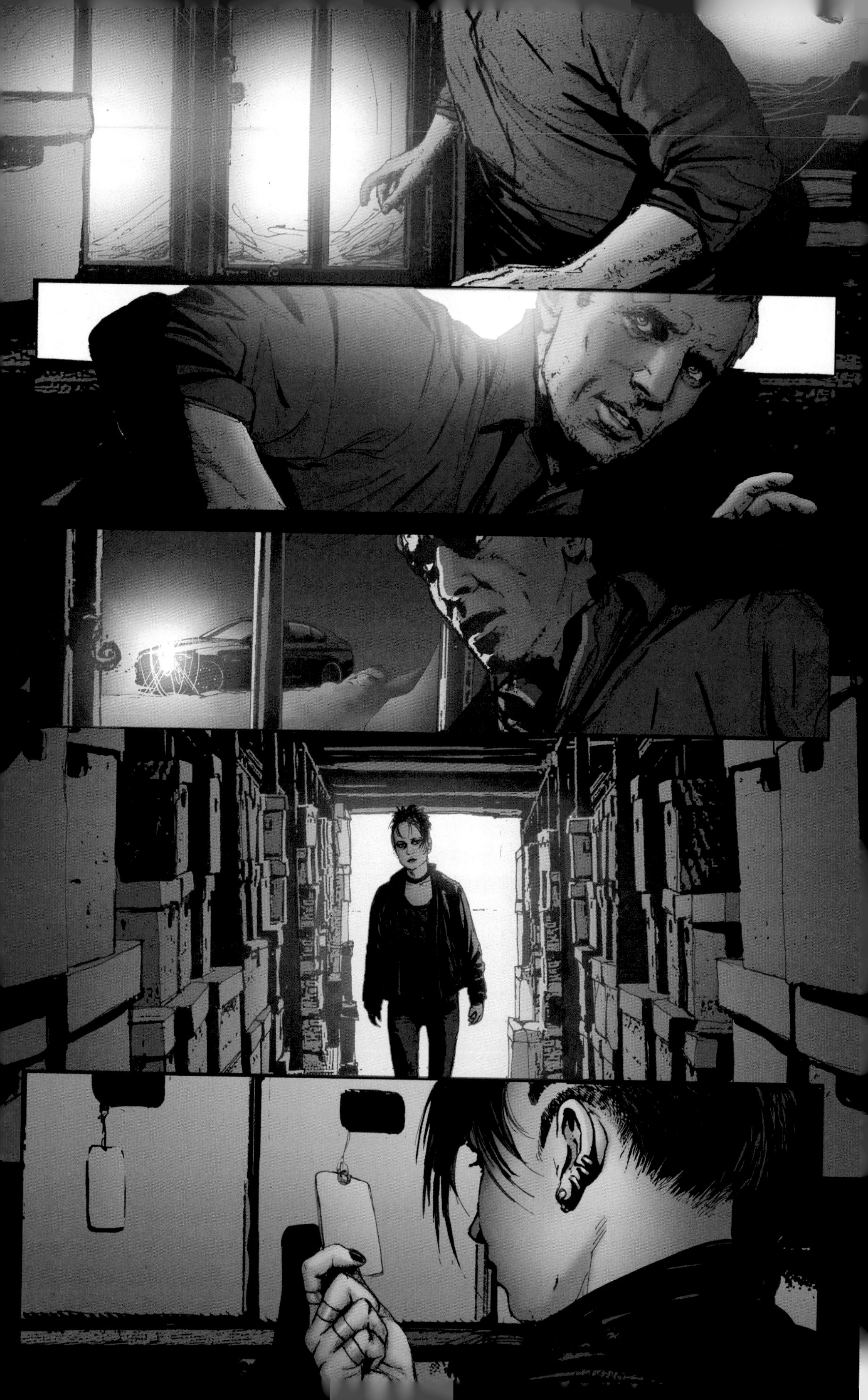

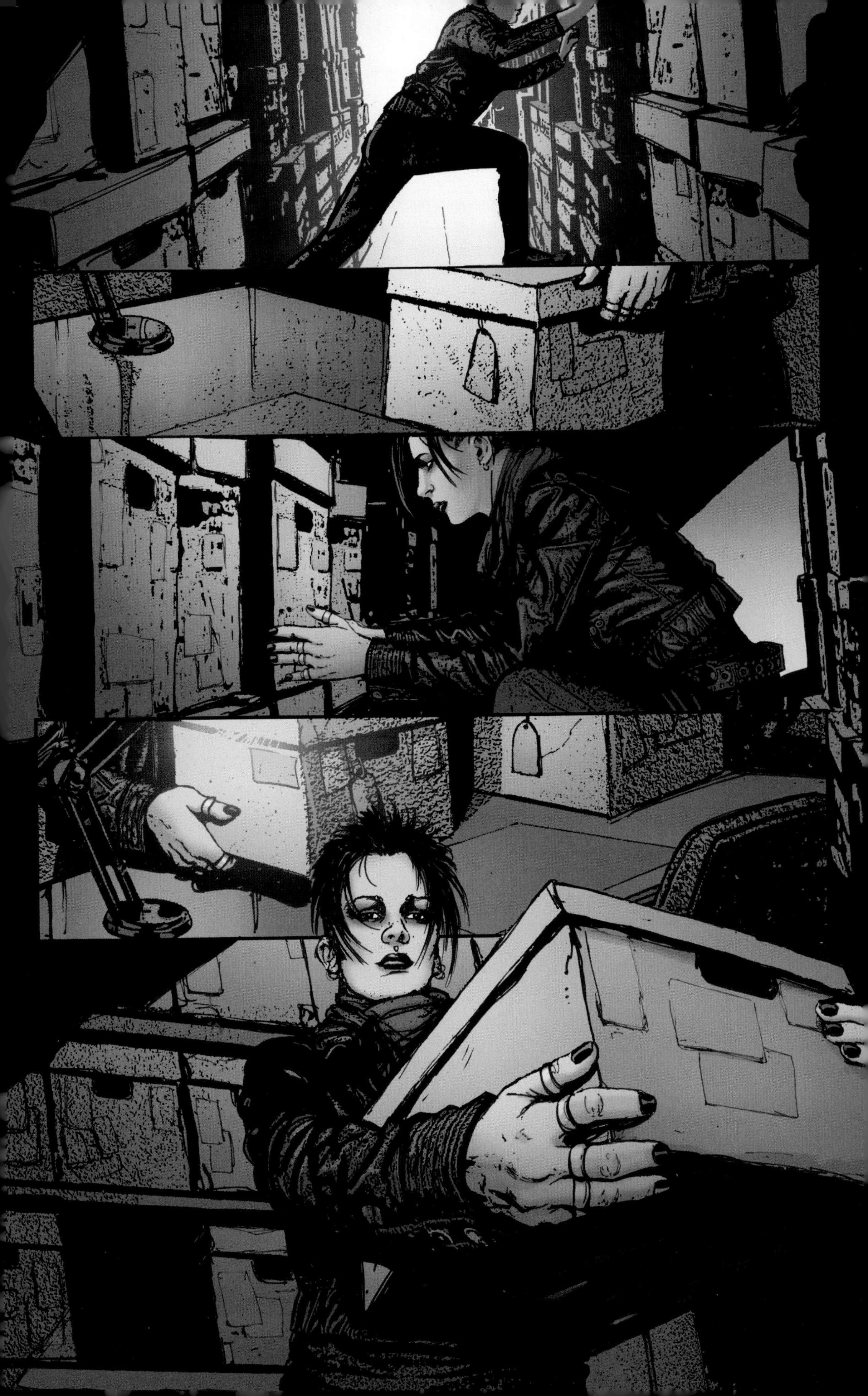

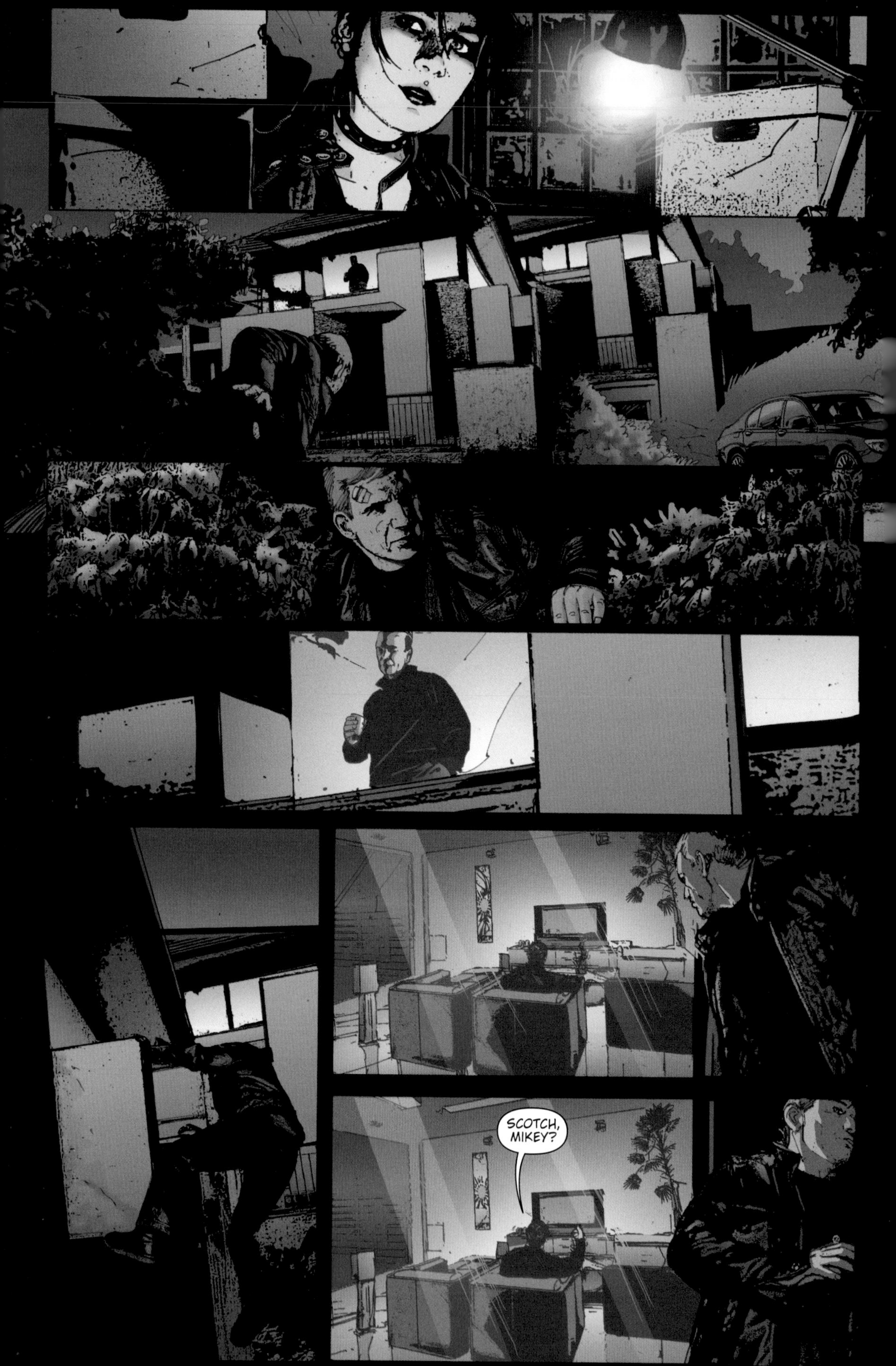
SCOTCH, MIKEY?

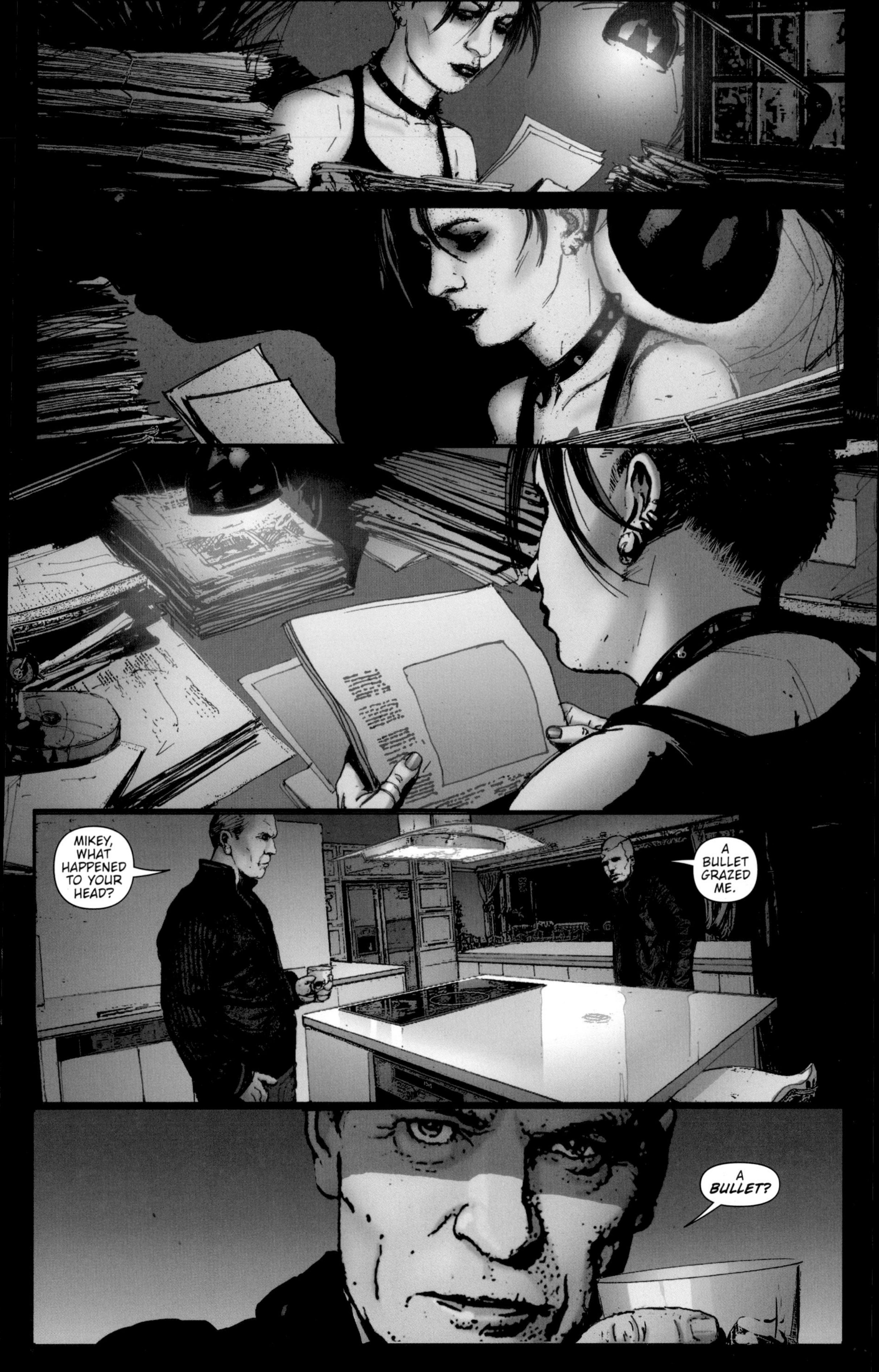
MIKEY, WHAT HAPPENED TO YOUR HEAD?
A BULLET GRAZED ME.
A BULLET?

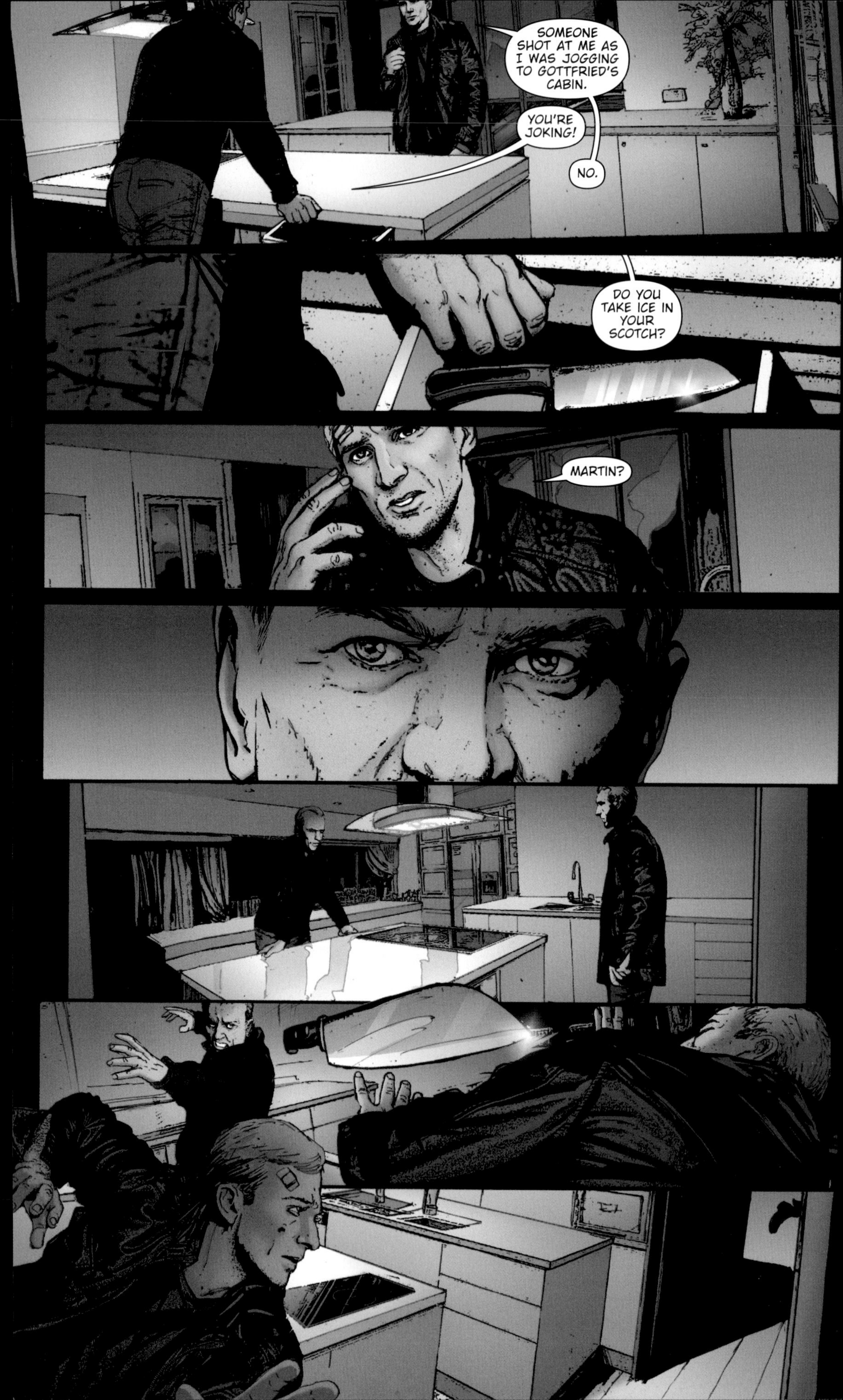
SOMEONE SHOT AT ME AS I WAS JOGGING TO GOTTFRIED'S CABIN.
YOU'RE JOKING!
NO.
DO YOU TAKE ICE IN YOUR SCOTCH?
MARTIN?

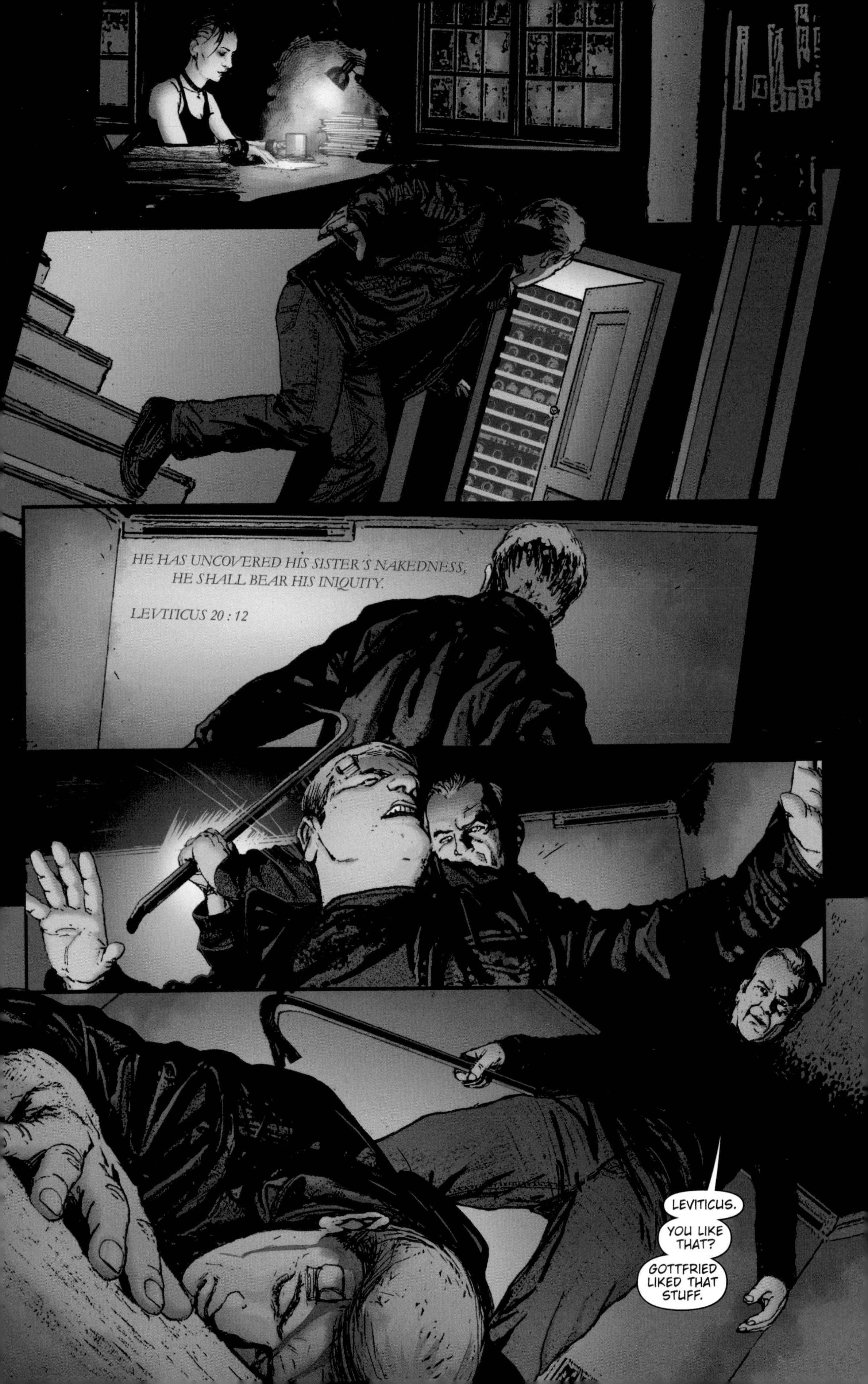
HE HAS UNCOVERED HIS SISTER'S NAKEDNESS, HE SHALL BEAR HIS INIQUITY.
LEVITICUS 20 : 12
LEVITICUS.
YOU LIKE THAT?
GOTTFRIED LIKED THAT STUFF.

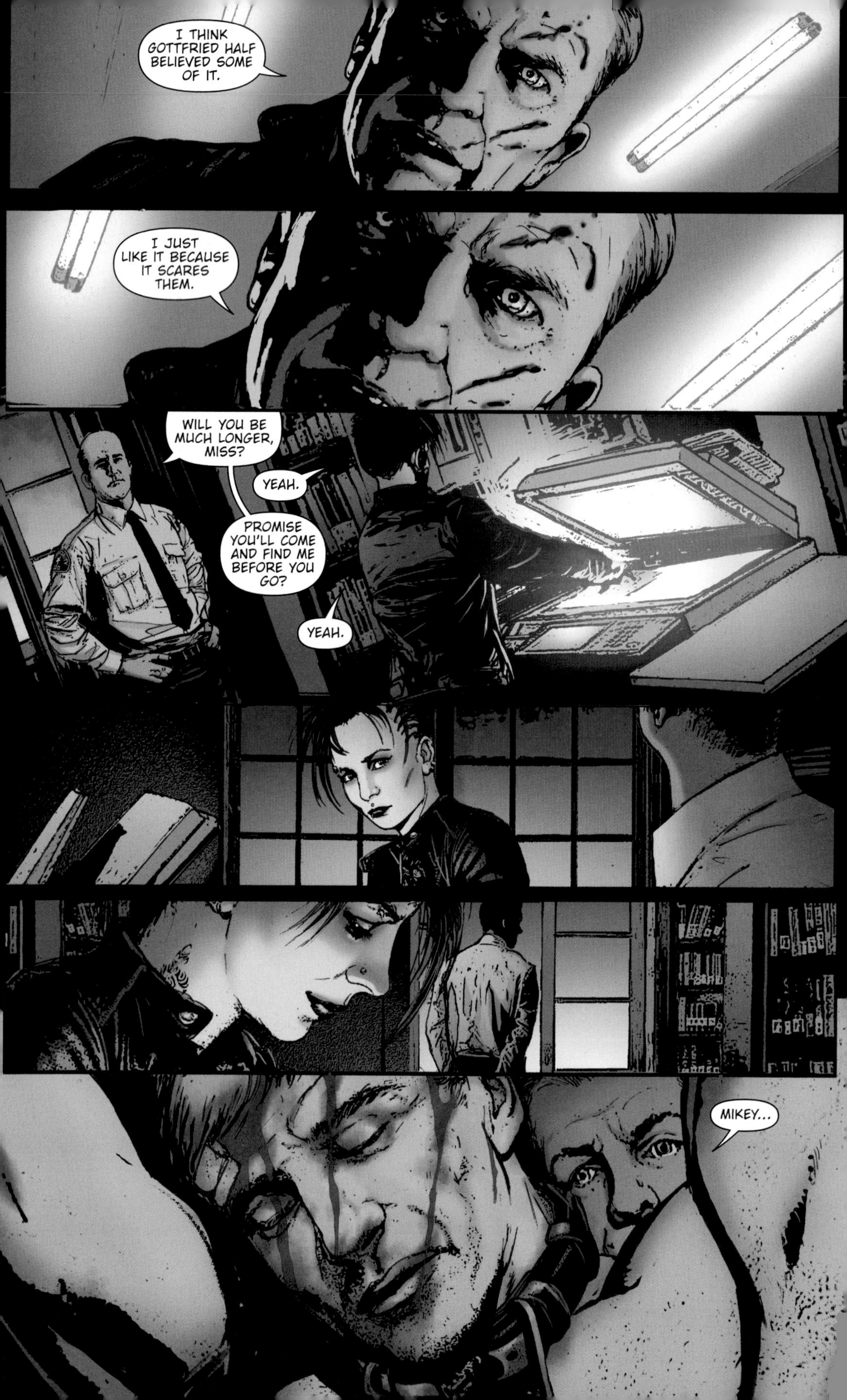
I THINK GOTTFRIED HALF BELIEVED SOME OF IT.
I JUST LIKE IT BECAUSE IT SCARES THEM.
WILL YOU BE MUCH LONGER, MISS?
YEAH.
PROMISE YOU'LL COME AND FIND ME BEFORE YOU GO?
YEAH.
MIKEY...

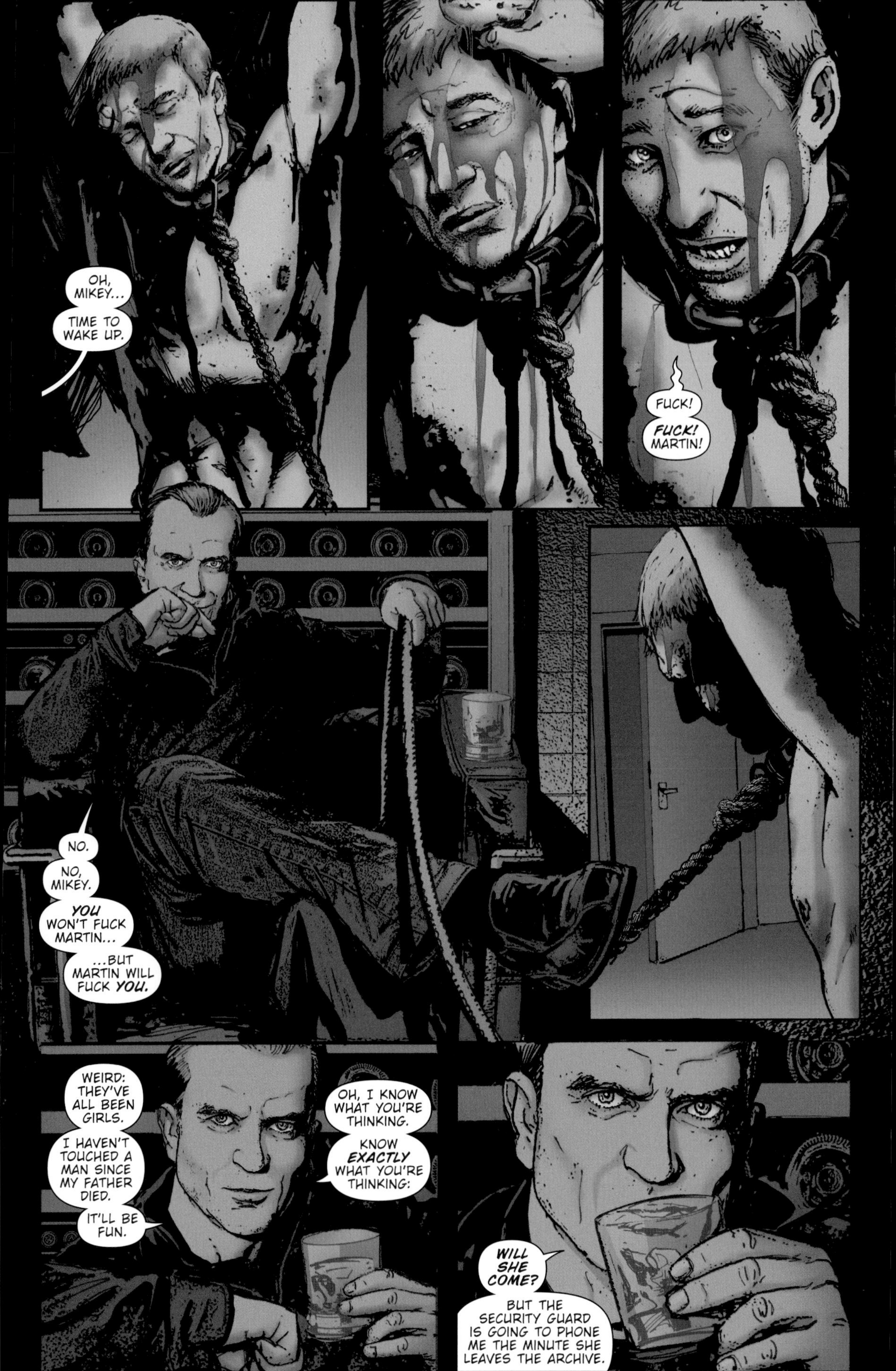
OH, MIKEY...
TIME TO WAKE UP.
FUCK!
FUCK! MARTIN!
NO.
NO, MIKEY.
YOU WON'T FUCK MARTIN...
...BUT MARTIN WILL FUCK YOU.
WEIRD: THEY'VE ALL BEEN GIRLS.
I HAVEN'T TOUCHED A MAN SINCE MY FATHER DIED.
IT'LL BE FUN.
OH, I KNOW WHAT YOU'RE THINKING.
KNOW EXACTLY WHAT YOU'RE THINKING:
WILL SHE COME?
BUT THE SECURITY GUARD IS GOING TO PHONE ME THE MINUTE SHE LEAVES THE ARCHIVE.

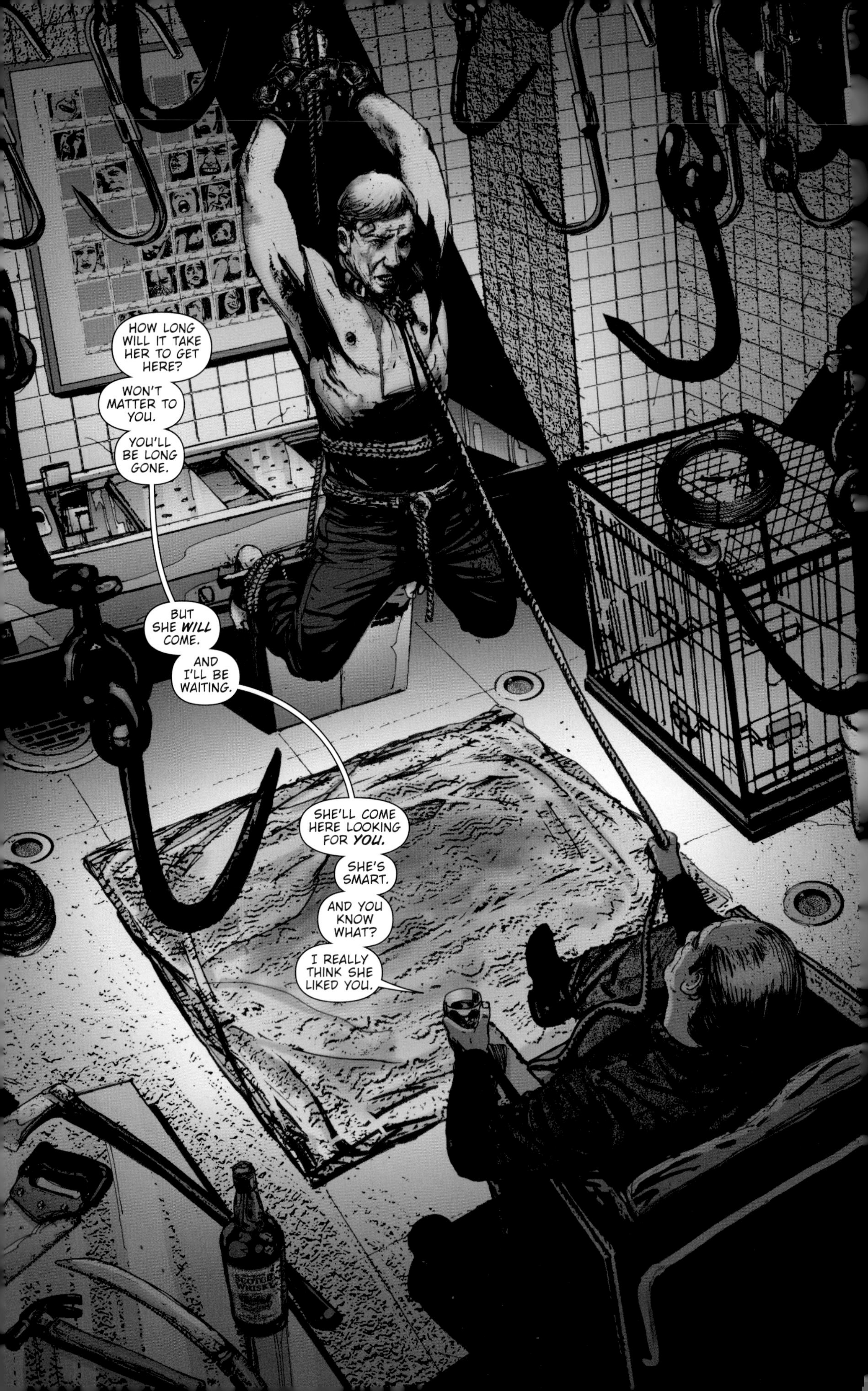
HOW LONG WILL IT TAKE HER TO GET HERE?
WON'T MATTER TO YOU.
YOU'LL BE LONG GONE.
BUT SHE *WILL* COME.
AND I'LL BE WAITING.
SHE'LL COME HERE LOOKING FOR *YOU.*
SHE'S SMART.
AND YOU KNOW WHAT?
I REALLY THINK SHE LIKED YOU.

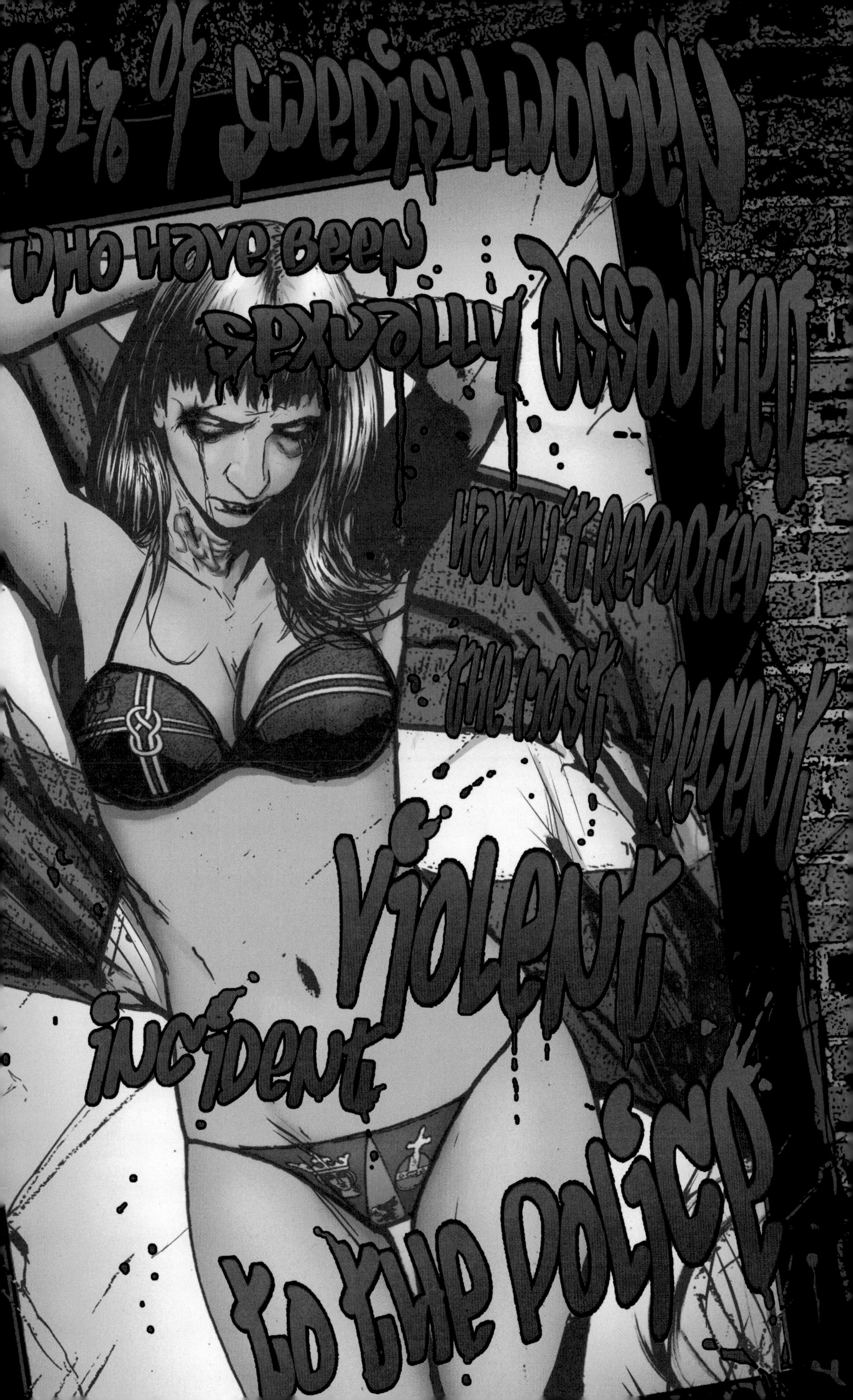
92% OF SWEDISH WOMEN
WHO HAVE BEEN SEXUALLY ASSAULTED
HAVEN'T REPORTED THE MOST RECENT
VIOLENT INCIDENT
TO THE POLICE

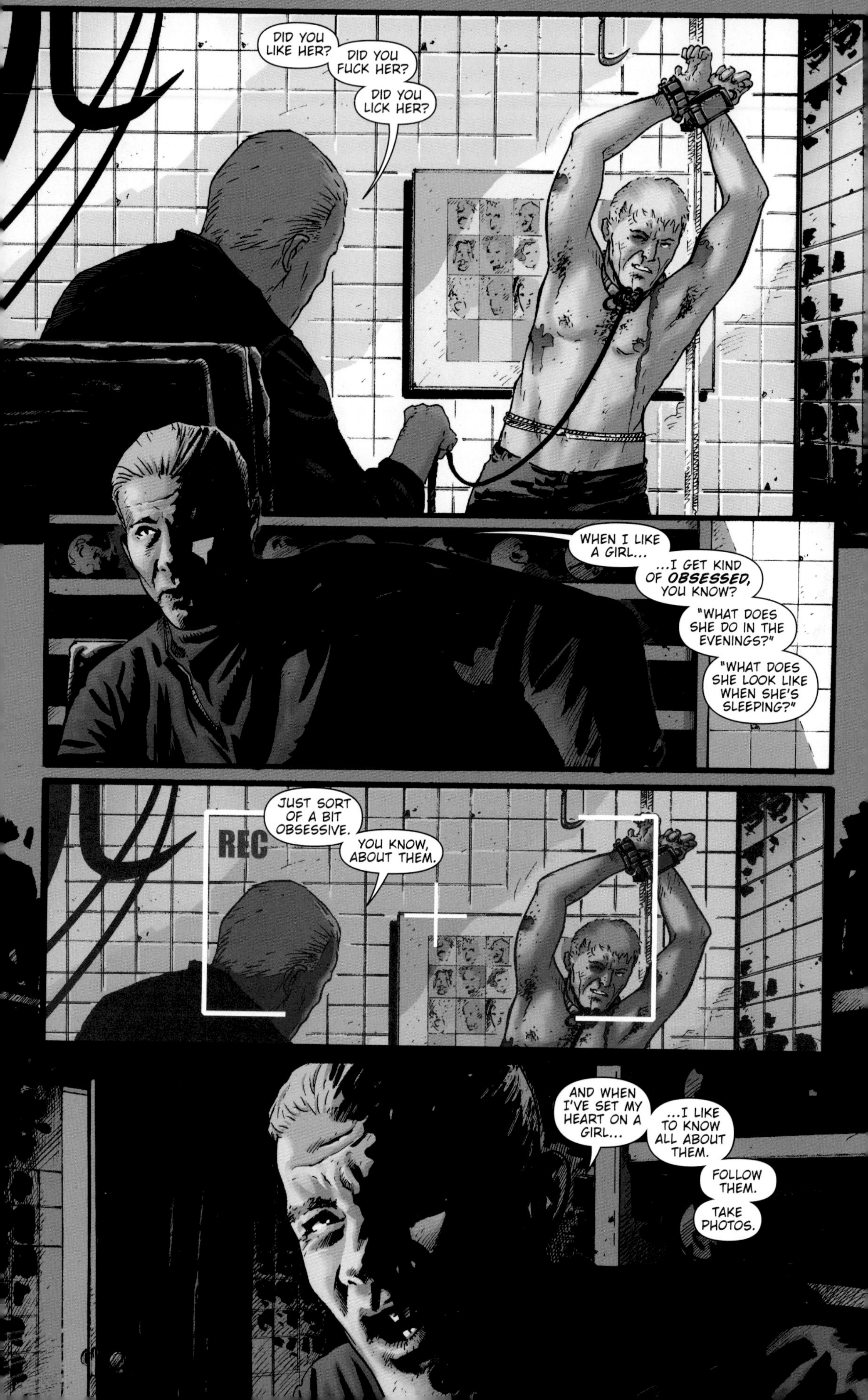
DID YOU LIKE HER?
DID YOU FUCK HER?
DID YOU LICK HER?
WHEN I LIKE A GIRL...
...I GET KIND OF *OBSESSED,* YOU KNOW?
"WHAT DOES SHE DO IN THE EVENINGS?"
"WHAT DOES SHE LOOK LIKE WHEN SHE'S SLEEPING?"
REC
JUST SORT OF A BIT OBSESSIVE.
YOU KNOW, ABOUT THEM.
AND WHEN I'VE SET MY HEART ON A GIRL...
...I LIKE TO KNOW ALL ABOUT THEM.
FOLLOW THEM.
TAKE PHOTOS.

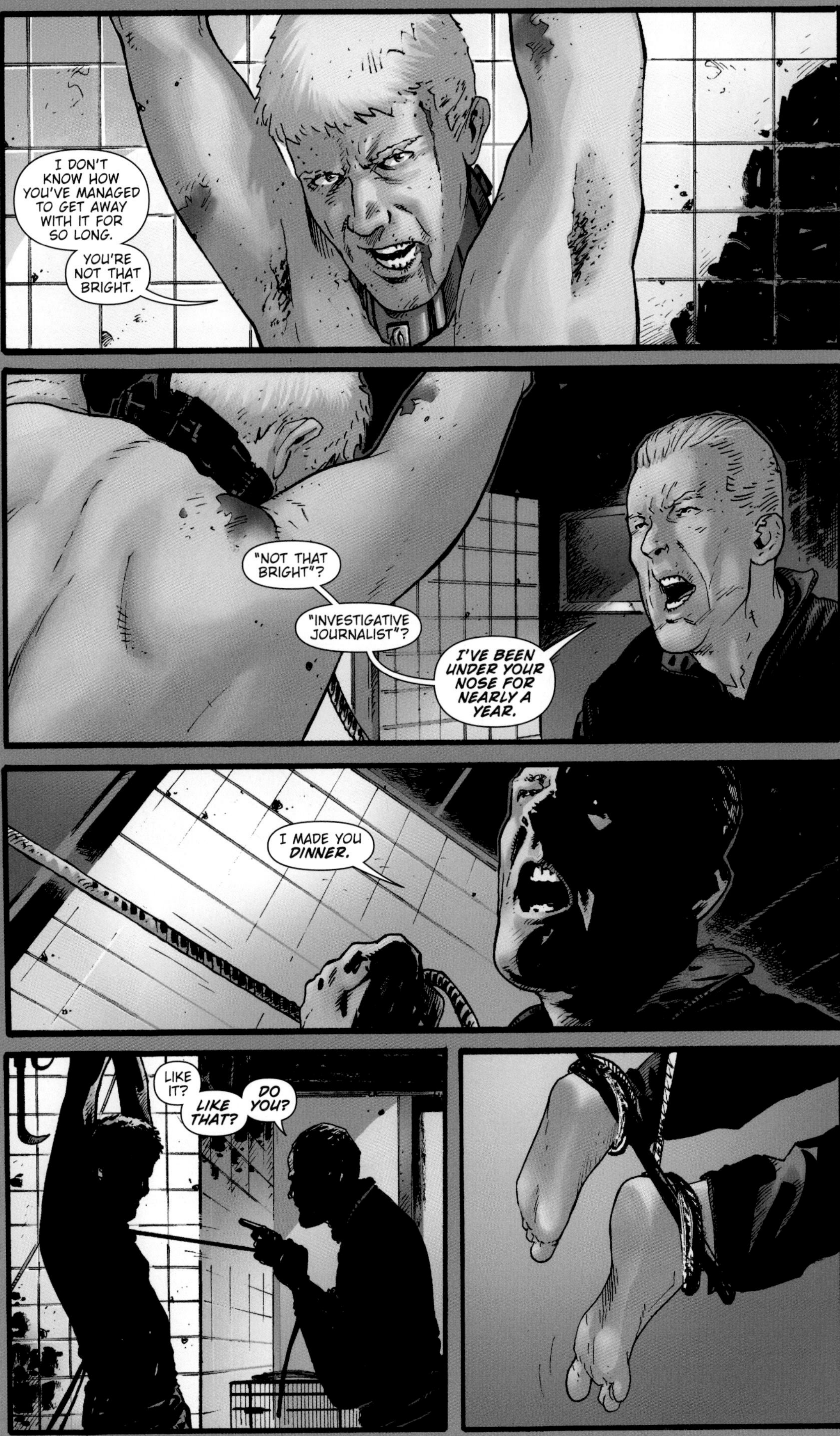
I DON'T KNOW HOW YOU'VE MANAGED TO GET AWAY WITH IT FOR SO LONG.
YOU'RE NOT THAT BRIGHT.
"NOT THAT BRIGHT"?
"INVESTIGATIVE JOURNALIST"?
I'VE BEEN UNDER YOUR NOSE FOR NEARLY A YEAR.
I MADE YOU DINNER.
LIKE IT?
LIKE THAT?
DO YOU?

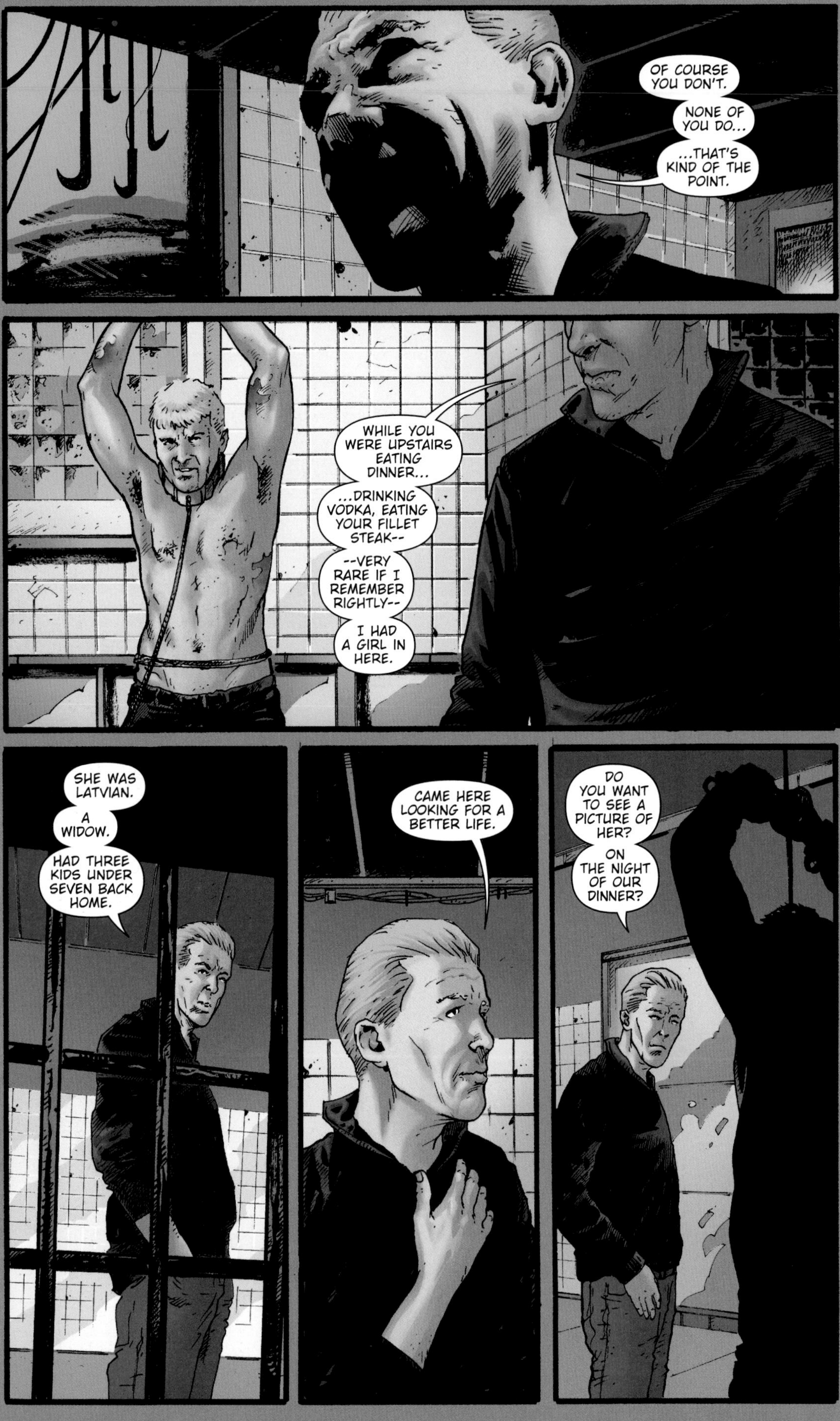

OF COURSE YOU DON'T.
NONE OF YOU DO...
...THAT'S KIND OF THE POINT.
WHILE YOU WERE UPSTAIRS EATING DINNER...
...DRINKING VODKA, EATING YOUR FILLET STEAK--
--VERY RARE IF I REMEMBER RIGHTLY--
I HAD A GIRL IN HERE.
SHE WAS LATVIAN.
A WIDOW.
HAD THREE KIDS UNDER SEVEN BACK HOME.
CAME HERE LOOKING FOR A BETTER LIFE.
DO YOU WANT TO SEE A PICTURE OF HER?
ON THE NIGHT OF OUR DINNER?

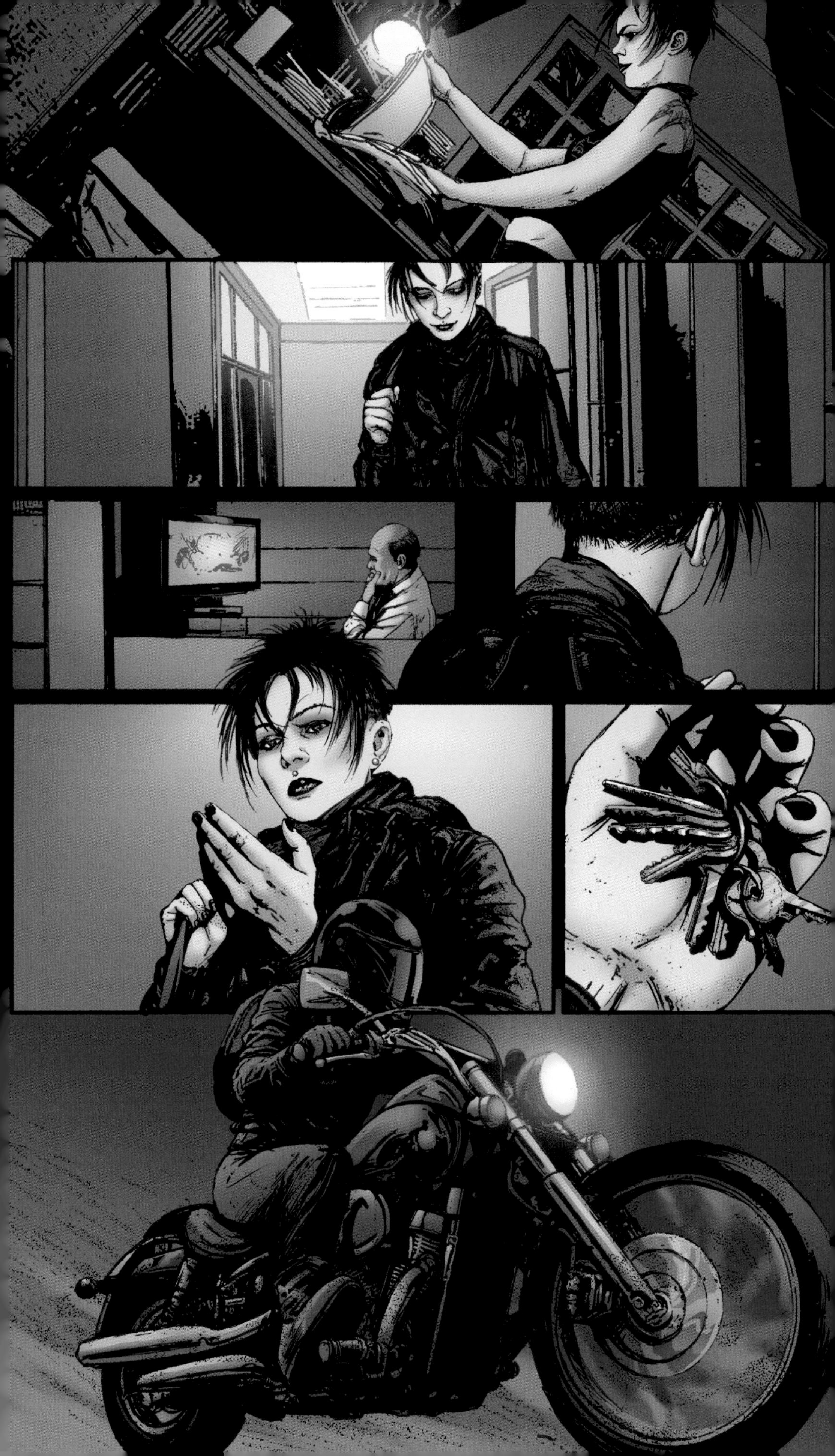

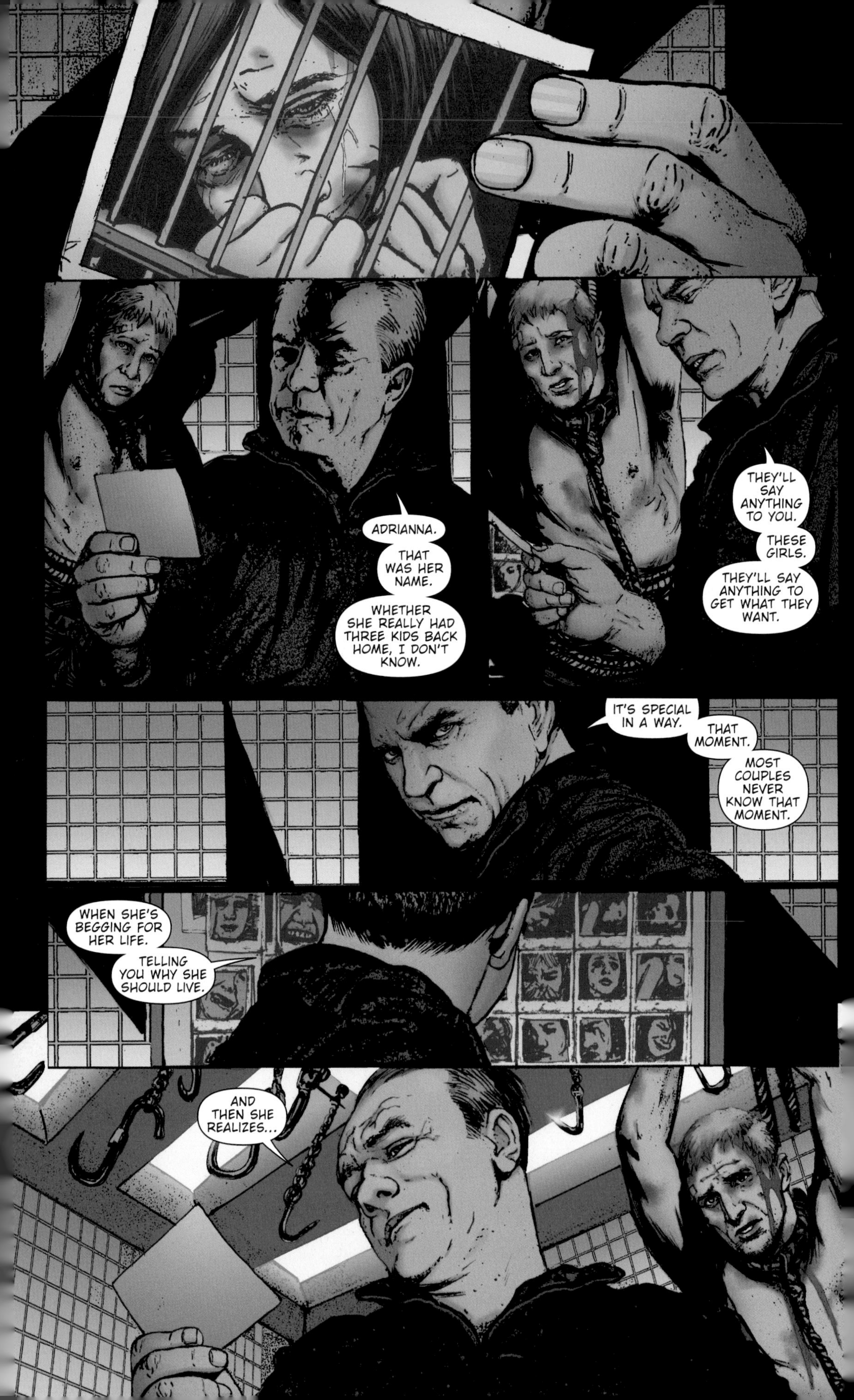

ADRIANNA.
THAT WAS HER NAME.
WHETHER SHE REALLY HAD THREE KIDS BACK HOME, I DON'T KNOW.
THEY'LL SAY ANYTHING TO YOU.
THESE GIRLS.
THEY'LL SAY ANYTHING TO GET WHAT THEY WANT.
IT'S SPECIAL IN A WAY.
THAT MOMENT.
MOST COUPLES NEVER KNOW THAT MOMENT.
WHEN SHE'S BEGGING FOR HER LIFE.
TELLING YOU WHY SHE SHOULD LIVE.
AND THEN SHE REALIZES...

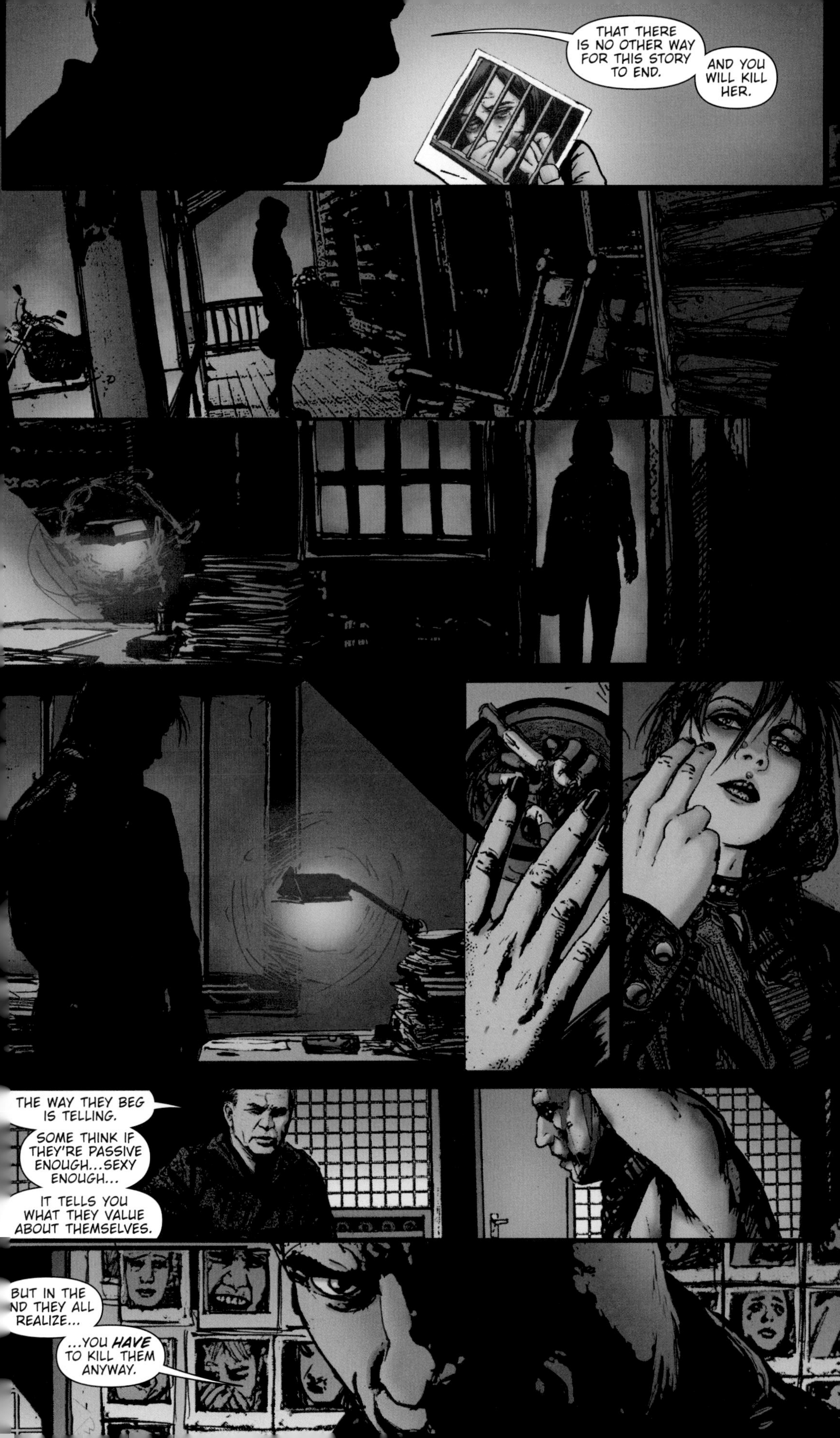
THAT THERE IS NO OTHER WAY FOR THIS STORY TO END.
AND YOU WILL KILL HER.
THE WAY THEY BEG IS TELLING.
SOME THINK IF THEY'RE PASSIVE ENOUGH...SEXY ENOUGH...
IT TELLS YOU WHAT THEY VALUE ABOUT THEMSELVES.
BUT IN THE ND THEY ALL REALIZE...
...YOU *HAVE* TO KILL THEM ANYWAY.

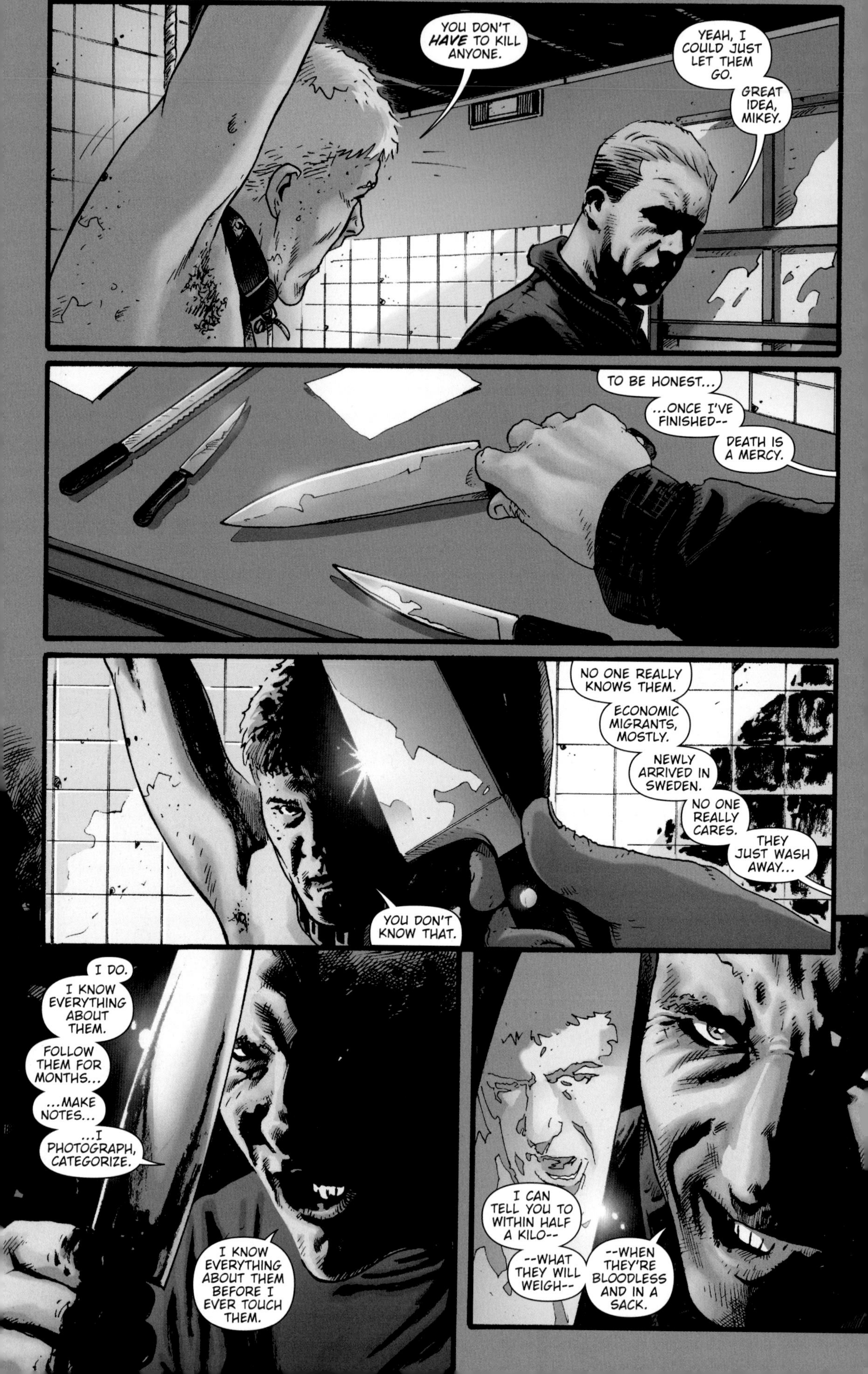
YOU DON'T HAVE TO KILL ANYONE.
YEAH, I COULD JUST LET THEM GO.
GREAT IDEA, MIKEY.
TO BE HONEST...
...ONCE I'VE FINISHED--
DEATH IS A MERCY.
NO ONE REALLY KNOWS THEM.
ECONOMIC MIGRANTS, MOSTLY.
NEWLY ARRIVED IN SWEDEN.
NO ONE REALLY CARES.
THEY JUST WASH AWAY...
YOU DON'T KNOW THAT.
I DO.
I KNOW EVERYTHING ABOUT THEM.
FOLLOW THEM FOR MONTHS...
...MAKE NOTES...
...I PHOTOGRAPH, CATEGORIZE.
I KNOW EVERYTHING ABOUT THEM BEFORE I EVER TOUCH THEM.
I CAN TELL YOU TO WITHIN HALF A KILO--
--WHAT THEY WILL WEIGH--
--WHEN THEY'RE BLOODLESS AND IN A SACK.

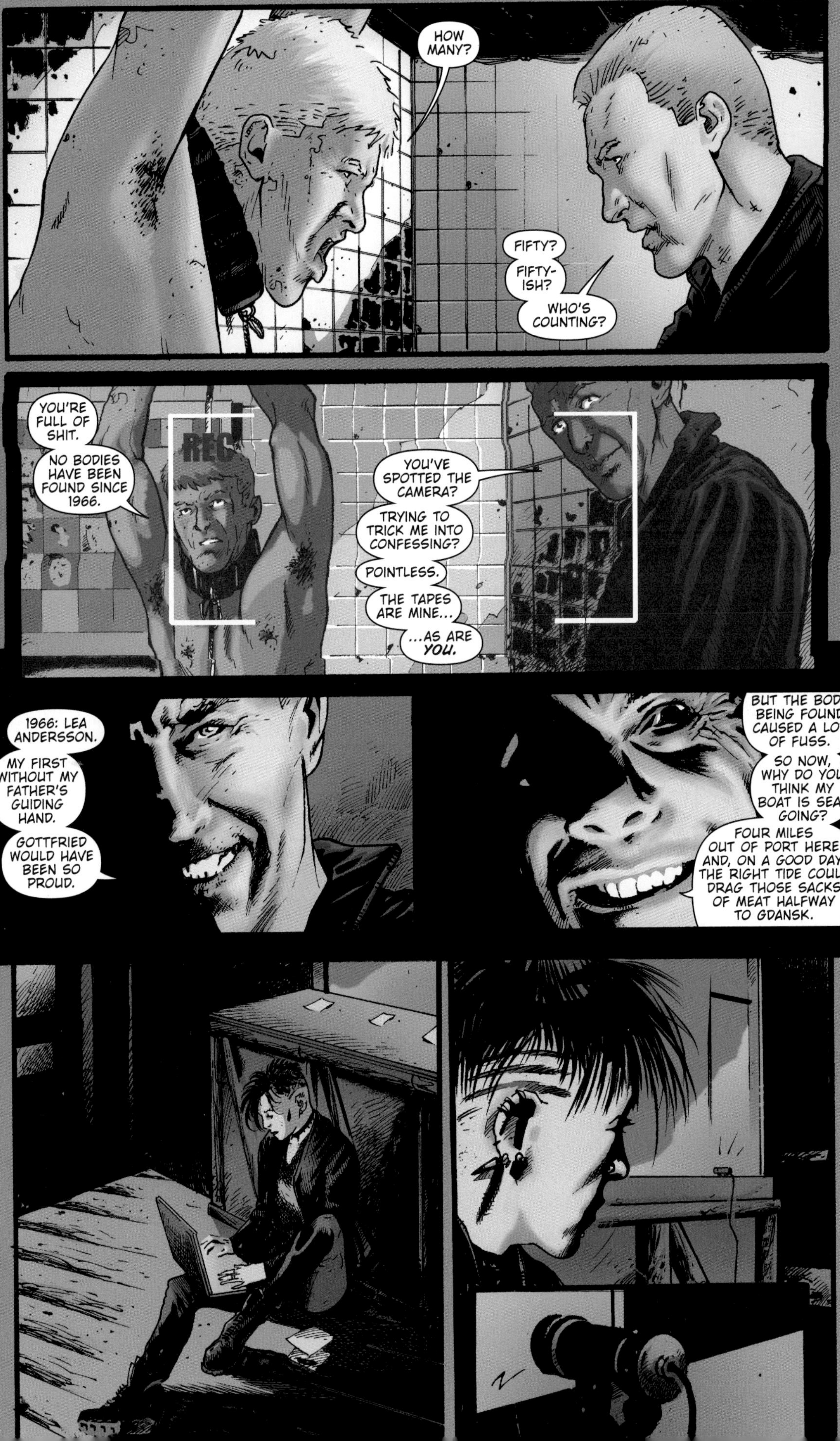
HOW MANY?
FIFTY?
FIFTY-ISH?
WHO'S COUNTING?
YOU'RE FULL OF SHIT.
NO BODIES HAVE BEEN FOUND SINCE 1966.
REC
YOU'VE SPOTTED THE CAMERA?
TRYING TO TRICK ME INTO CONFESSING?
POINTLESS.
THE TAPES ARE MINE...
...AS ARE *YOU.*
1966: LEA ANDERSSON.
MY FIRST WITHOUT MY FATHER'S GUIDING HAND.
GOTTFRIED WOULD HAVE BEEN SO PROUD.
BUT THE BODY BEING FOUND CAUSED A LOT OF FUSS.
SO NOW, WHY DO YOU THINK MY BOAT IS SEA-GOING?
FOUR MILES OUT OF PORT HERE AND, ON A GOOD DAY, THE RIGHT TIDE COULD DRAG THOSE SACKS OF MEAT HALFWAY TO GDANSK.

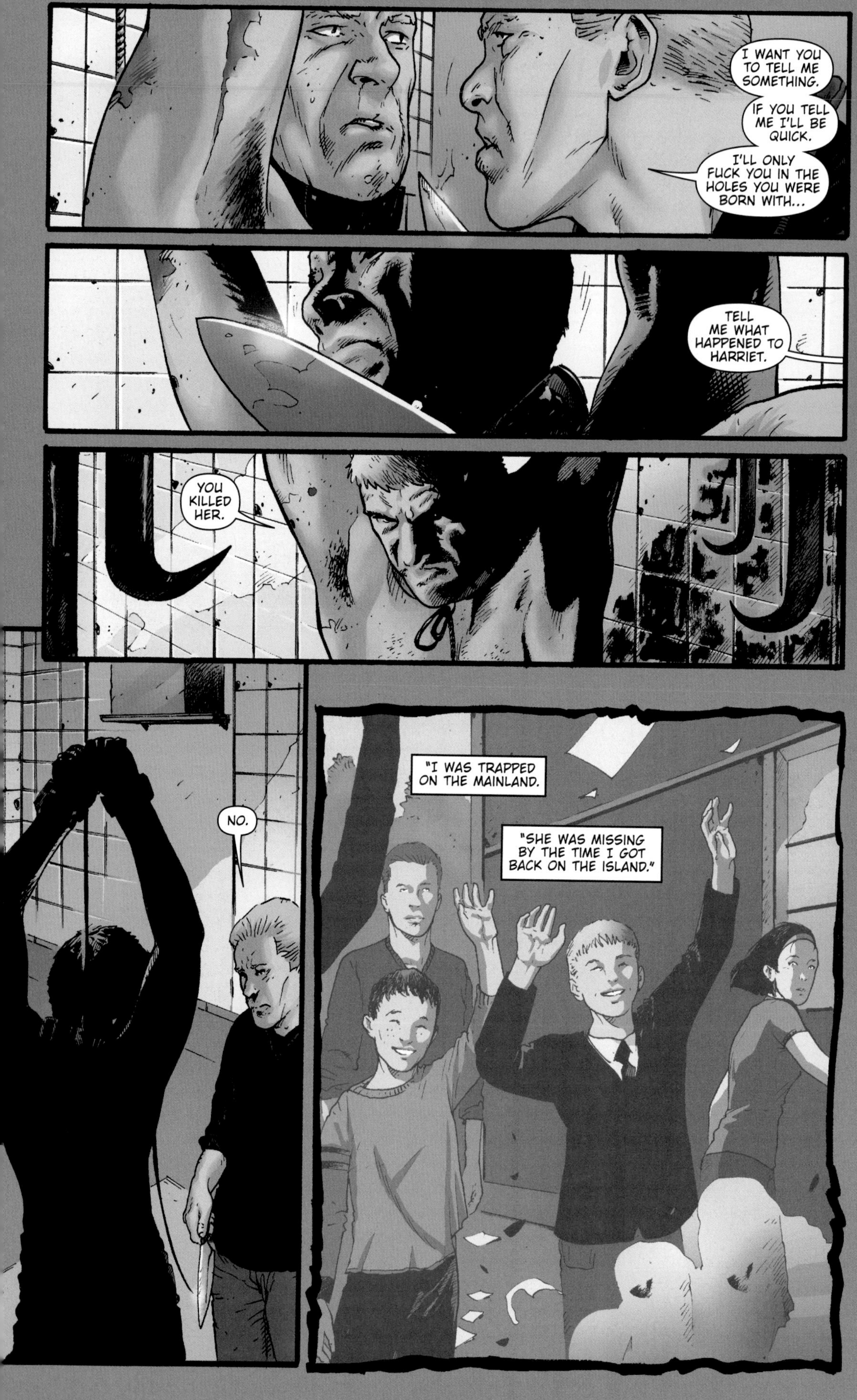
I WANT YOU TO TELL ME SOMETHING.
IF YOU TELL ME I'LL BE QUICK.
I'LL ONLY FUCK YOU IN THE HOLES YOU WERE BORN WITH...
TELL ME WHAT HAPPENED TO HARRIET.
YOU KILLED HER.
NO.
"I WAS TRAPPED ON THE MAINLAND.
"SHE WAS MISSING BY THE TIME I GOT BACK ON THE ISLAND."

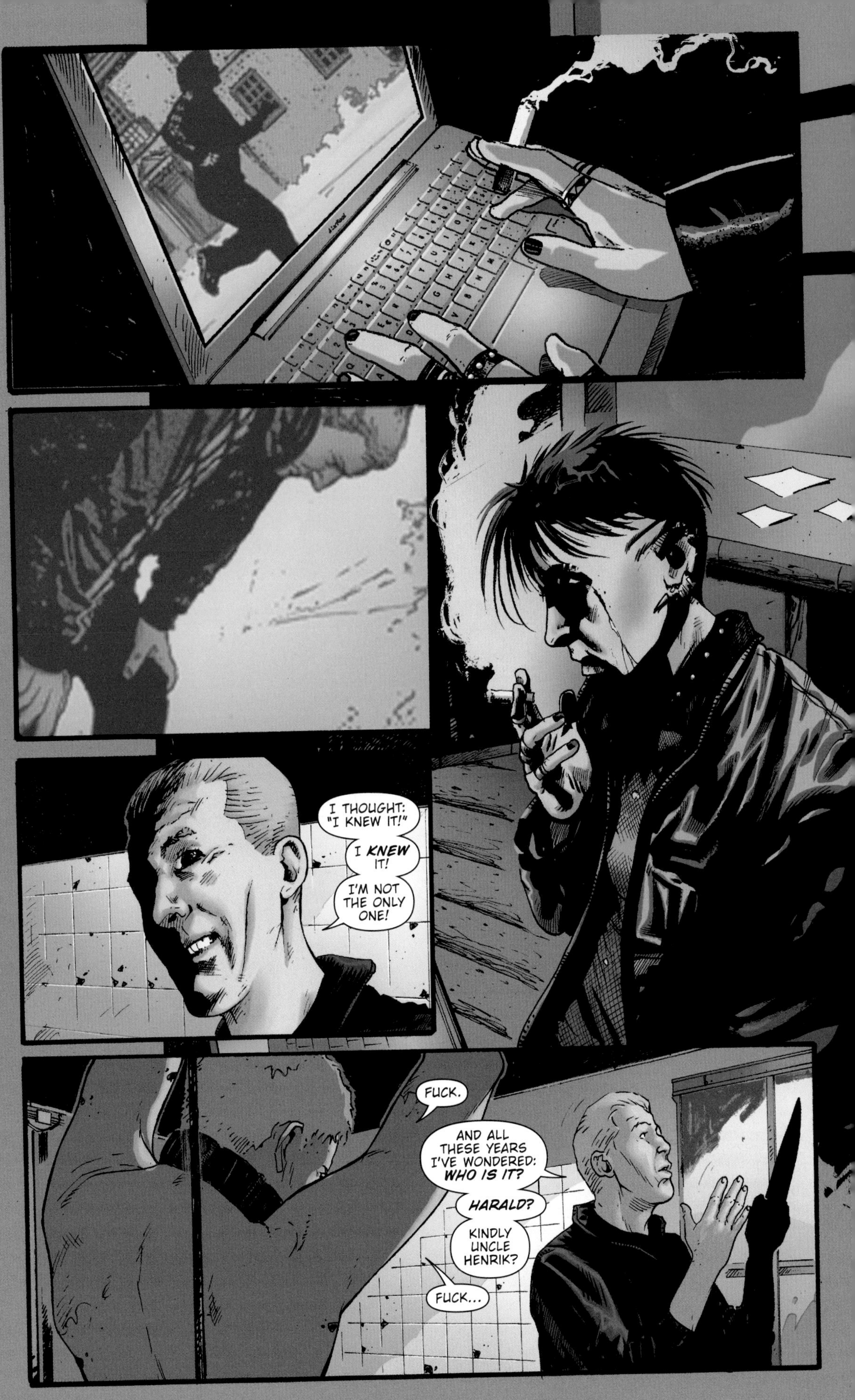
I THOUGHT: "I KNEW IT!"
I *KNEW* IT!
I'M NOT THE ONLY ONE!
FUCK.
AND ALL THESE YEARS I'VE WONDERED: *WHO IS IT?*
HARALD?
KINDLY UNCLE HENRIK?
FUCK...

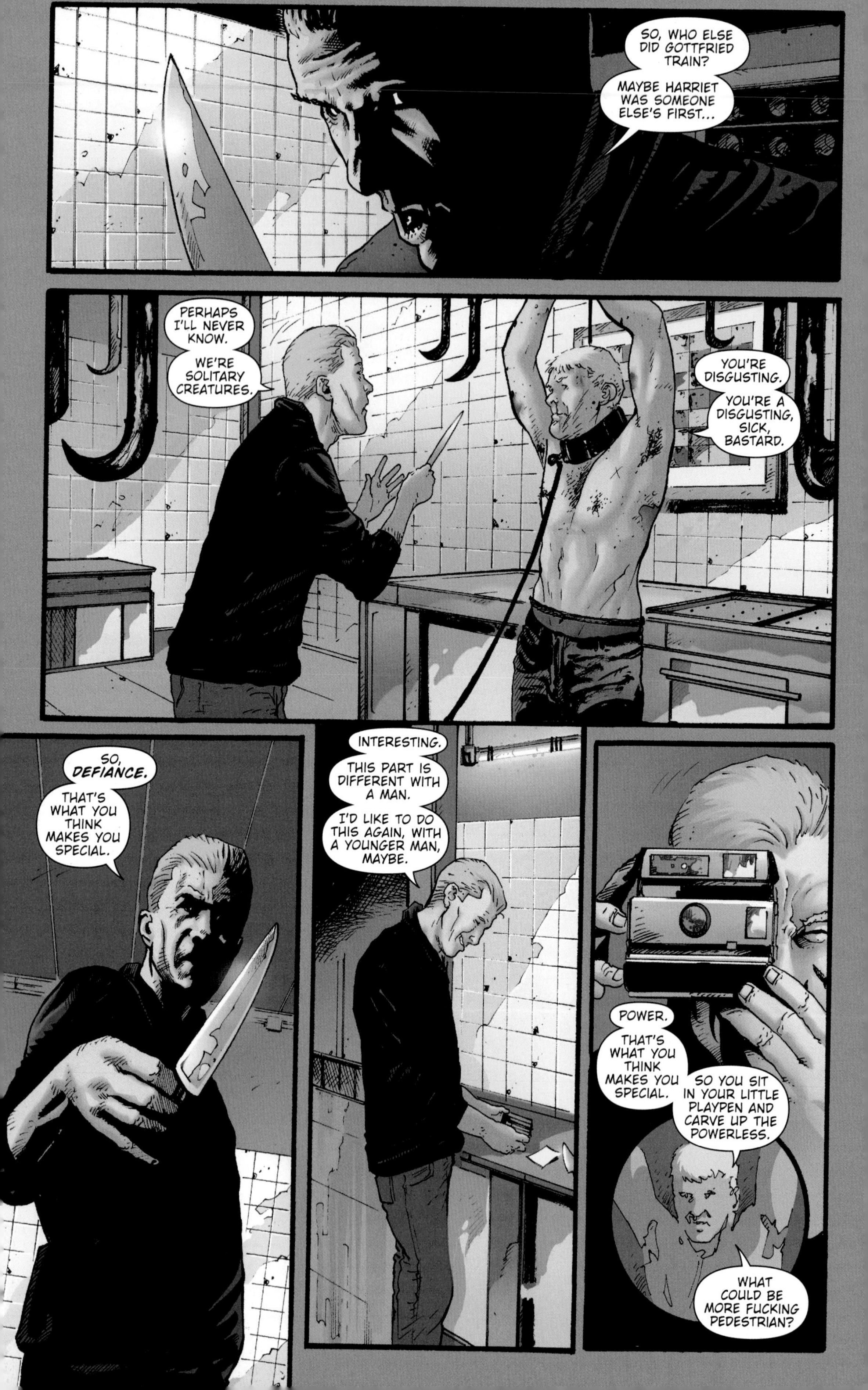
SO, WHO ELSE DID GOTTFRIED TRAIN?
MAYBE HARRIET WAS SOMEONE ELSE'S FIRST...
PERHAPS I'LL NEVER KNOW.
WE'RE SOLITARY CREATURES.
YOU'RE DISGUSTING.
YOU'RE A DISGUSTING, SICK, BASTARD.
SO, ***DEFIANCE.***
THAT'S WHAT YOU THINK MAKES YOU SPECIAL.
INTERESTING.
THIS PART IS DIFFERENT WITH A MAN.
I'D LIKE TO DO THIS AGAIN, WITH A YOUNGER MAN, MAYBE.
POWER.
THAT'S WHAT YOU THINK MAKES YOU SPECIAL.
SO YOU SIT IN YOUR LITTLE PLAYPEN AND CARVE UP THE POWERLESS.
WHAT COULD BE MORE FUCKING PEDESTRIAN?

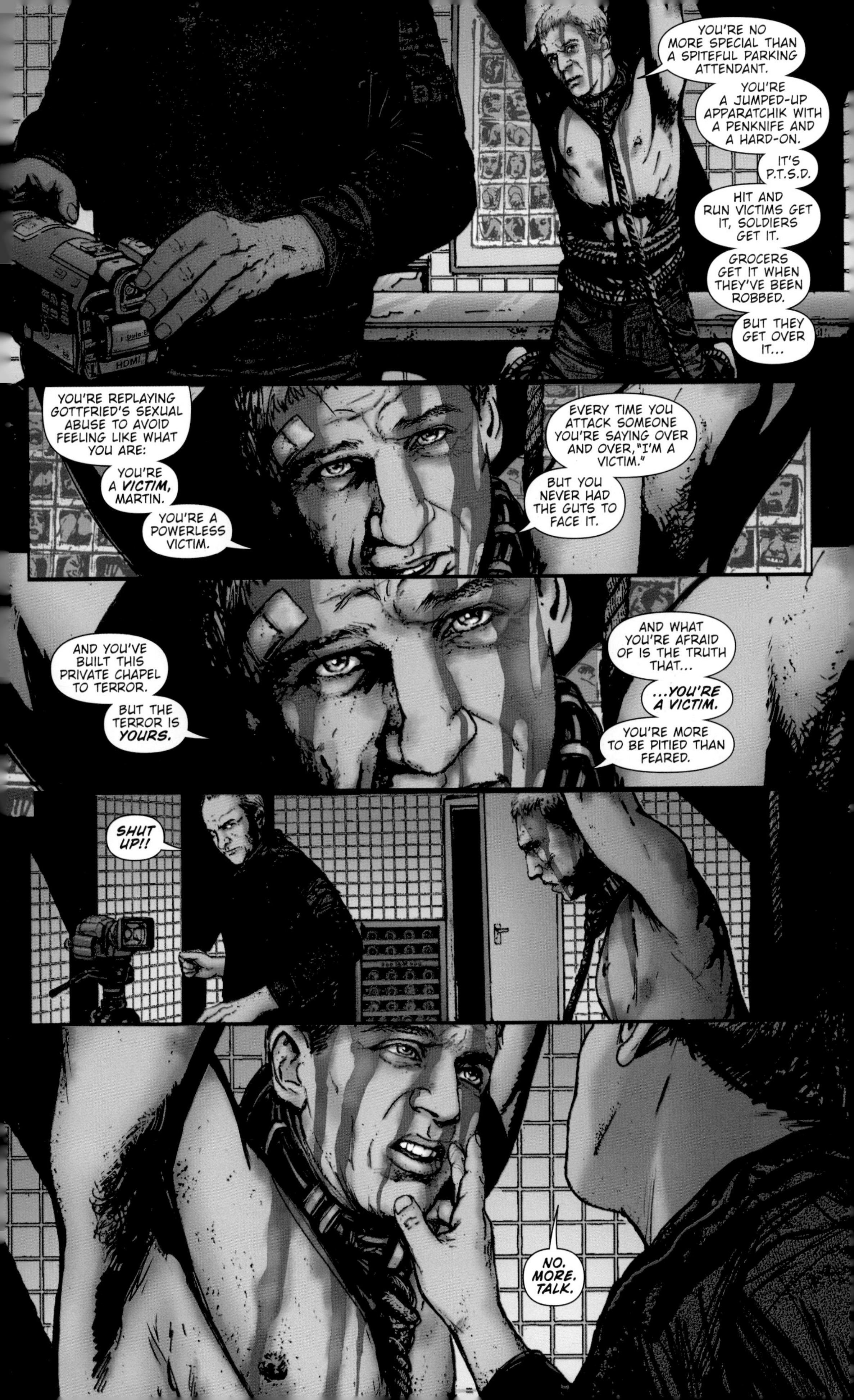
YOU'RE NO MORE SPECIAL THAN A SPITEFUL PARKING ATTENDANT.
YOU'RE A JUMPED-UP APPARATCHIK WITH A PENKNIFE AND A HARD-ON.
IT'S P.T.S.D.
HIT AND RUN VICTIMS GET IT, SOLDIERS GET IT.
GROCERS GET IT WHEN THEY'VE BEEN ROBBED.
BUT THEY GET OVER IT...
YOU'RE REPLAYING GOTTFRIED'S SEXUAL ABUSE TO AVOID FEELING LIKE WHAT YOU ARE:
YOU'RE A *VICTIM,* MARTIN.
YOU'RE A POWERLESS VICTIM.
EVERY TIME YOU ATTACK SOMEONE YOU'RE SAYING OVER AND OVER, "I'M A VICTIM."
BUT YOU NEVER HAD THE GUTS TO FACE IT.
AND YOU'VE BUILT THIS PRIVATE CHAPEL TO TERROR.
BUT THE TERROR IS *YOURS.*
AND WHAT YOU'RE AFRAID OF IS THE TRUTH THAT...
...YOU'RE A VICTIM.
YOU'RE MORE TO BE PITIED THAN FEARED.
SHUT UP!!
NO. MORE. TALK.

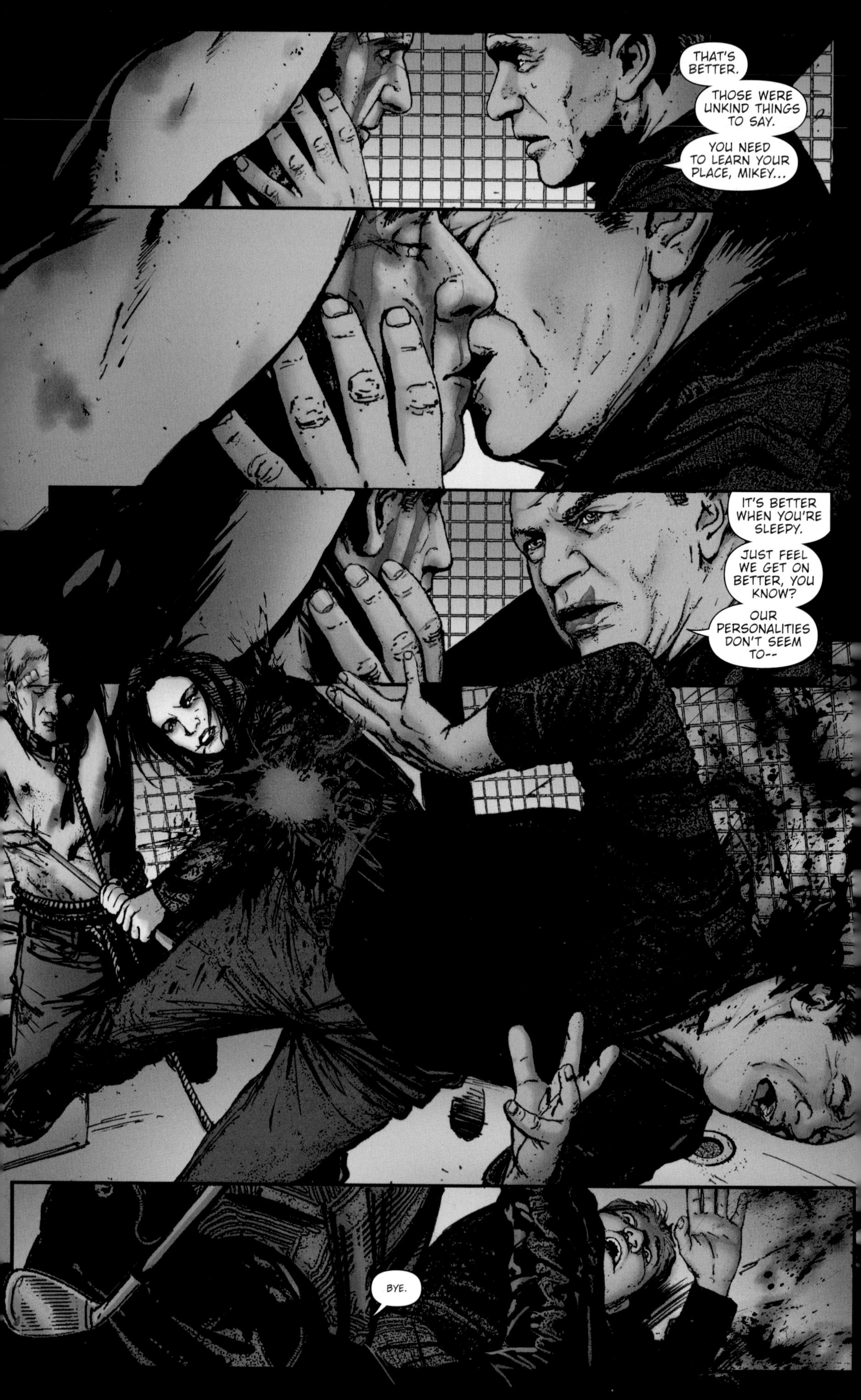
THAT'S BETTER.
THOSE WERE UNKIND THINGS TO SAY.
YOU NEED TO LEARN YOUR PLACE, MIKEY...
IT'S BETTER WHEN YOU'RE SLEEPY.
JUST FEEL WE GET ON BETTER, YOU KNOW?
OUR PERSONALITIES DON'T SEEM TO--
BYE.

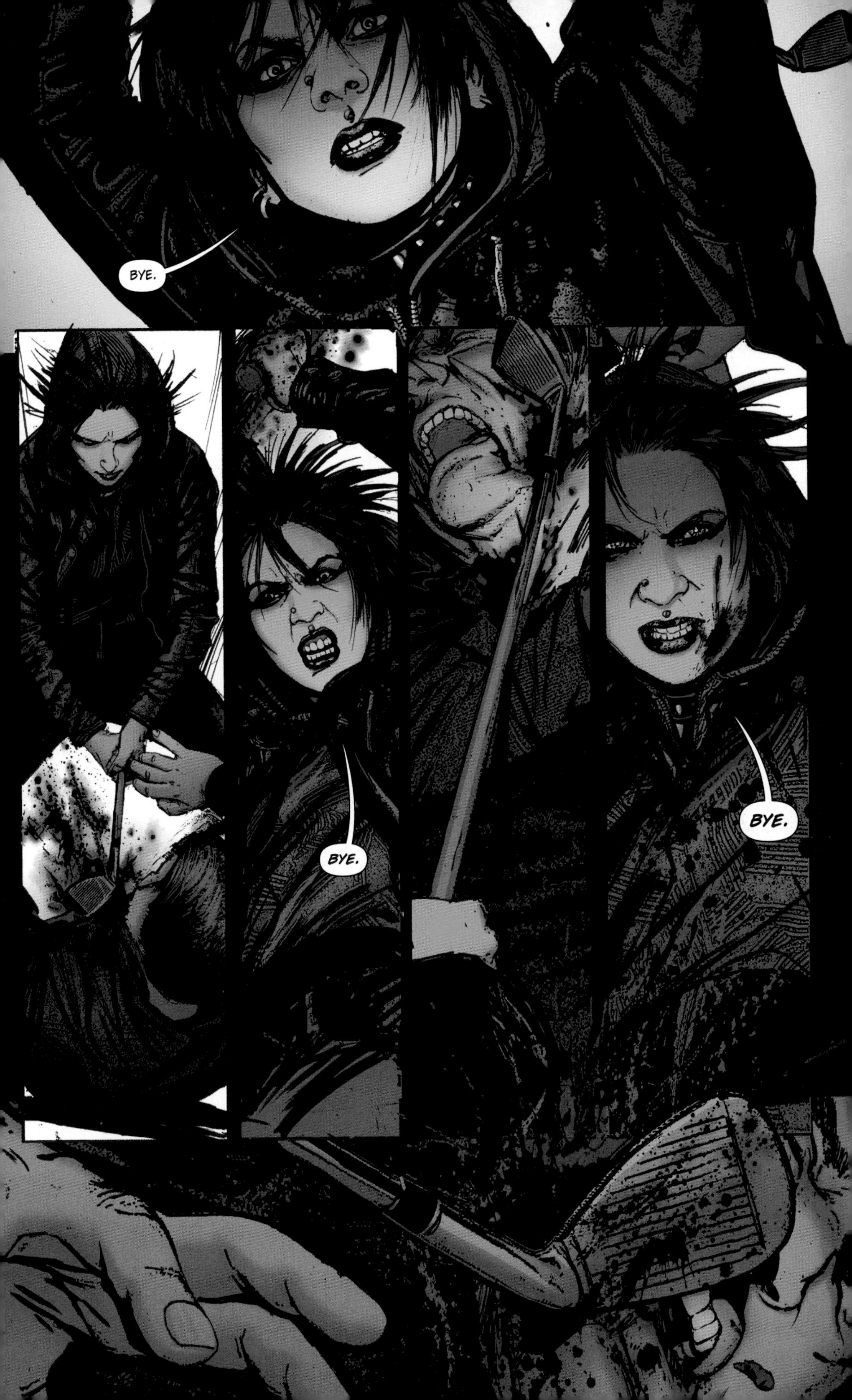
BYE.
BYE.
BYE.

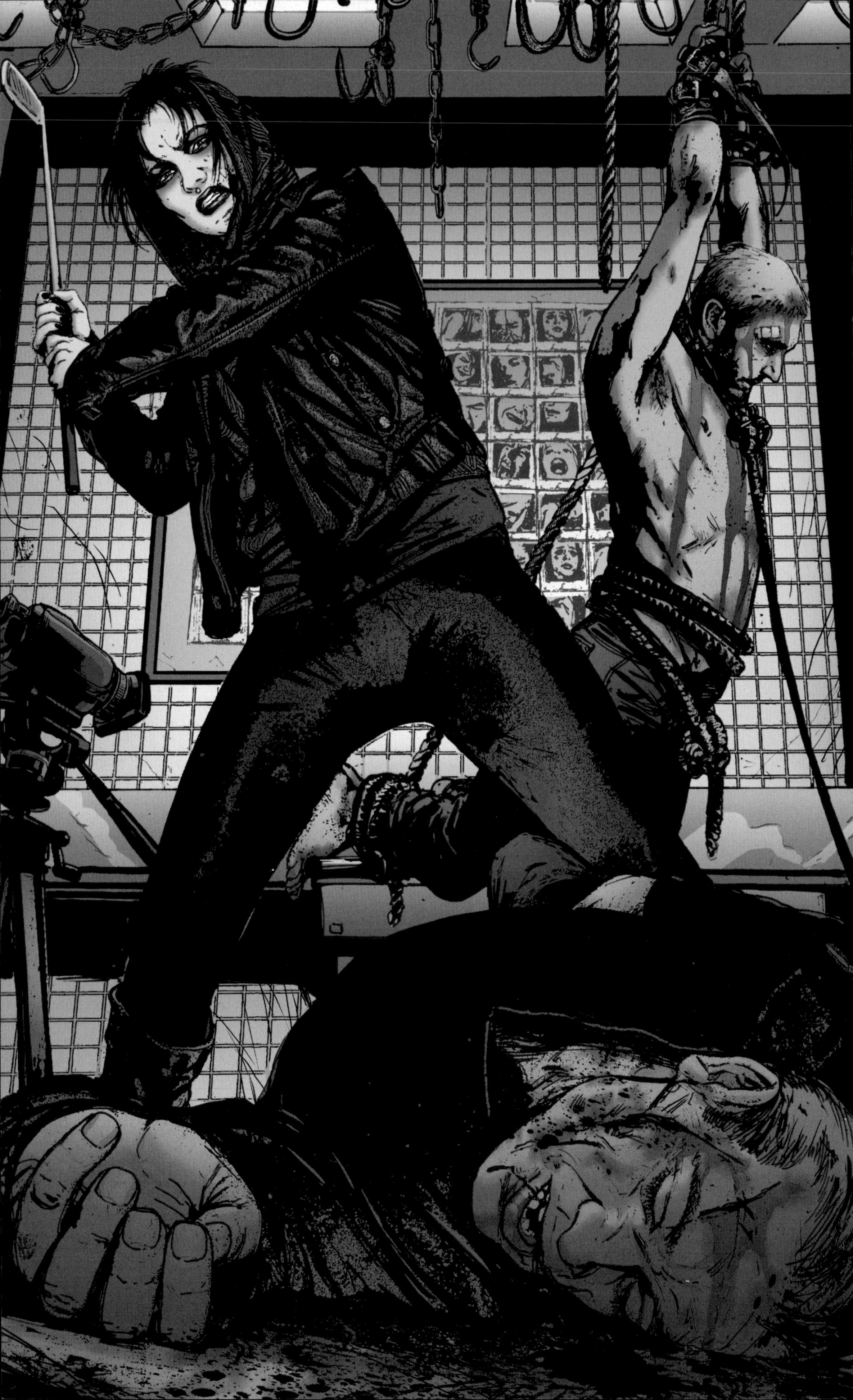

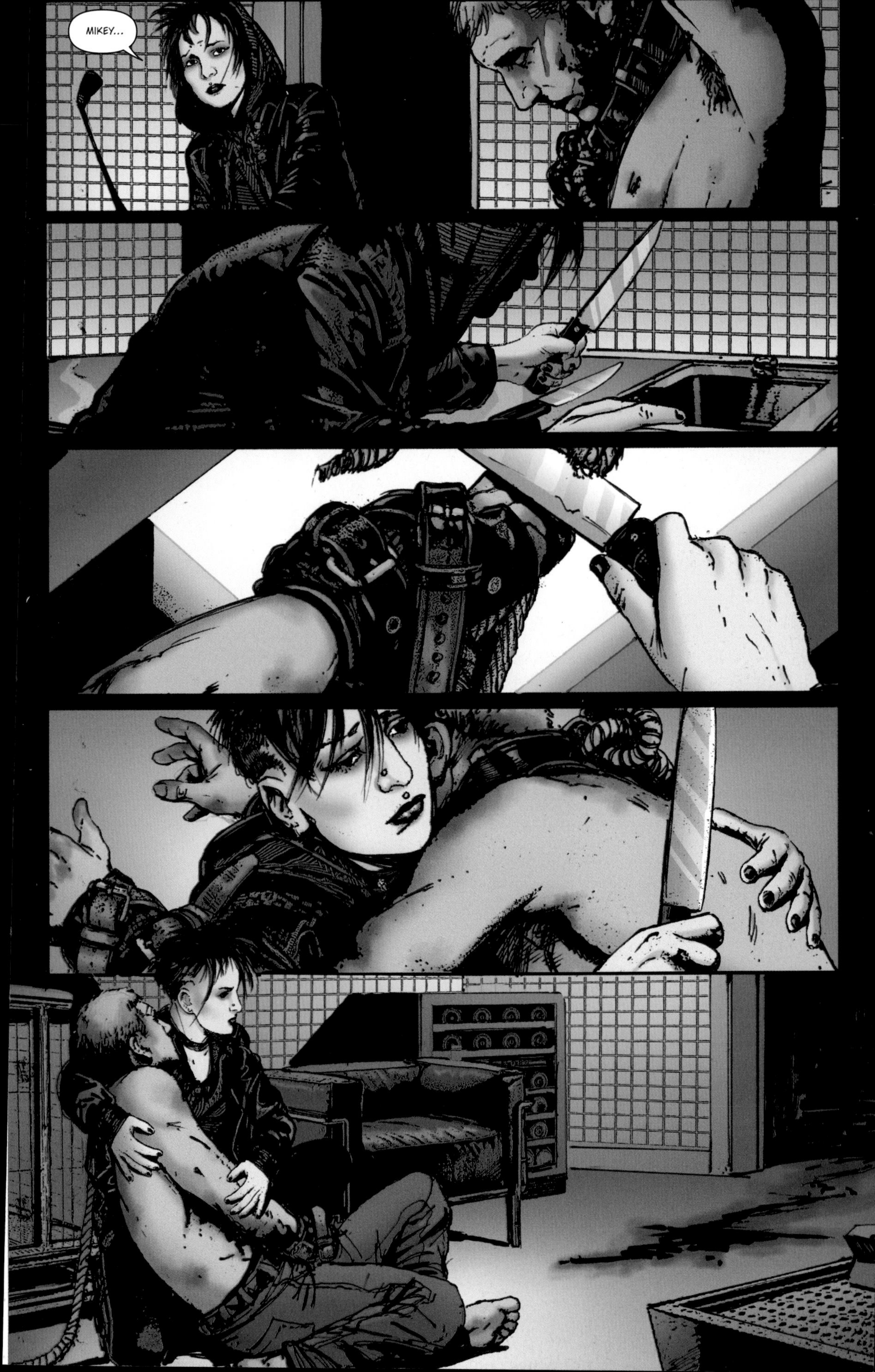
MIKEY...

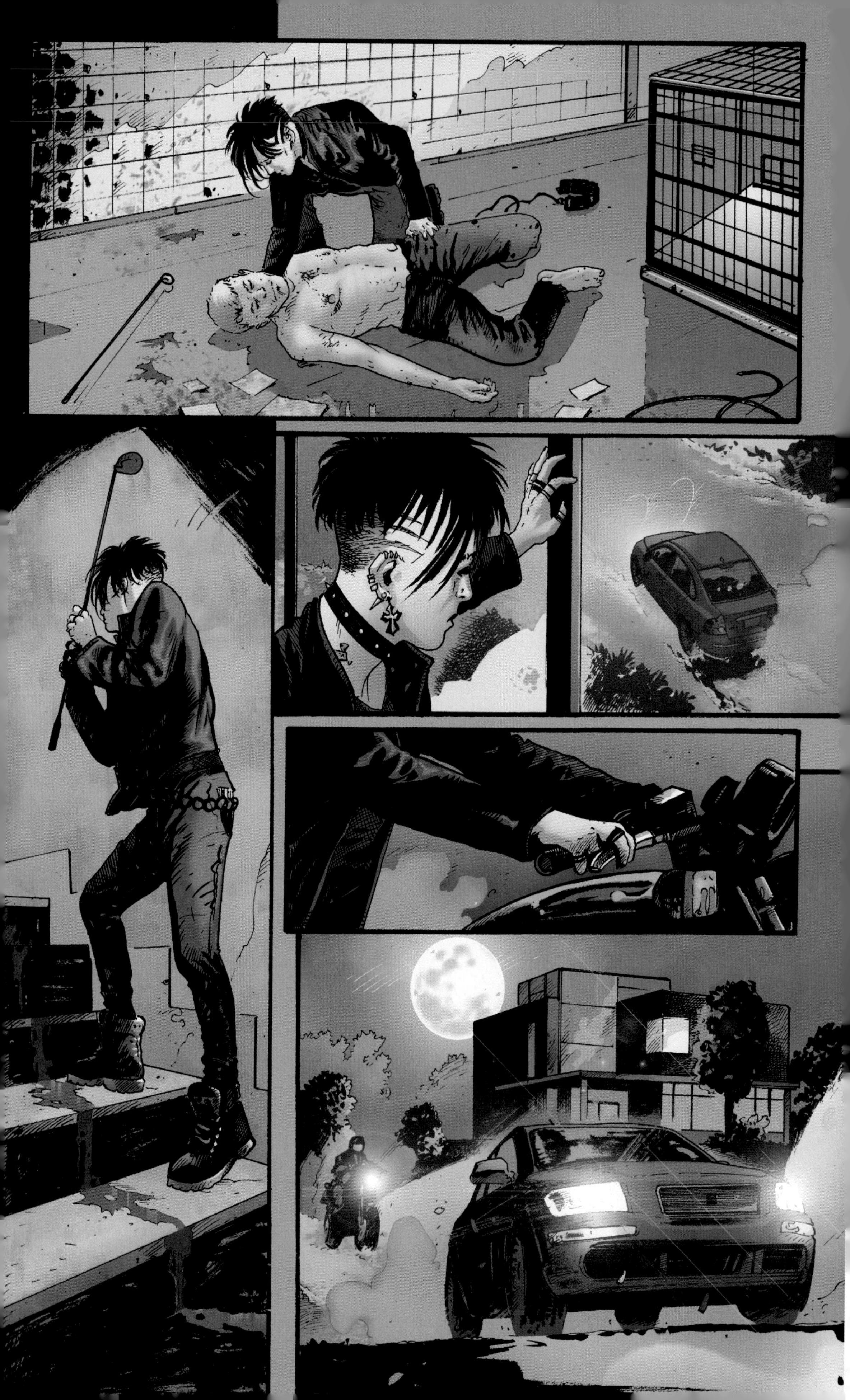

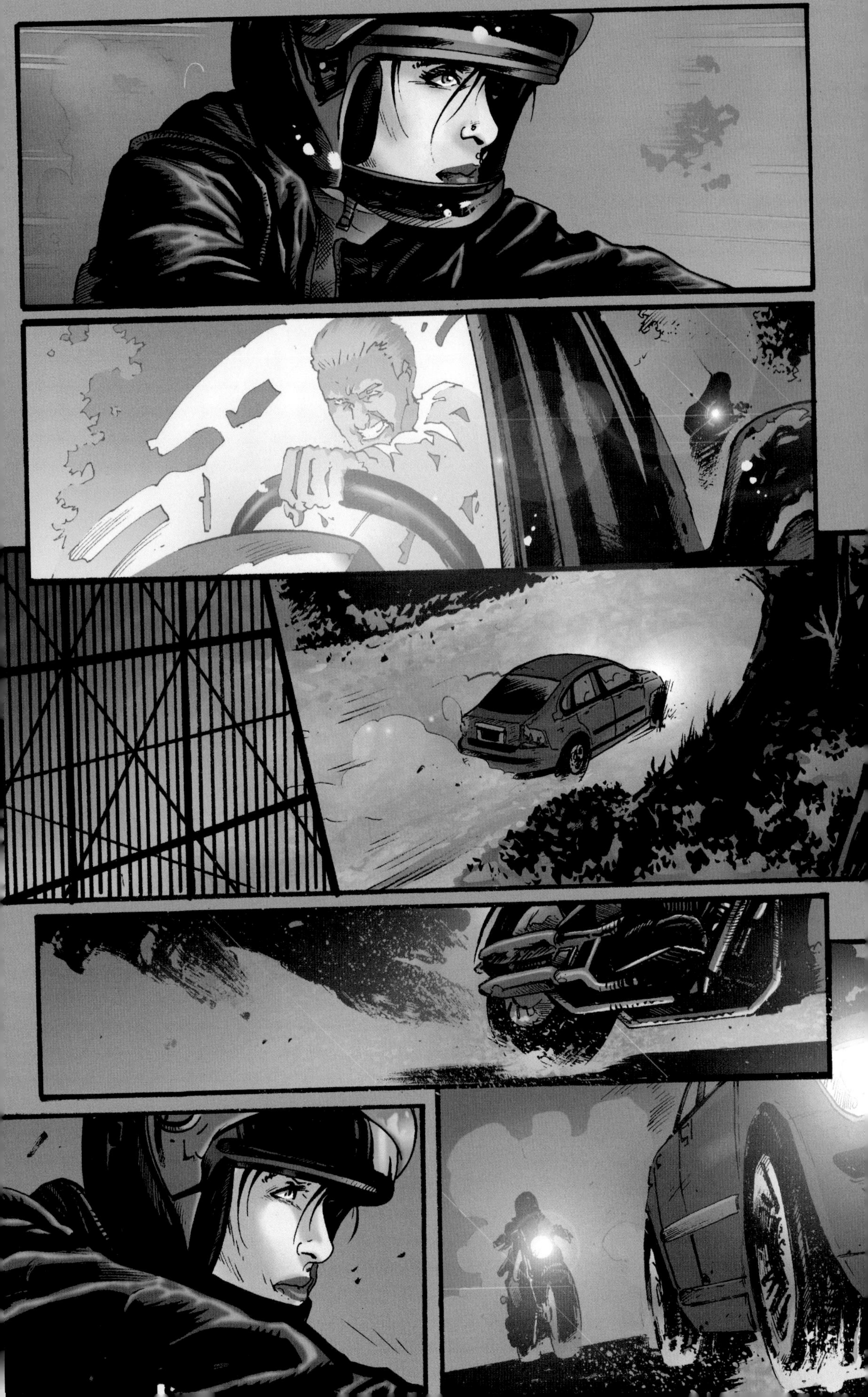

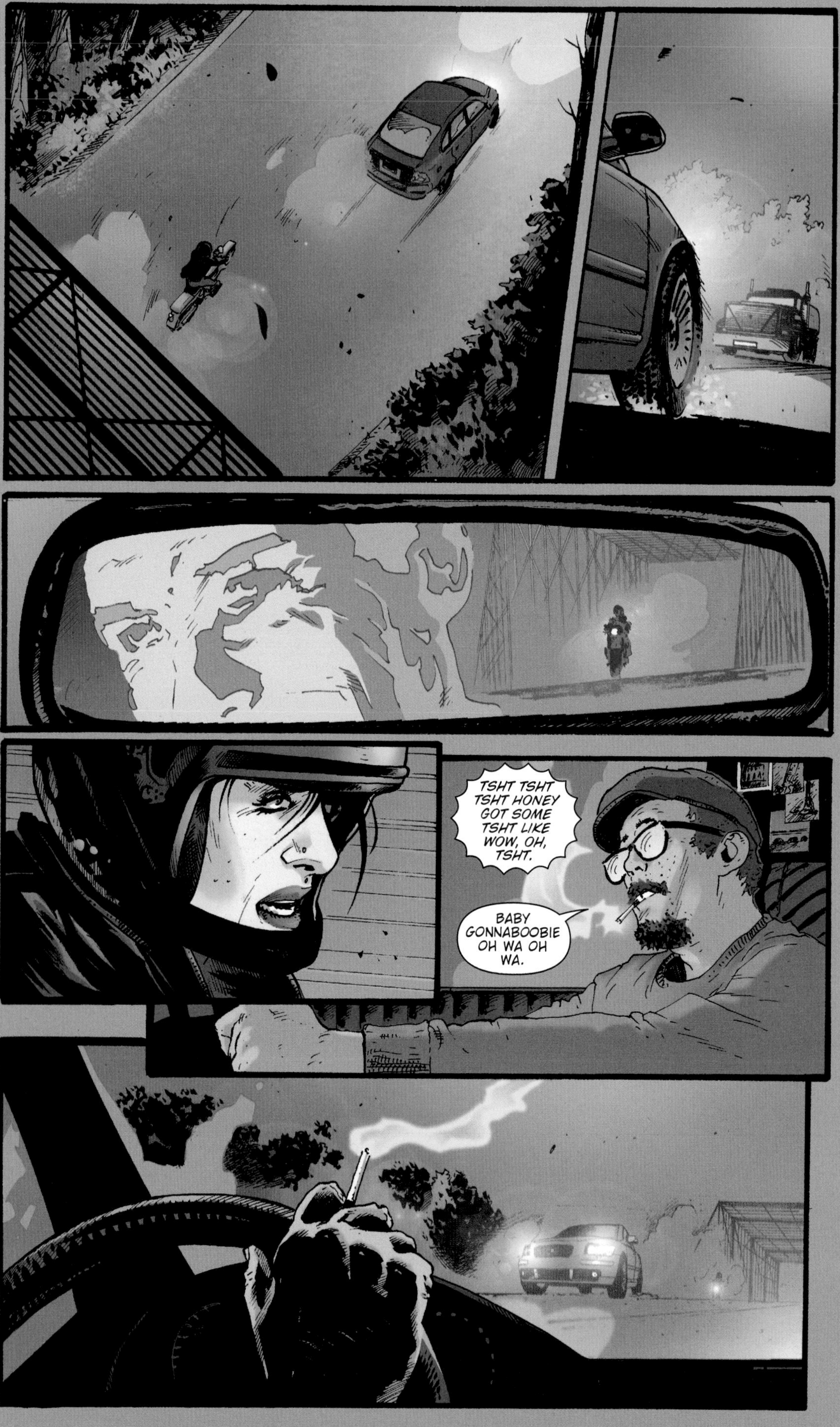
TSHT TSHT TSHT HONEY GOT SOME TSHT LIKE WOW, OH, TSHT.
BABY GONNABOOBIE OH WA OH WA.

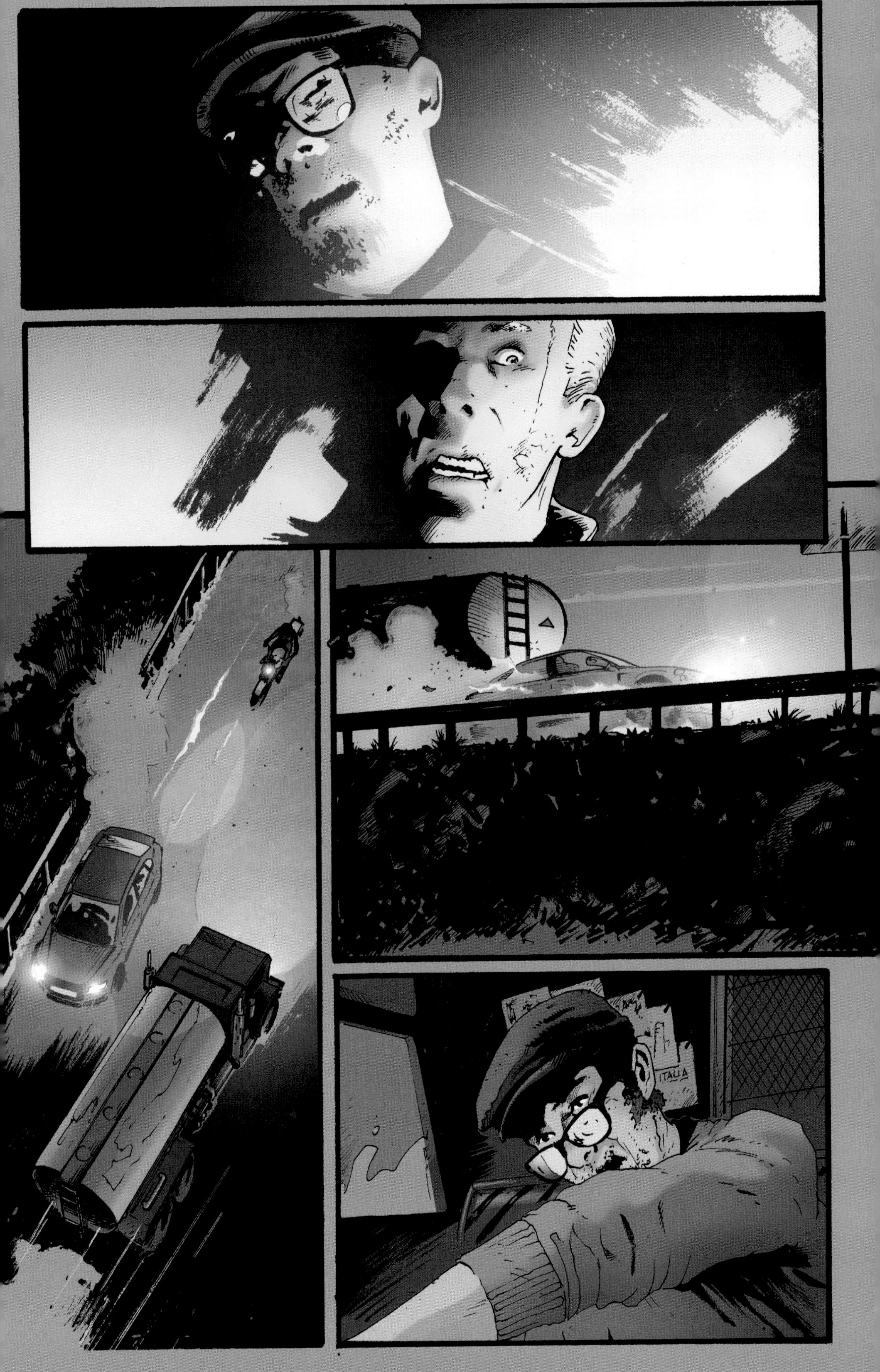
ITALIA

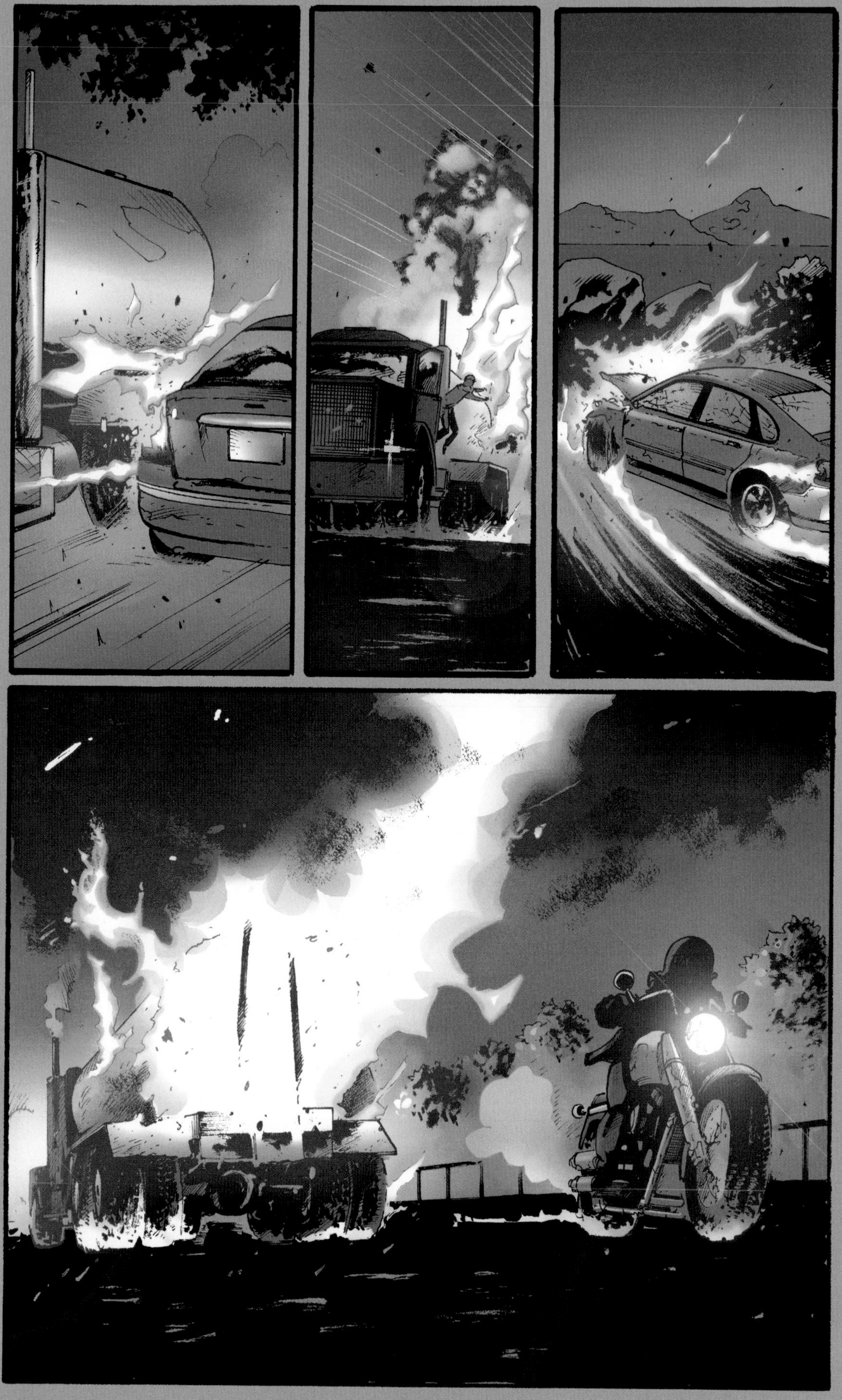

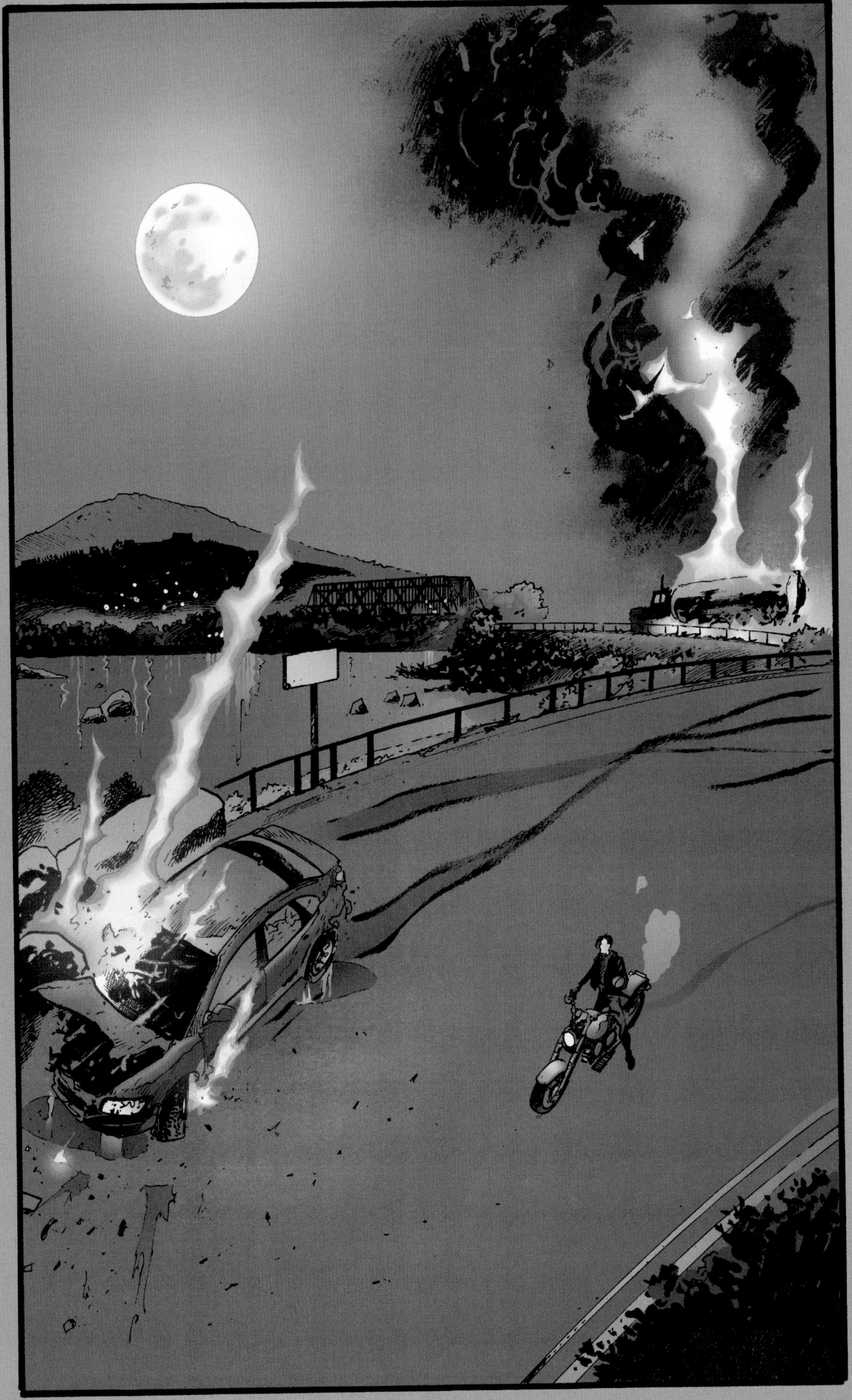

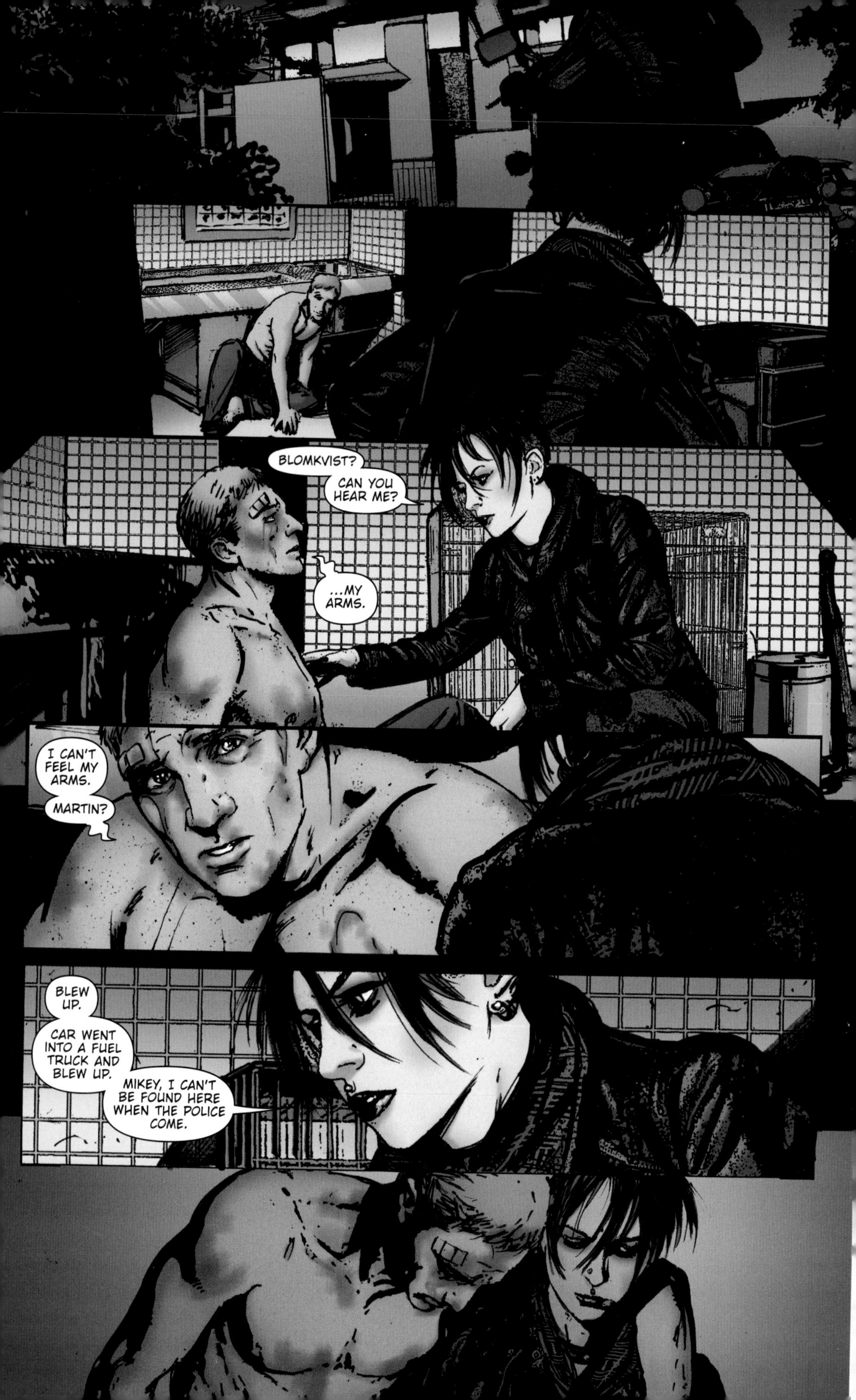
BLOMKVIST?
CAN YOU HEAR ME?
...MY ARMS.
I CAN'T FEEL MY ARMS.
MARTIN?
BLEW UP.
CAR WENT INTO A FUEL TRUCK AND BLEW UP.
MIKEY, I CAN'T BE FOUND HERE WHEN THE POLICE COME.

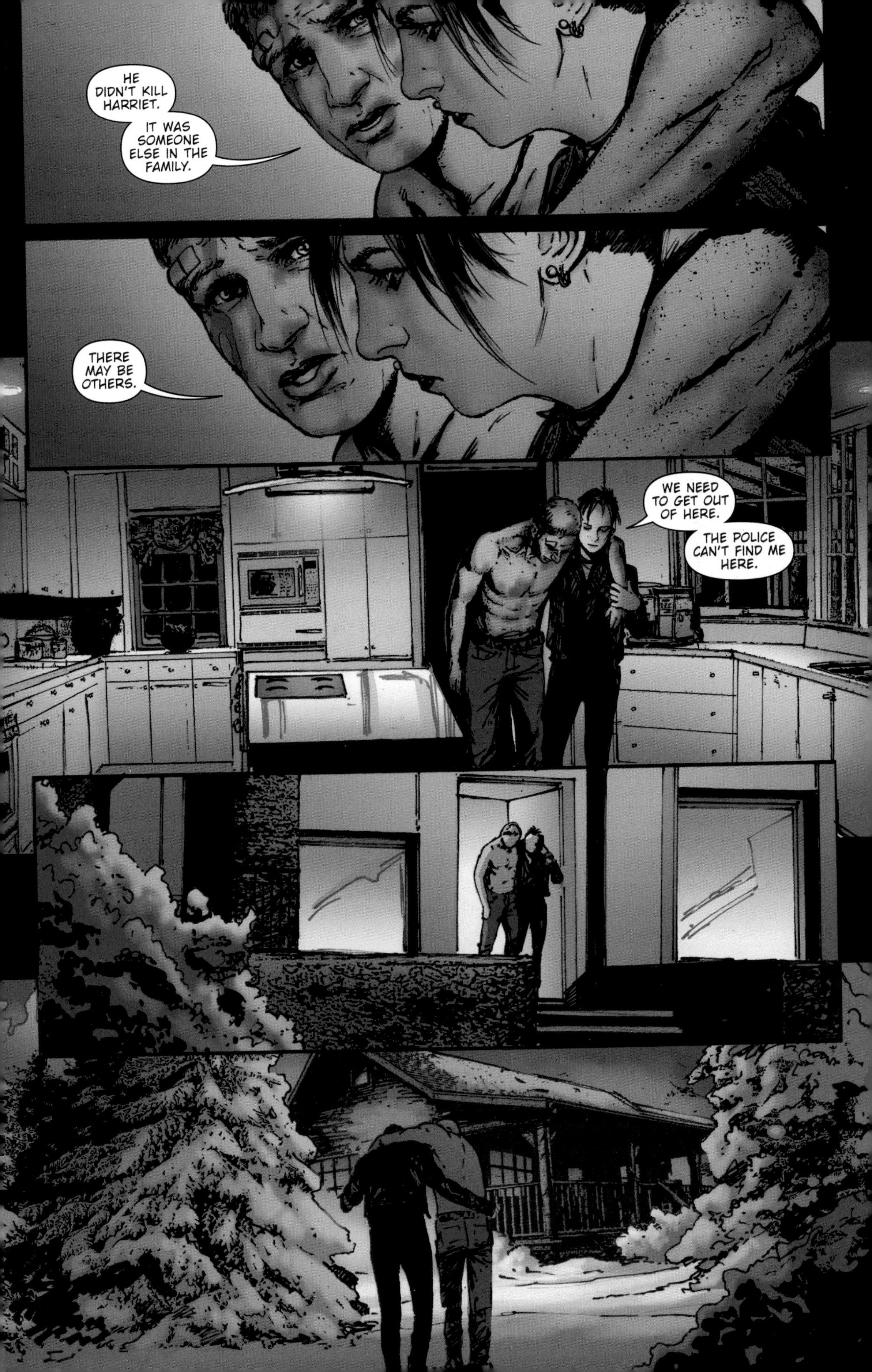
HE DIDN'T KILL HARRIET.
IT WAS SOMEONE ELSE IN THE FAMILY.
THERE MAY BE OTHERS.
WE NEED TO GET OUT OF HERE.
THE POLICE CAN'T FIND ME HERE.

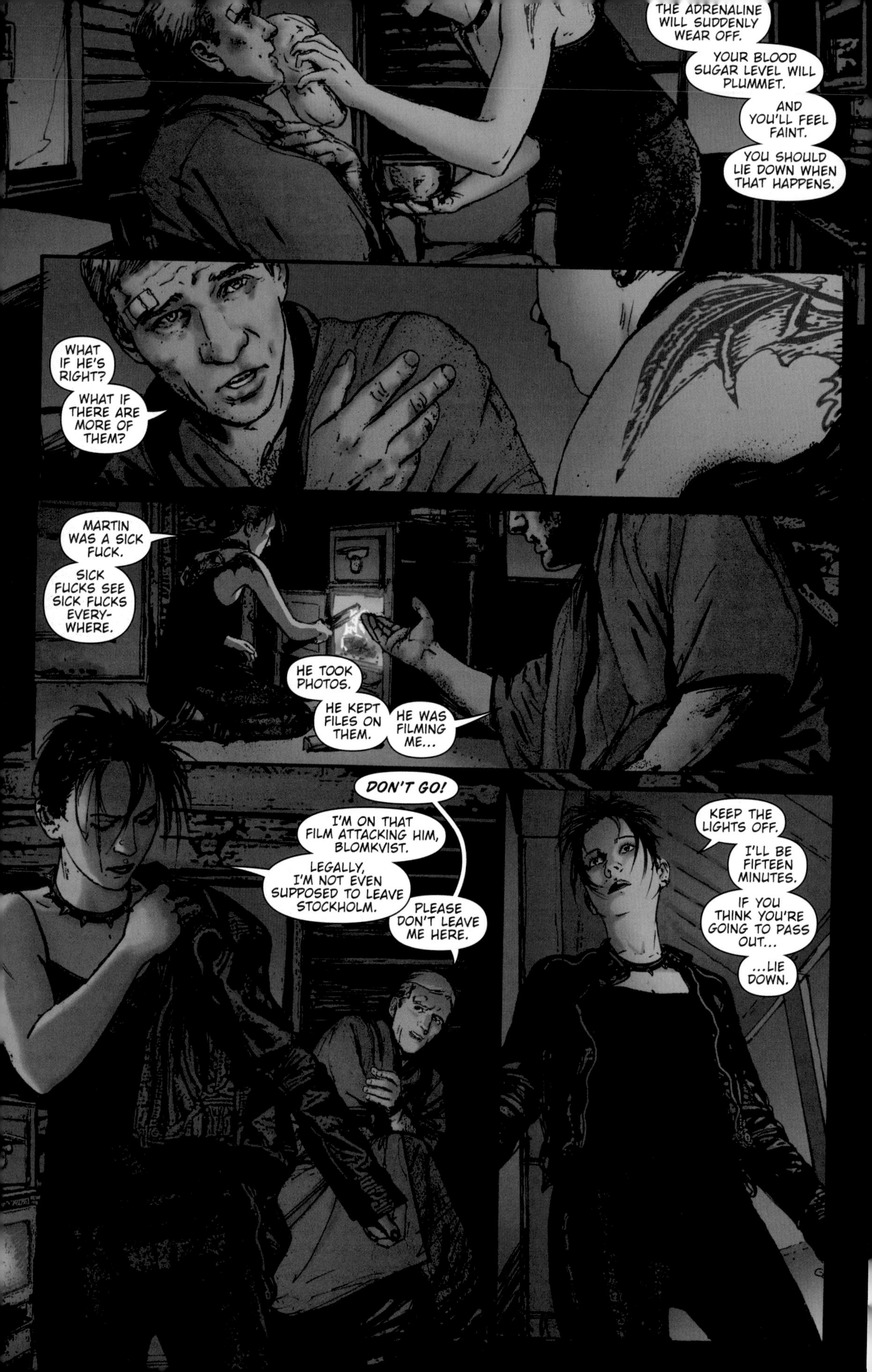
THE ADRENALINE WILL SUDDENLY WEAR OFF.
YOUR BLOOD SUGAR LEVEL WILL PLUMMET.
AND YOU'LL FEEL FAINT.
YOU SHOULD LIE DOWN WHEN THAT HAPPENS.
WHAT IF HE'S RIGHT?
WHAT IF THERE ARE MORE OF THEM?
MARTIN WAS A SICK FUCK.
SICK FUCKS SEE SICK FUCKS EVERY-WHERE.
HE TOOK PHOTOS.
HE KEPT FILES ON THEM.
HE WAS FILMING ME...
DON'T GO!
I'M ON THAT FILM ATTACKING HIM, BLOMKVIST.
LEGALLY, I'M NOT EVEN SUPPOSED TO LEAVE STOCKHOLM.
PLEASE DON'T LEAVE ME HERE.
KEEP THE LIGHTS OFF.
I'LL BE FIFTEEN MINUTES.
IF YOU THINK YOU'RE GOING TO PASS OUT...
...LIE DOWN.

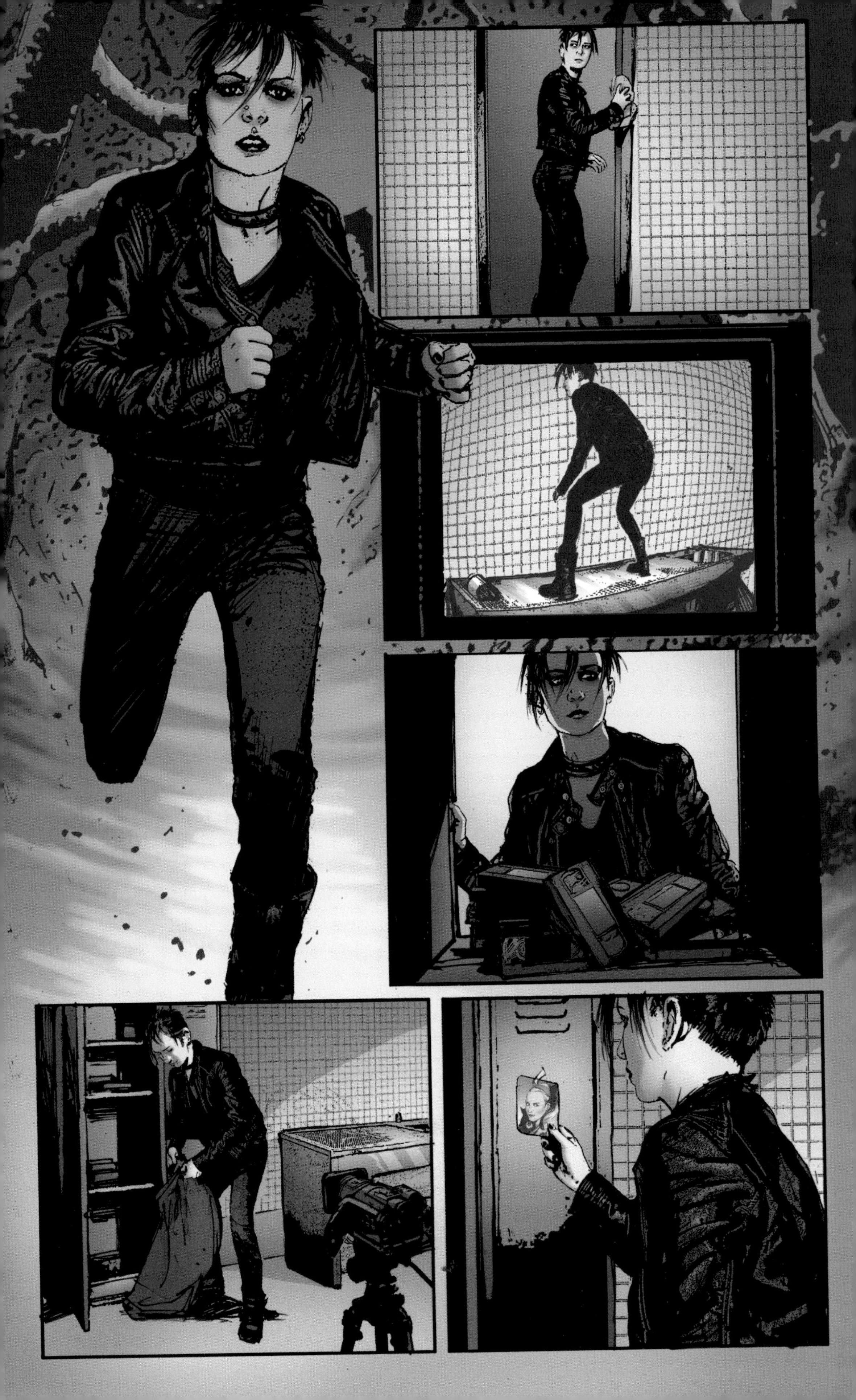

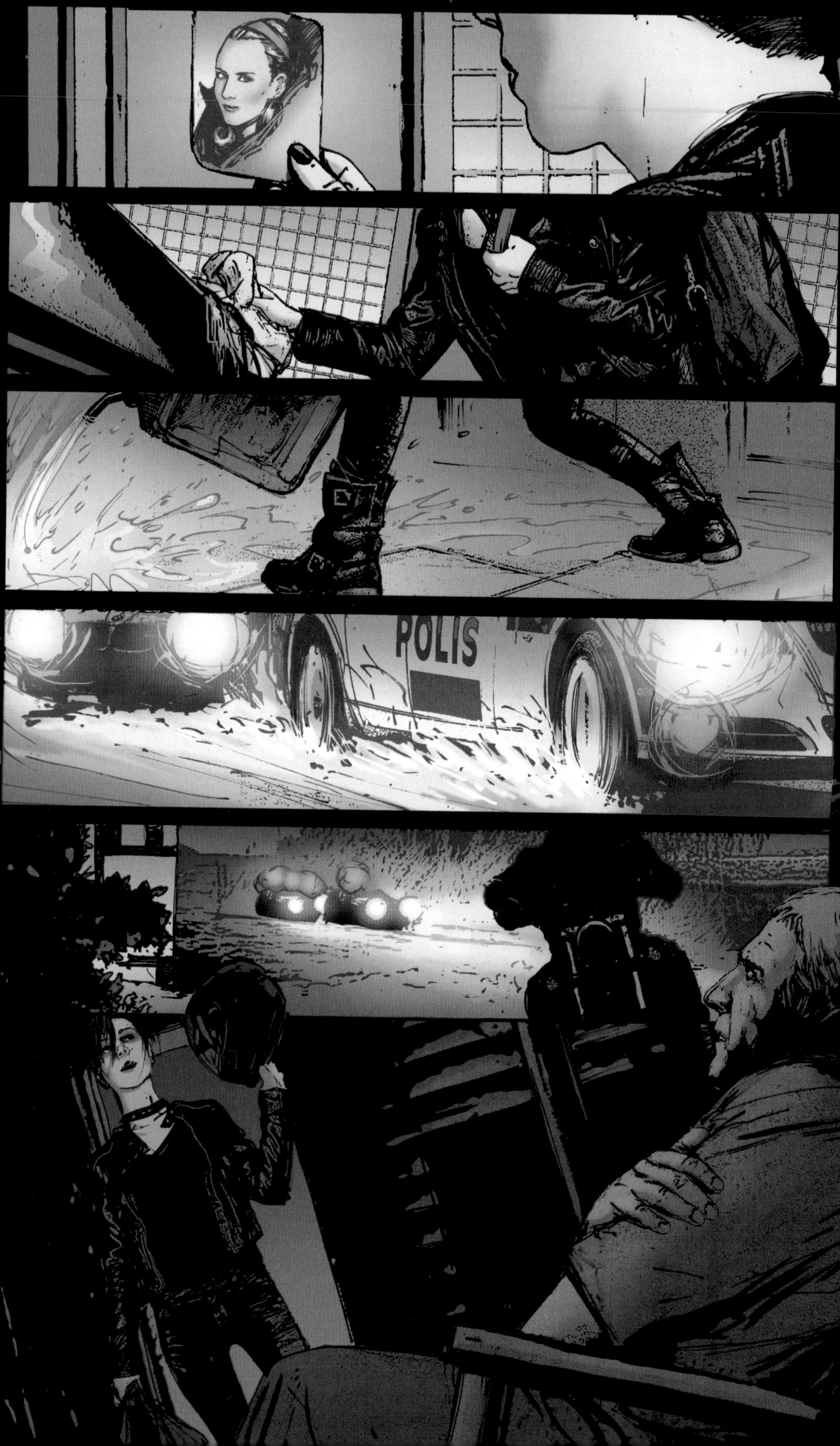
POLIS

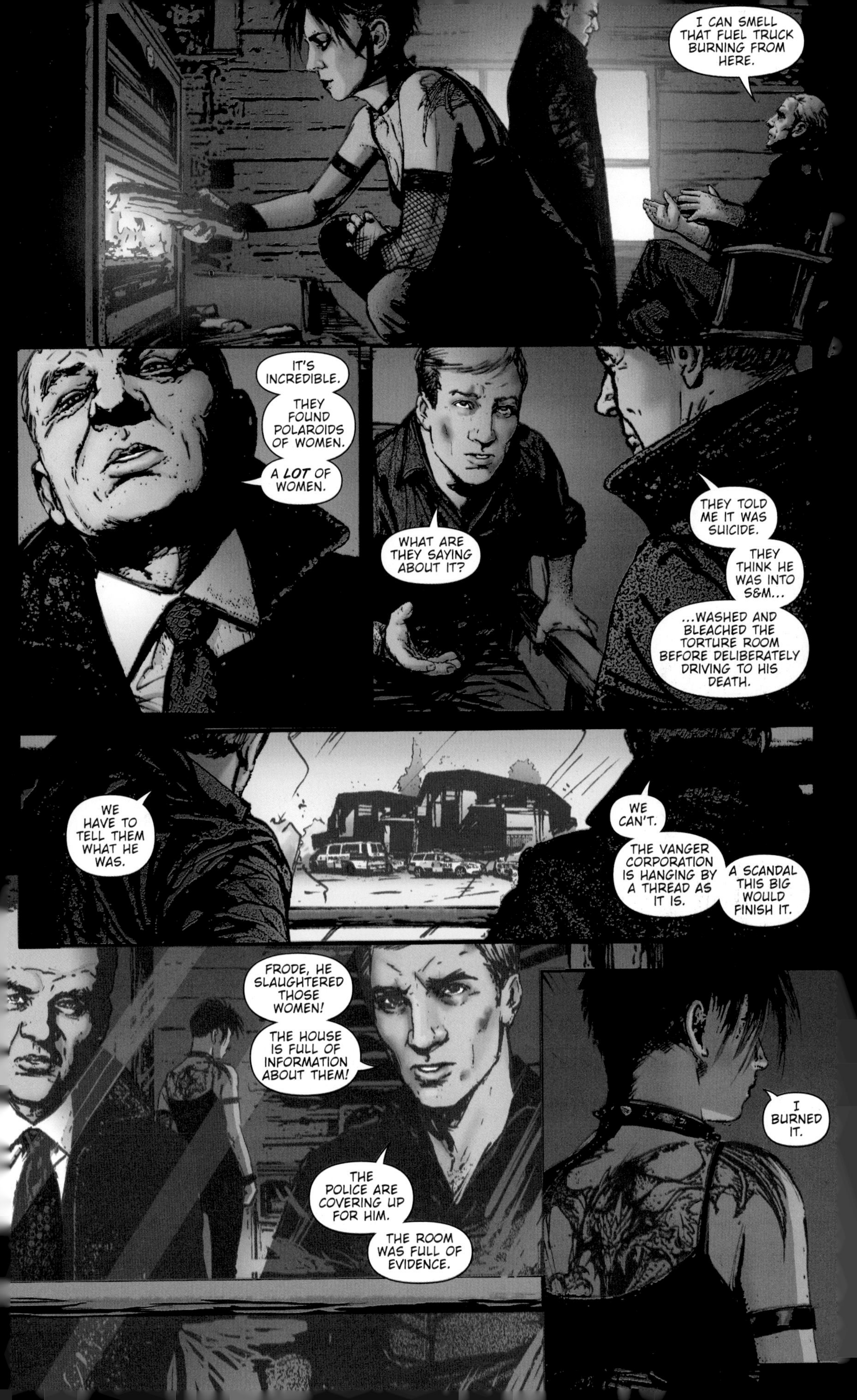
I CAN SMELL THAT FUEL TRUCK BURNING FROM HERE.
IT'S INCREDIBLE.
THEY FOUND POLAROIDS OF WOMEN.
A **LOT** OF WOMEN.
WHAT ARE THEY SAYING ABOUT IT?
THEY TOLD ME IT WAS SUICIDE.
THEY THINK HE WAS INTO S&M...
...WASHED AND BLEACHED THE TORTURE ROOM BEFORE DELIBERATELY DRIVING TO HIS DEATH.
WE HAVE TO TELL THEM WHAT HE WAS.
WE CAN'T.
THE VANGER CORPORATION IS HANGING BY A THREAD AS IT IS.
A SCANDAL THIS BIG WOULD FINISH IT.
FRODE, HE SLAUGHTERED THOSE WOMEN!
THE HOUSE IS FULL OF INFORMATION ABOUT THEM!
THE POLICE ARE COVERING UP FOR HIM.
THE ROOM WAS FULL OF EVIDENCE.
I BURNED IT.

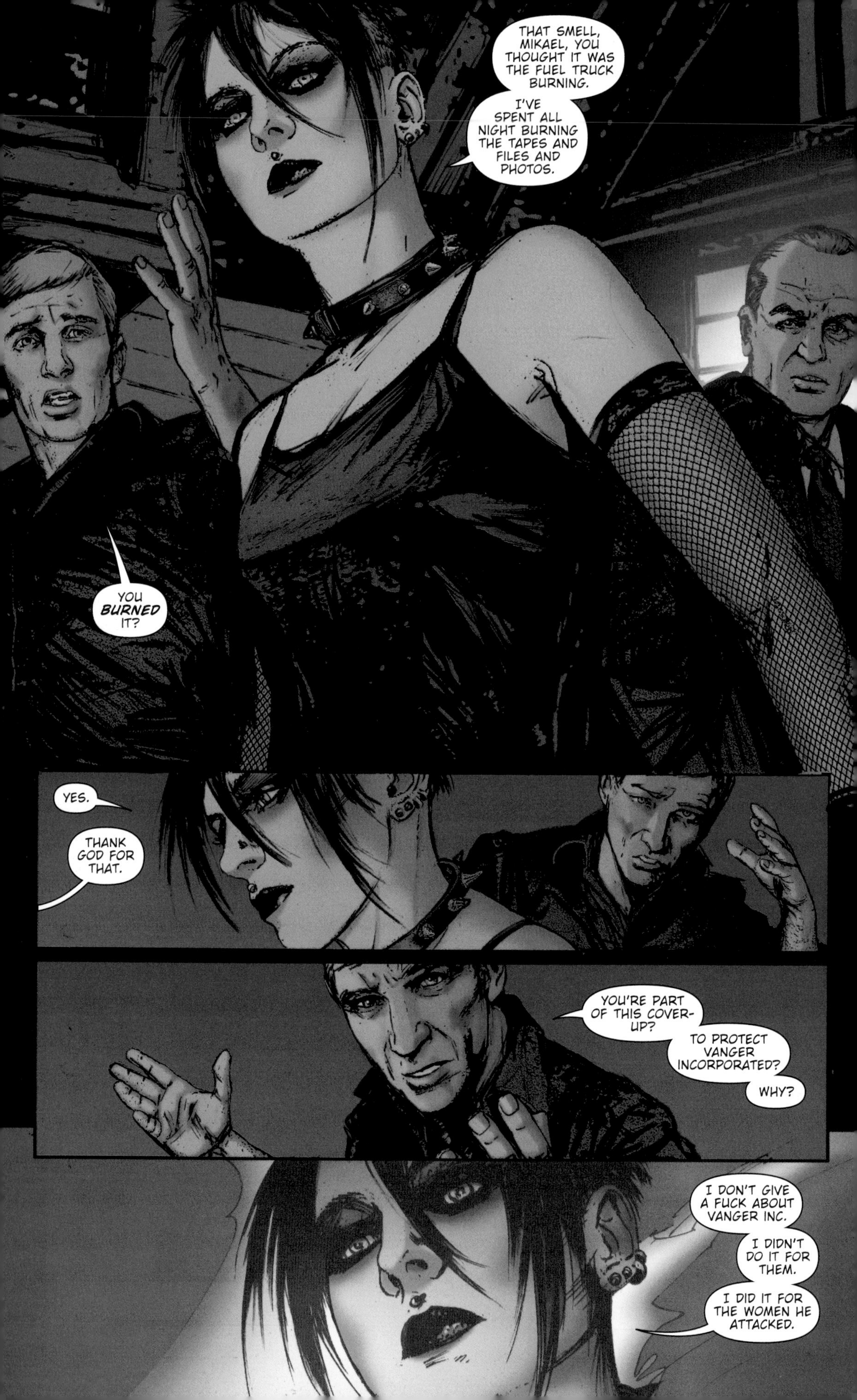
THAT SMELL, MIKAEL, YOU THOUGHT IT WAS THE FUEL TRUCK BURNING.
I'VE SPENT ALL NIGHT BURNING THE TAPES AND FILES AND PHOTOS.
YOU **BURNED** IT?
YES.
THANK GOD FOR THAT.
YOU'RE PART OF THIS COVER-UP?
TO PROTECT VANGER INCORPORATED?
WHY?
I DON'T GIVE A FUCK ABOUT VANGER INC.
I DIDN'T DO IT FOR THEM.
I DID IT FOR THE WOMEN HE ATTACKED.

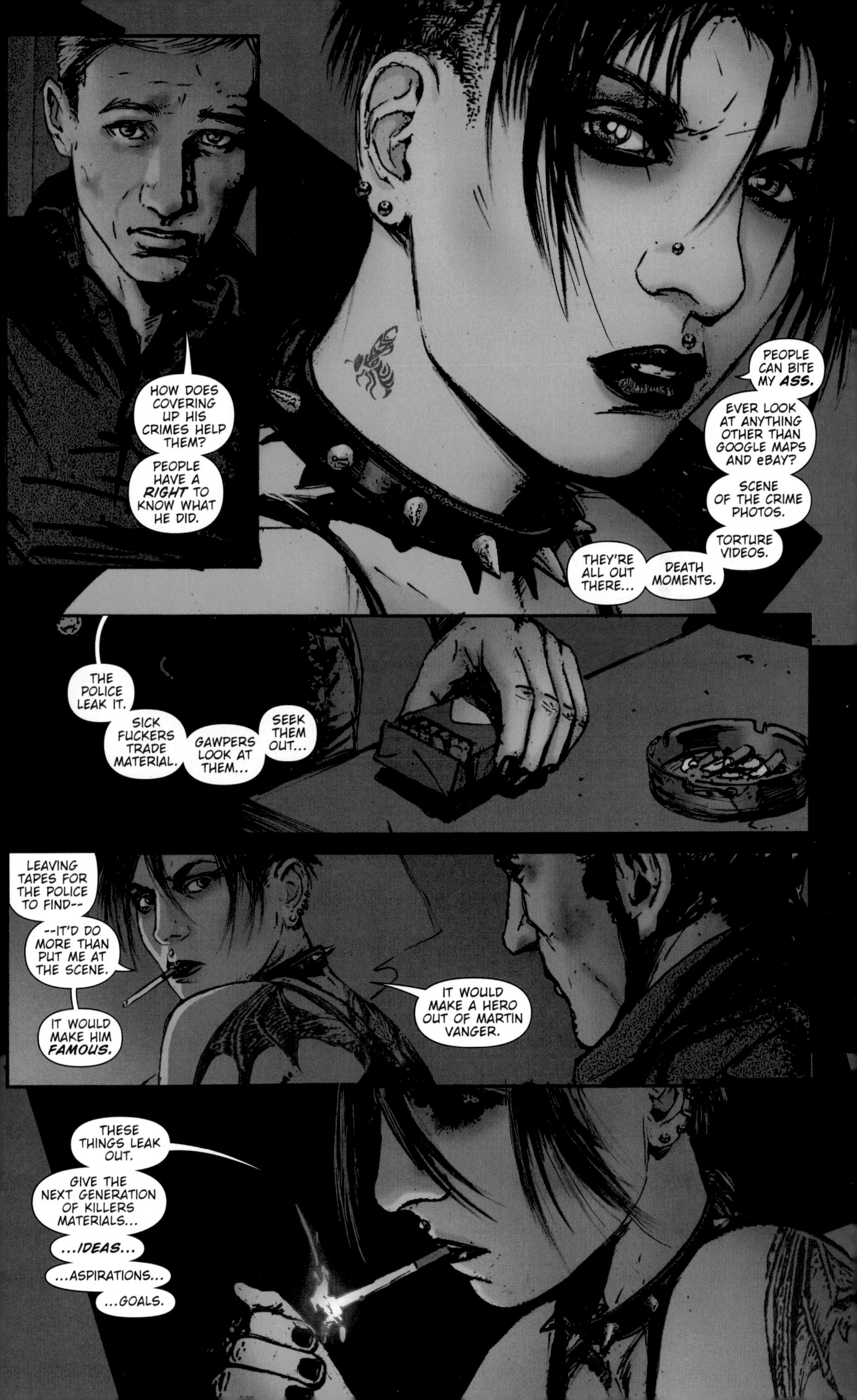
HOW DOES COVERING UP HIS CRIMES HELP THEM?
PEOPLE HAVE A *RIGHT* TO KNOW WHAT HE DID.
PEOPLE CAN BITE MY ***ASS.***
EVER LOOK AT ANYTHING OTHER THAN GOOGLE MAPS AND eBAY?
SCENE OF THE CRIME PHOTOS.
TORTURE VIDEOS.
DEATH MOMENTS.
THEY'RE ALL OUT THERE...
THE POLICE LEAK IT.
SICK FUCKERS TRADE MATERIAL.
GAWPERS LOOK AT THEM...
SEEK THEM OUT...
LEAVING TAPES FOR THE POLICE TO FIND--
--IT'D DO MORE THAN PUT ME AT THE SCENE.
IT WOULD MAKE HIM ***FAMOUS.***
IT WOULD MAKE A HERO OUT OF MARTIN VANGER.
THESE THINGS LEAK OUT.
GIVE THE NEXT GENERATION OF KILLERS MATERIALS...
...***IDEAS...***
...ASPIRATIONS...
...GOALS.

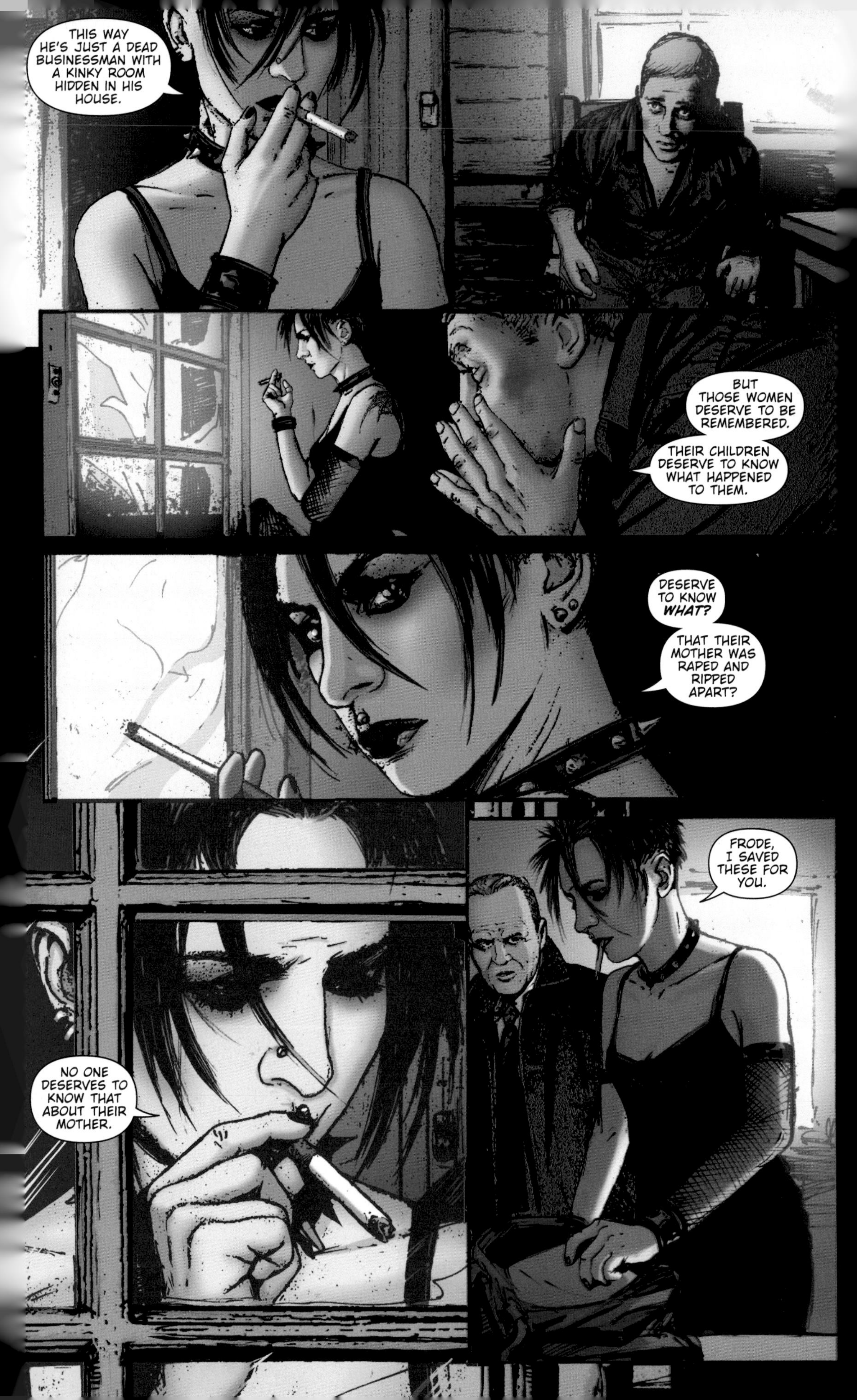

THIS WAY HE'S JUST A DEAD BUSINESSMAN WITH A KINKY ROOM HIDDEN IN HIS HOUSE.
BUT THOSE WOMEN DESERVE TO BE REMEMBERED.
THEIR CHILDREN DESERVE TO KNOW WHAT HAPPENED TO THEM.
DESERVE TO KNOW *WHAT?*
THAT THEIR MOTHER WAS RAPED AND RIPPED APART?
NO ONE DESERVES TO KNOW THAT ABOUT THEIR MOTHER.
FRODE, I SAVED THESE FOR YOU.

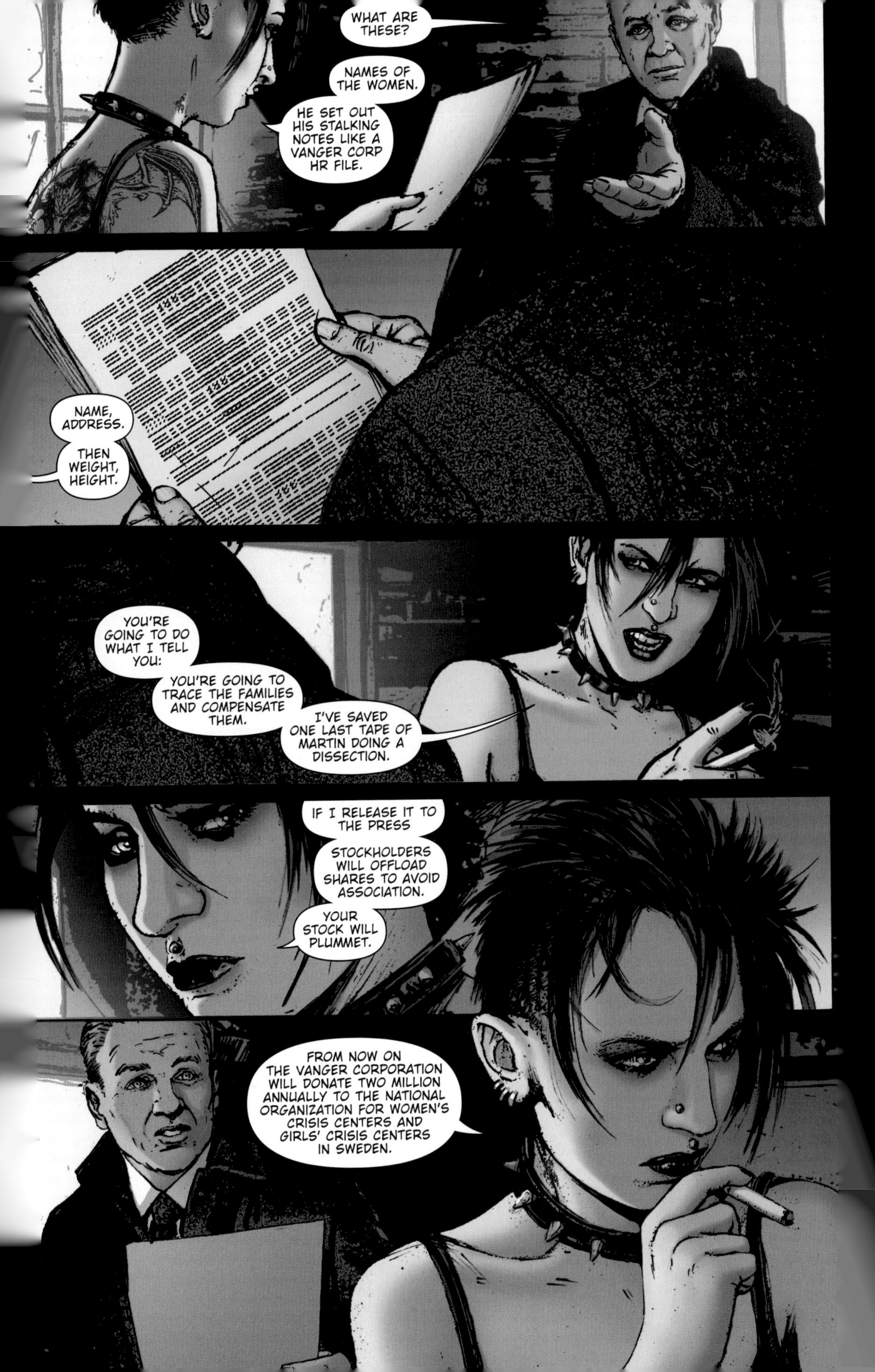
WHAT ARE THESE?
NAMES OF THE WOMEN.
HE SET OUT HIS STALKING NOTES LIKE A VANGER CORP HR FILE.
NAME, ADDRESS.
THEN WEIGHT, HEIGHT.
YOU'RE GOING TO DO WHAT I TELL YOU:
YOU'RE GOING TO TRACE THE FAMILIES AND COMPENSATE THEM.
I'VE SAVED ONE LAST TAPE OF MARTIN DOING A DISSECTION.
IF I RELEASE IT TO THE PRESS
STOCKHOLDERS WILL OFFLOAD SHARES TO AVOID ASSOCIATION.
YOUR STOCK WILL PLUMMET.
FROM NOW ON THE VANGER CORPORATION WILL DONATE TWO MILLION ANNUALLY TO THE NATIONAL ORGANIZATION FOR WOMEN'S CRISIS CENTERS AND GIRLS' CRISIS CENTERS IN SWEDEN.

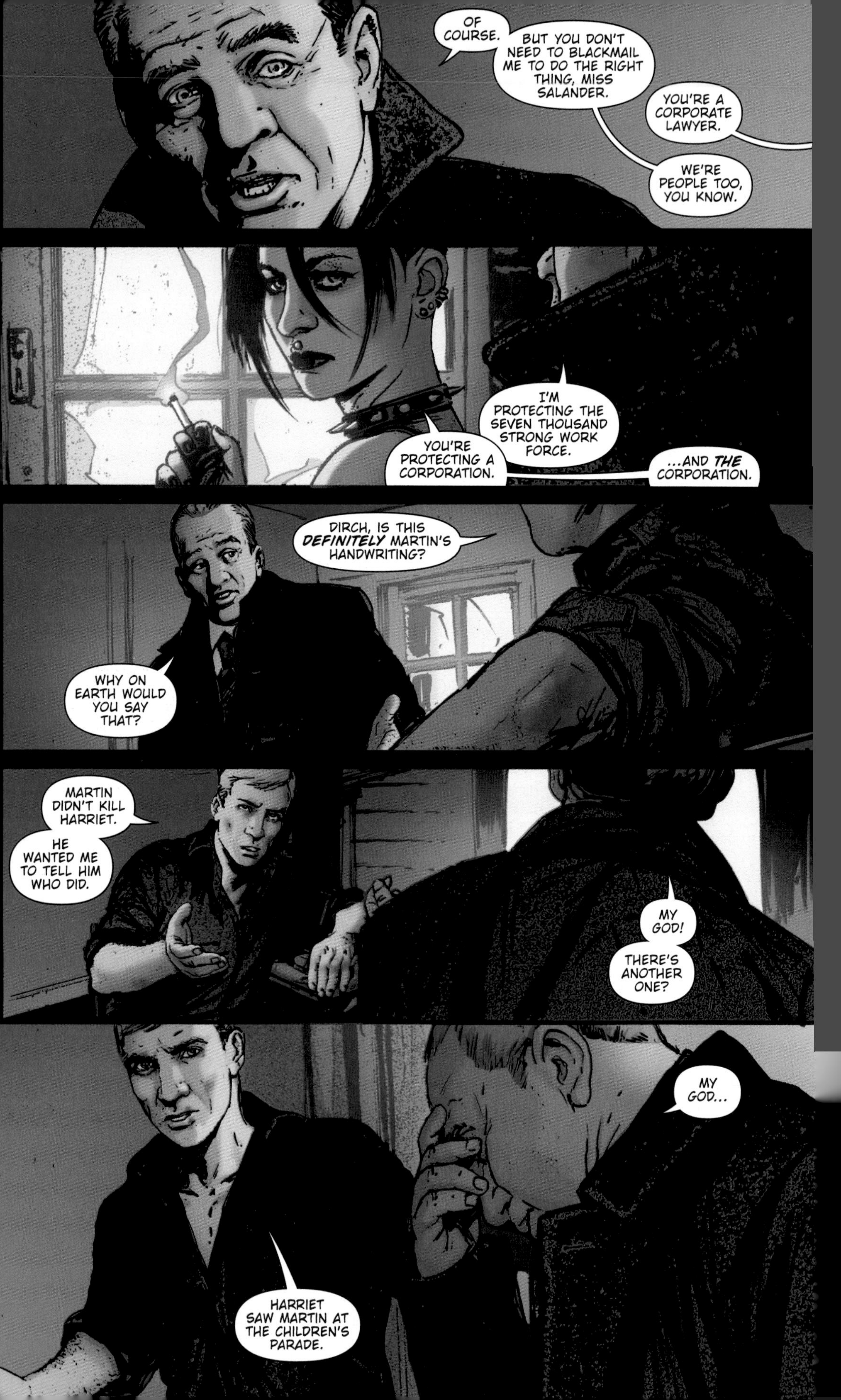
OF COURSE.
BUT YOU DON'T NEED TO BLACKMAIL ME TO DO THE RIGHT THING, MISS SALANDER.
YOU'RE A CORPORATE LAWYER.
WE'RE PEOPLE TOO, YOU KNOW.
I'M PROTECTING THE SEVEN THOUSAND STRONG WORK FORCE.
YOU'RE PROTECTING A CORPORATION.
...AND *THE* CORPORATION.
DIRCH, IS THIS *DEFINITELY* MARTIN'S HANDWRITING?
WHY ON EARTH WOULD YOU SAY THAT?
MARTIN DIDN'T KILL HARRIET.
HE WANTED ME TO TELL HIM WHO DID.
MY GOD!
THERE'S ANOTHER ONE?
MY GOD...
HARRIET SAW MARTIN AT THE CHILDREN'S PARADE.

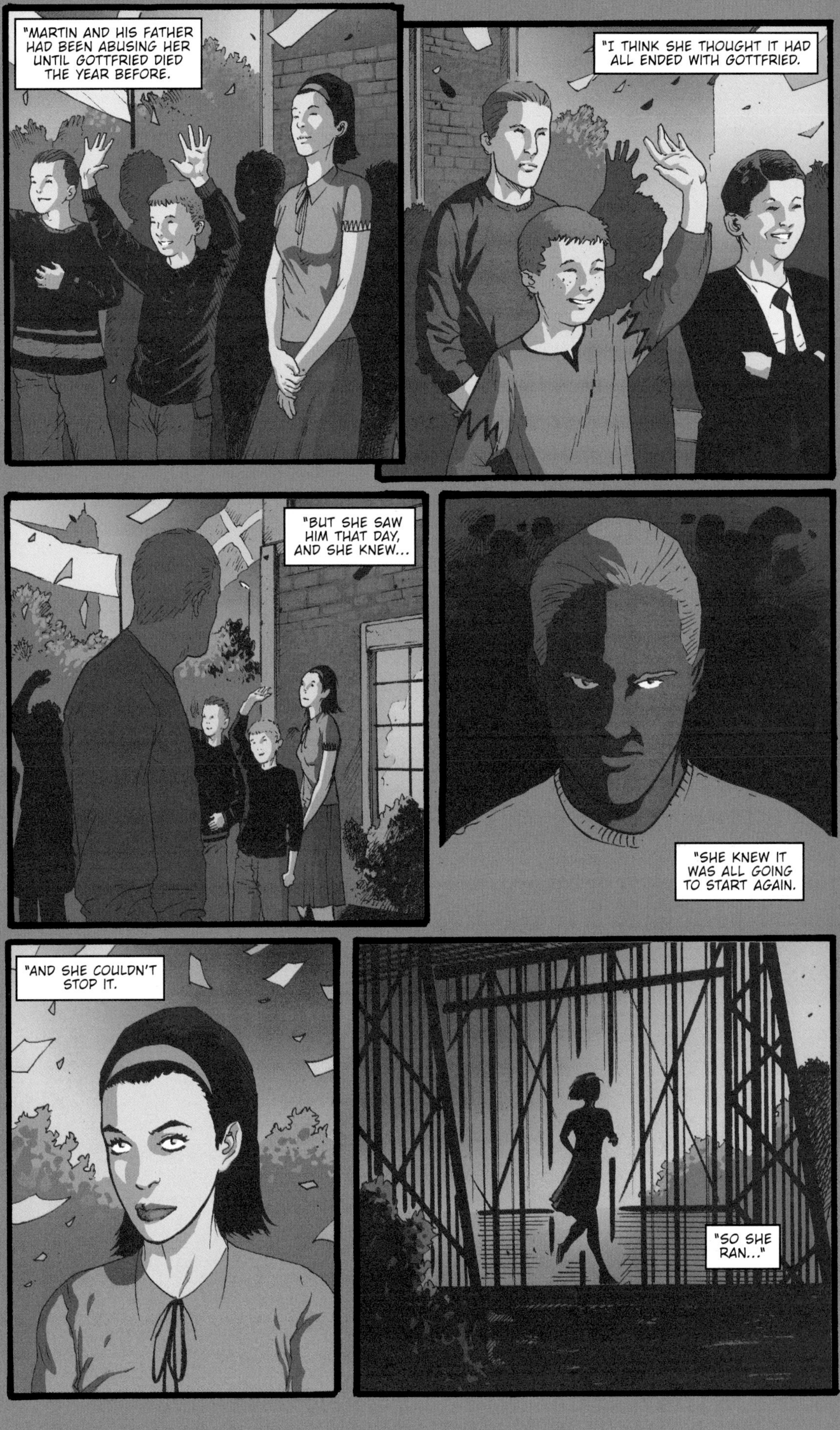
"MARTIN AND HIS FATHER HAD BEEN ABUSING HER UNTIL GOTTFRIED DIED THE YEAR BEFORE.
"I THINK SHE THOUGHT IT HAD ALL ENDED WITH GOTTFRIED.
"BUT SHE SAW HIM THAT DAY, AND SHE KNEW...
"SHE KNEW IT WAS ALL GOING TO START AGAIN.
"AND SHE COULDN'T STOP IT.
"SO SHE RAN..."

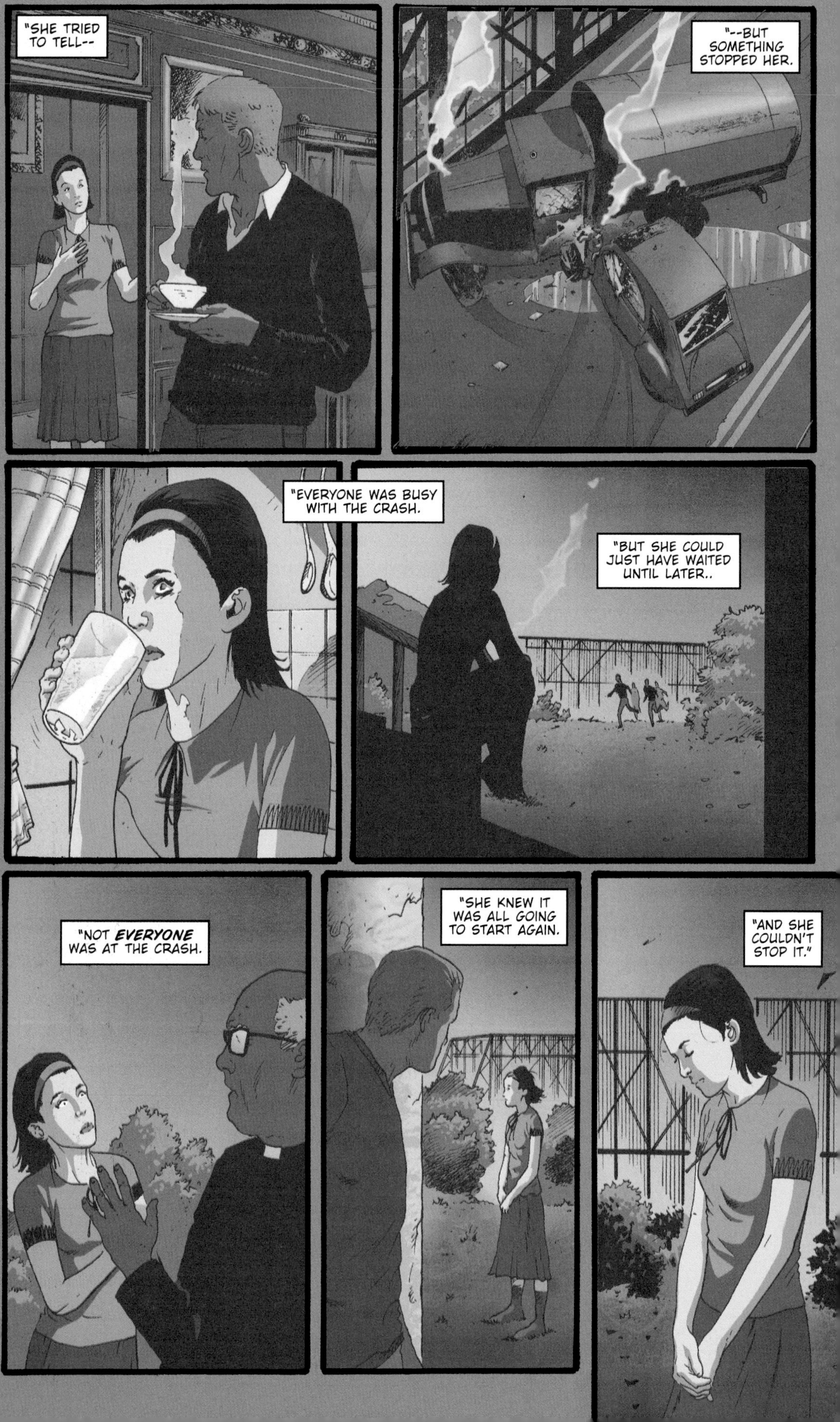
"SHE TRIED TO TELL--
"--BUT SOMETHING STOPPED HER.
"EVERYONE WAS BUSY WITH THE CRASH.
"BUT SHE COULD JUST HAVE WAITED UNTIL LATER..
"NOT EVERYONE WAS AT THE CRASH.
"SHE KNEW IT WAS ALL GOING TO START AGAIN.
"AND SHE COULDN'T STOP IT."

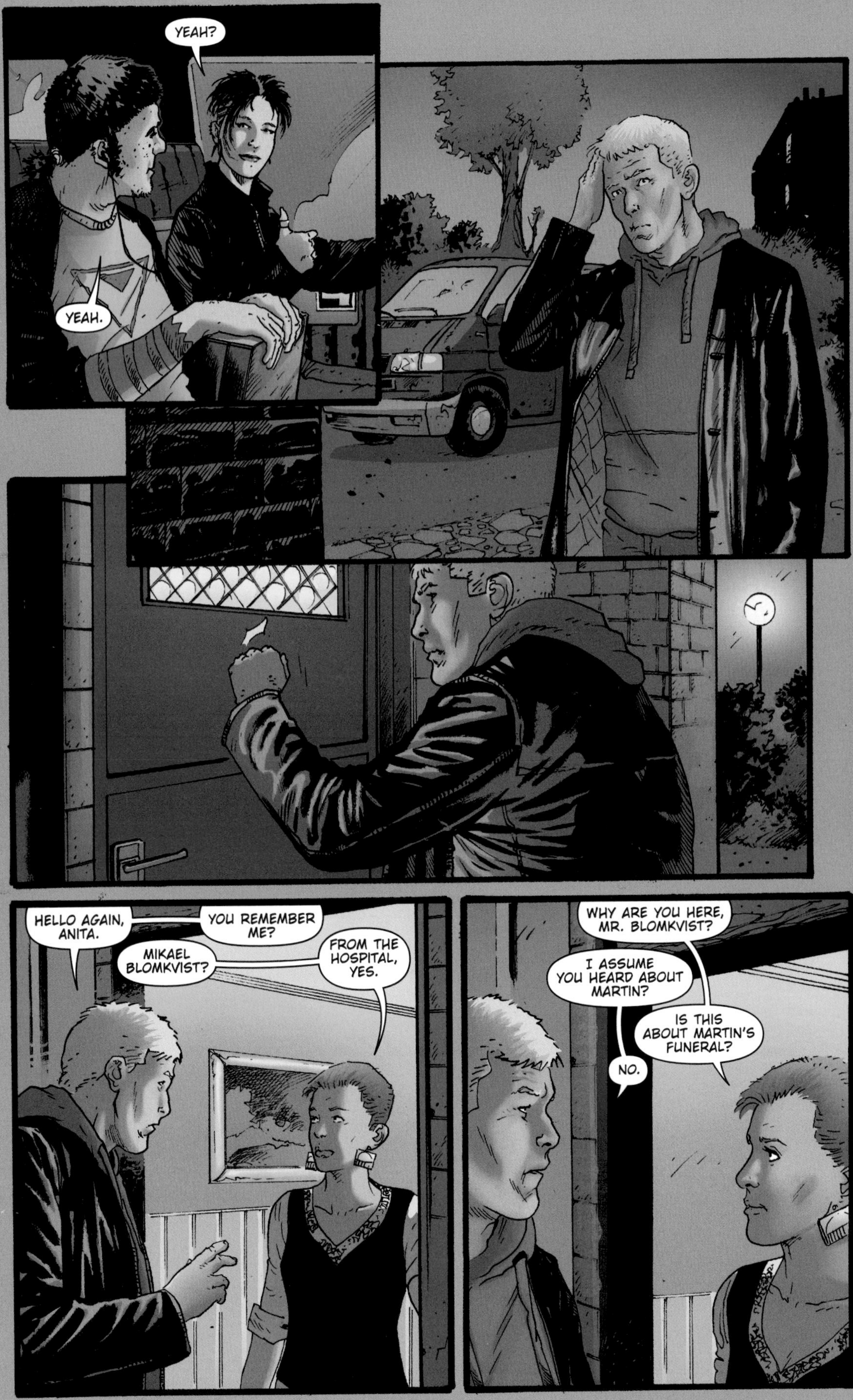
YEAH?
YEAH.
HELLO AGAIN, ANITA.
YOU REMEMBER ME?
MIKAEL BLOMKVIST?
FROM THE HOSPITAL, YES.
WHY ARE YOU HERE, MR. BLOMKVIST?
I ASSUME YOU HEARD ABOUT MARTIN?
IS THIS ABOUT MARTIN'S FUNERAL?
NO.

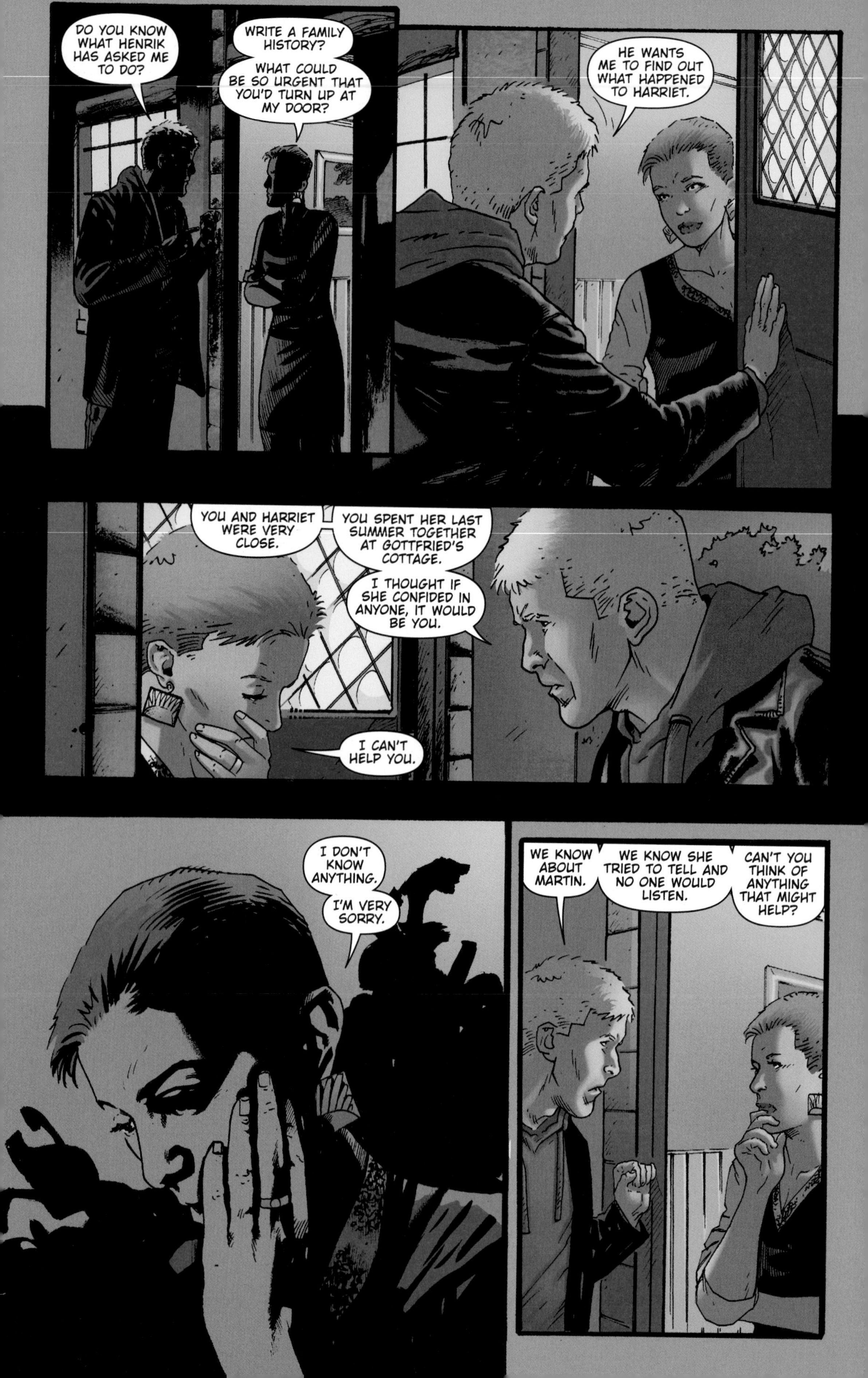
DO YOU KNOW WHAT HENRIK HAS ASKED ME TO DO?
WRITE A FAMILY HISTORY?
WHAT COULD BE SO URGENT THAT YOU'D TURN UP AT MY DOOR?
HE WANTS ME TO FIND OUT WHAT HAPPENED TO HARRIET.
YOU AND HARRIET WERE VERY CLOSE.
YOU SPENT HER LAST SUMMER TOGETHER AT GOTTFRIED'S COTTAGE.
I THOUGHT IF SHE CONFIDED IN ANYONE, IT WOULD BE YOU.
I CAN'T HELP YOU.
I DON'T KNOW ANYTHING.
I'M VERY SORRY.
WE KNOW ABOUT MARTIN.
WE KNOW SHE TRIED TO TELL AND NO ONE WOULD LISTEN.
CAN'T YOU THINK OF ANYTHING THAT MIGHT HELP?

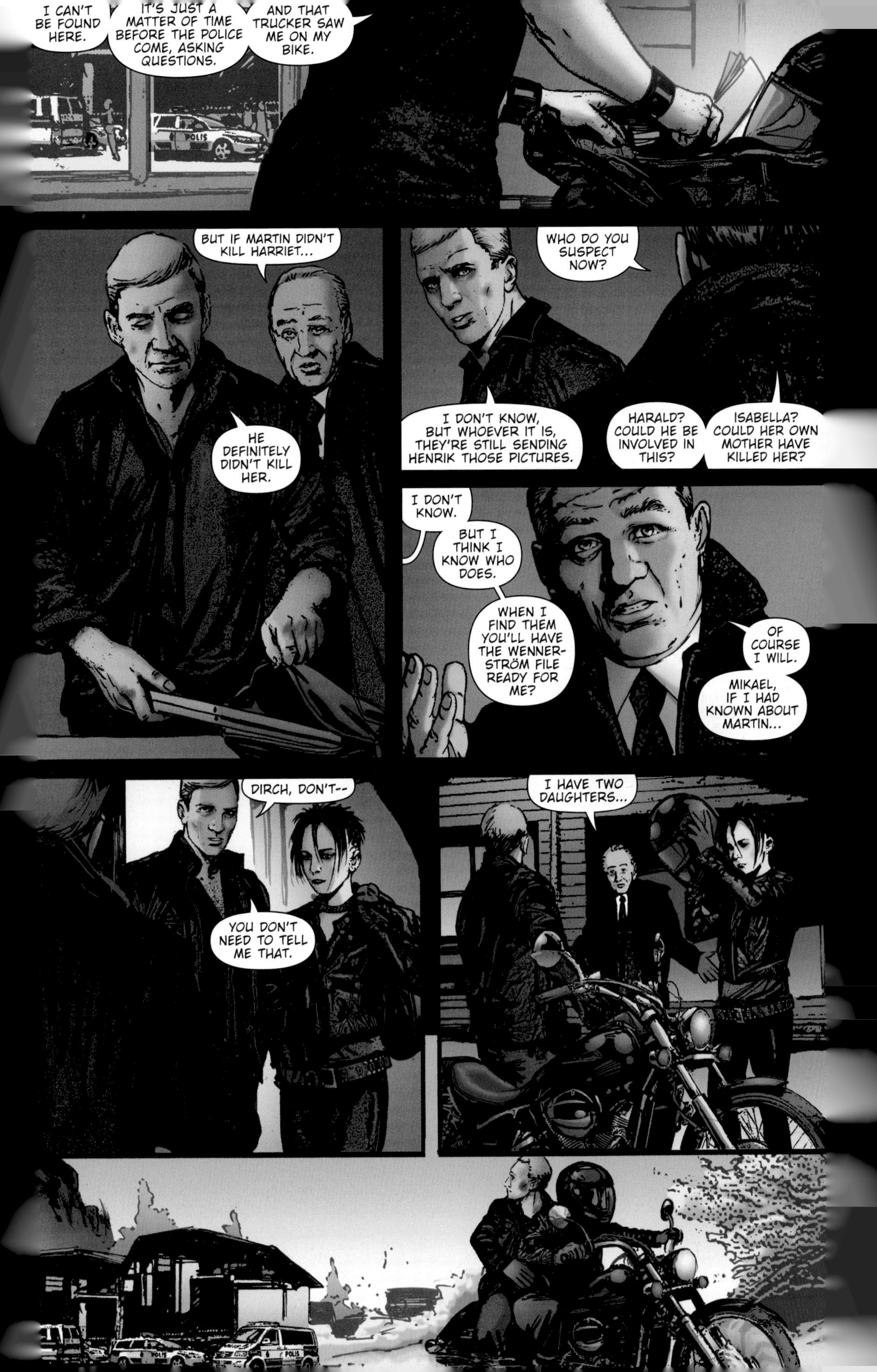
I CAN'T BE FOUND HERE.
IT'S JUST A MATTER OF TIME BEFORE THE POLICE COME, ASKING QUESTIONS.
AND THAT TRUCKER SAW ME ON MY BIKE.
POLIS
BUT IF MARTIN DIDN'T KILL HARRIET...
HE DEFINITELY DIDN'T KILL HER.
WHO DO YOU SUSPECT NOW?
I DON'T KNOW, BUT WHOEVER IT IS, THEY'RE STILL SENDING HENRIK THOSE PICTURES.
HARALD? COULD HE BE INVOLVED IN THIS?
ISABELLA? COULD HER OWN MOTHER HAVE KILLED HER?
I DON'T KNOW.
BUT I THINK I KNOW WHO DOES.
WHEN I FIND THEM YOU'LL HAVE THE WENNERSTRÖM FILE READY FOR ME?
OF COURSE I WILL.
MIKAEL, IF I HAD KNOWN ABOUT MARTIN...
DIRCH, DON'T--
YOU DON'T NEED TO TELL ME THAT.
I HAVE TWO DAUGHTERS...
POLIS

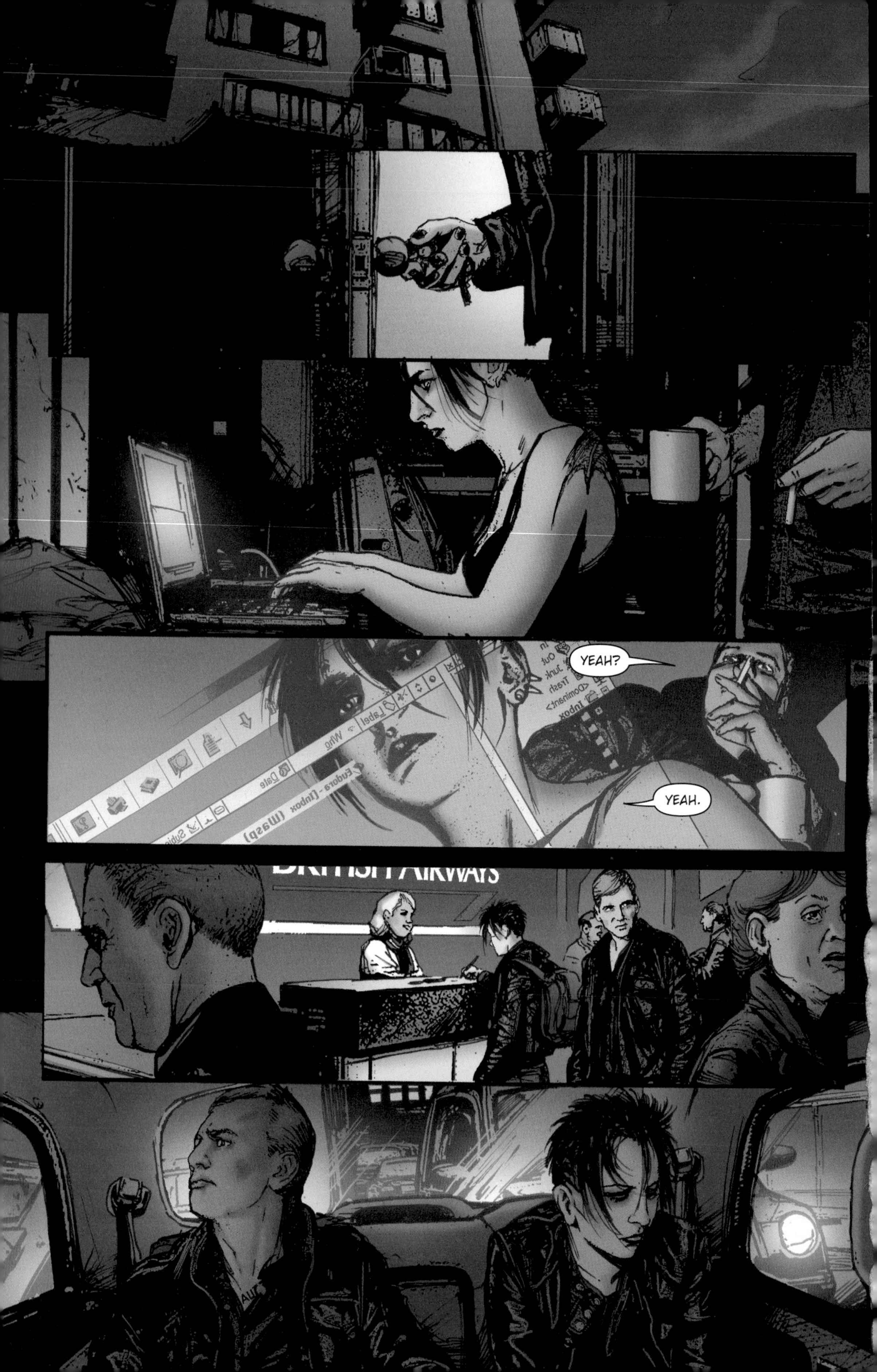
YEAH?
YEAH.

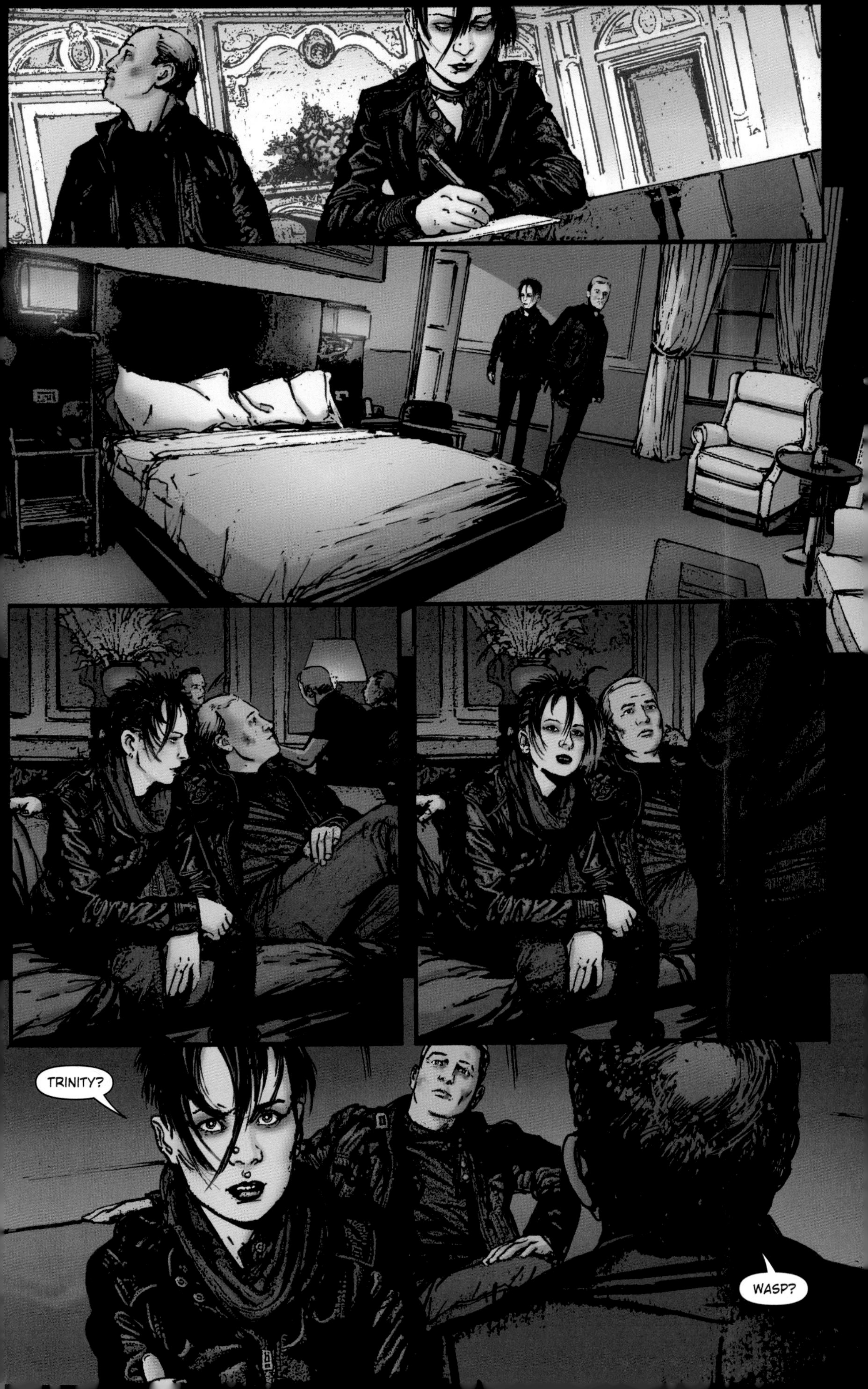
TRINITY?
WASP?

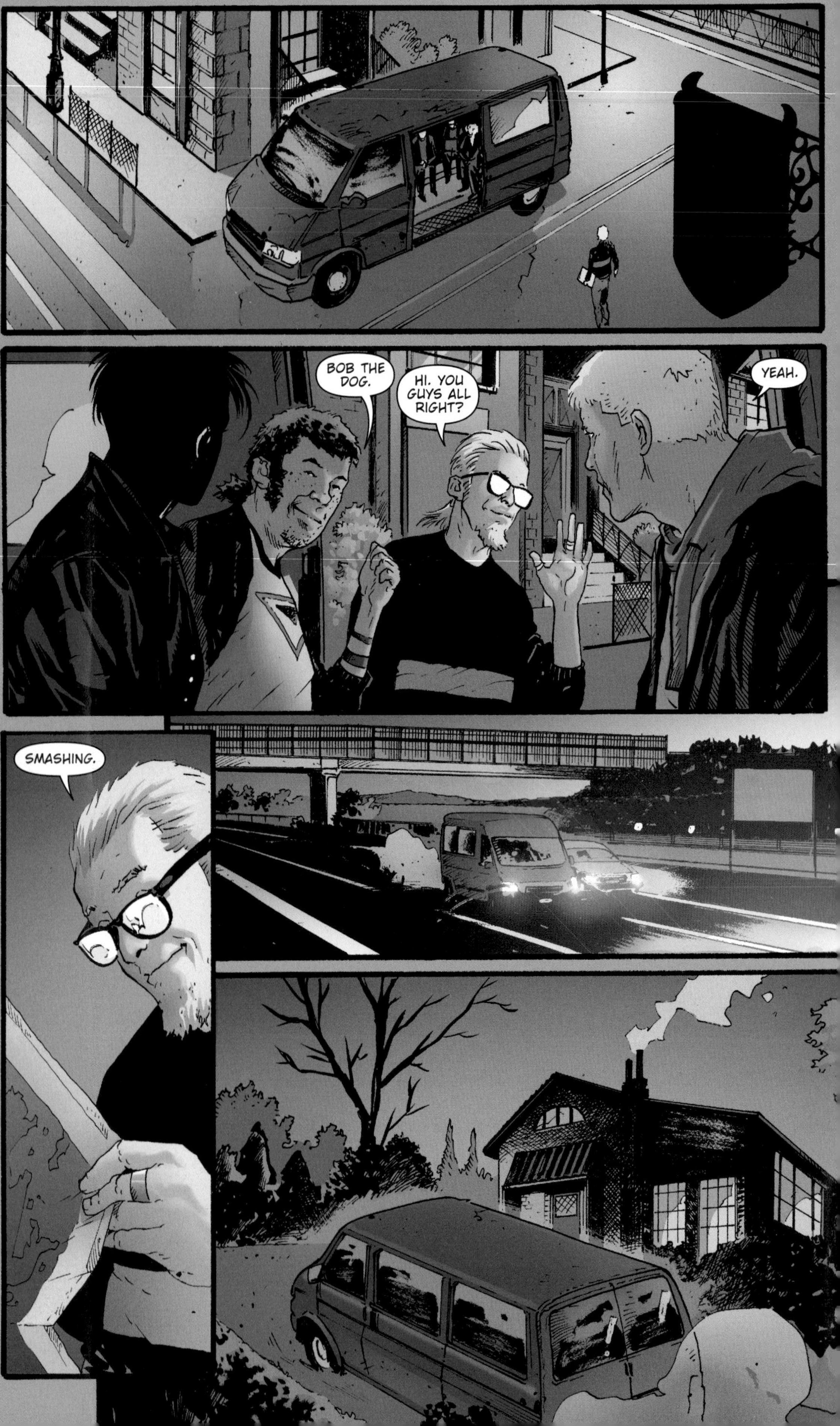
BOB THE DOG.
HI. YOU GUYS ALL RIGHT?
YEAH.
SMASHING.

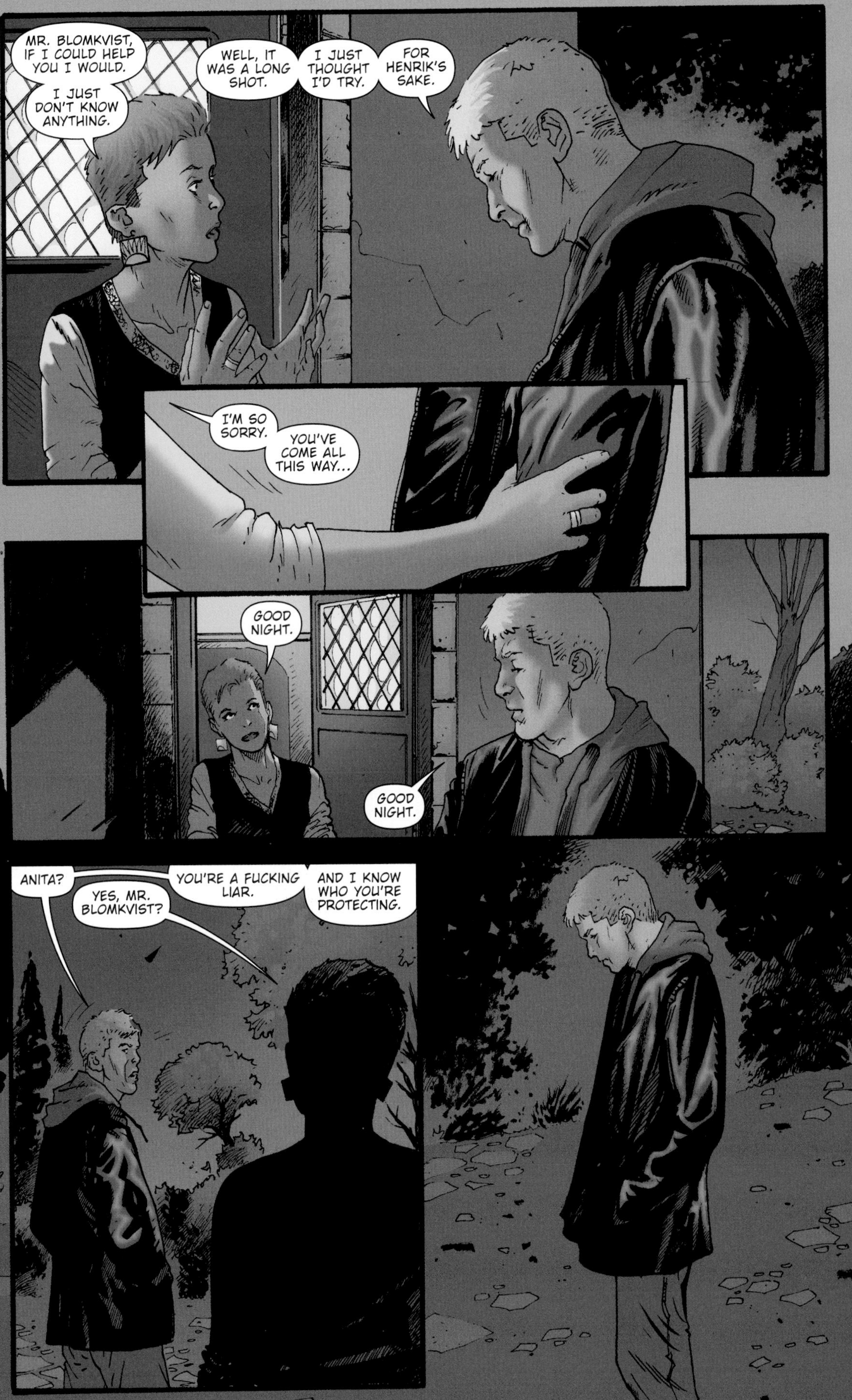
MR. BLOMKVIST, IF I COULD HELP YOU I WOULD.
I JUST DON'T KNOW ANYTHING.
WELL, IT WAS A LONG SHOT.
I JUST THOUGHT I'D TRY.
FOR HENRIK'S SAKE.
I'M SO SORRY.
YOU'VE COME ALL THIS WAY...
GOOD NIGHT.
GOOD NIGHT.
ANITA?
YES, MR. BLOMKVIST?
YOU'RE A FUCKING LIAR.
AND I KNOW WHO YOU'RE PROTECTING.

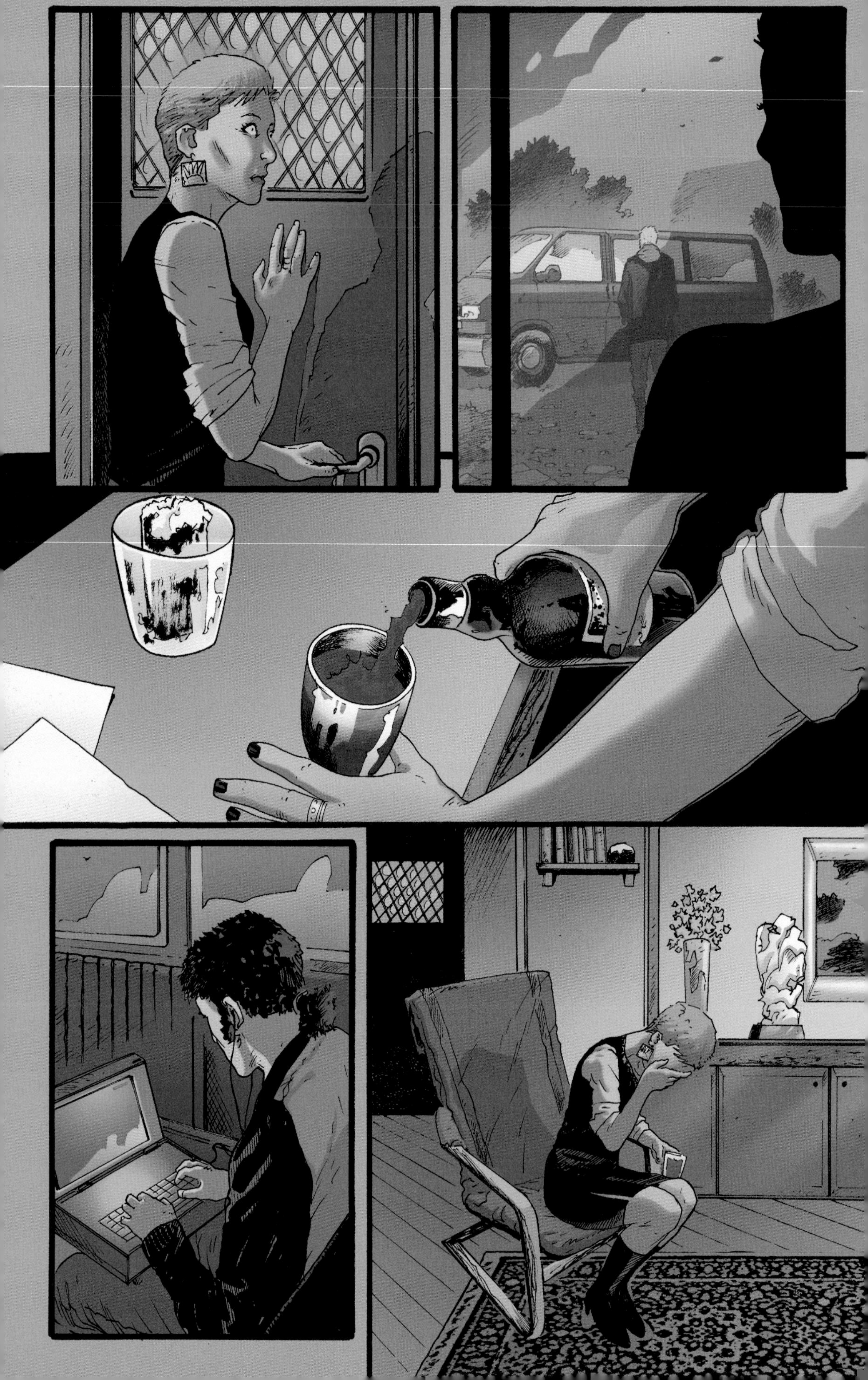

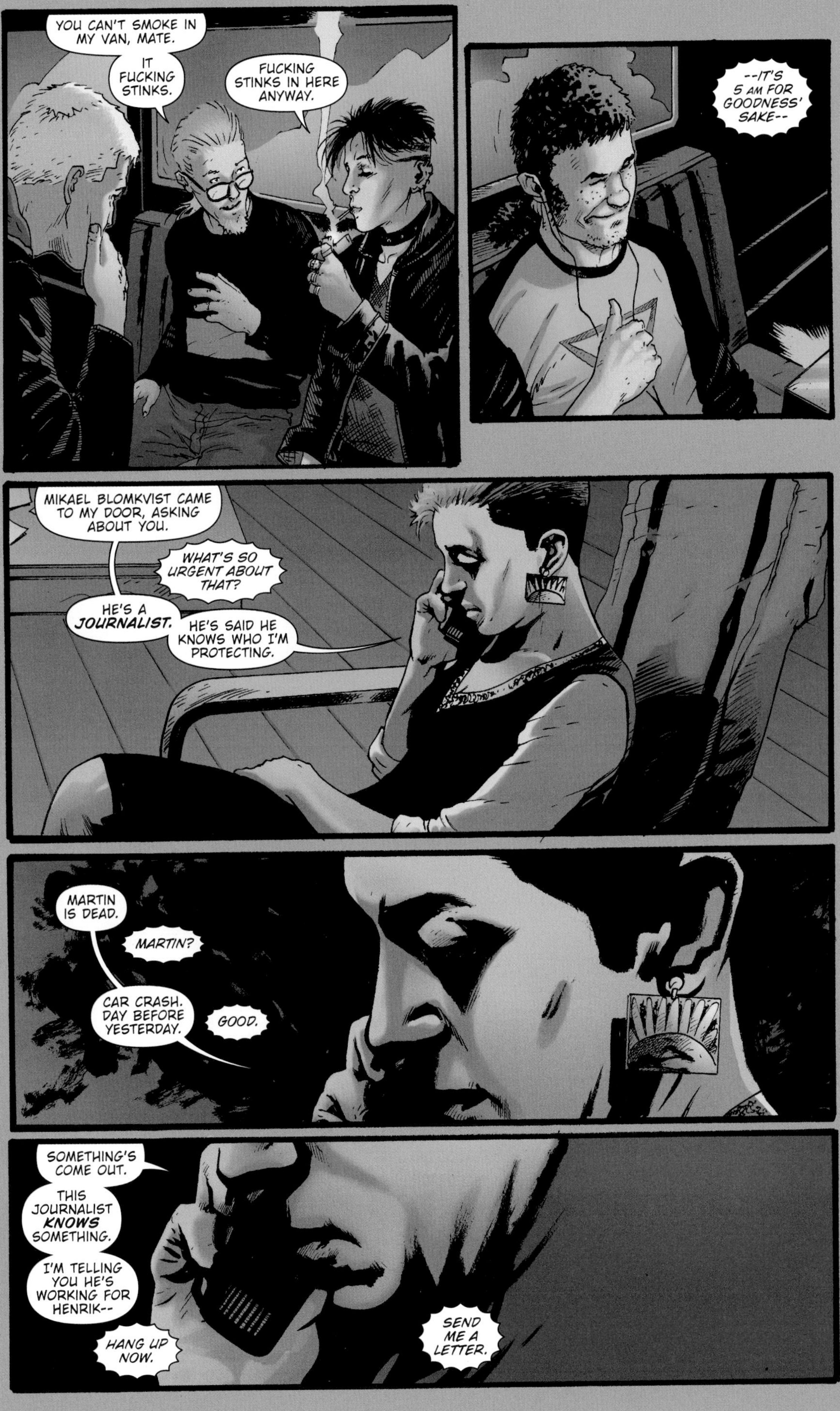
YOU CAN'T SMOKE IN MY VAN, MATE.
IT FUCKING STINKS.
FUCKING STINKS IN HERE ANYWAY.
--IT'S 5 AM FOR GOODNESS' SAKE--
MIKAEL BLOMKVIST CAME TO MY DOOR, ASKING ABOUT YOU.
WHAT'S SO URGENT ABOUT THAT?
HE'S A JOURNALIST.
HE'S SAID HE KNOWS WHO I'M PROTECTING.
MARTIN IS DEAD.
MARTIN?
CAR CRASH. DAY BEFORE YESTERDAY.
GOOD.
SOMETHING'S COME OUT.
THIS JOURNALIST KNOWS SOMETHING.
I'M TELLING YOU HE'S WORKING FOR HENRIK--
HANG UP NOW.
SEND ME A LETTER.

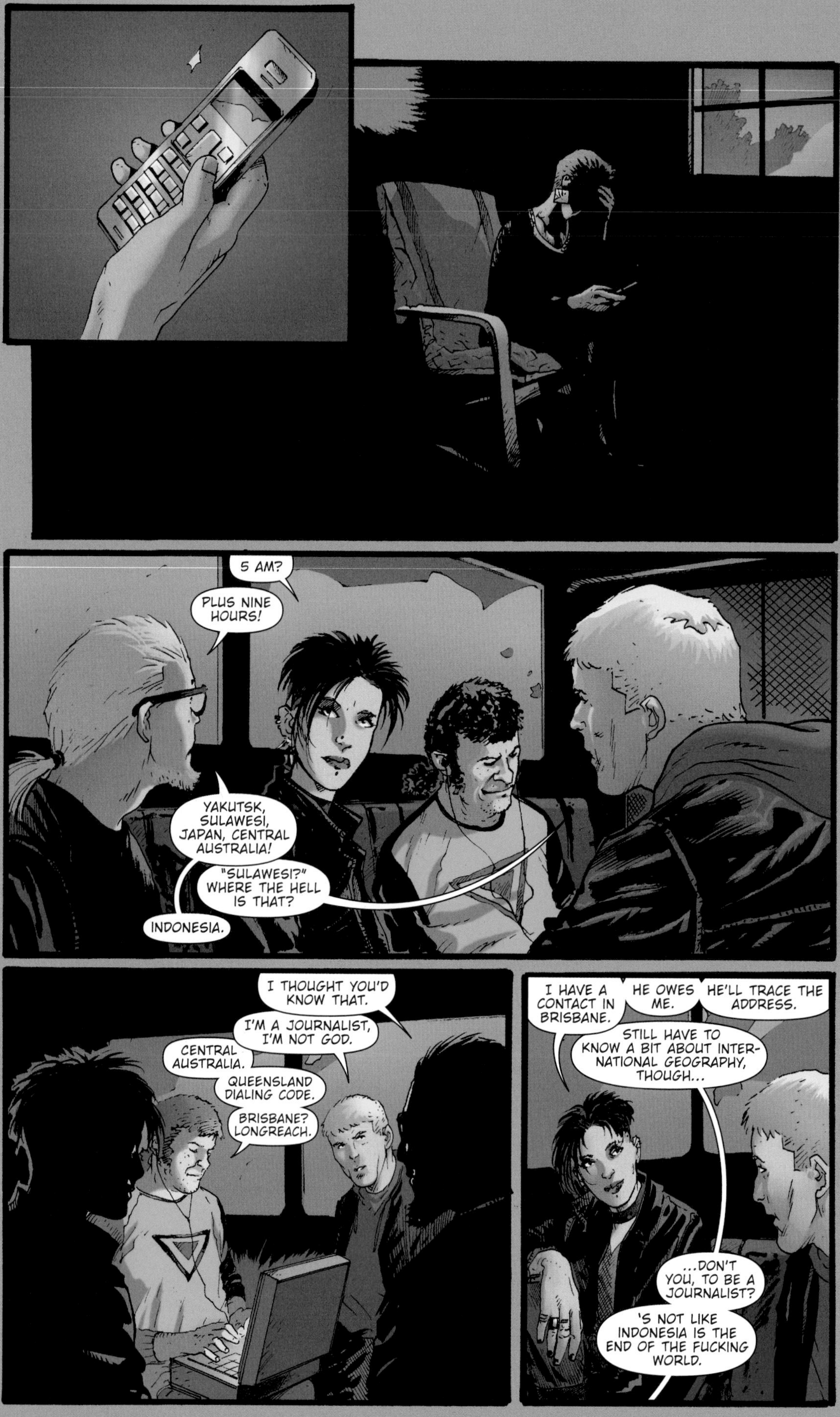
5 AM?
PLUS NINE HOURS!
YAKUTSK, SULAWESI, JAPAN, CENTRAL AUSTRALIA!
"SULAWESI?" WHERE THE HELL IS THAT?
INDONESIA.
I THOUGHT YOU'D KNOW THAT.
I'M A JOURNALIST, I'M NOT GOD.
CENTRAL AUSTRALIA.
QUEENSLAND DIALING CODE.
BRISBANE? LONGREACH.
I HAVE A CONTACT IN BRISBANE.
HE OWES ME.
HE'LL TRACE THE ADDRESS.
STILL HAVE TO KNOW A BIT ABOUT INTER-NATIONAL GEOGRAPHY, THOUGH...
...DON'T YOU, TO BE A JOURNALIST?
'S NOT LIKE INDONESIA IS THE END OF THE FUCKING WORLD.

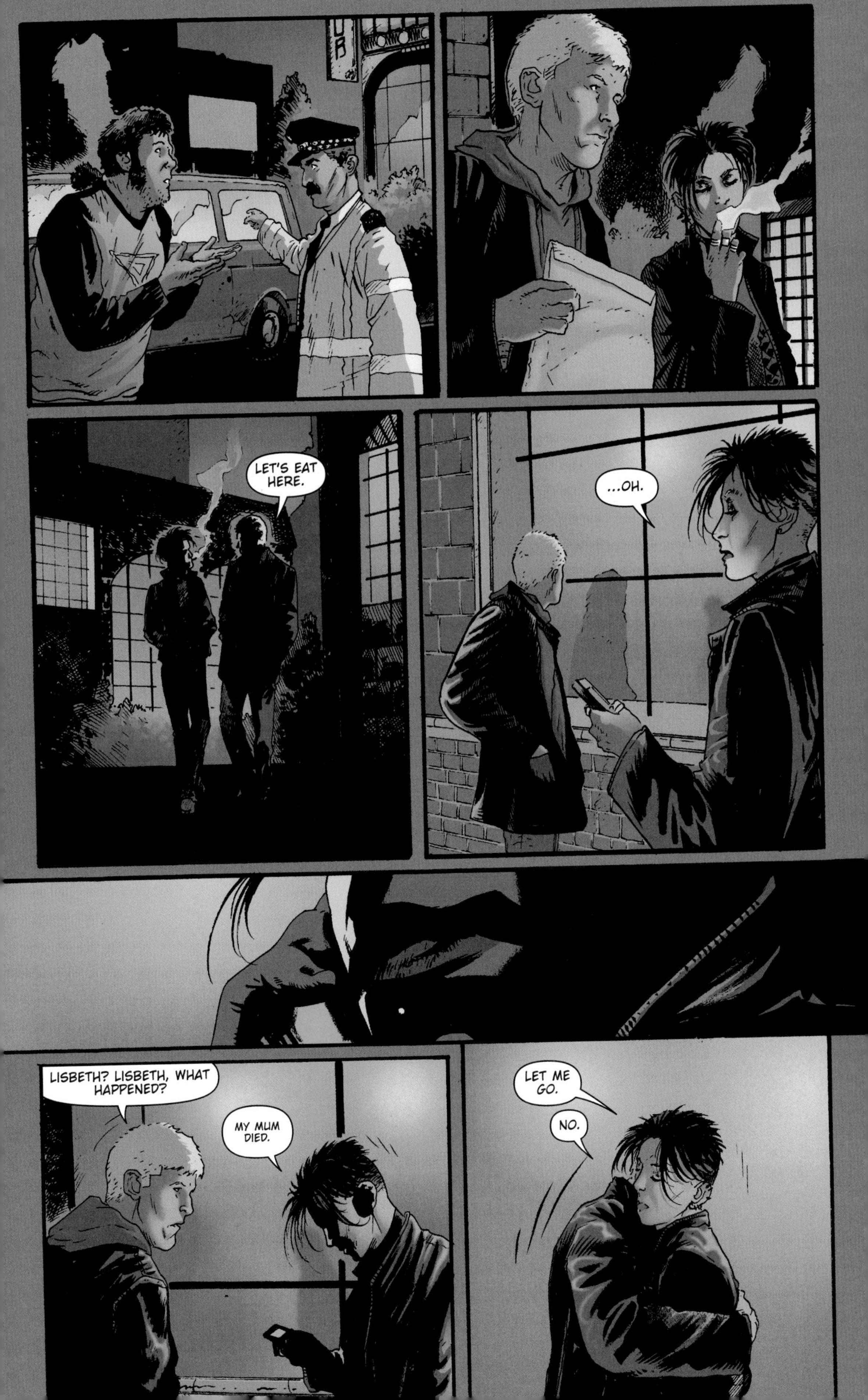
LET'S EAT HERE.
...OH.
LISBETH? LISBETH, WHAT HAPPENED?
MY MUM DIED.
LET ME GO.
NO.

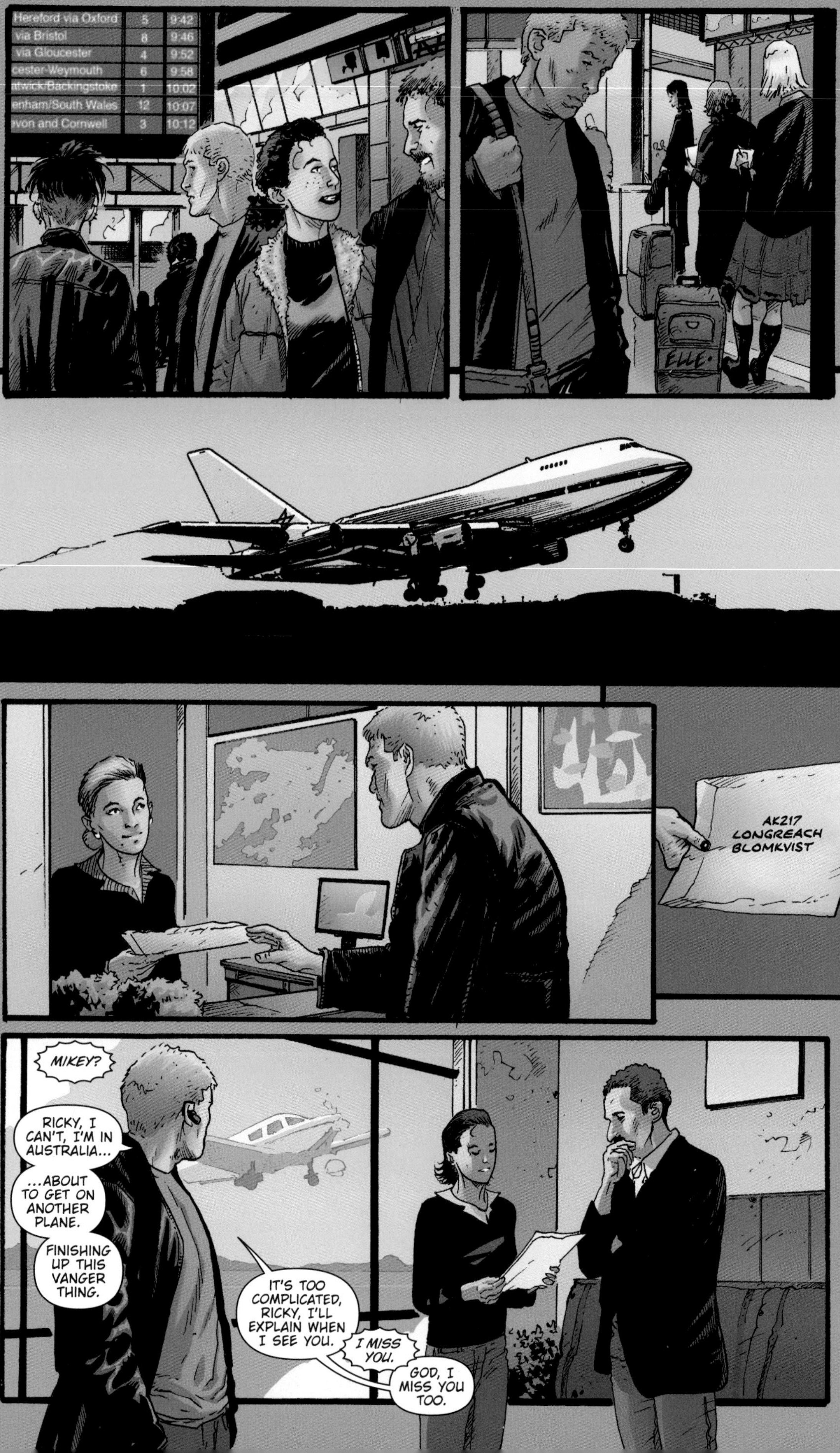
Hereford via Oxford 5 9:42
via Bristol 8 9:46
via Gloucester 4 9:52
cester-Weymouth 6 9:58
atwick/Backingstoke 1 10:02
enham/South Wales 12 10:07
evon and Cornwell 3 10:12
ELLE
AK217
LONGREACH
BLOMKVIST
MIKEY?
RICKY, I CAN'T, I'M IN AUSTRALIA...
...ABOUT TO GET ON ANOTHER PLANE.
FINISHING UP THIS VANGER THING.
IT'S TOO COMPLICATED, RICKY, I'LL EXPLAIN WHEN I SEE YOU.
I MISS YOU.
GOD, I MISS YOU TOO.

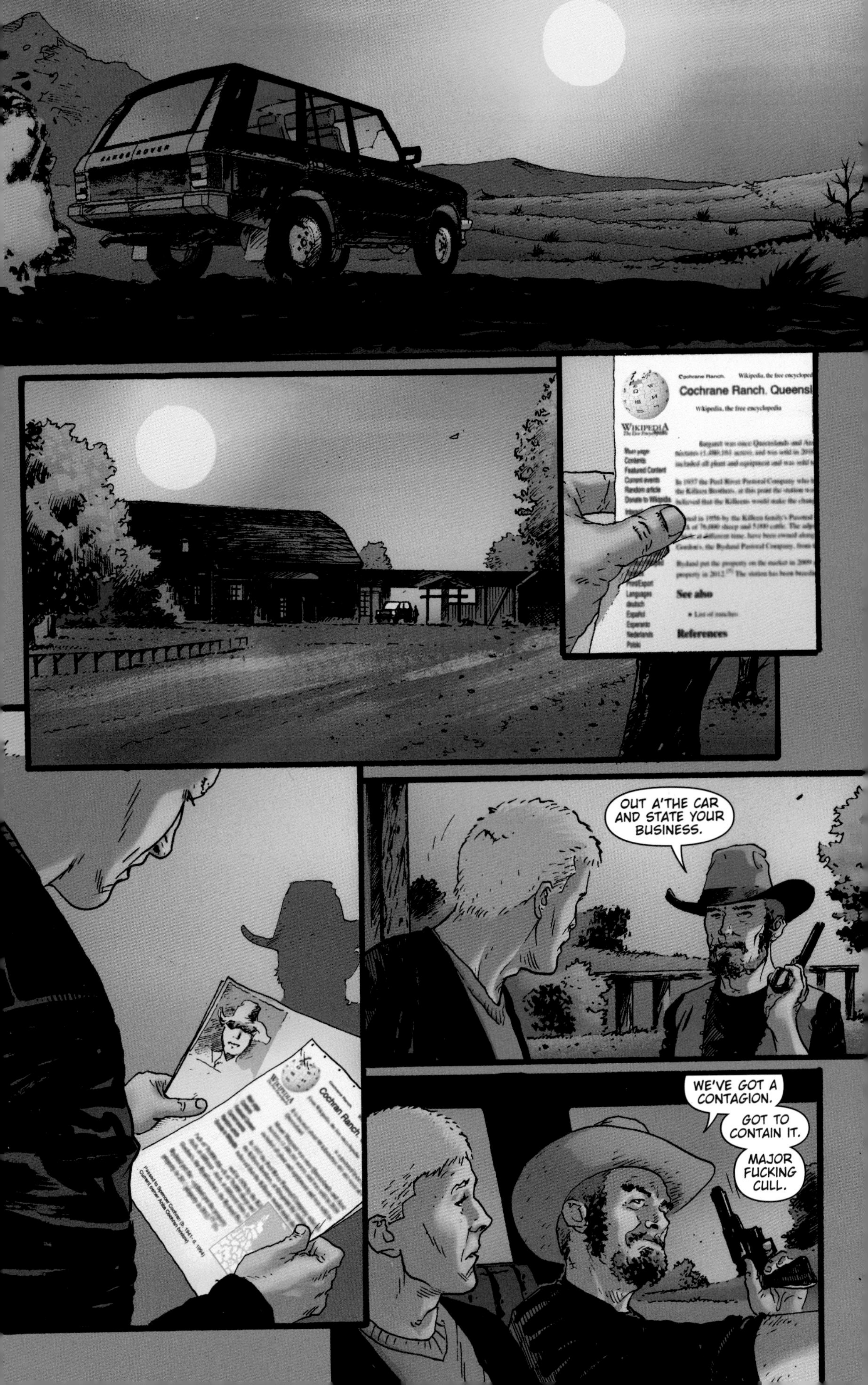
RANGE ROVER
Cochrane Ranch. Queensl
Wikipedia, the free encyclopedia
See also
References
OUT A'THE CAR AND STATE YOUR BUSINESS.
WE'VE GOT A CONTAGION.
GOT TO CONTAIN IT.
MAJOR FUCKING CULL.

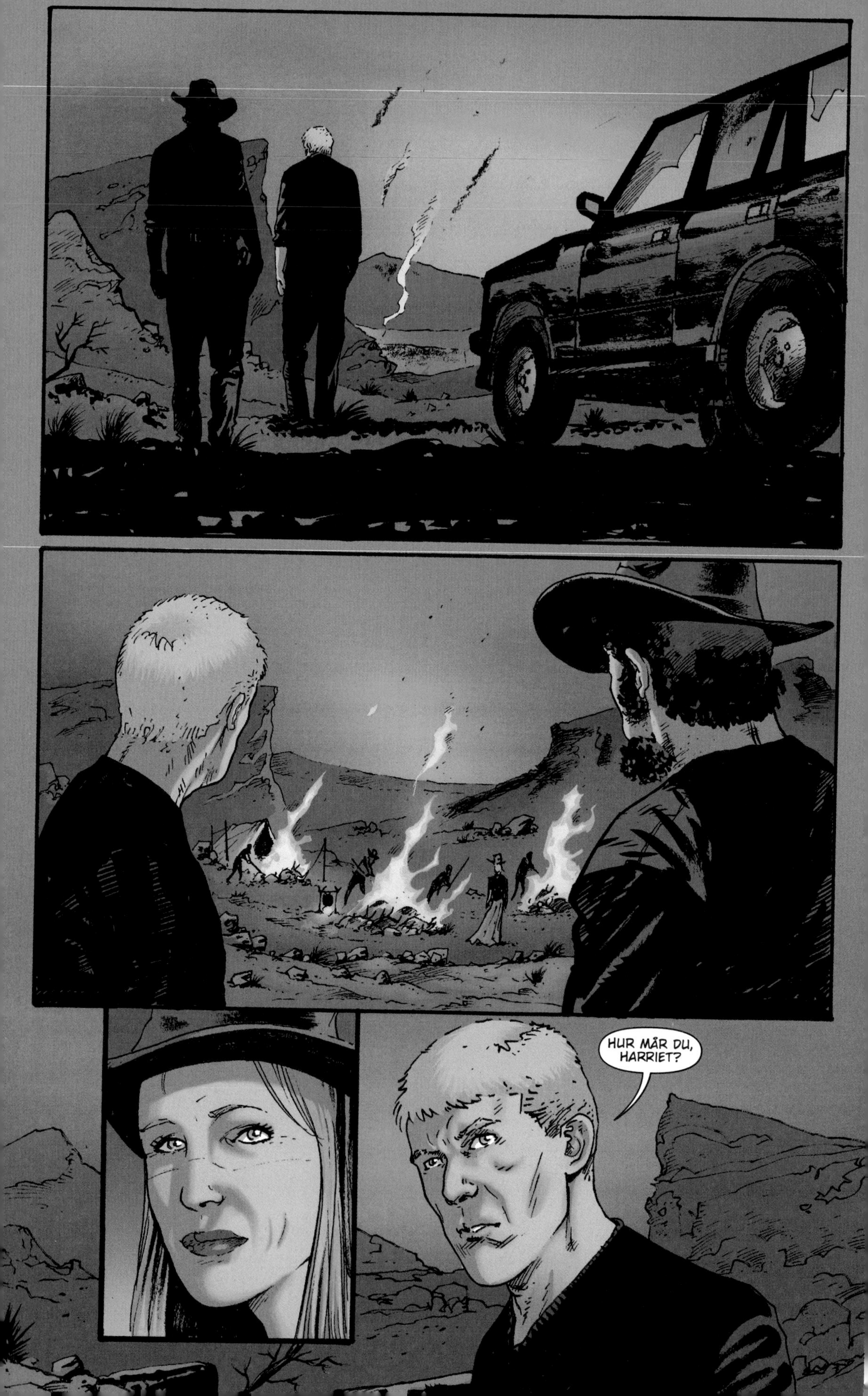
HUR MÅR DU, HARRIET?

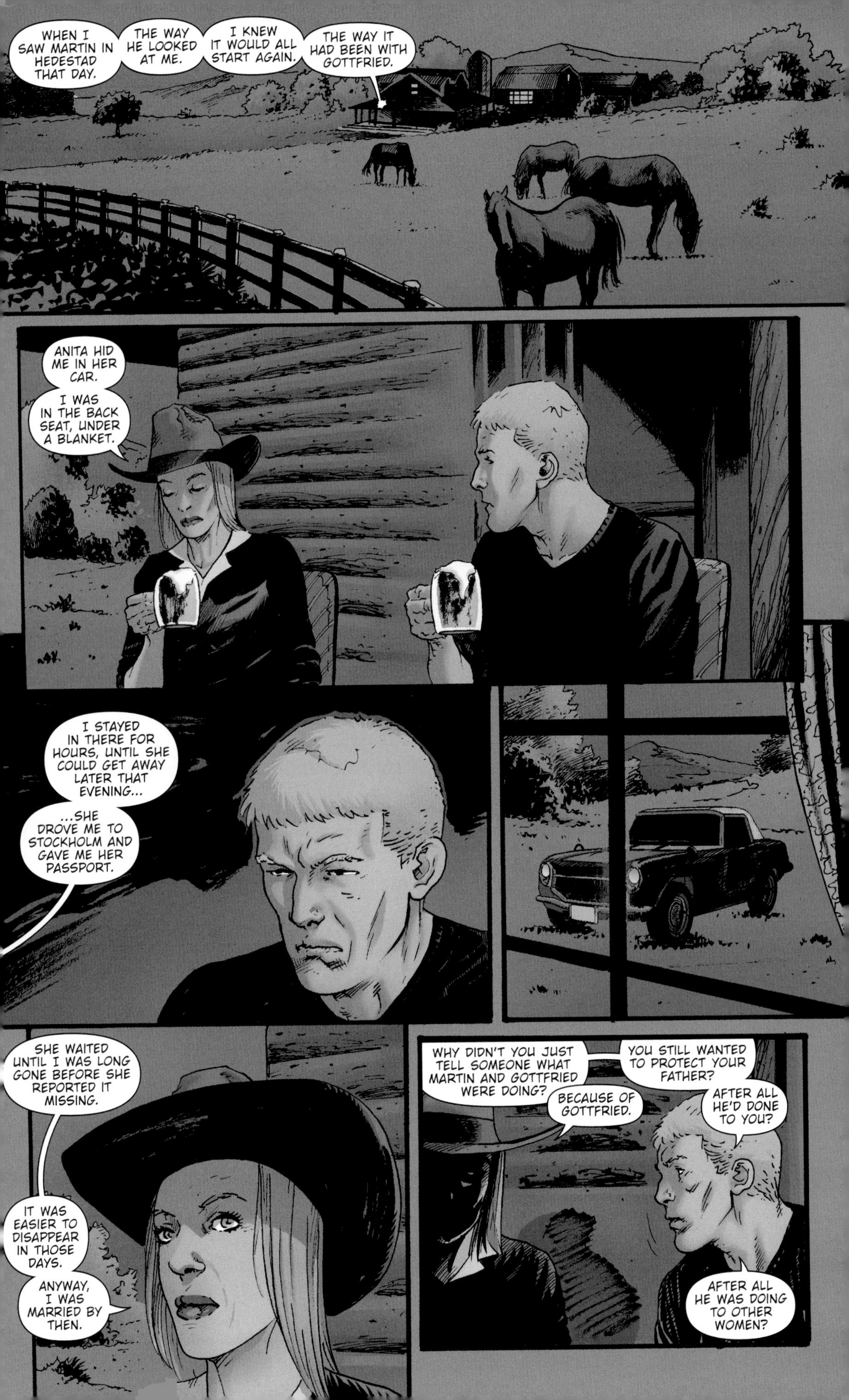
WHEN I SAW MARTIN IN HEDESTAD THAT DAY.
THE WAY HE LOOKED AT ME.
I KNEW IT WOULD ALL START AGAIN.
THE WAY IT HAD BEEN WITH GOTTFRIED.
ANITA HID ME IN HER CAR.
I WAS IN THE BACK SEAT, UNDER A BLANKET.
I STAYED IN THERE FOR HOURS, UNTIL SHE COULD GET AWAY LATER THAT EVENING...
...SHE DROVE ME TO STOCKHOLM AND GAVE ME HER PASSPORT.
SHE WAITED UNTIL I WAS LONG GONE BEFORE SHE REPORTED IT MISSING.
IT WAS EASIER TO DISAPPEAR IN THOSE DAYS.
ANYWAY, I WAS MARRIED BY THEN.
WHY DIDN'T YOU JUST TELL SOMEONE WHAT MARTIN AND GOTTFRIED WERE DOING?
BECAUSE OF GOTTFRIED.
YOU STILL WANTED TO PROTECT YOUR FATHER?
AFTER ALL HE'D DONE TO YOU?
AFTER ALL HE WAS DOING TO OTHER WOMEN?

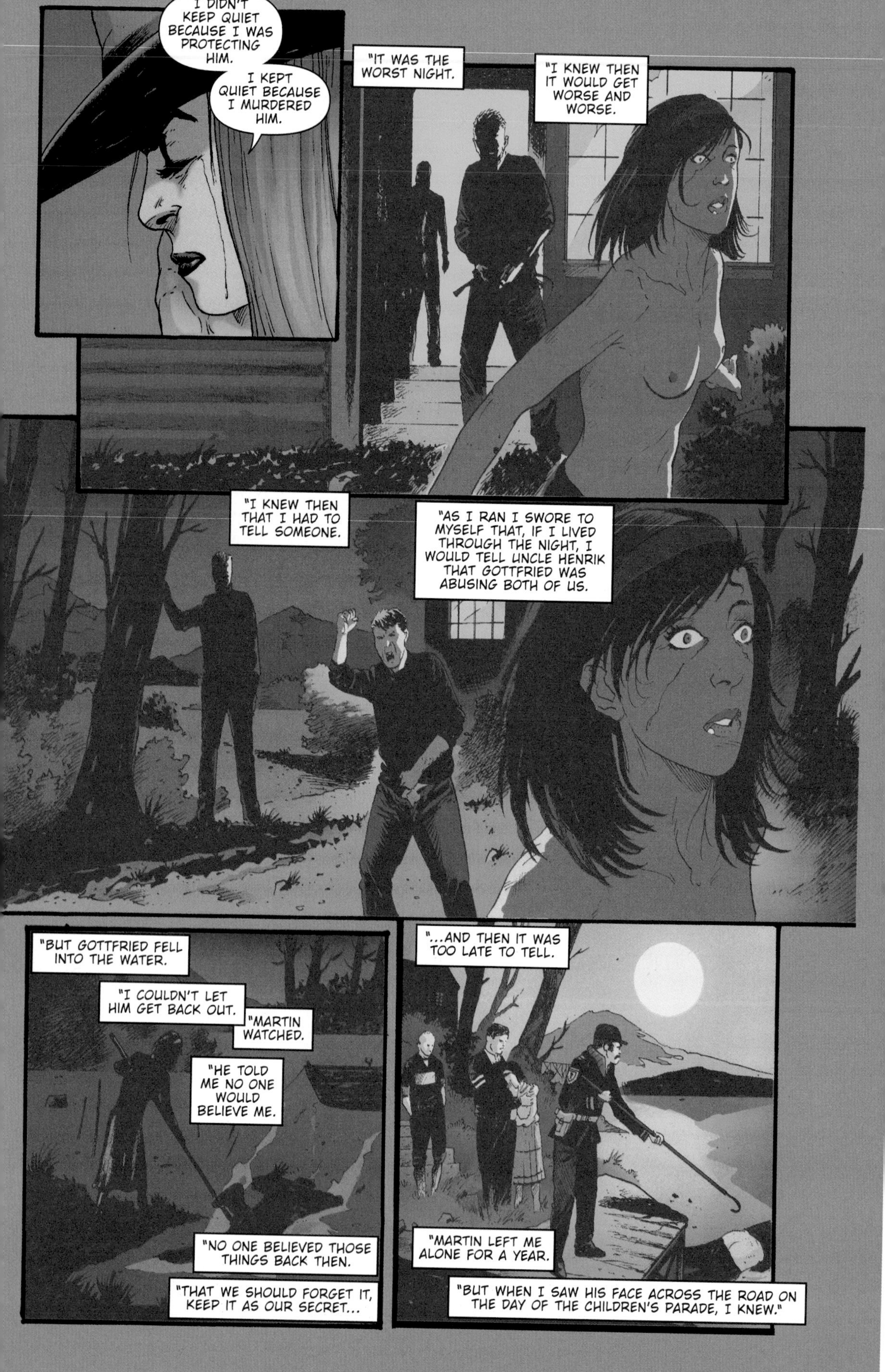
I DIDN'T KEEP QUIET BECAUSE I WAS PROTECTING HIM.
I KEPT QUIET BECAUSE I MURDERED HIM.
"IT WAS THE WORST NIGHT.
"I KNEW THEN IT WOULD GET WORSE AND WORSE.
"I KNEW THEN THAT I HAD TO TELL SOMEONE.
"AS I RAN I SWORE TO MYSELF THAT, IF I LIVED THROUGH THE NIGHT, I WOULD TELL UNCLE HENRIK THAT GOTTFRIED WAS ABUSING BOTH OF US.
"BUT GOTTFRIED FELL INTO THE WATER.
"I COULDN'T LET HIM GET BACK OUT.
"MARTIN WATCHED.
"HE TOLD ME NO ONE WOULD BELIEVE ME.
"NO ONE BELIEVED THOSE THINGS BACK THEN.
"THAT WE SHOULD FORGET IT, KEEP IT AS OUR SECRET...
"...AND THEN IT WAS TOO LATE TO TELL.
"MARTIN LEFT ME ALONE FOR A YEAR.
"BUT WHEN I SAW HIS FACE ACROSS THE ROAD ON THE DAY OF THE CHILDREN'S PARADE, I KNEW."

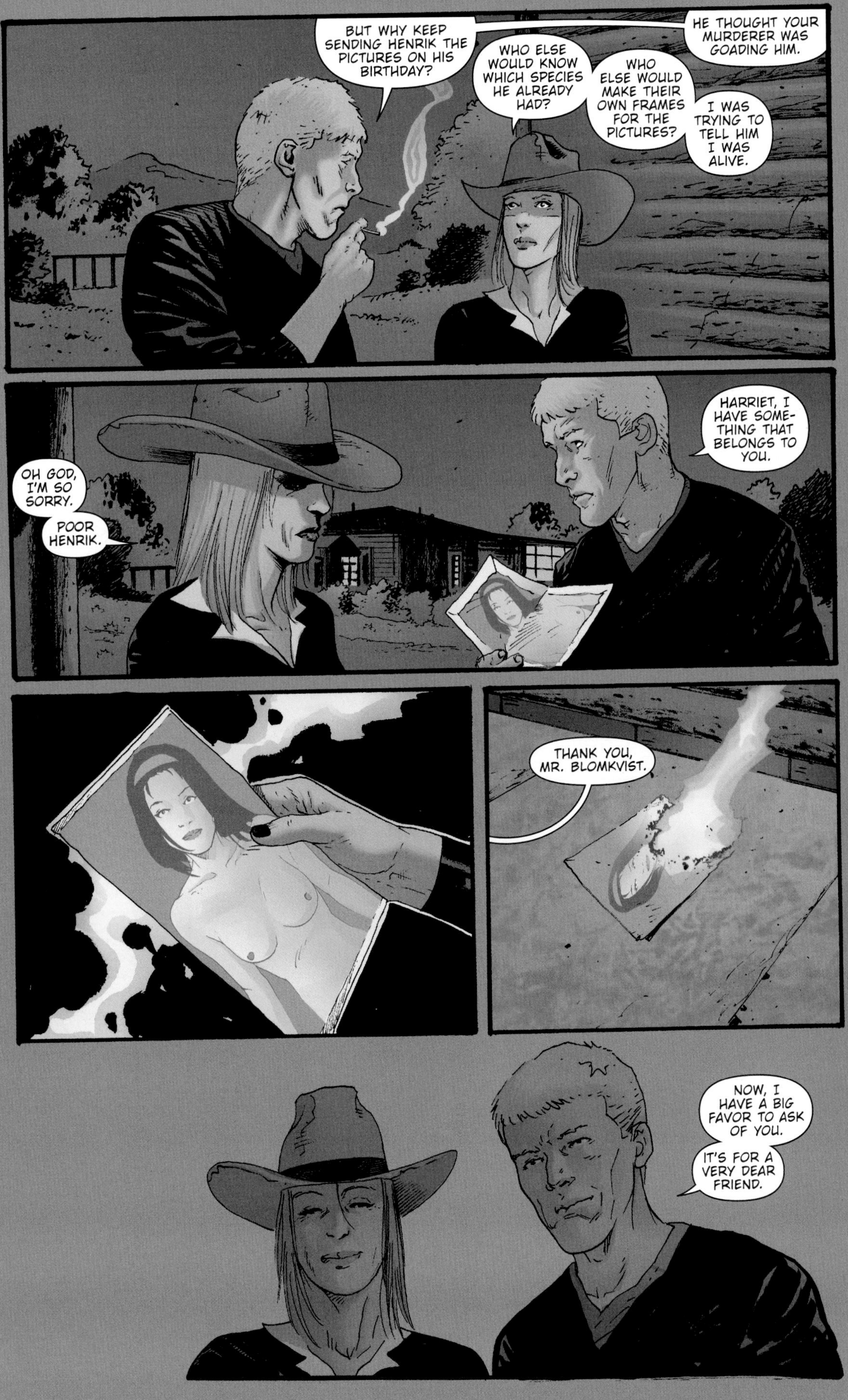
BUT WHY KEEP SENDING HENRIK THE PICTURES ON HIS BIRTHDAY?
HE THOUGHT YOUR MURDERER WAS GOADING HIM.
WHO ELSE WOULD KNOW WHICH SPECIES HE ALREADY HAD?
WHO ELSE WOULD MAKE THEIR OWN FRAMES FOR THE PICTURES?
I WAS TRYING TO TELL HIM I WAS ALIVE.
HARRIET, I HAVE SOME-THING THAT BELONGS TO YOU.
OH GOD, I'M SO SORRY.
POOR HENRIK.
THANK YOU, MR. BLOMKVIST.
NOW, I HAVE A BIG FAVOR TO ASK OF YOU.
IT'S FOR A VERY DEAR FRIEND.

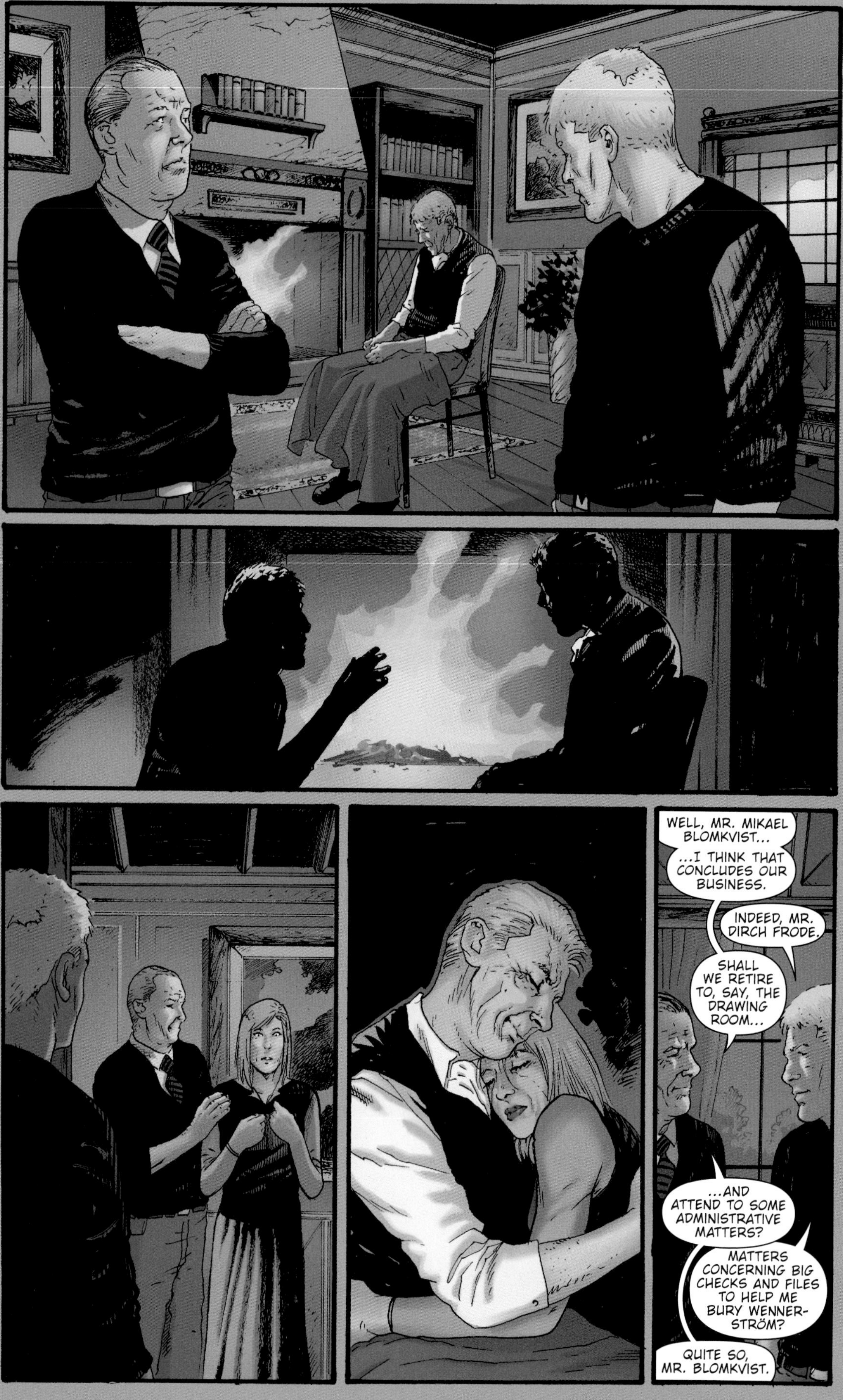
WELL, MR. MIKAEL BLOMKVIST...
...I THINK THAT CONCLUDES OUR BUSINESS.
INDEED, MR. DIRCH FRODE.
SHALL WE RETIRE TO, SAY, THE DRAWING ROOM...
...AND ATTEND TO SOME ADMINISTRATIVE MATTERS?
MATTERS CONCERNING BIG CHECKS AND FILES TO HELP ME BURY WENNER-STRÖM?
QUITE SO, MR. BLOMKVIST.

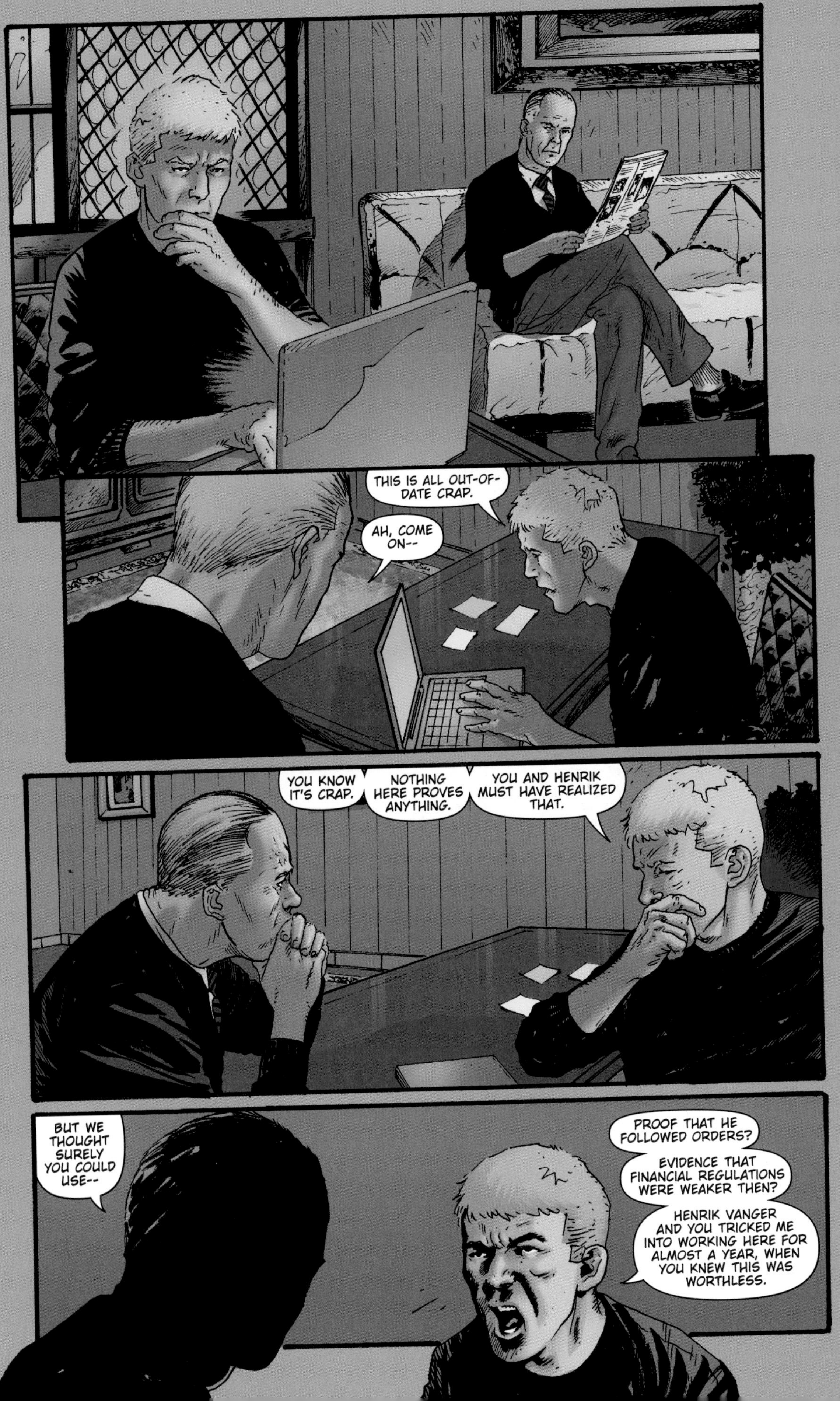
THIS IS ALL OUT-OF-DATE CRAP.
AH, COME ON--
YOU KNOW IT'S CRAP.
NOTHING HERE PROVES ANYTHING.
YOU AND HENRIK MUST HAVE REALIZED THAT.
BUT WE THOUGHT SURELY YOU COULD USE--
PROOF THAT HE FOLLOWED ORDERS?
EVIDENCE THAT FINANCIAL REGULATIONS WERE WEAKER THEN?
HENRIK VANGER AND YOU TRICKED ME INTO WORKING HERE FOR ALMOST A YEAR, WHEN YOU KNEW THIS WAS WORTHLESS.

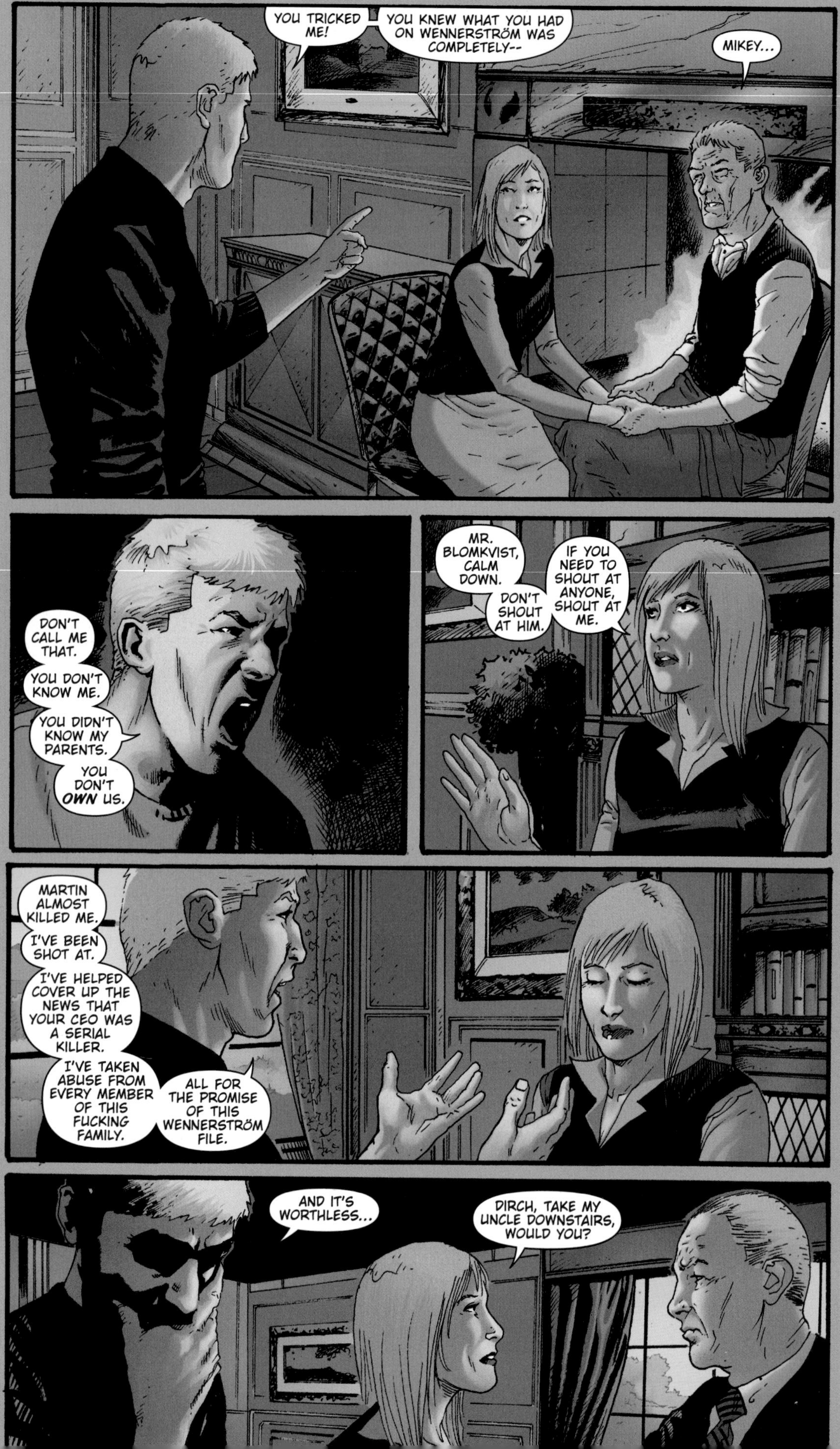
YOU TRICKED ME!
YOU KNEW WHAT YOU HAD ON WENNERSTRÖM WAS COMPLETELY--
MIKEY...
DON'T CALL ME THAT.
YOU DON'T KNOW ME.
YOU DIDN'T KNOW MY PARENTS.
YOU DON'T OWN US.
MR. BLOMKVIST, CALM DOWN.
DON'T SHOUT AT HIM.
IF YOU NEED TO SHOUT AT ANYONE, SHOUT AT ME.
MARTIN ALMOST KILLED ME.
I'VE BEEN SHOT AT.
I'VE HELPED COVER UP THE NEWS THAT YOUR CEO WAS A SERIAL KILLER.
I'VE TAKEN ABUSE FROM EVERY MEMBER OF THIS FUCKING FAMILY.
ALL FOR THE PROMISE OF THIS WENNERSTRÖM FILE.
AND IT'S WORTHLESS...
DIRCH, TAKE MY UNCLE DOWNSTAIRS, WOULD YOU?

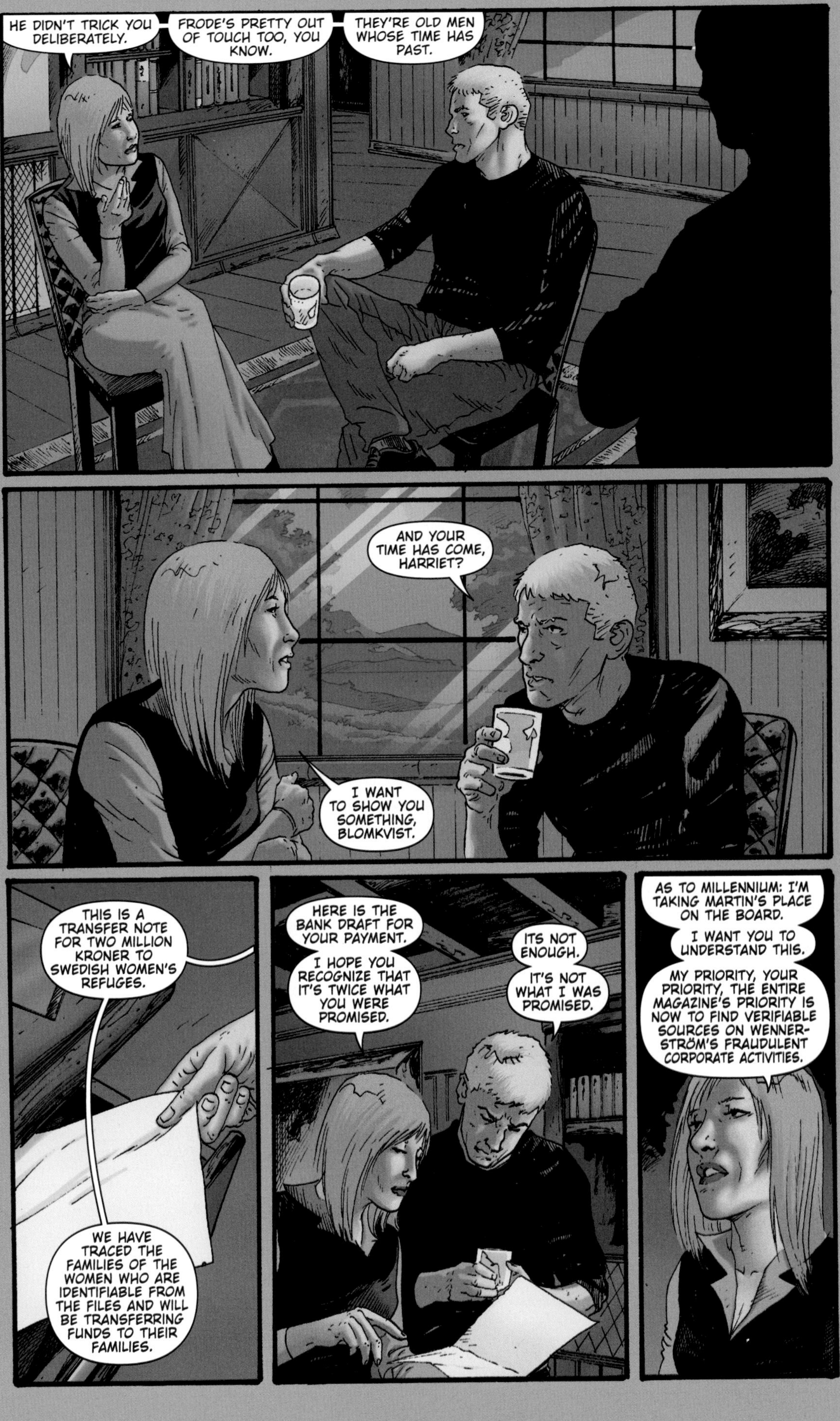

HE DIDN'T TRICK YOU DELIBERATELY.
FRODE'S PRETTY OUT OF TOUCH TOO, YOU KNOW.
THEY'RE OLD MEN WHOSE TIME HAS PAST.
AND YOUR TIME HAS COME, HARRIET?
I WANT TO SHOW YOU SOMETHING, BLOMKVIST.
THIS IS A TRANSFER NOTE FOR TWO MILLION KRONER TO SWEDISH WOMEN'S REFUGES.
WE HAVE TRACED THE FAMILIES OF THE WOMEN WHO ARE IDENTIFIABLE FROM THE FILES AND WILL BE TRANSFERRING FUNDS TO THEIR FAMILIES.
HERE IS THE BANK DRAFT FOR YOUR PAYMENT.
I HOPE YOU RECOGNIZE THAT IT'S TWICE WHAT YOU WERE PROMISED.
ITS NOT ENOUGH.
IT'S NOT WHAT I WAS PROMISED.
AS TO MILLENNIUM: I'M TAKING MARTIN'S PLACE ON THE BOARD.
I WANT YOU TO UNDERSTAND THIS.
MY PRIORITY, YOUR PRIORITY, THE ENTIRE MAGAZINE'S PRIORITY IS NOW TO FIND VERIFIABLE SOURCES ON WENNERSTRÖM'S FRAUDULENT CORPORATE ACTIVITIES.

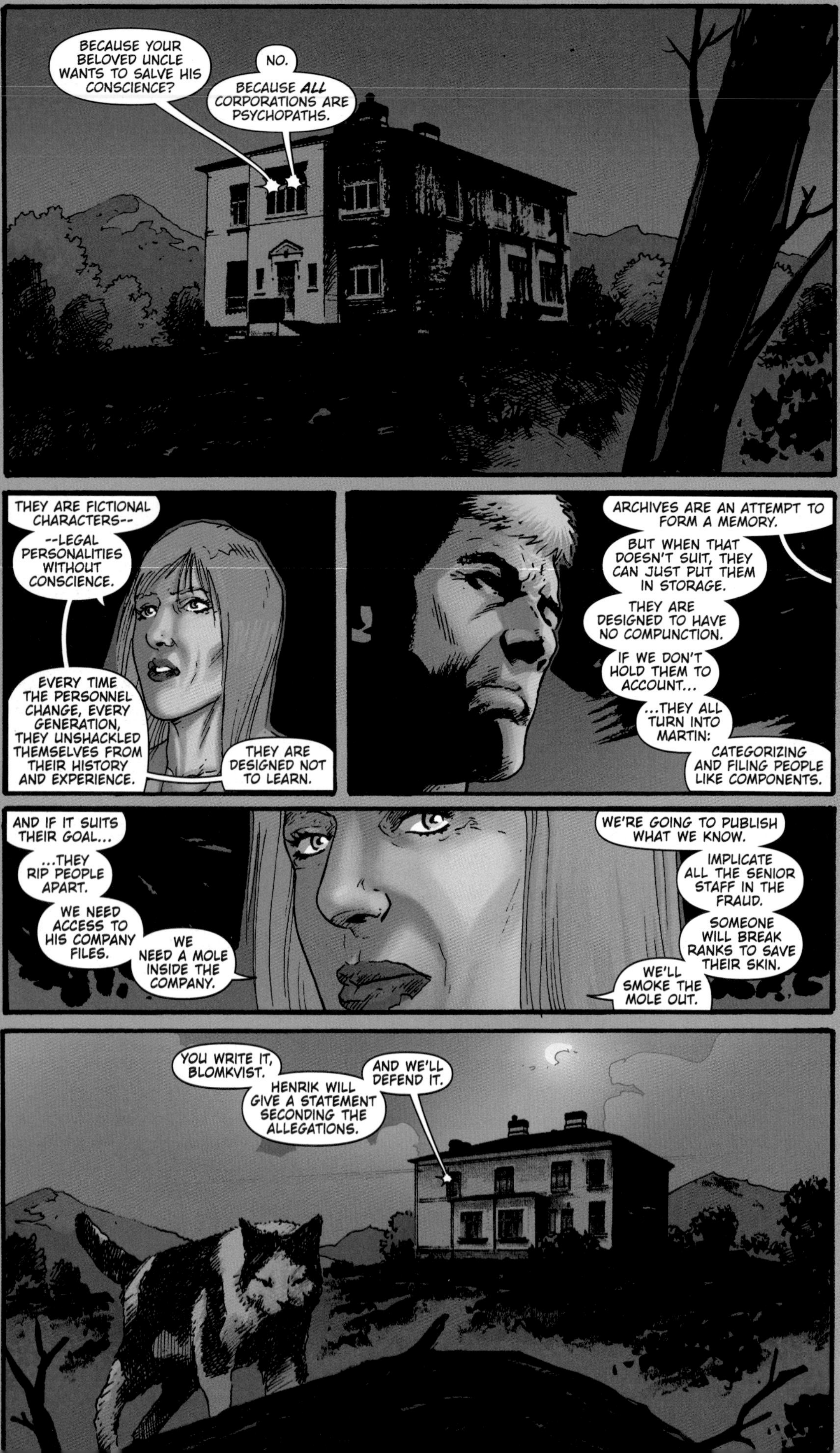
BECAUSE YOUR BELOVED UNCLE WANTS TO SALVE HIS CONSCIENCE?
NO.
BECAUSE ALL CORPORATIONS ARE PSYCHOPATHS.
THEY ARE FICTIONAL CHARACTERS--
--LEGAL PERSONALITIES WITHOUT CONSCIENCE.
EVERY TIME THE PERSONNEL CHANGE, EVERY GENERATION, THEY UNSHACKLED THEMSELVES FROM THEIR HISTORY AND EXPERIENCE.
THEY ARE DESIGNED NOT TO LEARN.
ARCHIVES ARE AN ATTEMPT TO FORM A MEMORY.
BUT WHEN THAT DOESN'T SUIT, THEY CAN JUST PUT THEM IN STORAGE.
THEY ARE DESIGNED TO HAVE NO COMPUNCTION.
IF WE DON'T HOLD THEM TO ACCOUNT...
...THEY ALL TURN INTO MARTIN:
CATEGORIZING AND FILING PEOPLE LIKE COMPONENTS.
AND IF IT SUITS THEIR GOAL...
...THEY RIP PEOPLE APART.
WE NEED ACCESS TO HIS COMPANY FILES.
WE NEED A MOLE INSIDE THE COMPANY.
WE'RE GOING TO PUBLISH WHAT WE KNOW.
IMPLICATE ALL THE SENIOR STAFF IN THE FRAUD.
SOMEONE WILL BREAK RANKS TO SAVE THEIR SKIN.
WE'LL SMOKE THE MOLE OUT.
YOU WRITE IT, BLOMKVIST.
AND WE'LL DEFEND IT.
HENRIK WILL GIVE A STATEMENT SECONDING THE ALLEGATIONS.

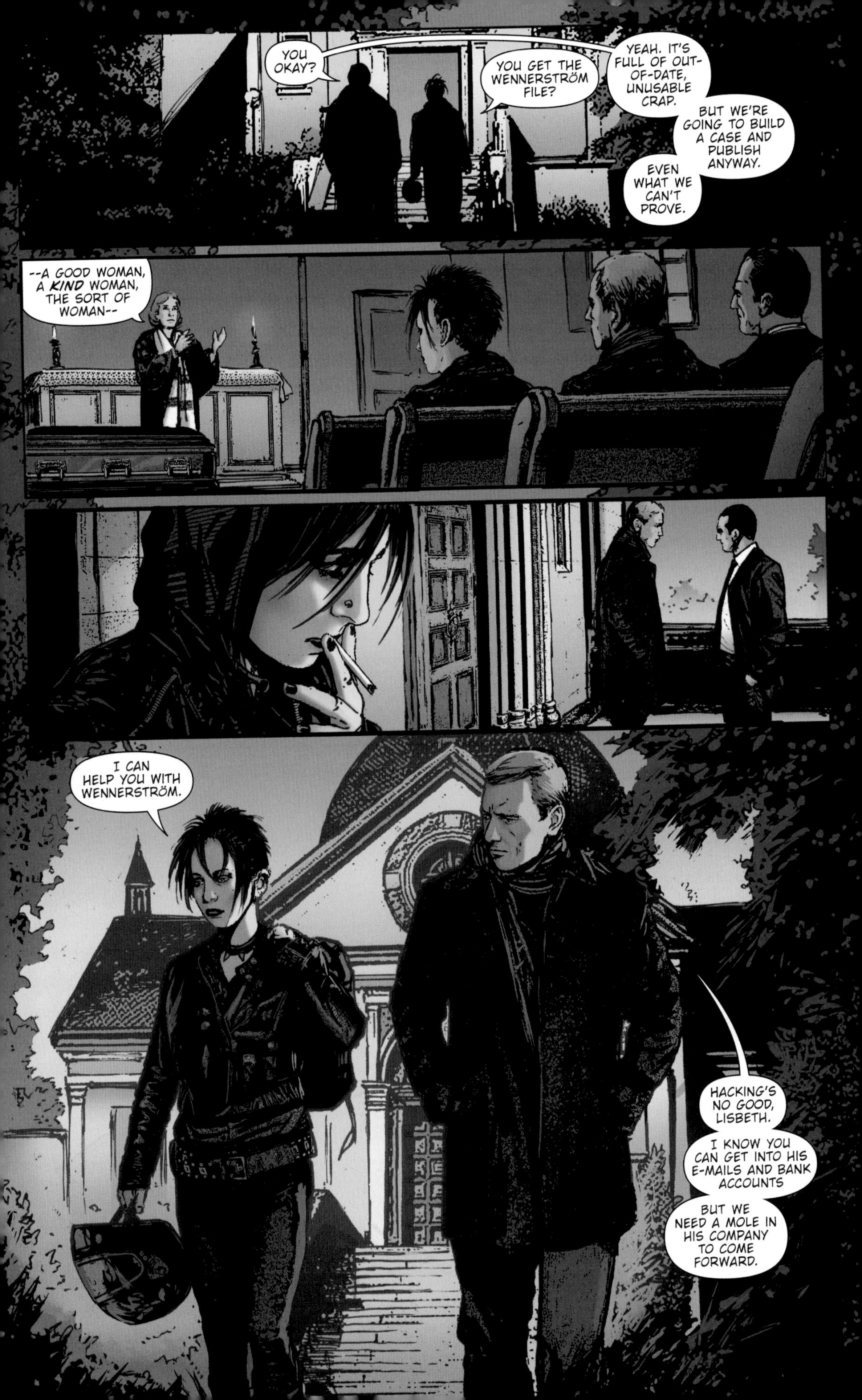
YOU OKAY?
YOU GET THE WENNERSTRÖM FILE?
YEAH. IT'S FULL OF OUT-OF-DATE, UNUSABLE CRAP.
BUT WE'RE GOING TO BUILD A CASE AND PUBLISH ANYWAY.
EVEN WHAT WE CAN'T PROVE.
--A GOOD WOMAN, A KIND WOMAN, THE SORT OF WOMAN--
I CAN HELP YOU WITH WENNERSTRÖM.
HACKING'S NO GOOD, LISBETH.
I KNOW YOU CAN GET INTO HIS E-MAILS AND BANK ACCOUNTS
BUT WE NEED A MOLE IN HIS COMPANY TO COME FORWARD.

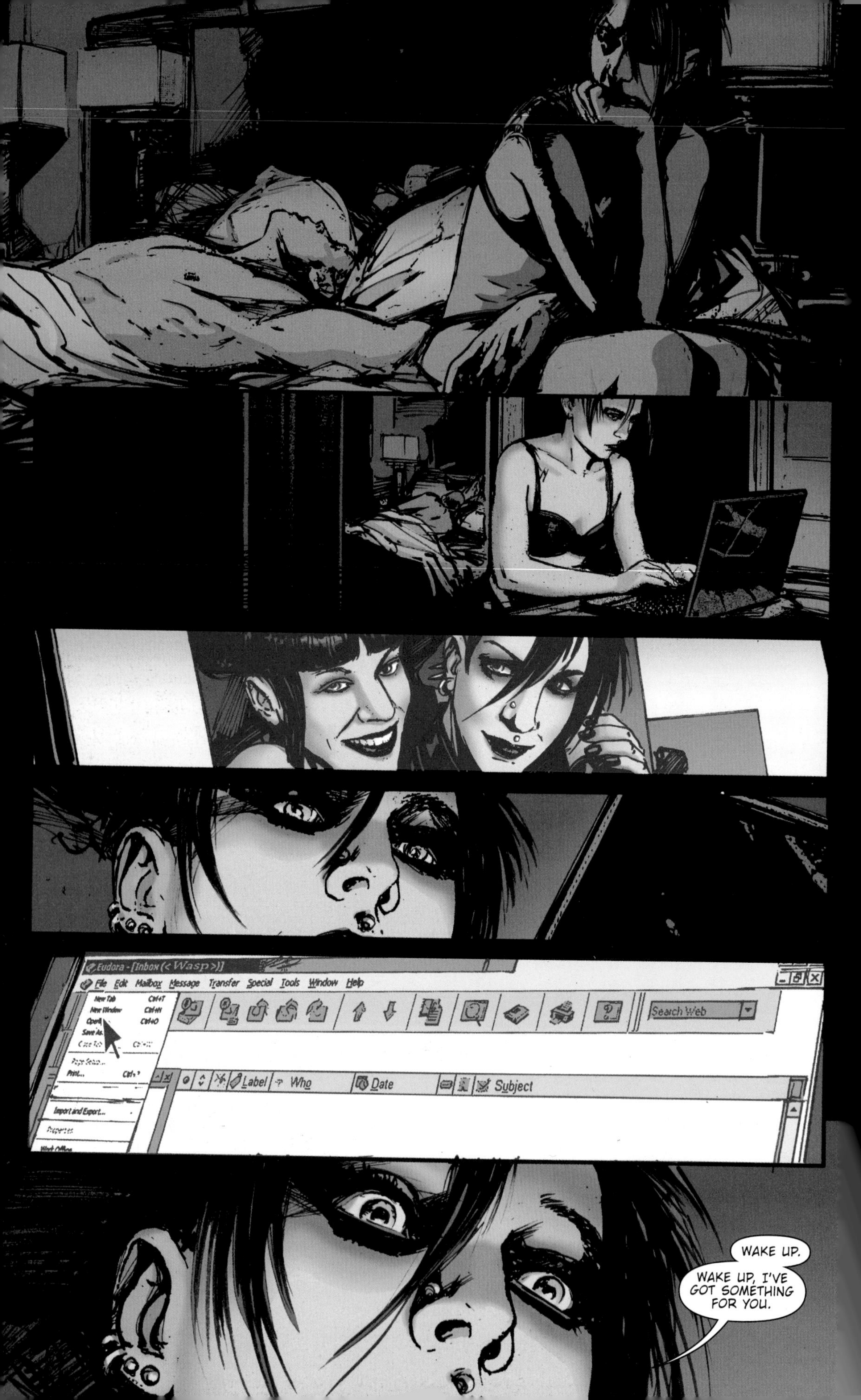
Eudora - [Inbox (< Wasp >)]
File Edit Mailbox Message Transfer Special Tools Window Help
New Tab
New Window
Save As...
Print...
Import and Export...
Search Web
Label Who Date Subject
WAKE UP.
WAKE UP, I'VE GOT SOMETHING FOR YOU.

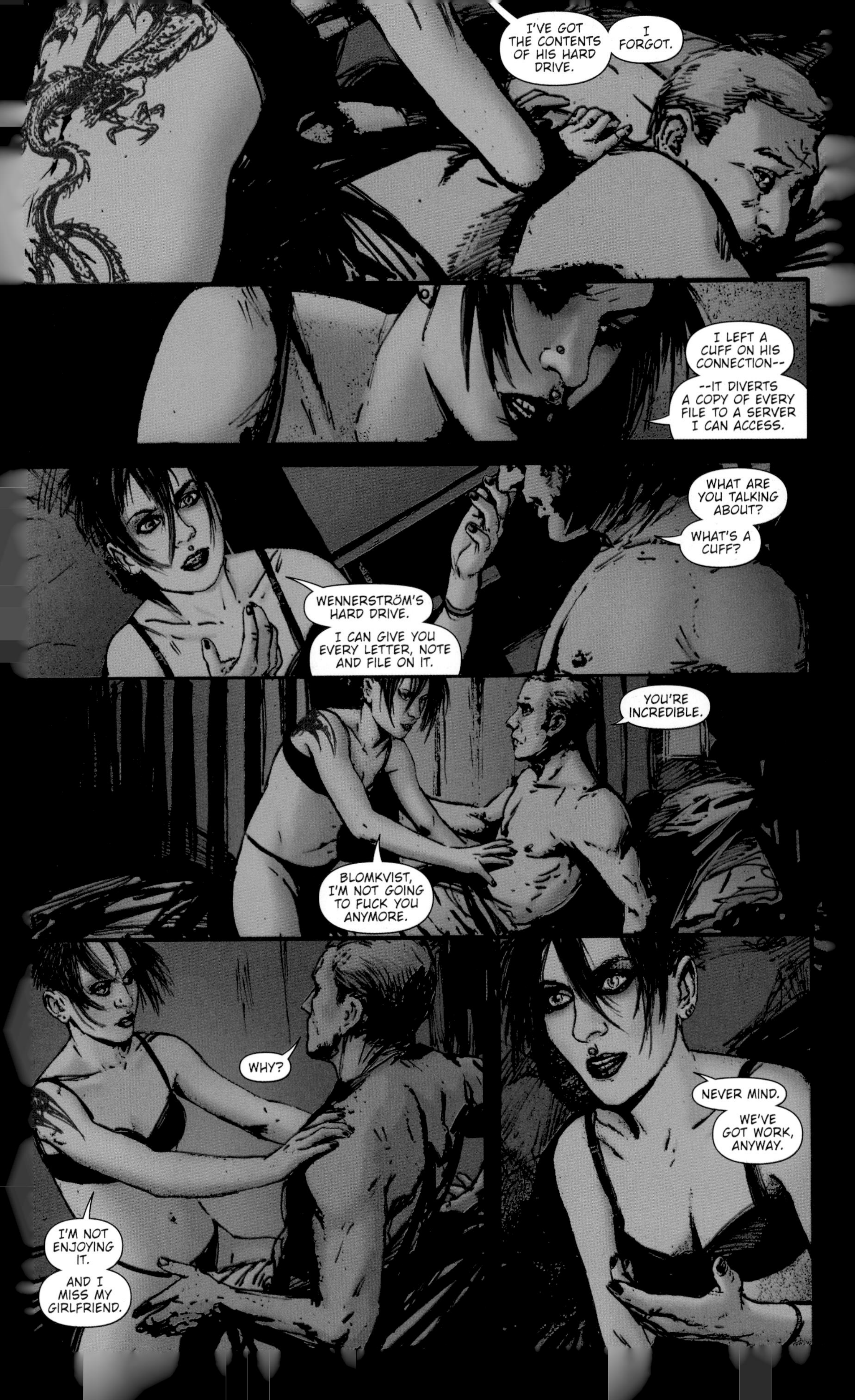
I'VE GOT THE CONTENTS OF HIS HARD DRIVE.
I FORGOT.
I LEFT A CUFF ON HIS CONNECTION--
--IT DIVERTS A COPY OF EVERY FILE TO A SERVER I CAN ACCESS.
WHAT ARE YOU TALKING ABOUT?
WHAT'S A CUFF?
WENNERSTRÖM'S HARD DRIVE.
I CAN GIVE YOU EVERY LETTER, NOTE AND FILE ON IT.
YOU'RE INCREDIBLE.
BLOMKVIST, I'M NOT GOING TO FUCK YOU ANYMORE.
WHY?
I'M NOT ENJOYING IT.
AND I MISS MY GIRLFRIEND.
NEVER MIND.
WE'VE GOT WORK, ANYWAY.

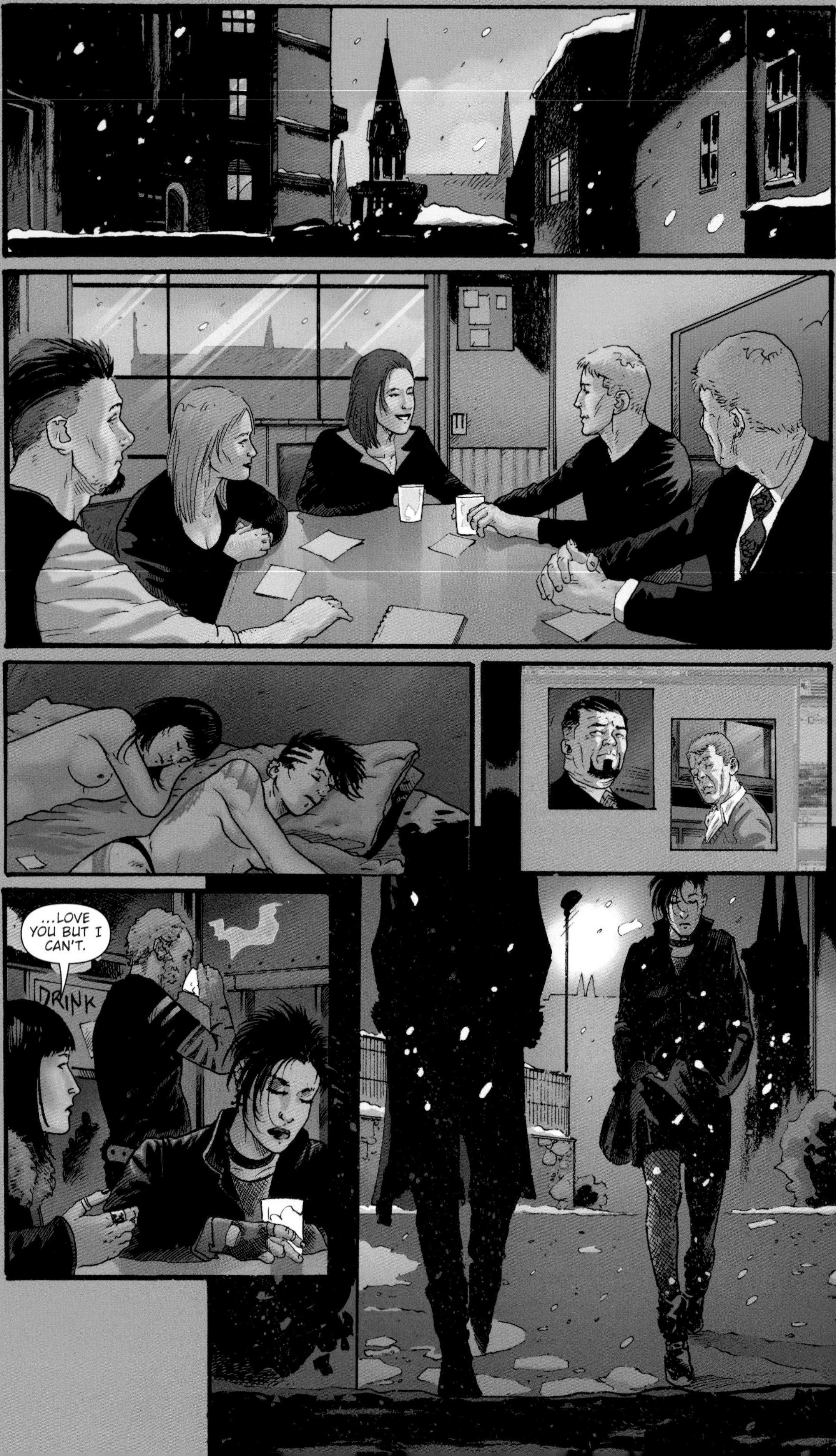
...LOVE YOU BUT I CAN'T.
DRINK

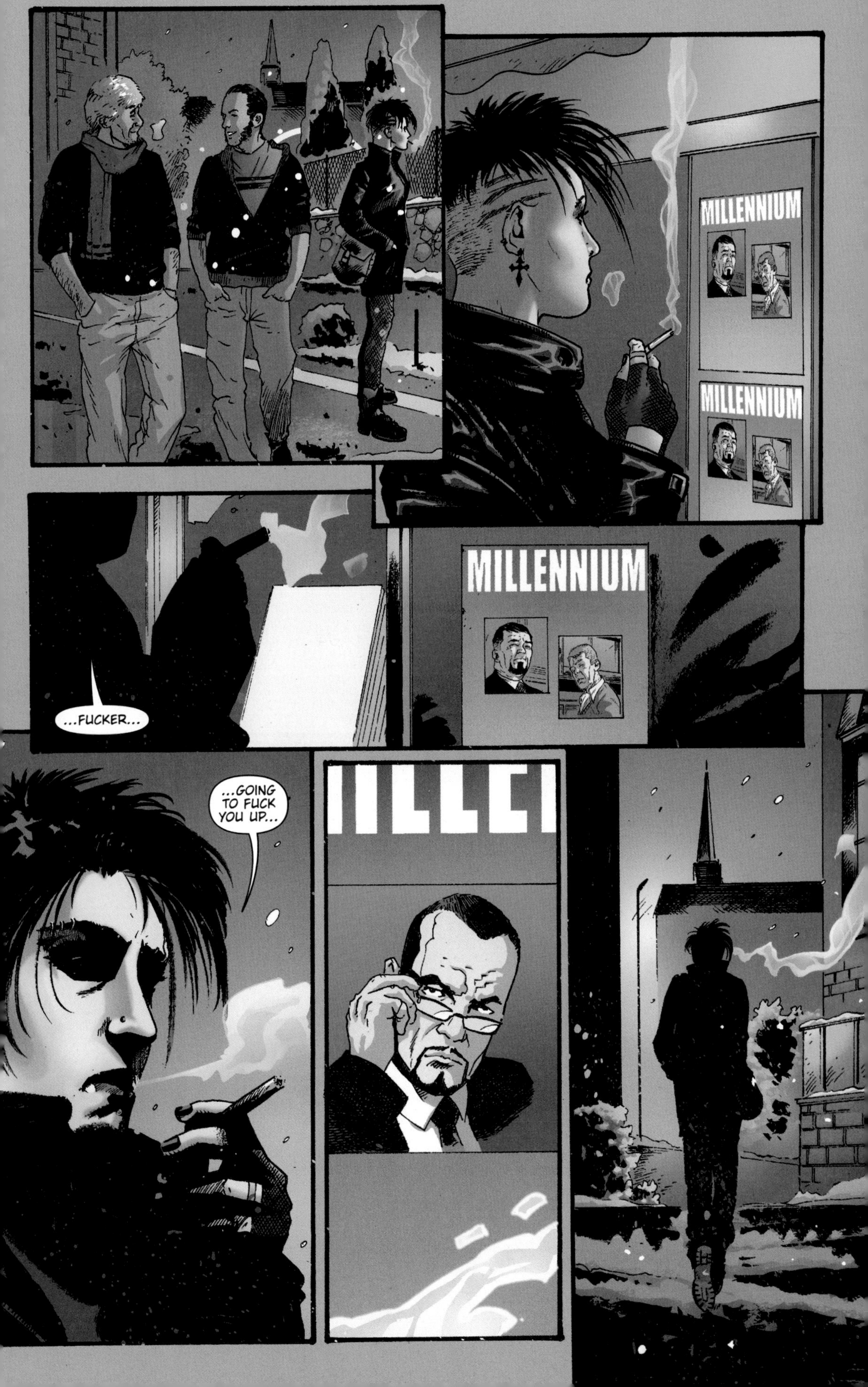
MILLENNIUM
MILLENNIUM
MILLENNIUM
...FUCKER...
...GOING TO FUCK YOU UP...
ILLEI

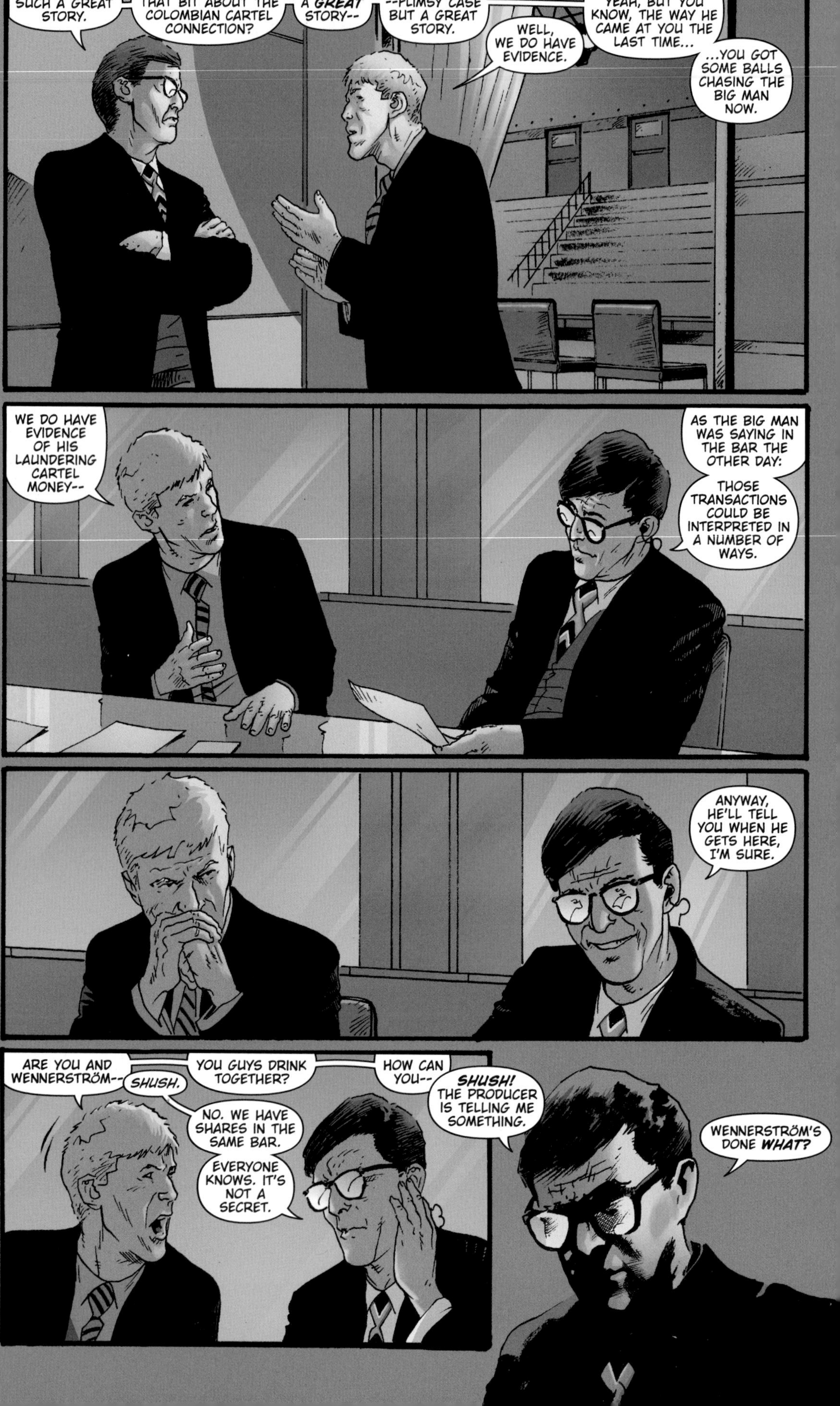
SUCH A GREAT STORY.
THAT BIT ABOUT THE COLOMBIAN CARTEL CONNECTION?
A GREAT STORY--
--FLIMSY CASE BUT A GREAT STORY.
WELL, WE DO HAVE EVIDENCE.
YEAH, BUT YOU KNOW, THE WAY HE CAME AT YOU THE LAST TIME...
...YOU GOT SOME BALLS CHASING THE BIG MAN NOW.
WE DO HAVE EVIDENCE OF HIS LAUNDERING CARTEL MONEY--
AS THE BIG MAN WAS SAYING IN THE BAR THE OTHER DAY:
THOSE TRANSACTIONS COULD BE INTERPRETED IN A NUMBER OF WAYS.
ANYWAY, HE'LL TELL YOU WHEN HE GETS HERE, I'M SURE.
ARE YOU AND WENNERSTRÖM--
SHUSH.
NO. WE HAVE SHARES IN THE SAME BAR.
EVERYONE KNOWS. IT'S NOT A SECRET.
YOU GUYS DRINK TOGETHER?
HOW CAN YOU--
SHUSH! THE PRODUCER IS TELLING ME SOMETHING.
WENNERSTRÖM'S DONE WHAT?

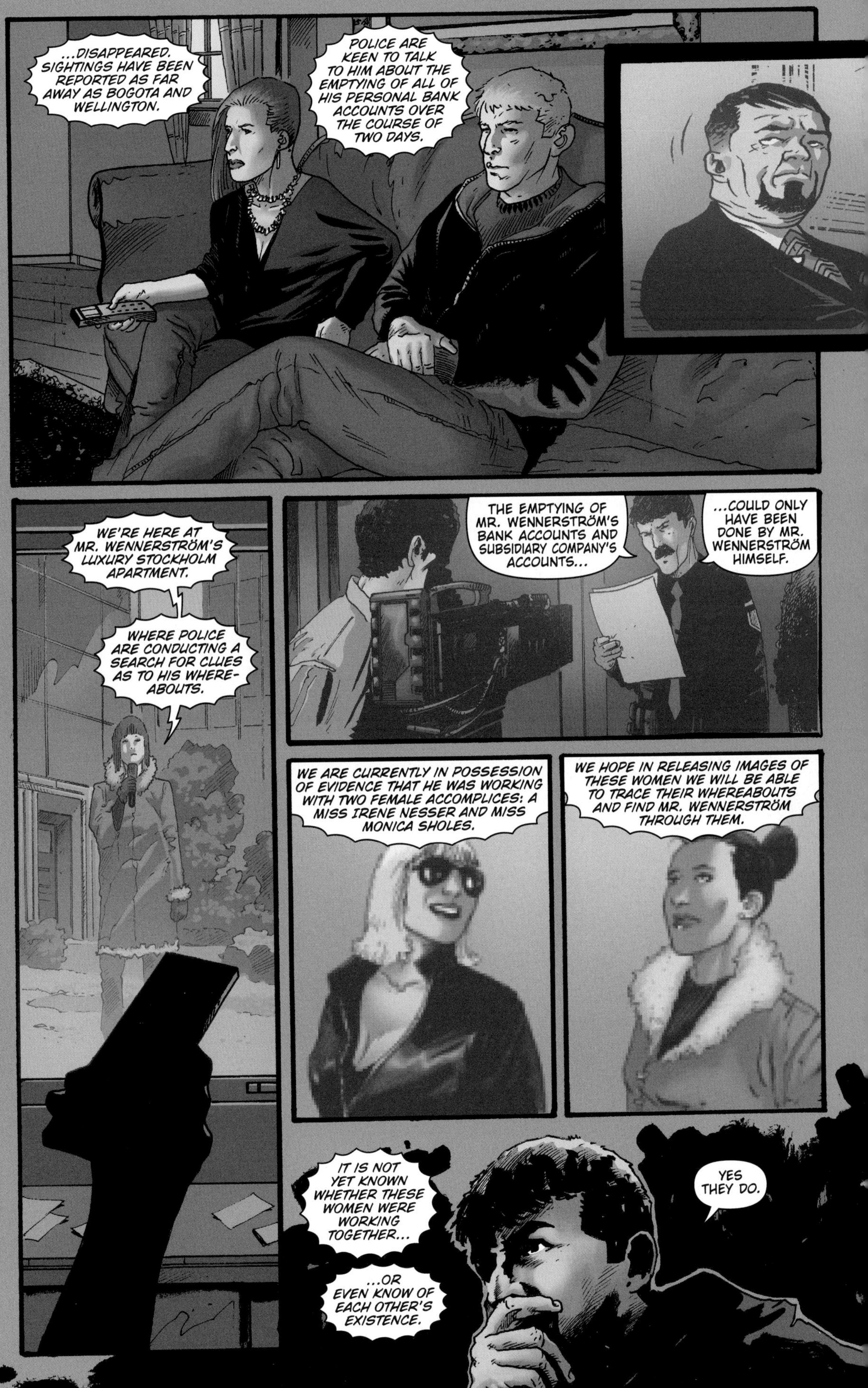
...DISAPPEARED. SIGHTINGS HAVE BEEN REPORTED AS FAR AWAY AS BOGOTA AND WELLINGTON.
POLICE ARE KEEN TO TALK TO HIM ABOUT THE EMPTYING OF ALL OF HIS PERSONAL BANK ACCOUNTS OVER THE COURSE OF TWO DAYS.
WE'RE HERE AT MR. WENNERSTRÖM'S LUXURY STOCKHOLM APARTMENT.
WHERE POLICE ARE CONDUCTING A SEARCH FOR CLUES AS TO HIS WHERE-ABOUTS.
THE EMPTYING OF MR. WENNERSTRÖM'S BANK ACCOUNTS AND SUBSIDIARY COMPANY'S ACCOUNTS...
...COULD ONLY HAVE BEEN DONE BY MR. WENNERSTRÖM HIMSELF.
WE ARE CURRENTLY IN POSSESSION OF EVIDENCE THAT HE WAS WORKING WITH TWO FEMALE ACCOMPLICES: A MISS IRENE NESSER AND MISS MONICA SHOLES.
WE HOPE IN RELEASING IMAGES OF THESE WOMEN WE WILL BE ABLE TO TRACE THEIR WHEREABOUTS AND FIND MR. WENNERSTRÖM THROUGH THEM.
IT IS NOT YET KNOWN WHETHER THESE WOMEN WERE WORKING TOGETHER...
...OR EVEN KNOW OF EACH OTHER'S EXISTENCE.
YES THEY DO.

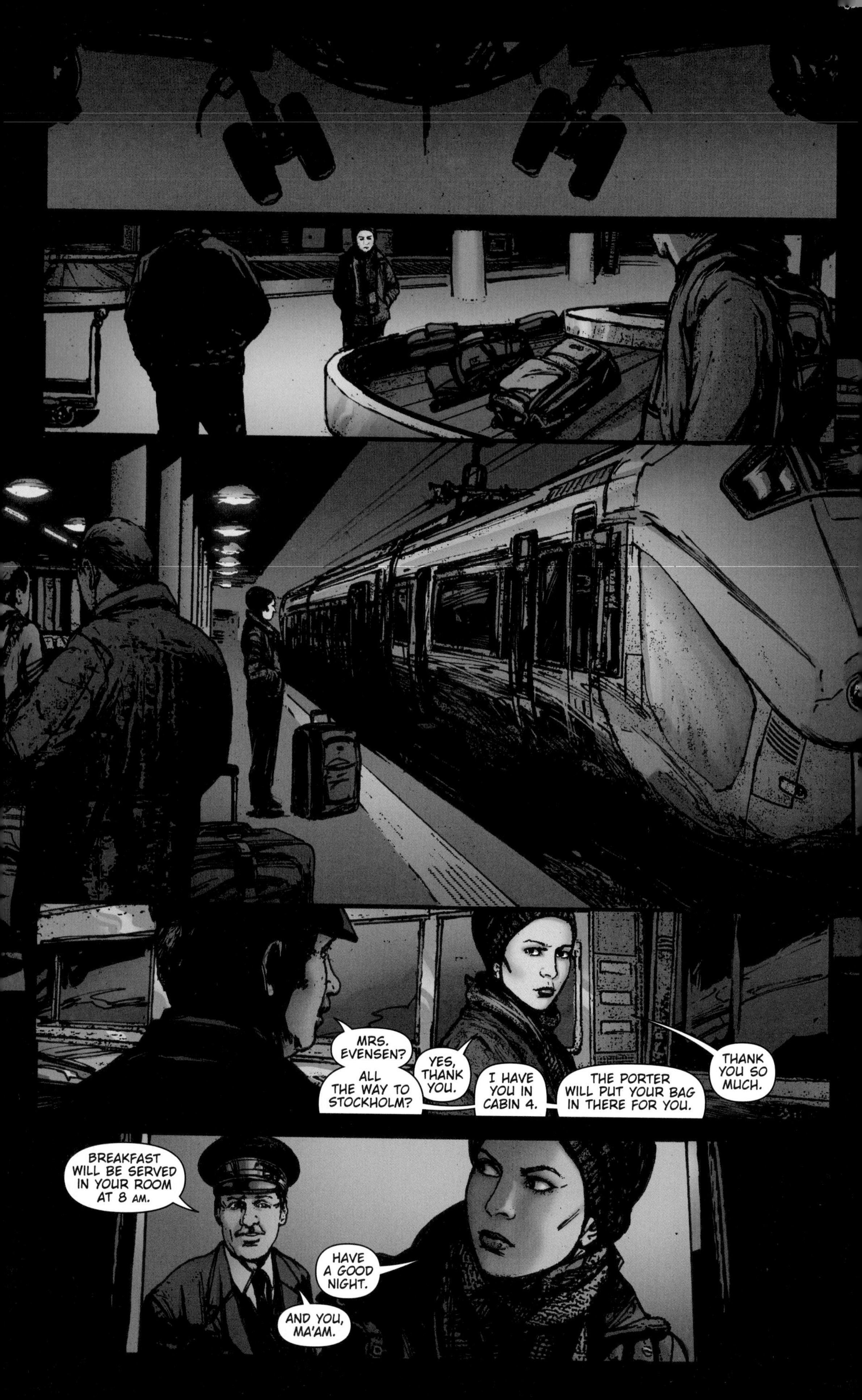
MRS. EVENSEN?
ALL THE WAY TO STOCKHOLM?
YES, THANK YOU.
I HAVE YOU IN CABIN 4.
THE PORTER WILL PUT YOUR BAG IN THERE FOR YOU.
THANK YOU SO MUCH.
BREAKFAST WILL BE SERVED IN YOUR ROOM AT 8 AM.
HAVE A GOOD NIGHT.
AND YOU, MA'AM.

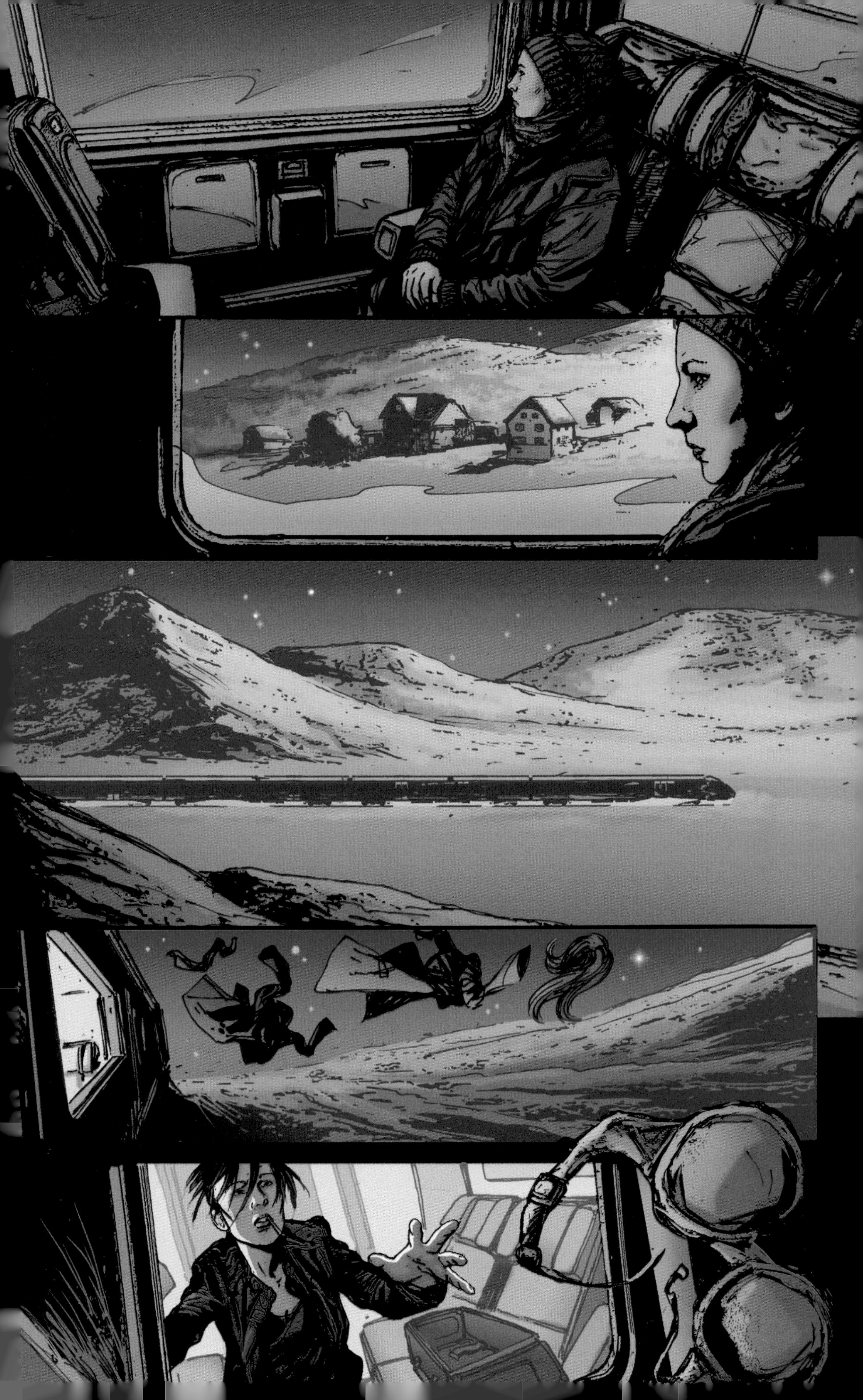

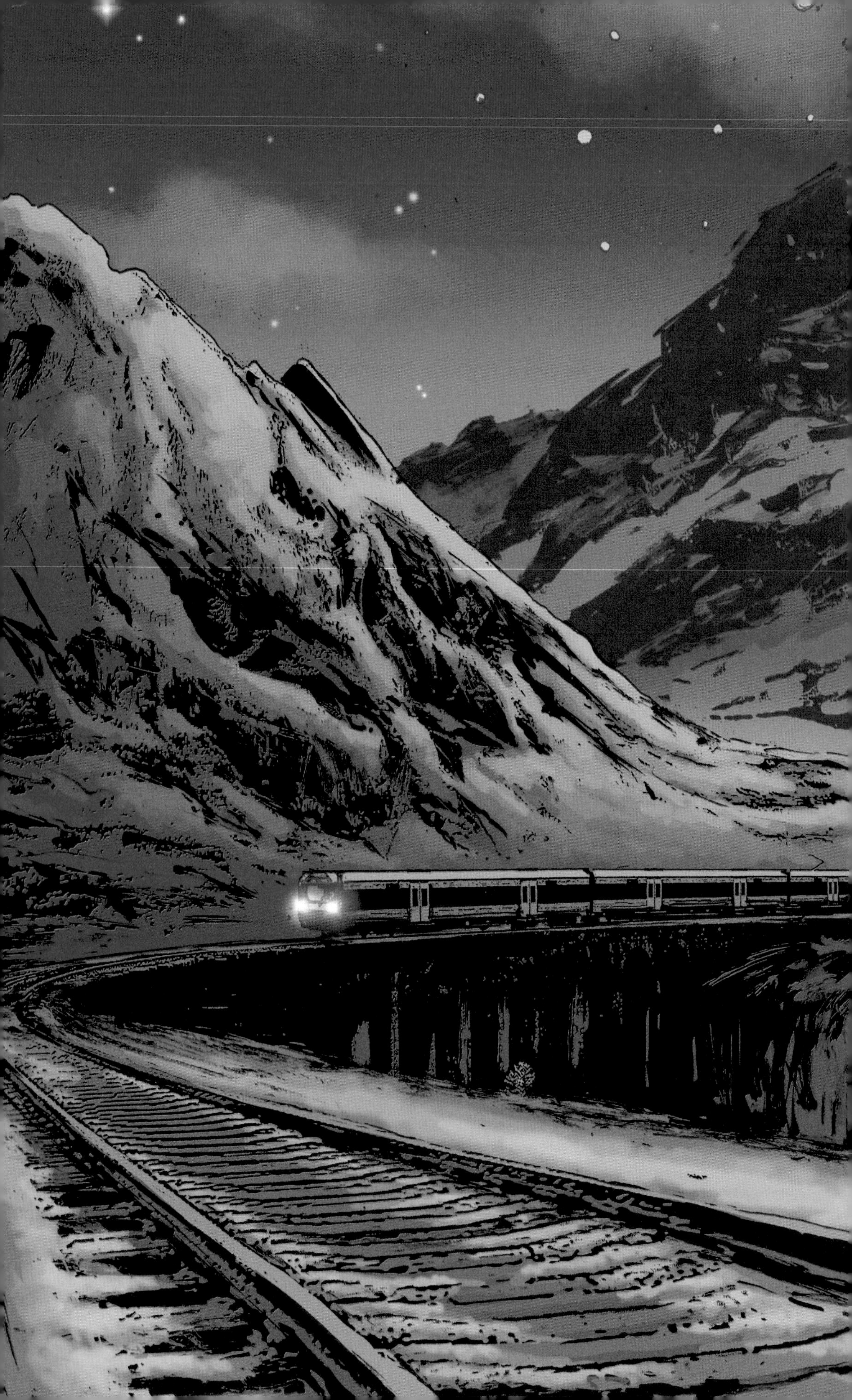

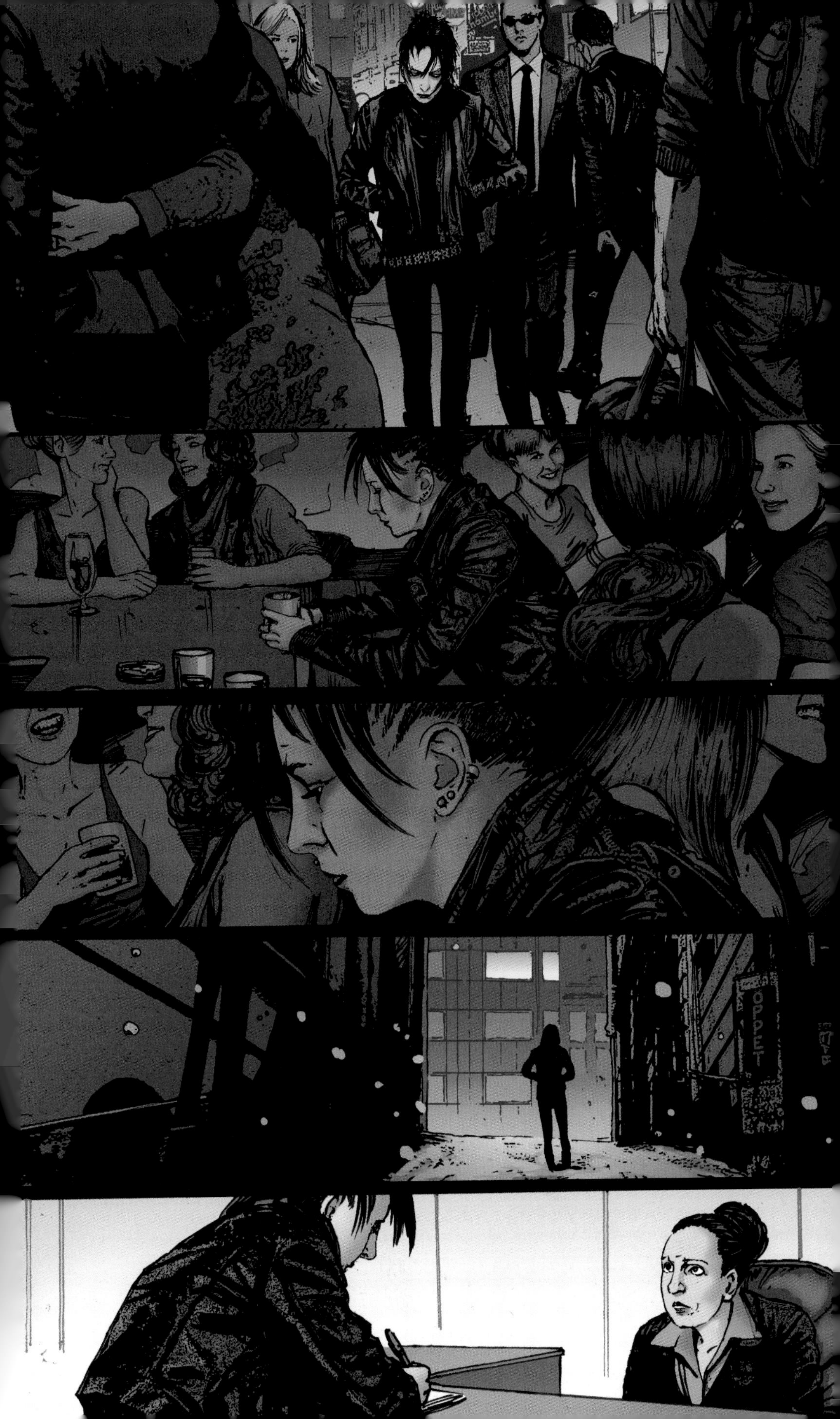
ÖPPET

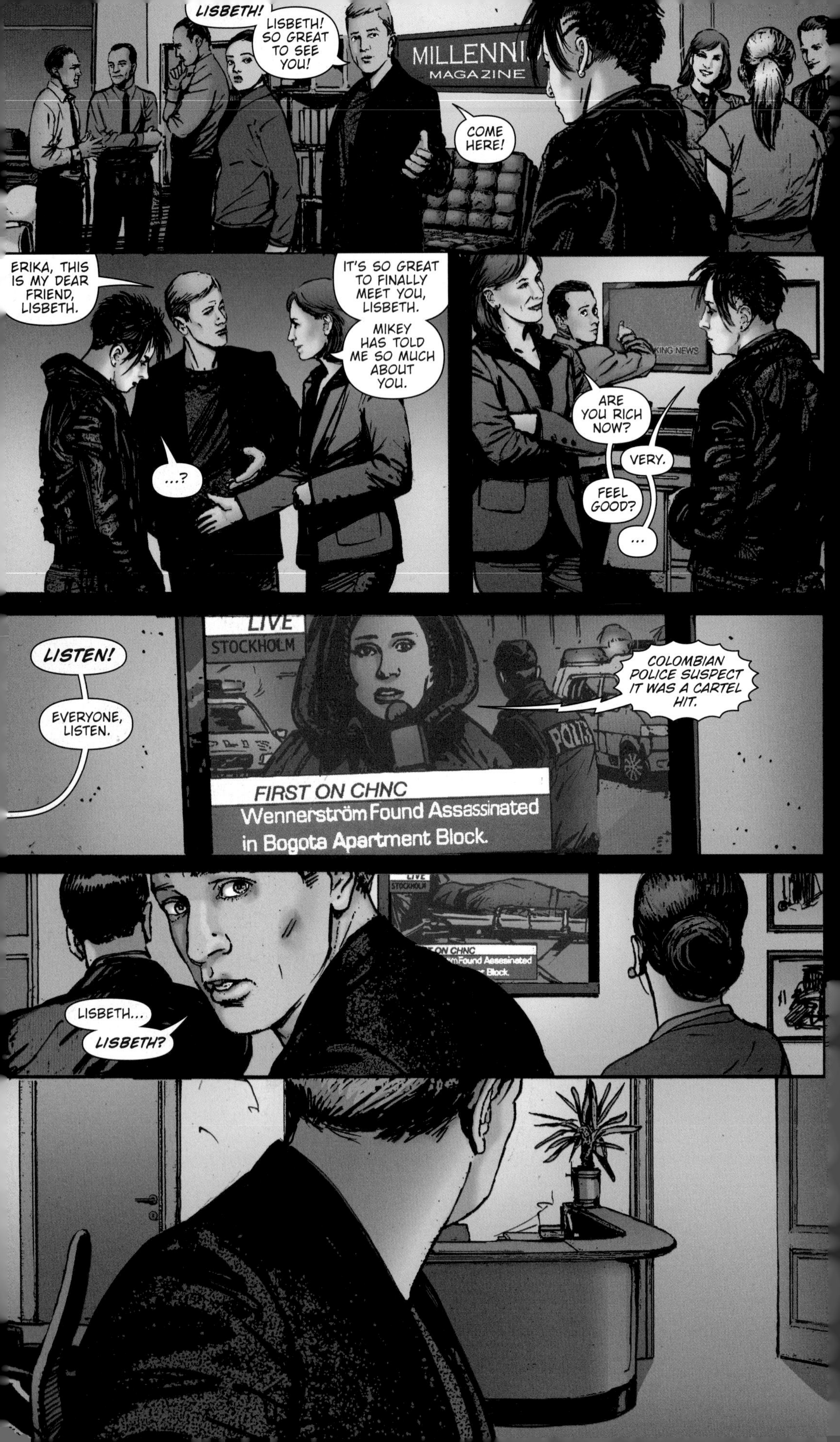
LISBETH!
LISBETH! SO GREAT TO SEE YOU!
MILLENNIUM MAGAZINE
COME HERE!
ERIKA, THIS IS MY DEAR FRIEND, LISBETH.
IT'S SO GREAT TO FINALLY MEET YOU, LISBETH.
MIKEY HAS TOLD ME SO MUCH ABOUT YOU.
...?
ARE YOU RICH NOW?
VERY.
FEEL GOOD?
...
LISTEN!
EVERYONE, LISTEN.
LIVE
STOCKHOLM
COLOMBIAN POLICE SUSPECT IT WAS A CARTEL HIT.
FIRST ON CHNC
Wennerström Found Assassinated in Bogota Apartment Block.
LISBETH...
LISBETH?

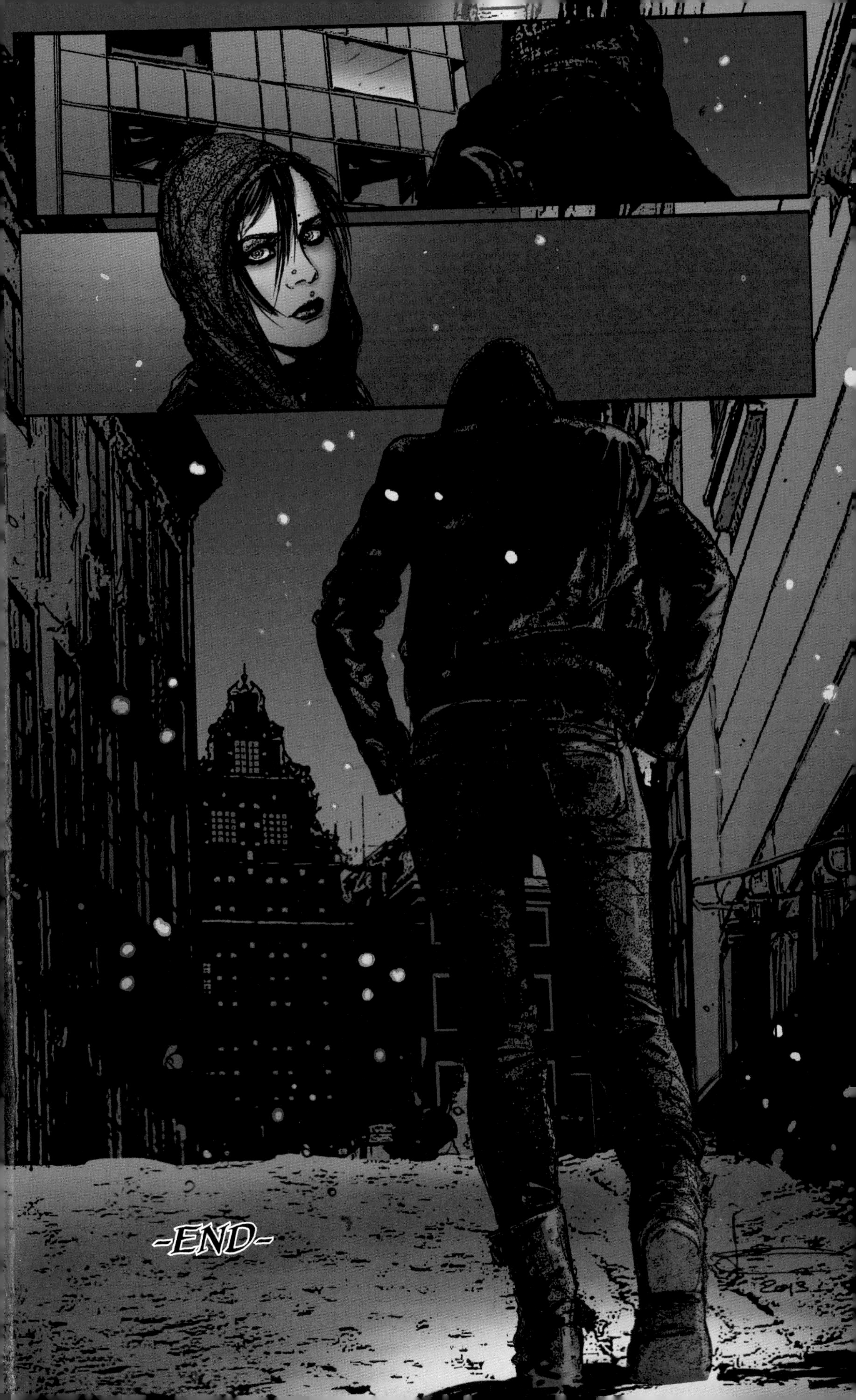
-END-

DENISE MINA is a Scottish crime writer and playwright. Her first novel, Garnethill, won the Crime Writers' Association John Creasy Dagger for the best first crime novel. She is also known for writing the DC Comics series **HELLBLAZER** and the graphic novel **A SICKNESS IN THE FAMILY.**

LEONARDO MANCO is an Argentine comic book artist and penciller best known for his dark and gritty style. Titles include Blaze of Glory, Apache Skies, Deathlok, and **HELLBLAZER.**

ANDREA MUTTI attended the International School of Comics in Brescia. He has worked extensively for the French market and is known for his work on the DC/Vertigo series **THE EXECUTOR** and **DMZ.**

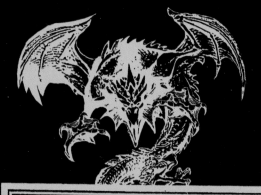

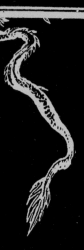